Studies in Church History

Subsidia

I

MEDIEVAL WOMEN

Photograph by YOGISH S. SAHOTO, A.I.I.P.

MEDIEVAL WOMEN

EDITED BY
DEREK BAKER

DEDICATED AND PRESENTED TO
PROFESSOR ROSALIND M. T. HILL
ON THE OCCASION OF HER SEVENTIETH BIRTHDAY

PUBLISHED FOR
THE ECCLESIASTICAL HISTORY SOCIETY
BY
BASIL BLACKWELL · OXFORD
1978

ISBN 0 631 19260 3

Printed in Great Britain
by Crampton & Sons Ltd, Sawston, Cambridge

PREFACE

The appearance of this volume inaugurates the Ecclesiastical History Society's second series of publications—*Studies in Church History: Subsidia*—published by the Society itself in collaboration with Basil Blackwell. It is a fitting occasion to acknowledge the harmonious and fruitful relationship established with Blackwell's by Mr J. K. D. Feather, and now continued under his successor, Mr David Martin, and the excellence of the services supplied by our printer, Mr Christopher Godden of Cramptons, and his staff. The British Academy, the Twenty-Seven Foundation and the Carnegie Trust for the Universities of Scotland have played important roles in establishing *Studies in Church History*, and all have generously supported this new venture. Much has also depended upon the commitment of the officers and members of the Society, in particular upon Professor Walter Ullmann, who until recently presided over the publications sub-committee, Professor W. R. Ward, Professor M. J. Wilks and the Reverend Professor J. K. Cameron, members of that committee, and Professor A. G. Dickens and Professor Geoffrey Elton who have given consistent support and encouragement to the Society's enterprises.

The publication of this volume is coincident with the seventieth birthday of Professor Rosalind M. T. Hill, who has devoted a lifetime of distinguished study to medieval ecclesiastical history, and is a founder member, and past-President of the Ecclesiastical History Society. It is with pleasure and gratitude that the Society present and dedicate this volume to her.

Derek Baker

PREFACE

The appearance of this volume inaugurates the Ecclesiastical History Society's second series of publications—*Studies in Church History: Subsidia*—published by the Society itself in collaboration with Basil Blackwell. It is a fitting occasion to acknowledge the harmonious and fruitful relationship established with Blackwell's by Mr J. K. D. Feather, and now continued under his successor Mr David Martin, and the excellence of the services supplied by our printers, Mr Christopher Goodden of Camelot Press, and his staff. The British Academy, the Twenty-Seven Foundation and the Carnegie Trust for the Universities of Scotland have played important roles in establishing *Studies in Church History*, and all have generously supported this new venture. Much, too, has depended during this period on the efforts of officers and members of the Society, in particular Professor Walter Ullmann, who until recently presided over the publications sub-committee, Professor W. R. Ward, Professor [illegible] and the Reverend Professor [illegible], successive members of that committee, and Professor A. G. Dickens and Professor [illegible], who have given [illegible] support and encouragement to the Society's enterprises.

The publication of this volume is coincident with the seventieth birthday of Professor Rosalind M. T. Hill who has devoted a lifetime of distinguished study to the ecclesiastical history, and is a founder member and past President of the Ecclesiastical History Society. It is with pleasure and gratitude that the Society present and dedicate this volume to her.

Derek Baker

CONTENTS

CONTENTS

LIST OF ILLUSTRATIONS

All photographs are by courtesy of the libraries concerned unless otherwise acknowledged. Dimensions refer to page size except for plate 26.

20 Stuttgart Landesbibl Cod Poet et Phil 2° 33 (Isidorus, *Etymologiae*. 327 × 240 mm) fol 31r detail: initial to book 3, xxiv: an astronomer.

21 Vienna Nat Bibl 1196 (Bible. 337 × 236 mm) fol 209r detail: initial to Proverbs: a teacher and pupil. (After Hermann)

22 Caxton's *Mirrour of the world*, London c1480, fol 21r detail: *rhetorica*. (After Prior)

23 Caxton's *Mirrour of the world* fol 22v detail: *musica*. (After Prior)

24 BN fr 14965 (Gossouin de Metz, *Image du Monde*. 220 × 145 mm) fol 30r: figures illustrating gravity.

25 BN fr 1607 (Gossouin de Metz, *Image du Monde*. 240 × 155 mm) fol 41v: figures illustrating gravity.

26 Berlin Staatsbibl Hamilton 675 (Thomasin von Zerclaere, *Welsche Gast*. Miniature 70 × 70 mm) fol 82v detail: *geometria* and Euclid.

27 Salzburg Univ Bibl MS M III 36 (Albertus Magnus *et al*. 407 × 281 mm) fol 239v: *dialectica* and Aristotle.

28 New Haven, Yale University, Beinecke Rare Book and Manuscript Library MS 404 ('*Rothschild Canticles*'. 120 × 83 mm) fol 6v: *grammatica*, *astronomia*, *arithmetica* and *geometria*.

29 New Haven, Yale University, Beinecke Rare Book and Manuscript Library MS 404, fol 7r: *musica*, *dialectica* and *rhetorica*.

30 Leipzig Univ Bibl MS 1253 (Boethius, *De consolatione philosophiae*. 225 × 160 mm) fol 3r detail: *philosophia*. (After Bruck)

31 BL Arundel 83 (De Lisle Psalter. 345 × 230 mm) fol 12r: *credo*, prophets and apostles. (Photo: Warburg Institute)

32 BL Add 15692 (Andreas Drutwyn MS. 310 × 210 mm) fol 24v: Priscian. (Photo: Warburg Institute)

33 BL Add 15692 fol 36v: *milicia sive armatura*. (Photo: Warburg Institute)

CONTRIBUTORS

DEREK BAKER
Lecturer in History, University of Edinburgh

BRENDA BOLTON
Lecturer in History, University of London, Westfield College

CHRISTOPHER N. L. BROOKE
Dixie Professor of Ecclesiastical History and Fellow of Gonville and Caius College, University of Cambridge

ROSALIND B. BROOKE
Honorary member of Lucy Cavendish College, University of Cambridge

GILES CONSTABLE
Director, Dumbarton Oaks, and Professor of History, Harvard University

CLAIRE CROSS
Senior Lecturer in History, University of York

MICHAEL EVANS
Warburg Institute, University of London.

JOHN FUGGLES
Research Assistant, The British Library

A. E. GOODMAN
Senior Lecturer in History, University of Edinburgh

BERNARD HAMILTON
Senior Lecturer in History, University of Nottingham

C. J. HOLDSWORTH
Professor of Medieval History, University of Exeter

JANET L. NELSON
Lecturer in History, University of London, King's College

JOAN NICHOLSON
University of London, Westfield College

DOROTHY M. OWEN
Keeper of the Archives and Fellow of Wolfson College, Cambridge

CONTRIBUTORS

SIR STEVEN RUNCIMAN
Fellow of the British Academy

JACQUELINE SMITH
University of London, Westfield College

PAULINE STAFFORD
Lecturer in History, Huddersfield Polytechnic

SALLY THOMPSON
University of London, Westfield College

STEPHEN E. WESSLEY
Assistant Professor of History, York College of Pennsylvania

'BOTH SMALL AND GREAT BEASTS': AN INTRODUCTORY STUDY

by CHRISTOPHER N. L. BROOKE

THE history of women in the middle ages is difficult to write.[1] Few women were literate; their opportunities to record their own thoughts and feelings and attitudes were restricted; the bulk of medieval records were written by men for men. Yet twelfth-century literature would be much impoverished in personal interest, and in human and intellectual content, if we lacked the writings of Heloïse and Hildegarde; and I remain stubbornly unconvinced that the letters of Heloïse were written by a man.[2] Some of the best poetry of this and other centuries was written by women; and the cult of womankind is the essential centre and focus of the whole romantic, courtly tradition. At the other extreme White Annays and her colleagues figure in innumerable court records. A part of the relative neglect of medieval women has been due to the neglect of the history of marriage. This is now past: the academic world is full of the sound of symposia and conferences on matrimony; and a much better balance of interests between the sexes is one evident result. Catherine Morland's gay jibe at history—'the men all so good-for-nothing and hardly any women at all'—had an edge to it in Jane Austen's day and in the early and mid-twentieth century; it will hardly be so true of the history we study in the 1990s.

It is doubtless true that women cannot be studied without their menfolk. It is common for members of a great partnership to be of far less interest in isolation: what could we make of Alcuin without Charlemagne, of Dunstan without Ethelwold and Oswald, of Eadmer

[1] No attempt at a bibliography is here attempted; nor is this paragraph intended to depreciate the rich literature on the subject. One must regret that Eileen Power never completed her great project in this field, though it is good that her surviving essays have been published in *Medieval Women,* ed M. M. Postan (Cambridge 1975); good too to learn that Dr Eleanor Searle is at work on her notes.

[2] Which is not to deny the serious nature of the argument about the authenticity of her letters, and of Abelard's. See esp the recent studies by [John] Benton, ['Fraud, fiction and borrowing in the correspondence of Abelard and Heloise'], *Pierre Abélard: Pierre le Vénérable,* Colloques Internationaux du Centre National de la Recherche Scientifique, 546 (Paris 1975) pp 469–511, and Peter Dronke, *Abelard and Heloise in Medieval Testimonies* (Glasgow 1976).

without Anselm, of Gilbert without Sullivan? If it is true that we cannot study wives without their husbands, by the same token we cannot study men without their wives. Alfred's version of the conventional division of mankind into those who fight, those who pray and those who work, strangely neglected those who bear children. Doubtless most women worked and many prayed; a few fought. Then as now they could have many specific occupations, though the opportunities open to them, most of the time, seem restricted today. But their specific function was to bear children, and there can be no doubt that this was normally taken for granted. In a society in which child-bearing was dangerous and infant mortality high, the future of a people evidently depended on a high birth rate; and a society based on land and war needed plentiful warriors and heirs to landed estates—or strong men to till them; warfare was slightly more dangerous even than childbirth.[3] In the present state of knowledge we must presume that in most European societies in most of the centuries of the middle ages the pattern now regarded as extra-European was normal: that is to say most women married young and only a tiny minority remained single. We may regard Margaret and Alice, daughters of Louis VII of France, affianced while still tiny children, as exceptional; but not their contemporaries, the English princesses, who were married between twelve and fifteen. Three centuries later the Lady Margaret Beaufort, mother of king Henry VII, was left a widow when she was 13, but already pregnant: this is a remarkable case, but yet in obvious ways the natural product of a society which accepted early marriage and reckoned women ready for it at twelve.

These propositions are sketchily and superficially stated, but contain enough truth to make the exceptions of special interest to us: the women whose careers are well documented, the women who fought and ruled, the women whose deep influence on those about them is recorded, the obscure women who are yet more than names on a legal record, those who escaped the marriage market to be nuns or dissenters, those who combined marriage with prophesy or heresy. This book tries to investigate a selection of princesses, queens, daughters, mothers, recluses, nuns, beguines, heretics, and humbler folk. We have been to palaces and convents, to the highways and the hedges, and invited

[3] Or so the only figures from the central Middle Ages known to me suggest: see [C.N.L.] Brooke, [*Medieval*] *Church and Society* (London 1971) p 52 n 14. But they relate only to the high nobility.

them to join in festive commemoration of the seventieth birthday of Rosalind Hill.

Our earliest guests, Brunhild and Balthild, were queens with a difference. Dr Nelson shows us two remarkable women playing the roles of men, with such success that their enemies in anger and admiration were compelled to regard them as Jezebels. But women they remained, and Brunhild's unique place in legend and literature serves to remind us of the fact; Balthild too in a very different way, for she is the only Anglo-Saxon female slave to earn a *Vita*, and she won her way to such renown, first by a feminine conquest; later, as a queen dowager who had served her time as queen regnant, she was free to become an abbess and a saint—a situation which would have hardly been open to her in her native England, where this dual role was reserved for princesses of the blood. Such English princesses are the central figures in Mrs Nicolson's lively survey of the ladies described by Bede. The story of Brunhild and Balthild is full of irony, which serves to sharpen our appreciation of the lessons they teach us: of the conventional norms of Merovingian life, which could be turned and altered for a time by women of exceptional character; and of the special nature of kingship among the Merovingian Franks, who were ready (as, in varying measure, were other barbarian peoples) to accept the queen and widow as a king.

Dr Stafford looks at Brunhild and her like, and a number of later Anglo-Saxon queens, from a rather different viewpoint. The opening antiphon of Edgar's coronation in 973, as of Elizabeth II's in 1953, was an echo of the anointing of Solomon; it was designed to draw attention to the role of the church, of Zadok the priest and Nathan the prophet, but it also reminds us of the queen mother, and the part which Bathsheba played in the court of David and Solomon; it was peculiarly appropriate to a society in which one man often had several queens, sometimes more than one at a time. Most of these queens had to play the part of king-maker, to ensure if they could the succession of their sons—or occasionally of a second husband. A few, like Brunhild, ruled. So also, in the very different context of the Byzantine court of the late eighth century, did the empress Irene, the Athenian, whose first role might be that of wife and mother, but who came to play the queen regnant, and to be condemned by her enemies as a tyrant. Sir Steven Runciman's elucidation of her strange story sets her in a more sympathetic light, and one is struck by the analogy with Brunhild. Dr Hamilton's crusading queens were likewise forced from time to time to reign. The Latin kingdom of Jerusalem is the extreme case in medieval Christendom of the feudal kingdom geared to war; for the western nobility was a small minority in an alien land surrounded by enemies. It occasionally happened in the west, but commonly in the crusading kingdom, that a queen was left in charge when men set off for war; and the curious case of Melisende shows how the queen's role appeared in sharper relief in the harsh world of desert warfare. Melisende brought the crown to her husband, and it is clear that the surface of a reasonably successful marriage was considerably ruffled for a time by disagreements as to who was king. To Melisende it doubtless seemed evident that she must be at least a partner with her husband; to him it was equally clear that mastery in the Latin kingdom was not woman's work. Melisende lived in the world of the empress Matilda, a consort in the empire but very nearly a queen in England, condemned in the end to be queen-mother, the woman by whose marriages the fate of Europe's kingdoms had been decided; and of queen Urraca of Castile, heiress of the king-emperor Alfonso VI, who tried with very mixed success to play the role of Melisende in her father's kingdom. It is pleasant to turn back for a moment to St Margaret, whose marriage to Malcolm of Scotland was as clear a union of opposites as medieval records will often reveal, who was a model of motherhood and piety, yet enjoyed to the full the gorgeous clothes to which her position and cosmopolitan background entitled her, and dominated the Scottish bishops of her day although she was not on speaking terms with most of them—in a quite literal sense, for she could not speak their language. We see a little of her image in her children, especially in Edith-Matilda, Henry I's queen, who stamped upon her veil to prove she was not a nun, yet washed the feet of lepers and taught her husband how to become the supreme monastic patron of his day[4]; and David, another of Matilda's pupils, who even with the limited resources of the Scottish crown was able to show himself a connoisseur of the monastic movements of the age, founding a house for almost every available order save that of Fontevrault.

From St Margaret to Robert of Arbrissel, founder of Fontevrault, seems a far cry; yet they had this in common, that neither accepted the spirit of the injunction in the First Epistle to Timothy, that women in church should be subservient to men, and be silent. Robert is a

[4] On Matilda, see Eadmer, *Historia Novorum,* ed M. Rule, *RS* (1884) esp pp 122–5; R. W. Southern, *St Anselm and his Biographer* (Cambridge 1963) pp 183–93; C. Brooke and G. Keir, *London 800–1216* (London 1975) pp 314–23.

spectacular example of a characteristic type of the age: the hermit, popular preacher, founder of an organised order, all in one; and, like his younger colleagues St Norbert of Premontré and St Gilbert of Sempringham, he attracted and encouraged the vocation of numerous women. A small number of holy women, sometimes aided, often discouraged by their families, had made the religious life for women a permanent part of the scene from the days of St Jerome. Yet they remained a minority. In the modern world there are roughly three female religious to every male; in the middle ages the ratio is impossible to calculate with any precision, but the evidence makes clear that the men greatly outnumbered the women, in most of Europe most of the time. Some of the causes lay deep in social organisation: it was assumed that women married, as is normal in poor societies with high death-rates, however obscure the mechanics of such societies may be to us.[5] Yet there were situations in which the number of women religious greatly increased: St Hilda's Northumbria was clearly one. In the early middle ages these cases are isolated, occasional, and ill-documented. The widening horizons of the late eleventh and early twelfth centuries opened new paths; many women rebelled against their enslavement to the marriage bed and their social inferiority, and in an age in which the celibate ideal flourished as never before or since in western Europe they sought escape in ways ascetic as well as carnal. Robert's career may only be exceptional in being well documented and in the scale of his success: out of the spiritual comradeship of the woods came the highly organised, aristocratic order of Fontevrault. In Fontevrault the difficult question—who should rule?—was answered adroitly by the founder: the Blessed Virgin in person; but Robert was a brave man, and insisted that at the earthly level the abbess was to govern both women and men. In the analogous situation of Heloïse and Abelard at the Paraclete a unique but equally characteristic solution was discovered: Abelard laid it down that a man should rule; after his death Heloïse ruled in fact and name.[6] The most ambitious attempt at a double order, though it never spread over a wide area, was St Gilbert of Sempringham's.

To us it may seem strange that the spiritual impulses of the twelfth

[5] Among the copious modern literature see esp the seminal paper of J. Hajnal in *Population and History*, ed D. V. Glass and D. E. C. Eversley (London 1965) pp 101–43.

[6] Hence, I would presume, the discrepancies between Abelard's 'Rule' and later practice at the Paraclete noted by Benton pp 475–6.

century led to so little collaboration in practice. The Gilbertine experience, in a world in which the notion that women were seductive and weak by nature—though the doctrine was not universally held—showed some of the difficulties. In the long run men and women were ruthlessly segregated. The extraordinary and tragic story of the nun of Watton, which Professor Constable has elucidated so incisively, suggests that relations in early days were easier, but that this could produce dangerous intimacy and powerful jealousies. The dangers and difficulties of the relations of Heloïse and Abelard have been celebrated in verse and prose, and the best interpreters, from Pope to Dronke,[7] have seen that their story and their letters presuppose—not only the romantic, tragic story of a woman seduced and her seduction fearfully avenged—but that they lived in a world in which the painful ascetic tradition that woman was man's worst enemy survived alongside a frank acceptance that men and women could be companions in love and friendship, and intellectual pursuits. It is above all characteristic of the twelfth century that it reveals to us the variety of its experience; St Ailred's tale of the nun of Watton, like the letters of Heloïse, would be an extraordinary document in any century; yet we can understand a little how it came to be written in the twelfth. Here we see earthy, human and sublime emotions in close juxtaposition, and they are shown to us by the two supreme masters of the century in the exposition of human feeling. It can be no mere chance that it is from the same period as Ailred's writings that one of the most remarkable of female biographies has survived, that of Christina of Markyate. Here are distilled in circumstantial detail, with many unexpected twists and turns, the struggles of a girl of rich burgess family who rejected the destiny of marriage her parents took for granted, won even her husband to her way of thinking, and became a recluse and the head of a small community of nuns. She inspired two great works of art, the biography and the St Albans Psalter; and the biography combines unusual revelation of the actual circumstances of a girl's life, with a powerful impression of an individual personality—an exceptionally good example of the growing interest in human emotion and individuality; perhaps a little marred for some of us by a sense that Christina, on whose reminiscences so much of it depended, was given to romancing—yet hardly so much as to destroy or even seriously affect the main lines of the picture and the story which emerges.

[7] See n 2.

Equally characteristic of the twelfth century is the treatment of the Blessed Virgin as an allegorical figure. Her place among the saints had been for many centuries—always perhaps—unique; yet in some senses her cult found new heights in the twelfth century. This was a natural corollary or an essential preliminary to the greatly increased interest in the human Jesus and his family. When Ailred of Rievaulx set on a new path traditional meditations on the human life of Jesus with his intensely vivid meditation on Jesus at the age of twelve, he explored the human feelings of His parents. We are naturally beguiled into seeing the Virgin as an essentially human figure; and as such doubtless many saw her, at any rate part of the time. But much even of Ailred's little tract is taken up with allegorical and moral interpretations of the tale; St Bernard found it natural to apply to the Virgin the erotic language of the Song of Songs, and the historian William of Newburgh wrote a commentary of immense ingenuity and dullness interpreting the Song of Songs as a hymn to Our Lady. Evidently she was a securely allegorical figure in these men's eyes; evidently too we reveal our literal-minded, twentieth-century assumptions in using such words. For it is deeply characteristic of the twelfth century that St Bernard can use his choicest rhetoric in such flights of allegorical fancy (as they seem to us) and of the whole of this period that so much artistic skill and ingenuity could be lavished on a whole hierarchy of allegorical women, as Dr Michael Evans' paper reminds us. Yet it was also the age which saw the rise of the romantic tradition, of courtly love and literature. Whatever its origin and background, however much its sentiments may be paralleled in earlier literature in Christendom and Islam, as a fashion generating a vast and flourishing literature it was something new, and reflects the inventiveness and variety of fashion and sentiment in the late twelfth and early thirteenth centuries. In the romance women are commonly the centres of a cult; and there will be speculation until the end of time what if anything this cult owed to the cult of the Virgin. They lived in the same world; they both had allegorical features; there are moments when the poets of courtly love evidently parody the cult of the saints. Yet a great gulf was set between them, manifest testimony of the wide range of sentiment of this age.

Thus it is not surprising to find that while the Cistercians fostered devotion to the sublime and allegorical Virgin to whom all their churches were dedicated, they strenuously rejected all contact with actual women. Some of Bernard's most moving letters are addressed to nuns; so are some of the most human of Ailred's tracts. But they and their colleagues steadfastly refused to follow Norbert and Gilbert and admit women to their orders or communities. Mrs Thompson's paper shows us the astonishing spectacle of the Cistercian order, ostrich-like, burying its head in the sand: denying that there were Cistercian nuns. In this enterprise they had an ironical alliance with the nuns of Las Huelgas, who insisted that they were Cistercian, but also—if we may read between the lines—refused submission to the chapter at Cîteaux because no women were admitted there. The paradox is striking: with all the strength of a male movement in an ascetic world dominated by men the Cistercian fathers rejected the admission of women; but in the thirteenth century they woke up to find that there were nuns in the order, and a larger number (perhaps) who called themselves Cistercian on account of their customs, or to win much sought after privileges; in thirteenth-century Germany more houses of women were founded than of men. The male reaction and the tide of female sentiment are evident in this story; though it is still far from clear why women religious of many different types were especially active in Germany and the Low Countries, and why this was the only area in Christendom where we have any reason to suppose that women religious ever in the middle ages came to be as numerous as men.

A remarkable witness of this world of activity and sentiment is found in the writings of Jacques de Vitry. He was a Frenchman by birth, best known perhaps for his work as bishop of Acre, who ended his life as a cardinal bishop. Yet his formative years were spent in the Low Countries, and it is characteristic of his interest and deep pastoral concern that he should be one of our chief witnesses on the early beguines, and also one of our most interesting witnesses of the early impressions made by St Francis and St Clare. In Francis and Clare the impulses of this world nearly produced a joint endeavour by men and women dedicated to helping each other; but Francis's devotion to prelates and priests in the end kept in check his wilder fancies, and it is sorrowful to observe—though the details are hidden from us—how here as elsewhere what began as a collaboration sought by Francis ended in strict segregation and Clare's enclosure. In the north, especially in the Low Countries, the impulse to the religious life among women seems to have been both more widespread and more varied; and by the very amorphous nature of their organisation the Beguines evaded the incarceration of the Clares, though they could not evade many other problems of practice and sentiment in a world which still tended to think that the place of women was in the home or in a convent—or a brothel. Yet in their different ways the cult of the Virgin, the cult of courtly love, the careers of Clare and the beguines, are striking evidence that a greater variety, and the possibility of a greater liberality, had entered into many folks' attitude to women and to women religious by the dawn of the thirteenth century. Of this the cult of the blessed Guglielma is an illustration: the good lady whom her followers regarded as a goddess is perhaps an excrescence on the history of medieval sentiment—a strange, extravagant, absurd episode; but also a very moving one, and important evidence of the range of ideas; an excellent example of an attitude which many historians would pronounce impossible if it were not clearly described in the inquisitors' records.

In these samplings of medieval women we began with Jezebel, and it is appropriate to recall that they were comparable powerful female figures dominating the male scene in late fourteenth-century England, especially Alice Perrers and Joan of Kent. Their world was not Brunhild's or Balthild's, but there are similarities in their situation, as well as the striking difference that these two were not anointed queens, Alice not in any sense a princess. They are examples of the force of personality in our story, and of something else. We know more of the fourteenth century than of the sixth and seventh, however, and can place them in a wider context. We know more of the context of ordinary married life, of the nurses and midwives, toys and distaffs, gossip and scandal, which surrounded the women of the late middle ages. To this the companions of White Annays bear witness, providing many remarkable details, especially of irregular marriages, from the court books. Our selection of the women of the late middle ages does not include any of the small band of wives who speak to us directly in their letters—the wife of the Merchant of Prato[8] or Margaret Paston, who open windows on the actualities of marriage in the fifteenth century and let in such floods of light as to blind us for a moment to their chief message, which is how little we know or can know of human relations at this level in earlier centuries. Our selection shows us women and wives in other roles, entering the ranks of the mystics in the person of Marjorie Kempe, playing their part in the spread and survival of dissent,

[8] Iris Origo, *The Merchant of Prato* (London 1957); compare Brooke, *Church and Society*, cap 12.

in the Lollard ladies; at the eve of the reformation Dr Cross reveals them engaged in moving and vivid religious instruction.

Had the opportunities for women increased over the centuries we have surveyed? The answer seems to be that they had, for some, grown far wider; but the same was true in even greater measure for men. Nor was it a story of even or regular advance. It is a tale full of vicissitudes, with local opportunities, such as those for religious women in the Low Countries and in Germany in the thirteenth century, not reproduced, or only dimly reflected, elsewhere. Yet at no point is it simply a story of male domination: men trembled before Brunhild; Heloïse emerges from her letters the very picture of the submissive wife who yet is the guide and leader of the partnership; the wife of the Merchant of Prato held her own against her older, domineering, fussy, tiresome, unfaithful husband. There are some notable sinners among our leading characters, but also numerous saints, and personalities enough to bring the subject to life and force us to ask new and deeper questions about the nature and diversity of women's roles in medieval Europe.

We have brought them together to join in the birthday celebrations of Rosalind Hill. When she retired as professor of history in the university of London in 1976, it was observed that she had completed exactly 39 years in the service of Westfield College, the perfect number for a distinguished Anglican serving an Anglican foundation. She is the symbol of academic *stabilitas*, and her life story is quickly told. She was brought up in the Wirral peninsular in Cheshire—or Merseyside—and in her other family home at Stockbridge in Hampshire; and in Stockbridge she still rules as lady of the manor, with mace and beadle and all the pomp of medieval seignorial authority, solving local disputes and (so legend has it) fining the geese who stray. She studied at St Hilda's, Oxford, where she also completed her first research; then went to Leicester, where she was the first to teach medieval history as a university subject. From Leicester she was summoned, in 1937, by a telegram from the principal of Westfield College; and at Westfield she stayed—teaching in Hampstead, in Oxford where the college lived in dignified exile in the second world war, in Hampstead again and in the university centre in Bloomsbury. But this bare recital of facts hides a life rich in enterprise and achievement. From her early years she has enjoyed climbing in the Lake District; in middle life she took to the Alps for her holidays; and after her retirement, when invited on one occasion to visit Cambridge, she explained that she would be in the Himalayas. Behind the mace at Stockbridge lies a story of quiet charity which will ensure that her name is remembered there. She has always set her standards high, and never ceased to climb; she has always remained the model of charity. She is a scholar of substantial achievement who has inspired two notable learned societies over many years; as lecturer, reader, professor and vice-principal at Westfield she has been in a special way associated with the quality of the college as a place of teaching and learning, a central figure to whom many generations of students look back with special gratitude and affection.

The register of bishop Oliver Sutton of Lincoln has reached its seventh volume, and two more await the printer; meanwhile her work (in collaboration) on the register of archbishop William Melton of York has begun to see the light; and we cannot but think that the bishops would be grateful to shine in the reflected glory of being edited by Rosalind Hill. Melton is being published in her own Canterbury and York Society, over which she has ruled first as editor and then as chairman years out of mind; much of her best work has been done in helping and inspiring other scholars to find her own enthusiasm and skill as an editor. The *Gesta Francorum* leads us to another of her interests, though it is a far cry from the world of the bishop's register—even if she has made us familiar with archbishop Melton setting forth to visit the remote and dangerous archdeaconry of Richmond as the Scottish raiders fell upon the border—to one of the most bloodthirsty of crusading chronicles. Her third field of interest is in Bede's Northumbria: in a series of papers she has shown how the shape of Northumbria and its hills has set its mark on the history of the Northumbrian church; and over a broader area, the way in which Christian influence worked, the actualities of life as the missionaries faced them.

Most characteristic of her is the blending of original work and teaching. Over many years her bishops have mingled with groups of students studying the institutions of the medieval church; the anonymous Norman knight who wrote the *Gesta* has led platoons of students on the first crusade; generations of third-year students have read Bede with her. They read him carefully and imaginatively, with a guide who knew his text from long years of study and meditation; then they went out and walked the Northumbrian hills and went down into the industrial suburbs of Tyneside to search out the remains of Jarrow, and made a pilgrimage to Lindisfarne. The quality of her teaching on Bede, the crusades and the medieval church is quite inseparable from the original work she has done in each field; and the freshness and enthusiasm which generation after generation of her pupils have enjoyed spills over from her teaching into her original papers and books. No doubt it is the union of this enthusiasm and the warmth and charm and kindness which all who come near her feel which explains the spell she has cast over many generations. When she retired as professor there were two great gatherings of students to do her honour: to one came a throng of former pupils, and friends and colleagues who would gladly claim to be her pupils, witnesses of how fresh and warm is her memory among those she has taught; and to the other the current generation of students, bringing clamorous witness that the power of her magic had not diminished.

Among the foundations of her success as a teacher were regular preparation, never stinted, sheer hard work, and a punctuality which could seem ruthless to those less disciplined. Nothing was ever allowed to interfere with the regularity of preparation and performance, save only an unhappy student or a sick animal. In a delicious way, her devotion to animals and to the middle ages are combined in *Both Small and Great Beasts* which she and Fougasse conspired to write for the University Federation for Animal Welfare. 'In a society which accepted without question the fact that Balaam's ass showed a good deal more perception and good sense than Balaam himself, there was much less pitying condescension towards the animal world than there is today' . . . 'As late as the eleventh century there were noble families which proudly boasted descent from a swan or a white bear.' The special care of some saints for animals she traced back behind St Francis to St Cuthbert and to St Pachomius who 'in Miss Waddell's charming phrase, "summoned crocodiles to ferry him as one would call a cab from a rank".' Her treatment of the wandering geese of Stockbridge can be traced to the medieval courts—'You could make a compact with an animal, and . . . could cite him to appear before the ecclesiastical courts if he broke it'. Nor does she disguise the more horrid side of medieval treatment of animals. 'In 1457 a sow was hanged . . for . . . murder . . .', but 'Her six piglets, found guilty of being accessories after the fact, were pardoned because of their extreme youth'.

Quite without sentimentality, brim full of humour, yet barely hiding a great depth of feeling and humanity; it is all very characteristic. Those of us who have been her colleagues in Westfield will count it among the delicious privileges of our lives. Those of us who have worked with her in the Ecclesiastical History Society will carry many vivid memories of her work for it: we have watched her over many years as secretary, president and senior citizen coping with everyone's needs and comfort, feeding us with the fruits of her scholarship, taking on herself, with the sweetest smile of apology, the responsibility for other folk's mistakes. No more congenial task could be found for the Society than to do her honour; and we who have worked with her, taught with her, sat at her feet, boasted that we are her friends, join in summoning Rosalind Hill herself to this festival, in which we celebrate her coming of age in the company of some of her predecessors, the notable women of the middle ages. It is a small token of a very large debt of gratitude, appreciation and warm affection.

University of Cambridge

FEMINAE GLORIOSAE: WOMEN IN THE AGE OF BEDE

by JOAN NICHOLSON

IN 655 king Oswy of Northumbria defeated and killed Penda of Mercia near the river Winwaed. The odds were heavily against Oswy. He faced Mercian forces some three times larger than his own, his nephew Ethelwald had defected and his son Egfrid was currently held hostage by queen Cynewise of Mercia. So depressed had Oswy's power become in the years leading up to 655 that he had even tried, unsuccessfully, to buy off Penda and although the favourable outcome at the Winwaed may have been assisted by the river's bursting its banks, Bede, recording the victory, was inclined to regard the unexpected success as heaven-sent request for fulfilment of a vow Oswy had made, in sheer desperation, to dedicate his daughter to God and to holy virginity if he were victorious. Thus, on a wet November day, the future of the infant Elfled was sealed. Barely a year old, she was consigned to the cloister at Hartlepool, where her aunt Hild presided, and shortly transferred to Hild's new foundation at Whitby where she grew up in the monastery which was to become pre-eminent in the north of England under the rule of its remarkable foundress.[1] The outlook for the tiny princess was not one of solitary gloom.

When Bede wrote his *Historia Ecclesiastica* he looked back, as he thought, to a golden age of monasticism. Self-admittedly concerned with relating good things of good people, he never doubted the piety of Elfled's aunt Ebba, abbess of Coldingham, who apparently did not know what was going on in her own monastery until an Irish ascetic reported that unofficial inspection had found most of the mixed community engaged in bibulous festivity.[2] It is only fair to add that Bede's picture of unmitigated dissipation aimed at accounting for divine retribution in the form of fire which destroyed the monastery after Ebba died and although Symeon of Durham, writing after the Norman reorganisation of the English church, attributed Cuthbert's

[1] Bede, *HE,* [ed C.] Plummer, [*Venerabilis Baedae Opera Historica*] (Oxford 1896) pp 177–8.

[2] *Ibid* p 265.

aversion to women to the immorality he found at Coldingham,[3] Bede, who was in a good position to know, records no such reaction. Nor was its reputation sufficiently bad to deter the saintly Ethelthryth from choosing to enter there.[4] Yet if religious houses were not dens of iniquity, neither were bare boards and hair-shirts the order of seventh-century mixed monasticism. Two of abbess Verca's priests were agreeably surprised by the excellent wine provided by Cuthbert at South Shields[5] and Guthlac, seeking austerity, soon abandoned Repton for the rigours of an antique grave-barrow in the fens, having made himself thoroughly unpopular with the community by setting an example of abstinence from intoxicating drink.[6] At Whitby, Caedmon fled to the stables rather than take his turn at singing to the harp in entertainments at dinner.[7] Ebba's nuns were charged with sewing stylish garments more fitting to brides of the world than to brides of Christ[8] and Aldhelm of Malmesbury warned the sisters at Barking to keep well away from manicures and curling tongs.[9] Austerity was difficult to impose on aristocratic youngsters accustomed to the sort of lifestyle reflected at Sutton Hoo and, in an age when monasteries performed the combined functions of orphanage and boarding-school, it is hardly surprising to find nuns like Ebba's committed to the cloister as children and subsequently lacking vocation. Although Boniface opted voluntarily for religious life aged four or five and was hindered thereafter only by his father's reluctance,[10] Wilfrid of Ripon dealt summarily with a mother who went back on a promise to give him her seven-year-old by sending his reeve to seize the boy by force.[11] Parents were readier to part with daughters and, before monastic facilities became available in England, shipped their girls off to France.[12] The princess Elfled was fortunate enough to be placed in her home

[3] Symeon of Durham, *Historia Ecclesiae Dunhelmensis*, ed T. Arnold, *RS* 75 (1882) 1 p 59.

[4] Bede, *HE* p 243.

[5] B[ede,] *V*[*ita Sancti*] *C*[*uthberti*], ed and trans B. Colgrave, *Two Lives of Saint Cuthbert* (Cambridge 1940) pp 264, 266.

[6] *V*[*ita Sancti*] *G*[*uthlaci Auctore*] *F*[*elice*], ed B. Colgrave, *Felix's Life of Saint Guthlac* (Cambridge 1956) p 84.

[7] Bede, *HE* p 259.

[8] *Ibid* p 265.

[9] *A*[*ldhelmi*] *O*[*pera*], ed R. Ehwald *MGH AA* 15 (Berlin 1919) p 318.

[10] *V*[*ita*] *B*[*onifatii Auctore*] *W*[*illibaldo*], ed G. H. Pertz *MGH SS* 2 (Hanover 1829) p 335.

[11] *E*[*ddius Stephanus*], *V*[*ita*] *W*[*ilfridi Episcopi*], ed and trans B. Colgrave, *The Life of Bishop Wilfrid by Eddius Stephanus* (Cambridge 1927). pp 38, 40.

[12] Bede, *HE* p 142.

country: Hild, electing to enter religious life in 647, had been prepared to join her sister at Chelles until Aidan persuaded her of the opportunities locally. Heiu, said to be the first Northumbrian woman to take the veil, had founded Hartlepool shortly before Hild took over and set the fashion for double monasteries ruled by royal or noble abbesses[13]

Augustine had brought Roman grandeur to Kent while Celtic asceticism flourished in the remote west. Two separately developed streams of religious culture collided in Northumbria, resulting in compromise. Under the rule of Hild, Whitby was no doubt better-run than Coldingham, although Elfled did not grow up in an environment detached from the secular world. Religious houses provided useful stopping-places for itinerant royalty and she probably saw her mother, queen Eanfled, from time to time: her father and brother were at Whitby for the fateful synod in 664,[14] Aidan frequently visited Hild, kings and princes came to her for advice. The monastery played a major intellectual role in a newly-literate society: eminent men received education and training under Hild's supervision.[15] When Caedmon was reported to have acquired a talent for composing religious verse in the vernacular, the abbess quickly took him under her wing, recognising a medium by which Christianity might be taught to the laity.[16] Hild had been among the first Northumbrian converts to receive baptism in 627 with her great-uncle, Edwin of Deira, at the hands of Paulinus, the Roman missionary who had come with Edwin's Christian bride from Kent.[17] By 664, much water had flowed along the Trent since the mass baptisms performed therein by Paulinus in sweeping but impermanent missionary enterprise. Change of dynasty in 633 from the Deiran to the Bernician royal line brought brief apostasy followed by Celtic missionaries in the wake of king Oswald, exiled in Iona during Edwin's reign.[18] Hild, baptised into the Roman church, was subsequently instructed by Aidan and, at the synod of Whitby, threw in her weight with the Celtic party against the ubiquitous Wilfrid who now questioned time-honoured customs on the authority of some remote man in Rome.[19] Wilfrid was a protégé of Eanfled who, raised in Kent, observed the lenten fast by the Roman

13 *Ibid* p 253.
14 *Ibid* p 182.
15 *Ibid* pp 253–4.
16 *Ibid* p 260.
17 *Ibid* p 252.
18 *Ibid* pp 127–8.
19 *Ibid* p 183.

calender while her husband feasted according to Celtic reckoning. Oswy, who had the final say, decided in favour of his wife's system of easter calculation, being persuaded that saint Peter would more willingly unlock the gates of heaven to those who did as the Romans do.[20] The pope, in his congratulatory letter to Oswy, appropriately enclosed a cross with a gold key for Eanfled.[21] Hild was obliged to accept the royal decision and thereafter Whitby observed Roman custom, but she continued to oppose Wilfrid to the end of her life, sending representatives to Rome in 679 when he appealed to the apostolic see against deposition.[22] Hild, then, was conservative although her attitude may have been influenced by family affiliations. Of the Deiran royal house, she had been born while the family was in exile during the reign of Ethelfrid of Bernicia and Oswy was Ethelfrid's son. Whatever lay behind her dislike of Oswy's friend Wilfrid, she passed on her prejudice to Elfled who was among those to whom archbishop Theodore wrote in 686 urging reconciliation with the prelate who had turned out to be something of a mixed blessing to the Northumbrian royal family.[23]

Elfled had succeeded as abbess of Whitby jointly with her mother after Hild died in 680.[24] Theodore's proscription of hereditary succession in monasteries received scant attention from a lay and ecclesiastical hierarchy who, adapting to the requirements of a new faith, proceeded to adapt its institutions to their own requirements.[25] Ethelthryth was succeeded at her foundation of Ely by her sister;[26] John of Beverley, arriving fortuitously at Watton, was able to cure a sick nun so that she might follow her mother as abbess.[27] Rulers adopted Christianity for the advantages which might accrue and one of these was the double monastery which provided the female element of the ruling caste with something to rule. The great abbess moving into the seat of power needed more than piety and vocation. Elfled had long training: Ethelthryth left her husband and the Northumbrian royal court for a one-year novitiate before becoming abbess at her own foundation and, in ruling Ely, her years as a reigning queen probably

[20] *Ibid* pp 188–9; *EVW* p 22.
[21] Bede, *HE* p 198.
[22] *EVW* p 116.
[23] *Ibid* p 88.
[24] Bede, *HE* p 267.
[25] [A. W.] Haddan and [W.] Stubbs, [*Councils and Ecclesiastical Documents*] (Oxford 1964) 3 p 195.
[26] Bede, *HE* p 244.
[27] *Ibid* p 286.

served her better than her years of prayer and chastity.[28] Although Coldingham, the only named religious house associated with scandal in Bede's writings, may not have been typical, the difficulties of maintaining order in communities of high-spirited girls were reflected at Wimborne where young nuns gleefully desecrated the grave of an over-zealous disciplinarian.[29] Rudolf, writing Leoba's *vita* many years after she died, described strict segregation at Wimborne where abbess Tetta, determined to preserve the purity of her female congregation, denied entry not only to laymen and clerics but even to bishops.[30] This may have been wishful hindsight: total segregation of the sexes is not typical of monastic scenes which Bede presents. Monks and nuns occupied separate living quarters—the plague hit the men's section first at Barking although the abbess was in no doubt that it would spread into the women's[31]—and Hild built a cell at Hackness where the sisters might go into retreat but the brothers who went there to report that Hild had died conversed directly with the sisters.[32] It was no use entering a monastery to get away from men and doubtful whether anyone really wanted to. Men and women worked together in the secular world and proceeded to do likewise in the cloister. Nuns staffed the nursery section;[33] men were needed for rough work on monastic lands. Caedmon looked after the stables at Whitby[34] and Cuthbert, dining with Elfled on one of her estates where he had come to dedicate a church, ruined a perfectly good meal by announcing that one of her shepherds had fallen to his death from a tree.[35] Men might set up in all-male houses but an isolated community of women only invited trouble in an age of violence and endemic warfare. One of Columba's miracles rested casually upon an incident when two clerics were unable to protect a girl from an armed pursuer.[36] If Cuthbert was able to take a solitary midnight dip in the North Sea,[37] a woman's

[28] *Ibid* pp 243–4.
[29] *V[ita] L[eobae Abbatissae Biscofesheimansis Auctore] R[udolfo] MGH SS*, ed G. Waitz, 15 (Hanover 1887) 1 p 123.
[30] *Ibid* p 123.
[31] Bede, *HE* p 219.
[32] *Ibid* p 257.
[33] *Ibid* p 220.
[34] *Ibid* p 259.
[35] *A[nonymous], V[ita Sancti] C[uthberti Auctore Anonymo]*, ed and trans B. Colgrave, *Two Lives of Saint Cuthbert* (Cambridge 1940) p 126; *BVC* p 262.
[36] *Ad[omnan,] V[ita] C[olumbani]*, ed and trans A. O. and M. O. Anderson (Edinburgh/London 1961) p 382.
[37] *BVC* p 188; *AVC* p 80.

safety depended on numbers which included the male element although religious houses were not always safe havens: Cuthbert had to provide village accommodation for nuns fleeing from a Pictish army.[38] If Bede, recording with horror Cadwallon's ravages, felt that women merited special consideration,[39] Ethelbert's code of law specified injury compensation for a single woman on a scale equal to a man's, which suggests female vulnerability as much as sexual equality.[40] Mixed monasticism was dictated by practical necessity although Bede's letter to his pupil Egbert, written shortly before he died, expressed the dangers inherent in the system. Lesser people than royalty came to see that they were on to a good thing: turning the family home into a monastery meant that they could pursue normal family life and at the same time evade the expense of military service.[41]

Half a century earlier Theodore had tried to discourage mixed houses but had been obliged to concede to established custom.[42] Founded initially by royalty and nobility whose anxiety to save their souls was matched by anxiety to see a decent return on capital investment, monasteries housed daughters who did not or would not marry; they fulfilled the functions of old people's homes where aging kings, worn out by battle, and noble dowagers no longer up to the itinerant life of the royal or aristocratic court might end their days in comfort and receive nursing care if needed. Bede was all in favour of virginity and some women may have agreed that celibacy was preferable to secular conjugality with its inevitable and dangerous pregnancies. In an age of arranged marriage, entry into religious life also provided respectable grounds for divorce from an unchosen and unattractive partner: Columba had to discourage a wife wishing to take the veil because she found her husband repulsive.[43] Theodore's *Penitential* allowed abandonment of marriage for the cloister provided both partners consented[44] and Offa of the East Saxons left his wife and went to Rome without any recorded marital opposition,[45] but it took king Sebbi of the East Saxons many years to persuade his queen to release him for

[38] *BVC* p 254.
[39] Bede, *HE* p 125.
[40] [*The Laws of the Earliest English Kings*, ed F. L.] Attenborough (Cambridge 1922) [Lawcode of] Ethelbert cap 74.
[41] *Epistola Bede ad Egbertum Episcopum*, ed Plummer, pp 415–16.
[42] Haddan and Stubbs 3 p 195.
[43] *AdVC* p 438.
[44] Haddan and Stubbs 3 p 200.
[45] Bede, *HE* p 322.

monastic vows, greatly to Bede's disapproval.[46] She may have had the interests of the kingdom in mind: there was a limit to how saintly a king was allowed to be. Sigebert of East Anglia, drawn reluctantly from monastic retreat to lead his army, lost the battle and the kingdom.[47] Bede was lukewarm when piety was carried to such excessive lengths as to interfere with kingly office but equally unenthusiastic when piety was thwarted. One Northumbrian woman who remained loyally at her husband's sick bed made no protest when recovering he promptly abandoned her for an eremitic life: she received a third-share of her husband's goods, which Bede regarded as fair compensation[48] and his ideal women were those like Ethelthryth who was given in marriage to Egfrid and spent the following twelve years adamantly refusing to consummate the marriage.[49] The bridegroom was only fifteen and Ethelthryth, who was older, had been married before. Thus her motives for taking the veil may have been mixed although according to Bede she became a pious abbess who abjured linen garments for coarse wool and restricted herself to three hot baths a year.[50] Such were expectations of piety in a society where the ruling caste confirmed its role by ostentatious display. Ethelthryth opted for austerity and, remorseful about worldly ornament incumbent upon her as a princess in Suffolk before she went north and met up with Celtic asceticism, attributed the neck tumour of which she died to unnecessary weight of jewellery worn in youth.[51] Iurminburg, second wife to Ethelthryth's divorced husband, played safe by appropriating Wilfrid's reliquary, which offered double benefit of personal adornment and medical protection, and even wore it in bed[52] but failed to provide Egfrid with an heir.

Infant mortality was high and infanticide was not unknown, although sources suggest that Christianity encouraged the practice rather than curbed it. Boniface, trying to reform the lascivious Ethelbald, condemned murder of illegitimate babies born to nuns[53] and the local women who found a dead infant in the river near Bischofsheim immediately accused the sisters.[54] Theodore's *Penitential* imposed

[46] *Ibid* p 225.
[47] *Ibid* p 163.
[48] *Ibid* pp 303–4.
[49] *Ibid* p 243.
[50] *Ibid* p 244.
[51] *Ibid* p 246.
[52] *EVW* p 70.
[53] Haddan and Stubbs 3 p 354.
[54] *VLR* p 128.

penance for infanticide but made concessions to poverty[55] and some deaths may have been caused by ignorance rather than by intent on the part of mothers given to such remedies as placing children on roofs and in ovens to cure fever.[56] Willibald, describing Boniface's childhood, took it for granted that his mother exercised normal watchful care[57]; Aldhelm of Malmesbury found an analogy he needed in that of the loving female caring for children[58] and, in general, contemporary writers display high expectations of parental love. Bede certainly cited parents as being loving of their children of either sex: Edwin was delighted when Eanfled was born and, not yet himself converted to Christianity but about to fight a battle, offered her for baptism with much the same sort of hopes as Oswy donating Elfled.[59] Might he have been less eager in the case of a son? If daughters might gainfully be used as propitiatory offerings, they were also useful political assets: at Hrothgar's court, Beowulf was entertained by queen Wealtheow who had established peace between peoples.[60] Hrothgar settled a feud by promising his daughter to the son of his one-time enemy but the perils attendant on a royal bride taking her retinue into a formerly hostile court were voiced by Beowulf. Wages of warfare being booty, if it turned up on the person of a retainer who had once fought on the other side, old resentments quickly flared up.[61] Vengeance for death of a kinsman was basic to Germanic tribal custom and churchmen struggled long and hard to substitute money compensation for bloodfeud. Northumbria and Mercia were old enemies and it seemed to Bede a great step forward when archbishop Theodore persuaded Egfrid to accept wergild from Ethelred of Mercia for a young brother killed in battle,[62] but Egfrid's sister Osthryth was married to Ethelred and some twenty years later she was murdered by the Mercian nobility.[63] Bede, not concerned with giving details of violent deaths unless they provided clear examples of divine vengeance, recorded her fate in a chronological summary but she was most likely a victim of human vengeance bedevilled by recollection of another of Oswy's daughters given in marriage to the Mercian prince Peada and involved, some three years

[55] Haddan and Stubbs 3 p 189.
[56] *Ibid* p 190.
[57] *VBW* p 334.
[58] *AO* p 501.
[59] Bede, *HE* p 99.
[60] [*Beowulf and Judith*, ed E. V. K.] Dobbie (New York 1953) line 2017.
[61] *Ibid* lines 2032–66.
[62] Bede, *HE* p 249.
[63] *Ibid* p 355.

after, in his murder by treachery.[64] The miseries of a wife persecuted by her husband's hostile kin were recorded in the *Wife's Lament*[65] and in a society clinging to tribal traditions based on kinship and vendetta, intermarriage among rival dynasties brought problems. Secular law-codes, attempting to substitute wergild for bloodfeud, still stressed the kinship responsibility for providing for children of widows,[66] but although Ethelberg fled to Kent after Edwin died, her brother offered no protection to his Deiran nephew, who was sent to Gaul for safety.[67] Eadbald was more interested in keeping well in with Oswald of Bernicia. He allowed his niece Eanfled to remain in Kent and later married her off to Oswald's brother and successor Oswy.[68] Thus Eanfled proved well worth her keep: Eadbald cemented the Kentish-Northumbrian alliance against the ever-threatening Mercia and Oswy got a bride of the Deiran royal blood.

Bede preferred to cite examples where conversion was a condition of acquiring a Christian bride, although dynastic marriages dictated by political factors do not reflect a race of downtrodden women. The bridegroom was in pretty much the same boat: young prince Egfrid was married off to Ethelthryth who firmly refused to have anything to do with him and Oswy, seeking a bride who would endear him to the Deirans, was obliged to take Eanfled whether he liked her or not. Secular codes of law regarded a wife as a valuable commodity, although replaceable. Purchase carried a legal guarantee of satisfaction or money back, and a man who committed adultery was obliged to supply the wronged husband with a substitute wife.[69] Bede, who considered heavenly espousal greatly preferable to secular marriage, probably had a good point: Elfled, married off to the heavenly bridegroom, may well have had the best of both worlds. The alternative, for a princess, was marriage to the earthly bridegroom chosen by the family. Conversion was incumbent on the heathen ruler who acquired a Christian bride and in this respect women played a major part in the propagation of Christianity, although they sometimes needed outside support. Elfled's great-grandmother, a Frankish princess, brought her own bishop with her to Kent but required Augustine with the weight of

[64] *Ibid* p 180.
[65] [*Anglo-Saxon Poetry*, trans R. K.] Gordon (London 1926) pp 79–80.
[66] Attenborough, Hlothere and Eadric cap 6, Ine cap 38.
[67] Bede, *HE* p 126.
[68] *Ibid* p 157.
[69] Attenborough, Ethelbert caps 30, 31.

the apostolic see behind him to achieve conversion of her husband.[70] She may have had a hand in the sending of Augustine: it is hard to believe that happy accident brought the Roman mission to the one place in England where they were not going to get the sort of reception Wilfrid got from the South Saxons some seventy years later.[71] Bede's famous account of the king, suspicious of the outlandish religion, interviewing Augustine in the open air, may be apocryphal,[72] but anyone who has walked from the walls of Canterbury to Saint Martin's church, where Bertha worshipped, would agree that her God had been put at a safe distance. After Ethelbert's baptism, the pope wrote to Bertha complaining that she had not converted him sooner,[73] but they were up against conservative opposition: even their son Eadbald, Ethelbert's successor, was heathen[74] and half a century later Eorconbert went down in history as the first English king to ban idols.[75] Eadbald was later converted, allegedly by bishop Laurentius employing miraculous aids which leave a yawning credibility gap,[76] although he also seems to have acquired a Christian wife,[77] which might have had something to do with his change of heart. He gave his sister Ethelberg Elfled's grandmother, in marriage to Edwin of Deira[78] who was, after considerable heart-searching and at least two narrow escapes from premature death, persuaded to adopt his wife's faith.[79] It is not possible to know how far Ethelberg influenced Edwin in this, although when king Redwald returned from Kent having been baptised, his pagan wife soon dissuaded him from such dangerous novelty.[80] Ethelberg was no fool: she took Edwin's treasure with her in the hasty flight to Kent after the king's death at Hatfield,[81] in which battle Eadfrid, son of Edwin's previous marriage, fought against his father.[82]

[70] Bede, *HE* p 45.
[71] *EVW* pp 26, 28.
[72] Bede, *HE* p 45.
[73] Haddan and Stubbs 3 p 17.
[74] Bede, *HE* p 90.
[75] *Ibid* p 142.
[76] *Ibid* pp 92–3.
[77] William of Malmesbury, *De gestis regum anglorum,* ed W. Stubbs, *Willelmi Malmesbiriensis Monachi, RS* 90 (1887) 1 p 15; Haddan and Stubbs 3 p 70. A spurious charter in which *Emma, Francorum regis filia, regis Eadbaldi copula* appears on the witness list seems to support William of Malmesbury.
[78] Bede, *HE* p 97.
[79] *Ibid* pp 106–13.
[80] *Ibid* p 116.
[81] *Ibid* p 126.
[82] *Ibid* p 124.

Oswy's son by an Irish marriage was kept well out of the Northumbrian scene until Eanfled's sons were all dead.[83] Mother and daughter may have been ambitious for their own children. The leaven of Christianity did not eliminate the wicked stepmother: Wilfrid left home to escape from his, although she probably found him as insufferable as Hild and Iurminburg did.[84]

The major role played by women in Germanic society impressed the Roman Tacitus in the first century AD and sources suggest that their descendants in seventh-century England were no less influential. Eanfled persuaded her husband to part with lands for a monastery in atonement for the death of his kinsman Oswini[85] although Oswy was not generous in gifts to the church: it was left to Wilfrid to restore the church Paulinus had built at York.[86] Redwald's wife dissuaded him from dishonourable betrayal of Edwin, granted asylum in the East Anglian court, to Ethelfrid of Bernicia.[87] Columba assured a fugitive that his persecutor would be persuaded by his wife to let him go free.[88] The feminine role is echoed in secular verse: gnomic poetry states that a noblewoman shall give wise council[89] and Hrothgar's queen reminded her husband of his obligations and graciously encouraged Beowulf.[90] Elfled, pleading on Wilfrid's behalf at the synod on the Nidd in 705, drew Eddi's praise as always the finest counsellor of the entire province[91] and king Egfrid listened meekly enough when his aunt Ebba rebuked him for his treatment of Wilfrid and proceeded to mend his ways.[92] Eddi saw Iurminburg as the evil genius at the root of Egfrid's hostility towards Wilfrid: there was no refuge for the prelate in Kent, where her sister was queen, nor in Mercia, where her sister-in-law reigned.[93] Biased as Eddi was against any who opposed Wilfrid, there may have been some truth in his allegations: after Osthryth died Ethelred of Mercia welcomed Wilfrid.[94] There was much scope for friction between Wilfrid and Iurminburg. Eddi charged her with jealousy of

83 *Ibid* p 268.
84 *EVW* p 6.
85 Bede, *HE* p 180.
86 *EVW* p 6.
87 Bede, *HE* p 110.
88 *AdVC* p 425.
89 Gordon p 311.
90 Dobbie lines 615–18.
91 *EVW* p 128.
92 *Ibid* p 78.
93 *Ibid* p 80.
94 *Ibid* p 92.

the prelate's wealth but she was a friend of Cuthbert and may well have disapproved of Wilfrid's ecclesiastical pomp and display. Wilfrid, who had himself turned down the offer of a noble wife in Gaul,[95] would certainly have encouraged Ethelthryth in her intention to leave Egfrid for religious life and, a purist, probably disapproved of the king's second marriage to Iurminburg, although canon law allowed it. Wilfrid's pious asceticism did not prevent his dabbling in secular matters when his influence was useful: he had a hand in restoration of king Dagobert II to the Austrasian throne and helped Cadwalla seize the West Saxon crown.[96] Religion and politics were inseparable. Queen Osthryth of Mercia transferred the bones of her uncle Oswald to her favourite monastery of Bardney in Lindsey and encountered opposition from a monastic community who recalled with resentment days of Northumbrian domination, but Osthryth succeeded in habilitating the relics of her sainted Northumbrian uncle in an independent corner currently under Mercian domination at a time when Mercia and Northumbria were trying to live at peace.[97] Eanfled and Elfled transferred to Whitby the relics of their renowned ancestor Edwin of Northumbria, a reminder of where local loyalties lay when royal succession was uncertain and Deira and Bernicia likely to split apart in the absence of an heir to Egfrid.[98] The abbess Elfled kept well in touch with Northumbrian politics, and when Cuthbert refused the bishopric of Lindisfarne offered by her brother Egfrid she persuaded the saint to leave his retreat and meet her on Coquet island, midway between Farne and Whitby, where discussion on the royal succession was concluded by a straight question from the abbess as to whether Cuthbert would reconsider his refusal of episcopal office.[99] She had good reason for concern. Egfrid had proved a hot-headed ruler in need of a strong restraining influence. Having invaded Ireland in the previous year, much against the advice of his councellors, he now proposed to march against the Picts, again against the advice of his counsellors who, significantly, included Cuthbert.[100] Churchmen, however saintly and reluctant, were inevitably drawn into matters of secular administration as advisers to rulers and Bede, writing a history of

[95] *Ibid* p 10.
[96] *Ibid* pp 54, 84.
[97] Bede, *HE* p 148.
[98] *The Earliest Life of Gregory the Great by an Anonymous Monk of Whitby*, ed B. Colgrave (Lawrence 1968) p 103.
[99] *BVC* pp 234, 236; *AVC* pp 102, 104.
[100] Bede, *HE* pp 266–7.

religion, produced a history of politics which nicely presents incubation of the situation which would later evoke the Gregorian reform movement. Cuthbert was consecrated bishop but it was too late. Egfrid over-reached himself shortly afterwards and died at Nechtansmere in battle against the Picts, during which time Iurminburg, taking advantage of the hospitality offered by her sister's monastery, was joined by Cuthbert at Carlisle. Advising her to retreat to Bamborough for her material safety, the bishop, ever-mindful of his spiritual responsibilities, added a warning against Sunday travel: hurry she must, but not until Monday.[101]

Even on weekdays it was probably safer to stay at home. *A roving woman causes words to be uttered* declared the all-wise gnomic poet.[102] An Irish ascetic might opt for the peripatetic life but a woman's place was in the home and it is precisely there that we find the secular women who crop up in the course of Bede's miracle stories, whether an earl's wife serving drinks to the men at dinner or a village dweller trying to persuade Cuthbert to break his fast and have a square meal before setting off into the wilderness.[103] Royal and noble women had several homes and travelled about locally: the abbess Elfled moved around the estates attached to Whitby,[104] queen Osthryth made a stay at Bardney,[105] Egfrid and Iurminburg were at Coldingham in the course of royal progress.[106] The monastery was a useful establishment in the pre-hotel era. By the late 680s kings were opting to go to Rome to die and in the following century a sufficient number of women were subscribing to the tourist trade for Boniface to ask archbishop Cuthbert whether matrons and nuns could possibly be restrained from making frequent trips to Rome.[107] Even the abbess Eadburga, a lady above reproach, received little encouragement when she wrote announcing her intention of going on pilgrimage. If she felt she absolutely must go, grumbled Boniface, at least she should delay until the Saracen danger abated.[108] To Cuthbert he was more candid about the nature of dangers threatening female pilgrims: *quia magna ex parte pereunt, paucis remanentibus integris.*[109]

[101] *BVC* pp 242, 244.
[102] Gordon pp 79–80.
[103] *BVC* p 168.
[104] *BVC* p 262; *AVC* p 126.
[105] Bede, *HE* p 149.
[106] *EVW* p 78.
[107] Haddan and Stubbs 3 p 381.
[108] *S. Bonifatii et Lulli epistolae*, ed E Dümmler, *MGH Epp* 3 (Berlin 1892) p 278.
[109] Haddan and Stubbs p 381.

The seventh-century abbesses of whom Bede wrote were not apparently subject to such temptations. Bernard of Clairvaux lay far in the future. Cuthbert's sanctity was never threatened by the women with whom he was so friendly: the misogynist seems to have emerged after some three hundred years of posthumous reflection. Felix of Crowland recorded Guthlac's life of solitude in the fens disturbed by a devil in the form of a male cleric who lusted for his blood, not a seductress lusting for his body.[110] Guthlac most gratefully accepted the coffin sent to him by abbess Egburh,[111] and his dying thoughts were for his sister Pega who, told of his death, fell to the ground unconscious with grief for an appropriate time although her brother had avoided her all his life—not, it should be added, from any aversion to women: he hoped to spend eternity with her in heaven.[112] Trumwine, forced to abandon Abercorn after Egfrid stirred up the Picts, made straight for Whitby and remained there assisting Eanfled and Elfled until he died.[113] Seventh-century saints had their problems no doubt but they were not the sort faced later by Perceval and Bors after responsibility for Adam's fall had been laid squarely on Eve's shoulders.

Bede, putting the finishing touches to his *Historia Ecclesiastica* in the eighth century might have been gratified to know that he would continue to be read in the twentieth, although the information which modern readers seek from his text is hardly that which he set out to give. Anyone interested in queen Osthryth and her difficulties with the Bardney community can only be disappointed to find a stark notice of her death in a chronological summary which tells little more than that life might be nasty, brutish and short no less for a queen than for a commoner. Bede's inclusion of Osthryth was solely for the purpose of recounting miracles connected with Oswald's relics and he was no more concerned with personality behind noble piety than Eddi describing Iurminburg as she-wolf, wicked Jezebel, sorceress and, in the same breath, perfect abbess and excellent mother of her community.[114] Polemic and praise suggest only that Iurminburg was a formidable women with a personality which might have clashed with that of Eanfled, the queen-mother, whose withdrawal to Whitby left the royal court clear for her reigning son's wife. Iurminburg herself

[110] *VGF* p 112.
[111] *Ibid* p 146.
[112] *Ibid* pp 154, 158.
[113] Bede, *HE* pp 267–8.
[114] *EVW* p 48.

retreated to a monastery after her husband's half-brother succeeded to the Northumbrian throne. Elfled, abbess of Whitby and princess-royal, displayed a keen interest in secular politics. Ethelthryth, whose iron will opposed the conjugal demands of Egfrid for twelve years, took herself off to Ely and Ebba, ready enough to give her nephew the length of her tongue, had Coldingham to keep her busy. The Anglo-Saxon double monastery, as orphanage, boarding-school, old people's home, hotel and, not least, avenue of occupation for meddlesome women, must have been the greatest single blessing bestowed by Christianity on God's seventh-century Englishmen.

University of London
Westfield College

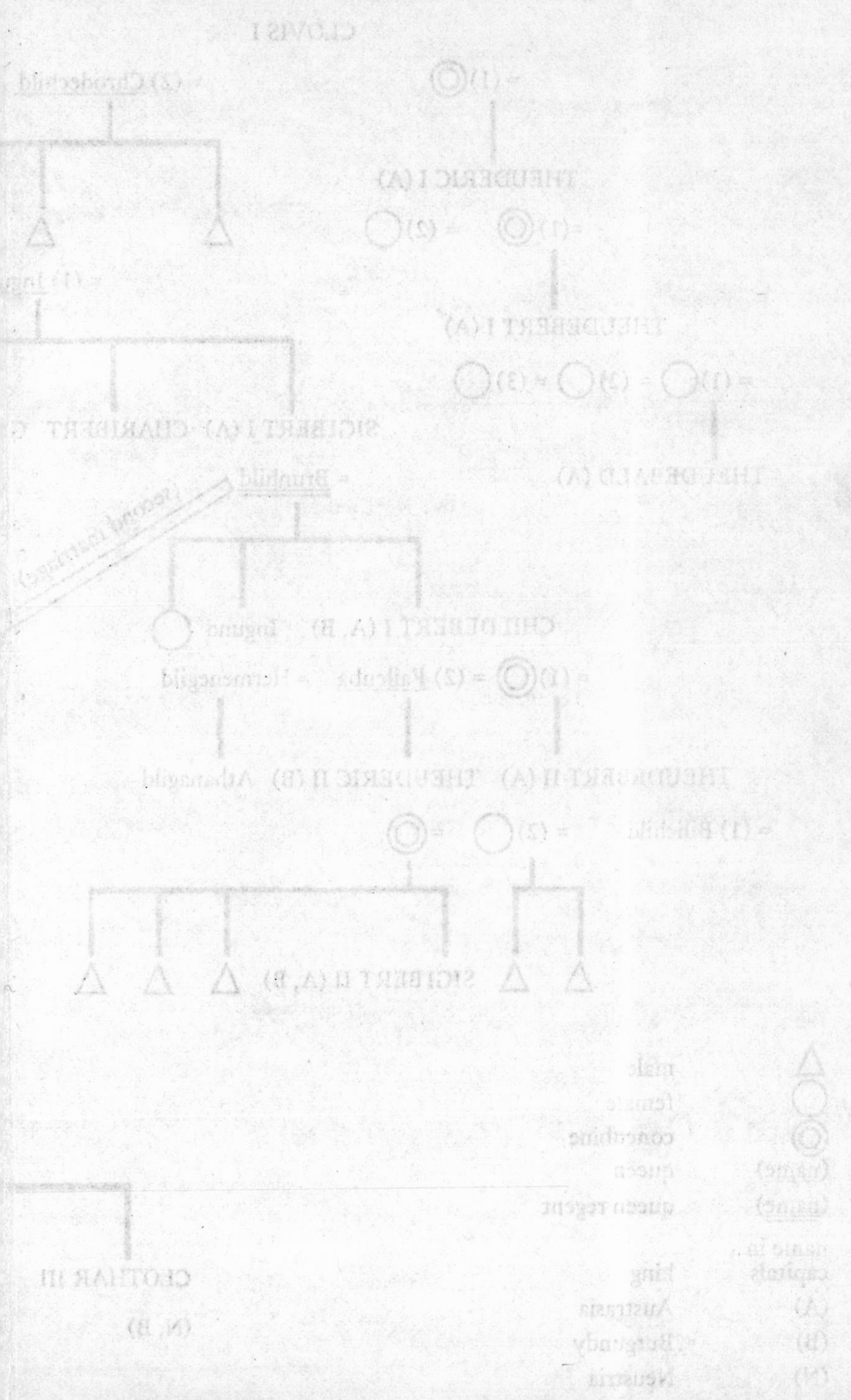

Table showing the Merovingians, their que

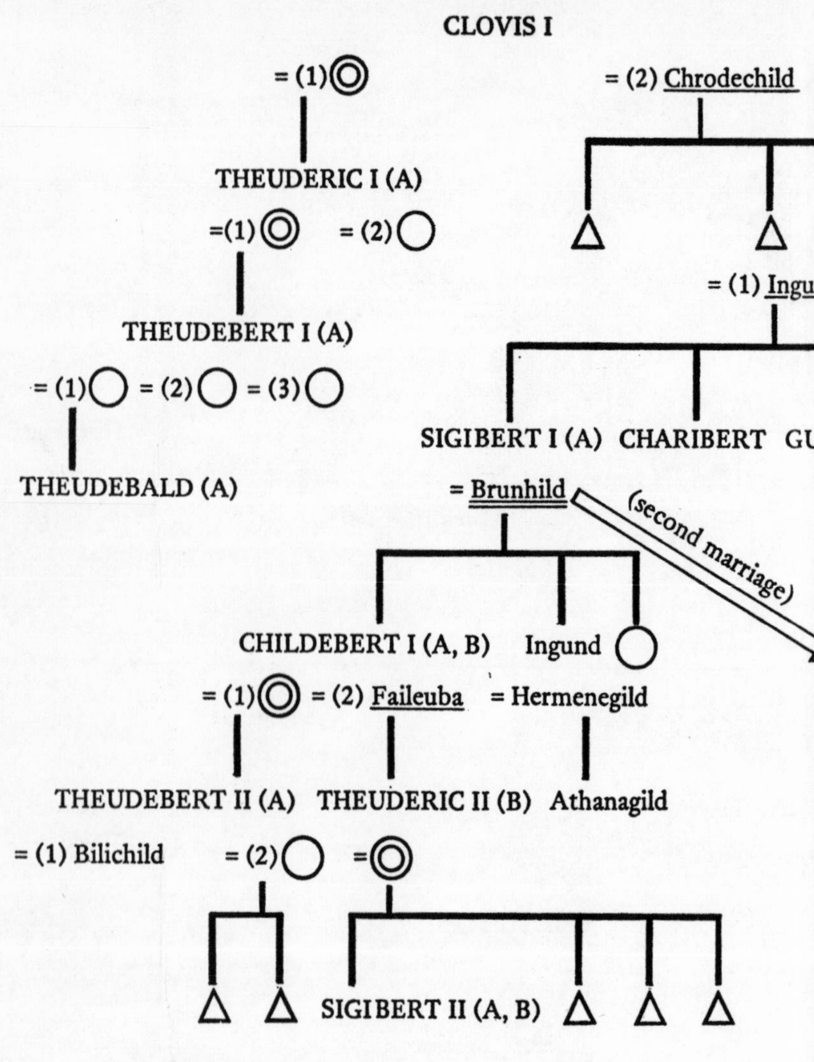

△	male
○	female
◎	concubine
(name)	queen
(name)	queen regent
name in capitals	king
(A)	Austrasia
(B)	Burgundy
(N)	Neustria

CLOTHAR III

(N, B)

s and concubines, dealt with in this paper.

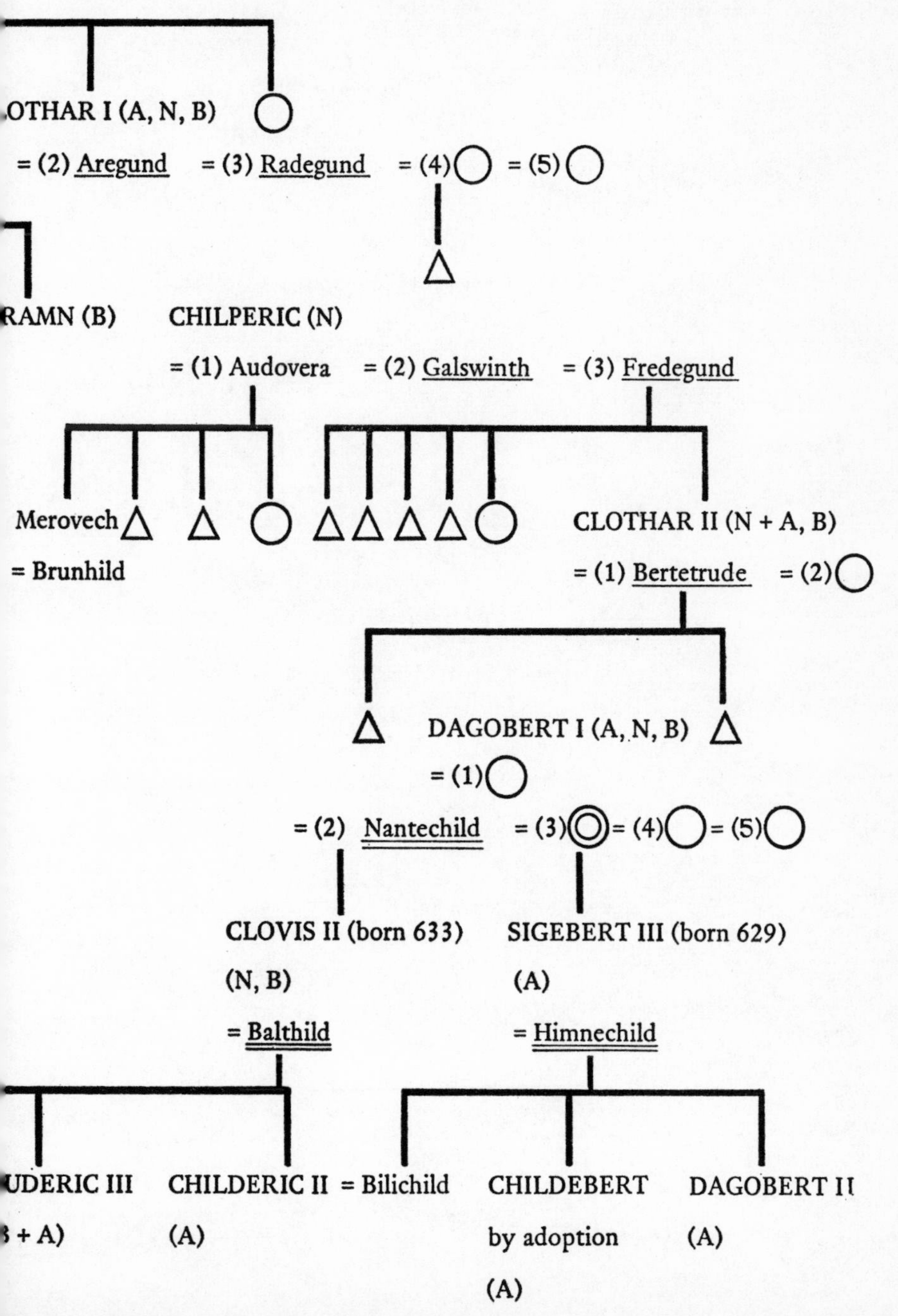

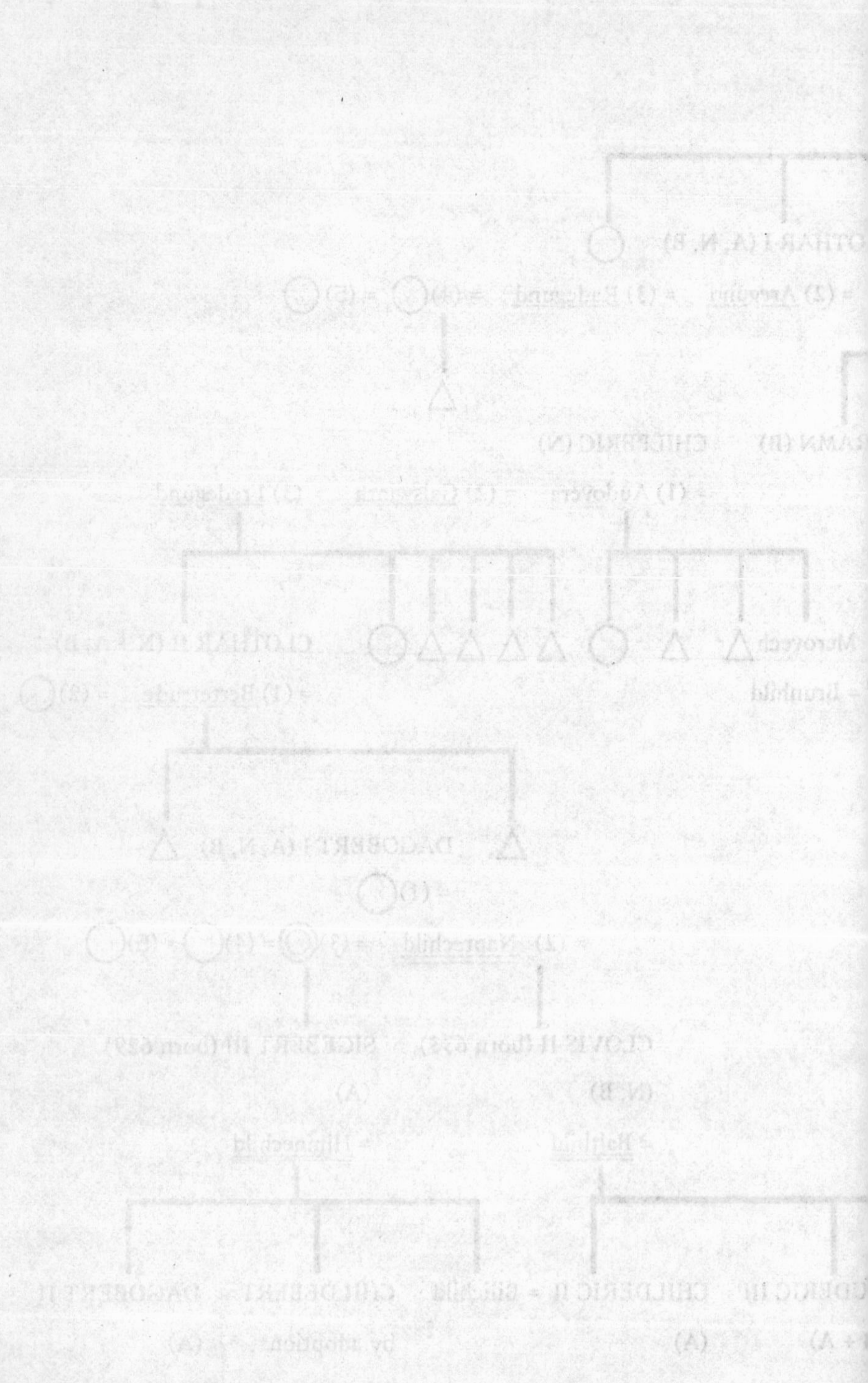

QUEENS AS JEZEBELS: THE CAREERS OF BRUNHILD AND BALTHILD IN MEROVINGIAN HISTORY.[1]

by JANET L. NELSON

SINCE they got a toe-hold in universities, the achievement of women in the field of medieval history has been high. Some female historiography may have been justly criticised for a certain breathlessness of style, a narrowness of concern, a subjectivity, even romanticism, of approach: faults produced, no doubt by the pressures of most women's early socialisation.[2] But the work of Rosalind Hill has shown an exemplary freedom from the faults and contributed substantially to the achievement. The combination of good sense and judgement with breadth of vision might perhaps have been expected from that rare person (of either sex) who can combine scholarly excellence with prowess in mountaineering. And so, despite its title, the paper that follows, in which I deal with the careers of two very active and intelligent women who commanded both the respect and the affection of many contemporaries (however unfairly posterity has treated them) will not, I hope, be thought a wholly inapt tribute.

That women played a 'large role' in Merovingian society is a commonplace of the historiography of the period. Queens Brunhild and Balthild[3] have been cited as cases in point. But if it is important to stress at the outset the obvious point that queens are not typical of women in this or any other period, it is also worth pursuing a little further the banal observation about the 'large role' of women to inquire *which* women appear as significant actors in the later sixth and seventh centuries, and why they do so. Some women sometimes found

[1] I am very grateful to Ian Wood, John Gillingham and Pauline Stafford for friendly criticism, and to Paul Fouracre for keen discussion of Merovingian matters.

[2] On some problems (if not the faults) of historical work by and about women, see the comments of [Susan Mosher] Stuard in her introduction to *Women* [*in Medieval Society*] (University of Pennsylvania Press 1976) pp 1–12. For some lively criticisms of the male-dominated historiography of women, see the remarks of Ria Lemaire in *CCM* 20 (1977) pp 261–3.

[3] For the sake of simplicity I have used anglicised spellings of these and other familiar names.

themselves in positions of wealth and potential power: they were those who belonged to a land-based aristocracy whose members generally married within their own ranks.[4] These women—as wives, bringers of dowries and receivers of bride-wealth, as widows and mothers (or stepmothers) custodians of family estates, as daughters heiresses to some or all of their parents' wealth—shared the status of their male kin, and had to be protected and provided for. If women loom so large in the history of Columbanan monasticism in seventh-century Gaul, this was not, I think, because 'women, especially, were seduced by the rigours of Columban's teachings',[5] but because, rather, these were new monastic structures eminently adapted to, and thus adopted by the managers of, land-based familial structures in which women already and necessarily occupied key positions. The number of sixth-century women's houses had remained low partly because monasticism on an

[4] This statement seems to me essentially true both for the Gallo-Roman and barbarian aristocracies in the period covered in this paper. On the former, see [K. F.] Stroheker, [*Der senatorische*] *Adel* [*im spätantiken Gallien*] (Tübingen 1948); on the latter, [R.] Sprandel, [*Der*] *merovingische Adel* [*und die Gebiete ostlich des Rheins*], *Forschungen zur oberrheinischen Landesgeschichte,* 5 (Freiburg-im-Breisgau 1957), and 'Struktur und Geschichte des merovingischen Adels', *HZ,* 193 (1961) pp 33–71; K. F. Werner, 'Bedeutende Adelsfamilien im Reich Karls des Grossen', in *Karl der Grosse, Lebenswerk und Nachleben,* ed W. Braunfels, 5 vols (Düsseldorf 1965–8) 1 pp 83–142, with full bibliography. The jural status of women differed as between Roman and various barbarian laws, but the long-term trend was towards heavy influence on the latter by the former and by canon law. Changes from the second half of the sixth century onwards made for an improvement in the status of women under the Salic law, especially in the matter of inheritance of ancestral land in which females could now share under certain circumstances, and in the women's control of her own *dos* or bride-price. On all this see [F. L.] Ganshof, '[Le] statut [de la femme dans la monarchie franque]', *Recueils Jean Bodin,* 12 (1962) pp 5–58, esp 15–17, 25–35. The specific political and social developments which, as Ganshof observes, (p 57) lie behind these legal changes have yet to be thoroughly examined. But see meanwhile F. Beyerle, 'Das legislative Werk Chilperics I', *ZRG GAbt* 78 (1961) esp pp 30–8. For particular aspects of women's legal position see K. F. Drew, 'The Germanic Family of the *Leges Burgundionum*', *Medievalia et Humanistica* 15 (1963) pp 5–14 and [J.-A.] McNamara and [S. F.] Wemple, '[Marriage and] Divorce [in the Frankish kingdom]', in Stuard, *Women,* pp 95–124. For a broader comparative view see two recent works of J. Goody: *Production and Reproduction* (Cambridge 1976), and his introductory chapter to *Family and Inheritance: Rural Society in Western Europe, 1200–1800,* ed J. Goody, J. Thirsk and E. P. Thompson (Cambridge 1976), both offering characteristically stimulating insights and analysis for historians as well as social scientists. See also his *Succession* [*to High Office*] (Cambridge 1966) esp pp 1–56.

[5] [P.] Riché, *Education* [*and Culture in the Barbarian West, Sixth through Eighth Centuries,*] trans J. J. Contreni (University of North Carolina Press 1976) p 329. For details of women's participation in monasticism, see [F.] Prinz, [*Frühes*] *Mönchtum* [*im Frankenreich*] (Munich/Vienna 1965); the good short survey in the first chapter of [G. A. de Rohan Chabot, marquise de] Maillé, [*Les Cryptes de*] *Jouarre* (Paris 1971). There remains, however, a basic problem of explanation.

urban, or suburban, episcopally-directed model could not readily be accommodated to the requirements (for solidarity and biological continuity) of aristocratic families: witness the complaint of the mother of Rusticula, her only child, who had entered the convent of St John at Arles: 'I look at the possessions of our house, the innumerable multitude of our *familia* and whom I shall leave it all to, I don't know . . . Who will look after me in my old age, now that the one daughter I had is lost?'[6] In the seventh century, Sadalberga, whose hagiographer writes glowingly of contemporary foundations *per heremi vastitatem* established her first convent *in hereditate paterna* having first conveniently converted husband and children to the monastic life;[7] while Moda, widow of the magnate Autharius, moved in with her own kin to take over control of her stepson Ado's recent foundation at Jouarre.[8] The importance of such family connexions is equally, and poignantly, shown in the case of Wulftrude, daughter of Grimoald and abbess of the Pippinid foundation at Nivelles, whose removal from office was attempted by Merovingian *reges* and *reginae* 'out of hatred for her late father', their family's enemy.[9]

No *Frauenfrage* of the deprived or alienated arises, then, in reference to the seventh-century nuns and abbesses of Gaul. It is rather a matter of families' deployment of their personnel. The one function that critically distinguished masculine from feminine roles, that of warfare, was conspicuously absent from the monastic life: monks like women were *inermes*. Conversely, within the monastery, a woman could transcend the 'weakness' of her sex and become, not perhaps 'virilised',[10] but desexualised. Thus the same literary and spiritual culture was offered in monasteries to both girls and boys; and in this same asexual milieu, a woman as abbess of a double monastery[11] could exercise the political authority which in the secular world, at all levels including the

[6] *MGH SSRM* 4, cap 5, p 342. See Riché, 'Note d'hagiographie mérovingienne: la *Vita S. Rusticulae*', *AB* 72 (1954) pp 369–77, showing this to be a seventh-century text.

[7] *MGH SSRM* 5, caps 8 and 12, pp 54, 56. For the site, a *villa* in the *pagus* of Langres, see Krusch's comments *ibid* pp 43, 56 n 2. Could paternal *saltus* be classed as *eremus*?

[8] J. Guerout, 'Les Origines et le premier siècle de l'Abbaye', Y. Chaussy *L'Abbaye royale Notre-Dame de Jouarre*, ed Y. Chaussy (Paris 1961) pp 1–67.

[9] *Vita Geretrudis*, cap 6, *MGH SSRM* 2, p 460. For *Sippenkloster* ('kin-group monasteries') as aristocratic cult-centres, see Prinz, *Mönchtum*, pp 489–503.

[10] So, Riché, *Education*, p 457, with, however, valuable comments on the place of women in monastic culture.

[11] See Guerout, 'Origines', esp pp 34 *seq*; also J. Godfrey, 'The Double Monastery in early English history', *AJ* 79 (1974) pp 19–32.

monarchic,[11a] was formally monopolised by men. The point to stress is the absence of any principle of matriarchy.[12] Aristocratic women propose and dispose *ex officio* in a context where their sex is irrelevant. If through the contingencies of mortality or inheritance they temporarily wield power in secular society, they do so primarily in virtue of, and by means of, biologically-ascribed status which marital status will normally match and reinforce.[13]

To all of this, the position of a Merovingian queen, at any rate from the later sixth century, stands in something of a contrast. For it *could* be (not necessarily, but usually—and the mere possibility is what matters here) achieved and constituted exclusively through her husband. This happened when it became royal practice, first in Burgundy, then in Austrasia and Neustria, to choose as consort a low-born woman or even a slave.[14] From this same period we have evidence that the birth or status (whether queen or concubine) of a king's bed-fellow could not affect the status or succession-rights of her sons,[15] and it may be that

[11a] Ganshof, 'Statut', p 54, stresses the inability of women, despite their *Rechtsfähigkeit* in private law, to receive or transmit royal power in their own right: Kingship was an *hereditas aviatica.* (For one small caveat, see below p 37). Ganshof's point must modify the notion that the Merovingians treated their realm simply as personal property, in view of the changes made in inheritance law by Chilperic I (561–84), on which see Ganshof, pp 34–5.

[12] This is certainly not to deny the importance of ties with and through maternal kin. See K. Leyser, 'The German aristocracy from the ninth to the early twelfth century', *PP* 41 (1968) pp 25–53, and 'Maternal kin in early medieval Germany: a reply', *PP* 49 (1970) pp 126–34, though Leyser deals with periods later than the Merovingian.

[13] This seems true of the seventh-century marriages on which details are given in hagiographic sources. I have found only one clear case of an asymmetrical marriage in Gregory of Tours' *L*[*ibri*] *H*[*istoriarum*] (the so-called *History of the Franks*) and here the mother's status is higher than the father's: see *LH* x, 8, ed B. Krusch and W. Levison, *MGH SSRM* I (2 ed Berlin 1937–51) p 489 (the parents of Tetradia - *nobilis ex matre, patre inferiore.*) For an alleged attempted exception to this conjugal matching by a Frankish aristocrat see below p 46.

[14] For details see [E.] Ewig, 'Studien [zur merowingingischen Dynastie]', *Frühmittelalterliche Studien* 8 (1974) pp 15–59 at 39 *seq. LH* iv, 25 and 26, pp 156–7, provides confirmation that low-born queens were not usual in the mid-sixth century.

[15] *LH* v, 20, p 228. See [Ian] Wood, 'Kings, [Kingdoms and Consent]', *Early Medieval Kingship,* ed P. H. Sawyer and I. N. Wood (University of Leeds 1977) pp 6–29 at p 14. On the distinction between queen (*regina*) and concubine (*concubina*) in Gregory and Fredegar, see Ewig, 'Studien', pp 38–9, 42–4. There is only once certain case of a concubine's son succeeding to the kingship in the later sixth century and through the whole later Merovingian period: Theudebert II. See below p 44. But Sigibert III is another probable case. Pauline Stafford rightly points out to me that the queen-concubine distinction is too simple, betraying an ecclesiastical perspective: matters were often more complicated. But in the light of the very scarce Merovingian evidence it seems impossible to say how much more so in the cases that have concerned me here.

the principle enunciated by Gregory of Tours reflected a new situation. Certainly, from the time of Guntramn and Chilperic, the typical Merovingian king expressed the uniqueness of his monarchic status, his freedom from the norms that constrained his aristocratic subjects, by marrying a woman who, far from bringing him potent affines or rich dowry, owed everything to her relationship with him. Even if the royal bride was, as occasionally in the sixth century, a foreign princess,[16] her situation in practice might be little different from the ex-serving maid's. Her dependence on her husband's generosity and favour, when her own kin were far away and her people reckoned, perhaps, the enemies of the Franks, might be similarly complete. A Visigothic princess (Spain being one source of foreign brides for Merovingians) might keep in touch with her fatherland, but dynastic discontinuity there might in the fairly short run cut her personal link with the reigning house.[17] The fate of the Spanish princess Galswinth at Chilperic's hands[18] was no different from that of the ex-slave Bilichild at Theudebert II's.[19] And Galswinth did not find her avenger in any Spanish king.

The wife of a Merovingian, then, enjoyed a position both dependent and precarious, resting as it did on her personal, sexual association with a husband whose interests or fancy could all too easily attach him to her supplanter. A Merovingian ex-wife often cuts a pathetic figure, especially if she was sonless, or if her sons quarrelled with, or predeceased, their father.[20] Radegund, opting for ascetic virtuosity,[21] is an exception that also proves the rule. A Merovingian wife might have the title of queen, but there is no evidence that she underwent any special inauguration ritual (apart, presumably, from the marriage-ritual itself) that would have paralleled her husband's to his kingship.

[16] Ewig, 'Studien', p 39.

[17] See below p 39.

[18] *LH* iv, 28, pp 160–1.

[19] [*The Fourth Book of the Chronicle of*] *Fred*[*egar*], ed J. M. Wallace-Hadrill (London 1960) cap 37, p 30.

[20] *LH* iii, 27 (Deuteria—though she did have a son, Theudebald); iv, 25 (Marcatrude—childless); iv, 26 (Ingoberg —sonless); v, 39 (Audovera—see below p 38 n 29). Nantechild, ex-wife of Dagobert, retained her queenly status and re-emerged to prominence at her husband's death because she had an infant son (Clovis II) for whom she became regent, whereas the two queens who superseded her in Dagobert's favours both seem to have been childless: *Fred* caps 60, 79, pp 50, 67.

[21] *LH* iii, 7, p 105. It is probably significant that Radegund was childless. On her spirituality see E. Delaruelle, 'Sainte Radegonde, son type de sainteté et la chrétienté de son temps', *Études Merovingiennes,* Actes des Journées de Poitiers, 1952 (Paris 1953) pp 65–74.

Yet the very limitations on the extent to which the queen was enmeshed in political and familial structures could also give her, under certain conditions, a paradoxical freedom. We can look at this under two aspects: the economic and the sexual-genetic. Whereas a female aristocrat usually inherited some wealth in land or retained a stake in family estates, a queen of low or servile birth acquired wealth exclusively from or through her husband; and because a fair proportion of such acquired wealth tended to be in movables,[22] there was probably rather less contrast in practice between the resources of a Bilichild and a Galswinth than the difference in original status might seem to suggest. The association of queens with treasure is a recurrent theme of Merovingian history, and the uses of treasure were manifold. First as gold-bringer or gold-receiver, then as guardian of the royal hoard in a primitive 'capital' during the king's absences at war, a queen could personally control sufficient treasure to support political activities on her own account. Fredegund was generous enough in deploying hers to taunt the Franks for their niggardliness;[23] plotters against Clothar II solicited his queen's alliance, asking her to send them secretly 'all the treasure she could[24]. Given the indispensability of treasure to political success in the Merovingian world, in the seventh and the eighth centuries no less than in the sixth,[25] the queen's access to such resources could put her in a strong position, despite her relative weakness in terms of the direct control of land. Politically as personally, a queen's

[22] This seems to have been true of the bride-price (*dos*—to be distinguished from dowry) in barbarian laws: see Ganshof, 'Statut', p 28 with nn 66–8. It is not clear from *LH* ix, 20, p 437 what proportion of the five *civitates* given to Galswinth by Chilperic constituted the *dos* and what was morning-gift. But it is clear that kings gave land as well as moveables to their wives: see *LH* vi, 45, p 318 (Fredegund). For Balthild's estates, see below, p 69 n 204.

[23] *LH* vi, 45, p 318. Compare *LH* iv, 26, p 159 (Theudechild), and vii, 4, p 328 (Fredegund again).

[24] *Fred* cap 44, pp 36–7. The bishop of Sion asks Bertetrude 'ut thinsauris quantum potebat secretissime ad Sidonis suam civitatem transferrit, eo quod esset locum tutissimum'. Perhaps episcopal treasuries had something of the function of banks. On the Burgundian background to this episode see Ewig, '[*Die fränkische*] *Teilreiche* [*im 7. Jahrhundert* (613–714)]', *Trierer Zeitschrift* 22 (Trier 1953) pp 85–144 at p 106.

[25] *Fred* cap 45, p 38; cap 67, p 56; cap 75, p 63; cap 84, p 71. The Continuator of Fredegar, *ibid* cap 9, p 88 shows the importance of treasure for Plectrude, widow of Pippin II, in 714–5. Hincmar, *De Ordine Palatii*, cap 22, *MGH Cap* 2, p 525, shows the continuing intimate connexion of the queen with treasure in the ninth century. See below n 234. For the continuance of taxation and tolls throughout this period, see F. Lot *L'Impot foncier et la capitation personnelle sous le Bas-Empire et a l'époque franque* (Paris 1928), and Ganshof, 'A propos du tonlieu sous les mérovingiens', *Studi in honore di Amintore Fanfani* (Milan 1962) 1, pp 291–315.

'rootlessness' might mean the advantage of greater freedom of manoeuvre.

The queen's initial offer to her husband of sexual services could obviously serve as a power-base as long as she retained his affections. Fredegund's is probably the best-documented case of a king's passion giving his consort long-term political ascendance.[26] Aside from such personal predilections, however, the strength of the conjugal bond—a point on which Germanic and ecclesiastical attitudes converged, though from different premises[27]—meant that a monarch's status rubbed off on his bed-fellow so that, while no queen could reign in her own right, a queen as widow could become a repository of royal powers for the time being apparently quiescent, a vehicle on which claims to the royal succession could be carried to a second husband. Admittedly, in every such case known to me, the queen was not low-born but herself of noble or royal family.[28] Still, her capacity to transmit a claim to rule seems to have arisen from her association with a reigning king; and in the interregnum created by his death, given an indeterminate succession system (whether dynastic or elective), the queen would function as an inhibitor of conflict if her second husband could make his claim stick.

[26] *LH* iv, 28, p 161; v, 18, p 240 (Fredegund had 200 pounds of silver to offer as a bribe); v, 34, p 220; etc. For a caution about Gregory's bias, see below p 40. Fredegund is vividly evoked in the novel of M. Brion, *Frédégonde et Brunehaut* (Paris 1935).

[27] Ganshof, 'Statut', pp 15 *seq*, cites evidence not only from the laws but from legal acts (wills; land-grants) showing the rights of wives and widows in conjugal property. Roman law here influenced barbarian laws. Of course divorce was allowed in barbarian as in Roman codes. But McNamara and Wemple, 'Divorce', pp 98 *seq*, seem to overstress both the disadvantaged position of wives as compared with that of husbands, and the importance of the divergence between barbarian and ecclesiastical law on this point. Divorce and inheritance need to be treated together, as do law and practice, in both areas. I am not convinced by those who argue that the cases of Clothar I (*LH* iv, 3) or Dagobert (*Fred* cap 60, p 50) show the practice of royal polygamy, though these two kings offer the most conspicuous examples of serial monogamy.

[28] For the Lombards, see *Fred* caps 51, 70, pp 42, 59; and the comments of [*K. A.*] Eckhardt *Studia* [*Merovingica*], *Bibliotheca Rerum Historicarum* 11 (Aalen 1975) p 141. For the Anglo-Saxons, the evidence is conveniently assembled by W. A. Chaney, *The Cult of Kingship in Anglo-Saxon England* (Manchester 1970) pp 25–8, though the inferences there drawn concerning matrilineal royal succession are quite unwarranted. For the Merovingians, see *LH* iii, 6, iv 9; and perhaps *Fred* cap 44, p 37; also below p 40. The men concerned in all these cases where information is available already had a claim to the kingship, which suggests that marriage with the late king's widow strengthened, but did not constitute, such a claim. See also [R.] Schneider, *Königswahl* [*und Königserhebung im Frühmittelalter*] (Stuttgart 1972) pp 246–8, where however the notion of *Einheirat* ('endogamy') seems of doubtful relevance.

In Gaul, however, unlike Lombard Italy or Visigothic Spain, filial succession remained normal. Thus the only way a queen could secure her position, both in her husband's lifetime and especially after his death, was to produce a son who survived.[29] Because of the frequent succession of minors, regents might govern for relatively long periods (even though the age of majority was fifteen)[30] and a queen-mother clearly had a strong claim to the regency. Hers was not the only claim: the role of *nutritor*, literally 'male nurse', which in fact contained that of a regent, thereby illustrating once again the political significance of personal closeness to the king even when he was a child,[31] was appropriated by mayors of the palace on several occasions in the sixth and seventh centuries.[32]. But a dowager queen could normally hope to act as regent for her own son. If a dowager queen were childless or had only daughters, then her husband's death would obviously mean her exclusion from power. But even if she had a young son, she might have difficulty in maintaining that physical proximity to him on which a regent's power depended. An infant prince might be reared on a country estate;[33] he would probably be in the care of a nurse. The moment of his father's death might find his mother far away. In any event, what determined a boy-prince's success in claiming the royal succession also directed his mother's future: namely, the attitude of the aristocracy, or, immediately, of a few well-placed aristocrats. A widowed queen was thrown back on the personal ties she had formed during her husband's lifetime, and on her own political skill: for on these depended how much treasure and influence (the two were not unconnected) she might be able to salvage.

[29] For the position of a widowed queen with only daughters, see *LH* iv, 20 (Ultrogotha). For the risks of sonlessness during the husband's lifetime see *LH* iv, 26 (Ingoberg) and possibly iii, 7 (Radegund). See also below p 47, and for another probable seventh-century example (Gomatrude), see *Fred* cap 58, p 49. There were the additional risks of very high infant mortality (Fredegund lost four sons in infancy) and of sons growing up to quarrel with their father and being killed on his orders (Audovera lost two of her three sons this way, and the third also predeceased his father).

[30] Ewig, 'Studien', pp 22–4.

[31] For the potential importance of the nurse's position, see *LH* ix, 38, pp 458–9, where a royal nurse and her male assistant conspire with powerful aristocrats.

[32] Venantius Fortunatus, *Carmina* vii, 16, *MGH AA* 4, pp 170–1 (Condan, preceptor of Theudebald and *de facto* mayor of the Austrasian palace); *LH* v, 46, p 256 (Gogo—see below p 41); *Fred* caps 86, 88, pp 72, 75 (Otto; Grimoald). On Otto see [H.] Ebling, *Prosopographie [der Amtsträger des Merovingerreiches (613–741)]* (Munich 1974) pp 66–7.

[33] *LH* vi, 41, p 314.

Throughout Merovingian history, the fates of widowed queens in interregna highlighted the persisting power of bishops and *leudes*.[34]

So far I have laid stress on the precariousness and contingency of queens' positions rather than any inherent advantages accruing from their associations with monarchy, and on the relatively small extent to which the queen's powers were integrated into ongoing political or social structures: beyond personalities, episcopacy, aristocracy, kingship can be said to have existed as institutions, but it is much harder to identify anything that could be called 'queenship'. I want now to consider in more detail two queenly careers, not simply to illustrate but to amplify, and perhaps qualify, the above generalisations, and by exploring more fully the mechanisms of queenly activity to get at what seem to me some of the main forces and fundamental continuities in Merovingian politics. I begin with some basic biographical information on each.

First: Brunhild.[35] A Visigothic princess who maintained links with Spain till her last years, Brunhild's kinship link with the ruling dynasty there was severed when Liuva II was murdered in 603. Sisebut (612–21) whose *Vita* of Desiderius of Vienne[36] is the earliest surviving source for Brunhild's regency and is also violently hostile, was therefore no relative of hers. Nor was Witteric (murderer of Liuva II) whose daughter Ermenberga was sought as a bride for Brunhild's grandson Theuderic in 607.[37] These facts, I shall argue, are relevant to the unfolding of Brunhild's Spanish connexion.

Born *c*545–50, Brunhild was sought in marriage by Sigibert (apparently continuing an Austrasian tradition of foreign dynastic marriages)[38] in 566. Her Arianism was no obstacle, and she swiftly abandoned it. Gregory of Tours, our chief source for Brunhild's life up to 591, has no unfavourable comment to make on her: he introduces her on her arrival at Sigibert's court as good-looking and shrewd with a

[34] *LH* v, 1, p 194; vii, 7, p 330. See Wood, 'Kings', pp 6–7, 10–11; also below pp 41, 48.

[35] The best scholarly study remains [G.] Kurth, '[La reine] Brunehaut', in *Études Franques*, 2 vols (Paris, Brussels 1919) 1, pp 265–356, with full references to the nineteenth-century literature. (Kurth's paper first appeared in 1891). See also Ewig, '[Die fränkischen] Teilungen [und Teilreiche (511–613)]', *AAWL*, Geistes- und Sozialwissenschaftlichen Klasse, 9 (Wiesbaden 1952) pp 689 *seq*. For the chronology of Brunhild's life, I have relied on Ewig, 'Studien'.

[36] *MGH SSRM* 3, pp 620–7. See below pp 56–7.

[37] *Fred* cap 30, p 20.

[38] Ewig, 'Studien', p 40.

large dowry of treasures.[39] But Gregory's view of Brunhild must be set in a literary as well as an historical context: Chilperic figures in Gregory's drama as 'the Nero and Herod of our time',[40] Fredegund is his female counterpart in villainy, and Brunhild for whose sister Galswinth's death the evil pair are responsible[41] is therefore an avenger on the side of the angels. Twenty years after Galswinth's murder, the mutual hatred between Brunhild and Fredegund was as strong as ever.[42] Clearly the pursuit of this vendetta is one main theme in Brunhild's whole life.[43]

But another, equally significant, is Brunhild's identification with the family into which she had married. Of the various aspects of her collaboration with her husband and, later, her son praised in the courtly verse of Venantius Fortunatus, none is more revealing than her patronage of the cult of St Martin, the Merovingians' *Reichsheiliger*.[44] It was said after Sigibert's death that she had 'held the realm under her husband.'[45] She had joined him on his last campaign against Chilperic, bringing treasure to him at Paris. She was there, with treasure and children, when the news of his assassination arrived.[46] But though deprived of this treasure and of the custody of her children and exiled to Rouen, she retained an impressive quantity of personal treasure[47] as well as the special association with kingship adhering even to the widow of a Merovingian king. Very soon, Merovech, son of Chilperic and stepson of Fredegund, came to Rouen and married her.[48] *Aima-t-elle réelement Merovée?*[49] Kurth's delightful question must remain unanswered. But it is not fanciful to guess that Merovech's motive was

[39] *LH* iv, 27, p 160: '. . puella elegans opere, venusta aspectu, honesta moribus atque decora, prudens consilio et blanda colloquio . . . cum magnis thesauris. .' For Gregory's own personal relations with Brunhild, see below p 42 n 59, and p 53. He is hardly, therefore, a dispassionate witness.

[40] *LH* vi, 46, p 319.

[41] *LH* iv, 28, p 161.

[42] *LH* ix, 20, p 439: '. . . odium, quod inter illas olim statutum est, adhuc pullulat, non arescit.'

[43] This is rightly stressed by [J. M.]Wallace-Hadrill, [*The*] *Long-Haired Kings* (London 1962) pp 134–5, 205.

[44] Venantius Fortunatus, *Carmina* x, 7, pp 239–41. See Prinz, *Mönchtum*, pp 32–3.

[45] *LH* vi, 4, p 268.

[46] *LH* v, 1, p 194.

[47] *LH* v, 18, p 221: Brunhild had left five bundles with the bishop of Rouen for safekeeping, of which two were alleged to be stuffed with 'species et diversis ornamentis . . . quae praeciebantur amplius quam tria milia solidorum; sed et saccolum cum nummismati auri pondere, tenentem duo milia'.

[48] *LH* v, 2, p 195.

[49] Kurth, 'Brunehaut', p 280.

the staking of a claim to Sigibert's kingdom.[50] As it turned out, Sigibert's young son Childebert proved more acceptable to a majority of the Austrasian magnates. Brunhild herself commanded enough personal loyalty from some of those magnates for them to request and get her liberation from Chilperic.[51] And Merovech's rejection by 'the Austrasians' when he attempted to rejoin Brunhild (577) may not, as Kurth surmised, have meant her humiliation but the carrying out of her wishes. For as long as her son was king, she could hope to retrieve her position. Kurth portrays the period 576–84, that is, until Childebert attained his majority, as 'eight years of humiliation' for Brunhild at the hands of the Austrasian aristocracy.[52] But there is no evidence that Childebert's *nutricius* Gogo was hostile to her: he may, indeed have been her appointee both in this capacity and in the royal chancery.[53] Brunhild could conduct her own relations with Spain, using the bishop of Châlons as an envoy.[54] Even the driving into exile of her 'faithful supporter' duke Lupus of Champagne was the work of a faction, not an 'anti-royal'aristocracy as a whole. Brunhild had been strong enough to prevent faction-fighting from erupting into open warfare in a threatened attack on Lupus when, in Gregory's fine phrase, 'girding herself manfully, she burst into the midst of the opposing ranks', and her *industria* prevailed. Against these facts, Ursio's taunt that Childebert's realm 'is being kept safe by our protection, not yours' should not be understood as implying Brunhild's eclipse.[55]

When Childebert reached his majority in 585[56] however, Brunhild's position became a commanding one. Dispensing with a 'tutor', she now took over her son's guidance herself,[57] and pope Gregory the

[50] Ewig, 'Studien', p 33.

[51] *LHF* cap 33 p 299. See Kurth, 'Brunehaut', pp 281–2.

[52] Kurth, 'Brunehaut', p 28.

[53] For the letter written for Childebert to the Lombard king Grasulf by Gogo, see *MGH Epp* 3, no 48, p 152. Riché, *Education,* p 222, suggests that Brunhild 'brought Gogo into the royal chancellery'. For Gogo as *nutricius,* see *LH* v, 46, p 256. According to the *Chronicle of Fredegar,* iii, cap 59, *MGH SSRM* 2, p 109, Gogo was one of the envoys sent to Spain to fetch Brunhild.

[54] *LH* v, 40, p 247. The date is 580.

[55] *LH* vi, 4, p 268: '. . ."Recede a nobis, o mulier. Sufficiat tibi sub viro tenuisse regnum; nunc autem filius tuus regnat, regnumque eius non tua, sed nostra tuitione salvatur . . . "Haec et alia cum diutissime inter se protulissent, obtenuit reginae industria, ne pugnarent.'

[56] Ewig, 'Studien', p 22.

[57] *LH* viii, 22, p 389: '. . . regina mater curam vellit propriam habere de filio'. As Ewig points out this did not, of course, involve a formal legal position, but rather a personal relationship.

Great would soon afterwards treat 'both the government of the realm and the education of your son' as evidence of Brunhild's qualities.[58] A family compact between the Austrasian and Burgundian branches of the dynasty was achieved at Andelot (586) where her continuing hostility to Fredegund is transparent.[59] Fredegar makes her responsible for Chilperic's assassination and names the man she hired for the job:[60] against this, the argument from Gregory's silence, given his bias, may not be as telling as Kurth supposed—which is only to say that Brunhild carried out her family duties according to her Germanic lights. Family duty marched with political interest within Austrasia: those Austrasian magnates who had opposed Brunhild not surprisingly found support in Neustria.[61] But now able to back her aristocratic supporters with the full weight of royal resources, the queen mother crushed her opponents within Austrasia, demonstrating then and later her capacity to exercise the eminently royal virtues of rewarding loyalty, avenging wrongs done to those under her protection, and revenging herself on personal enemies.[62] Her famous 'foreign relations' with Spain and with Constantinople were in fact extensions of family relations, on the one hand forging further links with the royal dynasty in Spain and, after her daughter Ingund's marriage to Hermenegild and his unsuccessful revolt against his father Leuvigild,[63] trying to recover her little grandson Athanagild from the Byzantine imperial protectors to whom he had fled;[64] on the other hand identifying with a new Frankish assertiveness expressed as clearly in Baudonivia's *Vita* of Radegund[65] as

[58] Gregory the Great, Ep vi, 5, in *MGH Epp* 1, p 383: 'Excellentiae vestrae praedicandam ac Deo placitam bonitatem et gubernacula regni testantur et educatio filii manifestat'. The date is 595.

[59] *LH* ix, 20, pp 434–9, for the text. For the date, see [W. A.] Eckhardt, '[Die] *Decretio Childeberti* [und ihre Uberlieferung]', *ZRG GAbt* 84 (1967) pp 1–71 at 66 *seq*. In the subsequent diplomatic exchanges between Guntramn and Childebert and Brunhild, Gregory of Tours himself served as the latter's envoy. This closeness to the Austrasian court is noteworthy.

[60] *Fred* iii, 93 in *MGH SSRM* 2, p 118: '. . . ab homine nomen Falcone'.

[61] *LH* ix, 9, p 421.

[62] *LH* ix, 9–12, pp 421–7. Brunhild's relations with Lupus, Ursio and Berthefried, illustrating the varieties of just deserts, should be compared with the earlier episode recounted in *LH* vi, 4, pp 267–8. Brunhild's concern for someone under her protection is shown in the story of Sichar, *LH* ix, 19, pp 433–4.

[63] See J. N. Hillgarth, 'Coins and chronicles: propaganda in sixth-century Spain and the Byzantine background', *Historia* 15 (Wiesbaden 1966) pp 483–508; and E. A. Thompson, *The Goths in Spain* (Oxford 1969) pp 64–73.

[64] The evidence is contained in the *Epistolae Austrasicae*, nos 25–48, *MGH Epp* 3, pp 138–53.

[65] *MGH SSRM* 2, pp 358–95, II cap 16 at p 388: in acquiring a piece of the true cross,

in the diplomatic exchanges of earlier Austrasian kings,[66] and now epitomised in Brunhild's appeal to the empress Anastasia (wife of Maurice) to join with her in bringing the benefits of peace 'between the two peoples'![66a]; Beneath the Roman verbiage of *pax* and *caritas* is a thoroughly gentile consciousness of Frankish-Roman parity.

Childebert, who had inherited Burgundy on Guntramn's death in 593, himself died aged only twenty-six in 596, leaving Austrasia to the ten-year-old Theudebert, Burgundy to nine-year-old Theuderic.[67] Brunhild as de facto regent for both young kings now entered the last and most active phase of her career. She and her son had had their Austrasian supporters. Now she needed, and found, support from members of a more southerly aristocracy, of mixed 'Roman' and barbarian origins, long used to collaboration with kings. Asclepiodotus, former head of Guntramn's chancery, had carried his expertise to Childebert, whose great *Decretum* of 596 he probably drafted, and he remained influential during Brunhild's regency.[68] I shall examine presently other bases of the old queen's continuing power, but here briefly consider her position in the royal family. She had vetoed Childebert's marriage to the Agilolfing Theodelinda (the pair had been betrothed before 589) presumably to counter the hostile influence of that princess's Austrasian and Lombard connexions.[69] But she seems to have approved Childebert's eventual marriage with his ex-mistress Faileuba, who may possibly have been a woman of low birth.[70] If this was so, and Childebert was following Guntramn in raising a low-born concubine to queenship, we might speculate that Brunhild assented the more readily because Faileuba, lacking powerful aristocratic connexions

Radegund tells King Sigibert she will act 'pro totius patriae salute et eius regni stabilitate'. 'Sicut beata Helena . . . quod fecit illa in orientali patria, hoc fecit beata Radegundis in Gallia', comments Baudonivia. Radegund commends her foundation, *ibid* p 389, 'praecellentissimis dominis regibus et serenissimae dominae Bronichildi'.

66 *MGH Epp* 3, nos 18, 19, 20, pp 131–3, esp no 20, p 133, where Theudebert I lists 'quae gentes nostrae sint, Deo adiutore, dicione subiectae', and asks Justinian 'ut . . . in communi utilitate iungamur'.

66a *MGH Epp* 3, no 29, p 140: ' . . . dum inter utramque gentem pacis causa conectitur, coniuncta gratia principum subiectarum generent beneficia regionum', and no 44, p 150, another appeal to the empress to return Brunhild's little grandson Athanagild 'et inter utramque gentem per hoc, proptitiante Christo, caritas multiplicetur et pacis terminus extendatur'. These letters date from 584 and 585.

67 *Fred* cap 16, p 11, Paulus Diaconus, *Historia Langobardorum* iv cap 11, *MGH SSRL* p 120: 'Brunichildis tunc regina cum nepotibus adhoc puerulis . . . regebat Gallias'.

68 Eckhardt, '*Decretio Childeberti*', pp 70–1.

69 *Fred* cap 34, p 22. I accept the interpretation of Ewig, 'Studien', p 40, n 145.

70 Ewig, 'Studien', p 42.

of her own, posed less of a threat to Brunhild's ascendance than a noblewoman might have done. Over the marriage of her elder grandson Theudebert II, a concubine's son,[71] Brunhild had no control. His coming-of-age in 600 saw, hardly coincidentally, her expulsion from Austrasia,[72] presumably because magnates hostile to her found the young king ready to assert himself. Soon after, he married Bilichild, a former slave of Brunhild herself with no kind feelings for her former mistress.[73] Once queen, Bilichild's position could not be affected by Brunhild's taunts about her base origin—so long as the Austrasian magnates approved of her. Had withdrawal of that approval, and perhaps also her lack of a son, anything to do with her murder in 611?[74] The case of Bilichild could show that a queen who was an ex-slave was just a bit more vulnerable to changing currents of aristocratic support than was a princess like Brunhild: certainly her fate was unusually harsh. Theuderic II (Faileuba's son)[75] provides a marked contrast to his half-brother. Having given a welcome to his grandmother when she sought his court in 600,[76] Theuderic remained close to her for the rest of his life. That he never married was due to Brunhild's influence (I see no reason to reject the evidence of the *Vita Columbani* on this point):[77] the raising of a concubine to queenly status would have created a new power in the *aula regis* and so weakened Brunhild's position in general and her freedom to choose Theuderic's heir(s) in particular. This freedom played a crucial part in the network of personal loyalties which upheld the old queen for loyalty required long-term prospects dependent, in turn, on predictions of who would control the royal succession. I shall return to this point below. Only one other action of Brunhild needs mentioning here: her renunciation in 613 of the allegedly 'traditional' practice of dividing a Merovingian's realm

[71] *L[iber] H[istoriae] F[rancorum]*, cap 37 *MGH SSRM* 2, p 306.

[72] *Fred* cap 19, p 12. The attempt of Kurth, 'Brunehaut', p 310, to gloss over this is unconvincing.

[73] *Fred* cap 35, pp 22–3. On the probable date of this marriage (601–2), see Ewig, 'Studien', p 26.

[74] *Fred* cap 37, p 30: 'Belechildis a Teudeberto interfecitur'.

[75] *LHF* cap 37, p 306. Both Theudebert and Theuderic were sons of Childebert according to *LH* viii, 37 and ix, 4. But there seems no reason to doubt that Brunhild goaded Theuderic to attack Theudebert by alleging that the latter was a gardener's son and thus no kin at all to Theuderic: *Fred* cap 27, p 18. If Theuderic believed this, his subsequent treatment of Theudebert and his sons is even less surprising: *Fred* cap 38, p 32, and *LHF* cap 38 pp 307–9.

[76] *Fred* cap 19, p 13.

[77] *V[ita] C[olumbani]* I, cap 18, *MGH SSRM* 4, p 86. This chapter and much of the next two are borrowed almost verbatim by *Fred*, cap 36, pp 23–9.

between his sons. Theuderic in 612 had defeated Theudebert and gained control of Austrasia. His sudden death just as he was marching against Clothar II of Neustria (Fredegund's son) created an interregnum of the usual dangerous kind. How did Brunhild respond? 'Her endeavour was to make Sigibert [Theuderic's eldest son, then aged eleven] his father's successor',[78] in other words, to maintain, at least for the time being, the union of Austrasia and Burgundy. By this date there was no question, I think, of dividing Theuderic's inheritance among his *four* sons. But why was the two-fold division of 596 (already foreshadowed in 589) not followed in 613? Should not Brunhild have bought off the Austrasian 'separatists' and so forestalled their alliance with Clothar? The answer, in my view, lies not in the old queen's alleged 'centralising' ambitions nor in her adherence to *Romanentum* against *Germanentum*,[79] but in a short-term bid to rally her old and new supporters among the Burgundian and Austrasian aristocracy in a final thrust against Clothar II. There is nothing to suggest that, had she won, she would have resisted the inevitable pressures—since young princes were available—to redivide the *regnum* by allocating kings to the Neustrians and Austrasians. Her supporters among them would surely have expected such a pay-off. Brunhild's mistake in 613 was, as Ian Wood has recently pointed out,[80] to overestimate the support she commanded among the aristocracy, especially and fatally the very Burgundian office-holders she had believed loyal. The politics were as ever those not of *raison d'état*[81] but of family interests, of self-preservation, of manoeuvring among shifting aristocratic loyalties. Brunhild's game was the old one, only now she made her first bad miscalculation and lost all.

Before looking more closely at some key aspects of Brunhild's

[78] *Fred* cap 40, p 32: 'Brunechildis . . . Sigybertum in regnum patris instituere nitens . . .

[79] So, Ewig, 'Teilungen', pp 705–8, 715. For a similar view, see H. Löwe, 'Austrien im Zeitalter Brunichilds. Kampf zwischen Königtum und Adel', H. Grundmann, *Handbuch der deutschen Geschichte* (9 ed, rev B. Gebhardt Stuttgart 1970) pp 124–7. This view seems standard in German historiography. The alleged evidence (the *chaussées Brunehaut*) for Brunhild as a 'Roman' road-builder or maintainer was demolished by Kurth, *Histoire poétique des Mérovingiens* (Paris 1893) pp 424 *seq.*

[80] Wood, 'Kings', p 13.

[81] So, Kurth, 'Brunehaut', p 306 and 350–1: 'elle prétendit soumettre à l'autorité d'une femme des gens qui ne reconnaissaient pas même celle d'un homme'. Kurth's contrast between the would-be despot Brunhild, an inevitable failure, and the *monarchie temperée* of the Carolingians seems to have had a strong influence on francophone historiography: see H. Pirenne, *Mohammed and Charlemagne,* trans B. Miall (London 1939) pp 265 *seq,* and F. Lot, in F. Lot, C. Pfister and F. L. Ganshof, *Les Destinées de l'Empire en Occident de 395 a 888* (2 ed Paris 1940–1) pp 265–6; 297–8; 314–15.

success, I turn now to Balthild,[82] and a sketch of her career which, much shorter than Brunhild's, is also less variously documented, the main source being the *Vita Balthildis* written soon after her death (in 680 or soon after).[83] Born in England probably in the early 630s, Balthild was brought as a slave-girl to Gaul and bought (in 641 or after) by Erchinoald, mayor of the palace of Neustria.[84] Her hagiographer's stress on her low birth (she was one of those 'poor' whom God 'raises from the dust and causes to sit with the princes of his people', and a 'precious pearl sold at a low price')[85] must be taken seriously, in view of the usual contemporary hagiographical delight in noble ancestry.[86] She was good-looking, (had doubtless caught Erchinoald's eye) and she was also canny—*prudens et cauta*.[87] Erchinoald himself is said to have wished to marry her after his wife's death, but this seems implausible, given all the other evidence of aristocratic marriage patterns.[88] The hagiographer introduced this detail, I suggest, in order to deploy the chastity motif obligatory in the *Vitae* of female saints[89] and otherwise unusable in the special case of Balthild. Divine providence caused the girl to spurn the king's minister so as to be saved for the king himself—Clovis II, son of Dagobert. Clovis probably married Balthild as soon

[82] The only usable biography remains [M. J.] Couturier, *Sainte Balthilde,* [*reine des Francs*] (Paris 1909) which, despite its devout and rather rambling style, should not be dismissed as by [L.] Dupraz, [*Le*] *Royaume* [*des Francs et l'ascension politique des maires du palais au déclin du VIIe siècle* (*656–680*)] (Fribourg en Suisse 1948) p 223 n 3. For useful preliminary remarks on Balthild, see [W.] Levison, *England* [*and the Continent in the Eighth Century*] (Oxford 1946) pp 9–10 with a full bibliography of the source materials at p 9, n 4.

[83] *MGH SSRM* 2, pp 475–508, version 'A', with the ninth-century reworking, 'B', in parallel columns. For the dates of both versions, see Krusch's introduction, *ibid* pp 478–9. The 'A' *Vita* was evidently written by a nun at Chelles, and commissioned by some monks—perhaps those of Corbie?

[84] *MGH SSRM* 2, cap 2, p 483.

[85] *Ibid.* These are standard topoi in references to low-born holy people: the references are to 1 Kings 2, 8 and Ps 112, 7, as is observed by [F.] Graus, [*Volk, Herrscher und*] *Heiliger* [*im Reich der Merowinger. Studien zur Hagiographie der Merowingerzeit*] (Prague 1965) pp 411–12. For another example, Gerbert writing of himself, see *Lettres de Gerbert, 983–887,* ed J. Havet (Paris 1889) no 217, p 229.

[86] See Prinz, 'Heiligenkult [und Adelsherrschaft im Spiegel merowingischer Hagiographie]', *HZ* 204 (1967) pp 529–44. Low birth was perceived as hard to reconcile with holiness. Version 'B' of the *Vita* makes Balthild into a noble lady: *claro sanguine*; and she was later depicted as belonging to an Anglo-Saxon royal family! See Couturier, *Sainte Balthilde,* p 2, n 2.

[87] *MGH SSRM* 2, cap 2, p 483; cap 3, p 485: 'prudens et astuta virgo'.

[88] *Ibid* cap 3, p 484. Ian Wood suggests to me, however, that Erchinoald, a kinsman of Dagobert on his mother's side, may have been deliberately imitating royal practice.

[89] Graus, *Heiliger,* pp 410 *seq.* The authoress of this *Vita* clearly had before her Venantius' *Vita Radegundis.*

as he came of age in 648.[90] 'Astute' as ever, Balthild had no illusions about her position. Pregnant in 649, she confided her anxieties to Eligius, most influential of Dagobert's courtiers and a holy man still evidently at the heart of royal affairs: what would happen to the realm (did she mean, to herself?) if she carried only a girl-child? Eligius reassured her that she would give birth to a son, and put his money where his mouth was: 'he had a piece of metalwork made which was suitable for a boy-baby and ordered it to be kept for his use until he was born'.[91] Balthild duly had her son—the future Clothar III, followed by Theuderic (III) and Childeric (II).[92] Already during her husband's lifetime, her great influence was evident: she seems to have organised the care of the king's entourage of young aristocrats at the court—that cradle of royal servants; and she controlled, with the help of her almoner Genesius, quantities of treasure for disbursement to the poor and other pious causes.[93] The hagiographer paints the picture of a *palatium* in which all revolves around the queen. Other sources stress the role of Erchinoald in maintaining peace throughout Clovis II's reign.[94] Balthild and her former master probably coexisted by each concentrating on different areas of activity, and the Neustrian aristocracy, whether dazzled still by Dagobert's glories or gratified by the restitution of his unjust exactions after his death during the conciliatory regency of Nantechild (died 641/2),[95] were satisfied. But the best argument from silence for Bathchild's strong position during Clovis II's lifetime might be that despite his womanising, he did not

[90] *LHF* cap 43, p 315. On the date, see Ewig, 'Studien', p 26.

[91] *Vita Eligii*, ii, 32, *MGH SSRM* 4, p 717. Riché, *Education*, p 231 with n 354, seems slightly to misinterpret this passage: I cannot see that Eligius's present for the baby can possibly have been 'a teething-ring' which would have been equally suitable for a boy or a girl.

[92] For the birth-order of the three boys, I follow that implied by the near-contemporary *Passio Leudegarii* I, cap 5, *MGH SSRM* 5, p 287, in preference to that given by *LHF* cap 44, p 317. See [L.] Levillain, '[Encore sur la] Succession [d'Austrasie au VIIe siècle]', *BEC* 105 (1945,6) pp 29–30 at p 305, n 1. The *filiola* who lived with Balthild at Chelles and died just before she did must, as the 'B' *Vita* and Krusch agree, have been a god-daughter. (After all, Clovis II had died in 657!) Although Clovis II is said to have had other women (*LHF* cap 44, p 316) he is not known to have had any children except by Balthild.

[93] *MGH SSRM* 2, pp 485–7. 'Auri vel argenti largissima munera' are disbursed. On the role of Genesius, see Ewig, '[Das Privileg des Bischofs Berthefrid von Amiens für Corbie von 664 und die] Klosterpolitik [der Königin Balthild]', *Francia* 1 (1973) pp 63–114 at pp 107–8 with n 86: '. . . eine Art Grand Aumônier'.

[94] *Fred* cap 84, p 71. Compare the aggressive and tightfisted Erchinoald depicted in the *Vita Eligii*, i, caps 20, 27, *MGH SSRM* 4, pp 711, 714.

[95] *Ibid* cap 80, p 68.

endanger her position (as Dagobert had done Nantechild's) by raising another woman to the status of queen.[96] Both the moral and the political backing of Balthild's ecclesiastical connexions must have helped her here.

Balthild's situation changed with the deaths of Clovis and, soon after, Erchinoald (657, 758/9).[96a] She now became regent for her son Clothar III, who significantly, succeeded to an undivided realm, excluding at least for the moment his two little brothers. The *Vita Balthildis* and the *Liber Historiae Francorum*[97] both stress the decisive roles of the Neustrian aristocracy. No doubt the many personal bonds forged during Balthild's years as 'nurse to the young men' in the *palatium* now stood her in good stead. The Neustrians' choice of Ebroin, a former *miles palatinus,* to succeed Erchinoald as mayor must have had Balthild's consent.[98] It has been alleged that Balthild and Ebroin between them pursued a systematic policy of reunifying the Merovingian *regnum,* first by imposing the Neustrian prince Childeric II on the Austrasians, then by abolishing the Burgundian mayoralty of the palace thus uniting Neustria and Burgundy.[99] On an alternative hypothesis, the unification-policy was 'only neustro-burgundian, not pan-frankish'.[100] Neither view offers an entirely convincing interpretation of the *Vita's* account of Balthild's actions. The complications surrounding the export of Childeric II boil down to Merovingian family politics with two dowager queens playing typical roles. It is possible that the coup of Grimoald and his son Childebert III was even part of the same family politics, in a broad sense, if indeed they too had Merovingian blood in them.[101] The most plausible reconstruction of

[96] *Ibid* cap 84, p 71.

[96a] Clovis II died between 11 September and 16 November 657: see Levison, 'Das Nekrologium von dom Racine', in *NA* 35 (1910) p 45. For the date of Erchinoald's death, see Dupraz, *Royaume,* p 245 with n 1.

[97] *Vita* cap 5, *MGH SSRM* 2, p 487; *LHF* cap 44, p 317.

[98] *LHF* cap 45, p 317; *Fred* (Continuator) cap 2, p 80, *Vita Balthildis,* cap 5, p 487. See [J.] Fischer, [*Der Hausmeier*] *Ebroin* (Bonn 1954) pp 82 *seq,* whose case for Ebroin's low birth seems, however, unproven and his explanation of Ebroin's rise therefore unconvincing. (His picture of the regent and 'her' mayor as two *Willensmenschen* risen from nothing through their own energies yet fated to clash because of the very strength of their wills, has a splendidly Wagnerian quality, at once romantic, epic and sexist: 'Früher oder später musste es zwischen ihnen zur entscheidenden Auseinandersetzung kommen, und der weniger Starke musste dem Stärkeren weichen'!)

[99] Dupraz, *Royaume,* pp 239 *seq,* 351 *seq.*

[100] Fischer, *Ebroin,* p 87. See also Ewig, 'Teilreiche', pp 121 *seq.*

[101] On the evidence for Grimoald's coup, Levillain, 'Succession', remains fundamental, and for a cogent restatement of his views in the light of subsequent research, see Ewig, 'Noch einmal zum "Staatsstreich" Grimoalds', *Speculum Historiale, Festschrift*

the events of 662, in my view, is that Childebert's childless death left Grimoald in a dangerously exposed position rather like that of a dowager queen. He had exiled Dagobert, son of Sigibert III, in 656[102] and to recall him would have been, at best, difficult and time-consuming for Grimoald. With Austrasian enemies to cope with, Grimoald had little time to afford. But he did have custody of Dagobert's sister Bilichild and perhaps also of her mother, Sigibert's widow Himnichild. To play this 'trump-card', Grimoald needed to find a Merovingian husband for Bilichild. There was no alternative but to seek him in Neustria. Thus the initiative in 662 was an Austrasian one,[103] and the outcome was a Merovingian family compact: the seven-year-old Childeric II was sent (perhaps it was Balthild's decision to choose her third in preference to her second son) to be betrothed to his first cousin Bilichild—a unique case of Merovingian in-marriage—while her mother assumed the regency,[104] all with the backing of a powerful section of the Austrasian aristocracy.[105] At this point, Grimoald became expendable and thus the sole victim of these arrangements. In him

J. Spörl (Munich 1965) pp 454–7. But in what follows I have accepted some revisions suggested by H. Thomas, 'Die Namenliste des Diptychon Barberini und der Sturz des Hausmeiers Grimoald', *DA* 25 (1969) pp 17–63, and further modified by Eckhardt, *Studia,* pp 152 *seq,* who also argues that Grimoald was descended in the maternal line from the Austrasian king Theudebald. But even if Levillain and Ewig are right, and Grimoald was killed in 657 rather than 662 (see following note) my view of Balthild's actions in the latter year would be unaffected.

[102] *LHF* cap 43, p 316: 'Decedente vero tempore, defuncto Sighiberto rege, Grimoaldus filium eius parvolum nomine Dagobertum totundit Didonemque Pectavensem urbis episcopum in Scocia peregrinandum eum direxit, filium suum in regno constituens. Franci itaque hoc valde indignantes Grimoaldo insidias preparant, eumque exementes ad condempnandum rege Francorum Chlodoveo deferunt. In Parisius civitate in carcere mancipatus, vinculorum cruciatu constrictus, ut erat morte dignus, quod in domino suo exercuit, ipsius mors valido cruciatu finivit'. Levillain argues that the *LHF* account must be accepted entirely: thus, Grimoald's death must precede Clovis (II)'s, in autumn 657. Those who argue that Grimoald's death must be dated to 662, on the grounds that his son Childebert III could not otherwise have been sustained as king in Austrasia until that date, must emend the *LHF*'s 'Chlod*oveo*' to 'Chlod*ochario*' or 'Chlo*thario*', that is, Clothar III. This emendation is not merely 'arbitrary' as Levillain alleges: for evidence of just this confusion of names in seventh- and eighth-century *diplomata,* see Dupraz, *Royaume,* pp 382–4.

[103] *Vita Balthildis* cap 5, p 487: '. . . Austrasii pacifico ordine, ordinante domna Balthilde, per consilium quidem seniorum receperunt Childericum, filium eius, in regem Austri'. Only by mistranslating 'ordinante' could Dupraz, *Royaume,* p 355, infer that Balthild 'gave orders' and 'imposed' her own solution. See further, Schneider, *Königswahl,* pp 163–4.

[104] Himnechild continued to subscribe Childeric II's *diplomata* until he came of age: see Ewig, 'Studien', p 23. For the assassination of Childeric and Bilichild in 675, see *LHF* cap 45, p 318.

[105] For the role of Wulfoald, see Ewig, 'Teilreiche', p 123.

Merovingian blood, if any, was much diluted. Perhaps the narrower family of Dagobert I's descendants closed ranks against more distant kin, the *indignatio* of the Neustrians against Grimoald was genuine, and his execution in Paris a kind of vengeance for the exile of Dagobert's grandson.[106] In all this, it is impossible to see Balthild as imposing her son—still less Neustrian control—on the Austrasians. She acts within limits defined by the Austrasians themselves, and her response restores harmony within both family and *regnum*. The *Vita's* depiction of her as a peace-bringer is not mere hagiographical convention.

As for her 'neustro-burgundian policy', it is possible to interpret Clothar III's succession in both Neustria and Burgundy as evidence of aristocratic interests in *both* regions, rather than only of royal design. The gradual cessation of the practice of dividing the realm in the course of the seventh century was not the result of kings' (or queens') decisions alone.[107] The *Burgundofarones* had something to gain from access to the *palatium* of a king who was theirs and the Neustrians' alike.[108] Nor can I see much evidence for a formal extinction of the Burgundian mayoralty by Balthild. It is arguable, anyway, that their laws and customs mattered more to the Burgundians than a mayoralty.[109] Scholarly discussion of the whole issue has turned on the interpretation of a phrase in the *Vita Balthildis:* 'The Burgundians and the Franks were made as one'.[110] What seems to have been unnoticed hitherto is that not merely this sentence but the whole final section of chapter 5 of the *Vita* echoes a remarkable passage in the Book of Ezechiel. The context (Ezechiel chapter 36) is a divine promise to the prophet that the *gentes* shall be put to shame and Israel renewed and exalted. In the following chapter, God sets Ezechiel down in the valley of the bones and brings them to life. He then tells the prophet to take two sticks, one to signify Israel and the other Judah:

> And join them one to another into one stick; and they shall become one in thine hand . . .

[106] Above n 102.

[107] This is a basic assumption in Dupraz's book. See also Ewig, 'Teilreiche', pp 110 *seq.*

[108] *Fred* cap 44, p 37; cap 55, p 46. For later Burgundian resistance to Ebroin because he denied them direct access to the *palatium,* see *Passio Leudegarii* I, cap 4, *MGH SSRM* 5, p 287.

[109] *Fred* cap 54, p 46: the Burgundians decide to do without a mayor of the palace after the death of Warnacher (626), preferring *cum rege transagere. Passio Leudegarii* I, cap 7, p 289, shows the Burgundians' concern to preserve their *lex vel consuetudo*. The Burgundian mayoralty seems not to have been revived after the death of Flaochad, a Frankish appointee of Nantechild, in 642. See also Ewig, 'Teilreiche', pp 106–7, 120.

[110] *Vita,* cap 5, pp 487–8: 'Burgundiones vero et Franci facti sunt uniti'.

And when the children of thy people shall speak unto thee saying, Wilt thou not shew us what thou meanest by these?

Say unto them, Thus saith the Lord God . . . Behold, I will take the children of Israel from among the heathen . . .

And I will make them one nation . . . and one king shall be king to them all: and they shall be no more two nations, neither shall they be divided into two nations any more at all . . .

Moreover I will make a covenant of peace with them; it shall be an everlasting covenant with them: and I will place them, and multiply them, and will set my sanctuary in the midst of them for evermore.[111]

The hagiographer's purpose throughout his fifth chapter is to show Balthild as the instrument of divinely-ordained concord between the once-warring kingdoms. The queen is presented, not as the author of specific new constitutional arrangements, but—in almost apocalyptic terms—as the inaugurator of a new era of peace. There is a significant contrast, as well as a similarity, here with the note caught by Ewig in the early eighth-century *Continuator* of Fredegar's identification of the Franks with Israel and of their war-leader Charles Martel with Joshua:[112] clearly the insistence on the Frank's providential role is a common theme, but a female ruler cannot be the lieutenant of a God of Battles. Here, in a warlike age, the obstacles to an ideology of 'queenship' are as evident as the hagiographer's ingenuity.

One final point to make here concerns Balthild's loss of power, which, as with Brunhild in Austrasia, coincided with her son's coming of age. Like Brunhild, Balthild found regency imposed its own time-limit and tenure was non-renewable. Balthild's retirement to her foundation of Chelles in late 664 or 665 was no voluntary move. Though her hagiographer glosses over it,[113] the threat of force is strongly suggested by the *Vita Eligii*.[114] Whether or not Ebroin was

[111] Ezechiel 37; 17–18, 20–2, 26 (Authorised Verion). The vulgate reading of verse 17 is: 'Et adjunge illaunam ad alterum tibi in lignum unum; et erunt in unionem in manu tua'.

[112] Ewig, 'Zum christlichen Königsgedanken im Frühmittelalter', *Das Königtum,* ed T. Mayer *Vorträge und Forschungen* 3 (Konstanz 1956) pp 7–73 at 51 *seq.*

[113] *Vita Balthildis* cap 10, p 495: 'Erat enim eius sancta devotio, ut in monasterio [Chelles] . . . conversare deberet. Nam et Franci pro eius amore hoc maxime dilatabant nec fieri permittebant . . . Et exinde . . . permiserunt eam subito pergere ad ipsum monasterium. Et fortasse dubium non est, quod ipsi principes tunc illud non bono animo permissisent . . .'

[114] *Vita Eligii* ii, 32, p 717: '. . . iure regio exempta'. The last of Clothar III's *diplomata* subscribed by Balthild is dated 6 September 664: *MGH DD* 1, no 40, p 38.

directly involved,[115] those responsible were clearly a powerful section of the Neustrian aristocracy. The very violence of these *principes'* reaction implies the reality of Balthild's power: as her *Vita* puts it, they had acted against her will and feared her vengeance.[116] But their success also showed how precarious was a queen-mother's position if those 'whom she had tenderly nurtured' should turn against her. Her elimination could be more decorously handled, but, like Grimoald, she had become expendable. The dowager's phoney vocation, the mayor's judicial murder, could be arranged without the political upheavals of an interregnum.

So far, I have portrayed two queens acting in a thoroughly secular context of kingly courts and counsels, treasure, armed force and aristocratic politics. But other, equally important, non-secular types of power in the Merovingian world must now be considered if we are fully to appreciate these queens' activities, or their posthumous reputations. The saints—the holy dead—were believed to incorporate supernatural power which could seem random, inexplicable in its operations.[117] Those who could claim to mediate such power, to render it intelligible, to enable 'human strategy [to be set] at work on the holy'[118] were the bishops, the holy men and the monks in the towns and countryside of Gaul. Both the power and the exponents thereof predated the Merovingians: Clovis and his successors had to come to terms with them. We must now examine how, first, Brunhild and then Balthild did so.

If the Frankish kings from the fifth century onwards wielded a territorial authority from city bases, the collaboration of bishops was

[115] Judgements on this point have been very subjective. See Fischer, *Ebroin,* pp 98–104.

[116] *Vita* cap 10, p 495: '. . . nec fieri permittebant, nisi commotio illa fuisset per miserum Sigobrandum episcopum, cuius superbia inter Francos meruit mortis ruinam. Et exinde orta intentione, dum ipsum *contra eius voluntatem* interfecerunt, metuentes *ne hoc ipsa domna contra eos graviter ferret ac vindicare ipsam causam vellet,* permiserunt eam subito . . .' etc (above n 113.) A few lines further on, p 496, the *Vita* gives a further revealing glimpse of Balthild's position: 'Habuit enim tunc non modicam querelam contra eos, quos ipsa dulciter enutriverat, pro qua re falso ipsi eam habuissent suspectam, vel etiam pro bonis mala ei repensarent. Sed et hoc conferens cum sacerdotibus citius, eis clementer cuncta indulsit . . .' For the Sigobrand episode, see below p 70.

[117] For a fine account, full of fresh insights, see now [P.] Brown, 'Relics [and Social Status in the Age of Gregory of Tours]', The Stenton Lecture for 1976 (University of Reading 1977), with references to previous work. Also indispensable is Graus, *Heiliger,* Brown's paper must be supplemented for the seventh century by Prinz, 'Heiligenkult', and *Mönchtum*; and Ewig, 'Milo [et eiusmodi similes]', *Bonifatius-Gedenkgabe* (Fulda 1954) pp 412–40, at 430 *seq.*

[118] Brown, 'Relics', p 14.

indispensable. Appointments of, and relations with bishops remained key aspects of royal action through the sixth and most of the seventh centuries:[119] and rulers had scope for action precisely because, though episcopacy was part of the 'Establishment', bishops, especially prospective ones, needed outside support to secure their local positions. Had 'senatorial blood, episcopal office and sanctity' *really* 'presented a formidable united front,'[120] Merovingian kings—and queens too—could never have been as formidable as they sometimes were. Brunhild is a case in point. As a consort, she, like other sixth-century queens had probably used her influence in episcopal elections, notably, according to Venantius, that of Gregory of Tours himself.[121] Better documented is her intervention at Rodez in 584, where her influence was invoked by one of the participants, count Innocentius, in a power-struggle in the nearby city of Javols. When the count transferred his interests to the see of Rodez, Brunhild's support secured him the bishopric in an election which scandalised even Gregory by the fierceness of the competition.[122] Brunhild's own interest here might have been connected, I suggest, with her continuing efforts to secure the restitution of her sister Galswinth's morning-gift which included the city of Cahors.[123] The dioceses of Rodez and Cahors were contiguous, and bishop Innocentius's harrassment of the neighbouring see[124] may have exerted some of the pressure which achieved the transfer of Cahors into Brunhild's possession in 586. Her continuing interest in this region, in which Frankish and Visigothic powers competed, and the key position of

[119] D. Claude, '[Die] Bestellung der Bischöfe [im merowingischen Reiche]', *ZRG KAbt* 49 (1963) pp 1–77. For some general aspects of episcopal collaboration, see Wood, 'Kings'. It is tempting to correlate the absence of queenly regencies in England in the seventh century (the year-long reign of Seaxburh, widow of Cenwalh of Wessex, apparently in her own right, in 672–3 is quite exceptional) or later, with the relative weakness of episcopal power there as well as with the ubiquity of warfare: there was no substitute therefore for an adult warrior king. An obvious further correlation would be with the persistance of dynastic discontinuity in the English kingdoms into the ninth century. See below p 75.

[120] So, P. Brown, *Religion and Society in the Age of Saint Augustine* (London 1972) p 131, quoted and renounced, with admirable open-mindedness, by Brown himself: 'Relics', p 17. See also his reservations, 'Relics', pp 19–20, about Prinz, '[Die bischöfliche] Stadtherrschaft [im Frankenreich]', *HZ* 217 (1974) pp 1–35, which, however, remains an important article.

[121] Venantius Fortunatus, *Carmina* v, 3, lines 11–15, p 106: 'Huic Sigiberchthus ovans favat et Brunechildis honori'.

[122] *LH* vi, 38, p 309. For the previous context at Rodez see *LH* v, 46.

[123] *LH* ix, 20, see above n 22.

[124] *LH* vi, 38, p 309.

Rodez are still evident twenty years later.[125] The other vital area for the queen's control of episcopal appointments after 600 was Burgundy proper. She must surely have been behind the elections of Aridius to Lyons and of Domnolus to Vienne in 603. She appointed Desiderius to Auxerre in 605.[126] Gregory the Great complained in 595 that no-one obtained a bishopric in the *regnum Francorum* without paying for it.[127] Assuming twelve to fifteen vacancies per annum, Claude has made the interesting calculation that the royal profits from simony over the *regnum* as a whole could have reached ten thousand solidi in the later sixth century.[128] Despite later accusations, I do not think that Brunhild's practice here was unusual, nor that she was responsible for a peculiarly bad attack of this 'contagion' in the late sixth century.[129] Of course the money was useful to her, as to the other strong rulers who profited from this source. But it was not the chief consideration. Whether or not they proved their devotion in hard cash, Brunhild needed episcopal allies and servants. They if anyone could control the cities, their very simony being proof of one vital attribute of power;[130] they could influence their aristocratic lay kinsfolk; and they could serve as counsellors and envoys, deploying their useful network of

[125] The evidence lies in three letters, two of them apparently addressed to the bishop of Rodez, by Bulgar, count of Septimania during the reign of the Visigothic king Gunthimar (610–2): *MGH Epp* 3, *Epp Wisigothicae* nos 11, 12 and 13, pp 677–81. The letters to the bishop of Rodez are violently hostile to Brunhild and Theuderic, accusing them of making an alliance with the pagan Avars, and making it clear that Gunthimar was sending money to Theudebert. The Auvergne region was, of course, an Austrasian enclave. Bulgar's third letter, evidently addressed to a Burgundian bishop (here Brunhild and Theuderic are *gloriosissimi reges*), reveals that Brunhild was negotiating with Gunthimar for two towns in Septimania which had been granted to her personally by her cousin king Reccared but taken back by the Visigoths, presumably after Reccared's death in 601 or his son's in 603. Brunhild was meanwhile holding two Visigothic envoys captive as a bargaining counter. For anti-Brunhild propaganda in this festering Visigothic-Frankish conflict, see below p 56. The treatment of Bulgar's letters by Kurth, 'Brunehaut', pp 313–4, is rather confused.

[126] *Fred* cap 24, p 15; cap 19, p 13 with Wallace-Hadrill's n 1. The case of Desiderius of Auxerre, and the inaccuracy of Fredegar's 'legendary' account, are discussed by Kurth, 'Brunehaut', pp 308–10.

[127] Ep v, 58, *MGH Epp* 1, p 369. Compare *Ep* ix, 213, *MGH Epp* 2, p 198.

[128] Claude, 'Bestellung der Bischöfe', p 59 n 290.

[129] *Vita Eligii* II, 1, p 694: 'Maxime de temporibus Brunehildis infelicissimae reginae . . . violabat hoc contagium catholicam fidem'. A similarly harsh view of Brunhild ('le mauvais génie de la maison de Sigebert . . .'!) is taken by E. Vacandard, 'Les elections episcopales', in *Études de Critique et d'Histoire* (Paris 1905) pp 159 *seq*.

[130] For a nice example from the 660s, of wealth as a qualification for episcopal office, see the contemporary *Passio Praejecti*, cap 12, *SSRM* 5, p 232: when Praejectus solicits the bishopric of Clermont, the *plebs* ask him 'si se sciebat tantam pecuniam auri argentique metalli habere, unde hoc opus queat subire'.

personal connexions. The bishops, for their part, could achieve no concerted action, could undertake no moral reform, without royal sponsorship. This pope Gregory understood very well when he directed his appeals to Brunhild.[131] The collaboration of queen, bishop and pope is apparent in Brunhild's foundations at Autun: a nuns' house dedicated to the Virgin, a *Xenodochium* associated with a male convent whose abbot was to be royally appointed, and a church dedicated to St Martin served by secular clergy and destined to provide the queen's tomb.[132] Brunhild's interest in Autun is significant. Continuing the eastward reorientation of the 'Burgundian' kingdom implicit in Guntramn's choice of Chalon for his *sedes regia*,[133] Brunhild, while cultivating links with the Rhone cities especially Lyons, also entrenched royal influence firmly in a major centre of sixth-century cult and culture, a point of articulation between the two broad zones of Martinian and Rhone-based monasticism, a citadel, finally, of Gallo-Roman aristocratic power which was close to the frontier with 'barbarian' Gaul.[134]

Brunhild's association with Syagrius of Autun is only the most striking instance of what must be seen as a characteristic and inevitable mode of royal government in the Merovingian *regnum*. Bishops were there in the *civitates*, and kings, from Clovis onwards, who wanted to govern in and from cities therefore had to work with bishops. This rather than any common commitment to *Romanentum* and Roman governmental principles, or any adherence to a '*parti romain*',[135] or any absolutist ambitions on the part of a cultured Visigoth grown into a 'Burgundian "lady-centralist" ',[136] accounts for Brunhild's relations with the bishops of the realms she ruled and, beyond them, with the pope. In Burgundy, naturally, the bishops were *Romani*, but it was not

[131] *Epp* viii, 4; ix, 213; xi, 46, *MGH Epp* 2, pp 5–8; 198–200; 318–9.

[132] *Epp* xiii, 11–13, *MGH Epp* 2, pp 376–81, where also the editor, L. M. Hartmann, convincingly defends the authenticity of these privileges, and suggests that Gregory based his wording on that of Brunhild in her original request. For Brunhild's tomb, see Kurth, 'Brunehaut', pp 347, 352–6.

[133] Ewig, 'Résidence [et capitale pendant le haut Moyen Age]', *RH* 230 (1963) pp 25–72, at p 48.

[134] See Gregory the Great, Epp ix, 214, 218 and 222 *MGH Epp* 2, pp 200, 205–10, 213–14 (contacts with Syagrius of Autun) and Epp ix, 208 and 230, pp 195–227 (contacts with Spain via Autun). Riché, *Education*, pp 179 *seq*, 268–70, with maps on pp 170 and 269; Prinz, *Mönchtum*, pp 60–1, 136, 140 with maps 5, 6 and 9; and Stroheker, *Adel*, pp 121–2, 163–4 (for the Syagrii and Desiderii).

[135] So, Delaruelle, 'L'Église romaine et ses relations avec l' Église franque jusqu'en 800', in *SS Spoleto* 7, i (1960) pp 143–84, at p 160.

[136] So, Prinz, *Mönchtum*, p 542.

their Romanity which determined Brunhild's favour, any more than ethnic affinity governed her choice of lay officials: her alleged partiality to 'Romans' is belied by the number of Frankish and Burgundian appointments mentioned by Fredegar.[137]

The exception to the record of harmony between Brunhild and her bishops is the case of Desiderius of Vienne, first exiled, later stoned to death, according to Fredegar on 'the wicked advice of Aridius of Lyons and of . . . Brunhild'.[138] If all we had was Fredegar's threadbare account of this apparently arbitrary action, it might be tempting to explain Desiderius' fate in terms of factionalism in the Burgundian episcopate and the traditional rivalry between Lyons and Vienne. But the remarkable *Vita Desiderii* written by the Visigothic king Sisebut (612–21), and a second *Vita* written in the eighth century by a cleric of Vienne throw more light on the affair.[139] Sisebut is violently hostile to Brunhild, not I think because he held her responsible for the dismissal of Theuderic II's Visigothic bride (who after all was no relation of Sisebut's)[140] nor through any genuine concern for the sanctity of Desiderius, but because he is writing propaganda for Septimanian consumption. His *Vita* is, as Fontaine has brilliantly shown, 'a hagiographic pamphlet' designed to show how a Toledan king could respect a Gallo-Roman aristocrat and to incite opposition to Frankish rule.[141] And here, significantly, as in the letters of count Bulgar of Septimania (written about 610)[142] Brunhild the 'nurse of discords' is completely identified with the Merovingians. Sisebut stresses the role of Brunhild's protégé, the mayor of the palace Protadius in bringing about Desiderius's exile and suggests that the terror of Brunhild and Theuderic at Protadius's death made them avenge themselves on

[137] *Fred* caps 24, 28, 29, pp 16, 19, mentions Protadius, Claudius and Ricomer as 'Romans by birth'; but he also mentions the promotions of the Franks Quolen (cap 18, p 12), and Bertoald (cap 24, p 15), while the constable Eborin and the chamberlain Berthar (caps 30, 38, pp 20, 31–2) were also presumably Franks. Duke Rocco, probably a Burgundian, served as Brunhild and Theuderic's envoy to Spain in 607 and only turned against her in 613. (caps 30, 42, pp 20, 34). Among bishops, the Austrasian Frank Leudegasius of Mainz was an ally of Theuderic in 612 (cap 38, p 31) while Lupus of Sens, deposed after 614 for his previous loyalty to Brunhild, came from a Frankish family in Orleans: *Vita Lupi, MGH SSRM* 4, caps 1, 11, p 179, 182.

[138] *Fred* cap 32, p 21.

[139] Both *Vitae* are edited by Krusch in *MGH SSRM* 3, pp 630–45.

[140] cap 30, p 20: Ermenburga was the daughter of Witteric, murderer of his predecessor and himself murdered by Gunthimar in 610.

[141] J. Fontaine, *Isidore de Séville et la culture classique dans l'Espagne wisigothique* (Paris 1959) p 841 nn 1 and 2.

[142] *MGH Epp* 3, pp 677–81, at 677: 'iurgiorum auctrix'.

Desiderius. The eighth-century *Vita* hints at popular opposition to Desiderius in Vienne. But both *Vitae* agree that the basic reason for Desiderius' loss of royal favour and eventual death was his sharp criticism of royal *mores*—specifically of Theuderic's concubines.[143] How credible is it that Brunhild would have let such an issue embroil her in an uncharacteristic conflict with a leading bishop? Why did she not ensure that her grandson took a wife and became respectable in the eyes of an ecclesiastical moralist? Such a marriage, argued Kurth, could not have endangered Brunhild any more than concubines already did: 'will anyone seriously maintain', he asked, 'that a sensual king submits more willingly to the influence of his wife than that of his mistress?'[144]

To understand Brunhild's motives, we must look at one more episode: her relations with St Columbanus. She must have met him long since, when he first arrived in the *regnum Francorum c*591 and found patronage from her son Childebert.[145] From the outset Columbanus' *peregrinatio* had a strong inner-worldly objective, namely the restoration (or application) of *religio* to *fides*,[146] which could only be achieved with political support. It was a matter of building up a network of personal relations and loyalties, of education: and this took time. The history of Luxeuil is obscure until quite late in Theuderic's reign but it is clear that some Austrasian and Burgundian aristocrats had been patronising the monastery in the 590s.[147] and there is no sign of any royal hostility. The first mention in the *Vita Columbani* of Theuderic's attitude to the saint stresses his veneration: 'he had often come to [Columbanus] at Luxeuil and with all humility begged the help of his prayers'.[148] Brunhild too recognised his support as worth having. Columbanus seems to have been in the habit of coming to visit Brunhild and the royal family. In 609 she sought the holy man's blessing for her great-grandsons, the eldest of them born in 602.[149] We should note the lateness of the evidence for conflict between the queen and the saint. If for years he had been complaining about Theuderic's failure to marry, it was only in 609 that the political consequences of

143 *MGH SSRM* 3, pp 635, 640–1.

144 Kurth, 'Brunehaut', p 322.

145 Jonas, *VC* cap 6, *MGH SSRM* 4, p 72 with Krusch's n 3. See [G. S. M.] Walker, [*Sancti Columbani Opera*], *Scriptores Latini Hiberniae*, 2 (Dublin 1957) introd, pp x–xi, xxi *seq*.

146 *VC* cap 5, p 71. Compare Columbanus's ep 2, Walker, pp 12–23.

147 *VC*, I, caps 10, 14 and 15, pp 76, 79 and 81. For another possible case (Agilus) see Prinz, *Mönchtum*, pp 126, 217, 356–7.

148 *VC*, I, cap 18, p 86; *Fred* cap 36, p 23.

149 *VC*, I cap 19, p 87. *Fred* cap 21, p14 gives the date of Sigebert's birth.

his objections became explicit when he denied the claim of Theuderic's sons to succeed to the kingship. Now and only now Brunhild appears as 'a second Jezebel',[150] her sin the primal one of pride: but it is pride of a specific kind, which fears to lose long-held status, power and wealth, and it has a specific manifestation of hostility to the *vir Dei* whose moralising threatens that position. Theuderic had nothing to lose by compliance and indeed, Brunhild 'could see that he was yielding to the man of God'. But for her, what might be at stake was control of the *aula regis,* the court, and thus the real power and influence which made a queen's position worth having. Columbanus's hagiographer Jonas, for all his bias, had hit the nail squarely on the head: being the king's bedfellow, even being the mother of his sons, was not at all the same thing as being queen. Brunhild knew this. She must have known it when in Childebert's reign she had had a queen as daughter-in-law. But in such situations, personalities counted for much, and Faileuba did not strike contemporaries as considerable. And in any case that was all long ago when perhaps Brunhild herself had had little choice. In the early 600s she was old, had long grown used to power and did not want to retire: there was no contemporary sentiment against gerontocracy. Her aim now was to secure the future for her line; thus to get Theuderic's sons accepted as his prospective heirs. And there was a final element in her motivation, perhaps still an essential one: Fredegund's son lived and ruled in Neustria. Could Theuderic be counted on, without Brunhild at his side, to pursue the vendetta to its necessary end? Desiderius had already been eliminated probably by means of an intended exile that went wrong.[151] Columbanus too must now be exiled—for Brunhild rightly judged that the abrasive old Irishman would never be pressurised into silence when he saw principle at stake. The initiative was hers. The allegedly 'fundamental' hostility of the bishops, or, alternatively, of 'the monasticism of the Rhone region', have in my view been exaggerated. Despite Columbanus's rudeness, despite the awkward dispute over the dating of easter,[152] the bishops of Brunhild's realm had left the Irish to their eccentricities; as for

[150] *VC,* I, cap 18, p 86: '. . . mentem Brunechildis . . . secundae ut erat Zezebelis, antiquus anguis adiit eamque contra virum Dei stimulatam superbiae aculeo excitat quia cerneret viro Dei Theudericum oboedire'. It is worth noting that Sisebut, despite his violent antipathy to Brunhild, does not label her a 'Jezebel'. But his *Vita* is stylistically very different from Jonas's work.

[151] Kurth, 'Brunehaut', p 329, argues this on the basis of the second *Vita Desiderii, MGH SSRM* 3, cap 9 p 641.

[152] Columbanus, epp 1–3, Walker, pp 12–25, with Walker's comments, pp xxv–vi.

'monasticism', the delay in the appearance of Luxeuil's influence in southern Gaul (neatly demonstrated in Prinz's maps) had more to do with pre-existing deep-rooted traditions and patterns of aristocratic patronage and monastic practice than with positive or principled 'opposition'.[153] Jonas should still be believed, I think, when he says that it was Brunhild herself who 'worked upon the bishops' and on the lay magnates and *auligae* as well as the king, to co-ordinate an anti-Columbanan front. It was natural for Jonas to see a parallel with the biblical archetype of the wicked queen who sought to destroy God's mouthpiece, the holy man. Knowing as he did the details of Brunhild's life and death, Jonas must have relished other reminiscences of Jezebel: like her, Brunhild was a foreigner and a king's daughter; like her, Brunhild attacked a personal enemy (Naboth=Desiderius) by bringing false charges against him and then had him stoned to death; like her, Brunhild met a dreadful fate—*et equorum ungulae conculcaverunt eam.*[154] Jonas's audience, likewise connoisseurs of the Books of Kings, could readily supply these motifs, once given the identification of Brunhild with Jezebel; and readers of the *Vita Columbani* who wrote about Brunhild subsequently gained access to useful new 'material'. In the *Liber Historiae Francorum*, the aged Brunhild titivates herself in a pathetic attempt to seduce her conqueror Clothar II, just like Jezebel who, hearing of king Jehu's arrvail, *depinxit oculos suos stibio et ornavit caput suum;*[155] while in the eighth-century *Vita* of Desiderius, Brunhild becomes Jezebel in this second context, *alone* responsible for the bishop's death in which the motif of stoning is emphasised.[156] So influential, indeed, was Jonas's work, so definitive his portrayal of Brunhild that in Frankish hagiography she came to rank with Ebroin as a stereotype of villainy.[157] If in one tenth-century *Vita* she appears in a less awful light when, struck by the saint's power she becomes his patron, this simply proves that a hagiographer could best show the greatness of *his* holy man by pitting him successfully against the wickedest of Wicked Queens.[158]

[153] Prinz, *Mönchtum,* p 148 and n 137, stresses this 'opposition'. Reservations similar to mine, though based on other evidence, are voiced by Ian Wood, 'A prelude to Columbanus: the monastic achievement in the Burgundian territories' (in the press). I am very grateful to him for letting me see this paper in advance of publication.

[154] 3 Kings 16: 31; 19: 1–2; 5–16, 23; 4 Kings 9: 30–37. For Jonas' use of typology in the *Vita Columbani,* see J. Leclercq, 'L'univers religieux de St Columban', *Aspects du Monachisme hier et Aujourd'hui* (Paris 1974) pp 193–212 at 201 *seq.*

[155] *LHF* cap 40, p 310, influenced by 4 Kings 9: 30–33.

[156] *MGH SSRM* 3, cap 9, p 641.

[157] Graus, *Heiliger,* pp 373–4.

[158] *Vita Menelei, MGH SSRM* 5, caps 3–11, pp 150–4.

Brunhild, then, had not been born bad, but nor had she exactly had badness thrust upon her: in the hagiographer's terms, she deserved her reputation and had indeed challenged the authority of a saint and opposed heavenly by earthly power. That this action was untypical of her, that it was forced on her in a particular time and situation by the need to survive politically, could not concern the monks who reviled her memory. That she was very unlucky to have crossed the path of the one great charismatic of her age and that her posthumous fate was in a sense accidental: none of this could concern the generations of monks in whose collective memory this Jezebel lived on. But it must concern modern historians and cause us to rethink some of the sweeping generalisations and value-judgements out of which our predecessors, two or three generations ago, fashioned their own improbable images of Brunhild as benevolent despot or great soul.

Balthild's image is, of course, timeless: she was and is a saint.[159] But she was also, for some contemporaries, a Jezebel. The paradox, and the apparent contrast with Brunhild, invite our attention. Balthild's *Vita* makes it clear that she had grasped the uses of piety, both as a means to secure personal status and as a political instrument. There is a touch of Uriah Heep about her oft-praised 'humility' but this may be the hagiographer's fault, not hers. What is new and remarkable here is the depiction of a specifically royal sanctity.[160] This is apparent first in her activities as Clovis II's consort. In the intimate atmosphere of the court, Balthild structures her personal relationships 'correctly' in terms both of the hagiographer's values and of her own interests: 'to the great men she showed herself like a mother, to the bishops like a daughter, to the young men and boys like the best sort of nurse.' In a rather wider context too, she has the right priorities, loving 'bishops as fathers, monks as brothers and the poor as their pious nurse'; she does not infringe the magnates' sense of status but accepts their counsels when appropriate, she encourages the young men to monastic studies, and uses her influence with the king 'humbly but persistently' on behalf of churches and the poor.[161] Clovis assigns her the chief of his palace

[159] *LThK* 2, col 50 (Ewig) *sv* 'Balthildis'. Her feast-day is 30 January. If we may trust Ewig, 'Klosterpolitik', p 62, she is still capable of making a nocturnal visit to reprove a detractor!

[160] This is most evident in her remission of the capitation-tax and her prohibition of the slave-trade in Christian captives: 'datasque praeceptiones per singulas regiones, ut nullus in regno Francorum captivum hominem christianum penitus transmitteret', *Vita* caps 6 and 9, pp 488, 494.

[161] *Vita* cap 4, pp 485–6.

clerks, his *fidelis famulus* Genesius, to administer her charitable works: as the *Vita's* term *assiduus* implies, he was a force to be reckoned with in the Neustrian palace at this time. Further promotion was assured: he would become bishop of Lyons, 'on Christ's orders' (and doubtless Balthild's) in 660.[162]

Already during Clovis's lifetime, Balthild had had close ties with Eligius, bishop of Noyon from 641, and probably also Audoenus (Dado), bishop of Rouen from 641.[163] These men were at the centre of a friendship-network which spanned the entire *regnum Francorum* and had a remarkable capacity to persist and to reproduce itself over generations—from the 620s through to the 660s and probably later.[164] In so far as it transcended the boundaries of the *Teilreiche,* it could be troublesome for a king: Sigibert III forbade Desiderius of Cahors to attend a council at Bourges because that was in his brother's realm, and Desiderius could invite only his Austrasian friendss to celebrate the foundation of the monastery of St Amantius at Cahors.[165] But Clother II and Dagobert had made the network work for them, using its members first as lay officials and close advisers, later as bishops in major *civitates.* A hefty attack on simony made by the bishops themselves was directed against local aristocratic, rather than royal malpractice.[166] Control of episcopal appointments, simoniac or otherwise, remained essential for rulers. It seems likely, for instance, that Chrodobert became bishop of Paris late in Clovis's reign because of his already close connexions with Audoenus and with Balthild.[167]

When Clovis died late in 657, Balthild as queen mother naturally had a good claim to the regency, but her established friendships, especially

[162] *Ibid* pp 486–7.

[163] *Vita Eligii,* ii, 32, p 727. See also Vacandard, [*Vie de*] *Saint Ouen,* [*evêque de Rouen*] (Paris 1902) pp 249–55.

[164] The main evidence lies in the letter-collection of Desiderius of Cahors (died 650) *MGH Epp* 3, pp 191–214. Audoenus survived until 684. For the friendship-circle, see Levison's introduction to the *Vita Audoini, MGH SSRM* 5, pp 536–7; Sprandel, *Adel,* pp 16–7, 33; Riché, *Education,* pp 236 *seq.* Wallace-Hadrill, *Long-Haired Kings,* pp 222–3.

[165] Desiderii, *Ep* ii, 17, p 212; *Ep* i, 11, p 199.

[166] Council of Chalon-sur-Saône (647–53) cap 16, *Concilia Galliae 511–695,* ed C. de Clercq, *CCSL* 148A (Turnhout 1963) p 306.

[167] He seems to have belonged to Audoenus' circle, if the 'bishop Chrodobert' to whom Audoenus sent a copy of his *Vita Eligii* can be identified with the then bishop of Paris: see Krusch's comments in *MGH SSRM* 4, pp 650–1 and Vacandard, *Saint Ouen,* pp 236–7. But Vacandard's apparent identification of the bishop with a Rodebert, mayor of the palace in 655, is mistaken for the latter was still addressed as mayor in 663: see Ebling, *Prosopographie,* pp 112–13. The mayor and the bishop could well be relatives however.

with Genesius, allowed her to make the claim effective. There is no evidence of any demand at this point for a division of the Neustro-Burgundian realm, which, while suggesting the absence of any strong Burgundian secessionist movement, could also indicate the smoothness of the transmission of royal power. Audoenus and Chrodobert are named in the *Vita Balthildis* as the key supporters of the regency,[168] and Ebroin's appointment as mayor some months afterwards must have been made on their, as well as the queen's, 'advice'. In 657-8, then, the *regnum Francorum* remained at peace—no mean tribute to the degree of governmental stability and continuity which episcopal underwriting helped ensure.

But the maintenance of royal power was not just a simple matter of keeping inherited episcopal allies. The trouble was, there were bishops and bishops: the 'good' ones, as the *Vita* engagingly terms them (they certainly included Eligius and Audoenus) urged the queen on to prohibit simony specifically in episcopal appointments,[169] where the 'bad' ones, by implication, preferred to work the familiar systems. Whatever financial profits this meant foregoing Balthild continued to exercise her power to appoint. Politics based on personalities, families and factions were the reverse of static: to remain in any sort of control, a ruler had to be able to place his/her supporters in key positions. Earlier Merovingians had been able to exercise considerable freedom in appointing patricians, dukes and counts. The development of hereditary offices, restricting the scope of royal action,[170] heightened the need to secure the right bishops. Against this background, the scanty evidence for Balthild's episcopal appointments becomes significant. Three cases are known. In the first is recorded only the bare fact that through her influence Erembert, who came originally from the Chartres region, became bishop of Toulouse.[171] Aquitaine was clearly not yet outwith the scope of royal intervention. The second and third cases relate to Burgundy which contained, in my view, not a separatist movement, but aristocratic factions operating in cities as well as countryside. As in Brunhild's time, Autun and Lyons were two key cities in the region.

[168] *Vita* cap 5, p 487: '. . . suscepit ilico . . . Chlotharius quondam Francorum regnum, tunc etenim precellentibus principibus Chrodobertho episcopo Parisiaco et domno Audoeno seu et Ebroino maiore domus . . .'

[169] *Vita* cap 6, p 488: '. . . exortantibus bonis sacerdotibus . . .'

[170] A. R. Lewis, 'The Dukes in the *Regnum Francorum*, A. D. 550–751', *Speculum* 51 (1976) pp 381–410 at 398–9; Sprandel, 'Struktur und Geschichte', pp 43–7, 60–1.

[171] *Vita Eremberti, MGH SSRM* 5, p 654. This *Vita* was composed *c*800, but its accuracy on this point is accepted by Ewig, 'Teilreiche', p 127.

In Autun, faction-fighting kept the see vacant for two years (probably 660–2)[172] until Balthild took the initiative. She had already provided herself with the man for the job when she summoned to the court a learned, experienced and above all *strenuus* man from Poitiers—Leudegarius. It is tempting to suggest that Balthild needed a replacement for Genesius in the royal chapel and, probably on Audoenus' advice, sought an 'outstanding teacher of clerics'. His subsequent move from chapel to bishopric replicated that of Genesius. In the short run he proved the wisdom of Balthild's choice by restoring Autun to peace and good government.[173]

Balthild's interventions in Toulouse and Autun evoked little contemporary comment. But the third case involved more complications: Genesius's appointment to Lyons followed a violent episode in which his predecessor was killed. According to *Acta* which seem to have a genuinely seventh-century base,[174] bishop Aunemundus and his brother, the prefect of Lyons, were sons of a previous prefect and the family had built up a virtual monopoly of local power through using their influence at the courts of Dagobert and Clovis II. There Aunemundus had had a typically successful career as a lay office-holder before being appointed to Lyons, surely with royal support, about 650 (he baptised the infant Clothar III who was born in that year). But the *Acta* stress envy in what sounds like a local context as the cause of Aunemundus' downfall.[175] The bishop and his brother were accused of treason *(infidelitas)* and summoned to appear before the boy-king Clothar and the regent Balthild at an assembly at Mareuil, a royal *villa* near Orleans. The brother appeared, was found guilty and executed.

[172] *Passio Leudegarii* I, cap 2, p 284.

[173] *Ibid* I, caps 2, 3, pp 284–6. See also Riché, *Education,* pp 363–4.

[174] *Acta sancti Aunemundi, AASS* Sept vii (Brussels 1760) pp 744–6. See A. Coville, *Recherches* [*sur l'histoire de Lyon du Vme au IXme siècle*] (Paris 1928) pp 366 *seq.*

[175] *Acta* p 744: '... nullusque de aliqua re ad suum profectum quidquam valebat impetrare, nisi sua suggestione (that is, Aunemundus's) Clotario tertio principi deportaret . . . Ideo dum sublimitatis suae gloriam ac brachium vindicaret extentum, nec non et a fratribus celsior videretur in coetu, cunctis incidit in odium. Qui tractare eum seditiose coeperunt sub clandestina accusatione dicentes, quasi regnum ejusdem Clotarii . . . evertere moliretur occulte . . .' Dupraz, *Royaume,* p 343 n 1, and Fischer, *Ebroin,* p 92, both state, citing the *Acta,* that the bishop's accusers were *maiores natu ducesque.* But what the *Acta* in fact say is that these magnates appeared at the assembly at Mareuil, as one would expect. The *Acta* imply, rather, the identity of accusers and *fratres*—presumably the 'brethren' of the church of Lyons. A few lines later, the *Acta* tell how Aunemundus asked forgiveness from the *fratres* at Lyons for any injuries he had done them, including unfair seizure of their goods. For further evidence of Aunemundus' local power, see below n 181.

When Aunemundus himself failed to appear, pleading illness, the regent sent *duces* with instructions to bring him to the royal court and to kill him only if he resisted. On their way there, near Chalon, Aunemundus was murdered one night by two armed men whose action was deeply regretted by the *duces* themselves.[176] Now the local tradition about these events had got fairly confused by the time the surviving (late-medieval) texts were written.[177] But the crucial points so far as Balthild is concerned are, first, that these *Acta* ascribe to her neither the initiative in Aunemundus' accusation nor the responsibility for his death, and second that the identity or gentile origin of Aunemundus's accusers is not stated. To erect on this basis a theory of a 'Burgundian autonomist party' who had 'conspired against the Neustrian *palatium*' in sharp reaction against Balthild's 'programme of compulsory "union" '[178] is to pile figment on fantasy. We simply know too little about the alleged treason of Aunemundus and his brother and have no indication that any others but these two were involved. It is more likely, I think, that the episode belongs in a context of family or factional rivalries in and around Lyons, and that the accusers of Aunemundus and his brother were other local aristocrats, not Neustrian centralists. The whole affair is reminiscent of a situation recorded in the *Passio Praejecti,* where a dispute over land in the Auvergne between the bishop of Clermont and a local magnate is brought to the king's court and settled, but the royal decision is soon followed by violence on the spot when the bishop is murdered by other local enemies.[179] The interplay, rather than conflict, between royal and aristocratic interests, the circulation of power from court to provinces and back, seem to me as characteristic of Merovingian politics in the 660s and 670s as in the days of Gregory of Tours. In our Lyons case, anyway, the death of Aunemundus left the way open for Balthild to appoint Genesius, who not only survived but established a strong base for intervention in the politics of the *regnum* over the next twenty years.[180]

Unmentioned in any contemporary Frankish source, apparently without repercussions in the history of the *regnum Francorum,* the

[176] *Acta* p 745. The *duces* had promised the abbot of Luxeuil that Aunemundus would be safe.
[177] Coville, *Recherches,* pp 372 *seq.*
[178] So, Dupraz, *Royaume,* pp 342–4, 352–4; Fischer, *Ebroin,* pp 90–8.
[179] *MGH SSRM* 5, caps 23, 24, pp 239–40.
[180] Genesius died in 679. For his career, see Coville, *Recherches,* pp 416–21.

Aunemundus affair might seem irrelevant to Balthild's reputation. But because the young Wilfrid happened to have established close relations with Aunemundus and to have stayed for three years in Lyons, whence he subsequently acquired some information about the bishop's death, the story was translated in a new 'Wilfridian' version to an Anglo-Saxon literary milieu.[181] Thus, strangely, Balthild who had begun life in England returned there in posthumous tradition, not as a saint—but as a 'malevolent queen . . . just like the most impious queen Jezebel'.[182] Eddius may have borrowed the motif from the *Vita Columbani,* but he could equally well have used it independently, for his *Vita Wilfridi* is rich in biblical typology. Jezebel was the obvious type for a queen who persecuted a holy man, and Eddius actually used the same motif again later in his work in reference to the 'wicked' queen Iurminburg, second wife of Ecgfrith of Northumbria and Wilfrid's violent enemy until her later *conversio.*[183] Eddius wrote over half a century after Aunemundus's death, and based his account of it upon Wilfrid's reminiscences. He asserts that the 'evil-wishing queen Balthild' persecuted the church of God; that she had nine bishops put to death ('not counting priests and deacons'!) and one of these was 'bishop Dalfinus' (=Aunemundus)[184] whom certain dukes had most malignly ordered to come before them; and that Wilfrid not only was present at the bishop's 'martyrdom' but offered himself to the same fate, only to be spared by the dukes when they learnt that he was 'from overseas, of the English race from Britain'. So, concludes Eddius, Wilfrid, though denied a martyr's palm, was already a confessor—'just like John the apostle and evangelist who sat unharmed in a cauldron

[181] Eddius, *Vita Wilfridi,* ed Levison, *MGH SSRM* 6, cap 6, p 199; ed [B.] Colgrave, p 14. Bede *H[istoria] E[cclesiastica gentis Anglorum]*, ed [C.] Plummer (Oxford 1896) v, 19, p 325. Plummer, vol 2, pp 316–20, established the chronology of Wilfrid's life. During Wilfrid's first visit to Lyons on his way to Rome in 653, the bishop of that city offered him his niece in marriage together with 'a good part of Gaul' (*bona pars Galliarum*); *Vita* cap 4, ed Levison, p 197.

[182] *Vita Wilfridi* cap 6, p 199 (Levison). One of the two manuscripts of Eddius gives the reading 'Brunhild' instead of 'Balthild', as do some manuscripts of Bede, *HE*: see Levison's comment here p 199 n 3, and Colgrave's, p 154. Colgrave's suggestion that this may be a reminiscence of the Brunhild of the Volsung saga is surely incorrect.

[183] *Vita Wilfridi,* cap 24, p 218 (Levison), p 48 (Colgrave). I am grateful to Joan Nicholson for reminding me of Eddius's other Jezebel.

[184] The name 'Dalfinus' is not, as often alleged, evidence of Eddius's inaccuracy. Coville, *Recherches,* pp 381–5, shows that Aunemundus's brother is not named at all in any early Lyons source, that Aunemundus, typically in this period, had two names, and that his second name (Dalfinus) was simply 'borrowed' for his brother by late medieval reworkers of the story.

of boiling oil . . .'[185] Eddius's aim here is not factual reporting,[186] but the establishment of Wilfrid's saintly credentials at an early point in his *Vita.*

Now if we date Aunemundus's death to 660 with Levison and Ewig,[187] there is clearly a chronological problem involved in accepting Eddius's story, for Wilfrid left Lyons, at the latest, in 658.[188] Further the details of place, time and circumstances recorded in the *Acta* (where of course Wilfrid is not mentioned at all) actually contradict those of Eddius's account. Levison observed these discrepancies but left the matter unresolved; while Coville claimed the discrepancies were insignificant and on Eddius's 'authority' dated Aunemundus' death to 658.[189] I suggest another conclusion, namely, that Wilfrid was not in fact present at Aunemundus's death, and that Eddius's account therefore derives from information which Wilfrid acquired on one of his subsequent visits to Gaul (or perhaps from some other *peregrinus*) on which either Eddius or Wilfrid himself superimposed the tale of Wilfrid's youthful heroism—satisfying to upholders of Germanic and monastic values alike.[190] The motivation behind this tale need not concern us further, though Wilfrid's later connexion with Dagobert II and Eddius' very hostile attitude to Ebroin[190a] are no doubt relevant. Here the point is simply that the *Vita Wilfridi,* and Bede who depends on it, while they explain Balthild's otherwise surprising 'bad name in her native country',[191] need not seriously affect our assessment

185 *Vita Wilfridi* cap 6, pp 199–200 with n 2 (Levison); p 14 (Colgrave, who gives a possible source of the St John anecdote in the note on p 155.)

186 For pertinent views on Eddius's method, see R. L. Poole, 'St Wilfrid and the see of Ripon', *EHR* 34 (1919) pp 1–22, and H. Mayr-Harting, *The Coming of Christianity to Anglo-Saxon England* (London 1972) pp 139 *seq.*

187 Levison, *Vita Wilfridi,* pp 163–4; Ewig, 'Teilreiche', p 95.

188 *Vita,* ed Colgrave, pp 14–5; Plummer at p 317 of Bede, *HE,* vol 2.

189 Coville, *Recherches,* p 389; also Fischer, *Ebroin,* pp 95–6. But there is a further difficulty in accepting that Wilfrid, if he had really experienced Balthild's malevolence at first hand, could have been consecrated bishop in 664 at the Neustrian royal villa of Compiègne, by courtesy of Clothar III and presumably also Balthild: Bede, *HE* iii, 28, p 194, with Plummer's notes, vol 2, pp 198, 317.

190 R. Woolf, 'The ideal of men dying with their lord in the *Germania* and in The Battle of Maldon', *Anglo-Saxon England* 5 (1976) pp 63–81; Graus, *Heiliger,* pp 63–4, 101.

190a *Vita,* caps 25, 27, 33, pp 219–20, 228 (Levison); 50, 52, 68 (Colgrave). Poole, 'St Wilfrid', pp 4 *seq,* notes some inaccuracies in Eddius' information on Frankish affairs.

191 Levison, *England,* p 10. Balthild might have been expected to have had a glowing reputation in England, given the close links of Chelles and Jouarre with various English houses: see A. Lohaus, *Die Merowinger und England, Münchner Beiträge zur Mediavistik und Renaissance-Forschung* (Munich) 1974 pp 53 *seq,* and P. Sims-Williams, 'Continental influence at Bath monastery in the seventh century', *Anglo-Saxon England* 4 (1975) pp 1–10.

of Balthild's regency and, more particularly, of her interventions in local politics and her relations with bishops. Ewig has seen 'the conflict between Aunemundus and Balthild' as signifying a new development in the Neustro-Burgundian realm: the diocese was changing from an 'area associated with an office' to 'the area of a lordship' and Balthild, so Ewig implies, was thus engaged in a new struggle against episcopal 'territorial politics'.[192] I have argued, however, that the fate of Aunemundus was the result rather of a local conflict than of one between centre and province; that Eddius should not be invoked to suggest, as Ewig does, that Aunemundus's case is typical of many others during Balthild's regency; and that the relationship between ruler and *civitas*-politics evident in this case is not a new but a rather traditional one. Evidence of a 'structural change' in the seventh century must be sought elsewhere.

One last aspect of Balthild's dealings with the holy, its custodians and interpreters, remains to be considered: her *Klosterpolitik*.[193] Since the evidence for it begins in 655 and continues throughout the regency, we can fairly assume that she was at least partly responsible for it already as Clovis II's queen. The extant text of the privilege of bishop Landericus for St Denis has been tampered with by later forgers, but its genuine parts can be supplemented by Clovis II's confirmation of it which has survived in the original dated 22 June 655.[194] Clearly the bishop gave up certain rights he had formerly exercised in respect of the monastery: he could no longer exact payment for certain liturgical functions, nor interfere in the disposition of the monastic revenues nor dip into the monastic treasury. What prompted such substantial concessions of wealth and power? Landericus is explicit enough: he grants his privilege 'because the request of the king is for us like a command which it is extremely difficult to resist'.[195] During Balthild's regency this episcopal privilege was complemented by a grant of royal immunity, whereby the king took the monastery under his protection

[192] Ewig, 'Milo', pp 430–3. (His terms are *Amtsgebiet, Herrschaftsgebiet* and *Territorialpolitik.*)

[193] On what follows, Ewig, 'Klosterpolitik', is fundamental, as also is his 'Beobachtungen zu den Klosterprivilegien des 7. und frühen 8. Jhdts', *Adel und Kirche. Festschrift G. Tellenbach* (Freiburg 1968) pp 52–65.

[194] Landericus' privilege: [J. M.] Pardessus, [*Diplomata, Chartae . . . et instrumenta aetatis Merovingicae*], 2 vols (Paris 1843,9) 2, no 320, pp 95–7. Clovis II's confirmation: *MGH DD* 1, no 19, pp 19–21; facsimile in P. Lauer and C. Samarin, *Les Diplomes originaux des Merovingiens* (Paris 1908) no 6.

[195] Pardessus, p 96: '. . . quia supradicti domni Clodovei regis petitio quasi nobis iussio est, cui difficillimum est resisti'.

and put himself under the saint's protection, in return for releasing the monastery from fiscal obligations and other public services, making it 'immune' to the entrance of public officials in the performance of fiscal or judicial functions.[196] What was taking place was a redistribution of resources between three parties, bishop, monastery and king. The bishop's loss was the monastery's gain: so much the privilege made clear. But when at the same time the monastery became an immunist, the king while reallocating the burdens of royal administration could also hope to gain in terms of close, permanent, mutually-beneficial relations with the monastery and more effective control through, for example, royal intervention in abbatial appointments.[197] Finally, and also of vital importance from the king's standpoint, the establishment of the *laus perennis* at St Denis, which Dagobert seems unsuccessfully to have attempted,[198] was achieved in 655 by the introduction there of the *sanctus regularis ordo,* that is, the mixed Benedictine-Columbanan Rule of Luxeuil.[199] The monks' prayers were the instrument by which their royal protector on earth sought the benefits of heavenly protectors: Ewig is surely right to stress the importance 'for the court, [of] the cultic-liturgical business of monasticism'.[200]

The new arrangements at St Denis not only foreshadowed but provided the model for a whole series of similar ones precisely during Balthild's regency. On the one hand, there were two new foundations: Corbie, founded by Balthild and Clothar III between 657 and 661 and granted a privilege by the bishop of Amiens in 664 at Balthild's 'pious request',[201] and Chelles, effectively refounded on a royal *villa* where Chrodechild (Clovis's queen) had long ago established a little convent of nuns and a church dedicated to St George.[202] For Corbie, Balthild had monks and abbot imported from Luxeuil, for Chelles, nuns and abbess

[196] For the significance of privilege and immunity, see Levillain, 'Études [sur l'abbaye de Saint-Denis a l'époque mérovingienne]', *BEC* 87 (1926) pp 21–73. Clothar III's concession of immunity during Balthild's regency is not extant.

[197] Explicitly stated in the privilege of the bishop of Amiens for Corbie, ed Krusch in *NA* 31 (1906) pp 367–72 at p 369: '. . . quem unanimiter congregatio ipsius monasterii . . . dignum elegerint, data auctoritate a praefato principe vel eius successoribus. . .'

[198] *Fred* cap 79, p 68.

[199] See Prinz, *Mönchtum,* pp 105–6, 167–9, and Ian Wood's forthcoming paper, 'A prelude to Columbanus'.

[200] Ewig, 'Klosterpolitik', pp 112–13.

[201] *NA* 31 (1906) p 367. *Vita Balthildis* cap 7, pp 490–1.

[202] *Vita Balthildis* cap 7, pp 489–90, cap 18, pp 505–6, *Vita Bertilae, MGH SSRM* 6, cap 4, p 104. Chelles' function of prayer for king, queen and *proceres* is stressed by the dying Balthild herself: *Vita,* cap 12, p 498, urging the abbess to maintain this

from Jouarre. On the other hand there was the reorganisation of the communal life of old basilicas by the introduction therein of the *sanctus regularis ordo*. The *Vita Balthildis*, remarkably detailed and explicit on this topic, lists the main basilicas and makes it clear that Balthild's actions were coherent and well-planned—in Ewig's word, a 'policy':

> throughout the senior basilicas of the saints, lord Dionisius [St Denis near Paris], lord Germanus [St Germain at Auxerre], and lord Medardus [St Medard at Soissons], and also St Peter [St Pierre-le-Vif at Sens] and lord Anianus [St Aignan at Orleans] and also St Martin [at Tours], and everywhere else that her attention affected, she commanded the bishops and abbots, persuading them for the sake of zeal for God, and directed letters to them to this end, that the brethren settled in these places should live under the holy regular discipline. And in order that they [that is, the brethren] might willingly acquiesce, she ordered that a privilege should be granted them, and at the same time she granted them immunities, so that it might please them the better to pray for the mercy of Christ the highest king of all on behalf of the king and for peace.[203]

If we accept Ewig's plausible suggestion that 'everywhere else' probably included St Marcel at Chalon-sur-Saone, St Symphorien at Autun, St Bénigne at Dijon, St Hilary at Poitiers, St Lupus at Troyes and St Sulpicius at Bourges,[204] then with the *Vita's* six we have a list of nearly all the major cult-sites of seventh-century Gaul. Brunhild had cultivated St Martin's patronage and Dagobert St Denis's. But Balthild was mobilising a whole regiment of saints, enlisting the forces of the holy in every *civitas*. Perhaps still more confidence-inspiring was the placing of such forces right within the *palatium* itself: Clovis II (at Balthild's instigation?) had appropriated the arm of St Denis for the palace-oratory, outraging the monks thus deprived;[205] and it may well have been Balthild herself who acquired St Martin's *cappa* for the royal relic-collection[206] (it is first documented there in 679)[207] though in

'consuetudo, ut ipsa domus Dei bonam famam, quam coeperat, non amitteret, sed amplius semper in affectu caritatis cum omnibus amicis . . . permaneret in dilectione . . .'

[203] *Vita* cap 9, pp 493–4.

[204] 'Klosterpolitik', p 111. with n 43. Balthild's generosity to a group of Norman monasteries in the diocese of Rouen, to Luxeuil and 'the other monasteries of Burgundy', to Jouarre and Faremoutiers, and to the monasteries of Paris itself is stressed in *Vita* cap 8, pp 493–4, listing forests, *villae* and *pecuniam innumerabilem*.

[205] *LHF* cap 44, p 316.

[206] So, Ewig, 'Klosterpolitik', p 112.

[207] *MGH DD* no 49, p 45.

this case no opposition is recorded. Thus in the burial-places of the royal dead[208] and in the home-base of the living king, direct contacts were made between the Merovingian family and the sources of supernatural power—contacts which superimposed new centripetal forces on a previously localised field.

Playing for such high stakes, Balthild knew the risks she ran. Not every bishop was enthused by the new monasticism; and even if a bishop happily granted privileges to his own new foundation in the countryside, it would be naive to assume that he granted the same privileges equally gladly to the ancient basilica on his own doorstep in or by the city.[209] I am struck by the documents' emphasis on the bishop's economic loss, especially the renunciation by bishop Landericus of what was evidently an existing practice of carrying off from the monastery and into the city gold and silver bullion and cash which had been placed in the monastery.[210] The bishop of Amiens expressly renounced the same practice in the Corbie privilege,[211] but in his case the profit or loss was hypothetical. The bishops of Paris, Auxerre, Soissons and the rest must have faced a real loss of resources. The *Vita Balthildis* gives no hint of any compensation. For the brethren who served the basilicas, on the other hand, the new obligations Balthild laid on them were offset by new 'freedoms' which included financial incentives.[212] Balthild's policy then, might have been expected to arouse opposition, if anywhere, from bishops, which would make royal control of episcopal appointments all the more essential. Perhaps it is in this context that Balthild's 'fall' should be understood. Sigobrand, presumably her appointee to the see of Paris, alienated some powerful aristocrats by his *superbia*:[213] was he trying to recoup some of the losses his see had suffered because of his predecessor Landericus's enforced concessions to St Denis? Did the 'commotion' which caused

[208] Their significance is indicated by Ewig, 'Résidence', pp 48–52.

[209] Ewig, 'Klosterpolitik', p 109, rightly stresses that bishops might perceive Balthild's demands as 'an unheard-of imposition'.

[210] *MGH DD* 1, no 19, p 20.

[211] *NA* 31 (1906) p 369. The broader economic context which these references hint at cannot be discussed here. But for some archaeological and artistic evidence that might suggest continuing Neustrian prosperity, see Maillé, *Jouarre,* pp 112–14, p 206 *seq.* and for other evidence, F. Vercauteren, 'La vie urbaine entre Meuse et Loire du VIe au IXe siècle', in *SS Spoleto* 6, ii (1959) pp 453–84 at 478–9.

[212] *Vita Balthildis* cap 9, pp 493–4, (quoted above) suggests that the inducements to the *fratres* were well-planned: '. . . ut hoc libenter adquiescerent, privilegium eis firmare iussit [!], vel etiam emunitates concessit, ut melius eis delectaret pro rege . . . exorare'.

[213] Above p 52, and n 116.

Sigobrand's death signify the limits set by aristocratic interests to Balthild's policy in a situation of fierce competition for scarce resources (especially around Paris)? Balthild's wealth was clearly vast, both in treasure and in land; but had she enough to sustain lavish generosity to monasteries all over Neustria and Burgundy and at the same time to maintain bishops in their powerful yet dependent positions as lynchpins of royal government? In the event, the precariousness of her position as mere regent was exposed, and those whom she had 'sweetly nurtured' in the palace—including, probably, Ebroin—decided to dispense with her. Personal bonds held only so long as they were reinforced by real or prospective benefits. Balthild's regime had not been anti-aristocratic, nor, if she had gained prestige, had she done so at the aristocracy's expense; but their benefits were not apparent. With deadly accurate irony, the 'princes', according to Balthild's hagiographer, now 'suddenly permitted her'[214] to retire to Chelles which she had so richly endowed. There she died, perhaps in 680, after fifteen years of exemplary humility in the convent;[215] there she soon found her hagiographer and there her memory was kept green and her cult defended against the sceptical.[216]

Balthild had attempted, as Ewig observes, 'a structural change in the Merovingian church'.[217] But this could not fail to have consequences also for non-ecclesiastical politics. To be sure of this, we need only recall the implications of the Carolingians' *Reichskirche* for their whole political position, especially in the ninth century when royal exploitation of the church's resources replaced, to a significant extent, an eroded secular power-base.[218] Ewig thinks that Balthild's fall made her attempted 'structural change' quite abortive.[219] I am not so sure. True, we lack the evidence which might show whether or not a Childeric II

214 Above *ibid*, and p 51 n 113. The role of the *sacerdotes* at this point is interesting: they intervene, not to save Balthild but to re-establish peace between her and the *seniores* and thus to nip in the bud her *non modica querela* (feud ?) against them. The implication is that she might have pursued the quarrel even in 'retirement'.

215 For the date, see Krusch's introduction to the *Vita*, p 476. In describing Balthild's convent years, her hagiographer lavishly deploys the motifs of female ascetisism: the influence of Venantius' *Vita Radegundis* is clear, and we are assured no less than thrice that Balthild was an *exemplum humilitatis* (caps 11, 12, 16, pp 496, 498, 502).

216 Their existence must be inferred from the reference in the *Vita* cap 1, p 482 to *detractores*. In caps 18–9, pp 505–7, the hagiographer tries to establish Balthild's saintly credentials by setting her in a line of holy queens: Chrodechild, Ultrogotha and Radegund.

217 'Klosterpolitik', p 113.

218 See C. -R. Brühl, *Fodrum, Gistum, Servitium Regis* (Cologne 1968) pp 50 *seq*.

219 'Klosterpolitik', p 113.

or even a Theuderic III landed himself and his court more often than his predecessors had done on the hospitality of monastic communities, or used monastic lands to reward trusty warriors, or dipped into monastic treasuries when need arose. We do know, however, that towards the end of the seventh century, there were 'organisational connexions' between Corbie and the royal chancery[220] and that there were similarly close and continuous links between the ruling dynasty and both St Denis[221] and Chelles.[222] After Balthild, there were still powerful Merovingians—the more powerful, I suggest, because of what she had done. The real threat to such rulers was not bad blood but assassination. Against that the only remedy in the early middle ages, so the Carolingians' experience implies, was the dynastic prestige that came of contact with supernatural power. Precisely that contact was what Balthild had effected so forcefully. But it took time and a more thorough Christianisation of Frankish society for sentiments of legitimacy to grow, and so the Carolingians reaped what Balthild had sown. It was apt enough, therefore, that in the time of Louis the Pious, the abbess of Chelles, who was also the emperor's mother-in-law, staged in the imperial presence a splendid *translatio* of Balthild's remains into a fine new church dedicated to the arch-protectress, the Virgin.[223] Ewig's claim that 'not constitutional or political but religious aspects primarily determined [Balthild's] actions'[224] seems to me in one sense a truism, in another misleading. For those 'religious' aspects were at one and the same time political: to appropriate relics, to commandeer prayers, to pressurise bishops, to make dependents and allies of urban as well as rural monastic communities—all this was to gain power at once this-worldly and other-worldly. Balthild's tenure of that power was brief, partly, at least, because of the inherent weakness of her position as a mere regent, a married-in woman. But in terms of what she attempted, she must be judged a rarely gifted and creative early medieval politician.

In sketching the careers of Brunhild and Balthild, I have tried to grasp both the fortuitous and the significant in their reputations as 'Jezebels'. I have therefore had to consider some aspects of royal power

[220] See Prinz, *Mönchtum,* p 174 and works cited there, n 114.

[221] Ewig, 'Résidence' p 52; Levillain, 'Études', *BEC* 87 (1926) pp 21–73 and 91 (1930) pp 1–65.

[222] B. Bischoff, 'Die Kölner Nonnenhandschriften und das Skriptorium von Chelles', *MStn,* 2 vols (1966) 1, pp 16 *seq* at 26–7.

[223] *Translatio Balthildis, MGH SS* 15, pp 284–5.

[224] 'Klosterpolitik', p 113.

and of its interrelations with what in the sixth and seventh centuries was believed to be the power of the holy. Though we in the twentieth century tend to place these two types of power in separate compartments, it is precisely their interrelations which make for some fundamental continuities in the Merovingian period. If it is hard to make 'a clear distinction between religion and politics'[225] in establishing the motivations of Brunhild, Balthild and their contemporaries, perhaps, without discarding useful categories, rather than seeking lines of division, we should look for points of intersection and ask how far we can understand the religious *as* political, and vice versa, in the Merovingian world. It is in the changing location of such points of intersection that we can find evolution, and a kind of dialectic. In the sixth century, there are important cult-sites mainly in *civitates,* in which royal and episcopal power mutually reinforce each other, in the early seventh century, land-based aristocratic power creates new religious centres in the countryside; and in the mid-seventh century royal power is redefined and extended (in intent, at least) in relation to rural as well as urban centres. Thus from the activities of Brunhild and Balthild, which serve so conveniently to identify two of these three phases, we can make some useful inferences about the modes of Merovingian royal power and its adaptation, by means of new religious forms, to economic and social changes.

Can we also make any useful inferences about women, or about royal women, in the sixth and seventh centuries? There is no simple answer. In comparing her position with that of a female aristocrat, we observed the queen's special character. And while her position had its disadvantages these are hard to attribute specifically to her femininity. The weakness of ineligibility for kingship she shared with all non-Merovingian men; that of the non-institutionalisation of her power, with even very powerful male contemporaries, including mayors of the palace. A queen who possessed the right personal qualities could command the loyalty of warriors, and if, as a woman, she could not wield armed force herself, she could direct armies in a strategic sense. Wallace-Hadrill once asked how women could have prosecuted a

[225] *Ibid,* where Ewig himself recognises the problem.

feud except by using hired assassins;[226] but I have suggested that her grandson's campaign against Clothar II may have been instigated by Brunhild precisely to prosecute her feud against the son of Fredegund. Balthild, on the other hand, used her power most effectively without recourse to armed force. All this prompts the question of whether the exercise in person of command on battlefields was always so indispensable a function of successful early medieval rulership as is usually assumed. Perhaps even a seventh-century Merovingian queen, like a Byzantine emperor (or, in the eighth-century, an empress)[227] or most modern rulers, could either like Brunhild have her battles fought for her, or like Balthild use political as an alternative to military action.

Our discussion of these two queens' careers has indicated, less the alleged drawbacks of a woman's position than a kind of strength inherent precisely in its domestic location. A king might win or confirm his power on the battlefield, but he exercised it in the hall, and this we have seen to be the prime area of the queen's activity. Here in the royal *familia* the distribution of food, clothing, charity, the nurturing of the *iuvenes*, the maintenance of friendly relations between the *principes*, the respectful reception of bishops and foreign visitors: all fell to the queen's responsibility. Thus the organisation of the household, the woman's sphere, became a political function in the case of the *aula regis*. The centrality of *Hausherrschaft* to early medieval kingship has long been recognised.[228] But its implications for the queen's position, perhaps less clearly appreciated hitherto, have emerged in strikingly similar ways in both Brunhild's and Balthild's careers: Brunhild braves even Columbanus's wrath to preserve all the *dignitates* and *honor* that only control of the *aula regis* has given her, while Balthild makes the *palatium* her power-house as long as she controls the network of friendships and clientage that radiates from it. In so far as later Merovingians remained powerful, it was their activity in the palace that made them so. Wallace-Hadrill lists the judgements, the confirmations, the arbitrations, the confiscations and the exemptions which had been, and in the late Merovingian period remained, the peacetime functions of kingship.[229] In all these queens could be active too:

[226] *Long-Haired Kings*, p 135. Men, including kings, used assassins sometimes: Gregory and Fredegar give several examples.

[227] See Sir Steven Runciman's paper in the present volume.

[228] W. Schlesinger, *Beiträge zur deutschen Verfassungsgeschichte des Mittelalters* (Göttingen 1963) 1, pp 9 *seq*, partly translated in F. L. Cheyette, *Lordship and Community in Medieval Europe* (New York 1968) pp 64 *seq*.

[229] *Long-Haired Kings*, pp 237–8.

Brunhild ransomed captives.[230] Balthild remitted taxes,[231] and behind the dry *diplomata* how often can a queen's influence be suspected? Praejectus owed to Himnechild the favourable outcome of his land-dispute.[232] Indeed episcopal *Stadtherrschaft,* and the whole complex of relations between bishops and rulers, need to be linked to the *Hausherrschaft* of kings and queens. When Chilperic sought the support of one bishop against another 'traitorous' one, the whole exercise was conducted through face-to-face contact in the palace; and though the king's first move was a threat to sabotage the bishop's local power-base in his own *civitas,* his second was a conciliatory offer of an alfresco snack of specially-cooked chicken and pea soup.[233] If banquets still play an important role in modern diplomacy, how much the more useful instruments were food-prestations and commensality to an early medieval king. The distinction between public and private action becomes redundant in the context of the royal hall. All this explains why in the case of a queen, domestic power could mean political power.[234] Their realisation and effective exploitation of this possibility go far to explain the achievements of Brunhild and Balthild.

But in the end, it is not just as female but as royal figures that the pair have commanded our attention. That both were able to function as regents at all is significant. In no other early medieval kingdom did queen regents recurrently rule as they did in the late sixth- and seventh-century *regnum Francorum.*[235] It could be argued that such regencies are symptomatic of aristocratic power. For whereas elective monarchy tends to produce a sequence of mature kings who may consolidate royal power at the expense of their magnates (and even of

[230] Paulus Diaconus, *Historia Langobardorum* iv, 1, *MGH SSRL,* p 116.

[231] *Vita* cap 6, p 488: the capitation-tax had apparently been causing parents to prefer infanticide to rearing offspring, so Balthild by removing the *impia consuetudo* also removed the inducement to an impious crime. Her financial loss would of course be compensated by a *copiosa merces* of a heavenly kind.

[232] *Passio Praejecti* cap 24, *MGH SSRM* 5, p 239–40.

[233] *LH* v, 18, pp 219–20.

[234] This equation, and its relevance to the queen's position, was made explicitly by Hincmar in reference to ninth-century *palatium* organisation, in his *De Ordine Palatii* cap 22, *MGH Capit* 2, p 525: 'De honestate vero palatii seu specialiter ornamento regali necnon et *de donis annuis militum* . . . ad reginam praecipue et sub ipsa ad camerarium pertinebat'. Thus the king could be freed 'ab omni sollicitudine *domestica vel palatina*' to turn his mind to the *status regni*! Here again, Carolingian arrangements show continuity with Merovingian.

[235] The contrast with seventh-century England was noted by Wallace-Hadrill, *Early Germanic Kingship in England and on the Continent* (Oxford 1971) p 92.

many magnates' lives)[236], hereditary monarchy, with son(s) succeeding father, though it may exclude princes who had hitherto been eligible, in practice ensures that there will be minorities during which those princes and other magnates can collaborate with the queen-mother in ruling the kingdom. On this view the regimes of Brunhild and Balthild would represent the product of aristocratic interests. But the very fact that those interests are centred still on the royal *palatium* suggests that our queens' regencies are also symptomatic of dynastic strength. The long-term Merovingian monopoly of Frankish kingship should be explained primarily in terms of concentrations of monarchic power from Clovis to Sigibert and Chilperic, and during the reigns of Clothar II and Dagobert, and only secondarily in terms of aristocratic reactions to that power. If magnates exploited minorities, they did not create the conditions for them: filial succession became normal as a consequence of the activity and the will of kings.

The careers of Brunhild and Balthild, therefore, highlight the Merovingians' monopoly of kingship, as well as some of the modes and potential resources of royal government in the Frankish realm which made that monopoly possible and conditioned its operation in practice. The extent of these queens' political success thus helps confirm what the work of Ewig and others have shown of the fundamental structures of Merovingian politics in *palatium* and *civitas*. At the same time, Brunhild and Balthild focus our attention on the ebb and flow of power through those structures, on the dynamic relationships and the personalities that shaped the course of Merovingian history. Both queens, acting in areas of life dominated by men, were depicted as having masculine traits: Brunhild defied a posse of armed enemies *viriliter*[237]—'like a man'—while to Balthild was attributed that most manly of virtues—*strenuitas*.[238] Each ruled like a Merovingian, with a Merovingian's authority. Each earned the ill-name of 'Jezebel' in certain quarters not because female rulership was seen as a monstrous incongruity but because these particular rulers in the exercise of their

[236] For the spectacular bloodbath following the accession of the Visigothic king Chindaswinth in 641, see *Fred* cap 82, pp 69–70. On the differing consequences of indeterminate and hereditary father-son succession, see Goody, *Succession*, pp 29 *seq*; compare also the remarks of Pauline Stafford, below pp 79–100. I am grateful to John Gillingham for discussion of this point.

[237] *LH* vi, 4, p 268.

[238] *LHF* cap 43, p 315: '. . . pulchram omnique ingenio *strenuam*'. Compare *Vita Bertilae* cap 4, *MGH SSRM* 6, p 104: '[Baltechildis] . . . *viriliter* gubernabat palatium'.

power offended particular influential men. If we want to redress the gross unfairness of their posthumous reputations, we shall do them less than justice to consider them *only* as women. Like their contemporary female saints[239]—or like any climber of the Matterhorn—they are distinguished as *homines:* as human beings.

University of London
King's College

[239] See the evidence assembled by Kurth, *Études Franques,* I, pp 161–7, for women *homines* in Merovingian texts.

SONS AND MOTHERS: FAMILY POLITICS IN THE EARLY MIDDLE AGES

by PAULINE STAFFORD

'IN this year (975) Edgar, king of the English, reached the end of earthly joys, chose for him the other light, beautiful and happy and left this wretched and fleeting life' (*ASC* MS A)[1].

Edgar died in his thirty-second year. He had ruled the whole of England for sixteen years, since the age of sixteen, and the northern parts of it at least since the age of fourteen. He left three known surviving children, each by a different mother. Eadgyth, his daughter, was abbess of the nunnery at Wilton, appropriately enough since she was the daughter of the nun Wulfthryth[2]. He left two sons. The eldest Edward the martyr was the son of his first marriage to a lady named Aethelflaed.[3] Edward's mother was dead or otherwise disposed of by 975. She had disappeared early in the reign, before Edgar took as his wife and queen the lady Aelfthryth in 964. Aelfthryth was the mother of two sons: Edmund, who pre-deceased his father in 972, and Aethelred, better known to history as Aethelred Unraed.[4] The reputation which has attached to the mild Aethelred would hardly apply to his mother, who involved herself with great purpose in the advancement of her two sons. Aethelred was at most nine years old in 975, making all possible allowance for the speedy consummation of his mother's marriage and the birth of his elder brother. We do not know the age of Edward, but he is called a 'child ungrown' in MS C of the *Anglo-Saxon Chronicle,* which should make him no more than twelve, the age of social maturity in tenth century England. These two children, or more accurately their supporters, immediately flung themselves into a battle

[1] References to the Anglo-Saxon Chronicle throughout are to the edition and translation of D. Whitelock, D. C. Douglas and S. Tucker (London 1961).

[2] William of Malmesbury, *De Gestis Pontificum,* ed N. Hamilton, *RS* 52 (1870) pp 188–9.

[3] Florence [of Worcester, *Chronicon ex Chronicis*], ed B. Thorpe (London 1848) 1 p 140.

[4] For her marriage see *ASC* MS D *sa* 965 *recte* 964. Her consecration as queen is described in the *Life of St Oswald, Historians of the Church of York and its Archbishops,* ed J. Raine, *RS* 71 (1879–94) 1 (1879) p 438.

for the throne.[5] Edward was reputedly his father's favourite and was supported by a group of powerful churchmen headed by archbishop Dunstan, and by sections of the nobility of southern England and East Anglia. Aethelred, the younger of the two, had the support of the Mercian nobility and perhaps most important of all, of his mother. Aelfthryth had reason for annoyance in 975. During Edgar's lifetime she had tried to secure some sort of designation for her own sons in preference to Edgar's other children. Her motives were straightforward. The position and role of a king's widow were minimal; a queen-mother was a power in the land. Aelfthryth's desire to have her own son rule was natural. Nor was she to be thwarted by the mere fact that Edward emerged victorious from the original dispute and was consecrated king. Aelfthryth was a driving force in the pro-Aethelred faction which struggled for over three years to get its candidate on the throne. And in the end it was Aelfthryth herself who succeeded where her supporters had failed; it was she who engineered the events which secured Edward the title of *martyr*. Early in 979 the young king was visiting his brother and step-mother at Corfe in Dorset. As Edward approached the house on horseback, Aelfthryth and a couple of henchmen went out to greet him with a drink, and as Aelfthryth held out the cup of welcome, her servant slipped a dagger between Edward's ribs. The young Aethelred was inconsolable with grief. Aelfthryth must have found this a poor recognition for her efforts and was so annoyed that she beat him with a candlestick, from which arose Aethelred's lifelong fear of candles. Edward was buried very unceremoniously in a hole at Wareham, and it was a year before the body was recovered and given decent royal burial. Edward's saintliness was already manifesting itself, in the form of a reluctant horse which refused to carry Aelfthryth to the funeral. But by then Aethelred was consecrated and established on the throne and Aelfthryth was a power behind it.

In the story of the death of king Edgar and the details of his children and their fates occur most of the themes which run through the history of the royal family in the early middle ages, and make it at once so complex and so important. The king's early death, leaving only minors to succeed him is common. Edgar's own brother, who ruled before him, can have been no more than eighteen when he died; his father Edmund was twenty-four, and his uncle Eadred no more than

[5] What follows is based on accounts in the *Passio Sancti Edwardi*, ed C. Fell (Leeds 1971), the *Life of St Oswald* pp 443–5, 448–51, and the *ASC*. I have discussed this question more fully in a forthcoming paper 'The reign of Aethelred'.

thirty-two.[6] Kings who ruled young and died young are a feature of the period. A young ruler is an easier prey to faction and perhaps more easily dominated by his family, and especially his mother. Similarly an early death is likely to leave minors to inherit, with more opportunities for the advancement of maternal kin. But members of a king's family are anxious to advance themselves in all ages. Two other factors exemplified by Edgar make for much extra trouble in these centuries. The first is the tendency to contract multiple marriages. The Merovingians were certainly polygamous.[7] Anglo-Saxon kings by the tenth century were, if not polygamous, committed serial monogamists and very adept at disposing of previous wives. Edgar with only three known wives was by no means immoderate in his habits. His grandfather Edward the Elder had gone through three wives,[8] and Edgar's much-maligned son Aethelred proved himself a worthy member of the dynasty at least in this direction by contracting at least two marriages.[9] But in this as in other respects the tenth-century English kings were but pale shadows of that great Frank, Charlemagne. Charlemagne managed to combine nine women with his other known healthy appetites, four wives approved by holy church, five rather more irregular.[10] He *was* a great king, but the pattern is general. Many wives means many mothers. Each mother wishes her own son to succeed to the throne. Each wife under a system of polygamy, and the last wife of a serial monogamist is anxious to be queen-mother and not royal widow. Different sons are likely to have different factions of maternal kin supporting them. Each queen will be anxious to advance her own son at the expense of his elder half brothers.

[6] Edgar was thirty when consecrated in 973, hence sixteen in 959. His brother Eadwig is unlikely to have been more than two years his senior. Edmund was eighteen on his accession in 940 (*ASC* MS A), twenty four at his death in 946, and Edmund's brother, Eadred, can have been no older than thirty-two or thirty-three in 956 since he must have been born 923/4.

[7] See J. M. Wallace-Hadrill, *The Long-Haired Kings* (London 1961) pp 134, 161, and on the Merovingian dynasty, its wives and children see E. Ewig, 'Studien zur merowingischen Dynastie', *Fruhmittelalterliche Studien* 8 (Berlin 1974) pp 15–59.

[8] *De Gestis Regum*, ed W. Stubbs, *RS* 90 (1887–9) 1 (1887) paras 137, 139.

[9] Aelred of Rievaulx tells us the name of Aethelred's first wife, Aelfgifu daughter of earl Thored. Florence 1 p 275 makes her the daughter of an otherwise unknown ealdorman Aethelberht. Are these garbled accounts of the same marriage or of two separate ones? The second known marriage was to Aelfgifu/Emma daughter of Richard of Normandy. Her first charter signature occurs in AD 1002 in Kemble no 1296.

[10] Einhard, [*Life of Charlemagne*], ed H. W. Garrod and R. B. Mowat (Oxford 1925) caps 18, 20.

Such advancement was still possible because the rules of primogeniture were not yet fully established. It is only during the tenth and eleventh centuries that rules of primogeniture began to emerge in the royal families of England and the Continent.[11] The emergence was gradual, rarely the result of any general decision or edict. Rather it was the sheer force of frequency and the development of custom which gradually established the fact that eldest son should succeed father. But the contrary custom was still strong. The Germanic peoples of western Europe from the sixth century onwards recognised that all male members of the royal family had rights in the succession to the throne. Eighth-century England demonstrates just how widely 'all male members' could be interpreted. In the kingdom of Mercia two kings ruled in the eighth century, Aethelbald and Offa. Neither was the son of the previous king. Aethelbald claimed the throne through his grandfather, who had been the *brother* of a king and had died over seventy years previously. Offa claimed through his great-great-grandfather, also only the brother of a king, who had died some century before.[12] Before the church spoke out against the idea, bastards and their progeny were also eligible, and even after the church had made its views felt they continued to succeed to rule. William the Conqueror is better known on the continent as William the Bastard, not a term of English nationalist opprobrium but a description of his birth.[13] This feeling for the importance of blood and the idea that all who possessed royal blood were in some way eligible to rule still persisted in the tenth and eleventh centuries. There were powerful forces at the same time working for primogeniture but this had by no means triumphed. It was still possible for a disappointed queen to find *legitimate* support for her son, whatever his position in the royal family. At the same time, almost all these dynasties recognised the greatest rights of succession within the close kin-group, thus focusing the inevitable tensions of the struggle for the throne within domestic relationships. These elements were combined with a degree of designa-

[11] See for example J. Dhondt, 'Election et Heredité sous les Carolingiens et les premiers Capetiens', *Revue Belge de Philologie et d'Histoire,* 18 (Brussels 1939) pp 913–53; J. Le Patourel, 'The Norman Succession, 986–1135', *EHR* 86 (1971) pp 225–50.

[12] *ASC* MS A, *sa* 716, 626 and 757. A necessary note of caution on the use of regnal lists and genealogies has been raised by D. Dumville, 'Kingship, Genealogies and Regnal Lists', *Early Medieval Kingship,* ed P. H. Sawyer and I. N. Wood (Leeds 1977) pp 72–104. But whatever the truth of these claims for Offa and Aethelbald, it was clearly felt that claims of such remoteness were worth making.

[13] For his birth see D. C. Douglas, *William the Conqueror* (London 1964) p 15 and pp 379–82.

tion. The reigning king, either formally through consecration or designation, or informally through simple favour, could influence the choice of his successor. The results of the combination of all these factors were the series of struggles over the succession not only on the deaths of kings, but also and just as important during their lifetimes: domestic quarrels; rivalry between wives; the attempts of wives to rid themselves of the children of other marriages and attempts to gain royal designation for their own sons, all these are features of these systems of succession and marriage. For princes this situation meant fear and suspicion of each other, especial dislike of their step-mothers, and particular resentment of a father's second marriage to some young beauty who was likely to outlive her spouse and fight fiercely for the position of herself and her kin. Family rivalries exacerbated by frequent marriages and open rules of succession and focused by the great prize of the throne itself are the stuff of the political role of the royal family in these centuries. And the period saw a procession of formidable personalities who exploited every possibility which the situation opened to them.[14]

At the centre of most documented intrigues in the royal family stands the queen. The West Saxons did not have queens in the early ninth century, so Asser informs us.[15] His statement cannot mean that all their kings were celibate; king Aethelwulf did not happen upon his five sons under gooseberry bushes around the royal palace at Cheddar. Asser is suggesting rather that the king's wife need not be a queen. She need not be given the prominence and power of that position. She would not necessarily be consecrated by the church and so given a formal and a proved place. The West Saxons had had an unfortunate experience with a previous queen, Eadburh. Eadburh was the daughter of Offa of Mercia, a woman of good birth and almost certainly given the formal position of queen, but her actions left the title in bad odour. Unable to dominate the court as she wished, she murdered many of the followers of her husband Beorhtric by guile or poison, and ended by poisoning the king himself. Since Wessex was too hot to hold her, she fled after her husband's death to the continent.

[14] On the whole question of succession rules and their relations to marriage patterns and family disputes see [J.] Goody, [*Cambridge Studies in Social Anthropology*] (Cambridge 1966) esp Goody's own introduction and the contribution of [M.] Southwold. Also [A. I.] Richards, *Journal of the Royal Anthropological Institute*, 91 (London 1961) pp 135–50. General discussion of the role of wives, mothers and sisters in Lucy Mair, *Primitive Government* (London 1962).

[15] Asser, ed W. Stevenson (Oxford 1904) pp 11–13.

Charlemagne himself received her and was so impressed by her that he offered her a husband. She refused, and Charles gave her a monastery instead. Her exploits here are left to the imagination, but things certainly did not work out. She was expelled and finally died in poverty at Pavia, a suitably moral ending. Because of all this, Asser tells us, the West Saxons were reluctant to give any king's wife the prominence which the position of queen entailed.

Much is involved in this question of an honorary title. In a situation in which a king had many wives, either simultaneously or in succession, the title of queen meant important things to its lucky possessor. The designation of a wife as queen can be one way of designating an heir and so eliminating the claims of other brothers. It may involve designating not the heir himself but the heir-producing consort, not the heir, but his mother.[16] To raise one woman as queen, especially under polygamy, enhances both her own position as mother of the prospective king and that of her children. Under a system of polygamy without such designation the status of all wives and dowagers is low, since none can certainly be said to be the future queen-mother, and the low status of most early medieval wives is a sure sign of the marriage practices of the royal dynasties. Even where kings took wives consecutively the designation of a queen might pre-empt the significance of subsequent marriages and so be undesirable. And the designation of an heir could cause problems by alienating other sons, and encouraging presumption on the part of the chosen. It was in a king's own interests to keep all his sons on tenterhooks, to give all 'hope and expectation', to have all courting his favour.

There might be reasons against the raising of any one wife to the position of queen, but they were not reasons endorsed by the lady in question. For her, to secure such designation for herself and her sons must be a prime aim, especially if she has any political ambitions and the personality to realise them. Many problems were caused by women who had been so designated. Sons were inevitably suspicious of such ladies. Aethelbald of Wessex, as will be seen, feared Judith, his father's second wife and queen. Some century and a half later Aethelred the Unready's son, Edmund Ironside, entertained similar feelings towards his stepmother Emma who had been designated *seo hlaefdige,* a real lady, unlike his own poor mother. Those who acquired the title, like Aelfthryth whom we have already encountered, may have done so partly because of their strong personalities. Is it surprising that such

[16] Goody p 33.

women could be a great trouble at court, centres of factions already building up around their sons who were assured of succession, anxiously working to realise the power of their position and to secure that succession. We do not know Eadburh's real crimes, but her attitudes towards the courtiers of Beorhtric may indicate scheming over the succession, and her possession of the treasure points in the same direction.

Eadburh's dynamic personality coupled with her high birth may have led to her formal consecration as queen. Asser tells the story of Eadburh in relation to another West Saxon queen, Judith. Judith was the daughter of Charles the Bald, king of the West Franks. King Aethelwulf of Wessex had met her on his way back from a pilgrimage to Rome and had become infatuated by her, a classic case of a middle-aged king, away from the restraints of home, taking a final fling with a princess less than half his age. He married Judith, who was consecrated as queen at Verberie in 856, and then brought her back to England, much to the chagrin of the West Saxons who had bitter experience of such ladies. Aethelwulf was not the safe bet Judith had thought him. His eldest son, Aethelbald, as will be seen, was already in revolt against him, partly because of this marriage itself, and succeeded in forcing him out of Wessex to become king in Kent. The situation was resolved by Aethelwulf's death within two years. Judith had learnt the realities of the West Saxon court by now, and immediately accepted an offer of marriage from that same eldest son. Within months of his father's death, Aethelbald had married his stepmother.[17]

Such a step was not without parallel. From the point of view of Judith it was a way of continuing her position, and incidentally avoiding the fate which befell most princesses, incarceration in a nunnery. There is a similar marriage in seventh-century Kent, when Eadbald, much to the disgust of Bede, married his father's widow, probably queen Bertha another Frankish princess.[18] Procopius has preserved a garbled story of a certain prince Radiger, son of the king of the Varni, who married his father's widow, a sister of king Theudeberht of the Franks, jilting an English princess in the process. In this case the marriage was said to have been contracted in obedience to his father's dying commands and by the advice of the chief men of the kingdom, none of which prevented the outraged princess from

[17] Asser pp 9–11, 16.

[18] Bede, *HE* ed C. Plummer (Oxford 1896) bk 2 cap 5.

revenging herself with a naval attack.[19] Much later, in 1017, the Danish conqueror of England, Cnut, took as his wife, as will be seen, king Aethelred's widow, the daughter of the duke of Normandy. There may be many elements involved in such marriages. It was a way of buying off the lady's faction. If she were a foreign princess, it meant retaining any links of which she was a symbol and neutralising hostility. Perhaps there is also an element of legitimation, and certainly a hopeful diversion of her loyalty to her own sons, potential threats to the new king.

Not every king's wife need be a queen. Some of them were hardly wives, at least as far as the church was concerned. The chroniclers, both contemporary and later, were all ecclesiastics. With their narrower view of what constituted marriage these Christian writers gave many of the wives of early kings very short shrift. Many of them are referred to as outright concubines, or wives at best after the Danish or pagan fashion. Thus the wife of Cnut, Aelfgifu of Northampton is a concubine according to Roger of Wendover, and the *Anglo-Saxon Chronicle* expresses amazement at Harold Harefoot's claim to be the son of her and Cnut. Cnut himself entertained no doubts of his paternity, assigning parts of his realms to both his sons by Aelfgifu. William of Malmesbury refers to Ecgwyna, first wife of Edward the Elder, as a concubine, but clearly his sources were ambiguous on Ecgwyna, since he goes on to call her both the daughter of a shepherd and an illustrious woman, though there is no evidence of a Romantic 'back-to-the-land' movement among the tenth-century nobility. When Edgar married his third wife Aelfthryth, archbishop Dunstan bearded him in his very marriage bed and accused him of adultery, a rash move in view of the character of Aelfthryth and one for which she never forgave him. Charlemagne himself was the son of a marriage not blessed by holy church.[20] Most of these ladies would not have been considered by their contemporaries as concubines. Many were of noble birth. The numerous marriages of these early kings are partly to be explained by a non-Christian or at best part-Christian view of marriage, one in which wives could be easily put aside, one which made serial monogamy much easier. Our sources are the products of

[19] [E. A.] Freeman, [*History of the Norman Conquest*], 6 vols (Oxford 1873) 1 p 567.

[20] *De Gestis Regum* paras 126, 139 on Ecgwyna; Gaimar, [*L'Estorie des Engles*], ed T. D. Hardy and C. T. Martin, *RS* 91 (1883) lines 3939 *seq.* on Aelfthryth. Aelfgifu of Northampton and 'Danish Marriages' are discussed by Freeman, 1 pp 733–5, 624–6. On such marriages and on Charlemagne's birth see [H.] Fichtenau, [*The Carolingian Empire*] (Oxford 1963) pp 38–9.

ecclesiastics who were struggling to establish Christian monogamy and have obscured the nature of many of these marriages.

A complex of factors thus determined the position of any royal wife: her birth, though this was normally high; the importance of her relatives and, as we shall see, her ability to produce sons; the question of formal designation involved in a consecration ceremony; and as time went on, whether her marriage had been blessed by holy church. Most imponderable but often most important, even when it came to the question of formal designation, was her personality.

The positions of Eadburh and possibly of Judith derived from their birth and personalities. Inevitably it was such women of royal birth or high position and strong personality who found the low status of king's wife most difficult to bear. They were princesses accustomed to the status of royal blood and struggled to achieve a position commensurate with their self-esteem. Eadburh in Wessex had memories of her royal upbringing in Mercia to spur her on. But strong personality mattered as much as birth, as the differing fates of two royal sisters in sixth-century Frankia shows. Brunhilda and Galswintha were the daughters of the Visigothic king, and married two brothers, the Merovingians Sigebert of Metz and Chilperic of Soissons.[21] In comparison with Brunhilda, Galswintha pales into insignificance, outclassed and outmanoeuevred by her rival, Fredegund, another of Chilperic's wives. But Brunhilda dominates the history of the sixth century, together with her arch-enemies, her brother-in-law, king Chilperic, and his third wife Fredegund. Brunhilda's husband was murdered by his brother's thugs, and she and her five year old son taken captive.[22] But Chilperic's prisons were not strong enough to hold such a woman. She escaped to Rouen, married Chilperic's disgraced son, and for the next twenty one years ruled as queen regent for her son, dominating him and his policies long after he came of age. She was instrumental in securing the accession of Childebert to Burgundy, and ended up helping her grandsons rule both kingdoms. The strength of her personality is written large over the chronicles of Gregory of Tours and Fredegar. She ruled with all the ruthlessness typical of the age. Opposition was inevitable. A conspiracy of her nobility took the usual form of a palace revolution, an attempt to set up her grandsons against her using their nurse and household nobles to plot against the queen.[23] When the plot was discovered the ringleaders

[21] Gregory [of Tours], ed and trans O. M. Dalton, 2 vols (Oxford 1927) bk 4 caps 27, 28.
[22] Gregory bk 5 cap 1. [23] Gregory bk 9 cap 38.

were captured and tortured, the nurse disfigured with red hot irons and sent away to a corn mill and the noble ringleader shorn of his hair and his ears and sent to do menial work in a vineyard. Brunhilda's political influence in Austrasia and Burgundy spread over forty years, especially after her son Childebert came of age, and during the rule of her docile grandson, Theuderic, but when that grandson died in 613 and she attempted to rig the succession for her great-grandson, another malleable child, the opposition broke loose. Her nephew, Chilperic's son, moved against her with the support of a large section of the nobility. Brunhilda was captured and tortured before her infamous death, tied to the tail of an unbroken horse which was lashed into fury.[24]

Brunhilda shows what a queen stood to gain, and to lose. It was not sufficient to have high born relatives, or even to achieve the status of queen; it was also necessary to have an obedient husband or son. Only through such could a queen realise her ambitions. Even for those two great sixth-century ladies, Brunhilda and Fredegund, their male relatives were all important. Thus Fredegund fought for the advance of her own infant son Lothair II, and, wishing to hit out at her enemy, Brunhilda, could find no better way than an attempt on the lives of Brunhilda *and* her son Childebert.[25]

To secure the succession of your son was of first importance, and such attempts explain many of the family troubles of the period. Louis the Pious, Charlemagne's son and heir came to grief largely through the schemes of his second wife. Louis' first wife Irmengard had provided him with a full complement of sons before his accession to the throne of the Carolingian Empire. Soon after his accession this first wife died and Louis, like Aethelwulf, married again to another beautiful young Judith, the Welf. It is difficult to get at the truth about Judith. The churchmen who wrote the chronicles and documents of Louis' reign had little love for her. But some things are clear: she was a great beauty who was suspected, or rather accused, of turning more heads than Louis'; she had a family and especially brothers eager for advancement at the court; and she had a son, the future emperor Charles the Bald. After the birth of Charles in 823 she had tried long and hard to get a kingdom allotted to him. The sons of Louis' first marriage resented any changes which could only be to their disadvantage, and doubtless feared the possible directions which Judith's

[24] *The Fourth Book of the Chronicle of Fredegar,* ed J. M. Wallace-Hadrill (London 1960) bk 4 cap 42.

[25] Gregory bk 8 cap 29.

plans for her son might take. The rest of the reign of Louis the Pious is one long confused history of plots and counterplots. Running through all is the name of Judith, accused of taking lovers and plotting with them to murder the king by magic, captured by her stepsons, endlessly in and out of captivity in nunneries. Inevitably, all the other resentments of the reign crystallised around this central issue of the succession to the throne. The fact that the major aim of her stepsons was to separate their father from his young wife is a measure of Judith's importance. When their revolt against Louis finally brought him to his knees in 833 she was whisked off to a nunnery, accused by the bishop of Lyons of being 'a monster of iniquity from whose machinations the palace was now cleansed. Louis, after first being separated from her, had constantly returned to his vomit . . . like king Achab, led astray by Jezebel, and Samson, who believed in an unjust woman and so lost his sight and his government'. All this trouble resulted from the desire of a second wife to ensure an adequate inheritance for her son.[26]

It was inevitable that where the rules of succession remained so open a second marriage was always conceived as a threat by the sons of the earlier union. Just as the problems of Louis the Pious date from his second marriage so the revolt of Aethelbald in Wessex against his father Aethelwulf arose at least in part from Aethelwulf's marriage to this same Judith's grand-daughter. Over a century later the revolt of Liudolf, son of Otto I's first marriage is related to Otto's Italian marriage,[27] and that of Edmund Ironside against his father Aethelred in 1015 was a response to the maturing of the sons of his own father's second marriage.[28] The threat was a very real one and the reaction of Louis the Pious's sons well justified by events in many parallel situations. Second wives had to plot the succession of their own sons, and were often very successful. In the absence through death or exile of former wives, the influence of these women is easy to understand. Almost every dynasty has its Thankmar, son of Henry the Fowler, passed over by his father in favour of Otto I, son of the second union.[29] Many have an Edward the martyr, disposed of by his stepmother. The situation is multiplied in the case of polygamous dynasties like the Merovingians. Fredegund, one of Chilperic's wives, engineered the

[26] See the account by L. Halphen (Paris 1947 repr 1968) bk 2 caps 3, 4.

[27] K. Leyser, 'The battle of the Lech', *History* 60 (1965) pp 9–10.

[28] See my discussion in 'The reign of Aethelred' (forthcoming).

[29] See J. Gillingham, *The Kingdom of Germany in the High Middle Ages* (London 1971) p 15.

murder of both his other known wives, Audovera and Galswintha, and acted against Clovis, Chilperic's son by Audovera.[30] The situation is complicated by the fact that fathers with adult sons felt a natural unease, and undoubtedly many of the actions which ecclesiastics have chosen to attribute to women like Fredegund are those of a king fearful of his own security. The second or third wife stood to gain much by cutting out, even wiping out the opposition to her own sons. Is it surprising that few princes viewed the acquisition of a step-mother with equanimity?

For these early royal wives as for many later ones, the first rule was produce your son. Kings were very disappointed if such progeny was not forthcoming. No wife's position was secure until a son was produced, and with wives such a disposable commodity haste was of the essence. Lothair II a king of Lotharingia, had already rehearsed Henry VIII's struggle with the papacy in the ninth century. Lothair had contracted one of the loose, Germanic style marriages with a noblewoman, Waldrada, but he had put her on one side to marry Theutberga, the sister of Hubert abbot of St Maurice. Waldrada had given him sons in plenty; Theutberga proved barren. But Lothair had made a great mistake. He had had his second marriage blessed with the full ceremonies of holy church, and although his native bishops proved accommodating, the pope was determined to make capital out of the situation. Lothair twisted and turned for over a decade. He had his own bishops condemn his second marriage, only to have his bishops excommunicated by the pope. To prove that his marriage was null, he accused Theutberga of every conceivable crime, including that of incest and unnatural relations with her brother Hubert, a crime which rendered her totally unworthy of the royal bed and fit only for a nunnery. But in spite of all his claims and protests the pope held out, and it was Lothair who had to give in.[31] Nor was it really papal pressure which forced him to submit, but the many uncles and cousins ready in the wings and only too anxious to profit from his embarassment to dismember his kingdom. Lothair's sorry plight illustrates the complications which the church's fostering of monogamy and a high view of marriage could produce, and the dangers of designating too formally any one wife.

[30] Gregory bk 5 cap 39, bk 4 cap 28.

[31] For the story of Lothair see Halphen bk 3 cap 4, and W. Ullmann, *A Short History of the Papacy in the Middle Ages* (London 1972) p 104.

The desire for a son was felt equally desperately by the wives themselves. Clearly there was a simple question of security and the future of their power depended on producing and securing the accession of a son. Where polygamy makes the status of a royal wife low, she depends on that of her children, who possess the all-important royal blood. Fredegund, who was blessed with children in her own mould, was taunted by her daughter for her lack of this vital commodity.[32] In such circumstances it needs little imagination to measure the depths of Fredegund's despair at the death of her own young sons, especially after all her efforts to be rid of rival wives and children.[33] Where it is little to be the wife of a king and everything to be his mother, any woman of ambition must have prayed devoutly for male offspring.

For the queen who had a son and succeeded in securing his accession, the problem then became that of realising her power. The remarkable fact, in view of the known tensions of family life, is that so many of them succeeded in wielding so much influence, especially in the early years of a reign. Charlemagne himself was sufficiently docile to his mother's desires as to marry the bride of her choice, although he repudiated the lady two years later.

His mother has been identified as one of the important figures in the first decades of his reign.[34] Where it was effective, the influence of the queen mother may be partly a function of the youth of so many kings. It has as much to do with the troubled accessions of most of them. The role of the queen-mother's faction and relatives might be crucial until the reign was well established. Aelfthryth for example was the driving force behind the group backing Aethelred in the succession dispute in 975. She was a dominating influence in the first half of Aethlered's reign. She was a well-connected woman, the daughter of an ealdorman of the south-west, where her family continued to be important.[35] She was related to Aelfhere, ealdorman of Mercia and Aethelred's most significant supporter in 975.[36] She was the dominant female at Aethelred's court until her death *c*1000, and her brother was a leading member of the royal household during the same period. An anointed

[32] Gregory bk 9 cap 34.

[33] Gregory bk 5 cap 34.

[34] Einhard cap 18, and F. L. Ganshof, 'Charlemagne', *Carolingians and the Frankish Monarchy* (London 1971) pp 17–27.

[35] *ASC* MS D, *sa* 965 *recte* 964.

[36] She was certainly related to his brother, ealdorman Aelfheah of Wessex, see his will, Whitelock, *Wills* no 9.

queen, she figures prominently in the witness lists of charters, was appealed to as a lady of influence in land disputes[37] and had a household of her own, where she was responsible for bringing up the sons of Aethelred's first marriage.[38] The reputation which she left behind her is an indication of her strength of character.[39] She and her husband Edgar are implicated in the death of her first husband Aethelwold.[40] At Ely she was remembered with ill will as the person responsible for the drying up of land grants to the house.[41] Her malice towards the house arose from an unfortunate incident involving abbot Brihtnoth, who while answering a call of nature in the woods, had come across the queen in the guise of a horse, disporting herself and 'satisfying her insatiable appetites' with a group of her minions. This only served to confirm the good abbot's suspicions that the queen was a practitioner of the black arts, and he was foolhardy enough to take her to task for her evil ways. She repaid him by murdering him by witchcraft and hardening her son's heart towards Ely. Such stories leave us in no doubt of the strong impression Aelfthryth made on her contemporaries. Whatever her earlier relations with the devil, she ended her life with a cautious investment in heaven. She was the foundress of Wherwell and retired there early in the eleventh century to end her days.[42]

Aelfthryth had been the dominant woman at Aethelred's court. She totally eclipsed his first wife, so much so that we are not even certain of her name. She brought up the children of the first marriage. It does not seem that there was room for more than one such lady at a time at court. Aelfthryth's position arose partly from the fact that she had been consecrated queen, a role which could not be duplicated. But such consecrations might themselves, as has been seen, be a result of force of personality. Aelfthryth's role is very like that of an earlier tenth-century queen, Eadgifu, similarly a *queen* but whose position can be related to her personality and to her capacity to influence her sons. Eadgifu was the third wife of Edward the Elder, and bore him two sons in the last years of his life. Edward was succeeded by his eldest son Athelstan, and during his reign Eadgifu disappears entirely from sight. Athelstan had no children and no wife, and on his death Eadgifu

[37] A. J. Robertson, *Anglo-Saxon Charters* (Cambridge 1956) nos 45, 66.
[38] Reference to this in the will of her grandson, Athelstan, Whitelock, *Wills* no 20.
[39] The many legends about Aelfthryth are discussed by C. E. Wright, *Cultivation of Saga in Anglo-Saxon England* (London 1939) pp 146–53, 157–71.
[40] *De Gestis Regum* para 157 and Gaimar lines 3649–731.
[41] *Liber Eliensis*, ed E. O. Blake, *CSer* 3, 92 (1962) pp 127–8.
[42] Kemble no 707.

reemerges. Her two sons ruled in turn; she is prominent during both reigns. Edmund married, but his wife played no political role. She is remembered as a saint,[43] significant when we consider the church's memory of Aelfthryth. The second son, Eadred, never married. When he died in 955/6, Eadgifu was loth to give up influence. She was mixed up in the succession dispute between her grandsons, and her fortunes collapsed when the eldest won. She was deprived of all her property and disappears again. But Eadgifu was undaunted; she continued to be involved in the plots in favour of Edgar, and when he succeeded to the throne was rewarded with full restitution of her lands and position.[44] Eadgifu had eclipsed the other royal women of the mid-tenth century as Aelfthryth was to eclipse Aethelred's wife at the end of it. Both dominated their sons to the exclusion of any other female influence.

This was the role which queen-mothers craved, but not all were so successful at achieving it. Emma of Normandy is a case in point. Emma was Aethelred Unraed's second wife. He married her at about the time of his mother's death, and she was certainly consecrated as queen. She was the daughter of duke Richard of Normandy and the mother of Edward the Confessor, Alfred and Godgifu.[45] Emma outlived Aethelred, and the circumstances of foreign conquest in which the reign ended effectively prevented her realising plans to enthrone her son Edward. Emma however secured the continuance of her own position by a marriage to the conquering king, Cnut, by whom she produced another son Harthacnut. Again Emma was a wife with a rival. She had to contend with Harold Harefoot, the son of Cnut's marriage to Aelgifu of Northampton. On Cnut's death in 1035, she seized the royal treasure at Winchester as part of a bid for power on behalf of her son Harthacnut.[46] Emma and her supporters struggled for nearly two years but Harold finally won in 1037, and Emma was banished to the continent.[47] There she remained, plotting her comeback. Harold's death provided her opportunity, and from 1040 till 1042 she and Harthacnut were back on the English throne. But Emma was

[43] *ASC* MS D *sa* 955.

[44] F. Harmer, *Select English Historical Documents of the Ninth and Tenth Centuries* (Cambridge 1914) no 23, an account of the estate of Cooling and of the vicissitudes of Eadgifu. On the position of the English queen in general see [A.] Campbell, [*Encomium Emmae Reginae*], *CSer* 3, 72 (1949) pp 62–5.

[45] On Emma see Campbell and [F.] Barlow, [*Edward the Confessor*] (London 1970) esp pp 28–32.

[46] *ASC* MS C *sa* 1035.

[47] *Ibid* MSS C and E *sa* 1037.

unfortunate. She seems to have had fears regarding the health of Harthacnut. He was dead within two years, cut down in mid toast while attending the wedding of Tofig the Proud.[48] How farseeing of Emma that she had persuaded him to invite back to England the son of her previous marriage Edward. Edward was on the spot and ready to succeed in 1042, but he proved less pliable that Harthacnut. He may have resented the mother who had virtually ignored him for twenty five years and had pushed the claims of his half brother in 1035 in preference to his own. She may have realised the worst when he returned to England, and there is a little evidence to suggest that she was plotting against him in 1042.[49] Edward was certainly not making a gesture of friendship and filial piety when he rode against her in 1043 and deprived her of all her lands, and also of the royal treasure which she had appropriated as some final desperate bargaining counter.[50] But the saints, in the person of saint Mildred, in whose legend we hear of Emma's problems, looked kindly upon her and she was restored to favour. But it was temporary and illusory. Emma had little influence over *this* son. When he married in 1044 she sinks into obscurity.[51] Edward packed her off to the nunnery at Winchester, where she had seven years to reflect on lost opportunities before she died in 1052.[52]

There was little point in pushing the claims of one's sons if one had little hold over them. Emma was clearly desperate by 1042. It was almost carelessness to have lost two royal husbands and one crowned son in twenty-five years. She had little to lose in pushing Edward, but part of the trouble was that she had little to offer him. She had no family faction to support her and throw into the balance; and in any case Edward lacked any major rival in 1042. His half brother was dead, his full brother murdered, his half-nephew as yet undiscovered in central Europe. There was no significant trouble for his mother to stir or from which she could help deliver him.

Edward was lucky, for brothers (and sisters) had their part to play in family politics. Growing sons and brothers, with their excellent pedigrees, were always a potential focus of discontent.[53] Many kings sensibly sent their sons away from court to keep them out of palace intrigue. Charlemagne despatched several of his sons at an early age.[54]

[48] *Ibid* MS C and Florence *sa* 1042. [49] Barlow p 58.
[50] *ASC* MSS D and E *sa* 1043.
[51] Her witnessing of charters ceases after this year.
[52] *ASC* MS E *sa* 1052.
[53] On the question of brothers and sons in general see Goody, Southwold and Richards.
[54] Fichtenau pp 39–43.

Edward the Elder's sons may have been brought up away from court—Athelstan was certainly raised in Mercia[55]—and Aethelred Unraed did not have his sons around him until late in the reign.[56] It was by no means a total answer. They were removed from court intrigue, but often placed in a position to build up their own faction to challenge their father's power. Many kings who had long and not entirely successful reigns suffered from rebellions of their sons. Even Charlemagne suffered a rebellion by his bastard, Pepin the Hunchback, and we have already encountered Louis the Pious's difficulties. For their fathers sons could be a mixed blessing, crucial to the survival of the dynasty, but eminently throne-worthy and liable to grow discontented, especially if they saw that throne-worthiness threatened in any way. Brothers gave their own share of trouble, since fraternal succession was as common as vertical (that is, father to son). Athelstan suffered revolt from his brother Edwin in 933, and Otto I's relations with his brother Henry were not always amicable.[57] Brothers were an especial problem at the beginning of a reign, challenging the succession, offering themselves as rival candidates. Charlemagne began his reign ruling jointly with his brother Carloman; but Carloman died after only two years. Abbot Cathwulf was later to write to Charles congratulating him on his good fortune in losing his brother so early.[58] The fewer full-grown male relatives a king had around him, the easier he slept at night. Royal princes posed such a threat that it is distinctly probable that in some dynasties they were not allowed to marry, or at least actively discouraged from marriage before their accession. Not a single tenth-century English king can be shown to have been married before his accession.[59] Indeed the marriage of a king's son before his father's death might be a sign of rebellion. The second son of Aethelred Unraed defied his father and married a widow in 1015. The act was part of Edmund's revolt at the end of his father's reign. His elder brother Athelstan, who had died when well turned twenty, was unmarried.[60]

[55] Athelstan was raised in Mercia and the signatures of Edward's other sons are rare in charters, only Aelfweard, who was probably the designated heir, appearing at all regularly.

[56] Up to AD 1001 the royal children only appear with their grandmother who was bringing them up. The only exception is their witness of Kemble no 700. From AD 1002 onwards the older sons are more regularly with their father.

[57] *ASC* MS E *sa* 933 and *De Gestis Regum* 1 para 139; for Otto's troubles see B. Hill, *Medieval Monarchy in Action* (London 1972) pp 25–9.

[58] Halphen bk 1 cap 3 on Charles' accession.

[59] The only exception is the case of Edward the Elder, married before Alfred's death.

[60] For a fuller discussion of the actions of Edmund see my 'The reign of Aethelred' (forthcoming).

Are the actions of a man like Merovech, Chilperic's son in the sixth century, in marrying Brunhilda also related to rebellion against his father?[61] The greater expectations of a married man with children are the reason for such a prohibition. Married men, with the support of their wife's kin, were more inclined to demand the realities of power. There was also a real danger of creating too many collateral lines before the next stage of the succession had been settled. Certainly at a slightly later date, the nobility were discouraging the marriages of young men, and these bachelors were sent off to the courts of kings and princes until they either acquired the family land or made their own fortunes.[62]

Sons were necessary to a king; they could pose problems, but lack of them posed even more. The situation of daughters was rather different, in that their marriages could pose a real danger. In the early part of our period Germanic custom was still strong. Such custom allowed the sister's son to make many demands on his uncle, and kings may have not been anxious to have too many sister's sons importuning them in this way.[63] But more important, and of significance throughout the period, a daughter carried royal blood out of the family and could carry claims to the throne with it. It is this danger which explains why so many princesses were forbidden to marry, found their way, perhaps unwillingly, into nunneries, or were married off to some suitably distant ruler, preferably overseas. It is a well-known fact that Charlemagne kept all his daughters constantly with him, technically unmarried. Their debaucheries are a feature of Carolingian history, and one which embarrassed their pious brother, Louis, who packed them all off to nunneries immediately after his accession. Charlemagne had kept them unmarried but had not been worried about their virginity. Einhard claims that they were kept constantly at court with their father because of his great love for them, and certainly he saved them from the fate of the veil. But political considerations should not be discounted: when the English king, Offa, made a treaty with Charlemagne, it was suggested that Offa's daughter should marry Charles' son. The negotiations broke down when Offa demanded that his son marry one of Charles' daughters in return.[64]

Dynasties which were becoming more aware of the problems likely

[61] Gregory bk 5 cap 3.

[62] G. Duby, 'Dans la France du Nord-Ouest au XIIe siècle, les jeunes dans la societé aristocratique', *Annales*, 19 no 5 (1964) pp 835–46.

[63] On such relations in general see J. Goody, 'The mother's brother and the sister's son in West Africa', *Comparative Studies in Kinship* (London 1969) pp 39–90.

[64] J. M. Wallace-Hadrill, *Early Germanic Kingship* (Oxford 1971) pp 115–16.

to be caused by their succession rules may have taken the precaution of restraining the marriage of their princesses to the great native nobility. In tenth and eleventh-century England there were only three known exceptions to this rule. Alfred married his eldest daughter Aethelflaed to Aethelred, lord of the Mercians. The circumstances were exceptional; they were jointly resisting the Danes and Aethelred's position was that of an independent ruler. Aethelflaed ended up ruling Mercia alone. But her brother Edward the Elder took no risks on her death. He marched straight into Mercia, established his rights to kingship there and captured his niece Aelfwyn, who was taken back to Wessex, presumably to suffer the normal fate of dangerous royal ladies with too much royal blood for their own good.[65] Athelstan married his sister to Sihtric of York, again as an alliance with an independent ruler. Eadgyth ended her days in the time-honoured fashion at the nunnery at Polesworth after Sihtric had cast her off.[66] Only in the troubled circumstances of the reign of Aethelred Unraed in the early eleventh century were three of the king's daughters married to great nobles, for very special reasons.[67]

Nunneries were emphatically the favoured way of disposing of surplus daughters. Perhaps it was more acceptable to have them in nunneries than debauching high ecclesiastics at court, even given the liberal moral attitudes of the day. In the nunneries they retained a full sense of their own dignity. When Edgar's daughter Eadgyth, abbess of Wilton, was taken to task by bishop Aethelwold for her costly garment she was ready with the sharp retort that as incorrupt a mind might be found beneath her own gold raiment as under his tattered skins.[68] Nunneries must have been full of the daughters of the best people. Might this explain why more than one pretender to the throne passes casually through a nunnery en route and carries off a nun?[69] There was certainly a lot of high blood cooped up in them, willing to add what legitimation it could to a shaky claim. Most of these princesses became abbesses and some figure prominently, like the famous abbess

65 *ASC* MS C *sa* 919 and F. Wainwright, 'Aethelflaed, Lady of the Mercians', *Scandinavian England,* ed H. P. R. Finberg (London 1975) pp 305–24.

66 *ASC* MS D *sa* 925 and Roger of Wendover, *Flores Historiarum,* ed H. O. Coxe (London 1848) *sa* 925.

67 For the marriages of Aethelred's daughters and their significance see my 'The reign of Aethelred' (forthcoming).

68 William of Malmesbury, *De Gestis Pontificum,* ed W. Stubbs, *RS* 91 (1891) para 87 p 189.

69 See for example the actions of Aethelwold in 900 *ASC* MSA *sa,* Edmund Ironside in 1015 *ASC* MS C *sa,* and Swegn in 1046 *ASC* MS C *sa.*

Hilda of Whitby, niece of king Edwin of Northumbria. She was hostess at the great debate between the Celtic and Roman churches in seventh-century Northumbria.[70] But life was not all feasts and synods, and there must have been many princesses galled by the fate of their sex, especially when their royal birth had raised them to such pride. We hear little of how most of them took to the life, only the odd reference which makes apparent their refusal to sink into obscurity. But there is one notable exception, who may give some insight into the impact of these royal maidens on the religious life.

In sixth-century Frankia the princess Chlotild, daughter of king Charibert, became a nun at St Radegund at Poitiers. With her in the same nunnery was her cousin Basina, daughter of king Chilperic, whose vocation was due to the wishes of her step-mother Fredegund.[71] Chlotild soon grew dissatisfied with the life at Poitiers. She tried to enlist the help of her royal relatives to improve her conditions there, but to no avail. They may have been reluctant to set precedents. So Chlotild took matters into her own hands and led a revolt against the abbess. At first her revolt was internal; she took over many of the estates of the nunnery, and when the abbess objected, threatened to throw her over the precinct wall. At this juncture many of the less belligerent sisters left the nunnery. Chlotild was excommunicated and expelled, but this royal lady was not to be so easily disposed of. She gathered around her 'a band of cut-throats, evil-doers, fornicators, fugitives from justice, and men guilty of every crime'. Together they attacked the nunnery, planning to take the abbess prisoner. The latter was suffering from an attack of gout, which made flight rather difficult, so she hid in the sanctuary of the Holy Cross in front of the reliquary. Here the cut-throats found her. They fell to squabbling among themselves over the prize, and in the confusion the prioress blew out the candle and tried to smuggle out the abbess under the altar cloth. The men, seeing what was happening, rushed forward, tore off the prioress's veil and, taking her for the abbess, carried her off by mistake. When they discovered their error, they rushed back, seized the abbess and looted the nunnery. All this happened at the beginning of holy week. Rioting between Chlotild's gang and that of the abbess continued all over easter, and was only quelled when the king sent an army to Poitiers under the local count. Chlotild, always mistress of the dramatic gesture, went out to meet them carrying a cross before her

[70] Daughter of Hereric, nephew of king Edwin, Bede, *HE* bk 4 cap 23.
[71] Gregory bk 9 cap 39, bk 10 cap 15.

and garbed as a nun, claiming the protection of her habit and her birth. At the ensuing trial she threw every conceivable accusation at the abbess: keeping a man dressed as a woman in the nunnery for her own use; castrating her servants—an element of mutual contradiction here; playing backgammon; eating with lay visitors; holding engagement parties in the nunnery and making a necklace for her niece out of the gold from the altar cloths. Nor had Chlotild found conditions at Poitiers up to four star standards. The food was bad, service terrible, and she had had to share a bathroom. The morals of the nuns had left much to be desired. Several were pregnant at the time of the trial, though the judging bishops generously excused this as the result of their being left to their own devices, without an abbess, and with the nunnery gates broken down. In spite of these accusations, the abbess answered all and was acquitted; she had relatives among the judges. Chlotild had gone too far, especially when, after attacking the nunnery, she had personally assaulted the bishop when he came to restrain her, treading him underfoot. She was returned to suffer the abbess's vengeance. There is much to the story of Chlotild, political overtones perhaps and a glimpse of the frustrations of the monastic life for a woman of spirit. But to have princesses in the nunneries in any numbers was to invite such troubles, and one must wonder how happy an abbess was when a royal lady arrived at the gates seeking the religious life.

Most of our information about these royal ladies comes from chronicles and from the occasional royal biography, such as Asser's life of king Alfred or Einhard's life of Charlemagne. The reality of the power of many of these queens is demonstrated in the witness lists of charters and in the objective pages of wills, accounts of legal cases and other record materials. But the colourful picture and the details of their actions derives from these chronicle sources. In almost all cases, the information has been refracted through the peculiar gaze of an ecclesiastic. It must have become obvious that the female members of the royal family, if they were at all forceful or played any role in political life, get a uniformly bad press. They are at best schemers and interferers, at worst, she-devils securing their ends through the practice of magic arts. The ecclesiastical writer had biblical models into which to fit his female types—Jezebel and Delilah are frequent comparisons—and he drew on ideas on witchcraft which were already part of European culture. The picture of these royal wives and princesses is often overdrawn and distorted, and blame is heaped on them which should have been shared more widely. It is certainly true, for example, that in the tense situations which characterised relations between fathers and sons many kings took actions which may have been blamed on their wives. Criticism of kings was always difficult, and their immediate family and especially its female members could be used as scapegoats. The hostility may be explicable in terms of the dominant biblical ethos and the low opinion of women which many of these societies shared. It has certainly made the role of many of these queens difficult to assess. At times the ecclesiastical bias has been positively misleading, when, for example, the desire to promote Christian views of marriage has obscured the status of many so-called concubines.

But recognition of the bias of the writers should not blind us to the important role of family politics in this period. These palace intrigues may appear to be a highly coloured picture of early medieval politics, but such intrigues did occur. They are the product of succession rules and marriage practices which exacerbated the intrigues and power struggles which are a feature of any personal monarchy. The nature of these family politics is illustrated by modern anthropological studies of kingdoms where similar circumstances obtained to those in early medieval Europe; hereditary rule without laws of primogeniture, the practice of polygamy and youthful rulers. The same uneasy family relationships and the same pattern of bitter succession disputes occur, with the mothers and kin of rival princes as leaders of the warring factions. As Gluckman has remarked 'politics are still dominated by rebellion in the royal family'.[72] The wicked stepmother is a common motif in western folklore, representing as she does a threat to her step-children's property rights. How much more of a threat are she and her children when the property in question is the throne itself?

Relationships within the royal family continue to be important long after the eleventh century, but their nature begins to change. The establishment of rules for the succession to the throne of a stricter nature and the more rigid Christian view of marriage reduced the room for manoeuvre and the occasions of dispute. In this early period, struggles for the throne could still be seen as legitimate, and with the stakes so high, it is small wonder that so many mothers and princes were prepared to risk a play in the game.

The Polytechnic
Huddersfield

[72] M. Gluckman, *Politics, Law and Ritual in Tribal Society* (Oxford 1965) p 163.

THE EMPRESS IRENE THE ATHENIAN

by SIR STEVEN RUNCIMAN

IN these days of women's liberation it must be a matter of satisfaction for the ladies of Athens to reflect that during the long Byzantine period the two most eminent native-born Athenians were both of them women. There was, in the early days, the scholar Athenaïs who became the pious empress Eudocia, and, in the high Byzantine era, Irene, the first woman in recorded European history to reign as a sovereign monarch. It is Irene whom I wish to discuss, as I think that she has been rather shabbily treated by historians. Her reign was a period of ecclesiastical, constitutional, diplomatic and economic importance, with herself at the centre of it all. Yet, so far as I know, no one has ever published a monograph on her or on her reign or given it more than cursory treatment. It must be admitted that the reason for this is not disapproval or contempt for the empress, but simply the inadequacy of the source material. Apart from the seventh oecumenical council, which is fully documented, the events of the reign

Bibliographical Note

The only original source that deals at all fully with the reign of the empress Irene is the chronicle of Theophanes. Theophanes had his strong prejudices, against the iconoclasts and, later, against Irene's successor, Nicephorus. But he was a conscientious and, as far as one can tell, a reliable recorder of facts. With regard to Irene he was writing about what had occurred in his own lifetime. His attitude towards her was a trifle equivocal but honest. He approved of her religious policy but was uncomfortable about her ambition and her dealings with her son. He can be accepted as a dependable witness for the reign. There are further references to the reign in the *Lives* of Theophanes, of the future patriarch Nicephorus I and of Theodore the Studite, and in Theodore's early letters. None of them add very much to our knowledge. Later chroniclers all follow Theophanes.

The proceedings of the seventh oecumenical council are given fully in Mansi's *Concilia,* volume 13, and are well summarised in Hefele's *Histoire des Conciles,* edited by Leclerc, volume 3, chapter 2. Such of the Acts and official documents of the reign as have survived are given in Zachariae von Lingenthal's *Jus Graeco-Romanum,* volume 3, in Dolger's *Regesten der Kaiserurkunden des Oströmischen Reiches,* volume 1, (nos 339–59), and in Grumel, *Les Regestes des Actes du Patriarchat de Constantinople,* volume 2. For the wars on the eastern frontier the most useful Arabic chronicler is Tabari, who wrote about a century later but copied earlier chronicles. For Charlemagne's coronation and its relation to Byzantium there is a useful discussion in P. Charanis, *Studies on the Demography of the Byzantine Empire,* (Variorum Reprints) chapter 22, which summarises the various views of historians on the question. There is no satisfactory study of Irene's economic policy, though her successor's counter-policy has been much discussed. See Ostrogorsky, *History of the Byzantine Empire,* trans Hussey, pp 166–8. I think that no one has tried to understand Irene's aims.

are covered by one original source only, the *Chronographia* of Theophanes. Later histories and chronicles depend almost entirely on his work. And Theophanes, though on the whole a conscientious and reliable historian, had his own views and prejudices, of which the most obvious was his hatred of iconoclasm. With regard to Irene his attitude has a certain ambivalence. He highly approved of her religious policy and was full of admiration for her piety. He seems on the whole to have admired her government but not to have had much liking for her ministers. But he cannot disguise his horror at her treatment of her son. This ambivalence carried a certain sincerity with it; but it may also have led to reticence on vital points. The rest of the evidence that we have for the history of the reign comes incidentally from other sources, much of it significant and valuable, but inevitably incomplete. There are many unexplained gaps in the story, many questions for which no answer now can be found.

The problems begin at the outset. Irene owed her career to her position as empress. But how and why did she become the bride of an emperor? She must have been born in about 753 AD. In 768 the great iconoclastic emperor Constantine V was searching for a bride for his son Leo IV, and his choice fell on her. But why did he choose her? We know nothing of her family, except that she had a niece who was married a few years later to the refugee Bulgar khan Telerik, and a much younger relative who after her death married the emperor Stauracius. It is most unlikely that it was a family of any political significance. Moreover, the Greek peninsula was one of the most obstinate centres of image-worship. Was the marriage intended to mollify the iconodules of Greece? That seems unlikely. I suspect that the marriage resulted from an early instance of the 'bride-show', that curious method for choosing imperial brides that was practiced in Byzantium from the late eighth to the early tenth century: which involved the mission of inspectors round the empire to select girls who measured up to the strictly listed standards of beauty, brains and health, and who were then summoned to Constantinople for the imperial bridegroom to make his choice from them. It is generally assumed that this somewhat oriental method was introduced to Byzantium by the Chazar Turkish princess whom Constantine V had married—the princess Cicek, or 'flower', whose other cultural achievement was to introduce the *tzitzakion,* a ceremonial garment derived from the mandarin robes of China. The Chazar-born empress was dead by now; but Constantine V may have used the method when choosing his own two subsequent wives and thought it suitable for his son by his Chazar wife. But the accounts that we have of a bride-show indicate that the successful candidate was married immediately after the show: whereas it is expressly stated that Irene came in pomp from Athens to her wedding. Perhaps she had been allowed to return home after the show; or perhaps she was so highly recommended by the inspectors that her personal attendance was not thought necessary. It is difficult to know how else to explain the marriage.

Constantine V did not live to see the results of the marriage. In his later years, perhaps under the influence of the Slav-born patriarch Nicetas I, his fury against the image-worshippers and the monasteries was slightly abated. He even allowed his last empress to keep a nun as her companion in the palace. But so long as he lived Irene could not air her own views. His death in 775 altered the atmosphere. The new emperor, Leo IV, was devoted to his wife; and she and the patriarch seem to have persuaded him to remove the disabilities imposed on the monasteries and even to revert to the former usage of appointing bishops from amongst the monks. But Leo was a nervous man whose health was poor. The tolerant patriarch Nicetas died early in 780; and Leo appointed a tougher iconoclast, Paul of Cyprus, in his place. A few months later a number of officials, including the palace chamberlain, Theophanes, were arrested for image-worshipping. They were flogged, tonsured[1] and cast into prison, where Theophanes died. A much later story told of Leo having found Irene paying reverence to two images, and his action was taken to show that his tolerance did not extend to the palace. The tale is probably untrue. Had Irene been so piously engaged the chronicler Theophanes would certainly have proudly reported it. But she may well have been trying quietly to fill the palace with inconodule sympathizers; and Leo was determined to stop it. He was too late. Within a few months he had died, in September, 780.

Leo had been anxious about the succession. He and Irene had only one child, Constantine, born in 770. But there were other members of the imperial family. By his third wife Constantine V had six children. The daughter, Anthusa, called after the nun who was her mother's friend, spent her life doing good works, founding and organizing orphanages and hospitals and becoming, surprisingly, considering her parentage, a devotee of holy images. The five brothers, the caesars Nicephorus and Christopher and the *nobilissimi* Nicetas, Anthimus and

[1] Tonsured in this context means the shaving off of the beard, not a monastic tonsure.

Eudocimus, lacked their sister's energy and purpose. They formed a tragi-comic troupe, weak and feckless, and inseparable. Leo had been kind to them but had no illusions about them. Early in his reign, in 776, he had insisted on the imperial coronation of his young son and on oaths of allegiance being taken to him by the court, the senate and representatives of the army and the people. Even so, there was soon afterwards a conspiracy to elevate the caesars. The conspirators, probably iconoclasts who resented the new tolerance and were alarmed for the future, were banished. The princes were unpunished; indeed, they may not have known of the plot. But they were discredited in popular eyes.

However, when his father died, Constantine VI was a backward boy of ten. A regency was necessary. Hitherto there had only been two cases since the foundation of Constantinople of emperors coming to the throne as minors. Constans II had been eleven when he became sole emperor. His step-grandmother, Martina, and her sons having fallen from power and his own mother being almost certainly dead, there was no adult to take over the regency; and the senate seems to have acted as regent till the boy reached the age of sixteen. In the earlier case, that of Theodosius II, both of whose parents were dead, the pretorian prefect of the east, Anthemius, acted as regent until the young emperor's eldest sister, Pulcheria, at the age of sixteen, had herself crowned Augusta (or empress) and took over the regency for two years till her brother reached sixteen. The idea of a female regent was not unknown. Indeed, Sophia had acted as regent when her husband Justin II went mad. It is true that Martina's attempts to rule had been greeted with horror and declarations that a woman could not administer the government. But Martina was personally regarded as accursed, having incestuously married her uncle, and she was seeking to overrule adult emperors. But since then there had been a change in family law. Leo III's legislation had given mothers equal rights with fathers over their children, and a widow was to be sole guardian of children not yet of age. Irene was therefore unquestionably the legal guardian of the young emperor; and her right to act as regent for him was generally accepted. Six weeks after Leo IV's death there was another conspiracy in the name of the caesars and the *nobilissimi,* organized by the captain of the imperial guard, the logothete of the course and the admiral of the Dodecannese, amongst others, all of them probably officials dating from Constantine V's time and suspicious of the empress's iconodule tastes. It was discovered; and the leaders were flogged, tonsured and banished. For the five princes subtler treatment was reserved. They were rushed through the stages of ordination, and on Christmas day they were obliged all together to adminster the sacrament in the great cathedral of Saint Sophia. All the world could see that they were now no longer qualified to sit upon the throne.

Nevertheless plots in their favour continued. In February, 781, Irene appointed a certain Elpidius as governor of Sicily. She must have believed him to be an iconodule to send him to so iconodule a province. In April she learnt that he had proclaimed the caesars there. An official sent to fetch him home was thwarted by the Sicilians. She imprisoned his wife and children who were in Constantinople; but it was not till next spring that she could send a fleet, under an able eunuch general, Theodore, to recapture the province. On its coming Elpidius fled to the Moors in Africa, together with the duke of Calabria. There he was received as Roman emperor, but, it seems, never came back from his exile. In later centuries it was rumoured in the east that he had been exiled because the young emperor had found him in a compromising position with Irene. It is hard to know how the rumour arose. Elpidius was already in Sicily when he defected. Constantine, aged eleven, was unlikely to have taken vigorous action against him: while Irene, though her sins were many, was never accused of physical lust.

Irene still had to move cautiously before she could settle down to her main aim, the restoration of image-worship. In 781 her troops had driven back an Arab attack on the eastern frontier with great success. But when the Arabs attacked again next year, one of her best generals, Tatsates, commander of the Bucellarian theme, went over to the enemy, inspired, it seems, by jealousy of Stauracius, the eunuch whom Irene had made her chief minister. The main imperial army had gone to Sicily; so Tatsates's defection obliged the Byzantines to sue for a truce. Stauracius hastened to the frontier with fellow-delegates to fix the terms. They rashly came to the meeting-place without having arranged for hostages. The Arabs treacherously took them prisoner; and Irene was obliged to pay 70,000 dinars a year for three years to secure their release.

The peace was expensive, but it was worth while; and Stauracius redeemed his reputation by conducting next year a successful campaign against the wild Slav tribes of northern Greece, for which he was honoured with a triumph. As a sign that order was restored Irene and her son went on a ceremonial journey along the Balkan frontier as far as Berrhoea, which the Slavs had half ruined and which was restored and rechristened Irenoupolis. Meanwhile Irene secured her position in the west. After a half-hearted attempt to incite the Lombards of southern Italy against the Franks who were overrunning the peninsula, she saw that it would be wise to make friends with the great Frankish monarch, Charles, She sent him an embassy suggesting a marriage between one of his daughters and the young emperor. Charles was delighted. He selected his daughter Rotrud, whom the Greeks called Erythro; and at his request Irene sent to his court at Aachen a scholar monk, Elisaeus, to teach the girl the Greek language and the usages of polite society.

By 784 the ground seemed ready for the re-introduction of image-worship. The empire was at peace. Irene had, it seems, by now replaced most of the old officials and generals by men sympathetic with her views; and she had an able chief minister in the eunuch Stauracius, the logothete of the course. One difficulty remained—the iconoclastic patriarch Paul. Irene had carefully avoided any confrontation with him. Instead, she seems to have exercised her charm on him, with some success. Despite her obvious iconodule tastes he neither plotted nor protested against her. Suddenly in August, 784, he fell ill and announced that he had seen the error of his iconoclastic ways and was retiring to a monastery. Irene hastened to his bedside, where he reaffirmed his repentance. She them summoned all the senators and patricians whom she believed to have iconoclastic sympathies to join her; and Paul solemnly told them that they would not be saved unless there were an oecumenical council to restore the unity of Christendom. Soon afterwards Paul died, in the odour of sanctity.

A new patriarch could be elected. With excellent judgment Irene decided upon the imperial secretary, Tarasius, a man well versed in diplomacy but also well educated in theology. A synod was summoned to the Magnaura Palace, where, though there were a few voices raised against the appointment of a layman (which, though not uncommon later, was still unusual), he was elected by a large majority. He protested his unworthiness and his unwillingness to preside over a see separated from the other great sees of Christendom; but his protests were easily overruled. On Christmas day, 784, he was consecrated patriarch.

Soon after his election Tarasius prepared letters of enthronization, containing his own statement of belief, to be sent, according to the ancient custom, to the pope and the three eastern patriarchs. It is unlikely that the eastern patriarchs ever received their letters. The Arab authorities were at the time blocking communications between them and the Byzantine court. But indirect contact was made. The letter to the pope, Adrian I, was eventually sent on 29 August, 785, together with a *divalis sacra* from Irene and her son, asking the pope to fix the date for an oecumenical council to settle the doctrine of images and begging him, if he could not attend it in person, to send suitable representatives. Irene had intended to send the missives by the hand of the Sicilian bishop of Leontini, whom she had interviewed in Constantinople and found to be acquainted with the pope. But he seems to have fallen ill on the way; and the letters were delivered by the bishop of Catania, accompanied by a priest from Constantinople. The pope replied on 27 October. He gave his support for a council, while telling the empress that she should return to the patrimony of Saint Peter the provinces annexed by Leo III, and reproving her for giving the title of oecumenical to the patriarchate of Constantinople. Writing to Tarasius he congratulated him on his orthodoxy but suggested doubts of the canonicity of his appointment.

The council was planned to open in the church of the Holy Apostles in Constantinople on 17 August, 786. The eastern churches were represented by the *syncelli* of Alexandria and Antioch. Owing to the difficulty of communications they had no official papers; but their presence indicated the co-operation of the eastern patriarchates: who have always regarded the council as being oecumenical. The pope was represented by his steward, Peter the priest, and by Peter, abbot of Saint Sabba. The bishops of the empire attended in full force.

But among the bishops there were still several devoted iconoclasts who were determined to wreck the council. In early August, when the delegates were arriving, the court was touring in Thrace; and the dissidents were able to plot with the military garrison of the city and the imperial guard. Tarasius forbade them to hold meetings, but he could not stop their intrigues. On 17 August the delegates all assembled in the great church, the empress and her son sitting in the catechumens' seats. Hardly had the proceedings begun when a mass of soldiers rushed into the church with drawn swords, threatening death to all image-worshippers. The empress and her ministers were powerless to calm them. It was only when the iconoclast bishops rose in a body, shouting 'We have won', that the soldiers withdrew. The council then dispersed in some disorder, and many of the delegates prepared to return home, including the papal legates.

Irene was dismayed but undefeated. Next month, when news came of an Arab raid across the frontier, she announced that there was to be a great campaign against the Arabs, and she and the Court moved to Malagina, the garrison city in Bithynia where it was customary for the imperial army to assemble for an eastern expedition. The regiments in Constantinople came willingly to the meeting-place. Meanwhile Stauracius went to Thrace and there collected the European troops whom he knew to be loyal—doubtless the troops that had fought under him against the Slavs.[2] Some of them he left to garrison the capital and the palace. With the others he marched on Malagina and surrounded the regiments there. Taken by surprise they submitted without a struggle, and were disbanded and disarmed, and sent home to their villages.

The council could be convoked again. In May of next year summons went out to the delegates telling them to re-assemble; and a ship was sent to bring back the papal legates, who had gone as far as Sicily. But the council was to meet not in Constantinople but in the hallowed city of Nicaea, away from the dangers of popular riots. In the meantime Irene seems to have seen to the retirement and replacement of the more obstinately iconoclastic bishops. The iconoclasts who came to the council came in a state of repentance and recanted their errors. Irene and her son did not attend the meetings in Nicaea when they opened on 24 September. On the presidential throne an open gospel was placed. The papal legates were given the first place, followed by the priests representing the eastern churches. But Tarasius in fact acted as chairman. Some three hundred bishops and abbots were present, most of them coming from sees in Asia Minor.

This is not the place for discussing the proceedings and the findings of the seventh oecumenical council, which restored and defined the doctrine of the reverence due to holy images. But one point must be noted. Tarasius, with the undoubted approval of Irene, was anxious to make things as easy as possible for repentant ex-iconoclasts. After admitting past errors they were allowed to take their seats. This was not to the liking of many of the monks who were present, led by Sabas, abbot of Studion, even though the most formidable of the abbots, Plato of Saccudion, seems to have supported Tarasius. The monkish party had led the opposition to the iconoclastic emperors. Now, though orthodoxy was restored, they still were ready to oppose a church that seemed to them too much under the control of the state.

[2] The 'Penaiotikoi' troops were the European troops, not (as Bury and others have supposed) the Asiatic.

They held that the church should be independent even of the divine emperor himself.

Nevertheless, it was a document signed by all the delegates which was brought to the eighth and final session of the council, held in the Magnaura Palace in Constantinople on 23 October, to be presented to the empress and the emperor. After suitable speeches by the patriarch and by Irene she signed the document, followed by her son.

Had Irene died at this juncture or had she retired from power, she would have been remembered in history as an able and sagacious ruler who had restored to the empire a doctrine that the majority of her subjects desired, and had done so without vindictiveness or rancour. She had moreover been a correct regent, always accompanied by her son and putting his name before hers in all official documents, even if she did sign the *oros* of the council before him. Indeed, she should have resigned; for Constantine was now seventeen; and an emperor had always been held to come of age at sixteen. Constitutionally, however, the position was vague. If the young emperor chose to continue to associate his mother with him in official acts, there was no reason why he should not do so, nor even why he should not let her continue to interview and direct the ministers of state. This was in fact the situation. Constantine was a backward boy who was showing no interest in politics and seemed willing as yet to leave things to his mother. She for her part clearly liked power; and doubtless the compliments that she received from the church as a result of her restoration of image-worship inclined her to believe that she was divinely ordained to exercise power. Moreover she seems to have had little confidence in her son's abilities. She remained at the helm.

But Constantine was growing up, and next year he began to show signs of dissatisfaction. He had looked forward to his marriage with the daughter of Charles the Great. The idea of the exotic Frankish princess appealed to him. But by 788 relations between the courts of Constantinople and Aachen had worsened. Charles's invasions of southern Italy in 786 and of Venetia in 787, in the course of which he blockaded Venetian trade in which the Greeks were interested, roused resentment at Constantinople; and Charles himself came out strongly against the findings of the council of Nicaea, largely owing to the fact that the translation of the *oros,* made for him in the papal secretariat, was, where it was at all intelligible, completely inaccurate. Whether it was he or Irene who broke off the marriage treaty is uncertain. By 788 there was no longer any question of it.

The princess Rotrud never married, though she bore a son out of wedlock to the count of Maine. But a wife was found for Constantine. In the summer of 788 inspectors were sent out from Constantinople to collect young maidens for a bride-show. Detailed instructions were given about the required qualities and even physical measurements of face and feet. Amongst the candidates was a girl called Maria, the grand-daughter of a wealthy but saintly farmer at Amnia in Paphlagonia. It was on her that the choice fell: but it was Irene, not Constantine, who made the choice. Maria's features may have been of the correct proportions, but she lacked charm in her husband's eyes. After one child, a daughter, was born he treated her with neglect.

His resentment against his mother and especially against her minister Stauracius increased. They allowed him no part in the government. Early in 790 a group of his friends, counting on the support of most of the army, planned a *coup d'état* which should overthrow Stauracius and exile him to Sicily. But a sudden and severe earthquake upset the conspirators' time-table, and Stauracius, who was well-informed, was able to strike first. The ringleader John the protospatharius, who had perhaps been the emperor's tutor, was banished to Sicily, and the patrician Damian to Apollonias, both after scourging and tonsure. The other conspirators were put under house arrest. Irene herself had an angry interview with her son, in which she lost her temper and struck him on the face. Soon afterwards orders were sent to the army ordering all the regiments to take an oath never to replace Irene as supreme ruler by her son so long as she lived. The order was obeyed except by the soldiers of the Armeniac theme, in central Anatolia. Irene sent the drungarius of the watch, Alexius Musele, to bring the Armeniacs to obedience. But he went over to their side. The soldiers appointed him as their commander in place of the lawful *strategos;* and he set about seducing the other regiments from their allegiance to the empress. By October, 790, all the thematic regiments, under commanders of their own choice, assembled at Atroa, in Bithynia, and demanded that Constantine be sent to them. Irene had to let him go. They proclaimed him sole emperor and Irene deposed from power. In December Constantine returned triumphantly to the capital. Stauracius was scourged and tonsured and sent in exile to the Armeniac theme. Irene's other ministers were degraded; and she herself was confined to a palace which she had built, the House of Eleutherios, on the slope overlooking the harbour of Eleutherios and the sea of Marmora.

Constantine was not suited to be an emperor. He longed for military glory. But when he led a campaign against the Bulgarians early next year, both armies after making contact fled in terror during the night. Later in the year he made a raid into Arab territory as far as the walls of Tarsus; but it achieved nothing. Civil administration clearly bored him, and he had no ministers whom he could trust. It was probably for that reason that, surprisingly, in January, 782, he recalled his mother to the palace. He probably felt secure in the support of the army. He could therefore afford to let her take over the tedious civil administration, even though it meant the return of Stauracius, while he won glory on his campaigns.

The Armeniac regiment, to whom Constantine owed his power, was not prepared to accept Irene's restoration. Its commander, Alexius Musele, was summoned to Constantinople; and when he refused to fall in with Constantine's wishes, he was thrown into prison. Another of Constantine's few friends, Theodore Camulianus, was sent in his place to command the regiment, in the vain hope that he would make it change its mind. In the meantime, in July, the emperor sought military glory in a campaign against the Bulgarians. It was a disastrous failure. His army was severely beaten and retreated in confusion, leaving horses and armaments as well as the royal tent and treasure in the hands of the Bulgarians. To many of the generals Constantine now was as unacceptable as Irene. But whom could they elevate in their stead? They thought of the five miserable princes, Constantine's uncles. A plot was hatched to put the eldest, Nicephorus, priest though he was, on the throne. The plot was easily detected and the conspirators punished; and on Constantine's orders the caesar Nicephorus, who was probably innocent of the intrigue, was blinded, and his four brothers had their tongues slit. The cruelty of the action deeply shocked the people of Constantinople.

Irene, who had never forgiven Alexius Musele for his part in her downfall, persuaded her son that he was involved in the plot. He was blinded. When the news reached the Armeniac regiment the soldiers blinded their commander, the emperor's friend Theodore Camulianus. Constantine had to go in person to suppress the revolt. He succeeded, only because a number of Armenian mercenaries who were supporting the Armeniacs, changed sides, expecting a large reward: which in fact they did not receive; so they went over next to the Arabs.

For the moment relations between the emperor and his mother were correct, if not cordial; but their collaboration was fragile. To assume that Irene was purely motivated by the love of power is, I think, unfair to her. Iconoclasm was still a strong force in the empire, particularly in the army. An emperor whose support was based on the army might well find it prudent to adopt iconoclasm. Irene, whose piety was without doubt genuine, was suspicious of her son's intentions, not without reason.

In the summer of 795 Constantine conducted a campaign against the Arabs which was, for once, successful. He won a victory over their frontier forces. This may not have pleased Irene overmuch. But soon afterwards he was distracted from his military ambitions. He had fallen in love with one of his mother's ladies-in-waiting. Irene was thought to have encouraged the affair; her admirer the chronicler Theophanes even believed that she did so to embroil Constantine with the church. One may question whether she would have taken a line that might well drive him into the arms of the iconoclasts. More probably she thought that love would distract him from all political enterprise, and, perhaps, that the girl, Theodote, would be a good influence on him; for she was a close relation of Plato, the pious abbot of Saccudion. In January, 795, he had divorced the empress Maria, who was sent to a convent on the island of Prinkipo, together with her little daughter: who as the nun Euphrosyne was to emerge some thirty years later to be the bride of the emperor Michael the Amorian. In September the emperor announced his intention of marrying Theodote. There were doubts over the canonicity of Maria's divorce—the church's position as regards marriage-laws was not yet defined—if she became a nun the annulment of the marriage might be permissible. But the patriarch Tarasius refused either to accept Maria's vows or to perform the marriage with Theodote. Constantine was furious and, it seems, threatened Tarasius that if he did not have his way he would go over to the iconoclasts. Tarasius, who was temperamentally inclined to compromise, allowed an unnamed catechist to tonsure Maria and an abbot, Joseph, to perform the marriage ceremony: after which Constantine crowned Theodote empress.

At once there was an outcry amongst the pious, especially amongst the monks, headed by Theodote's own relatives, Plato of Saccudion and his nephew Theodore, the future Studite. Tarasius, they said, should unfrock Joseph and excommunicate the emperor. Constantine angrily ordered any monk who criticised him to be exiled from Constantinople. Irene, disappointed, no doubt, in Theodote, made it clear that she shared the pious view. This won her the devotion of the monasteries but somewhat chilled her relations with Tarasius.

Outwardly she remained on friendly terms with her son. In the autumn of 796 they went to Brusa together with the court to take the waters. While they were there a message came to Constantine to say that Theodote had borne him a son in Constantinople. He galloped off at once to see the baby, who in fact died two months later. As soon as he was gone Irene collected all the officials and generals at the court and, we are told, by her blandishments won them to her side. It is a little difficult to believe that she could have done so without some good reason. The solution must be that she could provide them with proof that Constantine was flirting with iconoclasm. Iconoclasm was still a force within the empire, and its triumph would be a disaster for every member of the present court. The fear of iconoclasm would also explain why Tarasius the patriarch, for all his humanity and tolerance, never lifted a finger on behalf of Constantine. Irene's warnings, flatteries and gifts won her the support of the court. She waited for the moment to strike. Next spring the emperor led an expedition against the Arabs. Irene's friends in the high command did all that they could to hamper him; and he did not have the strength of character to overrule them. The campaign was a fiasco, and it lost him what remaining respect he commanded in the army.

At the end of July, as Constantine was proceeding through the city, a group of soldiers fell on his party and tried to assassinate him. It was thought that they had been hired by Stauracius. The emperor managed to escape; but he realized that his life was in danger. He fled with a few friends in the imperial launch across the Bosphorus, intending to make his way into central Anatolia where he hoped to find troops that would support him. But his companions were false. When they were warned that their double-dealing would be exposed they brought the emperor back under guard to Constantinople. He was immured in the Purple Chamber in which he had been born; and there on 15 August 796 his eyes were savagely put out. He did not die. He lived on in darkness for some eight more years. But he could no longer reign as emperor.

The plot had been arranged by Stauracius; and it is possible that he ordered the blinding and faced Irene with the *fait accompli*. But it was generally believed that she herself had given the order. In horror at the deed heaven was darkened for seventeen days; and the pious noted that it had been five years to the day since Constantine had put out his uncle's eyes.

The elimination of the emperor left Irene in sole control of the government. But what was her constitutional position? Since early

Byzantine times it had been accepted that in default of an emperor—a rare occurrence owing to the custom of crowning co-emperors—the senior empress or augusta was the depository of imperial power; that is to say, it was for her to nominate the next emperor. Pulcheria nominated Marcian, Ariadne nominated Anastasius, and Sophia, when her husband was incapacitated by madness, nominated Tiberius. If Irene chose not to nominate an emperor but to remain the depository of imperial power, was she acting unconstitutionally? The church should perhaps have objected, since the emperor was a semi-priestly figure with religious duties to perform. But the church was not going to oppose so pious an empress. The army did object, for the emperor was its commander-in-chief. But its objections were ineffectual. The lawyers were a little worried. The only pieces of legislation to survive from her reign run in the name of Irene the pious emperor. But in general her autocracy was accepted. It ended only when she could no longer exercise it efficiently.

There were minor plots against her rule, in favour of her five brothers-in-law. In November, 797, the princes heard of such a plot and fled to the sanctuary of Saint Sophia to avoid involvement. The conspirators were easily detected and punished without severity; and the princes were sent to a comfortable exile in Athens. There a year later a similar plot was unearthed and suppressed; and the princes were left unharmed. After Irene's fall they were moved to Sicily but were eventually brought to the island of Aphasia in the Sea of Marmora, where they died.

It was not, perhaps, a very glorious reign; but it was not as disastrous as historians like to pretend. Her economic policy has been criticized. She made it her business during the next years to reduce taxes and tolls. The reliefs that she accorded to the monasteries were perhaps due more to piety than to fiscal good sense, though they ensured her popularity with an influential and very vocal section of society. But her repeal of the municipal tax paid by the people of Constantinople, which was heavy and greatly resented, must have helped to re-animate municipal life. Byzantium was more heavily over-taxed than any other medieval state; and to reduce the burden, though it might lessen the revenue, was not necessarily bad for the economy. Similarly, her reduction of the duties to be paid by merchants at Hieron and Abydos on their way to and from Constantinople, while again it might lessen the revenue, undoubtedly stimulated trade. With wealth in western Europe rapidly increasing under the Carolingian government, it was useful to attract merchants to Constantinople. Otherwise they might be tempted to buy their oriental goods in Arab markets. It was known that Charles the Great was in diplomatic contact with the caliph Harun ar-Rashid. After her fall her successor Nicephorus re-imposed and added to the taxes, for the sake of revenue. But as he had been her minister of finance he must have condoned her policy of freer trade at the time.

Foreign affairs were less happy. Irene could not trust the army and had, it seems, disbanded much of it. She therefore sought for peace with the caliphate; but it was only after an Arab raid in 798 that devastated Anatolia as far as Malagina that Harun consented to a truce of four years, for which Irene had to pay a large yearly subsidy. The Byzantines saw nothing inherently disgraceful in applying for peace. It was usually cheaper than mounting expensive military expeditions and suffering the damage caused by foreign raids. But the army, remembering the glorious wars of the iconoclastic emperors, was not content under her rule.

More galling to Byzantine pride was the ceremony that took place at Saint Peter's in Rome on Christmas day, 800, when Charles, king of the Franks, was crowned emperor by pope Leo III. We cannot discuss here the background to the event nor what the chief actors really felt about it. There seems to be little doubt that Charles, while pleased to be emperor, was doubtful of the legality of his title. To satisfy him some of his friends pointed out that there was now no emperor reigning in Constantinople, only a woman. If New Rome failed to fill the vacancy in the *imperium,* it was legally justifiable for Old Rome to do so. But Charles himself remained desperately anxious to receive recognition from Constantinople. It was to secure recognition that he sent an embassy to Constantinople in 802 with the remarkable suggestion, so it was said, that he should marry the empress. It is difficult to believe that the suggestion was serious. But Charles may have contemplated a purely nominal marriage, which would give Irene the excuse for nominating him as emperor, though each would continue to govern his and her territory, possibly occasionally meeting in Constantinople or in Rome. Irene may have liked the idea; but her ministers were horrified. After all, it could mean that on her death Charles would be legitimate emperor of the east as well as the west and entitled to reign in Constantinople, or, more probably, send some Frankish prince to be his co-emperor there. They saw to it that the negotiations came to nothing.

The ministers had cause for worry; for Irene's health was failing. She had her last moment of glory on easter day, 799, when she drove round the city in a chariot drawn by milk-white horses, while four high officers of state walked by her side, and the populace cheered. But she seems to have grown to dislike the Great Palace, with its sombre memories and to have spent more and more time in her own pleasant House of Eleutherios. An autocrat cannot afford ill-health; and it is especially dangerous for an autocrat who has no obvious heir. Anyone who aims to secure the succession for himself or a friend does not want to be taken by surprise by the death of the sovereign. It is wiser to anticipate that event. Irene's ministers began to think of the future. Stauracius was still at the helm; but she was placing increasing reliance on a rival eunuch, Aetius. Irene's employment of eunuchs was natural. It obviated any rumour of scandal; and a eunuch could not aspire to the imperial throne, though Stauracius is said to have dreamed of it. He had been a highly efficient and loyal minister but now he was impatient. In May, 799, Aetius reported to Irene that Stauracius was plotting against her. Knowing the rivalry between the two eunuchs, Irene contented herself with warning Stauracius that she knew of his intrigues. Early next year she fell ill, and Stauracius plotted again. In February he was put under house arrest in the palace and no one connected with the army in which he had friends was allowed to see him. But he was dying of a kidney disease. So, though he continued to intrigue, believing pathetically in a soothsayer who had promised him supreme power, she let him die in peace. His death occurred in June. Aetius was now chief minister; and he began to work for the elevation to the throne of his brother Leo, a man of no particular distinction. To balance Aetius the empress began to show favour to another eunuch, Nicetas. But his hatred of Aetius was greater than his loyalty to his mistress. He collected a group of officials and generals together in secret; and they decided to secure the succession of the grand logothete, the minister of finance, Nicephorus, a man whom they all respected.

In the autumn of 802 Irene fell ill again and retired to the House of Eleutherios. Early in the morning of 10 October Nicetas and his friends, having sent a detachment of troops that they could trust to surround the House of Eleutherios, went to the palace, demanding admittance in the name of the empress, saying that she had unearthed a plot by Aetius, and that she therefore wished to elevate Nicephorus. The palace guard was convinced. Once they had secured the palace the conspirators proclaimed Nicephorus emperor at the Augusteum. The patriarch Tarasius was aroused and hastily crowned Nicephorus. He may have thought that he was carrying out Irene's wishes; or he may have acted out of dislike of her support of the monkish party, with which he was now on bad terms. Once crowned Nicephorus went to visit Irene, to announce that he had taken over, and to ask her where she kept the stores of imperial treasure. Byzantine autocrats knew how to accept disaster with dignity, because they genuinely believed that sins were punished in this world as well as in the next. Irene made a short and suitable speech, accepting divine retribution, and handed over the keys of her treasury, asking only that she should be allowed to spend her remaining days in the House of Eleutherios. Nicephorus promised to leave her undisturbed; but, as soon as he was in possession of the treasure, he had her conveyed to the island of Prinkipo, to a convent that she herself had founded. She was kept there for a month. But the populace of Constantinople showed more sympathy with her than he liked. He moved her in November to the island of Lesbos. Later legend said that she had to earn her keep there by spinning; but it seems that she lived in adequate comfort till her death in the following August. Her body was buried in the convent that she had founded on Prinkipo.

I have given this account of Irene's life and reign at some length because if we are to judge her we must examine all that is known about her. It is true that the chief witness, Theophanes, had a qualified bias in her favour. But, allowing for that, I still do not think that she was the monster that historians like to depict. For the first years of her regency she was a prudent and tactful ruler who managed to reintroduce image-worship with the minimum of bitterness or fuss. She clearly liked power, but she probably convinced herself that her authority was needed to maintain the religious settlement, about which she trusted her son less and less. Her blinding of him—or her consent to his blinding—was a crime that shocked even her admirer Theophanes. But she may have thought that her duty to God, as she saw it, took precedence over her duty as a mother. Apart from that crime, and perhaps the blinding of Alexius Musele, she was remarkably lenient to conspirators and traitors. Scourging and house-arrest, and in extreme cases exile, were the punishments that she imposed, in contrast to the ferocity of the iconoclastic emperors. When her old friend Stauracius turned against her, she allowed him to die in peace. And I do not think that her administration was as bad as historians like to suggest. Her reign was not glorious as regards foreign affairs; but I am not convinced that her internal government and in particular her fiscal policy was disastrous. I doubt if we really know enough to pronounce on it. All in all I believe that she did more good than harm to the empire; and I think that womanhood has no reason to be ashamed of this remarkable and glamorous Athenian, whose memory I salute.

Elshieshields

'A NURSERY OF SAINTS': ST MARGARET OF SCOTLAND RECONSIDERED

by DEREK BAKER

WRITING of the early and impressionable years spent by Ailred in the household of king David of Scotland, Knowles, in a felicitous phrase, remarked that the Scottish court had been 'something of a nursery of saints'[1] during the previous half-century. The conduct, character and traditions of that spiritual kindergarten he associated with 'that *âme d'élite*', the 'exquisite St Margaret',[2] and the contrast between the Scotland of king David and that of his father Malcolm Canmore, the proliferation of religious vocations and works of practical piety which followed the marriage of Malcolm and Margaret, make his claim self-evident. Within the royal circle if the careers of David and Edith/Matilda, and in the next generation of Waldef and Ailred, supply conspicuous testimony they do not stand alone. For Ailred, writing *c*1153/4, Malcolm's oldest surviving son Edgar was *homo . . . dulcis et amabilis, cognato suo regi Edwardo* [the Confessor] *per omnia similis*,[3] while his successor Alexander 'the fierce', was 'humble and loving to clerks and monks'.[4] *Litteratus*, according to Ailred, his active interest in the conduct of church life, and his piety reflect the interests and example of his mother. As earl he was the only layman present at the opening of St Cuthbert's tomb in 1104,[5] while his father, allegedly, was present at the foundation of the new cathedral at Durham in *c*1093.[6] Even Malcolm Canmore

[1] Knowles, *MO* p 242.

[2] *Ibid* pp 170, 242.

[3] [Ailred, *Genealogia Regum Anglorum,* ed R.] Twysden, [Historiae *Anglicanae Scriptores Decem*], cols 347–70 (London 1652) col 367.

[4] *Ibid* col 368.

[5] [Symeon of Durham], *H*[*istoria*] *R*[*egum*], *sa* 1104: 'praesente Alexandro comite, postea Scottorum rege'. Alexander is the only named layman present, and although the *HR* account continues 'et multis aliis' the full account given in chapter 18 of the anonymous *Historia Translationum Sancti Cuthberti* makes it clear that these, numbering forty, included no laymen—see [*Symeonis Dunelmensis Opera et Collectanea*, ed Hodgson] Hinde, 1, *SS* 51 (1867) p 195. For additional comment on Alexander's presence, which is not mentioned by any Scottish source, see F[lorence of] W[orcester, *Chronicon*], *sa* 1104.

[6] See *HR sa* 1093, where the date is given as 11 August. This account records the initiative of the bishop of Durham and names Malcolm III and prior Turgot as those

himself was affected, though his metamorphosis was posthumous. At the translation of Margaret's body to her shrine in the new church at Dunfermline the intransigence of Malcolm's remains obtained him, so it was said, a place beside the shrine of his newly-canonised wife, and a dubious share in her sanctity.[7]

Whatever the reputations of her spiritual protégés only Margaret herself achieved a formally-recognised sanctity[8]—though it is often mistakenly claimed, Ailred was never canonised, whilst Waldef, despite the efforts made on his behalf, never progressed beyond a local reputation.[9] It is, in fact, something of a paradox that of all these early twelfth-century figures only William of York, the discredited, deposed archbishop of York, opposed by Ailred, Waldef and the saintly William, first abbot of Rievaulx, and threatened by the distant thunders of saint Bernard, should be recognised as a saint, while his English opponents were not.[10]

William of York was canonised some twenty years before Margaret,[11] and the queen's process, like the archbishop's, can be related to the interests of the church which housed her relics. It was on 27 July 1245 that Innocent IV instructed the bishops of St Andrews, Dunkeld and Dunblane to inquire diligently into the life, merits and miracles of the queen, and to report their findings to him.[12] Three months earlier the pope, *ad preces regis Scotiae*, had mitred the abbey, and a series of papal privileges followed.[13] These were the years when

---

responsible for laying the first foundation stones. Symeon's *H*[*istoria*] *D*[*unelmensis*] *E*[*cclesiae*], however, under the same date, makes no mention whatsoever of Malcolm; see also Ritchie p 59; the family devotion to St Cuthbert is clearly demonstrated by Edgar (king 1095–1107) who terms him 'my lord' in one of his writs, and if his early generosity to Durham was later scaled down it remained substantial—see [A. A. M.] Duncan, [*Scotland, the Making of the Kingdom*] (Edinburgh 1975) pp 125–8; for the foundation of Coldingham see *MRHS* pp 55–6.

[7] See [J.] Pinkerton, [*Lives of the Scottish Saints*], revised and enlarged W. M. Metcalfe, 2 vols (Paisley 1889) 2 pp 189–92.

[8] See Potthast 2 p 1142, nos 13800 (16 September 1249), 13807 (21 September 1249); Pinkerton 2 pp 189–90.

[9] For some discussion of Waldef see [Derek] Baker, ['Legend and reality: the case of] Waldef [of Melrose'], *SCH* 12 (1975) pp 59–82, and Baker, 'Patronage in the early twelfth-century church: Walter Espec, Kirkham and Rievaulx', *Traditio, Krisis, Renovatio aus theologischer Sicht*, ed B. Jaspert and R. Mohr (Marburg 1976) pp 92–100.

[10] For the York election dispute see Baker, 'San Bernado e l'elezione di York', *Studi su San Bernardo* (Florence 1975) pp 85–146, and the references there given. A separate study of the canonisation process of William of York is projected.

[11] In 1226.

[12] Potthast 2 p 999, no 11753 (*Reg Dunf* no 281).

[13] Potthast 2 p 987, no 11632a, 24 April 1245.

the abbey church of Dunfermline was being rebuilt, and it is clear that the proposed canonisation of Margaret must be associated with this process of royal patronage and monastic development. Initially, as with William of York, the inquisition does not seem to have gone well. On 13 August 1246, some thirteen months after its inception, Innocent IV wrote to the bishops of St Andrews and Glasgow complaining of the inadequacy of the report sent to him, and instructing them to inquire as fully as possible into the truth.[14] The details of this inquiry are not known, but it was another three years before the pope wrote to the abbot of Dunfermline, on 16 September 1249, about the investigation,[15] five days later granting an indulgence of forty days for those attending the church of Dunfermline on the feast of *saint* Margaret.[16] The translation of the saint's relics followed nine months later, presided over by the young Alexander III, who had been king for less than a year.[17]

Margaret followed William of York and Edmund of Canterbury[18] into the calendar of saints—the third British addition in less than a generation—and if her process of canonisation was purely Scottish, it should not be seen in too narrow a context. Duncan has remarked on the parallel devotion of the English royal house to Edward the Confessor and the Scottish to Margaret,[19] and the process of inquiry and canonisation of Margaret had as a broader context the grandiose project for the rebuilding of Westminster Abbey as a more splendid shrine for the relics of the Confessor. Henry III's attachment to his saintly ancestor was not simply the result of canonisation or tradition, but an intense and individual personal devotion which cannot have gone unnoticed in Scotland, or elsewhere.[20] What wider motives, if any, inspired Dunfermline to seek canonisation for Margaret in 1245 cannot be known. It may be suggested, however, without devaluing the approach, that it bears some relation to Alexander II's other attempts to enhance his regality vis-à-vis his English 'lord', and to the renewed interest in the Confessor.[21]

[14] Potthast 2 p 1037, no 12252, 13 August 1246 (*Reg Dunf* no 285).

[15] Potthast 2 p 1142, no 13800 (*Reg Dunf* no 290).

[16] Potthast 2 p 1142, no 13807 (*Reg Dunf* no 291).

[17] Duncan p 558, for the succession of Alexander III see pp 552–60.

[18] 21 April 1245. [19] Duncan p 558.

[20] See [F. M.] Powicke, *Henry III and the Lord Edward,* 2 vols (Oxford 1948) 2 pp 163–7; Powicke, *The Thirteenth Century* (Oxford 1954) pp 102–5; *A House of Kings,* ed E. Carpenter (London 1964) pp 170–85. See also B. Harvey, *Westminster Abbey and its estates in the middle ages* (Oxford 1877).

[21] See Duncan pp 552–60; [Gordon] Donaldson, [*Scottish*] *Kings* (London 1967) pp 11–12.

Whatever the truth here it was fitting that the two cults should be associated in the mid-thirteenth century, linked as they had been from their inception in the early twelfth, with Margaret then, in fact, achieving a more rapid recognition than Edward. It took almost a century for the reputation and cult of the Confessor to become established. 'In the later eleventh century', Barlow has remarked, 'the abbey was for the most part uninterested in Edward, even, perhaps, hostile to his cult',[22] and as late as *c*1122 'we are in the presence of uncertainty over which of the abbey's patrons deserved special honour'.[23] In spite of the energetic advocacy of Osbert of Clare in 1138 canonisation only finally came in the changed political circumstances of 1161.[24] The translation of the Confessor to his new shrine took place on 13 October 1163, and Ailred, who ten years earlier (1153/4) had found nothing to say of the Confessor's sanctity in his *Genealogia regum Anglorum*,[25] set the seal on the process in his rewriting of Osbert of Clare's account in a new *Life* of the Confessor, achieving 'the proper banality of characterisation',[26] though still, it would seem, retaining some reservations about the new saint.[27]

The decisive moment in this whole process, however, which owed nothing to Osbert of Clare, had come sixty years earlier with the opening of the Confessor's tomb in the presence of a motley and undistinguished gathering, and the discovery of his incorrupt body.[28] There can only be speculation about the reasons for this inspection of the Confessor's remains in 1102,[29] but it is tempting to associate it with Henry I's marriage two years earlier, shortly after his accession, to Edith/Matilda, the daughter of Margaret, and difficult to supply a

[22] [*The Life of King Edward the Confessor,* ed F.] Barlow (London 1962) p 113.

[23] *Ibid* p 122, referring to the mortuary roll of Vitalis of Savigny.

[24] Alexander III's bull of canonisation was issued on 7 February 1161, without recourse to a general council, see Barlow pp 130–3; for an admirable overall account of the development of the cult *ibid* pp 112–33.

[25] *Ibid* p 130. Barlow remarks of the chapter headed 'De sancto Edwardo rege confessore et virgine' that 'this must be a later addition, for the text ignores the king's sanctity, virginity and miracles'.

[26] *Ibid* p xxxv.

[27] In the preface addressed to abbot Laurence of Westminster, *Vita S. Edwardi regis, PL* 115 (1854) cols 737–90 (at cols 739–40); also printed in Twysden pp 369–410; see also Barlow pp xxxv–vii, 130.

[28] *Ibid* pp 1, 113–15: 'the company which assembled in 1102 . . . had come together for mixed reasons and without much confidence. It could not have been a very splendid or public ceremony'. Compare the sceptical reaction of those not present at the initial inspection of St Cuthbert's remains two years later.

[29] See Barlow's comments pp 114–15, 119–23.

plausible alternative. It has been customary, in this context, to stress the Ailredian line on the union of the Saxon and Norman houses in the persons of a king, alone amongst the sons of the Conqueror in being born after his father's assumption of royalty, and a queen who personified not merely the antiquity of English kingship but its piety. Recently, more narrowly material motives have been suggested for Henry I's enthusiasm for the union, and his early hostility to the English has been emphasised,[30] but if these reservations qualify and limit the broader view they also serve to lay greater stress on the individual initiative and sponsorship which by the latter part of the reign had achieved a more general awareness of the significance of the union.[31] Here the figure of Edith is important, whatever spectacular postures Osbert of Clare might later strike. Her early upbringing—until about the age of thirteen—had been at the nunnery of Wilton, 'the most famous refuge of English noblewomen after the Conquest' and 'one of the greatest repositories of English tradition in the country'.[32] She had probably accompanied her aunt Christina there in 1086, and it was Christina who directed and disciplined her. 'Good queen Maud' Edith might become, but it is clear that these years at Wilton were disturbed and unhappy, and there is little sign of the future queen's later piety. 'I . . . went in fear of the rod of my aunt Christina . . . and . . . she would often make me smart with a good slapping and the most horrible scolding, as well as treating me as being in disgrace'.[33] It was Christina who, to protect her niece, put a veil on her head. Edith's reaction matched her father's fury—'I did indeed wear [it] in her presence, but as soon as I was able to escape out of her sight, I tore it off and threw it on the ground and trampled on it and in that way . . .

[30] [R. W.] Southern, [*St Anselm and his Biographer*] (Cambridge 1963) pp 188–90: 'It was not, as is sometimes thought, a grand plan of national appeasement that led Henry to seek a marriage with Matilda. In his early policy he was markedly hostile to the English and an alliance with a princess of the old stock would not in itself have appealed to him. The English could not harm him, but the Norman baronage presented difficulties of alarming proportions. In these circumstances a marriage with the sister of the king of Scotland probably offered the best means of protecting his rear'. Compare Barlow p 121. It need hardly be said that the advancement of Edith/Matilda should not be considered apart from the subsequent favour shown to her sister Mary and brothers Alexander and David.

[31] See, for example, [William of Malmesbury], *G*[*esta*] *R*[*egum*], bk 5, cap 418; *ASC sa* 1100; [Eadmer], *H*[*istoria*] *N*[*ovorum in Anglia*], trans G. Bosanquet (London 1964) bk 3, p 126.

[32] Southern pp 182–3; on Wilton see also Barlow pp 91–101.

[33] *HN* p 127.

I used to vent my rage and the hatred of it which boiled up in me'.[34] The incident, in conjunction with others, led to Edith's departure from Wilton in the company of her father, but within months both Malcolm and Margaret were dead, and Edith was an exile in England.

In any real sense Edith lacked parents, and though this may have been something of a commonplace, there are indications that this affected her deeply. It is most clearly evident in her overpowering attachment to Anselm, rather unsympathetically viewed by Southern,[35] but there are signs, too, in the life and patronage described, and criticised, by William of Malmesbury,[36] which did not, perhaps, simply reflect her temperament. To this high-spirited girl Wilton and her aunt had been not altogether satisfactory surrogate parents, and it is scarcely surprising that she should seek fuller information about the mother she had scarcely known, and the line and traditions she would have heard so much about in the hot-house atmosphere of Wilton, and which recalled in the names of its kings her own family. Edith's four elder brothers recapitulate with their names the last century of West Saxon kingship, and she herself displayed a strong attachment to the Confessor, choosing—unless we accept the protests of the Aldgate Augustinians—to be buried close beside him, on 1 May 1118.[37] While there is no indication that she was present at the opening of the Confessor's tomb, nor any clear evidence that she instigated it, it would be surprising if she had not been concerned and involved, and the *Life of St Margaret*, in its longer form, makes her role explicit—'you desire not only to hear of the queen your mother . . . but also to have it constantly before you in writing: so that although you knew but little your mother's face, you may have more fully the knowledge of her virtues'.[38] As Ritchie rightly remarked of the opening section of

[34] *Ibid*, see Southern pp 182–93.

[35] Southern pp 191–3.

[36] *GR* bk 5, cap 418.

[37] *Ibid*; see Barlow pp 121–2. For the Aldgate account of the seizing of her body by the monks of Westminster, so that it should not be buried at the Augustinian priory, see *The Cartulary of Holy Trinity Aldgate*, ed G. Hodgett, *London Record Society* 16 (1928) p 997.

[38] Haec iussa et haec vota ego libens amplector; amplectens, multum veneror; venerans, vobis congratulor, quae a Rege Angelorum constituta Regina Anglorum, vitam matris Reginae, quae semper ad regnum anhelabat Angelorum, non solum audire, sed etiam litteris impressam desideratis iugiter inspicere; ut quae faciem matris parum noveratis, virtutum eius notitiam plenius habeatis, Pinkerton 2 p 159. An English translation of the *Life* is included in *E*[*arly*] *S*[*ources of*] *S*[*cottish*] *H*[*istory*], trans A. O. Anderson, 2 vols (Edinburgh 1922) 2 pp 59–60.

this *Life*, there is a 'heavy insistence'[39] on the Confessor, and on Margaret's relationship to him, but the awkward genealogical preamble to the text[40] demonstrates merely a 'spiritual genealogy': 'the ancestry described is Edward's not Margaret's'.[41] It is all intended to 'attach a cult of Margaret to the already formed cult of Edward',[42] and though this cannot, I think, be understood quite in the way that Ritchie intended,[43] there it no doubt that it does reflect the purpose of the *Life* in its longer form. Written, it would seem, not long after the opening of the tombs of the Confessor and St Cuthbert, and barely a dozen years after Margaret's death, by an intimate acquaintance, from his own and other first-hand evidence, at the behest of her daughter the new queen of England, it is anchored, however uncomfortably, on the reputation of the Confessor, 'brother (by his father only) of king Edmund, whose son's daughter Margaret, with the glory of her merits greatly adorns the glorious line of her ancestors'.[44] The king, remarked the *Anglo-Saxon Chronicle*, married Edith 'the daughter of Malcolm, king of Scotland, and of Margaret the good queen, the kinswoman of king Edward, and of the true royal race of England'.[45] There are few saints whose lives have been so quickly and circumstantially recorded, and accorded such a central contemporary significance, as in this 'simple but exquisite life',[46] 'which must take a high place amongst the biographies of the time'.[47]

'The new Queen', declared Donaldson in 1954, 'represented the culture of England and the continent . . . and she encouraged the tendency of the Scots to strengthen their links with the south . . . Margaret was a woman of outstanding ability who knew how to use her position for political as well as religious ends'.[48] For Burleigh, a few years later, 'it was his marriage with Margaret that gave to Malcolm's reign its importance for Scottish history',[49] while Barrow,

39 [R. L. G.] Ritchie, [*The Normans in Scotland*] (Edinburgh 1954) p 396.

40 *Vita* [*S. Margaritae Reginae Scotiae*], cap 2; Pinkerton 2 pp 160–5. Chapters are given in conformity with Hinde 1 p 235: Pinkerton's tabulation differs.

41 Ritchie p 397. 42 *Ibid* p 396.

43 See Barlow pp 112–33.

44 *ESSH* 2 p 64; ex solo . . . patre frater Edmundi Regis; cuius filio Margarita exor ta, claritate meritorum claram peronat seriem progenitorum, Pinkerton 2 p 162.

45 *sa* 1100.

46 Knowles *MO* p 170; see the comments of [Bruce] Webster, [*Scotland from the eleventh century to 1603*] (London 1975) pp 40–2.

47 Knowles *MO* p 499.

48 Donaldson, [*The*] *Scottish Church* [*from Queen Margaret to the Reformation*] (London 1954) p 5.

49 [J. H. S.] Burleigh, [*A Church History of Scotland*] (London 1960) p 41.

writing in the same year, is emphatic about Margaret's role: 'no history of Scotland in the eleventh and twelfth centuries would be adequate if it failed to recognise that in associating Lanfranc with her reforming activity in Scotland, in introducing under Cantuarian auspices, a wholly new kind of religious life north of the Forth, above all in inspiring in her sons, her husband's successors, a zeal and devotion towards the forms of religious life and ecclesiastical observance familiar in Norman England and on the continent, Queen Margaret was knowingly and deliberately instigating changes which for both Church and Nation were of fundamental, far-reaching significance'.[50] To the court, church and people of Scotland Margaret brought, it seems, her cosmopolitan cultural and spiritual standards and experience, acquired in 'the intense piety of the court of St Stephen' and at 'the equally pious court of Edward the Confessor',[51] and applied them in the broader context of the kingdom, with Malcolm's backing, and in the domestic setting of her own household. A recent judgement characterises her as 'a somewhat severe lady, who checked mirth at court and dominated her husband, none of whose children was given a Scottish name'[52] . . . 'one of these strong, interfering, pious and persistent women of whom England has successfully bred a considerable number'.[53] Despite the disapproving tone there has never been any doubt as to her influence: 'no history', declared William of Malmesbury referring to Edgar, Alexander and David, 'has ever recorded three kings, and at the same time brothers, who were of equal sanctity, or savoured so much of their mother's piety'.[54]

It may seem churlish to cavil at such a consensus, consistently maintained since Turgot's articulation of the events of queen Margaret's career in his *Life*, 'a paean on Queen Margaret's character and virtues',[55] but it is noticeable how unanimity disintegrates, unease and equivocation creep in, once the accounts pass from the general to the particular.[56] Burleigh, having remarked that 'even the critical eye of so

[50] [G. W. S.] Barrow, [*The Kingdom of the Scots*] (London 1973) p 196. Chapter 6 (pp 188–211), 'Benedictines, Tironensians and Cistercians', is a revised version of 'From Queen Margaret to David I: Benedictines and Tironensians', *Innes Review* 11 (1960).

[51] Burleigh p 43.

[52] *Who's Who in Scottish History*, ed Gordon Donaldson and Robert S. Morpeth (Oxford 1973) p 5.

[53] *Ibid*, quoting Eric Linklater, *The Lion and the Unicorn* (London 1935) p 36.

[54] *GR* bk 5 cap 400. [55] Webster p 40.

[56] For example, Webster pp 40–1: 'it gives a fairly detailed statement of the reforms which she wished to introduce into the Scottish church, which had obviously fallen

good a Catholic as Queen Margaret could only detect minor failings'[57] in the unreformed Scottish church, declared 'it is clear that Margaret undertook no drastic reform of the Scottish Church',[58] and asserted that the careful upbringing of her children 'may be regarded as the most important part of Margaret's work'.[59] MacEwen, denying Margaret and Malcolm any part in the creation of a diocesan system, or the reform of native Scottish monasticism, described Margaret as 'a reformer of religion rather than a reformer of the Church, [who] influenced the tone of Christianity rather than its ordinances'.[60] Donaldson, in a series of works, progressed from cautious reservation to blunt finality—'Margaret's programme had at the best been a limited one . . . and she did nothing, apart from bringing a few Benedictine monks to Dunfermline, to foster and endow new institutions . . . The achievement of Margaret which was most influential on the Scottish church and the Scottish nation was the achievement uncommon in saints, of producing six sons and two daughters'.[61] It was to this judgement that Barrow responded in his 1973 revision of a distinguished essay which had first appeared over a decade earlier.[62] If, however, his undermining of Donaldson's judgement on Margaret, by its absurdity when transferred to the apparently parallel case of Ethelbert of Kent,[63] is a nicely taken and entertaining debating point it cannot be regarded as anything more. Barrow's study establishes the discussion of Margaret, and her sons, at a new critical level, but he cannot altogether avoid traditional generalisations, nor, in championing Margaret, the tendency to associate the achievements of the sons with the apparent intentions of the mother.[64] Most recently Cowan and

---

out of line with the rest of Christendom in a number of ways. It is interesting that Turgot is very concerned with points of observance and ritual . . . and only in passing with what we often take to be the great contemporary issues'.

[57] Burleigh p 37.

[58] *Ibid* p 44.

[59] *Ibid* p 43.

[60] [A. R.] MacEwen, [*A History of the Church in Scotland*] (London 1913) p 160.

[61] Donaldson, [*Scotland*:] *Church and Nation* [*through sixteen centuries*] (London 1960) pp 18–19. Compare Donaldson, *Scottish Church*, pp 5–6; *A Source Book of Scottish History*, ed W. Croft Dickinson, Gordon Donaldson and Isabel A. Milne, 1 (2 ed 1958) pp 57–8; Donaldson, *Kings* p 14.

[62] See above n 50.

[63] 'It would not be entirely untrue to say of Ethelbert, the heathen king of Kent, that his programme had at the best been a limited one, and that he did nothing, apart from bringing a few Benedictine monks to Canterbury, to foster and endow new institutions', Barrow pp 195–6.

[64] For example, pp 165, 193, 196, 211. Compare Donaldson, *Kings* p 14 'for it was the

Easson, though accepting Barrow's assessment of the significance of the arrival of the Benedictines *presumably* at Dunfermline,[65] are quite clear that 'her "innovations", significant as they may have been for the future, were modest contributions towards the alignment of Scottish ecclesiastical institutions with those of Western Christendom'.[66]

It is clear that it is no easy matter to assess the achievement of Margaret of Scotland, even with the assistance of a virtually contemporary *Life*—and in part, of course, because of it. In the face of Turgot's 'indifference to topographical detail and proper nouns of every sort'[67] Barrow's description of the author as 'exasperating' seems remarkably temperate. In its account of Margaret's spiritual and charitable exercises, of her influential piety, and of one minor miracle, the *Life* is in the mainstream of hagiography, but it is not sufficient simply to explain and dismiss it in such a fashion. The author is an eye-witness, the confidant of the queen, yet nowhere in the *Life*, not even in the recapitulation of the set-piece arguments of one of Margaret's 'councils', is there any hint of 'the great issues and personalities that were shaping the history of the universal church at this time', and which were 'surely a deeper cause for anxiety in Margaret' than practices none of which 'appears to have touched the fundamentals of eleventh century catholic doctrine'.[68] If the approach to Lanfranc and the possible introduction of Benedictines to Dunfermline are amongst the most significant acts of her reign,[69] then it is extraordinary that neither are mentioned in the *Life*,[70] and it is difficult to equate Turgot's account of her reform of the manners and dress of court and people[71] with the record of Malcolm's munificent and splendid reception and despatch of Edgar Atheling, twice, in 1075.[72] It may be, as Webster claims, that 'Ailred and Turgot specifically regarded native Scottish ways as barbaric or backward, and even the

---

English Margaret who impressed so many of her views and aims on her sons and descendants'.

[65] *MRHS* p 5.

[66] *Ibid* p 4.

[67] Barrow p 190.

[68] *Ibid* p 192.

[69] *Ibid* p 193, *MRHS* p 5.

[70] The *Life* simply records—postquam ergo culmen ascenderat honoris; mox in loco ubi eius nuptiae fuerant celebratae, aeternum sui nominis et religiositatis erexit monumentum . . . nobilem ibi ecclesiam in Sanctae Trinitatis aedificavit honorem (Pinkerton 2 p 163, *ESSH* 2 pp 64–5): Dunfermline is not mentioned by name.

[71] *Vita* cap 7, Pinkerton 2 p 166, *ESSH* 2 p 68.

[72] *ASC* D. *ASC* E places it under 1074; FW and *HR* give 1073: see Ritchie pp 46–7.

authors of Melrose and Holyrood would probably have shared their views',[73] but Turgot, at any rate, was writing during the reign of Margaret's eldest surviving son, and for an audience which knew Malcolm's court—nor was he in any sense an Ailred.[74] Attractive as the *Life* is as hagiography, in its portrait of the painstakingly pious queen within her household, it is less satisfactory in its portayal of an active Scottish queen—the only one to achieve a personal presentation before the later fifteenth century.[75] There is no clean interface between *Life* and reality, and it is from this mismatch, and the attempts to reconcile it, that the problems arise.

It may be as well then to take a further look at Turgot's *Life* itself. The *Life* was edited by Papebroch *ex Membraneo nostro MS Valcellensi*[76] and printed in the second volume for June of the *Acta Sanctorum*.[77] It was this text which was reprinted by Pinkerton in his *Lives of the Scottish Saints*.[78] Neither Papebroch nor Pinkerton give any description of the manuscript, which is now said to be lost. In 1868 the *Life* was printed for the Surtees Society, in the edition of Hodgson Hinde,[79] as an appendix to the first volume of the works of Symeon of Durham, on this occasion from a fire-damaged Cottonian manuscript ascribed by Hinde to the latter part of the twelfth century.[80] In his brief account of the *Life* Hinde mentions in passing an abridgement of it included in another damaged Cottonian manuscript, dated to the early fourteenth century.[81] This abridgement, printed by Capgrave, and reprinted by Surius, was included by Pinkerton in his collection.[82] 'Both works', remarked Hinde, 'have been carefully collated with the MSS by Mr Raine for the present edition: [and] all variations between the original and the abridgement are pointed out'.[83] Such a claim, difficult to sustain in the face of the manuscript evidence, has probably

[73] Webster p 42.

[74] For some account of the relations between the English and Scottish courts see Ritchie pp 29–60, Southern pp 182–5.

[75] For the inclusion of Margaret of Denmark (died 1486), the wife of James III, in the catalogue of Scottish saints see A. P. Forbes, *A Calendar of Scottish Saints* (Edinburgh 1872) p 391.

[76] *ASB* June 2 p 324A; compare p 316F—ex membraneo Codice Valcellensis in Hannonia monasterii, nunc nostro.

[77] Paris/Rome 1867.

[78] Pinkerton 2 pp 135–82.

[79] Hinde 1 pp 234–54; see *ibid* pp lvii–lx.

[80] BL Cotton Tiberius D 3, Hinde 1 p lvii.

[81] BL Cotton Tiberius E 1, Hinde 1 p lviii.

[82] Pinkerton 2 pp 199–209.

[83] Hinde 1 p lviii.

been instrumental in directing subsequent attention away from the abridgement.

It is the Bollandist edition which supplies the name of the author, Theodericus, where the Cottonian manuscript simply has the initial T. It is, however, impossible to validate the Bollandist ascription in the absence of the manuscript, and other opinion concurs in preferring Turgot, in spite of protracted dispute, and continuing uncertainty, since the seventeenth century.[84] Though doubts still remain, it is probably as well to accept this ascription as the most likely hypothesis. The dating of the *Life* in its longer version depends not upon its author, but upon its dedication to Margaret's daughter, *queen* Matilda,[85] and its reference to Margaret's son Edgar as still reigning.[86] This outlines the period 11 November 1100 to 8 January 1107, but a passing reference to the incorrupt body of St Cuthbert indicates a date of composition subsequent to the opening of the saint's tomb in 1104.[87] At this point, however, it is necessary to be quite clear as to what has been established, and what has not. On the basis of an apparently later twelfth-century manuscript a *Life of Saint Margaret* can be dated to the early years of the twelfth century, may be ascribed, on circumstantial evidence, to Turgot, and is explicitly connected with a commission from Margaret's daughter Matilda. The text is also, it may be added, disturbingly anachronistic: as Ritchie remarked, 'in Turgot's mind [Margaret] was already a saint',[88] and though he accepts the *Life* as it stands his brief account of it displays a full awareness of its difficulties and inconsistencies.[89]

It is here that the so-called abridged version of the *Life* seems to me to be important, particularly if it is viewed not as an abridgement, but as a text in its own right, closely related to the longer version, but not completely identical with it, even where the two accounts coincide. These lesser differences apart, large parts of the longer version do not

[84] For a resumé of the discussion of the authorship of Turgot see Hinde 1 pp lviii–lx, Ritchie pp 395–9. Though Selden's ascription of the *Historia Regum* to Turgot is now generally discredited there remain considerable problems in connection with the text and its ascription to Symeon of Durham. The new edition of the works of Symeon being prepared by Mr Bernard Meehan should clarify these and other matters.

[85] *Vita*, prologue: Excellenter honorabili et honorabiliter excellenti, Reginae Anglorum Mathilda . . .

[86] Interea filius eius, qui post patrem Regni gubernacula iam nunc in praesenti tenet . . ., *Vita* cap 13; Pinkerton 2 p 180, *ESSH* 2 p 84.

[87] *Vita* cap 13; Pinkerton 2 p 179; *ESSH* 2 p 82.

[88] Ritchie p 396.

[89] *Ibid* pp 395–9.

appear in the shorter. There is no prologue and dedication; virtually nothing of the elaborate genealogy for Margaret, and no reference whatsoever to the Confessor; much edifying detail of her life at court, of her influence over the king and his companions, of her pious works is absent; the reference to the encouragement of foreign merchants and the enhanced presentation of the monarch vanishes; her 'frequent councils' for the reform of religious life became *multa consilia,*[90] and her lone battle *contra perversae consuetudinis assertores*[91] is less dramatically conveyed. There is no reference to her establishment of *habitacula* for pilgrims to St Andrews;[92] her relations with local hermits read rather differently; the miracle associated with her gospel book is reduced to three lines, and the account of her edifying death is much abbreviated.

Amongst all these omissions, however, attention may be directed specifically to those which affect our consideration of the *Life* as a whole. Towards the end of the *Life*, where the longer version refers to Edgar as king, the shorter simply has *filius eius . . . Edgarus*;[93] earlier in the same chapter all references to the priest *ad sepulchrum incorrupti corporis sanctissimi Patris Cuthberti suscipiens habitum monachi*[94] are missing, and in the absence of a prologue and dedication there is no reference to queen Matilda. On this evidence it could be argued that the *Life* in its shorter version represents a text composed much earlier than usually assumed, after Margaret's death on 16 November 1093 and before the summer of 1095 when Edgar was, probably, invested as king. Such a hypothesis, associated with a text which removes many of the difficulties of the longer version, is worth consideration. In circumstances which Duncan has described as 'calamitous for . . . alien influences',[95] with the 'Margaretsons', to use Ritchie's not entirely felicitous description,[96] in exile, with Turgot already at Durham,[97] this is likely to have been a time when thought would have been given to the preservation of Margaret's memory and reputation—and if the *Life* is to be associated with Edith/Matilda at all this period, immediately following her mother's death, is surely more likely than after her

[90] *Vita* cap 8; Pinkerton 2 p 168; *ESSH* 2 p 70. Compare Pinkerton 2 pp 201–2.
[91] *Vita* cap 8; Pinkerton 2 p 168; *ESSH* 2 p 70.
[92] *Vita* cap 9; Pinkerton 2 pp 173–4; *ESSH* 2 p 77.
[93] Pinkerton 2 p 207.
[94] *Vita* cap 13; Pinkerton 2 p 179; *ESSH* 2 p 82.
[95] Duncan p 124. For Edgar's 'investiture' see p 125.
[96] Ritchie p 236.
[97] See Ritchie pp 52–3, 58.

coronation as queen of England almost exactly seven years later for the commissioning of a memorial of the mother she had scarcely known.

In the absence of a thorough re-examination of the *Life* in its various versions, of the manuscripts themselves, such a hypothesis can be no more than speculation. What can, I think, be asserted, however, is that the shorter version of the *Life* cannot be dismissed simply as an abridgement of the longer, which itself shows all the signs of having passed through a succession of editorial hands, amongst them perhaps, those of Ailred. Certainly it displays the influence of the developing cult of the Confessor in the twelfth century. Its final form, as demonstrated in the Cottonian and Bollandist texts, should perhaps be linked with the canonisation process in the thirteenth century, for the Cottonian manuscript, dated by Hinde to the later twelfth century, has more recently been ascribed by Levison to the thirteenth.[98] Here again a new examination of the manuscripts may assist, and until that has been done it is necessary to reserve judgement on the *Life*, its authorship, date of composition and versions, and its relationship to other contemporary writings, particularly those of Ailred. Even within these restrictions, however, it seems reasonable to suggest that the core of the *Life* is an eye-witness account of Margaret by someone who knew her well, and it may be that that account was composed significantly earlier than present discussion of the *Life* allows. It must also be stressed that however the accepted text of the *Life* may be criticised and pruned the essential message and testimony of the earlier version is not compromised by the later revisions it appears to have undergone.

Suspension of judgement on the *Life*, doubts about the evidence as normally considered, need not inhibit further discussion of queen Margaret, and it may be useful to review other aspects of her life briefly here. In particular her Hungarian background demands consideration. The most recent historian of Malcolm Canmore's reign makes no reference to Margaret's birth and childhood in Hungary,[99] but others have laid stress upon the influences exerted by the newly Christianised court of St Stephen—'the new Queen represented the culture of England and the continent—she had spent part of her early life in Hungary',[100] 'not only was she familiar with English usage and

[98] W. Levison, 'Conspectus Codicum Hagiographicum', *MGH SRM* 7 (1918) pp 527–706, at p 600, no 283.

[99] Duncan pp 119 *seq.*

[100] Donaldson, *Scottish Church* p 5.

organisation, but she had a zeal which may have owed something to her experience of Hungary, a country which had been converted to Christianity only a generation earlier',[101] and, for Burleigh, 'the intense piety of the court of St Stephen'[102] acted strongly upon Margaret. It is an emphasis wholly lacking in the *Life* itself, and as Ritchie pointed out 'none of the authorities even mention the name of Stephen',[103] canonised in 1083, and Turgot and Ailred, amongst others, are unlikely to have ignored Margaret's relationship to a king and saint, even if she was not, as has unconvincingly been argued, Stephen's granddaughter.[104]

Family relationships apart, however, it may be doubted whether the atmosphere at the Hungarian court was quite as evangelical as the association with St Stephen implies. Dvornik's classic survey asserts that 'the oldest feature of Hungarian Christianity was Byzantine',[105] the baptism of Butzu and Gylas *c*950 predating the Hungarian kingdom by half a century. Gylas, ruling eastern Hungary, was fervent in the new faith, and his formidable daughter, 'who held the kingdom [*sic*] in her hand'[106] married duke Geiza, the father of the future king Stephen. Geiza himself boasted that 'he was rich enough to afford sacrifices to all the gods, Christian as well as pagan',[107] recalling the East Anglian Redwald almost four centuries earlier, but conversion did proceed, and the elements of a church were established, under him. If his consort was given much of the credit for the conversion of the Hungarians, Geiza was not idle, and it is at this period that St Adalbert of Prague becomes *apostolus Hungarorum*.[108] It is against this background, and in the context of complicated political and ecclesiastical manoeuvrings that 'the final Christianisation of the Magyars should go to the credit of Stephen I'.[109] It was a process that turned Hungary from the Byzantine to the western world, from orthodoxy to catholicism, justifying Gregory VII's later claim that 'the kingdom of Hungary belongs to the Church of Rome'.[110] This

101 Donaldson, *Church and Nation* p 15.

102 Burleigh p 43; see also Ritchie p 10.

103 Ritchie p 390.

104 See Ritchie pp 389–92.

105 [F.] Dvornik, [*The Making of Central and Eastern Europe*] (London 1949) p 149.

106 *Ibid* p 155.

107 *Ibid*

108 On Adalbert see Dvornik pp 95–135, and, for an assessment of his work in Hungary, pp 151–6.

109 *Ibid* p 156: Stephen I (1000–38).

110 See Dvornik p 156; *Register* bk 2 no 13, *MGH Ep Sel* 1, ed E. Caspar (1920) p 144.

was the crux of the matter. There is an inevitable emphasising amongst western writers of the significance of St Stephen's role, but these party preoccupations should not lead us to ignore the earlier background of Christianity in Hungary, nor to over-dignify the religious life of early eleventh-century Hungary.[111] The turbulent mixture of secular and ecclesiastical politics survived St Stephen, and the 'fervent piety of the court of St Stephen' is perhaps better exemplified in the person of his mother. Fervent Christian though she was, Thietmar of Merseburg had it that 'the white lady' was a heavy drinker and experienced horsewoman, who killed a man who provoked and angered her with her own hands.[112]

The Hungary of St Stephen was not perhaps altogether unlike the contemporary kingdom of the Scots, but it can have had little to contribute to the making of the future St Margaret, particularly to a child born after the death of St Stephen, who left the country at the age, perhaps, of seven, perhaps of eleven, to travel to Anglo-Saxon England.[113] More important in her upbringing, it would seem, was the period of nine years at 'the equally pious court of Edward the Confessor',[114] and so it has been asserted. Yet here again too much should not be claimed. The legend of the Confessor is a later creation, its birth not easy, and 'it emasculates a passionate, active and resourceful man, ... mass followed by hunting seems to have been his usual day'.[115] His queen, Edith, was renowned for her piety, but her charity was on occasion suspect, she was ambitious, hard and tenacious and 'she could even be accused of political assassination'.[116] Overall, the most recent and judicious judgement of the Confessor is damning—'despite the suggestion of a high moral tone in the household, the ecclesiastical policy was rather worldly . . . the leadership was uninspiring . . . The court was probably to some extent the victim of circumstances. The

[111] See Dvornik pp 159–60, 165. Dvornik's comment on 'the slow but steady progress of Hungary's ecclesiastical status'—in contrast to the claims made in the Legend of St Stephen—is underlined by recent work in Hungary on the establishment of a parochial system, its emphasis on the role of the local families in early ecclesiastical government and administration, and the consequent qualification of the role assigned to Stephen. Compare *In memoriam Sancti Stephanic Hungariae Apostolici Protoregis (937–1038)*, ed E. Lukinich (Budapest 1938).

[112] Dvornik pp 155–6.

[113] Margaret's date of birth is variously given—see Ritchie p 8 n 2, 'it is generally accepted that she was born in 1046'; *ODCC* gives *c*1045; the fifth revised edition of *The Book of Saints* (London 1966) *c*1050.

[114] Burleigh p 43; Compare Ritchie pp 8–11.

[115] Barlow, [*The*] *English Church* [*1000–1066: a Constitutional History*] (London 1963) pp 51, 52. [116] *Ibid* p 52.

monastic revival was almost spent, foreign monks were politically unacceptable, and use had to be made of inferior material . . . It is doubtful indeed whether Edward had a policy . . . what can appear systematic . . . was only the chance effect created by the interplay of the various interests within an ancient and strong tradition. The English church was ruled by the king but to little purpose and to no true ecclesiastical end'.[117] That the church which Margaret encountered in England was radically different in tradition, diffusion and sophistication from that which she had left in Hungary cannot be denied, and there can be no doubt that her piety was shaped by Anglo-Saxon forms and conventions. But whatever the differences the type was the same—courtly, king-centred, compromised by the interests and factions of the magnates in church and state from the king downwards, conventional in its attitudes and devotions. We should look for no more in the future queen of the Scots, whatever the undoubted strength of her personal piety, and in this perspective there is no need to remark upon her failure to implement or to argue 'Hildebrandine' policies in her Scottish environment, policies of which she must have been unaware when she left England in 1067, and to which in all probability, like Lanfranc, she would have been unsympathetic.

The Scotland she entered in the company of her brother the atheling, her mother and her sister in 1067 would certainly have seemed foreign to members of the west Saxon royal house, but perhaps not much more foreign than York or Durham. When William of Malmesbury talks of the future king David of Scotland as 'a youth more courtly than the rest, polished from his boyhood by his intercourse and friendship with us', and in consequence 'rubbing off the tarnish of Scottish barbarity',[118] it is as well to recognise that the comparison is between Scotland and Anglo-Norman, not Anglo-Saxon, England. As the kings of the Scots recognised in their titles and their claims, there was no clear line to be drawn between the Scottish and Anglo-Saxon kingdoms, not in territorial or personal

[117] *Ibid* pp 52, 55. This is not of course to place in question the Confessor's concern for the young Hungarians, and the much later comment of Orderic Vitalis that he brought them up 'benignly as though they were his own offspring' is entirely acceptable. There is, however, no direct evidence for Ritchie's assumed French education for Margaret (p 10)—though her attempt to recruit Theobald of Étampes to the Scottish court is interesting in this connection (see below n 131)—nor, for all her alleged inclinations towards a regular life, is there any evidence for her association, or her sister Christina's association, with any English community before the Conquest.

[118] *GR* bk 5 cap 400.

affiliations, not in social or political conditions, not in cultural accomplishments, and not in ecclesiastical organisation. There was no regular Benedictine house north of Ely, and the cult of St Cuthbert was an isolated outpost of pre-Viking traditions in a province still only beginning the painful process of reconstruction under the last Anglo-Saxon archbishops.[119] It is misleading in these circumstances to over-emphasise the peculiarities of Scottish society. That there were peculiarities is plain, but the sanctuary sought in Scotland by the Anglo-Saxon refugees is itself testimony to the accessibility of the northern kingdom, and its culdee communities can perhaps be taken to witness to a more flourishing religious life than was to be found south of the Forth and beyond the Tweed.[120]

However much the biographer of queen Margaret might seek to highlight the barbarous and primitive ways of the court and people whose queen she became, it was an alliance at which no contemporary commentator looked askance—an important political alliance between royal houses long and directly acquainted, and to whose political implications the Conqueror reacted with decision.[121] That Margaret entered fully into this Scottish life is apparent, even if the indications are slight. With her husband she appears as the patron of culdees,[122] and however the passage is evaluated her *Life* testifies to her attachment to native Scottish hermits.[123] On the negative side, as has been remarked, there seems to have been no attempt to restructure the existing bishopric of St Andrews.[124] She was a partner in a successful marriage and a strong reign, but not quite the dominant, superior partner that the *Life* implies. She was a strong queen, a queen to be remembered, and it would have been surprising had she not attempted to graft on to the Scottish court and household over which she presided some of the greater sophistication of the Anglo-Saxon court at which she had been brought up. Equally, it would have been surprising if she had not expressed views on, or sought to change, some of the religious customs to which she was unaccustomed. Here, interesting confirmation of the sort of local customs she is alleged to have opposed in her 'councils' is provided by two letters of Paschal II

[119] Knowles *MO* pp 165–71; Barlow, *English Church* pp 226–31 and *passim*; [Donald] Nicholl, [*Thurstan, Archbishop of York (1114–1140)*] (York 1964) pp 1–40.

[120] See *MRHS* pp 1–4, 46–54.

[121] See Ritchie pp 21–38; Duncan pp 117–20,

[122] See Barrow pp 190–1; *MRHS* pp 4–5.

[123] *Vita* cap 9; Pinkerton 2 pp 173, 205; *ESSH* 2 pp 76–7.

[124] See Barrow pp 192–3.

written to Turgot in his position as bishop of St Andrews in 1113, but the letters also demonstrate the continued acceptance of such customs in Scotland twenty years after Margaret's death.[125]

So it is with the other hard evidence. If it is certain that Margaret approached Lanfranc and persuaded him to send Goldwine and two other 'brethren' to Scotland it is necessary to note that the most recent commentators can only date the transaction before '1089' and presume a settlement at Dunfermline.[126] Nor it must be remembered, do three monks constitute a community, and Lanfranc's concluding remarks in his letter to Margaret—'if you can or should wish to fulfil your work through others, we greatly desire that our brothers should return to us, because their services are needed by our church. But let it be according to your will'—deserve more consideration than they appear to have received.[127] What happened to this Canterbury group in the reaction after the death of Malcolm and Margaret it is impossible to say, but it is unlikely that they escaped, and it appears that Edgar later sought monks from Anselm.[128] Barrow's establishment of confraternity links between Dunfermline and Canterbury in the time of Eadmer, though a fascinating glimpse of early twelfth century Scottish society, adds nothing for the earlier period.[129] It may be that Margaret did place Goldwine and his companions at Dunfermline, but it is by no means certain, and the confraternity links of the ladies Estrild and Ligiva with Canterbury appear to accord better with the period of Anselm and Eadmer than with the pontificate of Lanfranc, with the reign of Edgar than with that of his father. As far as the abbey of Dunfermline is concerned, here, as in so much else, David is the effective founder, drawing an abbot and community from Canterbury 'a few years after his accession'.[130]

The quintessence of Margaret's aspirations and achievements at the Scottish court can be distilled from her other recorded contact with Lanfranc in the course of her unsuccessful attempt to obtain the services of the Norman master Theobald of Étampes at her court.[131] It is,

[125] See Denis Bethell, 'Two Letters of Pope Paschal II to Scotland', *SCHR* 49 (1970) pp 33–45; Barrow pp 191–2; Duncan pp 129–30.

[126] *MRHS* pp 5, 58; compare Barrow pp 195–6.

[127] Quoted Barrow p 194.

[128] *MRHS* pp 5, 58; Barrow p 194.

[129] Barrow pp 196–8.

[130] *MRHS* pp 5, 58; Barrow p 195. Though perhaps some connection may be sought between Estrild and Ligiva and the 'feminae . . . natu nobiles, et sobriis moribus probabiles' of the *Life*: *Vita* cap 4; Pinkerton 2 p 164; *ESSH* 2 p 65.

[131] R. Foreville and J. Leclercq, 'Un débat sur le sacerdoce des moines au XIIe siècle',

within the limitations of the evidence, an isolated and personal approach, and its significance may be found less in what might have been achieved had he arrived in Scotland than in its demonstration of Margaret's determination and resource. On the death of Malcolm and Margaret in 1093 there was, it appears, a reaction against alien influences, and without imputing too chauvinistic a motive to events which had their basis in local political and dynastic conditions,[132] it may be accepted that the recruitment of men like Theobald of Étampes, the settlement of a relatively substantial English entourage—of which Estrild and Liviga may be representative—the modification of court ceremonial and local religious custom, and the introduction of alien institutions did induce resentment and opposition in a society whose sole focus was the royal court. MacEwen's description of Margaret as 'a thorough Teuton'[133] is brutally unkind, but there is no escaping the queen's strength, perhaps a rather over-bearing and intolerant strength, wherever one looks in the sources. Of this the most obvious, and most remarked, indication is to be found in the names of her sons, none of them Scottish, and the first four repeating the genealogy of West Saxon kingship.[134]

Faced with the difficulty of defining Margaret's actual role in the Scotland over which she reigned writers, from Turgot and Ailred onwards, have laid stress upon her influence over her children—hence Knowles' 'nursery of saints'. Even here, however, it is necessary to qualify the assessment. Edward, the eldest (born *c*1071), died within three days of his father in 1093,[135] Edmund, the second son (born *c*1072), was, according to Malmesbury, 'the only degenerate son of Margaret'.[136] He seems to have backed his uncle Donald III in the overthrow of Malcolm Canmore's son, Duncan, by his first marriage, but fell when Edgar, with Rufus's help, replaced Donald III.[137] Ethelred, Margaret's third son (born *c*1073) followed family tradition and succeeded to 'the family abbey at Dunkeld'.[138] Thus far there is

SA 41 (*Analecta Monastica* 4 series) (1957) pp 8–118, at pp 9–14; R. Foreville, 'L'École de Caen au XIe siècle, et les origines normandes de l'université d'Oxford', *Etudes Médiévales offertes à M. le Doyen Augustin Fliche* (Paris 1953) pp 90–100; A. L. Poole, *Domesday Book to Magna Carta* (Oxford 1951) p 237; Ritchie pp 71, 74.

[132] SeeDuncan pp 122–6.

[133] MacEwen p 155.

[134] See Ritchie pp 393–4.

[135] *Ibid* p 393.

[136] *GR* bk 5 cap 400.

[137] See Duncan pp 125–6; Ritchie pp 60–6, 87.

[138] *Who's Who in Scottish History* p 4; *MRHS* p 47.

little evidence of outstanding piety, let alone sanctity: nor is there any great change with Edgar (*c*1074–1107). If he sought monks from Anselm[139] he allowed the bishopric of the Scots at St Andrews to remain vacant from the death of bishop Fothadh in 1093 to the appointment of Turgot in 1107,[140] 'and there was no sign of episcopal activity anywhere in Scotland'[141] during his reign. It is only with Alexander, the fourth son (born *c*1077), who succeeded Edgar as king early in 1107, that a more active piety becomes apparent. Earlier, he had been the only laymen present at the opening of Cuthbert's tomb,[142] and one of his first acts was to appoint Turgot, prior of Durham, to the vacant see of St Andrews. Under him, it has been wrongly said, the bishoprics of Dunkeld and Moray were reconstituted *c*1110,[143] but his bringing of Augustinian canons to Scone in *c*1120 now seems to be accepted,[144] thereby establishing an important link with the Yorkshire house of Nostell, even if the foundation of Inchcolm has had to be placed substantially later.[145] Yet if he was 'a lettered and godly man' who 'clearly inherited some of his mother's solicitude for the church',[146] it is as well to remember that he could be as harsh as any of his predecessors, and it must be remarked that the range of his activity and patronage during his seventeen years as king was neither extensive, nor altogether satisfactory—if it is unfair to blame him for the difficulties created by the developing quarrel between St Andrews and York[147] it is clear that neither Turgot nor Eadmer were particularly happy choices for the see of St Andrews.

Of all Margaret's children it is the youngest, David (born *c*1084) who comes most readily to mind in any discussion of Scottish ecclesiastical developments during the lifetime of Margaret's children. There is no need here to rehearse the range of his patronage, so burdensome on the crown, from the days before his accession, when he ruled the lands south of the Forth under his brother, to his final years: it is admirably delineated elsewhere.[148] Suffice it to say that it concerned the whole spectrum of the religious life—reconstituting,

[139] *MRHS* pp 5 n 2, 58.

[140] See Ritchie p 170; Barrow pp 169, 191–2, 198. But see Donaldson, ['Scottish bishops] sees [before the reign of David I]', *Proceedings of the Society of Antiquaries of Scotland* 87 (1952–3).

[141] Burleigh p 51. For a more extended account of Edgar see Ritchie pp 87–121.

[142] See above p 119.

[143] A. H. Dunbar, *Scottish Kings 1005–1625* (Edinburgh 1899) p 51; Donaldson, 'sees'.

[144] *MRHS* pp 5, 97. [145] *Ibid* p 91. [146] *Who's Who in Scottish History* pp 7–8.

[147] See Nicholl pp 78–84, 93, 97–107.

[148] See Barrow pp 165–211 *passim*.

perhaps creating, a diocesan structure; establishing the new orders of monks and canons; extending earlier initiatives at Dunfermline, and strengthening relations with Durham; setting a sufficient personal example for Ailred to stress his sanctity, and creating an atmosphere in his household conducive to the formation of the vocations of Ailred and Waldef—however much it may be necessary to qualify Jocelyn of Furness's portrayal of the latter.[149]

It is small wonder that the flowering and fulfilment of Margaret's endeavours and ideals has been seen to be achieved in the pious works of David, and of his elder sister Edith—the 'good queen Maud' of Henry I's court. Yet Margaret's direct influence on these two can only have been very slight. There is no need to recapitulate Edith's career, but David can only have been nine when his mother died and he went into exile, and though it has been suggested that he played a part in the establishment of his brother Edgar on the Scottish throne[150] his upbringing and education took place in England—as Malmesbury indicated. Styled 'brother of the queen of the English', his marriage in 1114 to an English heiress made him one of the greatest of English feudatories,[151] and his role as coadjutor to his brother Alexander extended his influence.[152] As his early patronage of Tiron[153] indicates he is to be numbered amongst the great patrons of the Anglo-Norman state—indeed, when his overall career is viewed he was probably the greatest of them all, and if there is little sign of the sanctity that Ailred discerned amid this massive conventional piety the depth and consistency of his religious commitment cannot be doubted. It was this which distinguished him from most of his contemporaries, and it is relevant to ask whence it sprang.

The direct influence of his mother cannot have been very great, but in the person of his sister Edith, both before her marriage in 1100, and afterwards as queen, he encountered a formidable personality and a restless piety. It would not be unreasonable to suggest that Edith was the most formative influence upon David's development and upbringing at the Anglo-Norman court over which she presided. Further, it seems likely that in Edith David encountered a personality and devotion evocative of Margaret. Both, as contemporaries record, controlled and set the tone for their households, their entourages, and

[149] See Baker, 'Waldef'.

[150] See Duncan p 126; Ritchie pp 65–6; *ESSH* 2 pp 89–91; *GR* bk 5 cap 400.

[151] See Ritchie pp 139–151; Barrow p 173; Baker, 'Waldef' pp 73–5.

[152] See Ritchie pp 166–75; Duncan pp 134–5; Barrow pp 173–9.

[153] See Barrow pp 174–7, 199–210.

their husbands. With neither of them is it really possible to talk of policy in their dealings with the church and religious life, but their Christian devotion, their range of pious work and charitable benefactions, is undeniable. Both left the impress of their personalities upon contemporaries, and appear more vividly, more humanely, in their accounts than, for example, the Conqueror's Matilda or the Empress. Both were successful not as innovators, but in dealing with things as they found them, and resemble, in this respect, the mother of Stephen of Hungary, and the wife of the Confessor. Edith was very much her mother's daughter, and I think it unlikely that the mother did not possess that hauteur, passion and irascibility which the daughter displayed. For the apparent differences here Margaret's *Life*, even in its earliest form, is to blame. It set out to record the practical piety of a woman at once the latest representative of the eclipsed West Saxon line, and the matriarch of the emergent medieval Scottish monarchy, and for Edith there was no such contemporary witness. In this process Edith herself played a decisive part—to whatever point in it we should ascribe her participation—and it is clear that she was deeply influenced by the mother she hardly knew, not merely in simple hereditary terms, but by the reputation and legend that she encountered. Margaret was a remarkable woman in a turbulent age and society, no more a saint, I would suggest, than her daughter[154] or her youngest son, but no less, and like them in temper and attitude. If any final, definitive assessment must await the critical reappraisal of the sources, and in particular of Turgot's *Life*, and if her life was less dramatically and practically influential than is sometimes claimed, we may yet agree with Turgot—

> Let others admire in others the signs of miracles; I esteem much more in Margaret the works of mercy. Signs are common to the good and to the bad, but works of true piety and love are peculiar to the good . . . Let us more worthily hold her in awe, because through her devotion to justice, piety, mercy and love we contemplate in her, rather than miracles, the deeds of the ancient fathers.[155]

University of Edinburgh

[154] For a vivid account of Edith, and en passant references to Margaret, see Ritchie pp 109 *seq*. Edith's claims to sanctity are dismissed in *ASB*, April 3, p 730.

[155] *Vita* cap 11, Pinkerton 2 p 176; *ESSH* 2 p 80. A new edition and translation of the *Life* is in preparation.

WOMEN IN THE CRUSADER STATES: THE QUEENS OF JERUSALEM (1100–1190)

by BERNARD HAMILTON

THE important part played by women in the history of the crusader states has been obscured by their exclusion from the battle-field. Since scarcely a year passed in the Frankish east which was free from some major military campaign it is natural that the interest of historians should have centred on the men responsible for the defence of the kingdom. Yet in any society at war considerable power has to be delegated to women while their menfolk are on active service, and the crusader states were no exception to this general rule. Moreover, because the survival rate among girl-children born to Frankish settlers was higher than that among boys, women often provided continuity to the society of Outremer, by inheriting their fathers' fiefs and transmitting them to husbands many of whom came from the west.

The queens of Jerusalem are the best documented group of women in the Frankish east and form an obvious starting-point for any study of the role of women there. There is abundant evidence for most of them in a wide range of sources, comprising not only crusader chronicles and documents, but also western, Byzantine, Syriac and Armenian writers. Arab sources very seldom mentioned them: the moslem world was clearly shocked by the degree of social freedom which western women enjoyed[1] and reacted to women with political power much as misogynist dons did to the first generation of women undergraduates, by affecting not to notice them. Despite the fulness of the evidence there is, so far as I am aware, no detailed study of any of the twelfth century queens of Jerusalem with the notable exception of Mayer's article on Melisende.[2] For reasons of brevity only the queens of the first kingdom will be considered here.

Godfrey of Bouillon, the first Frankish ruler, was a bachelor and no woman occupied a central position in the state until his brother,

[1] *The Autobiography of Ousâma,* trans G. R. Potter, (London 1929) p 177.

[2] [H. E.] Mayer, ['Studies in the History of Queen Melisende of Jerusalem',] *DOP* 26 (1972) pp 93–183.

Baldwin I, count of Edessa, succeeded him in 1100. Baldwin's wife, Godvera, had accompanied him on crusade, but had died at Marasch in October 1097.[3] Soon after this Baldwin married the daughter of the Armenian prince Thoros, brother of Constantine the Roupenian. Paoli called her Arda, and it is convenient to use this name, although it is given in no source known to me.[4] She was an only child, and potentially a great heiress[5] and was promised a dowry of 60,000 bezants which her impoverished husband sorely needed to raise troops to defend his county, while he also benefitted from the advice and alliance of his father-in-law.[6]

When he was summoned to Jerusalem in 1100 Baldwin travelled there by the hazardous land-route, but his wife and her ladies waited at Antioch for a ship to take them south.[7] Possibly the queen did not make the journey that winter: she would have needed a strong naval escort, since most of the coastal cities were still held by the moslems. Certainly she does not seem to have been present at Bethlehem when Baldwin was crowned there on Christmas day. By 1101 Arda had reached Jaffa, possibly escorted by a Genoese fleet which had wintered at Laodicea.[8] When the battle of Ramleh was fought in September 1101 she was still at Jaffa, and when a false rumour reached the garrison that the king had been killed she took charge and sent a message by sea to Antioch asking Tancred for help.[9]

Nothing more is known about her until the king repudiated her. William of Tyre implies that this happened before 1105, but Guibert of Nogent, a contemporary source, places it more exactly immediately after Arda's arrival in the kingdom. He tells a romantic story of how the king put away his wife because she had been raped by pirates on the

[3] A[lbert of] A[ix, *Historia Hierosolymitana,*] bk 3, cap 27, *RHC Occ* 4, p 358; H. Hagenmeyer, *Chronologie de la première Croisade (1094–1100)* (Paris 1902) no 196, pp 101–2. compare Orderic [Vitalis, *Historia Ecclesiastica,*] bk 5, cap 13, ed A. Le Prévost, L. Delisle, 5 vols (Paris 1838–55) 2, p 404.

[4] C. [du Fresne] Du Cange, [*Les Familles d'Outremer,* ed E. G. Rey] (Paris 1869) p 11.

[5] W. H. Rüdt-Collenberg, *The Rupenides, Hethumides and Lusignans. The Structure of the Armeno-Cilician Dynasties,* Calouste Gulbenkian Foundation Armenian Library (Paris 1963) table 1 and p 50 no 7.

[6] AA bk 3, cap 31, *RHC Occ* 4, p 361 places the marriage before Baldwin reached Edessa in March 1098; W[illiam of] T[yre, *Historia rerum in partibus transmarinis gestarum,*] bk 10, cap 1, *RHC Occ* 1, p 402 places it after he came to Edessa.

[7] WT bk 10, cap 5, *RHC Occ* 1, p 407; Guibert [of Nogent, *Gesta Dei per Francos,*] bk 7, cap 48, *RHC Occ* 4, p 259.

[8] F[ulcher of] C[hartres, *Historia Hierosolymitana (1095–1127),*] bk 2, cap 8, [ed H. Hagenmeyer] (Heidelberg 1913) pp 393–4.

[9] *Ibid* bk 2, cap 14, p 421.

voyage south.[10] William of Tyre is more cautious: some people, he says, believed that the queen had been unfaithful, but others supposed that the king wished to make a more advantageous marriage. Fulcher of Chartres who, as Baldwin's chaplain, was in a unique position to know the truth about the separation, is totally silent. This suggests that the rumours about the queen's unfaithfulness were not true, since if they had been the king's repudiation of his wife would have met with general sympathy. Fulcher's silence implies that the king's action was criticised, and circumstantial evidence suggests that Baldwin's motives were political rather than moral: the marriage to a Roupenian princess which had been politically advantageous to him as count of Edessa was valueless to him as king of Jerusalem; the bride's father had only paid a fraction of the dowry;[11] and the queen was still childless after several years of marriage.[12] All these factors suggest that Baldwin's chief concern was to marry a richer wife who would bear him an heir. The marriage was not annulled. William of Tyre states that the separation took place 'without due process of law', and the queen was forced to take the veil at Saint Anne's Jerusalem.[13] She lived as a nun for some years and then asked permission to visit her kin in Constantinople on a fund-raising mission. Once there she abandoned the religious habit and, according to William of Tyre, lived promiscuously,[14] though this may be doubted since the king later professed his readiness to take her back.

A suitably rich replacement for Arda was not immediately available, and Jerusalem was without a queen for some years. Then in 1112 the patriarch Arnulf persuaded Baldwin to seek the hand of Adelaide, countess dowager of Sicily, who must have been in her late thirties.[15] Since the death of her husband, Roger I, in 1101, she had acted as regent of Sicily until Roger II came of age in 1112.[16] An alliance with

[10] Guibert, bk 7, cap 48, *RHCOcc* 4, p 259.

[11] 7,000 of the promised 60,000 bezants, AA bk 3, cap 31. *RHC Occ* 4, p 361.

[12] Orderic bk 9, cap 11, 3, p 570.

[13] Although this was later a Latin convent it may have been an eastern rite community at this time, since Arda was an Armenian Christian. B. Hamilton, 'Rebuilding Zion: the Holy Places of Jerusalem in the twelfth century', *SCH* 14 (1977) p 111.

[14] WT bk 11, cap 1, *RHC Occ* 1, pp 451–2.

[15] She married Roger I in 1089 as a young woman and had probably been born in *c*1074. Her marriage settlement shows that she was not considered to be above the age of child-bearing in 1113 and there seems no reason for crediting Orderic Vitalis's report that she was a wrinkled old hag when she married Baldwin, Orderic bk 13, cap 15, 5, p 36.

[16] For an account of her regency see J. J. Norwich, *The Normans in the South* (London 1967) pp 280–9.

Sicily, the nearest western power to the crusader states, and one which had a strong navy, was attractive to Baldwin, and so was the countess's wealth, of which his penurious kingdom stood in great need. He therefore instructed his envoys to agree to any conditions which the Sicilian court might make: these were onerous, for it was required that not only should any child born of the marriage be heir to the kingdom, but also that if the union were childless Roger II of Sicily should succeed Baldwin. The countess reached Acre in August 1113 with a large dowry[17] and also, according to Albert of Aix, with a thousand men-at-arms in her suite and a company of Saracen archers. It is a matter of conjecture whether her ship-of-state was so ornate as Albert reports, since he was writing from hearsay.[18]

Initially the countess's money eased the financial problems of the state, but she failed to produce the heir that the king needed.[19] The prospect of the succession of the count of Sicily, which became more likely as the countess passed the age of childbearing, was not viewed with enthusiasm by some of the Jerusalem baronage. They attacked the marriage-settlement indirectly through the patriarch. Arnulf was very vulnerable: he was accused of simony and concubinage, and was also denounced for solemnising a bigamous marriage between Baldwin and Adelaide while the king's first wife was still alive at Constantinople. The case finally went to Rome where, as his opponents had perhaps correctly calculated, Arnulf was able to clear himself of all the charges made against him except that relating to the Sicilian marriage where the facts were beyond dispute. In July 1116 Paschal II re-instated him as patriarch[20] on condition that he secured the separation of Baldwin and Adelaide.[21] That proved easy, because in the winter of that year Baldwin fell gravely ill and was persuaded by his clergy that he had contracted a bigamous marriage. He therefore vowed to dismiss Adelaide and recall Arda, a decision which seems to have been motivated solely by religious conviction, since he would have gained nothing from a reconciliation with his long-estranged wife.[22]

Life in the royal household must have been strained in the Lent of

[17] WT bk 11, cap 21, *RHC Occ* 1, pp 487–9; FC bk 2, cap 51, pp 575–7 relates her arrival but says nothing about her dowry.

[18] AA bk 12, cap 13, *RHC Occ* 4, pp 696–7.

[19] WT bk 11, cap 21, *RHC Occ* 1, p 489.

[20] FC bk 2, cap 54, p 591; WT bk 11, cap 26, *RHC Occ* 1, p 499; Paschal II's bull of 19 July 1116 in [E.] de Rozière, [*Cartulaire de l'Église du Saint-Sépulchre de Jérusalem*], *Collection des documents inédits sur l'histoire de France,* 1 ser, 5 (Paris 1849) no 11, pp 11–13.

[21] AA bk 12, cap 24, *RHC Occ* 4, p 704.

[22] FC bk 2, cap 59, p 601; WT bk 11, cap 29, *RHC Occ* 1, p 506.

1117. The queen was highly indignant at the treatment she had received, and had to undergo the further humiliation of having her marriage annulled by a church synod at Acre.[23] Moreover, though she lost her husband and her royal status she did not recover her dowry, which had been spent. On Saint Mark's day 1117 she finally sailed to Sicily,[24] vowing to build churches to Saint Anne and the Blessed Virgin if she made the journey in safety. She fulfilled this vow,[25] but she did not long enjoy the peace of Sicily, where she died on 16 April 1118.[26] The ill-treatment accorded to her was not only inhumane, it was also politically ill-advised. Her son never forgave the insult to his mother or the disregard of his own rights of succession under the terms of her marriage settlement. Writing some fifty years later William of Tyre laments that the rulers of Sicily, alone of all the kings of the West, had never sent help to Jerusalem.[27]

Queen Arda did not return to her husband after Adelaide's departure, and when Baldwin I died in 1118 there was no queen in Jerusalem. He was succeeded by his cousin, Baldwin II, count of Edessa, who had come to Jerusalem on pilgrimage and arrived there by chance in time for his predecessor's funeral.[28] Baldwin II had also married an Armenian wife after he became count of Edessa, probably in 1100. She was Morphia, daughter of Gabriel of Melitene who, though an Armenian, was Orthodox in religion. The alliance of Gabriel was initially valuable to Baldwin, as, no doubt, was the large dowry which his wife brought him.[29] Unlike his royal cousin, Baldwin II was happily married; it was as well for Morphia that this was so, since she signally failed to meet two of the chief requirements in the wife of any medieval ruler: her father's principality was conquered by the Turks soon after her marriage, so that no long-term political advantage accrued to her husband from the match; and she failed to produce a male heir. When Baldwin became king the couple had three daughters, Melisende, Alice and Hodierna, and the queen subsequently gave birth to a fourth girl,

[23] AA bk 12, cap 24, *RHC Occ* 4, p 704.
[24] FC bk 2, cap 60, p 602.
[25] [H. F.] Delaborde, [*Chartes de la Terre Sainte provenant de l'abbaye de Notre-Dame de Josaphat,*] *B*[*ibliothèque des*] *É*[*coles*] *F*[*rançaises d'*] *A*[*thènes et de*] *R*[*ome*], 19 (Paris 1880) no 20, pp 38–40.
[26] FC bk 2, cap 63, p 608 and n 14.
[27] WT bk 12, cap 29, *RHC Occ* 1, p 506.
[28] *Ibid* bk 12, cap 2, *RHC Occ* 1, pp 512–13; FC bk 3, cap 1, p 616.
[29] WT bk 10, cap 24, *RHC Occ* 1, p 437, places this marriage before the arrival of Jocelyn Courtenay in the east with the crusade of 1101.

Yveta.[30] Matthew of Edessa remarks that Baldwin was devoted to his wife[31] and this is borne out by the fact that he delayed his coronation for almost eighteen months, until Christmas day 1119, so that she could travel to Jersualem and be crowned with him.[32]

Perhaps as a result of the oriental environment in which she had grown up the queen took no part in the public life of the kingdom: her name is never associated with Baldwin's in any of his acts. Nevertheless, she was capable of taking the initiative in political affairs when necessary. When the king was captured by Nur-ad-Dualah Balak in 1123 Morphia is alleged to have hired Armenians who disguised themselves as Turks and infiltrated the garrison of Kharpart where the king was held.[33] She certainly took a central part in the negotiations leading to Baldwin's release in 1124, travelling to north Syria, and handing over her youngest daughter, Yveta, as a hostage to stand surety for the payment of the king's ransom.[34] Paradoxically, although the exact day of Morphia's death is known—it was 1 October—[35] the year is not, although it took place before 1129. She was buried in the shrine church of our Lady of Josaphat at Jerusalem.[36]

Neither Morphia nor either of the wives of Baldwin I had taken any public part in the government of the kingdom, but because Baldwin II had no sons he recognised his eldest daughter, Melisende, as his heir, and towards the end of his reign she began to be associated with him in official documents. In March 1129 she witnessed a grant which the king made to the Holy Sepulchre and took precedence over all the clergy,[37] while in another document from about the same period she

[30] *Ibid* bk 12, cap 4, *RHC Occ* 1, p 517.

[31] M[atthew of] E[dessa, *Chronique d'Arménie,*] cap 76, Armenian text with French translation, *RHC Arm* 1, p 119.

[32] FC bk 3, cap 7, p 635.

[33] Armenian infiltrators certainly played some part in Baldwin's escape attempt. WT bk 12, cap 18, *RHC Occ* 1, pp 538–9; Morphia's involvement is recorded by Orderic, bk 11, cap 26, 4, pp 250–1.

[34] ME cap 91, *RHC Arm* 1, p 139.

[35] Entry in the calendar of queen Melisande's psalter, ed [H.] Buchtal, [*Miniature Painting in the Latin Kingdom of Jerusalem*] with liturgical and palaeographical chapters by F. Wormald (Oxford 1957) pp 124–6.

[36] [C.] Kohler, ['Chartes de l'abbaye de Notre-Dame de la vallée de Josaphat en Terre Sainte (1108–1291). Analyse et extraits'], *R*[*evue de l'*] *O*[*rient*] *L*[*atin*], 7 (Paris 1899) no 21, p 128, which was drawn up before Melisende's marriage in June 1129. Compare de Rozière no 46, pp 85–6, in which Baldwin II remits some customs charges on pilgrims in the port of Acre for the repose of Morphia's soul.

[37] de Rozière no 44, pp 81–3. This is dated the fourth indiction, March 1128. The indiction has certainly been wrongly transcribed. As the patriarch Stephen was present on this occasion, and only took office in 1128, it seems likely that the new year

styled herself *filia regis et regni Jerosolimitani haeres*.[38] She married count Fulk V of Anjou, an experienced ruler, and a widower with grown sons who had been chosen as her husband by Louis VI of France. The wedding took place at whitsuntide 1129. Mayer argues that Baldwin II had originally promised Fulk sole right of succession, implying that Melisende was only to be queen-consort, but that on his deathbed he altered the terms of the settlement and associated Melisende and the infant Baldwin III with Fulk as joint-heirs, fearing lest after his death Fulk should repudiate Melisende and make one of the sons of his first marriage his heir. This is not convincing, since the accounts which William of Tyre gives of the terms of the marriage settlement and of the king's dying wishes are not incompatible: in the account of the marriage settlement there is nothing to suggest that Baldwin was intending to exclude Melisende from power. An important indication of Baldwin's intentions in the matter of the succession is the grant which he made to the Holy Sepulchre in 1130–1, in which he associated both Fulk and Melisende with him, which implies that from the time of the marriage he treated them as joint-heirs of the kingdom.[39] In 1130 Melisende gave birth to the future Baldwin III, and thus the succession was assured before the death of her father on 21 August 1131. On Holy Cross Day, 14 September, an important feast in the crusader kingdom, Fulk and Melisende were crowned in the church of the Holy Sepulchre.[40]

After her father's death Melisende did not enjoy the power which she had previously possessed: she is not associated with Fulk in any public act in the first five years of his reign. The revolt of Hugh II of Le Puiset, count of Jaffa, which Mayer convincingly argues took place in 1134, happened in this period. The facts of this *cause célèbre* are known only through William of Tyre. The king took a strong dislike to Hugh who was thought to be having a liaison with the queen. Some time later Hugh's stepson accused him of treason in the curia regis, and Hugh retired to Jaffa, allied with the moslems of Ascalon and defied the royal army which was sent against him. Peace was mediated by the patriarch, who obtained lenient terms from the king: the rebels were to be exiled

reckoning employed began on March 25 and that in modern style the document should be dated March 1129.

[38] Kohler, *ROL* 7, no 21, p 128.

[39] de Rozière no 43, pp 80–1. The marriage settlement is in WT bk 13, cap 24, *RHC Occ* 1, p 594: the account of the dying king's wishes *ibid* bk 13, cap 28, *RHC Occ* 1 pp 601–2. See Mayer, *DOP* 26, pp 99–102.

[40] WT bk 14, cap 2, *RHC Occ* 1, pp 608–9.

for three years, but at the end of that time they might return and resume their fiefs. But before Hugh left, an unsuccessful assassination attempt was made on him, which was commonly supposed to have been instigated by the king, although his collusion was never proved. Hugh then went to Apulia, where he died before his sentence had run its term, but the queen bitterly resented the way Hugh had been treated and the slight on her own honour. As a result, the king's supporters went in terror of their lives, and even the king himself did not feel safe among the queen's suite. Finally peace was mediated between Fulk and Melisende and, concludes William of Tyre, the king 'did not attempt to take the initiative, even in trivial matters, without her knowledge'.[41]

Mayer is undoubtedly correct in discounting the love element in this story: if Fulk had been a wronged husband a strong section of public opinion, led by the church, would have sided with him, not, as it did, with the queen, in a matter which might concern the royal succession. Mayer rightly sees the conflict as a dispute between the king's supporters, and those whose loyalties lay with the queen as Baldwin II's daughter. Hugh of Le Puiset, who was Melisende's second cousin, and the only great nobleman of the blood royal in the kingdom, was the natural leader of the queen's party.[42] There was evidently widespread resentment among some sections of the nobility and the church about the way in which the queen was being treated. I am not convinced by Mayer's argument that Fulk was trying to implement the terms of his marriage settlement and set aside the dying wishes of the old king, since I would suggest that the two settlements did not differ; but whichever interpretation is correct, the consequence was the same: Fulk excluded Melisende from power.[43] This was not simply a matter of protocol, but also one of patronage: unless the queen had some effective share in the affairs of state she could not reward her supporters with appointments and land. Hugh's revolt failed because he made the tactical error of allying with the saracens, thereby alienating many of his own supporters, but at this point Melisende first

[41] *Ibid* bk 14, caps 15–18, *RHC Occ* 1, pp 627–33; on the dating see Mayer, *DOP* 26, pp 104–6.

[42] In *c*1129 Hugh of Le Puiset witnessed a charter of Baldwin II immediately after the princess Melisende, Kohler, *ROL* 7, no 21, p 128.

[43] Mayer *DOP* 26, pp 102–13. I can find no evidence to support Mayer's view that Fulk may have wished to repudiate Melisende and set aside the claims of Baldwin III in favour of Elias, the younger son of his first marriage. He seems only to have wished to reduce Melisende to the status of a consort.

showed her considerable powers of initiative. She rallied her supporters, particularly the churchmen, obtained lenient terms for the rebel count, and, when an attempt was made to infringe this settlement, made life so unpleasant for the king that he was forced to recognise that he could only continue to rule with her co-operation.

The reconciliation of Fulk and Melisende took place before 1136 when their younger son, Amalric, was born.[44] Thereafter the queen was regularly associated with her husband in official documents relating to the kingdom of Jeruselam.[45] The scale on which she was able to dispense patronage in those years was expressed in a spectacular way in 1138. Of her three sisters, Alice had been married to Bohemond II of Antioch in her father's lifetime, and Hodierna to Raymond II of Tripoli earlier in Fulk's reign, but her youngest sister, Yveta, had become a nun at Saint Anne's. Melisende, who did not consider it fitting that a king's daughter should be a simple choir-sister, founded a convent at Bethany so that when she was old enough her sister could become abbess there.[46] Recent excavations have revealed the extensive scale of the building operations at Bethany [47] and the house received endowments commensurate with its status as a royal abbey, including the fertile plain of Jericho. The queen also supplied rich furnishings and liturgical vessels to the house, wishing 'that it should not be inferior to any community of men or women in the kingdom in wordly wealth.'[48]

In the later years of Fulk's life Melisende might justly be described as co-ruler, and from 1138 the child Baldwin III was associated with his parents in some of their acts.[49] No woman had previously enjoyed such power in the kingdom, but it was to grow greater. In 1143 Fulk

[44] Amalric was seven when Fulk died in 1143, WT bk 15, cap 27, *RHC Occ* 1, p 702,

[45] The first of these relates to the gift of Bethgibelin to the Hospital in 1136. *C[artulaire] G[énérale de l'] O[rdre des] H[ospitaliers de St.-Jean de Jérualem (1100–1310).* ed J. Delaville Le Roulx], 4 vols (Paris 1894–1906) 1, no 116. As Mayer points out, Melisende is not associated with Fulk in documents which he issued as administrator of Antioch, *DOP* 26, pp 109–10.

[46] de Rozière no 33, pp 60–5. Bethany belonged to the canons of the Holy Sepulchre, who were given Thecua in exchange. As Yveta was only about eighteen in 1138 an elderly abbess was appointed on the understanding that the princess would succeed her.

[47] S. J. Saller, *Excavations at Bethany (1949–1953), Publications of the Studium Biblicum Franciscanum* 12 (Jerusalem 1957).

[48] WT bk 15, cap 26, *RHC Occ* 1, pp 699–700.

[49] For example, de Rozière no 32, pp 58–60; [A.] de Marsy, ['Fragment d'un cartulaire de l'Ordre de St.-Lazare en Terre Sainte',] *A[rchives de l'] O[rient] L[atin]*, 2 vols (Paris 1884) 2, no 2, p 124.

was killed in a hunting accident: Melisende made the public demonstration of grief which her position as chief mourner required; then she took over the government. Baldwin III was only thirteen, and Melisende is commonly said to have acted as regent for him. This is not what she considered her position to be, nor is it what William of Tyre believed her to have done: he writes, *reseditque regni potestas penes dominam Melisendem, Deo amabilem reginam, cui jure hereditario competebat.*[50] Melisende was not a regent, but the queen regnant.

Baldwin III and Melisende were crowned on Christmas day 1143.[51] The association of the boy Baldwin with his mother shows the strength of feeling in this feudal society that there should be a male head of state, but while Baldwin was under age all power was in the hands of the queen. By reason of her sex she could not command the army, so she appointed Manasses of Hierges, her cousin, who had only recently arrived from the west, as constable of the kingdom, the officer who deputised for the king in military affairs.[52] In this way she avoided giving too much power to one of her subjects, which might have weakened the royal authority. As co-ruler with a thirteen year old child Melisende had no alternative but to take the measures she did: what surprised her contemporaries was that she showed no signs of relinquishing power to him when he came of age in 1145, an occasion which was marked by no public solemnity.

It would be otiose to describe the build-up of tension between Baldwin and Melisende since Mayer has discussed the evidence so thoroughly.[53] A breach had clearly occurred between them by 1150, when Melisende began to issue documents in her own name without reference to Baldwin.[54] No complaint was made about the quality of the queen's government: she seems to have been a good administrator and to have ruled wisely; but Baldwin and his supporters resented the fact that he had no share in power and was not allowed to make independent decisions. The king blamed the constable Manasses for alienating his mother from him, and matters reached a crisis in 1152

[50] WT bk 15, cap 27, *RHC Occ* 1, p 702 dates Fulk's death 1142, but since he also states that Baldwin III was then thirteen Fulk must have died in 1143. Melisende and Fulk were not married until Pentecost 1129 (Whitsun fell on June 2 in that year), so Baldwin cannot have been born before March 1130.

[51] WT bk 16, cap 3, *RHC Occ* 1, p 707.

[52] He was in office by 1144 when he led the royal relief force to Edessa, *ibid* bk 16, cap 4, *RHC Occ* 1, p 710.

[53] Mayer *DOP* 26, pp 114–66.

[54] de Marsy, *AOL* 2, no 8, p 129, no 10, pp 130–1; de Rozière no 49, pp 90–2, no 48, pp 87–9.

when Baldwin demanded to be crowned in the Holy Sepulchre on easter day without his mother's being present. The patriarch Fulcher refused to agree to this, so on easter Monday, 31 March, the king staged a solemn procession through Jerusalem, wearing a laurel wreath as a symbol of royal power, presumably because the patriarch refused to let him use the crown jewels.[55]

Baldwin then summoned the high court and demanded that the kingdom should be divided between his mother and himself. The request was criminally irresponsible, for the small kingdom could only maintain its defences satisfactorily if its military resources were under a unified command. Melisende agreed, presumably because she thought that such a solution would be less dangerous to the state than a civil war: she kept Samaria and Judaea while Baldwin held the north.[56] Melisende has often been criticised for not resigning power gracefully to her son at this time: it is difficult to see what justification she would have felt for doing so; she obviously had the support of the church and of most of the southern lords; she was not a regent clinging tenaciously to power after the heir had reached his majority, but the acknowledged co-ruler of the kingdom; she had governed well, but her son was inexperienced and had shown little capacity for government hitherto. The most important need of the kingdom was to avert a civil war, so she acquiesced in the demands of Baldwin and the northern baronage who supported him.

Mayer is surely right in asserting that this situation lasted only for a few weeks.[57] The king retired to the north, raised an army and invaded his mother's half of the kingdom. He defeated and deposed the constable, siezed Nablus, and was admitted to Jerusalem by the citizens. Melisende was deserted by many of her vassals, perhaps because the king had now proved himself to be a competent general, which the state needed, and they feared to prolong the civil war in case their enemies took advantage of it. But some of her followers remained loyal to the queen, notably Rohard the Old, castellan of Jerusalem, Philip of Nablus, and her younger son, Amalric, count of Jaffa. The queen and her supporters fortified themselves in the tower of David, to which Baldwin III laid siege. This unedifying spectacle of son fighting mother and brother was brought to an end by the intervention of some unnamed peacemakers, perhaps churchmen. It might have been

[55] WT bk 17, cap 13, *RHC Occ* 1, p 781.
[56] *Ibid* bk 17, cap 14, *RHC Occ* 1, p 781.
[57] *DOP* 26, pp 166–71.

expected that Melisende, who had no hope of winning against such unequal odds, would have been allowed to retire with dignity to live with her sister in the convent of Bethany, but she held out for better terms: the city of Nablus and its adjacent lands were granted to her for life and the king swore a solemn oath that he would not disturb her peace.[58] This shows that although the queen had lost the war she still had powerful allies, for sixteen years of authority had enabled her to exercise a great deal of patronage. The patriarch and the church as a whole took her side and so did her younger son, Amalric, who was now sixteen and heir-presumptive to the throne.

The queen's initiative was not exhausted as she showed soon after this. The king was anxious about the government of north Syria where the power of Nureddin was growing. Antioch was ruled by his cousin Constance, a widow since the death of Raymond of Poitiers in 1149, and he wanted her to re-marry in order to provide the state with a new military leader. This need was all the more pressing now that he had sole charge of the kingdom of Jerusalem and could less easily absent himself than he had formerly done to deal with trouble in the north. He therefore summoned a general assembly of the crusader states to meet at Tripoli in the early summer of 1152.[59] This was attended by the princess of Antioch and the chief clergy and barons of her state, the high court of Tripoli, and the chief vassals of the king. Queen Melisende also came to Tripoli. The ostensible reason for her visit was to straighten out the marital difficulties of her sister, the countess Hodierna, and Raymond II of Tripoli. It was an astute move, since the queen could not be prevented from paying a visit to her sister, yet when she was there she had to be invited to the assembly since the chief business on the agenda was the marriage of her niece, Constance of Antioch. Neither the assembly nor the royal aunts, Melisende and Hodierna, could persuade Constance to choose a new husband, and Melisende was unsuccessful in

[58] WT bk 17, cap 14, *RHC Occ* 1, pp 781–3.

[59] *Ibid* bk 17, cap 18, *RHC Occ* 1, p 790, places this event after his account of the deposition of Melisende, but gives no date. It is in a section of his work which relates to events in north Syria, some of which occurred before 1152. Some scholars have therefore placed the assembly of Tripoli before the civil war, for example, [S.] Runciman, [*A History of the Crusades*], 3 vols (Cambridge 1951–4) 2, p 333. I accept the date given by Mayer, because the reasons he gives are convincing in the light of a piece of evidence recently discovered, J. Riley-Smith, 'The Templars and the Castle of Tortosa in Syria: an unknown document concerning the acquisition of the fortress', *EHR* 84 (1969) pp 278–88. Mayer's date is also convincing because Baldwin would have been in no position to summon a general assembly unless he had been sole ruler, *DOP* 26, p 160.

her attempts to reconcile the count of Tripoli and his wife. Soon after the council the count was murdered by members of the sect of the assassins, and Hodierna became regent of Tripoli for her young son, Raymond III. After the count's funeral Baldwin III escorted his mother home. By attending the council Melisende had asserted the strength of her influence in north Syria. Henceforth, if the king wished to preserve some measure of control over Tripoli and Antioch, which the rising power of Nureddin and the absence of an adult male ruler in the Christian states of the north made desirable, he would have to treat his mother with outward respect, since the regent of Tripoli was her sister and the regent of Antioch her niece, and any harsh treatment of Melisende by Baldwin might cause tension between the king and the northern states.[60]

Indeed, as Mayer has shown, the king continued to pay his mother every sign of outward respect. There was a short period of coolness between them, which is scarcely surprising in view of the recent civil war, and during this time the king asserted his sole authority. But once he had established his position as a military leader by conquering Ascalon in 1153 he made peace with his mother. From 1154 onwards she was associated with him in many of his public acts, and he also ratified the grants which she had made by her sole authority during the time of their estrangement.[61] Melisende's involvement in state affairs after her retirement to Nablus was not always confined to internal matters, such as the transference of land. In 1156, for example, the king made peace with the merchants of Pisa *concessione Melisendis reginae, matris . . . meae.*[62] In 1157 when Baldwin was campaigning in Antioch Melisende took a military initiative. According to William of Tyre, the important cave-fortress of el-Hablis, which controlled the lands of Gilead beyond the Jordan, was recovered from the moslems 'through the planning and zeal of Melisende the queen'.[63] In the same year the patriarch Fulcher of Jerusalem died, and the appointment of his successor, Amalric of Nesle, was thought to have been due to the intervention of the king's half-sister, Sybil, countess of Flanders, and one of his aunts, perhaps the abbess of Bethany. Again it is significant

60 WT bk 17, caps 18, 19, *RHC Occ* 1, pp 789–92.

61 *DOP* 26, pp 172–5.

62 *Documenti sulle relazioni delle città toscane coll'Oriente cristiano e coi Turchi fino all'anno 1531*, ed G. Müller, *Documenti degli archivi toscani* 3 (Florence 1879) no 5, pp 6–7.

63 WT bk 18, cap 19, *RHC Occ* 1, p 851.

that this important appointment was decided in the circle of the queen, not by the king.[64]

On 30 November 1160 Melisende gave her assent to a gift made by her son Amalric to the Holy Sepulchre.[65] Soon after this she had what appears to have been a stroke: her memory was impaired and she could take no further part in the affairs of state. Her sisters, the countess of Tripoli and the abbess of Bethany, nursed her for several months. She died on 11 September 1161 and was buried, like her mother, in the shrine of our Lady of Josaphat.[66] Among her bequests, as befitted the daughter of queen Morphia, she left property to the Orthodox monastery of Saint Saba.[67]

Throughout her life she had been a great benefactor of the church. In addition to founding the convent of Bethany she had also given endowments to the Holy Sepulchre, our Lady of Josaphat, the *Templum Domini*, the order of the Hospital, the leper hospital of Saint Lazarus, and the Praemonstratensians of Saint Samuel's, Mountjoy.[68] It is not to be wondered at that a good churchman like William of Tyre considered that the eternal salvation of this pious queen was assured.[69] Her contemporaries do not remark on it, but she was evidently a cultured as well as a devout woman. The psalter which bears her name and which is now in the British Museum is evidence of her interest in the fine arts. Buchtal, who argues that it was executed for the queen in the lifetime of Fulk, has detected the presence of Byzantine, western and south Italian traditions in the illuminations, and concludes: 'Jerusalem during the second quarter of the twelfth century possessed a flourishing and well-established scriptorium which could, without difficulty, undertake a commission for a royal manuscript *de grand luxe*.'[70] Melisende must be given credit for being an important patron of the artists of the young Latin kingdom.

[64] *Ibid* bk 18, cap 20, *RHC Occ* 1, p 854; the king's aunt who is mentioned could also have been Hodierna of Tripoli.

[65] de Rozière no 58, pp 115–17. [66] WT bk 18, caps 27, 32, *RHC Occ* 1, pp 867, 877.

[67] de Rozière nos 140, 144, pp 256, 262–8.

[68] Holy Sepulchre: de Rozière nos 32, 48, pp 58–60, 87–9; Josaphat: Delaborde, nos 33, 34, 36, pp 80–4; *Templum Domini*: F. Chalandon, 'Un diplôme inédit d'Amaury I roi de Jérusalem en faveur de l'Abbaye du Temple-Notre-Seigneur', *ROL* 8 (1900–1) pp 311–17; Hospital: *CGOH* I, nos 175, 191, 244; Saint Lazarus: de Marsy, *AOL* 2, nos 10, 16, pp 130–1, 135; Saint Samuel's: H. E. Mayer, 'Sankt Samuel auf dem Freudenberge und sein besitz nach einem unbekannten diplom König Balduins V', *QFIAB* 44 (1964) pp 35–71.

[69] 'Sepulta est autem inclytae recordationis domina Milissendis, angelorum choris inferenda, in valle Josaphat', WT bk 18, cap 32, *RHC Occ* 1, p 877.

[70] Buchtal p 14.

She was a truly remarkable woman who for over thirty years exercised considerable power in a kingdom where there was no previous tradition of any woman holding public office. William of Tyre's comment, that 'she was a very wise woman, fully experienced in almost all spheres of state business, who had completely triumphed over the handicap of her sex so that she could take charge of important affairs', has a patronising ring to a twentieth-century ear. Few, however, would disagree with his judgement that, 'striving to emulate the glory of the best princes . . . she ruled the kingdom with such ability that she was rightly considered to have equalled her predecessors in that regard'.[71]

When she died there was already another queen in Jerusalem. In 1157 the high court had debated the king's marriage, and had finally decided to seek a Byzantine bride. It was hoped that Manuel Comnenus would provide a large dowry, and Jerusalem was extremely short of money; but it was also hoped that he might give the crusaders military help against Nureddin.[72] Baldwin III's envoys were kept waiting in Constantinople for months. The Byzantine emperor was less wealthy than the crusaders supposed: the marriage which they proposed would involve the emperor in great expense and it would be of no value to him unless he could follow it up with a military campaign. In 1157 he could not take his armies to the east because he feared an attack from the Normans of Sicily, but the situation changed in 1158 when the Sicilians made a thirty years truce with Byzantium against their common enemy, Frederick Barbarossa.[73] Negotiations with Baldwin III's ambassadors then went ahead smoothly. The bride chosen was the emperor's niece Theodora, daughter of the sebastocrator Isaac, who left Constantinople in the late summer of 1158.[74] The marriage fulfilled all the Franks' hopes: the emperor brought his army to north Syria to fight Nureddin;[75] the bride was given a dowry of 100,000 gold *hyper-eroi*, a trousseau worth a further 14,000, and 10,000 *hypereroi* to defray the expenses of the wedding. There was also the uncovenanted bonus

[71] WT bk 16, cap 3, *RHC Occ* 1, p 707.

[72] *Ibid* bk 18, cap 16, *RHC Occ* 1, p 846.

[73] [F.] Chalandon, [*Les Comnènes. Études sur l'empire byzantin au XIe et XIIe siècle.* I. *Essai sur le règne d'Alexis Ier Comnène (1081–1118).* II. *Jean II Comnène (1118–43) et Manuel Ier Comnène (1143–80)*] (Paris 1912) 2, pp 380–1.

[74] She reached Tyre in September 1158, WT bk 18, cap 22, *RHC Occ* 1, pp 857–8; Chalandon 2, p 441.

[75] Gregory the Priest, *Continuation of the Chronicle of Matthew of Edessa*, cap 123, *RHC Arm* 1, p 186.

that Theodora, who was twelve, was exceptionally beautiful. The emperor, of course, also made conditions: the bride should receive as her dowry from Baldwin Acre, the greatest city in the kingdom, to hold for life if she were widowed;[76] and the king solemnly vowed to secure the recognition of Byzantine overlordship in the principality of Antioch.[77] On her arrival the queen was taken to Jerusalem where she was solemnly anointed and crowned before being married to the king. Baldwin, whose life-style had previously been a cause of scandal to his more staid subjects, became a reformed character, and the marriage seems to have been a happy one.[78]

The alliance between the crusaders and Byzantium achieved what both sides had hoped it would do: Manuel by a show of military force restrained the aggression of Nureddin, and Antioch acknowledged Byzantine overlordship. Yet although she was so politically important as the chief link in this alliance, Theodora enjoyed no public exercise of power in the crusader kingdom. She was not normally associated with the king in his public acts, and it is arguable that the forceful character of queen Melisende made her sons reluctant to give any share in state affairs to their wives. The two documents in which Theodora is associated with the king are exceptional: one relates to sugar plantations at Acre and was made with the queen's assent presumably because Acre was her dower-fief;[79] the other was the charter of 31 July 1161 in which the king arranged with Philip of Milly to exchange his lands at Nablus for the great fief of Outre-Jordan. This was agreed to by all the members of the royal family, the queen, the king's brother, Amalric, his aunt, Hodierna, countess of Tripoli, and her children, Raymond III and Melisende, which indicates how important the transaction was considered to be. Queen Melisende was dying: her lands at Nablus would revert to the crown, and if the other great landowner there were bought out the whole of Samaria would become part of the royal domain.[80] Theodora seems to have enjoyed complete freedom in disposing of her

[76] WT bk 18, cap 22, *RHC Occ* 1, p 858.

[77] This is not recorded by William of Tyre but is in Gregory the Priest, cap 125, *RHC Arm* 1, p 189.

[78] WT bk 18, cap 22, *RHC Occ* 1, p 858.

[79] S. Pauli, *Codice diplomatico del sacro militare ordine Gerosolimitano, oggi di Malta*, 2 vols (Lucca 1733–7) 1, no 50, pp 50–1.

[80] [E.] Strehlke, [*Tabulae Ordinis Theutonici*] (Berlin 1869) no 3, pp 3–5. Mayer *DOP* 26, pp 179–80, argues that Baldwin III was punishing Philip for his support of Melisende in 1152. This is not convincing: the fief of Outre-Jordan was greater than Philip's fief at Nablus. The exchange was to Philip's advantage and was only of benefit to the king because he could integrate Philip's lands with his mother's lands.

own lands: in 1161 she granted a house in Acre to her usher, Richard the Englishman, without reference to her husband.[81]

Theodora brought her husband money, prestige, political security and a happy marriage but, perhaps on account of her youth, she bore him no children. When he died on 10 February 1163[82] his widow was only seventeen. She retired to Acre and became the first dowager queen of Jerusalem; and for some years she remained the only queen.

Baldwin III was succeeded by his brother Amalric who had in 1157 married his third cousin, Agnes of Courtenay, daughter of Jocelyn II of Edessa.[83] Agnes was a widow: her first husband, Reynald of Marasch, had been killed in battle alongside Raymond of Antioch in 1149.[84] It is not known how old Agnes then was, but since the canonical age of marriage for girls was twelve, she may have been born in *c*1136 and therefore have been the same age as Amalric. After the loss of western Edessa in 1150 she and her mother came to live in Jerusalem, but when Amalric wished to marry her the patriarch Fulcher objected that they were related within the prohibited degrees and the couple seem to have waited to be married until after the patriarch's death in 1157.[85] No objection was made by anybody else, including Amalric's mother, the pious queen Melisende. It must have appeared a most suitable marriage; Agnes, it is true, had no dowry, since her family had lost all their lands, but there was no woman of better birth in the kingdom. She bore her husband a daughter, Sibylla, and then, in 1161, a son, the future Baldwin IV, to whom Baldwin III stood godfather.[86]

In 1163 the high court refused to recognise Amalric as king unless his marriage was annulled. It is difficult to establish the true reasons behind this request, which would be unusual in any age, since all three accounts of it are hostile to Agnes: William of Tyre never forgave her for preventing him from becoming patriarch; the thirteenth century *Estoire d'Eracles* is heavily dependent on William of Tyre for its early

[81] de Marsy, *AOL* 2, no 20, pp 138–9. Two Greeks are among the witnesses: Michael Grifo, *panetarius*, and Dionisius *miles*, who was presumably a member of Theodora's bodyguard.

[82] William of Tyre dates this 10 February 1162, 'regni ejus anno vicesimo . . . aetatis vero tricesimo tertio', bk 18, cap 34, *RHC Occ* 1, p 880. The twentieth year of Baldwin's reign would not have begun until 25 December 1162, his thirty-third birthday cannot have been earlier than March 1163 (see note 50 above). It is therefore generally agreed that he died on 10 February 1163.

[83] *Chronicles of the Reigns of Stephen, Henry II and Richard I*, 4, *The Chronicle of Robert of Torigni*, ed R. Howlett, *RS* 82, 4 (1889) p 194.

[84] WT bk 17, cap 9, *RHC Occ* 1, p 775.

[85] *Ibid* bk 19, cap 4, *RHC Occ* 1, p 889.

[86] *Ibid* bk 18, cap 29, *RHC Occ* 1, p 871.

material; while the chronicle of Ernoul was written by a supporter of the Ibelins[87] who held Agnes responsible for excluding them from the royal succession. William of Tyre and the *Eracles* give substantially the same account of the annulment: that the patriarch refused to crown the king because his marriage contravened canon law.[88] William adds that the annulment was made by a papal legate, but that the children of the marriage were declared legitimate.[89] The chronicle of Ernoul, however, gives what purports to be the objection raised by the lay members of the high court: *Car telle n'est que roine doie iestre di si haute cite comme de Jherusalem.*[90] This implies a slight on Agnes's moral character, but this can only be substantiated by instances which this same biased source gives of her lapses from virtue. Although the marriage was annulled on grounds of consanguinity, it is difficult to credit that this was the real reason for objecting to it: the relationship between Agnes and Amalric was such a distant one that William of Tyre, who had been studying overseas when the annulment took place, had to ask the abbess of Sainte Marie-la-Grande to explain the grounds for it to him.[91] There are two possible reasons why Agnes was unacceptable to the high court: they may have thought that the king could make a more politically and financially advantageous marriage, as he ultimately did; or they may have suspected that Agnes, like queen Melisende, would try to take too active a part in state affairs, as she was later to do.

Agnes kept the title of countess which she had held when Amalric was count of Jaffa and Ascalon. Almost immediately after the annulment she married Hugh of Ramleh, the eldest of the three ambitious Ibelin brothers, a marriage which may, as Ernoul relates, have been arranged by the king himself:[92] it certainly relieved him from the duty of making provision for his penniless ex-wife. Although she was never a crowned queen of Jerusalem, Agnes of Courtenay was the wife, mother, mother-in-law and grandmother of kings, and an influential person in the state for twenty years, and must therefore be included in this study.

[87] M. R. Morgan, *The Chronicle of Ernoul and the Continuations of William of Tyre, Oxford Historical Monographs,* (Oxford 1973) pp 41–6.

[88] [*L'Estoire d'*] *Eracles* [*Empereur et la Conqueste de la Terre d'Outremer*], bk 23, cap 3 *RHC Occ* 2, p 5.

[89] WT bk 19, cap 4, *RHC Occ* 1, p 889.

[90] [*La Chronique d'*] *Ernoul* [*et de Bernard le Trésorier,* ed L. de Mas Latrie] (Paris 1871) p 17.

[91] WT bk 19, cap 4, *RHC Occ* 1, pp 889–90.

[92] Ernoul p 17; *Eracles* bk 23, cap 3, *RHC Occ* 2, p 5; WT bk 19, cap 4, *RHC Occ* 1, p 890.

It was not until 1165 that Amalric began negotiations for a second marriage. The chief aim of his foreign policy at that time was to prevent the weakened Fatimid caliphate of Egypt from falling under the control of Nureddin, and to achieve this he needed Byzantine military and financial help. On the advice of the high court he therefore sent an embassy to Constantinople to seek a bride from Manuel Comnenus.[93] The discussions dragged on for two years because, as Byzantine sources make clear, Amalric wished the emperor to relinquish his claims to sovereignty over Antioch. Amalric eventually gave way about this[94] and the emperor's great-niece Maria, daughter of the protosebastos John, came to Syria and married the king at Tyre on 29 August 1167.[95] From the vagueness of Frankish sources it may be inferred that her dowry was not so great as that of her cousin Theodora had been, while the silence even of her supporters about her beauty is equally suggestive.

At the time of Amalric's marriage to Maria the dowager queen Theodora was still living in retirement at Acre. She had not remarried: she could only do so with the king's consent, and Amalric was unlikely to give this, since he would not wish Acre, the greatest city in the kingdom, to pass into other hands, whereas if Theodora remained a widow it would revert to the crown at her death. Her life must have been very boring: she was cut off by background and language from the Frankish nobility among whom she lived, and such ceremonial precedence as she had enjoyed would come to an end with the king's remarriage. In the winter of 1166–7, when Theodora was twenty-one, there came to the kingdom a distant kinsman of hers, Andronicus Comenus, the emperor Manuel's first cousin. He was an unusual figure in the hieratic court of Byzantium, an adventurer, who would have been temperamentally more at home as a freelance knight in the feudal world of western Europe. His early life had been a series of political and amorous scandals, but in 1166 the emperor had appointed him governor of Cilicia. He soon became bored by his official duties and went to Antioch where he seduced the princess Philippa, a tactless choice, since she was the emperor's sister-in-law, and the resulting scandal was so great that he was forced to leave in haste.[96] Armed with

[93] Ernoul pp 17–18.

[94] [John] Cinnamus, [*Epitome Historiarum*], bk 5, cap 13, *CHSByz* (Bonn 1836) pp 237–8.

[95] WT bk 20, cap 1, *RHC Occ* 1, pp 942–3; Ernoul p 18.

[96] For Andronicus's early life see [C.] Diehl, ['Les romanesques aventures d'Andronic Comnène, *Figures byzantines*], (5 ed Paris 1918) pp 86–106.

the revenues of Cyprus and Cilicia, which he had had the forethought to collect,[97] he went to Jerusalem. The king was absent on campaign in Egypt, but, as courtesy demanded, Andronicus called on his kinswoman, the dowager queen. Despite the great disparity in their ages, (Andronicus was in his late forties) Theodora was attracted to him and they became lovers. When Amalric returned from Egypt he was impressed by this distinguished and seemingly rich visitor, who had great charm, and bestowed the fief of Beirut on him. But, in the delightful phrase of William of Tyre, Andronicus behaved to the king 'like a mouse in a wallet' (*more muris in pera*): for he invited Theodora to visit him in Beirut and, while she was travelling there, abducted her and carried her off to the court of Nureddin at Damascus.[98]

The Franks did not know the reason for this extraordinary behaviour, but an explanation is given by the Byzantine writer, Nicetas Choniates. The emperor Manuel, who had learned of Andronicus's intrigue with Theodora, presumably from one of the noblemen who had escorted queen Maria to Syria, feared that this scandal might jeopardise his carefully constructed Syrian policy. There was no hope of regularising the liaison, for Andronicus had a wife in Constantinople. The emperor therefore sent orders to his agents in Syria to blind Andronicus, which he hoped would satisfy the Franks that he took this slight on the honour of their royal house seriously, but a copy of his letter was seen by Theodora, who informed Andronicus of his danger, and he persuaded her to elope with him.[99] The defection of a first cousin of the Byzantine emperor and a dowager queen of Jerusalem to moslem Damascus was, as may be imagined, very welcome to the entire islamic world. The couple were received with enthusiasm throughout the moslem near east, and appear to have lived happily together, having two children, a son, Alexis, and a daughter, Irene. Their subsequent adventures are not relevant to this paper, but Theodora, it would seem, died before 1182 when Andronicus made himself Byzantine emperor.[100] Contrary to Manuel Comnenus's fears the crusader states do not seem to have paid very much attention to this scandal: the Byzantine alliance was assured through Amalric's marriage to Maria, and, as a result of Theodora's elopement, the dower lands of Acre could revert to the crown.[101]

[97] Cinnamus bk 6, cap 1, p 250. [98] WT bk 20, cap 2, *RHC Occ* 1, pp 943–4.

[99] Nicetas Choniates, *Historia, De Manuele Comneno*, bk 4, cap 5, *CHSByz* (Bonn 1835) p 185.

[100] For Andronicus's subsequent career see Diehl, pp 107–33.

[101] Ernoul p 15.

Maria Comnena took no part in affairs of state during her husband's lifetime. In this regard Amalric followed the example of his elder brother and, like him, had no wish to allow a new queen Melisende to contest his authority. Maria bore the king two daughters, Isabella, who was born in 1172, and another girl who died in infancy.[102] The lack of a male child was a misfortune not only for the queen, who proved to be a most ambitious woman, but also for the kingdom. For Baldwin, the son of the king's first marriage, had leprosy, and there seems little doubt that had Maria borne the king a son he would have succeeded to the throne. As it was, when Amalric died in 1174 the thirteen year old leper child became king Baldwin IV.

On his deathbed the king granted Maria his mother's former lands of Nablus as a dower fief.[103] She and her daughter Isabella withdrew from public life, because the unusual situation existed in the new reign that the dowager queen was not the king's mother and had no natural place at court because Baldwin IV's own mother, the countess Agnes, was still living. In 1169 Agnes's third husband, Hugh of Ibelin, had died.[104] The marriage was childless, and she subsequently married Reynald, son of Gerald, lord of Sidon: William of Tyre places this event in king Amalric's lifetime. A mystery surrounds Agnes's fourth marriage: William of Tyre relates that Gerald of Sidon solemnly swore that the couple were related within the prohibited degrees (he carefully does not specify how), and that the marriage was consequently annulled.[105] Gerald may have objected to Agnes on moral grounds as a daughter-in-law since, with or without foundation, rumours were certainly circulating about her indiscretions.[106] William's account makes it plain that the annulment occurred while Gerald was still alive. This must have been before 1173, for in that year Reynald first appears in charters as lord of Sidon, which shows that his father had died.[107] Yet when William of Tyre describes the release of Jocelyn of Courtenay from prison in 1175–6 he attributes this to the efforts of 'the countess Agnes, wife of Reynald of Sidon'.[108] Moreover, the list of witnesses to a charter issued in 1179 by Agnes's daughter, Sibylla

[102] *Itinerarium* [*peregrinorum et gesta regis Ricardi I,* ed W. Stubbs], bk 1, cap 46, *Chronicles and Memorials of the reign of Richard I,* 1, *RS* 38,1 (1864) p 97.

[103] Ernoul p 31.

[104] Hugh is last mentioned in a document of 1169 (together with Agnes), de Marsy, *AOL* 2, no 25, pp 142–3.

[105] WT bk 19, cap 4, *RHC Occ* 1, p 890.

[106] Ernoul pp 59, 82.

[107] *CGOH* 1, no 551.

[108] WT bk 21, cap 11, *RHC Occ* 1, p 1023.

countess of Jaffa, is headed by *domina magna comitissa Sagite* and *dominus Reinaudus Sagite*.[109] Although the lady of Sidon is not given a Christian name in this document it clearly refers to Agnes, for she was the only wife of a lord of Sidon who was entitled to be styled countess: it was, moreover, natural that as Sibylla's mother she should have taken precedence over all the other witnesses. From this it must be concluded that if the annulment was ever granted it was reversed on appeal after Gerald of Sidon's death, and that Agnes remained the wife of Reynald of Sidon probably until her death, but certainly until 1179. It is equally clear that William of Tyre did not regard the marriage as valid, and this may account for the disfavour with which Agnes regarded him.

Up to the time of Amalric's death Agnes had little contact with her children: Baldwin IV had grown up at his father's court and Sibylla was brought up in the convent of Bethany by her great-aunt Yveta, queen Melisende's sister.[110] Nor does Agnes seem to have had any *entrée* to the court during her son's minority, which ended in 1176, during which Raymond III of Tripoli was regent. The regent's chief concern was to find a suitable husband for Sibylla, who could take over the government in the event of the king's death or incapacity, since it was evident that, because of his leprosy, the king could not himself marry and beget an heir. The man chosen for the princess was William Longsword of Montferrat, who married Sibylla in the autumn of 1176 and was created count of Jaffa and Ascalon. He died in the following June, leaving his wife pregnant with the future Baldwin V, and countess of Jaffa and Ascalon in her own right.[111]

Agnes seems to have taken no part in the negotiations for the Montferrat marriage, but she was clearly anxious to obtain power at court. Her first step was to arrange for the ransom of her brother, Jocelyn III, titular count of Edessa, who was a prisoner-of-war at Aleppo, for which purpose she raised the considerable sum of 60,000 dinars.[112] The sick young king came of age in 1176 and Raymond of Tripoli's regency ended, but Baldwin IV had a great shortage of male kin to whom power could be delegated. Jocelyn III was his uncle, and

[109] J. Delaville Le Roulx, *Les archives, le bibliothèque et le trésor de l'Ordre de Saint-Jean de Jérusalem à Malte*, *BEFAR* 32 (1883) no 53, pp 144–5.

[110] WT bk 21, cap 2, *RHC Occ* 1, p 1006.

[111] *Ibid* bk 21, cap 13, *RHC Occ* 1, pp 1025–6.

[112] *Ibid* bk 21, cap 11, *RHC Occ* 1, p 1023; details of the ransom in *Chronique de Michel le Syrien, patriarche jacobite d'Antioche (1166–99)*, bk 20, cap 3, ed with French translation, J. B. Chabot, 4 vols (Paris 1899–1924) 3, pp 365–6.

when he arrived at Jerusalem he was given the important office of seneschal of the realm.[113]

Shortly after William of Montferrat's death count Philip of Flanders, the king's cousin, came to Jerusalem on crusade and claimed the right to arrange marriages for both the king's sisters to his own vassals. The high court refused to agree to this, and Baldwin of Ibelin publicly insulted the count, who was offended and left the kingdom to campaign in Antioch.[114] Ernoul says that Baldwin acted in this way because he wished to marry Sibylla himself, and this may well be true although Ernoul's chronology is very confused at this point in his narrative.[115] The Ibelin brothers were certainly very ambitious: in the autumn of 1177 the king gave his consent for the queen dowager, Maria Comnena, to marry the youngest Ibelin brother, Balian, who thus carried on the family tradition of marrying king Amalric's former wives.[116] By this marriage the Ibelins gained control of the dower-fief of Nablus and custody of the king's younger sister, Isabella. An English source, admittedly one which is very hostile to Maria, gives an unflattering portrait of this marriage: the queen found in Balian, the writer says, 'a husband whose character matched her own . . . where he was savage, she was godless; where he was shallow-minded she was fickle; where he was treacherous she was scheming'.[117]

The Ibelin marriage excluded the possibility that Maria could, as the king's stepmother, fulfill the duties of queen at Baldwin IV's court. This function was performed by the countess Agnes, whose influence over both her children grew more marked in the following years. When the constable of the kingdom, Humphrey II of Toron, was killed in battle in 1179 Agnes secured the appointment of Amalric of Lusignan as his successor. In Ibelin circles it was rumoured that he was her lover, but, whether this was true or not, he was clearly not chosen simply for that reason, for he was an extremely able man who was later to become an outstanding king both of Jerusalem and Cyprus.[118] But

[113] He held that office by 1176, *CGOH* 1, no 496; R. L. Nicholson, *Joscelyn III and the Fall of the Crusader States (1134–1199)* (Leiden 1973) p 73, n 173.

[114] WT bk 21, caps 14, 15, 18, *RHC Occ* 1, pp 1027–30, 1034–5; Ernoul p 33.

[115] Ernoul p 33 places Philip of Flanders's arrival before Sibylla's marriage to William of Montferrat instead of after William's death: this is certainly wrong. He adds that Baldwin had separated from his first wife in order to be free to marry Sibylla, but that when she married William he married the widow of the lord of Caesaraea, pp 47–8. This also is wrong, since Baldwin had married that lady by 1175, *CGOH* 1, no 470; Du Cange p 365.

[116] WT bk 21, cap 18, *RHC Occ* 1, p 1035.

[117] *Itinerarium* bk 1, cap 63, p 121. [118] Ernoul p 59.

the Ibelins hated Agnes and the Lusignans, whom they held responsible for thwarting Baldwin of Ibelin's plans to become king. It is difficult to establish the truth about this, because the Ibelin assertion rests on the uncorroborated and highly romanticised story told by Ernoul. He relates that Baldwin of Ibelin was captured in battle by Saladin in 1179 and that while he was a prisoner-of-war the princess Sibylla wrote to him suggesting that he should marry her when he was released. Baldwin was at that time a widower, and therefore free to contract a new marriage, and, as the events of 1177 had showed, he had already aspired to Sibylla's hand. Moreover, Saladin, according to Ernoul, demanded a king's ransom of 200,000 bezants for him, which adds colour to the story. Baldwin was released on security, but since he would have been ruined if he had attempted to pay the ransom himself, he went to Constantinople to ask the help of the emperor Manuel. It may be supposed that Maria Comnena, who was Baldwin's sister-in-law and the emperor's kinswoman, was behind these negotiations, and that she informed Manuel that Baldwin had every prospect of becoming king of Jerusalem. The emperor, who had always had a strong interest in the crusader states, paid the ransom without raising any difficulty, presumably because he regarded the goodwill of the future king as a sound long-term investment.[119] The improbable element in this story is the account of Sibylla's indiscretion in writing to Baldwin while he was in prison: possibly Baldwin had previously reached some understanding with her, which was generally known, and which would explain both the size of the ransom which Saladin demanded and Manuel's readiness to pay it.

The weakness of Ernoul's account is that it treats the whole matter in terms of personal relationships, whereas the marriage of the king's sister and heir was a matter of state. Sibylla was not free to marry whom she chose: the final decision rested with the king and his advisers, and no source suggests that any formal marriage contract had been made between the princess and Baldwin of Ibelin. In fact Baldwin's hopes were frustrated, but for reasons which had nothing to do with Courtenay antipathy towards the Ibelins. The ascendancy of the king's mother and of his uncle, Jocelyn of Courtenay, was challenged by the only other members of the royal house in Syria. The king's health was known to be deteriorating, and at Easter 1180 his cousins, Raymond III of Tripoli and Bohemond III of Antioch, entered the kingdom, it was

[119] Maria Comnena's influence is implied by Ernoul who relates that Manuel offered to pay Baldwin's ransom *pour l'amour de Balyan son frere*, p 58. See Ernoul pp 56–60.

believed with the intention of choosing a husband for Sibylla, and thus of choosing the next king. Faced by this possible *coup d'état* the king, acting on his mother's advice, used his prerogative and arranged for Sibylla to be married to the constable's brother, Guy of Lusignan, who had recently arrived from the west. Contemporaries considered that this marriage took place with indecent haste, but it served its purpose by rendering any attempt at intervention by Raymond III and Bohemond III futile. But when, later that year, Baldwin of Ibelin returned from Constantinople, he found that Sibylla was already married.[120]

The Ibelins were angered by this, and do not seem to have considered that if Sibylla had not married Guy she would have been forced to marry somebody other than the absent Baldwin of Ibelin by Raymond III and Bohemond III. Their chief grievance was that they had lost a claim to the throne, and their chances of exercising even indirect power at court became even more remote when the king made formal arrangements for the marriage of his younger sister Isabella, Balian of Ibelin's stepdaughter. She was only eight years old, and therefore below the age for canonical marriage, but a marriage contract was drawn up in October 1180 between her and Humphrey IV of Toron, stepson of Reynald of Châtillon, lord of Outre-Jordan, who was a firm adherent of the Courtenays and the Lusignans.[121] Runciman sees in this a conciliatory gesture on the part of the king, intended to heal the division between the Ibelins and the Courtenays,[122] but it is arguable that it was, on the contrary, designed to deprive the Ibelins of the right to choose a husband for this alternative heir to the throne in the event of the king's death. This marriage too, like that of Sibylla, was almost certainly arranged by Agnes of Courtenay who was the chief immediate beneficiary, for by the terms of the marriage settlement Humphrey surrendered to the king the fiefs of Toron and Chastel-neuf which he had inherited from his grandfather[123] and Baldwin IV gave them, either then or later, to his mother.[124] For the first time in her life the king's mother became a great landowner in her own right. William of Tyre's judgement that she was 'a woman who was hateful to God and a shameless money-grabber' therefore seems unduly harsh.[125]

120 WT bk 22, cap 1, *RHC Occ* 1, pp 1062–3.
121 *Ibid* bk 22, cap 5, *RHC Occ* 1, pp 1068–9.
122 Runciman 2, p 424.
123 WT bk 22, cap 5, *RHC Occ* 1, p 1069.
124 [*The travels of*] *Ibn Jubayr*, [trans R. J. C. Broadhurst] (London 1952) p 316.
125 WT bk 22, cap 9, *RHC Occ* 1, p 1078.

But William had reason to hate her, for when the patriarch Amalric died in October 1180 and the canons of the Holy Sepulchre met to choose a successor and submitted two names to the king, Agnes persuaded her son to choose Heraclius, archbishop of Caesaraea, in preference to William of Tyre.[126] Predictably both Ernoul and the *Eracles* attribute Heraclius's success to his having slept with Agnes, but since the *Eracles* places the beginnings of this affair in king Amalric's reign, and attributes Heraclius's first major appointment, that of archdeacon of Jerusalem, to Agnes's favours, the story must be viewed with some mistrust, since the king would surely have been reluctant to bestow office on his former wife's lover. [127] It is simpler to suppose that Agnes as the king's mother, like queen Melisende before her, was merely exercising rights of church patronage in the patriarchal election, and a reason has already been suggested for her dislike of William of Tyre.

Agnes was clearly a remarkably clever woman. Starting from a position of no power at king Amalric's death, she had secured the appointment of her nominees to the chief lay and ecclesiastical offices in the kingdom by 1180: those of seneschal, constable and patriarch; and had arranged the marriages of both the king's sisters to husbands of her own choosing. The territorial power which she and her supporters commanded was equally great: the king held the great cities, Jerusalem, Acre and Tyre; Sibylla and Guy held the counties of Jaffa and Ascalon; Agnes's supporter, Reynald of Châtillon was lord of Outre-Jordan and Hebron; her husband was lord of Sidon; and she held Toron and Chastel-neuf in her own right. Her opponents could not move against her, and when Raymond of Tripoli wished to see the king in 1182 Agnes was powerful enough to refuse to allow him to enter the kingdom.[128]

Her influence was greatest while Baldwin IV was well enough to rule in person, for she was then virtually uncrowned queen. When the king's health grew worse in the summer of 1183 and he appointed Guy of Lusignan as regent Agnes's ascendancy was not threatened, for Sibylla was under her influence and Guy owed his advancement to Agnes. That autumn the princess Isabella, who was now fully of

[126] *Ibid* bk 22, cap 4, *RHC Occ* 1, p 1068, reports the election without comment. Full detail in *Eracles* bk 23, cap 38, *RHC Occ* 2, pp 58–9; Ernoul pp 82–4.

[127] *Eracles* bk 23, cap 39, *RHC Occ* 2, pp 59–60; Ernoul p 82. Heraclius is first mentioned as archdeacon of Jerusalem in a document of 1169, de Rozière no 167, pp 301–5.

[128] She later relented under pressure from members of the high court, WT bk 22, cap 9, *RHC Occ* 1, pp 1077–9.

marriageable age, was sent to Kerak of Moab to be married canonically as well as legally to Humphrey of Toron. The festivities were, however, marred by the arrival of Saladin's army, which laid siege to the castle while the wedding-breakfast was in progress.[129] Baldwin IV meanwhile had been offended by the conduct of Guy of Lusignan as regent and chose the occasion of mustering his host to march to the relief of Kerak to depose Guy from the regency. This was the opportunity for which Agnes's opponents had been waiting, since the king was evidently too ill to live much longer, and as Guy had been excluded the only other serious contender for the regency was Agnes's enemy, the count of Tripoli. With great presence of mind, Agnes advanced a compromise solution which met with general approval. The king should not appoint another regent, but should hold power directly himself: this guaranteed the continuance of Agnes's own ascendancy. But the king should also designate his heir, and exclude Guy of Lusignan from the succession: this conciliated the barons who were hostile to Guy. The heir she suggested was the child Baldwin, whom Sibylla had borne to William of Montferrat: his claim to the throne was impeccable, for he was the king's nephew, but he was also Agnes's grandson, and if he became sole king her position at court would still be assured. The child Baldwin V was duly crowned and the baronage did homage to him.[130] As a final act of humiliation to the boy's stepfather, Guy of Lusignan, and as a conciliatory gesture to the Ibelins, which cost nothing, the boy was carried in the coronation procession by Balian of Ibelin, who was the tallest member of the high court.[131] Only when this was done did the royal army march to the relief of the wedding party at Kerak of Moab.[132]

Agnes's opponents therefore gained no immediate advantage from the disgrace of Guy of Lusignan. The leper king ruled in person for the last years of his reign despite his ill-health; while the Ibelins lost any influence which they may formerly have had over the princess Isabella since Humphry of Toron, acting on his mother's advice, refused to allow his young wife to visit her mother, Maria Comnena.[133] Agnes

[129] Ernoul p 103; WT bk 22, cap 28, *RHC Occ* 1, pp 1124–5.

[130] WT bk 22, cap 29, *RHC Occ* 1, pp 1127–8.

[131] *Les Gestes des Chiprois*, cap 38, *RHC Arm* 2, p 658, which wrongly date this event 1181.

[132] I propose to publish elsewhere my reasons for supposing that the relief of Kerak was delayed by the deposition of Guy de Lusignan. It is implicit in William of Tyre's account, bk 22, caps 28–30, *RHC Occ* 1, pp 1124–30.

[133] *Eracles* bk 25, cap 11, *RHC Occ* 2, p 152.

could not prevent the king from pursuing his vendetta against Guy: he sought, with the help of the patriarch, to have Sibylla's marriage annulled, but Guy and Sibylla foiled this attempt by shutting themselves in Ascalon and refusing to leave even when the king summoned them in person. Since proceedings in a matrimonial case could not be heard in the absence of the contracting parties the case was abandoned.[134] This happened in the early months of 1184. The countess Agnes did not intervene, although she was still alive then, for when Ibn Jubayr, secretary of the moorish governor of Granada, passed near Toron in September of that year he remarked with the tolerant courtesy which characterises moslem writings about Christians in that period: Toron 'belongs to the sow known as queen who is the mother of the pig who is lord of Acre—may God destroy it.'[135]

It is not known whether Agnes was still alive when Baldwin IV died in 1185 and Baldwin V became sole king under the regency of her chief enemy, Raymond of Tripoli. If she was, her influence, although diminished, would not have been at an end, since her brother Jocelyn was the personal guardian of the young king. Her death occurred before the late summer of 1186, for she took no part in the succession crisis which arose then, and on 21 October king Guy acknowledged that count Jocelyn, who was her executor, had satisfactorily discharged the provisions of her will.[136] Agnes was, in many ways, a worthy daughter-in-law of queen Melisende. She lacked, it would seem, her mother-in-law's piety, but she shared her desire for political power and had a more decisive influence on the history of the first kingdom than any other woman except Melisende herself. It was her misfortune to have bad relations with the press: all contemporary sources are hostile to her, but they are not unprejudiced and it is arguable that her influence was not as baneful as the Ibelins and the archbishop of Tyre would like posterity to suppose.

Any hope that the coronation of Baldwin V would resolve the tensions of the kingdom was rendered ineffectual by the young king's death in the late summer of 1186. Raymond of Tripoli had only consented to be regent on the understanding that should Baldwin V die a minor the chief rulers of the west should be asked to adjudicate between the claims of his two sisters to the succession.[137] Accordingly

[134] WT bk 23, cap 1, *RHC Occ* 1, p 1133.
[135] Ibn Jubayr p 316.
[136] Strehlke no 32, p 20.
[137] Ernoul pp 116–17; *Eracles* bk 23, cap 4, *RHC Occ* 2, pp 6–7.

when Baldwin V died Raymond summoned the high court to Nablus to discuss the succession, while Jocelyn of Courtenay, as the dead king's guardian, made arrangements for his burial in Jerusalem. Guy and Sibylla attended the funeral with a strong armed escort with which they garrisoned the city. It is too well-known to need repeating here, how Sibylla, with the help of her supporters, who were, for the most part, the old supporters of Agnes of Courtenay, stole a march on the high court of Nablus and was crowned queen. Two points are worth emphasising: first Reynald of Châtillon gained popular support for Sibylla by affirming that she was *li plus apareissanz et li plus dreis heirs dou roiaume*; secondly that the patriarch crowned Sibylla alone, and that she conferred the crown on Guy. There was no real doubt, following the precedent of Melisende, that Sibylla, as the elder daughter of king Amalric, had the best claim to the throne; equally, there could be no doubt after the ceremony that Guy only held the crown matrimonial.[138]

Humphrey of Toron and the princess Isabella were present at Nablus, and when news reached the high court there of the coronation of Sibylla and Guy the barons wished to crown Humphrey and Isabella in opposition to them. Humphrey wrecked this plan by going to Jerusalem and taking the oath of fealty to Sibylla: he had never liked the Ibelins and, it may be argued, had no wish, in the event of a civil war, to fight against his mother and stepfather, both of whom supported Guy. Once they were deprived of an alternative candidate most of the barons at Nablus made their submission to Sibylla and Guy.[139] But Maria Comnena never forgave her son-in-law for depriving her daughter of the chance to be queen, a chance which would have led to the restoration of Maria herself to a position of power.[140]

Had Sibylla lived in more peaceful times she could have exercised a great deal of power since her husband's authority so patently derived from her. In the first few months of the reign, indeed, she was associated with Guy in some of his acts.[141] But the conquest of Saladin, which occurred within a year of the coronation, brought Guy and Sibylla's joint rule to a speedy end. When Guy was taken prisoner at Hattin, Sibylla was in Jerusalem, where she was joined by her stepmother,

[138] Ernoul pp 130–4; *Eracles* bk 23, cap 17, *RHC Occ* 2, pp 26–9.
[139] *Eracles* bk 23, caps 18–21, *RHC Occ* 2, pp 30–3; Ernoul pp 134–9.
[140] *Eracles* bk 25, cap 11, *RHC Occ* 2, p 152.
[141] Strehlke nos 20, 21, pp 18–19.

Maria Comnena. Both ladies were treated courteously by Saladin: Sibylla was allowed to join her husband, who was in detention at Nablus,[142] and Maria Comnena and her children were allowed to go to Tripoli, despite the fact that Balian of Ibelin failed to keep the oath which he had sworn to the sultan not to take up arms against him when Saladin gave him permission to go to Jerusalem to escort his wife to safety.[143] After Jerusalem had fallen Guy was taken to Damascus, but Sibylla was allowed to join queen Maria in Tripoli.

She stayed there until she was joined by Guy on his release from captivity in 1188.[144] The only city in the kingdom of Jerusalem which remained in Christian hands was Tyre, but when Guy and Sibylla marched there in 1189 they were refused entrance by Conrad of Montferrat, who had taken charge of its defence. After some months spent outside the walls, Guy led the vanguard of the third crusade, newly arrived in Syria, to lay siege to Acre,[145] and among those who followed him there were Humphrey of Toron and the princess Isabella, and Balian of Ibelin and Maria Comnena. It seemed as though former differences had vanished in the face of a common disaster. How illusory this unity was became apparent when Sibylla died of an epidemic in the camp at Acre on 25 July 1190, together with her two little daughters, Alice and Maria.[146]

Guy's enemies, and there were many who blamed him for the defeat of Hattin, claimed that as he only had the crown matrimonial his kingship ended with the death of his wife. The only other candidate for the throne was the princess Isabella, but her husband Humphrey was a friend of Guy's and unwilling to set himself up as king in opposition to him. Conrad of Montferrat, hero of the defence of Tyre, was an ambitious man who wanted to become king, and who found a ready ally in Maria Comnena. She deposed before the archbishop of Pisa, the pope's legate, and the bishop of Beauvais, that her daughter's marriage was invalid because she had only been eight when it was contracted, and had been forced into it by Baldwin IV against her wishes. Isabella, who was happily married and had no wish to be separated from her husband, was browbeaten into agreeing with this

[142] Ernoul p 185.

[143] *Ibid* pp 186–7; *Eracles* bk 23, cap 46, *RHC Occ* 2, pp 68–71.

[144] Ernoul p 252; *Eracles* bk 24, cap 11, *RHC Occ* 2, pp 120–1.

[145] *Eracles* bk 24, caps 13, 14, *RHC Occ* 2, pp 123–5; Ernoul pp 256–7.

[146] Sibylla had borne Guy four daughters. It is not clear whether they all died at the same time as their mother or whether two had predeceased her: Ernoul p 267; *Eracles* bk 25, cap 10, and see also variant readings C and G, *RHC Occ* 2, pp 151, 154.

statement by her strong-willed mother. The legate annulled the marriage; Isabella was then crowned, and immediately restored to Humphrey his fiefs of Toron and Chaste-neuf (an academic piece of justice since they were in enemy occupied territory); then she was married to Conrad.[147] Maria Comnena had had to wait for sixteen years to see her daughter made queen, but her patience was finally rewarded. As her conduct in the matter of the annulment shows, there was some truth in her opponents' view that she was a ruthless and scheming woman.[148]

Maria bore Balian of Ibelin four children: John, who became the 'old lord' of Beirut; Philip of Ibelin, who later became *bailli* of Cyprus; Margaret, who married successively Hugh of Tiberias, and Walter III of Caesaraea; and Helvis, who, ironically, married Reynald of Sidon, former husband of the queen's old rival, Agnes of Courtenay. When Balian died in about 1194[149] Maria did not remarry. She continued to take an active part in forwarding the interests of her family: in 1208 she helped to arrange the marriage of her grand-daughter Alice to king Hugh I of Cyprus.[150] She apparently died in the summer of 1217, for in October of that year Hugh I of Cyprus confirmed the endowment made by her son, Philip of Ibelin, for masses to be said in Nicosia cathedral for the repose of the soul of his mother *inclite recordationis*.[151] She had lived to see her great-grand-daughter, Isabella II, become queen of Jerusalem, and all the kings of Jerusalem and Cyprus, together with many of the higher nobility in both states in the thirteenth century, were descended from her.[152] By the time of her death she was the sole survivor of any consequence from the first kingdom of Jerusalem. She had occupied a central position in the state for twenty years before its fall. Perhaps the reputation which her son, the 'old lord' of Beirut, acquired as a repository of knowledge about the laws and customs of the first kingdom owed much to the memory of his long-lived mother.

[147] *Eracles* bk 25, caps 11, 12, *RHC Occ* 2, pp 151–4; *Itinerarium* bk 1, cap 63, pp 119–22; Ernoul pp 267–8 does not mention Maria's involvement.

[148] See note 115 above.

[149] He is last recorded in a document of that year, CGOH 1, no 954.

[150] Alice was the daughter of Maria's eldest child, queen Isabella, by her marriage to count Henry of Troyes. G. Hill, *A History of Cyprus,* 4 vols (Cambridge 1940–52). 2, p 75.

[151] L. de Mas Latrie, *Histoire de l'Ile de Chypre sous le règne des princes de la Maison de Lusignan,* 3 vols (Paris 1852–61) 3, pp 608–9.

[152] See the genealogical table at the end of Runciman 3.

Maria Comnena had great resilience and considerable powers of adaptation. She became queen of Jerusalem because that state needed the alliance of the powerful Byzantine empire. After 1180 Byzantium had ceased to be a world power, and before her death it had almost ceased to exist at all as a result of the fourth crusade. The kingdom of Jerusalem likewise had dwindled into the kingdom of Acre, yet Maria's influence increased rather than diminished under these adverse conditions. Like Agnes of Courtenay and queen Melisende, Maria Comnena had a central interest in power, though she was more concerned with the realities and less with the external trappings of power than they had been, and in consequence was more devious in her methods of attaining it.

All eight queens who reigned in the first kingdom made a serious impact on its development: this is true even of those of them who were a-political, like Theodora, whose dowry strengthened the inadequate finances of the state, and who was the personal link by which the Byzantine alliance was forged, which held the threat of Nureddin in check. Further investigation would probably show that women were equally influential at other social levels in this outwardly male-dominated feudal state.

University of Nottingham

ROBERT OF ARBRISSEL: *PROCURATOR MULIERUM*

by JACQUELINE SMITH

AT the close of the eleventh century the region of north west France experienced a revival in popularity of the eremitical movement.[1] Men and women seeking retirement from the world, withdrew to the seclusion of forests and wastelands where, dwelling in crudely constructed huts[2] and living only on small provision, they devoted themselves to a life of voluntary poverty and simple piety. Robert of Arbrissel provides an example of one following the eremitical life.[3] Having retired to the forest of Craon he lived under conditions of extreme austerity, seeking solitude and dedicating himself completely to the contemplation of God.[4] While still practising his austerities in the forest he began his mission of preaching and very soon gathered around him people eager to hear his message.[5] It is not the purpose of this paper to discuss the influences and personal motivations which were at work in determining Robert's career as a hermit and wandering preacher, aspects which I have examined elsewhere,[6] but to provide an analysis of the impact Robert's career may have had on others, and on women in particular.

Women formed a large proportion of the vast crowds which

[1] For discussions on the wider implications of the growth of the eremitical life at this time see *L'eremitismo* [*in occident nei secoli XI e XII*], Pubblicazioni dell' Universita cattolica del Sacro Cuore, *Miscellanea del centro di studi medioevali*, 4 (Milan 1965); [L'] Raison and [R.] Niderst, ['Le mouvement érémitique dans l'Ouest de la France à la fin du XIe siècle et au début du XIIe siècle'], *Annales de Bretagne* 55 (Rennes 1948). North west France was not unique in experiencing this phenomenon, see J. B. Mahn, *L'ordre cistercien et son gouvernement 1098–1265* (Paris 1945) pp 26–8 for a similar movement in northern Italy. For the causes of the revival see [J.] Smith, [unpubl MA] diss, University of London (1977).

[2] *Vita Bernardi*, *PL* 172 (1895) col 1381; [L.] Gougaud, *Ermites et Reclus*: [*ètudes sur d'anciennes formes de vie religieuse*] (Ligugé 1928).

[3] On Robert see J. von Walter, *Die ersten Wanderprediger Frankreichs* (Leipzig 1903 and 1906); R. Niderst, *Robert d'Arbrissel et les origines de l'ordre de Fontevrault* (Rodez1952); Smith, diss.

[4] [Baudry], *Vita* [*Roberti*] *I*, *ASB* February III (1658) 10, 11. On the practise of contemplation as a means to perfection see L. Gougaud, 'La Theoria dans la Spiritualité Medievale', *Revue d'ascétique et de mystique* 3 (Toulouse 1922).

[5] *Vita* 1: 10.

[6] Smith, diss.

accompanied Robert,[7] and consequently, presented him with a number of immediate problems. Groups of men and women living in irregular and unstable communities without the guidance and discipline of an established rule of life were viewed with suspicion by the church authorities, particularly when these communities included among their members prostitutes, harlots and others of ill-repute.[8] Such a heterogeneous group of followers rendered Robert vulnerable to severe criticism, which was forthcoming in the letters of Marbod, bishop of Rennes, and Geoffrey of Vendôme,[9] and after which he had no alternative but to accept the ultimate solution: institutionalisation. Always anxious to avoid scandal[10] he sought a suitable refuge, separated the men from the women and initiated the construction of the first simple dwellings of the house of Fontevrault.[11] His foundation was an immediate success, and this inspired a popular view of Robert as *procurator mulierum*, a protector of women and a guardian of their interests.[12] It is the purpose of this paper to examine this view and see how far the term *procurator mulierum* can be justified, to consider the depth of Robert's concern for the women among his followers, and to determine whether he was induced to make certain decisions by the force of circumstances.

Robert of Arbrissel's work with women has, in the past, received a variety of interpretations. In the mid-nineteenth century, Jules Michelet, in his voluminous *Histoire de France*, described Robert as a romantic hero who, working within a movement which Michelet

[7] *Vita* 1: 16, 17, 19; Letter of Marbod to Robert, *PL* 171 (1895) cols 1481–2; Letter of Geoffrey of Vendôme to Robert, *PL* 157 (1858) cols 181–3.

[8] *Ibid.* It is interesting to compare Robert's earlier career with that of a contemporary, Henry of Lausanne, who was in appearance pursuing a similar career and attracting vast crowds, including women. See R. I. Moore *The Birth of popular Heresy* (London 1975) pp 30–60.

[9] Marbod, *PL* 172 cols 1480–6; Geoffrey, *PL* 157 cols 181–4. On the letters of Geoffrey and Marbod see [J.] Petigny, [Robert d'Arbrissel et] Geoffroi [de Vendôme], *BEC*, 3 ser 5 (1853/4).

[10] *Vita* 1: 10, 16.

[11] *Ibid* 16, 17.

[12] The most adamant in this belief was [J.] Michelet, [Histoire de France] (Paris 1870) 1, pp 285–6. Sharing this romantic view of Robert's activities is R. Bezzola, *Les origines et la formation de la littérature courtoise en Occident 500–1200*, (Paris 1944–63) 2, 2, p 286. Other historians who view Robert's career in connection with the problem of women are Grundmann, and to a lesser extent, [E.] Werner, [*Pauperes Christi*] (Leipzig 1956).

called the *restauration de la femme*, endeavoured to remove the stigma of 'the dangerous Eve', a term attached to women by certain groups who considered them to be the source of all evil.[13] The views of J. de Petigny follow similar lines to those of his contemporary, Michelet, although they are expressed in less romantic terms.[14] Nevertheless, he still recognised in Robert's activities an attempt to raise women from their low status believing that Robert saw in them the emblem of redemption of human kind and the personification of the Virgin Mary. Unlike Michelet, however, he made no attempt to seek connections with a wider movement, but held the opinion that Robert worked independently, inspired only by a 'feeling of pious and tender compassion for the female sex'.[15] In more recent times there has been much research into the status of, and the problems encountered by, women in the middle ages, and many historians have chosen to examine Robert of Arbrissel's career in this context.[16] This has resulted in the presentation of Robert as a protector of women, who, against a background of social instability, shifting allegiances and spiritual upheaval,[17] consciously worked to safeguard their interests and provide a retreat for those wishing to retire from the world. Simultaneously, a different theory has been expounded suggesting that Robert had an ulterior motive in his concern for women. Based on the evidence of two accusatory letters[18] it has been claimed that Robert was seeking a form of martyrdom through his extreme and rigorous practices, in which women played an important role as the instruments of temptation of the flesh.[19] This theory has been developed a stage further by Dominique Iogna-Prat who concludes that the *mulierum consortia*, along with the other ascetic practices, was an essential part of the penitential design, and that it was within this framework that Robert overcame

[13] Michelet pp 285–6. For a discussion on virginity and woman as the source of evil see J. Bugge, *Virginitas: An Essay in the History of a Medieval Ideal* (The Hague 1975) esp caps 1, 2.

[14] Petigny, *Geoffroi* p 14.

[15] *Ibid.*

[16] Grundmann pp 40–50; Werner pp 53–72.

[17] [J.-M.] Bienvenu, 'Robert d'Arbrissel et la fondation de Fontevraud 1101', *Cahiers d'histoire* 20 (Quebec 1975) discusses the social and economic implications surrounding the foundation of a religious house; see esp pp 227–33. For a more detailed discussion of Anjou at this time see Bienvenu, 'Pauvreté, misères et charité en Anjou aux XIe et XIIe siècles', *Moyen Age*, 72 (1966), 73 (1967).

[18] Marbod, *PL* 172 cols 1480–6; Geoffrey, *PL* 157 cols 181–4 and Petigny, *Geoffroi*.

[19] L. Gougaud, 'Mulierum Consortia: Étude sur le syneisaktisme chez les ascètes celtiques', *Eriu: Journal of the School of Irish Learning*, 9–10 (Dublin 1921–3).

temptation and thereby proved that he was truly 'dead to his sex.'[20] All these interpretations reveal three common factors; that there is a tendency to regard Robert's whole career as being centred upon his concern for women; that much emphasis is placed on the presence of large numbers of prostitutes among his followers, and that there is a relative silence on the activities of Robert's contemporaries, implying that he was unique in the pursuit of his vocation. However, a re-examination of the evidence suggests a reconsideration of these interpretations.

At the time of Robert's decision to enter the forest of Craon in order to lead the life of an ascetic, north-western France was experiencing a growth in the revival of the eremitical movement. The harsh solitudes of the forests and woodlands found in the region of Brittany, lower Normandy, Maine and Anjou provided a popular retreat,[21] and the rapid establishment of cells and hermitages earned the region the title of the 'new Thebaid'.[22] Just as the hermits of fourth-century Egypt found that their search for peace and solitude in the desert would inevitably be broken by those wishing to hear their teachings or share their experiences, so the ascetics of France found themselves surrounded by large crowds of men and women who wished to join them in the forest and strive with them to attain the ultimate goal of perfection. It was not practical, however, that such large numbers of followers should continue without a degree of organisation and administration,[23] the hermits, therefore, took upon themselves the responsibility of providing some form of shelter, nourishment and discipline.[24] In this way the foundation of a number of religious houses was occasioned,[25] many of which attempted to make some provision for the inclusion of women. One of the most renowned of these foundations is undoubtedly Fontevrault, but Robert of Arbrissel was not alone in his achievement. Vitalis of Mortain also

[20] D. Iogna-Prat, 'La femme dans la perspective penitentielle des ermites du Bas-Maine (fin XIe début XIIe siècles)', *Revue d'histoire de la spiritualité* 53 (Toulouse 1977) p 61.

[21] R. Musset, *Le Bas-Maine* (Paris 1917) pp 231–2; Werner pp 31 *seq.*

[22] For evidence of the existence of hermitages see *Vita Bernardi*, *PL* 172 col 1380. Raison and Niderst, pp 5–7; [Abbe] Angot, *Dictionnaire historique*, [*topographique et biographique de la Mayenne*] 3 vols (Laval 1901–2), see articles under Alleaume, Bernard of Tiron, Aubert, Habit, Fontaine-Gèrard, Trinité.

[23] The church authorities viewed such activity with suspicion.

[24] Gougaud, *Ermites et Reclus*, discusses in detail the organisation established by the hermits themselves; see also Raison and Niderst p 21.

[25] Raison and Niderst p. 6 For a detailed list of houses established in the region see Angot, *Dictionnaire historique* as listed in note 22 above.

welcomed women among his followers and in 1105 he built a retreat for them at a place called Prise-aux-Nonnes.[26] After some dispute he moved the women to the gates of Mortain, sometime around 1120, and established them in the convent of The Trinity at a place called Neufbourg. The convent was later given the name of La Blanche because of the colour of their habits.[27] Norbert of Xanten was similarly occupied with the housing of women and he established at Prémontré, in 1121, a monastery/convent where the women were subjected to a severe discipline and were primarily responsible for the care of the poor and sick.[28] In the valley of Etival-en-Charnie Alleaume established a double monastery in 1109. In the same year Salomon built an abbey at Noiyseau to house his women, and in 1112 Ralph de la Futaie founded St Sulpice near Rennes for the same purpose.[29] Although Fontevrault precedes these foundations in date by a few years, it is clear from the number of female houses and double monasteries which were erected, that Robert of Arbrissel was not alone in recognising the difficulties which surrounded women who sought a religious life in retreat. It was a problem common to all hermits, not to Robert alone.

The extent to which Robert concerned himself with the question of provision and care for women has, however, been much overestimated. The foundation of Fontevrault took place in the year 1100 when Robert was already forty years of age[30] and it is of some significance to this discussion that he had led a substantial career prior to his alleged interest in women. Robert, a native of Brittany, went to Paris to study during the pontificate of Gregory VII (1073–1086), and while at Paris he must have been ordained because after his return to Rennes he is referred to as an archpriest.[31] He served bishop Sylvester in this role for four years and played a leading part in attempting to rid the church of corruption and abuse. His activities won him many enemies

[26] *Gal C* 11 (Paris 1870) Instr p 108.

[27] Raison and Niderst p 38; *Gal C* 11 Instr p 111.

[28] Werner p 56; Grundmann pp 44–50; U. Berliére, *Les monasteres doubles aux XIIe et XIIIe siècles*, Academie de Belgique Classe de Lettres et des Sciences morales et politiques, 18 (Brussels 1931) pp 22–3.

[29] On Etival-en-Charnie see extensive discussion by Dom Guilloreau, 'L'abbaye d'Etival-en-Charnie et ses abbesses, 1109–1790', *Revue historique et Archéologique du Maine* 49 (Le Mans 1901), For brief histories of the smaller houses see Raison and Niderst pp 35 *seq*.

[30] For a discussion on the controversial subject of Robert of Arbrissel's date of birth see Smith, diss p 9.

[31] *Vita* 1: 5, 9.

and he finally fled to Angers where he established himself in the cathedral school and continued his studies. During the two years he spent at Angers he became renowned for his persistence in ascetic practices and was already beginning to earn a reputation as an orator. Robert eventually entered the forest of Craon where he began his career as a hermit and wandering preacher. In 1096, at the age of thirty six, he established his first foundation, the Augustinian house of La Roe, and in the same year he was requested to preach before the pope, Urban II, at the dedication ceremony of the church of St Nicholas. It was at this ceremony that he was, apparently, awarded the honour of *Seminiverbium*, the permission to preach the word of God.[32] A further four years were to elapse before he established the first dwellings which were to form the foundation of his house for women, Fontevrault.

It can be seen, therefore, that it was not Robert's original intention to establish a permanent house for women, but that the need to do so was thrust upon him by the force of circumstance. He was, like all the other hermits and wandering preachers, concerned for the welfare, both physical and spiritual, of all his followers, whether male or female, rich or poor, good or bad, and felt that he had a responsibility to provide for them all.[33] The various dwellings which constitute the house of Fontevrault testify to this. A building dedicated to the Virgin Mary housed the virgins, widows and matrons; penitents were placed under the guidance of St Mary Magdalene, the sick lived in a house dedicated to St Lazarus and the men were placed in a house dedicated to John the Evangelist, an act symbolic of the subservient role men played at Fontevrault.[34] Baudry, the author of the first life of Robert, emphasises the heterogeneous nature of the community of Fontevrault, which resulted from Robert's reluctance to turn anybody away.[35] Despite his initial involvement in the establishment and organisation of Fontevrault, Robert was not to be tied to his foundation.

[32] There is some dispute as to what this honour actually entailed in Robert's case. It has been understood by many historians that he had been given permission to preach the first crusade but there is no evidence supporting this claim, neither is there any document in existence to certify pope Urban II's bestowal of honour on Robert. However, it appears that permission to preach was commonly awarded to orators of great renown, Norbert of Xanten and Vitalis of Mortain were both similarly honoured.

[33] *Vita* 1: 16, 18.

[34] Petigny, *Geoffroi* p 9. It has been suggested that Robert subjected men to the obedience of women after the example of John the Evangelist, who after the death of Jesus, constantly attached himself to the Virgin Mary.

[35] *Vita* 1: 16, 18, 19 and 22 refer to the heterogeneity of the crowds. *Vita* 1: 20, 22 and 24 describe the various dwellings and how the members of the community were divided.

He had been granted a commission to preach and this was to remain his primary concern throughout the rest of his life. After establishing a house of canons at La Roe he had detached himself from the responsibility of administration and with the consent of the local bishop 'went away freely, that he could be free to preach'.[36] Again, having supervised the organisation of Fontevrault, Baudry informs us that 'he did not wish, nor was he able to assist with works, for he had to preach to many nations'. He, therefore, selected Hersende, mother-in-law of the lord of Montsoreau, to govern the community in his absence.[37] Once again he had freed himself from the responsibility of administration in order to continue his cherished mission of preaching throughout regions 'neighbouring and distant'.[38] The depth of Robert's concern for the women and for the house he had established is therefore to be questioned.

After the initial foundation of Fontvrault the character of the house changed markedly and rapidly. In the years immediately prior to its foundation, and for a short while afterwards, Robert had been surrounded by a mixed group which found shelter in simple huts and basic sustenance from the land. Very little is known about Robert's followers at this stage apart from the fact that this communal living of men and women inspired Marbod of Rennes to compose his long condemnatory letter.[39] It is this letter which provides the basis for those who favour the opinion that Robert fulfilled the role of *procurator mulierum*, but it is important to emphasise that Robert's followers consisted at all times of both men and women, and that the scandal lay in both sexes living together; Robert's fault was in allowing this to happen. Marbod's condemnations concerning women were simply that he should beware of encouraging prostitutes and harlots among his followers.[40] Furthermore, Marbod's criticisms were less concerned with the problem of women than with Robert's whole way of life.[41] He

[36] *Ibid* I: 15.

[37] *Ibid* I: 21.

[38] *Ibid.*

[39] Marbod, *PL* 172 cols 1480–6.

[40] *Ibid* cols 1481–2.

[41] There was at this time a controversy concerning the merits of the eremitical life as opposed to the monastic. Marbod had made similar accusations in letters to a hermit Engelger, the fear being that once freed from the stable, secure community of a monastery, temptation from the secular world would lead to corruption and consequently damnation. The argument is pursued in an article by G. Morin, 'Rainaud l'ermite et Ives de Chartres. Un épisode de la crise du cenobitisme au XIe siècle', *RB* 40 (1928) pp 99–115. Peter Damian was an advocate of the merits of the eremitic life but

criticised his costume, the content of his preaching, the fact that he led parishioners away from their priests and that he had abandoned his first establishment of La Roe.[42] Marbod did not condemn Robert solely for his alleged activities with women but was bitterly opposed to Robert's form of the eremitical life and the dangers it involved.[43] Details from this letter, together with those from Baudry's account, reveal that the early groups were of both sexes, consisting of a variety of people, but drawn, in all probability, mainly from the lower echelons in society.[44] With the establishment of a regular institution the whole character of this gathering changed. The house was quickly adopted by members of the aristocracy who desired to show their generosity as patrons, and as the abbey grew larger and wealthier through this generosity, so it became an even greater attraction to widows, spinsters and younger daughters, all of aristocratic background, who wished to spend the remainder of their lives in retreat from the world. From the simple, crude constructions which had sufficed in the early years, and which became unattractive because of their insecurity, instability and non-conformity, grew an abbey of great complexity, marked by its respectability, traditionalism and aristocratic character.

After selecting Hersende as a woman capable of governing and administering the house, Robert increasingly withdrew from the supervision of Fontevrault. From evidence in charters and the occasional chronicle reference, it seems Robert spent the remainder of his life wandering and preaching throughout the provinces of France, returning to Fontevrault at intervals to preach or impart some advice to the sisters he had left in charge. His role is therefore far from being adequately described as a *procurator mulierum*. It is unlikely that Robert saw himself as a male patron, and there is no evidence that he consciously set out to solve the problems of women seeking help and advice. However, he does appear to have had a certain affinity with some women of nobility, the most notable being Ermengarde, duchess

---

was also aware of the need for sound preparation before becoming a solitary, however, he was always prepared to admit recruits direct to the life of the hermitage rather than via the possibly harmful interlude of cenobitic preparation. See P. McNulty, *St. Peter Damian: Selected Writings on the Spiritual Life* (London 1959) pp 33–47.

[42] Marbod, *PL* 172 col 1486.

[43] It appears Geoffrey of Vendôme was more vehemently opposed to women and the dangers involved. Petigny, *Geoffroi* p 14.

[44] As with the majority of contemporary histories it is the members of the higher classes in society who are fortunate enough to have their names and lives recorded. Information on people of lower status is rarely forthcoming.

of Brittany and daughter of Fulk le Rechin, count of Anjou.[45] Following the failure of her first marriage to William VII, count of Poitiers, she became the wife of Alan Fergent, count of Brittany. However, after a number of years Ermengarde fled to Fontevrault to seek help in obtaining a dissolution of her marriage, and it was the disappointing decision of the church authorities that there were no grounds for a divorce which inspired Robert to compose the *Sermo* advising her to submit to the church's ruling and to continue to fulfil her role as a mother and a princess. He exhorted her to have patience and courage and to pass her time in prayer and devotion, and he incorporated into his *Sermo* a short rule of life compatible with her role in the secular world. As she had much to occupy her time she should keep her prayers short, but she should hear the canonical hours and the hours of the holy Virgin every day. He exhorted her to love voluntary poverty, and in the midst of all the riches and honours surrounding her she should remember that she was a poor mendicant and that the Lord would take care of her, further, and of great importance, she should have care to be merciful to the poor and give alms. In her daily life Ermengarde was advised to be moderate in all things, but to be sure to eat, drink and sleep sufficient to support the body from fatigue, because, as Robert explained to her, to kill the flesh was to kill the soul which lives within it.[46] Unfortunately, this is the only document of Robert's own composition that has survived, and it is, therefore, impossible to say whether this intimacy with Ermengarde was exceptional.

With the change in character of Fontvrault Robert out of necessity found he had more dealings with women of aristocratic background, but even then his involvement was strictly limited to that of adviser and spiritual guide, the administration of Fontvrault being firmly placed in the hands of a capable abbess. In Petronilla Robert had found the ideal head to govern his house. A remarkable lady of great determination, she energetically defended Fontevrault from all hostile attacks and bitterly fought to defend its rights.[47] The administration was given over entirely to her, thus enabling Robert to pursue his peregrinations throughout the countryside. His connections with

[45] For an account of her life see Petigny, 'Lettre [inédite de Robert d'Arbrissel a la Comtesse Ermengarde]', *BEC* 3 ser, 5 (1853/4). The *Sermo* is translated and edited pp 225–35.

[46] Petigny, 'Lettre' pp 225–35.

[47] For an example of Petronilla's determination in safeguarding Fontevrault's rights see J. de la Martinière, 'Une falsification de document au commencement du XIIe siècle', *Moyen Age*, 2 ser 17 (1911) pp 1–45.

Fontevrault were not severed completely. He and Petronilla communicated frequently, probably in matters of a spiritual or administrative nature, but towards the end of Robert's life they shared a close companionship. The abbess accompanied him on his last journey, was at his side when he died,[48] and was responsible for the recording of his life, for which she commissioned Baudry.[49] As with Ermengarde, Robert fulfilled the role of friend and adviser, but through Petronilla, he may have had an influence on decisions made concerning his foundation. Nevertheless, it is clear from his mobility and long absences that he had no desire to be tied or burdened with the duties of organising a growing foundation or to take on the responsibilities of safeguarding its rights.

From the evidence available it is immediately clear that while Fontevrault came to enjoy success and popularity, Robert, its founder, had played a comparatively small part in this achievement. His original design had been to search for solitude, aiming for a perfection which could only be attained in the eremitic life, and his mission was solely to preach the word of God to all peoples. The foundation of Fontevrault, as with La Roe, was Robert's rational solution to a problem which increasingly caused him embarrassment and became a hindrance to his original design and his mission of preaching. This does not deny his awareness of the problems of religious women amid the social circumstances and pressures of his time, but he certainly did not consider them a priority in his chosen field of work. *Procurator mulierum* is not, it may justifiably be argued, applicable to Robert of Arbrissel, but an element of incidental and accidental success in this role can be attributed to him in that his foundation, although its character changed remarkably after his death, continued to flourish as the 'pearl of abbeys' for many centuries.[50]

University of London
Westfield College

[48] Andrew, *Vita Roberti II ASB* February III (1658) pp 608–16.
[49] *Vita* 1: 1–3, the prologue is addressed to Petronilla.
[50] Raison and Niderst p 33.

CHRISTINA OF MARKYATE

by CHRISTOPHER J. HOLDSWORTH

IN the middle ages any man, or woman, who wished to discipline themselves according to the principles developed in the early days of monasticism in Egypt had to withdraw from the world. This was true whether the experiment of asceticism was to be pursued in community or in isolation, as hermit, anchorite or recluse. Yet however extreme was the degree of withdrawal from contact with society, the world affected, and was affected by, the one who withdrew. This general thesis is amply illustrated by the surviving evidence for the life of Christina of Markyate who first spent some sixteen years as a recluse and then perhaps as many as thirty five as a nun, after her profession at St Albans around 1131. In one way or another she renounced the world for over fifty of her allotted three score years and ten.

Surviving evidence about her can be divided into four categories, three of considerable complexity and solidity, one restricted to a single record, but each throwing light on her position in society. In the first place is the considerable body of evidence which shows that at the place where she first settled with the hermit, Roger around 1118, a community had sprung up which became formally recognized as a priory of nuns dependent on St Albans by at least 1145.[1] Secondly, there is one book, the so-called St Albans psalter which was almost certainly made for her use.[2] Thirdly are the historical works written within or soon after her life-time which mention her, of which by far the most important is the anonymous *Vita* preserved in a unique fourteenth-century manuscript which was much damaged in the Cottonian library fire, and last of all is the entry on the pipe roll of 1155-6 which records that during that year Henry II ordered the payment of fifty shillings for Christina's support.[3] All of this evidence has been discussed before,

[1] *Early Charters* [*of the Cathedral Church of St. Paul's London*], ed M. Gibbs, *CSer*, 3 ser 58 (1939) nos 154, 156, pp 119–22. Both are reproduced in *The St. Albans Psalter* (see below) plates 169, 172.

[2] [*The St. Albans*] *Psalter*, ed Otto Pächt, C. R. Dodwell, Francis Wormald (1960). besides being greatly indebted to the work of these editors I owe much to the stimulation and erudition of a paper by P. R. L. Brown, 'The Rise and Function of the Holy Man in Late Antiquity', *JRS* 61 (1971), pp 80–101. I have also been helped by the comments of Professor Brooke.

[3] [*The*] *Life* [*of Christina of Markyate*], ed and translated C. H. Talbot (Oxford 1959);

most notably by the editors of the psalter, and by Talbot, the editor of the *Vita*, but it is my hope to discover from it some new insights, none of which would be possible were it not for their pioneering work. The evidence stimulates this re-evaluation because of its intrinsic interest, but more especially because it concerns a woman. Probably far fewer women than men may have been religious, but the evidence in our hands about even the external life of their communities or of isolated individuals is extremely sparse, whilst that which sheds light on the life within those communities, or of the inner life of individuals, is rare to a degree.

Markyate priory is in some respects the most solid evidence which can be connected with Christina; as a direct result of her life a community came into existence which survived until the dissolution.[4] Generations of nuns must have looked back on her as their foundress and patron, and perhaps for some time at least considered her a saint. Yet when she first went to stay with the hermit Roger around 1118 the idea of founding anything must have been far from her mind.[5] Her main intention was to hide from her husband who still hoped to track her down and persuade her to live with him as a married woman. There she stayed for the rest of her life, apart from two years or so, say 1122–3, when she had to leave the hermitage after Roger died. She was not without invitations to move permanently elsewhere; Thurstan, archbishop of York, and keen promoter of the religious life, tried to persuade her to become superior of the house for nuns which he founded in York, and when she refused, offered to send her to the great Cluniac priory at Marcigny, or to the more recently-founded double house at Fontevrault. But she, we are told, was devoted to the memory of Roger and to St Albans where he had been a monk, where he was buried, and with whose abbot, Geoffrey she had already formed a friendship.[6] So it was at St Albans that she made some form of monastic profession, perhaps in 1131, and became formally dependent on that community, as she had been informally hitherto, through her association with Roger. Roger during his lifetime had been the leader of a group of five hermits who lived with him, but they seem to have

Gesta Abbatum Monasterii Sancti Albani, ed T. H. Riley, *RS* (1867) pp 98–105; *Pipe Roll 2–4 Henry II,* ed Joseph Hunter (Record Commission 1884) p 22.

[4] There is a brief account in *VCH Bedfordshire,* 1 pp 358–61; see also *MA* 3 pp 370–3, and Tanner, *Notitia Monastica* (Cambridge 1787) under Bedfordshire cap 14.

[5] I have adopted Talbot's dating of the main events, of which he gives a useful summary) *Life,* pp 14–15.

[6] *Life* p 126; Donald Nicholl, *Thurstan Archbishop of York* (York 1964) cap 7, esp pp 195–9.

had no formal connection with each other.[7] Neither the *Vita*, nor any other record, help us to trace the process by which Christina gathered round her a community; there must have a been a priest who visited to celebrate mass from time to time from the start, and the life mentions her maidens before it tells of her profession.[8] By the end of the incomplete *Life* she is surrounded by a community of nuns who have a church, a small cloister and some other buildings.[9] The only clearly dated stage in this process is the earliest surviving agreement between the abbot of St Albans and the canons of St Paul's, London, about the land on which the priory was built in 1145, the year, too, in which Alexander the Magnificent, bishop of Lincoln consecrated the priory church.[10] So, long before Christina's death a properly constituted regular nunnery had grown up around the place where she had been a recluse.

No doubt she was happy with this development, since she seems to have wished to join an established nunnery from very tender years.[11] Much later, after she had been made to go through a ceremony of marriage, she reasserted her determination under circumstances not without their bizarre side. Her parents had, they believed, succeeded in making her drunk at a feast of the guild merchant in Huntingdon, and her husband, Burhred, that night managed to get into her bedroom. Everyone expected that the marriage would be consummated, but Burhred (for whom one feels some sympathy in the whole story) found Christina sitting sober on the bed where she regaled him with the story of St Cecilia and her husband, Valerian, and finally suggested that they should live chastely together and after three or four years agree each to enter the religious life.[12] She was, of course, unable to do this without his consent, and needed besides some form of a dowry if she were to be accepted by a regular community. So, for her, the sixteen years as a recluse may have been something of a second best.

But the change from hermitage to organised community was one which was taking place in many parts of England and indeed across the whole western Christian world during her life-time. Near to Christina, for instance, a group of recluses living at Eywood, turned into a priory at Sopwell, further away monks in Yorkshire absorbed a hermit

[7] *Life* p 108.
[8] *Ibid* pp 128, 146.
[9] *Ibid* pp 120, 152, 178.
[10] *Early Charters.*
[11] Her vow of virginity seems to have been made in her early teens, *Life* pp 36, 38.
[12] *Ibid* pp 48 *seq.*

community at Kirkstall, and in Europe from a group of hermits in the woods near Langres, sprang the monastery of Molesmes.[13] Genicot has called this process the slide to cenobitism and usefully distinguished two complementary sides to it.[14] As a hermit, or recluse, attracted others to join him by the force of his personality there came inevitably a need to supply both the spiritual and economic needs of the community. What a visiting priest could supply occasionally to one or two, needed to be provided on a more regular basis, likewise a larger group needed agreed rules by which to organise their life, and so some form of spiritual hierarchy was needed. On the other hand, whereas a single hermit, or two or three, could grow most of their own requirements on a scrap of waste land, this was not so easy for a larger group. Failing the possibility of living on alms, which would have meant in the conditions of the twelfth century, basing the community on a town and so making withdrawal from the world that much more difficult, the group had to seek gifts of land or revenues if they were to survive. There were, then, almost inevitable needs within a growing hermit or recluse group which would turn it to an organised community. From outside there were pressures too, for many a hermit had been a monk in community, as St Benedict himself had envisaged could be the case in his day, and their parent communities kept some sort of an eye over them.[15] Such was the case with Roger, Christina's teacher and supporter, and it is not surprising that she should become in turn friends with the abbot, professed at the monastery and ultimately head of a priory dependent on it. The gains to the monastery 'absorbing' such a community may have been more spiritual than economic where the hermit or recluse had created no cult, left no shrine. Godric at Finchale, for example, may have meant a real material gain to the cathedral monastery at Durham which finally turned his cell into a priory, but Christina's group must have been a very different affair.[16] Certainly the hints are clear in the *Vita* and in the *Gesta Abbatum* that some at St Albans resented the amount which the abbot spent on their

[13] *Ibid* p 29; *MA* 5 pp 530–1; Knowles *MO* p 198.

[14] Léopold Genicot, 'L'érémitisme du XI siècle dans son contexte économique et social', *L'Eremitismo* [*in Occidente nei Secoli XI e XII*], *Miscellanea del Centro di Studi Medioevali* 4, Contributi—serie terza, varia 4 (Milan 1965) pp 45–69, esp p 66 'L'anachorétisme a ainsi glissé fréquemment vers le cénobitisme . . .'

[15] *Reg*[*ula S.*] *Ben*[*edicti*], cap 1. *L'Eremitismo* has examples from all over Europe, and a full chapter by Hubert Dauphin on England.

[16] For Godric see principally Reginald of Durham, *Libellus* [*de Vita et Miraculis S. Godrici Heremitae de Finchale*], ed J. Stevenson, *SS* 20 (1847). Talbot discussed him and Christina in *The Month*, 215 (1963) pp 272–88.

support.[17] Another outside group who may well have encouraged this absorption of hermit communities was the episcopacy, who seem to have regarded them as a rather disturbing element in the church, and to have been trying by one means and other, if not to eliminate them, to control them more closely.[18]

Certainly the most beautiful object surviving to tell us something about Christina is the psalter now in Hildersheim which appears to have been made for her. The arguments to support this conclusion are convergent; there is no *ex libris* or other mark of ownership which could settle the matter beyond doubt, yet I think few could not be convinced that here is a book marked by Christina's life.[19] The manuscript begins with a calendar and here the deaths of many people connected with Christina—her father and mother, her two brothers, Roger the hermit, abbot Geoffrey her friend—are clear to see. The wording of the entry for Roger certainly suggests that he meant a lot to whoever made (or had made) the entry, and the fact that the hand which made it is not the same as the hand of most of the calendar may have significance in dating it.[20] But it is the contents of the rest of the volume which point perhaps even more strongly towards Christina.

A psalter is a psalter, as Gertrude Stein might have said, but this one is preceded by the calendar, four other items, and then followed by the creeds, litany and other prayers.[21] Immediately following the calendar comes a remarkable series of whole-page drawings illustrating the life of Christ, beginning with the fall and expulsion (which make, so to say, the incarnation necessary) and ending with the descent of the Holy Spirit at pentecost: thirty nine scenes in all.[22] None of them have rubrics, none of them have explanatory words inserted into the pictures. Then comes a full page drawing of David as a musician, which is followed by the *Chançon d'Alexis* in French and here the text begins with a drawing representing the first stage of the story.[23] The third

[17] *Life*, pp 172–4; *Gesta Abbatum*, I p 103.

[18] This subject would repay some study. Certainly by the thirteenth century the vocation of an anchorite was examined in some way; compare *Ancrene Wisse*, ed Geoffrey Shepherd (1959), pp xxxiv–v, and the discussion by G. le Bras of the peculiar status of hermits, *Institutions ecclèsiastiques de la Chretienté médiévale*, I, *FM* 12 (1959), pp 196–7.

[19] *Psalter* pp 5–6 for a summary. Compare *Life* pp 22–7.

[20] *Psalter* plate 10, and pp 193–5 below.

[21] *Psalter* pp 3–5 list the contents.

[22] *Psalter* plates 14–33. One scene from the life of St Martin of Tours is inserted between the incredulity of Thomas and the ascension. The reason for this has not yet been explained. I suspect that if we had a complete text of Christina's *Life* the answer would be there. See *Psalter* pp 94–5.

[23] Plate 35.

item is a brief extract from a letter of pope Gregory I defending the use of images, first in Latin, then in French, and lastly before the psalter, three whole-page drawings illustrating Christ's appearance to the disciples on the road to Emmaus: in this case a shortened form of the account in St Luke is written within the frame of the first picture.[24] The psalter occupies nearly three quarters of the volume, and is embellished with a remarkable series of historiated initials, as are the canticles, prayers and creeds which follow it. At the end are two full-page pictures of the martyrdom of St Alban, and of David and his musicians. Each part of the book has extraordinary features which gain point when the reader imagines Christina using it.

The calendar has already been discussed, but it is worthwhile noting that Christina appears to have harboured no lasting ill-will towards her parents who had treated her so very unsympathetically.[25] The psalter was the typical base upon which a recluse or hermit, like a monk, based his or her prayer life.[26] Godric at Finchale, for example, repeated it by day and night and probably, since he lacked formal schooling, had learnt it by heart by imitation, either from one of those he had lived with before he settled at Finchale, or during the period he had spent as a supernumerary at one of the churches in Durham.[27] The initials are decorated in such a way as to help the reader see the spiritual implications of the text and more especially the implications for one living a Benedictine way of life.[28] For example, in the course of psalm 118 (vulgate numbering), the sentence *Septies in die laudem dixi tibi* (v. 164) is illustrated by the figure of Christ looking down from heaven at David, wearing a crown, who points to the text. Anyone brought up knowing St Benedict's *Rule* would know that he uses the same verse at the beginning of his chapter on how the liturgy is to be performed during the day, and that he adopted a seven-fold pattern of services.[29] The usefulness of the pictures of Christ's life in meditation scarcely needs labouring, but it is worth noting that in this form, without any text, it is an innovation.[30] Mayr-Harting has already drawn attention to the way that the actual arrangement of the figures

[24] Plates 37–40.

[25] Her father and mother are remembered on January 11 and June 7 respectively, compare plates 2, 7.

[26] J. Leclerq, L'érémitisme en Occident jusqu' à l'an mil', *L'Eremitismo* p 39.

[27] *Libellus* pp 40, 45, 59–60.

[28] *Psalter* pp 181–97.

[29] *Psalter* p 255 and plate 82c: *Reg Ben* cap 16.

[30] *Psalter* p 138.

in one scene, the representation of the deposition of Christ from the cross, is recalled by the words with which Ailred of Rievaulx advised his recluse sister to meditate on the event.[31] The abbot of Rievaulx and the artist of the large pictures in the psalter belonged to a world which concentrated on many of the same episodes in Christ's life, and did so in a way which echoes the same preoccupations. Yet whereas Christina appears to have enjoyed this magnificent series of pictures (to use the educationalists' jargon and call it 'a visual aid' would be gross indeed), Ailred actually advises his sister to have only an image of the cross in her cell, and disparages her adorning it with pictures.[32] It is surely not beside the point to recall here the Cistercian, perhaps one should more accurately say Bernardine attitude, to the decoration of churches and books.[33] Ailred and Christina belonged to different traditions at this point. Her tradition is clearly indicated by the short *pièce justicative* on images which comes after the Alexis story.[34]

The appositeness of the story of Alexis, the bridegroom who leaves his bride on his marriage night to wander the world, to what actually happened to Christina has been well discussed by others. As Pächt put it the story was introduced into the volume 'as a symbolic memento of the owner's personal story'.[35] He also saw how singularly appropriate to Christina was the sole illustration provided for the *Chancon*, showing the couple in bed, and then Alexis setting out.[36] Normally the *Chancon* is accompanied by a drawing of an episode at the end when the old Alexis returns unrecognised to die at home.

The editors of the psalter recognised too a link between the *Chancon* and the Emmaus pictures in that in both the heroes, Alexis and Christ, are only recognised after they have left the world, and that in both the hero is a poor pilgrim.[37] The force of this last needs emphasising for those not brought up on the vulgate where the stranger who joins the disciples is *peregrinus*.[38] Behind the way the artist depicts Christ, bare-

[31] [H.] Mayr-Harting, ['Functions of a Twelfth-Century Recluse'], *History*, 60 (1975) p 351; *Psalter* frontispiece b, and pp 110–11; [*De*] *Inst*[*itutione*] *Incl*[*usarum, Aelredi Rievallensis Opera Omnia*, ed A. Hoste and C. H. Talbot], *CC* 1 (1971) pp 671–2. The work appears separately ed by Talbot in *ASOC* 7 (1951) pp 167–217.

[32] *Inst Incl* para 24, p 656.

[33] Knowles, *MO* pp 210, 646.

[34] Gregory's letter occurs in bk 11, ep 13 *Gregorii I Registrum*, ed L. M. Hartmann, *MGH* (1889) pp 269 *seq*.

[35] *Psalter* pp 137, 135–40.

[36] *Ibid* pp 139–40.

[37] *Ibid* pp 74–9; the words quoted come from p 78.

[38] Luke, 24, 18, 'Tu solus peregrinus es in Jerusalem' etc.

footed, wearing a tunic and a cap on his head, Pächt suggested lay the instructions for the clothing of Christ in the Peregrinus Play performed at St Benoît-sur-Loire. For him 'the Emmaus miniatures have to be read as a kind of pictured gloss on Alexis', and the wandering of Alexis is 'an imitatio Christi Peregrini'. This may be true, but what this explanation seems to lack is the sort of link with Christina's life which the Alexis story itself has. But in fact, such a link does exist as the final pages of the surviving *Life* make clear.

The anonymous account of Christina's life breaks off less than a folio after it has told of three appearances of a 'certain pilgrim' to Christina.[39] The first time he comes he is received hospitably but goes on his way. 'After a while' he returns again, talks with her, and sits down whilst she and her sister prepare refreshment for him. This he scarcely tastes, but after blessing them he goes on his way. The two sisters are left longing to see more of him; finally he turns up the day after Christmas day, attends services with the nuns and then disappears, although the church door had been locked so that no one could get in or out. At this point the author who has already drawn parallels between the behaviour of the pilgrim and the two sisters to that of Jesus with Mary and Martha, adds 'Who else could we say he was, except the Lord Jesus or one of his angels?', and appeals in justification to the vision which Christina had had on Christmas night of a crowned figure approving the way the monks at St Albans were singing Mattins.[40] His account breaks off with the tantalising phrase *In die vero sub perigrini sed maturioris viri specie videri voluit quia qualiter* .. and then four lines are missing. So Christina had had her 'Emmaus' experience in the same way as she had had an 'Alexis' experience, and therefore these illustrations had peculiar meaning for her, reminding her of the 'beloved pilgrim'.[41] The fact that the artist provided not just the normal two illustrations of the Emmaus story, one of the meeting on the road, and one of the meal, but added a third in which Christ disappears skywards to the astonishment of the two at meat with him, would have reminded her of the strange way her pilgrim vanished. As far as is known the artist had here no model to guide him, though the way only Christ's calves and feet are left is reminiscent of his drawing of the ascension, where he drew on an Anglo-Saxon tradition.[42]

[39] *Life* pp 182–8.
[40] *Ibid* p 188. I have slightly amended Talbot's translation here.
[41] *Ibid* p 186.
[42] *Psalter* pp 73, 56, and plates 40, 33a.

The St Albans psalter can be seen to be in every part a book 'made' for Christina, it reflected her own experience, and provided for her a means of reflecting on it. It is worth emphasising what rich material it gave her: the great corpus of the psalms enriched with drawings to stimulate meditation, pictures of Christ's life which combined features of Anglo-Saxon and Byzantine iconography in a new form, a newly translated poem from the Byzantine world, and the Emmaus series, taking up the pilgrim theme dear to Christina, besides having other meanings in her world. Such a rich blending of diverse elements needed an imaginative artist able to draw on a rich cultural background and there seems little doubt that St Albans was the place where this took place. The calendar has some features shared with St Albans, though not all, which is not surprising considering that Christina had links with other East Anglian centres, and the hand of the *Chancon d'Alexis* appears in at least one other St Albans manuscript.[43] But when was it produced? Here there is a disagreement.

The evidence which has to be considered is of two kinds, paleographic, and such deductions as can be made from the contents of the psalter. Wormald distinguished three principle hands, that which wrote the calendar, that of the psalter, canticles, litany and prayers, and that of the *Chancon Alexis* which also is found in other places, of which the most important are the extract from Gregory on images, the text in the first Emmaus drawing, and the obit for the hermit Roger. He also found two other hands which made additions to the calendar after the death of Christina, since she is among them.[44] The first two hands were, he believed, contemporary, and therefore the actual dating and wording of the obit for Roger the hermit are of some importance. This reads against the date *II Idus Septembis* (that is, 12 September) *Obitus Rogeri heremite monachi sancti Albani; apud quemcunque fuerit hoc psalterium fiat eius memoria maxime hac die.*[45] From this Dodwell concluded 'The fact that this entry is not in the original hand would indicate that Roger's death took place after the writing of the calendar, and of the psalter, which is referred to in the entry'.[46] And because Roger's death can be placed fairly securely before 1123 he argued that the manuscript as a whole was written by then. Wormald

[43] *Ibid* pp 5–6, summarises the evidence.
[44] *Ibid* pp 6, 275–7.
[45] *Ibid* p 278 and plate 10.
[46] Compare his more cautious words on p 280, 'if the entry of his obit in the calendar ... in writing different from that of the main hand, does indicate that the manuscript itself was written before his death, then one can say that it was written before 1123'.

wrote rather more cautiously and divided the creation of the book into three stages: the writing of psalter and calendar not before 1119 when Geoffrey started his abbacy, the addition of Roger's obit 'probably shortly after 1123' by the scribe of the Alexis poem and its attendant shorter pieces, although 'whether these were added at the same time as the obit it is impossible to say', and finally the addition of saints and obits after 1155.[47] A great deal depends here upon the identification of the hand of the obit for Roger with the hand of the Alexis poem, which was argued by Pächt to be also the hand of the artist of the cycle of pictures of the life of Christ, the Alexis drawing and the Emmaus cycle.[48] Basically however the editors of the psalter appear to be agreed that most of the psalter came into existence between 1119 and a date not long after 1123.

Talbot was prepared to consider a much later date, possibly after 1155 and for two separate reasons. He drew attention in the first place to an illustration after the Athanasian creed in which six nuns with an abbot hold up two books upon which are written the opening requests of the litany, each addressed to a separate person of the Trinity, and which end *Sancta Trinitas unus Deus miserere*. He saw here an allusion to the name by which Markyate priory was known, *Sancta Trinitas de Bosco*, and believed that the allusion would only have point after the priory had come into formal existence with the dedication of the church in 1145.[49] Secondly, he believed that the presence of St Margaret in the litany (and one other liturgical oddity) would not be likely before she was inserted into the litany at St Albans which only occurred under abbot Robert Gorham, the successor but one to Christina's friend, Geoffrey, and he therefore gave the whole volume a date 1155 plus.[50]

Neither of these solutions seem to me wholly satisfying. In the first place I remain sceptical about the identity of the hand which wrote the hermit's obit with so much else in the second to fifth gatherings of the manuscript. Wormald characterised this hand by three features; a specially twisted ampersand, a 'ct' ligature and a form of the letter 'g'.[51] Only one of these features is in the obit sentence, and I am unwilling to put so much weight on one short entry of seventeen words. Once this connection is cut it becomes possible to argue that

[47] *Ibid* p 277.

[48] *Ibid* p 49.

[49] *Life* p 25. The illustration is in *Psalter*, plate 96b, discussed p 271 where this deduction is not made.

[50] *Life* p 26. [51] *Psalter* p 276.

Roger's name could have been added some years after the psalter was completed. But I would also argue that a date for most of the volume *pre* 1123 seems to me to come too early in Christina's life and her relationship with St Albans, and everyone is agreed that the book was in one sense 'made' for her. The manuscript must have cost a good deal to produce, and it is scarcely credible that such a gift should have been made at a time which, according to the *Life*, precedes the beginning of her friendship with abbot Geoffrey. She had only been at Markyate since *c*1118 and her first recorded contact with the abbot was not until *c*1124.[52] On the other hand, if my explanation of the presence of the Emmaus pictures is correct then the psalter must come after the pilgrim incidents had occurred.[53] The *Vita* seems to tell an unfolding story in chronological order, and these events come after its account of the three occasions on which abbot Geoffrey had been asked to visit the Roman Curia—of which the last can be dated *c*1140–1.[54] I do not find it necessary to push the completion of the psalter much further than this as Talbot does. The allusion to the priory seems a forced one which the editors of the psalter did not see, whereas the presence of St Margaret in the litany can surely be explained on the basis that this was the name saint of Christina's own sister, and that she also plays a part in the one and only healing miracle told of Christina.[55] All in all I believe the evidence points in the direction of the psalter having been produced *after* 1140–1, and before the death of Christina's great friend, abbot Geoffrey, who was known to have given rich books to his own monastry, and who died in 1146.

The historical works which concern Christina are few, principally the *Life*, and Matthew Paris's *Gesta Abbatum* written at St Albans.[56] It is clear that the author of the first was a monk at St Albans (he refers more than once to it as 'our monastery') and one who knew Christina extremely well. He writes a good deal of direct speech and most of it reads as though she had told him, perhaps many times, what had happened, doubtless somewhat embroidering the original events with each repetition.[57] The fact that the fourteenth-century

[52] *Life* pp 14–15.

[53] Compare p 192 above.

[54] *Life* p 15.

[55] *Psalter* p 271; *Life* p 118: Margaret occurs a good deal, see particularly pp 140–2, p 182.

[56] For the composition of the *Gesta* see Antonia Gransden, *Historical Writing in England c. 550–c. 1317* (London 1974) p 357.

[57] *Life* pp 38, 126, and Talbot's discussion of the authorship and dedicatee, pp 5–10. The place which refers to an earlier omitted passage is on p 162. The question of

scribe did not copy out all the material he had in front of him is clear at one point, and since the prologue and/or dedicatory letter did not interest him we can not know for whom the book was destined. It seems reasonable to believe it was written soon after Christina's death, and very probably for Geoffrey's successor-but-one as abbot, Robert de Gorham, who died in 1166. The *Gesta Abbatum* seems to depend on the original *Vita* and refers anyone who wants to know more to the book kept then at Markyate. It adds nothing significant about Christina, though it does throw light on the feeling at St Albans that abbot Geoffrey was spending too much on the support of Christina and her companions.[58]

This friendship between the recluse/nun and the French abbot of one of the richest abbeys in England is one of the three themes of the *Vita* to which I want to draw attention. It is tied up with the other two: Christina's struggle to maintain her chastity, and the way that at every important crisis or decision point of her life she was reassured by visions or dreams. All of them are very twelfth-century themes, that is to say they deal with matters which were of wide-spread concern, and they were ones which almost inevitably arose out of the life of a female recluse.

During Christina's life-time some of the greatest and most articulate minds in Europe wrote on the theme of friendship: St Bernard and Ailred of Rievaulx stand out in the list.[59] The form their discussion took was deeply influenced by the *De Amicitia* of Cicero, a book which came to be in most monastic libraries.[60] It is interesting, therefore, to find Christina struggling at her own very unsubtle level with how her relationship with Geoffrey fitted in with her love of herself and her love of God. 'She began', we are told, 'to examine more often and more closely in the depths of her heart whether anyone can love another more than himself, at least in matters that pertain to the love of God.'[61] Typically, too, the answer came to her in the form

Christina's own veracity is a difficult one about which different views may be held (see note 68 below). Professor Brooke has said she 'romanced more than a little'; in his lecture in *Cathedral and City, St. Albans, Ancient and Modern*, ed R. Runcie (St Albans 1977) pp 60–1. I am convinced by the simple directness of most of her account.

[58] *Gesta Abbatum* 1 pp 95, 103, 105.

[59] Compare the typically nuanced discussion by Aelred Squire, *Aelred of Rievaulx* (London 1969) pp 98–111.

[60] R. M. Wilson, 'The Contents of the Mediaeval Library', *The English Library before 1700*, ed Francis Wormald and C. E. Wright (London 1958) p 98.

[61] *Life* p 180. The audition and vision continue to p 182.

of a mental discussion and then a vision. In the first she came to feel she ought to offer Geoffrey as a sacrifice for God in the same way that Abraham had offered Isaac. In the subsequent vision she saw Jesus standing at an altar facing Geoffrey and herself, and whilst she was on the Lord's right, honourable side, was alarmed to see that he was at the left, or dishonourable side.[62] For a time she wished for her friend to be moved, but finally realised she had to be content with what she had got. Afterwards she told Geoffrey 'that there was only one thing in which a person should not place another before self, God's love'. By a rather direct, simple route she had dealt with an area which was much discussed. But the *Life* makes perfectly clear too that their sweet conversations and exchanges of messages, did not occur without other people being shocked, or as the author puts it being 'pierced with the lance of envy'. It must have been difficult for other religious not to have been envious as they heard of gifts and endowments being given to the priory so that they called 'the abbot . . . a seducer, and the maiden a loose woman'.[63] The writer goes on to say that many changed their views in time, but the account gives good reason for seeing why Ailred writing to his recluse sister around 1163/4, about the time Christina died, warned her against such special relationships.[64] But the need for someone like Christina to have good advice is obvious, for how else was she to deal with some of her problems and difficulties?

The torment for Christina was a sexual one; she suffered the distractions which often strike those who had decided to renounce the exercise of a very fundamental part of their existence. A vow of chastity was part of the private vow which she took as a young girl, and she stuck to it through thick and thin when all the wiles of her family who wished her to behave like a sensible girl and submit to marriage, failed. The early part of the *Life* is dominated by the theme, which reaches its climax after the hermit Roger's death when archbishop Thurstan puts her in charge of a priest who then falls desperately in love with her, and she becomes evidently deeply attracted by him. The scars she suffers in this struggle are healed by a visionary

[62] The difference between those on the two sides of Christ at the final judgement is graphically brought out by Ailred, *Inst Inclus* cap 33, pp 678–9.

[63] *Life* pp 172–4. Giles Constable links the relationship with the wider problem of the popularity of syneisactism in twelfth century England (p 220 *seq* below). Christina's sojourn with the hermit Roger (compare p 186 above) is a much clearer example of it than her friendship with the abbot.

[64] *Inst Inclus* cap 7, pp 642–3.

experience in which the Christ child stays with her a whole day.[65] Perhaps as long as eight years later when she was about to make her profession at St Albans, she still had doubts as to whether her virginity 'had escaped unscathed', and again the matter was set at rest by a vision, this time of three youths who come to crown her.[66]

Here again in her own way Christina was working out a solution to a problem which concerned very serious minds and passionate individuals. Sex even within marriage was still, in general, considered unsuitable for a spiritually-minded person, and marriage was hardly given a more positive value in her life-time.[67] No doubt this partly reflected very crude social conventions, typified in Christina's own life by the attempt which a bishop, Ranulf Flambard, made to rape her.[68] It was scarcely, perhaps, surprising that St Bernard could not imagine that a man and a woman could be left together without their engaging in sexual relations.[69] But Christina was not just troubled by the issue whether she could have given way in deed, but whether she had given way to lust in her will, although she was not aware of having erred in either respect (*etsi nusquam meminerit se neque actu neque voluntate lapsam fuisse*).[70] Her awareness of the importance of the will in consenting to sin shows that she and her counsellors were aware of some of the discussion on *intention* which was going on in the schools, notably, of course, stimulated by Abelard.[71]

No one reading the *Life* can fail to be struck by the frequency with which visions or auditory experiences occur. Altogether forty two are mentioned, including in this total one reference to a considerable number of undescribed 'seeings', and this means that the reader of the original manuscript would have met almost one on each side of each of the twenty two folios now occupied by the *Life*.[72] Over two-thirds are reported as having been enjoyed by Christina herself, no one else gets much of a look-in, save Geoffrey the abbot, who has three. The

[65] *Life* pp 114–18.

[66] *Ibid* pp 126–8.

[67] [C. N. L.] Brooke, *The Twelfth Century Renaissance* (London 1969) pp 83–9, 182–3, and Brooke, *Europe in the Central Middle Ages* (London 1964), pp 345–7; Brenda M. Bolton, 'Mulieres Sanctae', *Sanctity and Secularity, SCH* 10 (1973) esp pp 77–80.

[68] *Life* pp 40–2. H. S. Offler has doubted the veracity of the story: *Durham Episcopal Charters 1071–1152, SS* 179 (1968) p 105.

[69] *Sermones* [*super Cantica Canticorum*], 65, para 4, [*S. Bernardi*] *Opera,* [ed J. Leclercq, C. H. Talbot, H. M. Rochais] (Rome 1958) 2, p 175.

[70] *Life* p 126.

[71] Compare *Peter Abelard's Ethics,* ed D. E. Luscombe (Oxford 1971) pp xv–xxxvii, esp xxxii *seq.*

[72] *Life* p 170.

balance are distributed evenly among her 'friends' and 'enemies'; for instance Roger the hermit, her servants, her mother, her husband and the priest hopelessly inflamed by her beauty. In every case the modern reader can understand how the vision helped the author and Christina to explain a change of heart by someone else, or a change in Christina's own intentions and feelings which they lacked the means of explaining in any other way. They belonged to a thought-world in which it was perfectly natural for people to explain what we might call their insights (using, incidentally, a word derived from the language of vision) in terms of something seen or heard. That a woman recluse turned nun should have a considerable number of these flashes compared with say, a male monk like Ailred or an archbishop like Anselm, at least as far as we can tell from reading the *Lives* about them, is scarcely surprising. Christina lacked that discernment which wide reading and training in argument might have been gained in the schools by a man.[73] And too she lived a life which, at least until Thurstan took an interest in her, was very much on the edge of the permissible and the impermissible from the point of view of the church. She 'needed' therefore, reassurance herself 'coming straight from the sanctuary' and others also needed to have her seriousness authenticated in the same way.[74]

The account of Christina's first contact with the man who became her great friend, is peculiarly significant in this respect. We are told that the two had not met when she was suddenly moved by a vision of a dead monk at St Albans, to warn him against doing something without consulting his chapter. She warned Geoffrey by a messenger and he, not unnaturally one may feel, was annoyed and advised her 'not to put her trust in dreams'. At this she prayed to God to avert the abbot from his plan in some way, and the following night the dead monk and others stood about his bed and attacked him until he promised to change his plans and to obey Christina's messages in future. What really seems to have convinced him next morning that the whole thing was not a night-mare, was the fact that the marks of his punishment were real: *vera namque fuerant flagella*.[75] He was moved by the apport, in the same way as long ago Jerome had been after his dream concerning his love of pagan literature, or (much nearer to Christina's

[73] Compare Leclercq's remark about St Hildegarde 'elle dit sous formes de "visions" ce que d'autres disent autrement'. J Leclercq, F. Vandenbroucke, Louis Bouyer, *La Spiritualité du Moyen Age* (Paris 1961) p 222.

[74] The phrase is A. D. Knock's: *Conversion* (Oxford ed 1961) p 107.

[75] *Life* pp 134–8.

time) as Wulfstan at Worcester had been by the foreign monk who had suffered in a dream from having told Wulfstan it was not a monk's job to preach.[76] Even Christina herself was sure that the second of her visions, a dream of the Virgin clothed like an empress, had been real, because she found in the morning her pillow was wet with the tears which she had shed in the dream.[77]

The anonymous author was at pains to make clear that the sometimes bizarre visions he recounted were genuine experiences and drew some interesting distinctions. Abbot Geoffrey has at one stage a waking vision of Christina which he 'saw clearly (for it was no dream)', whereas he writes of the recluse's own experiences that they were not fantastic visions or dreams, but were seen by her 'with the true gaze which is enjoyed by those who have spiritual eyes'.[78] In using the words *Neque enim phantastice erant visiones*, he was echoing the terminology of the *Somnium Scipionis* by Macrobius, where the *fantasma*, the dream seen between sleeping and waking, is dismissed as valueless.[79] Likewise of one of Christina's auditory experiences he writes *sed quibus auribus nescio vox auditur divina.*[80] It is clear, however, that he didn't have a well-judged standard by which he judged the quality of the experiences which he recounted, for when telling of Christina's vision of herself at St Albans seeing Christ approve the way the monks were singing, he applies to this the well-known phrase which St Paul used of his own undescribable vision in the Second Epistle to the Corinthians, 'But whether she saw these things in the body or out of the body (God is her witness), she never knew'.[81]

Whatever the modern reader may conclude about this part of the *Life*, we have to recognise that Christina and her biographer were dealing with some experiences which she and he could only describe in terms of being aware of the presence of Christ and the Virgin, and occasionally other saints. Nonetheless the historian can observe with interest the sort of behaviour which is said to have occurred. The

[76] Jerome, *Epistola 22, ad Eustochium*, para 30: *PL* 22 (1857) cols 416–17; *The Vita Wulfstani of William of Malmesbury*, ed Reginald R. Darlington, *CSer*, 3 ser 40 (1928) pp 13–15.

[77] *Life* pp 74–6.

[78] *Life* pp 152, 170.

[79] The distinction comes in bk 1, cap 3 (trans W. A. Stahl, New York, 1952, pp 87–92). There was a copy of the work at St Albans, now Corpus Christi College, Cambridge, MS 71.

[80] *Life* p 130.

[81] *Ibid* p 186: the allusion is to 2 Cor. 12.3.

Virgin, in Christina's first vision of her, may be arrayed like an empress to whom one should curtsey, but before the experience ends she has come to rest with her head in Christina's lap and allows her face to be gazed upon. Christ for his part gives her a gold cross, appears in the guise of a small child who stays in her arms a whole day 'not only being felt but seen', he joins her hands to help her hold her beloved Geoffrey, he stands at the altar with them, and he appears as a pilgrim.[82] They appear that is to say, in approachable, graspable, human guise, who welcome her gaze and not as distant, terrifying figures. At this point too Christina reflects wider changes in her world, particularly that tender quality which had been coming into devotion ever since Anselm's time at least, and which the Cistercians (with whom she had no recorded contact) advanced so much.[83] St Bernard would have understood what lay behind her hopes for the return of the pilgrim, which kept bubbling up in her mind (*ab eius corde huius modi exciderent*) *O qua hora veniet Dominus? O quomodo veniet? Quis videbit venientem? Quis eius glorie visionem dignabitur? Qualis quantave illa erit gloria? Quale quantumve gaudium erit intuentibus?*[84] And Christina, herself, no doubt would have enjoyed those taut rhymes of the Cistercian poet writing soon after her death, who exclaimed

quam bonus te quaerentibus—
sed quid invenientibus!

and later on his question

Desiderate millies,
mi Iesu, quando venies?
quando me laetum facies?
me de te quando saties?[85]

The fourth and last piece of evidence about Christina is the bald record on the pipe roll for 1155–6 which indicates that Henry II was responsible for seeing that she was paid fifty shillings that year. Admittedly by this stage Christina was not a recluse, but a nun, yet such a payment, as Mayr-Harting has pointed out was by no means exceptional.[86] In any one year the king might be supporting to some degree half a dozen hermits and any bishop might have another six on his roll of charitable gifts. But why should the great of the world wish

[82] *Ibid* pp 74–6; 106, 118, 168, 180–2, 182, 186–8.
[83] R. W. Southern, *The Making of the Middle Ages* (London 1953) pp 219–57.
[84] *Life* p 184. I have in mind Bernard, *Sermones* 74 II 5, *Opera* 2 pp 242–3.
[85] *The Oxford Book of Medieval Latin Verse*, ed F. J. E. Raby (Oxford 1959) pp 348, 350.
[86] *Pipe Roll 2–4 Henry II*, p 22, and Mayr-Harting p 337.

to patronise those who had so utterly withdrawn from the world? What was it about Christina which induced the abbot of St Albans to take her under his wing and set her financially on her feet?

In Christina's case the evidence seems to clearly point to the abbot valuing her advice and counsel, besides, undoubtedly finding her a fascinating person. Their first contact, as we have seen, came about because she warned him not to do something, and the very final words of the surviving text say that she watched over his affairs in prayer, interceding with 'God, the angels, and other holy folk in heaven and on earth, sensibly reproving him when his actions were not quite right . . .' (*que minus recte videbatur gerere sapienter increpando*).[87] From the start she was able to convince him of her power to foresee future events, and the *Life* gives examples of her ability to discern what was going on at places far distant, and to see into the minds of people present.[88] We do not have to accept the miraculous explanation which these abilities then received; the important fact is that such things impressed contemporaries. We may decide that Christina was no more than someone who used her common sense, and imagination, deriving, no doubt, much help from the way a community like hers must have accumulated gossip about a wide circle, rather like the old-style village shop used to do. In the twelfth century such percipience seemed miraculous. Apart from one healing miracle and a hint that her ill-wish had power, Christina was not a striking holy woman but she definitely belongs with a whole group of hermits, recluses and anchorites who whilst seeking their own salvation yet served the needs of society around them.[89]

The *Life* of Christina points clearly to one characteristic of this group: they were predominantly drawn from the non-Norman *strata* of society.[90] Christina's own parents were Anglo-Saxon burghers of a solid quality. The canon who strengthened her resolve as a girl was called Sueno; the first person she fled to was Ælfwen, a recluse: another hermit Eadwin helped her to escape: the list is considerable of people with Anglo-Saxon or Anglo-Scandinavian names. And the same is true if we look at the five other surviving *Vitae* for hermits, those for Wulfric of Haselbury, Henry of Coquet, Godric of Finchale, Bartholomew of Farne and Robert of Knaresborough, most of whom

[87] *Life* p 192.
[88] *Ibid,* see three stories pp 190–2.
[89] *Ibid,* pp 118–20; 172.
[90] Compare Mayr-Harting p 338; *Life* pp 12, 17.

were practising different forms of eremetic life between *c*1115 and *c*1170, exactly contemporary with Christina. Henry admittedly was a Dane, but all the others, including those with non-Saxon names came from the 'submerged majority'.[91] So it can I think be argued with conviction that the authority, position, of these people had some connection with their nationality. By and large they were ministering to the people who were not at home with the Anglo-Norman culture, and who may well have found it hard to make themselves understood by their new French-speaking lords.[92] Christina, whose main link was with a foreign-born abbot is something of an exception here, but it is clear that she had an Anglo-Saxon background, and that her training by Roger had a very native character. He, after all, called her his 'Sunday's child' (*myn sunendaege dohter*).[93]

But how had Christina and her contemporaries achieved a position where they could act as advisers, peace-makers, prophets and healers? They had done so by living in at least three senses on the margin, or frontier, of society where they could stand on ground which they had in a sense made their own, or to put the metaphor rather differently, where they had won a space which owed little to the authorisation or control of others.[94] In the first case the cell or hermitage where they retired was removed to some degree from the ordinary cross-currents and pressures of society; even an anchorite living in a cell built against a parish church attached himself to the one building in the typical village which had a large space, the grave-yard, round it. Christina fled from her family; every hermit rejected the normal calls of family responsibility, and in adopting chastity turned his back on the proper way of ensuring the survival of the family, and the whole way of life he or she adopted, fighting with the powers of the devil in loneliness by prayer, was poised as it were on the edge of life and death. This idea comes across clearly in the earliest rituals for inclusion which are based on the burial service and liken the recluse to a dead person, and it was expressed by Ailred when he reminded his recluse sister that she was buried with Christ in the tomb.[95] In these

[91] References to all the lives not already mentioned are given by Dauphin in *L'Eremitismo*, pp 274–5.

[92] The point comes across strongly in a story of Wulfric of Haselbury, whose life by John of Ford is edited by Maurice Bell, *Somerset Record Society*, 47 (1932) p 29.

[93] *Life* p 106.

[94] I hope to return to these sides of hermit life, elsewhere.

[95] For example, *The Pontifical of Magdalen College*, ed H. A. Wilson, *HBS* 39 (1910) pp 243–4 and a Soissons Rite (*c*1176) ed E. Martène, *De Antiquis Ecclesiae Ritibus* (Antwerp 1763) 2 p 178. Ailred, *Inst Inclus* 14, p 649.

senses at least we can recognise that the hermit or recluse had taken on what the anthropologist V. W. Turner called 'a permanent condition of sacred "outsiderhood"' and it was this that partly gave him or her a status felt to be full of power which could flow out into the world.[96]

For not only was England in the twelfth century a conquered country where those who might have exercised the functions of lordship were often absent from the village communities who needed them, but it shared with the whole of western Christendom a sense of unease about the old centres of power in the church.[97] Both parish clergy, the bishops, and the old cultic centres guided over by monastic bodies were under attack from those who sought new standards of behaviour, even though their novelty was often disguised as a return to old, apostolic practice or to the life of the desert fathers. Robert of Arbrissel's lament to the countess Ermengarde *Simoniachi sunt doctores, episcopi et abbates et sacerdotes, principes iniqui et raptores, adulteri et incestuosi, populi ignorantes legem Dei* . . . may stand as typical of this unease.[98] Where, then, was the Christian in need of advice to go? Some may have listened to the wandering preachers, some to have linked themselves to new foundations practising a stricter form of monastic life. But some, undoubtedly, made their way to the hermit, who by rejecting the world had come to fill a very special niche in it. Christina represents the gentler face of this place with her presents of embroidery, her advice and her flights of fancy, but she shows too how dependent upon that wider society she was, and how she was, albeit often unknowingly, playing a part in wide-spread movements, not only in devotional practices and the world of ideas, but in the settling down of a society under new controls.

University of Exeter

[96] Victor W. Turner, *The Ritual Process* (ed London 1974) p 103.

[97] Reginald Lennard, *Rural England 1086–1135* (Oxford 1959) p 390; compare p 33.

[98] *BEC* 3 ser 5 (1854) p 228. Dissatisfaction and new practises are discussed by M. D. Chenu 'Moines, clercs, laics au carrefour de la vie évangelique', *La Théologie au Douzième Siècle* (Paris 1957) pp 225–51.

AELRED OF RIEVAULX AND THE NUN OF WATTON: AN EPISODE IN THE EARLY HISTORY OF THE GILBERTINE ORDER

by GILES CONSTABLE

ALTHOUGH the story of the nun of Watton by Aelred of Rievaulx was published by Twysden in the seventeenth century and reprinted by Migne,[1] it has never been studied in detail for the light it throws on religious life and attitudes in the twelfth century and on the history of the order founded by St Gilbert of Sempringham. This neglect has been the result less of ignorance than of the nature of episode, which was described as 'disgraceful and fanatical' by Dixon, 'distressing' by Eckenstein and by Graham, 'painful' by Powicke, 'strange' by Knowles, 'of almost casual brutality' by Nicholl, and as 'curious' and 'unsavoury' by Aelred Squire.[2] The central events have recently been analyzed from the point

[1] Roger Twysden, *Historiae anglicanae scriptores x* (London 1652) pp 415–22, reprinted in *PL* 195 cols 789–96, which will be cited here by column and section only; compare [Anselm] Hoste, *Bibliotheca [Aelrediana]*, *Instrumenta patristica* 2 (Steenbrugge/The Hague 1962) p 121. Twysden took his text from the only known manuscript, now Corpus Christi, Cambridge, MS 139 fols 149^r–51^v (see n 12 below), of which photographs were kindly sent me by Professor C. R. Cheney, to whom I am also indebted for checking some readings. The printed text is on the whole accurate. Among the more important corrections from the MS are *uiridior* for *nitidior* (791D line 6), *ut* for *vero* (791D line 15), *intente* for *attente* (792B line 8), *temptas* for *tentans* (792B line 15), *uel denudauit* for *evoluit* (793A line 9), *oporteret* for *oportet* (795A line 6), *respicientesque* for *respicientes* (795B line 14), and *etiam* for *et* (796D line 9).

[2] W. H. Dixon, *Fasti Eboracensis: Lives of the Archbishops of York*, ed James Raine, 1 (London 1863) p 220; [Lina] Eckenstein, *Women [under Monasticism]* (Cambridge 1896) p 218; [Rose] Graham, *[S.] Gilbert [of Sempringham and the Gilbertines]* (London 1901) p 40; Walter Daniel, *[The] Life [of Ailred of Rievaulx]*, ed [F. M.] Powicke, *[Nelson's] Medieval Classics* (Edinburgh 1950) intro p lxxxi (compare Powicke, *Ailred of Rievaulx and his Biographer Walter Daniel* [Manchester 1922] p 59, where he said that the tract 'shows the monastic attitude at its worst'); Knowles, *MO* p 257 and p 263, compare p 207, where he cited this work (somewhat paradoxically) as evidence for the universal praise of Gilbert's nuns; [Donald] Nicholl, *Thurstan [Archbishop of York (1114–1149)]* (York 1964) p 33; [Aelred] Squire, *Aelred [of Rievaulx: A study]* (London 1969) p 118. Through the courtesy of Professor C. N. L. Brooke, I have seen the unpublished chapter on the Gilbertines by David Knowles, intended for his *Monastic Order*, in which he referred to the story of the nun of Watton as 'repellent to modern sentiment' and said of it and Gerald of Wales's story about Gilbert (see pp 221–2 below)

of view of psycho-history,[3] and Sharon Elkins studied it in her unpublished Harvard dissertation on religious women in England in the twelfth century;[4] but it deserves to be examined in itself and as a whole.

The account is brief—somewhat over two and a half thousand words in length—and consists of four sections, including a short introduction, separated by three parenthetical passages, each coming at a critical point in the story and serving as a commentary on the situation at that point. The first and third of these end with explicit statements by Aelred that he is returning to his purpose, showing that he introduced them consciously as divisions in the story.[5]

In the introduction Aelred stressed the importance of making known miracles and other manifestations of Divinity and cited the evidence of his own eyes and of reliable witnesses as proof of the truth of the present story. Then in the first parenthesis he gave a brief account of the origins of the nunnery of Watton in Yorkshire and of its reform by 'the venerable man' Gilbert, who renewed 'the ancient religion' and 'the ancient miracles' in that place. The nuns were dedicated not only to manual labour and psalmody but also 'to spiritual offices and heavenly theories,' Aelred wrote, 'so that many [of them] . . . are often taken in ineffable raptures and seem to participate in the heavenly choirs'. They continued to offer prayers for a deceased member of the community until they were assured of her salvation by a visible apparition, of which Aelred gave as an illustration the appearance at mass of a particular nun in order to prove to a friend that she was saved.

Returning to his main purpose, Aelred then related how a girl of about four years of age had been received at Watton at the request of

---

that, 'The only two anecdotes which show him in contact with the nuns obscure rather than reveal the picture'. The principal sources for the history of Gilbert and his order are the *Vita* and sets of *Constitutiones* and *Capitula* printed (in an incomplete and not entirely satisfactory edition) in a separately paginated section (following p 945) of *MA* 6, 2 pp v*–xcvii*, which appear as v*–lix* in the 1846 reprint, which will be cited here.

[3] [Francesco] Lazzari, *Esperienze* [*religiose e psicoanalisi*] (Naples 1972) pp 39–64 ('Peccato e redenzione in un testo monastico'). I am indebted to Dom Jean Leclercq for sending me a copy of this chapter.

[4] Some of my own views concerning the episode were developed in the course of fruitful discussions with Dr Elkins, the distinctiveness of whose approach will be clear when her thesis is published.

[5] 'His extra propositum praemissis, ad ea quae proposuimus enarranda transeamus' (791B); 'Sed ut ad propositum redeamus' (794B).

archbishop Henry of York 'of holy and pious memory'.[6] She grew up into a frivolous and lascivious young woman, who resisted all efforts at correction and remained without inclination for monastic life or love for God even after she became a nun. One day some of the brothers 'to whom the care of external affairs was entrusted' entered the nunnery to do some work, and she was attracted to one of them whom Aelred described as 'more comely than the others in features and more flourishing in age'. Nods between them led to signs, signs to words, and they arranged to meet at night 'at the sound of a stone which the unhappy man promised to throw onto the wall or roof of the building where she was waiting.'

At this point Aelred inserted the second parenthesis, beginning with a series of questions addressed to Gilbert and asking about his vigilance in guarding discipline and about his careful devices (*exquisita machinamenta*) designed to exclude all opportunity for sin. No one can save those whom God will not save, however, Aelred continued, addressing the nun, and he grieved that she was kept from such a sin neither by fear, nor by love, nor by reverence for the congregation or for the memory of archbishop Henry. After two unsuccessful efforts she managed to meet the young man. 'O close your ears, Virgins of Christ, cover your eyes,' Aelred said, returning to the story. 'She went out a virgin of Christ, and she soon returned an adulteress.'

The lovers continued to meet until, some time later, the suspicions of the nuns were eventually roused by the repeated noise of the stones thrown by the young man, and the senior sisters (*matronae sapientiores*)[7] challenged the woman, who confessed her sin. Aelred then described the consternation of the nuns, who seized and beat the culprit, tearing the veil from her head, and were prevented only by the senior sisters from burning, flaying, or branding her. She was chained by fetters on each leg, put in a cell, and fed with bread and water. Even then she was saved from yet harsher punishments only by the fact that she was pregnant and also, perhaps, by her seeming remorse for her misdeeds.

[6] The Cistercian Henry Murdac was archbishop of York from 1147 (enthroned 1151) until his death on 14 October 1153, during which period he remained abbot of Fountains: William Hunt, in *DNB*, 2 ed (London 1908–9) 13 cols 1218–20; *HRH* p 132. As archbishop of York, he confirmed the foundation of Watton: *MA* 6, 2 p 955.

[7] It is uncertain whether or not these were specific officials of the community, but they may correspond to the three 'religious and discreet' nuns who were entrusted with particular functions in the later *Institutiones ad moniales pertinentes* cap 3, in *MA* 6, 2 p xliv* (compare cap 12 p xlvi*).

The young man meanwhile fled from the monastery and returned to secular life, but the nun, inspired by the hope of being handed over to him, revealed when and where he could be found, and he was seized and beaten by some brothers sent by Gilbert, one of whom impersonated the nun by wearing a veil while the others lay in wait nearby.[8] Then came the most terrible part of the story, of which the following is a literal translation:

> Some [of the nuns], who were full of zeal for God but not of wisdom and who wished to avenge the injury to their virginity, soon asked the brothers to let them have the young man for a short time, as if to learn some secret from him. He was taken by them, thrown down, and held. The cause of all these evils [that is, the nun] was brought in as if for a spectacle; an instrument was put into her hands; and she was compelled, unwilling, to cut off the virus with her own hands. Then one of the bystanders snatched the parts of which he had been relieved and thrust them into the mouth of the sinner just as they were befouled with blood.[9]

At this dramatic point Aelred inserted the third parenthesis, praising the zeal of those who sought chastity, persecuted immodesty, and loved Christ above all things. 'You see,' he wrote, addressing the reader, 'how by mutilating him [and] by censuring her with disgraces and reproaches they avenged the injury of Christ'. He then cited the biblical parallels of Simeon and Levi, Phineas, and Solomon, but added, showing his disapproval, that, 'I praise not the deed but the zeal, and I approve not the shedding of blood but so great a striving of the nuns against evil.'[10]

The young man was returned to the brothers (and from this point on

[8] According to Powicke, in his introduction to Walter Daniel, *Life,* p lxxxi, the nuns lay in wait for the young man and captured him, but the text says that the *magister congregationis* (that is, Gilbert of Sempringham) sent out some brothers (793C).

[9] According to Squire, *Aelred* p 117 the young man was forced to mutilate himself, but the text leaves no doubt on the point. The use of the plural suggests that the testicles were removed and not the penis, as the interpretation of Lazzari requires (see p 216 below). The removal of both the penis and testicles under such circumstances would in all probability have been fatal.

[10] 'What would they not suffer,' he continued, 'what would they not do to preserve chastity, those who could do such things to avenge it?' These statements, and the previous one that the nuns acted 'full of zeal for God but not of wisdom', tend to refute the opinion of Powicke, in his introduction to Walter Daniel, *Life* p lxxxii that, 'Ailred himself does not seem to have been shocked.' Aelred's words (*Non laudo factum sed zelum*) echo the famous words of Bernard in his *Sermo super Cantica* 66, 12 (*Approbamus zelum, sed factum non suademus*) in *Sancti Bernardi Opera,* ed Jean Leclercq and H. M. Rochais (Rome 1957–) 2 pp 186–7.

disappears from the story), and the nun was put back in her prison. Then came what was for Aelred certainly the heart of the story, showing Christ's forgiveness of sins and attention to the prayers of the nuns, who implored Him, after their zeal had calmed down, 'to be mindful of their virginal shame, to counteract the infamy, and to ward off the danger' that threatened them and their house. Meanwhile they prepared for the birth of the nun's child, or children, since it looked as if she might be bearing twins. Shortly before that event, however, archbishop Henry, clad in the monastic habit and with the pallium, appeared to the nun in her sleep and asked her why she daily cursed him. After an initial denial, she replied that she did so because he had given her to this monastery where so much evil had befallen her. He then instructed her to confess her sins and to recite certain psalms and returned the following night, when she was about to give birth, accompanied by two beautiful women, who took away the baby. The following morning her custodians, finding her healthy and girlish, 'not to say virginal', in appearance, immediately accused her of doing away with her baby, and they and the other nuns who came were amazed when, after inspecting both her person and the cell, they found no trace of the birth. They were reluctant to make any decision about the matter 'without the authority of the father', however, that is, of Gilbert of Sempringham, who was apparently not there at the time, and meanwhile the chains by which she was held and one of the fetters fell off. After Gilbert was informed of these events, he decided to consult Aelred, who came from Rievaulx, visited the nun in her cell, and saw at once that she could have been freed, as he put it, 'neither by others nor by herself without the strength of God,' and he therefore decided that it would be impious to restore the fetters. This decision was confirmed, soon after he returned to Rievaulx, by a letter from Gilbert saying that the other fetter had fallen off. 'What God hath made clean, do not thou call common,' wrote back Aelred in the words of Acts 12.9, 'and what He has absolved, thou should not bind,' adding by way of conclusion that he had written these things 'in order both to deprive the envious of an opportunity and yet not to keep hidden the glory of Christ.'

The account is written in the form of a treatise, not of a letter, but at two points in the text it is addressed to a 'most beloved father' and to 'my dearest friend who is far removed from these parts'. The identity of this addressee is unknown.[11] The text survives in only one

[11] Eckenstein, *Woman* pp 218–19 said that it was addressed to Gilbert himself; Powicke,

manuscript, which was once at Westminster and is now at Corpus Christi College, Cambridge, and which was probably written in the late 1160s at the abbey of Fountains and moved in the early thirteenth century to Sawley in the West Riding of Yorkshire.[12] The events it describes must date from the late 1150s or early 1160s,[13] since Henry Murdac was archbishop of York from 1147 until 1153 (and enthroned only in 1151) and the nun, who was four years old when she entered Watton, cannot have become a nun and borne a child much before 1160.[14] Nothing is known about her family, but the facts that Henry took an interest in her and that she apparently became a nun (rather than a lay sister) at an early age suggest that she was not from the lowest ranks of society.

Aelred's involvement in the affair presumably arose both from a long-standing connection between Gilbert and the abbey of Rievaulx, of which the first abbot advised Gilbert concerning his original foundation,[15] and from Aelred's personal prestige and friendship with Gilbert,[16] whose order he praised not only in this account but also in his second sermon *De oneribus*, which was written about the same time,

---

in his introduction to Walter Daniel, *Life* p lxxxi proposed either prior John of Hexham or abbot Simon of Wardon.

[12] Bale, *Index* p 13; Peter Hunter Blair, 'Some Observations on the *Historia Regum* Attributed to Symeon of Durham', *Celt and Saxon: Studies in the Early British Border*, ed N. K. Chadwick (Cambridge 1963) p 116; Squire, *Aelred* pp 73–4; and especially [Derek] Baker, 'Scissors and Paste: [Corpus Christi, Cambridge, *MS* 139 Again]', *SCH* 11 (1975) pp 83–123. It was assigned to Hexham, however, by Hoste, *Bibliotheca* p 121 and by [Alberic] Stacpoole, 'The Public Face [of Aelred, 1167–1967]', *DR* 85 (1967) p 320.

[13] Hoste, *Bibliotheca* p 39 (dating the work 1158/65) and p 121 (dating it *c*1160); Stacpoole, 'The Public Face', p 320 (*c*1160); Squire, *Aelred* p 117 (about 1160); Baker, 'Scissors and Paste' p 97 ('between 1155–7 and 1158–65 (probably 1160)').

[14] She must have been born between 1143 (or more probably 1147) and 1149. Aelred's terminology is not very helpful, since he referred to her as 'puella quaedam quatuor ut putabatur annorum . . . Quae mox ut infantilem excessit aetatem, cum puellaribus annis puellarem induit lasciviam' (791B). Among boys, a *puer* might be up to twenty-eight years of age, according to Adolf Hofmeister, '*Puer. Iuvenis. Senex.* Zum Verständnis der mittelalterlichen Altersbezeichnungen', *Papsttum und Kaisertum . . . Paul Kehr zum 65. Geburtstag dargebracht*, ed Albert Brackmann (Munich 1926) pp 287–316. On the later ages of reception in the Gilbertine order, see the *Institutiones ad moniales pertinentes* cap 35, in *MA* 6, 2 p li*.

[15] *Institutio de exordio* cap 1, in *MA* 6, 2 p xix*.

[16] On Aelred's friendship with Gilbert, see [Brian] Golding, 'St Bernard and St Gilbert', *The Influence of Saint Bernard*, ed Benedicta Ward, *Fairacres Publication* 60 (Oxford 1976) p 48. Aelred referred to Gilbert as 'vir venerabilis ac Deo dilectus pater et presbyter' (789D); Compare his *Sermo 2 de oneribus*, in *Maxima bibliotheca veterum patrum* (Lyons 1677) 23 col 12F, which is called the 'only satisfactory' edition by Squire, *Aelred* p 169 n 15.

or somewhat earlier, and in which he described a Gilbertine house (very likely Watton) where the nuns 'daily transmit to heaven the abundant fruits of chastity' and where a particular nun had a mystical vision of Christ on the cross.[17] In 1164 Aelred was one of seven Cistercian abbots who witnessed the agreement between the chapters of Cîteaux and Sempringham.[18] Further evidence of the close relations between the Cistercians and Gilbertines, especially at Watton, is the fact that after the first abbot of Meaux resigned in 1160, according to the chronicle of the abbey, 'He enclosed himself at Watton, [which was] at that time a new monastery of virgins, and intended henceforth to devote himself to God alone, choosing to lead the life of an anchorite. And he remained enclosed there until at length, after seven years, the church next to [*sub*] which he lived caught fire, and he returned to his monastery of Meaux after he was rescued from the fire.'[19] It was therefore natural for Gilbert to turn to Aelred, as an old friend and abbot of a neighbouring Cistercian house, to arbitrate in the awkward affair of the nun of Watton.

It is less clear why Aelred decided both to write and to send to a distant friend an account which by modern standards seems to be both unedifying and derogatory to Gilbert and his order and in which he expressed openly his disapproval of the nuns' behaviour and of Gilbert's apparent negligence in allowing the young man and woman to meet. To Aelred, however, the act of adultery and the subsequent punishments were less important than the miraculous delivery of the child and freeing of the nun from her fetters, which clearly showed God's desire to protect the community from the bad effects of the behaviour of two of its members. He may also have been happy to enhance the reputation of the Cistercian archbishop Henry of York, in whose controversial election he had himself played a leading part.[20]

[17] Compare Squire, *Aelred* p 139 and, on the date of these sermons, Hoste, *Bibliotheca* p 55 (1158–63) and Stacpoole, 'The Public Face' p 321 (1158–63). This reference was thought to apply to Gilbert of Swineshead (Holland) by Mabillon (*PL* 184 cols 9–10), who was followed by Frédéric van der Meer, *Atlas de l'ordre cistercien* (Amsterdam/Brussels 1965) p 298; but this was disapproved by, among others, Edmond Mikkers, 'De vita et operibus Gilberti de Hoylandia', *Cîteaux* 14 (1963) p 34. I am indebted to the Reverend Lawrence C. Braceland for these references.

[18] Graham, *Gilbert* pp 128–9; Knowles, *MO* p 263.

[19] *Chronica monasterii de Melsa,* ed E. A. Bond, *RS* 43 (London 1866–8) 1 p 107; compare *Memorials of the Abbey of St Mary of Fountains,* ed J. R. Walbran, I, *SS* 42 (Durham 1863) p 97 n 7 and Nicholl, *Thurstan* p 161.

[20] On St William of York, see David Knowles, 'The case of St William of York', published in 1936 and reprinted in a revised form in his *The Historian and Character* (Cambridge 1963) pp 76–97 and Charles H. Talbot, 'New Documents in the Case of

There is no reason to doubt that Aelred fully accepted the authenticity of the events he described or to discuss here possible alternative explanations of the alleged miracles.[21] It is easy to speculate that the delivery and breaking of the fetters were in fact carried out by members of the community, or that the pregnancy turned out to be false. Aelred himself was aware of the possibility of a non-miraculous explanation of these occurences, since he inspected the fetters in order to establish to his own satisfaction that they could not have been broken without divine assistance. The story loses much of its interest for historians if it is regarded simply as a fraud, since its supernatural character was certainly accepted by most, if not all, of the participants.

Of the two miracles involved in the affair, that concerning the delivery of the child was probably less impressive to contemporaries than the freeing from the fetters,[22] which was one of the oldest and best-established types of miracles and therefore convincing testimony both of God's favour and of Henry Murdac's powers of intercession.[23] The miraculous delivery, on the other hand, was an almost unprecedented event in the first half of the twelfth century and is therefore particularly interesting from the point of view of the phenomenology of miracles. No exactly comparable miracle appears in the repertories of Brewer, Gunter, or Thompson.[24] The closest parallel is the story of

---

Saint William of York', *CHJ* 10, 1 (1950) pp 1–15. His apparent murder in 1154 contributed to the rise of a popular cult (and eventual canonization), which was doubtless a source of embarrassment to his opponents, the supporters of Henry Murdac.

[21] Compare R. C. Finucane, 'The Use and Abuse of Medieval Miracles', *History* 60 (1975) pp 1–10.

[22] These events seem to have taken place successively: first the delivery of the child; second, in two or three stages, the freeing from the fetters.

[23] On miraculous freeing from fetters and prisons (with which is associated opening of doors) see Otto Weinreich, *Gebet und Wunder* (Stuttgart 1929) pp 34 [200]—286 [452] esp 143–75 on the Acts of the Apostles and 261–3 on various saints down to the twelfth century; C. Grant Loomis, *White Magic: An Introduction to the Folklore of Christian Legend, Medieval Academy of America Publication* 52 (Cambridge, Mass., 1948) p 89; Heinrich Günter, *Psychologie de la légende,* trans. J. Goffinet (Paris 1954) pp 33–4 and 156–8; A. J. Festugière, 'Lieux communs littéraires et thèmes de folk-lore dans l'hagiographie primitive', *Wiener Studien* 73 (1960) pp 123–52; and [Stith] Thompson, *Motif-Index* [*of Folk-Literature*] (2 ed Bloomington/London 1975) 5 p 278 (no R 121).

[24] E. Cobham Brewer, *A Dictionary of Miracles* (Philadelphia nd) and n 23 above. There is a note in a seventeenth-century hand at the end of the text in Corpus Christi, Cambridge MS 139 fol 151^{v}: 'Talis fabula narratur de quodam monacho de Euesham tempore Ric. primi A^{o} 1196. Consimilis fabula narratur et asseveratur per fratrem Philippum de clara villa, de quadam puella, nomine Elizabeth, in monasterio vocat. Erkenrode in territorio Leodicensi. monasterium erat virginum Beati Bernardi. Vide

the abbess delivered of her child by the Virgin Mary,[25] of which the earliest known version is in the collection of Mary miracles compiled by Dominic of Evesham, probably in the early 1120s. According to this version, an abbess became pregnant 'by the inspiration of the Devil and her own weakness', and the fact became known, through the indiscretion of a confidante, to the community, the archdeacon, and the bishop. There was an outcry against her, but the Virgin took pity on her and relieved her of the child, who was taken by angels to a faithful devotee. At the public investigation before the bishop, therefore, the abbess was found to be without child, and he ordered her accusers to be burned. After hearing her story, however, he found the child, who was later brought to his court and eventually succeeded him as bishop.[26]

A substantially similar and at points verbally identical version of this story appeared some twenty years later, about 1143, in William of Malmesbury's *De laudibus et miraculis sanctae Mariae.*[27] This work had

---

in Alexandro Essebiensi pag[a] 185[a]'. This should be compared with the parallel note in MS 4 (Oxford, Bodleian MS Selden supra 66) of the vision of the monk of Eynsham, in *Eynsham Cartulary*, ed H. E. Salter, *OHS* 49, 51 (Oxford 1907–8) 2 p 371. But I can find no closely parallel miracle either here or in the *Vita* of Elizabeth of Erkenrode by Philip of Clairvaux, published in *Catalogus codicum hagiographicorum bibliothecae regiae Bruxellensis* (Brussels 1886–9) 1 pp 362–78.

[25] See *Catalogue of Romances in the Department of Manuscripts in the British Museum* (London 1883–1910) 2 (ed H. L. D. Ward) pp 720 (11) and 740 (3) and 3 (ed J. A. Herbert) pp 69 (109), 326 (xv), 333 (1), 341 (13), 395 (371), 523 (43), 547 (100), 565 (75), 575 (13), 626 (6), 676 (7), 691 (59), 696 (6), 716 (12), and 717 (41); Albert Poncelet, 'Index miraculorum B. V. Mariae quae in latine sunt conscripta', *An Bol* 21 (1902) p 245 (no 4) and p 284 (no 605); J. A. Herbert, 'A New Manuscript of Adgar's Mary-Legends', *Romania* 32 (1903) pp 415–21, saying that the abbess delivered was 'one of the most popular of all the Mary-Legends, and practically all the great Latin collections include it'; *Liber de miraculis sanctae dei genitricis Mariae,* ed Thomas F. Crane, *Cornell University Studies in Romance Languages and Literature* 1 (Ithaca/London 1925) pp 51–5 and 99. Compare intro pp xii and xxiii; Frederick C. Tubach, *Index Exemplorum: A Handbook of Medieval Religious Tales, F[olklore] F[ellows] Communications* 204 (Helsinki 1969) p 9 (nos 2 and 4); and Thompson, *Motif-Index* 5 p 383 (no T 401.1).

[26] Printed from Balliol College, Oxford, MS 240 fol 147 by [Hilding] Kjellman, *[La] deuxième collection anglo normande des miracles de la Sainte Vierge et son original latin* (Paris/Uppsala 1922) pp 60–1 and in the unpublished 1958 Oxford dissertation of J. Jennings, 'Prior Dominic of Evesham and the Survival of English Tradition after the Norman Conquest' pp 200–3, of which copies have kindly been sent me by Sister Benedicta Ward.

[27] José M. Canal, *El libro 'De laudibus et miraculis sanctae Mariae' de Guillermo de Malmesbury, OSB († c. 1143)* (2 ed Rome 1968) pp 154–6; compare R. W. Southern, 'The English Origins of the "Miracles of the Virgin" ', *Mediaeval and Renaissance Studies* 4 (London 1958) pp 200–1. Sister Benedicta Ward informs me that this work has also been edited by Peter Carter in his unpublished 1959 Oxford dissertation, 'An

only 'a local repute', however, according to Southern, and it was principally from Dominic's collection (or its sources) that the story of the abbess passed first into the collection of canon Alberic of St Paul, then into the Old French version of William Adgar, and so into almost all the Latin and vernacular collections of Mary legends.[28] It was probably not well-known in the middle of the twelfth century, however, and William of Malmesbury emphasized the novelty of the events. 'Who ever heard of such a miracle?' he asked. 'It is unheard of for a woman to give birth in her sleep.' Nor is it likely that Aelred knew the story, in view of the substantial differences between the two accounts. But the similarity of type, in addition to the fact that they both appeared in England during the first half of the twelfth century, suggests that they both arose out of the needs of women in religious institutions at that time.

The miracle served the double end both of disposing of an unwanted child in an acceptable way (though Aelred, unlike Dominic and William, did not specify how) and of providing a basis for reconciliation in a religious community after a shattering challenge to its most cherished norms. Aelred laid particular emphasis on this process of vengeance and reconciliation. The terrible punishments meted out to the culprits were not in themselves exceptionally harsh, judged by the standards of the time.[29] Death was a recognized penalty for adultery and fornication in both the ancient and the medieval world. According to Gregory of Tours, a woman who committed

---

Edition of William of Malmesbury's Miracles of the Virgin Mary', where he lists as sources for this story, in addition to Dominic of Evesham, Aberdeen MS 137 fol 107, Cambridge MS Mm. 6.15, and Toulouse MS 482. William's version is about a fifth longer than Dominic's and includes more biblical citations and passages of direct address, especially a long speech of the indignant nuns directed against their peccant abbess. William described at less length than Dominic the appeal of the abbess to the Virgin and omitted Her requirement that the abbess confess and make a vow before receiving Her assistance.

[28] See the articles by Herbert and Southern cited nn 25 and 27 above. The Latin collection was made either by or for Alberic, who appears as a canon of St Paul's between 1148 and 1162. On the later Old French versions, see Kjellman, *Deuxième collection* pp 60–7 and intro pp xli–xlii and Erik v. Kraemer, *Huit miracles de Gautier de Coinci, Annales Academiae scientiarum Fennicae* B 119 (Helsinki 1960) pp 9 and 64–77.

[29] Later Gilbertine legislation (possible influenced by this episode) laid down that in cases of incest the man should be imprisoned immediately, even if the master was absent, or expelled from the order and that the woman should be condemned forever to solitary confinement: *Scripta de fratribus* cap 28, in *MA* 6, 2 p xliii*.

adultery with a priest was burned to death by her own family,[30] and in Dominic of Evesham's version of the story of the pregnant abbess, some of the nuns urged that she should be burned. In the thirteenth century Bracton wrote that, 'In past times, the defilers of virginity and chastity suffered capital punishment . . . But in modern times the practice is otherwise and for the defilement of a virgin they lose their members;' and examples of the castration of clerics for sexual offences can in fact be found in England as late as the fifteenth century.[31]

The most remarkable feature of the punishment at Watton was not therefore either the beating and imprisonment of the nun or the castration of the man but the performance of the deed by the woman herself and the subsequent insertion into her mouth of the severed members *sicut erant feda sanguine*, of which the precise meaning is uncertain. As translated above, it may mean literally 'just as they were befouled with blood', but if *feda* is taken as a noun rather than an adjective it may refer to the *sanguis foederis* [blood of the covenant] of Exodus 24.8 and imply a process of expiation in which the severed parts were considered to be covenants in blood. At the very least, the

[30] Gregory of Tours, *Historia Francorum* 6, 36, ed W. Arndt and B. Krusch, *MGH SRM* 1 (Hannover 1884–5) 1, 1 p 276, compare 5, 32 *ibid* pp 224–5. On the barbarian law-codes, see *The Burgundian Code,* trans Katherine F. Drew (Philadelphia 1972) pp 60 (LII, 5) and 68 (LXVIII) and *The Lombard Code,* trans Katherine F. Drew (Philadelphia 1973) pp 93 (Rothair 212) and 201 (Liutprand 130); and on the practice in Mediterranean and middle eastern societies of killing unwed mothers before the birth of their children, see [Jacob] Black-Michaud, *Cohesive Force* (Oxford 1975) pp 218 and 226–7. The right of a husband, brother, or son to attack an adulterer was repeated in the *Leges Henrici primi* cap 82, 8, ed L. J. Downer (Oxford 1972) pp 258–9.

[31] Bracton, *On the Laws and Customs of England,* ed George E. Woodbine and trans Samuel E. Thorne (Cambridge, Mass., 1968) 2 p 415 (fol 147); compare Frederick Pollock and Frederic W. Maitland, *The History of English Law before the Time of Edward I* (2 ed Cambridge 1898) 2 pp 490–1 and 544 n 1, and Thomas A. Green, 'Societal Concepts of Criminal Liability for Homicide in Mediaeval England', *Speculum* 47 (1972) pp 679–80. Thompson, *Motif-Index* 5 pp 232 (no Q 451.10) and 313 (no S 176) cites some examples of castration as a punishment. Abelard is only the best-known of several examples from the twelfth century and later. Geoffrey of Anjou is said to have had the bishop-elect of Séez, Gerard, and a number of his clerics emasculated and to have had the *membra euneuchatorum* brought before him in a basket: William Fitz-Stephen, *Vita s Thomae* cap 55 (where some of the barons at Northampton in 1164 contemplated the same treatment for Thomas Becket) in *Materials [for the History of Thomas Becket]*, ed James C. Robertson, *RS* 67 (London 1875–85) 3 p 65; compare Gerald of Wales, *De principis instructione* cap 3 in *Opera,* ed J. S. Brewer, J. F. Dimock, and G. F. Warner, *RS* 21 (London 1861–91) 8 p 301 and *The Letters of Arnulf of Lisieux,* ed Frank Barlow, *CSer* 3, 61 (London 1939) intro p xxxiv. Among later examples (for which I am indebted to professor John Beckerman) see *Wykeham's Register,* ed T. F. Kirby, Hampshire Record Society 11 (London/Winchester 1896–9) 2 pp 379–80, 478, and 534 and *The Register of Henry Chichele, Archbishop of Canterbury 1414–1443,* ed E. F. Jacob (Oxford 1943–7) 3 p 73.

gesture must have added to the shame of the nun and also have associated her with the punishment of her lover. There is a parallel, to which Nicholl has drawn attention, in the *Vita* of William of York, which includes a description of a judicial combat between a man falsely accused of arson and his jealous enemy, who defeated and then castrated and blinded his innocent victim. 'Furthermore, like a sharp dagger making a wound,' the *Vita* continued, 'his bestial savagery viciously cut off the virile members from the man, and after they had been torn out by the roots, which was horrible to see, he publicly threw them, together with the pupils of his eyes, amongst the people, while the great and small people wondered at his rage and the judges abhorred his cruelty and accorded their consent on account more of their official position than of their agreement.' The lost parts were subsequently restored to the victim through the power of St William, which was the real point of the story; but it shows that events of this nature, involving judicial castration and abuse of the dismembered parts, were not unknown in the north of England in the twelfth century.[32]

For Lazzari, who gave a Freudian interpretation of the story of the nun of Watton, this event was a sign of the suppressed desire of the nuns to identify with their fallen sister and was in particular an expression of their wish to possess what they all secretly wanted. He described the act as 'the object of the collective rêveries of the monastery' and considered the savage behaviour of the nuns (which he called sadistic and erotico-anal) to be the result of the guilt generated by their unconscious temptations.[33] This interpretation certainly helps to explain in modern terms certain aspects of the story, but it is not the only possible explanation. Freud himself was very sceptical about the possibility of applying his theories to individuals who could not actually be observed, and he warned against conclusions about the unconscious attitudes and motives of people far away in time and space.[34]

[32] *Vita s Willelmi auctore anonymo*, in *The Historians of the Church of York and its Archbishops*, ed James Raine, *RS* 71 (London 1879–94) 2 pp 289–90; compare Nicholl, *Thurstan* p 33. Two other cases of judicial castration and blinding are found in William of Canterbury, *Miracula s Thomae* cap 2, 3 in *Materials*, 1 pp 156–8—also in Melville Bigelow, *Placita anglo-normannica* (London 1879) pp 260–1—and Benedict of Peterborough, *Chronicle of the Reigns of Henry II and Richard I*, ed William Stubbs, *RS* 49 (London 1867) 1 pp 79–80.

[33] Lazzari, *Esperienze* pp 47–8. Later (pp 50–4) he interpreted the account at the beginning of the story of the visions of the nuns at Watton as evidence of their own sublimated, and of Aelred's suppressed, homosexuality.

[34] Sigmund Freud, *Briefe 1873–1939*, 2 ed Ernst and Lucie Freud (Frankfurt a. M. 1968) p 399 (letter to Lytton Strachey in 1928).

The conscious concern of the nuns was above all with revenge, and Aelred used the term *ulciscor* and its derivatives five times in his description of the punishments of the two lovers. In many traditional societies the sexual modesty or shame of women is considered the counterpart of the honour of men, and its loss represents an intolerable affront not only to the individual but also to the community, which has an obligation as well as a right to claim vengeance for violated chastity.[35] The reaction of the nuns and canons can therefore be seen as an expression not so much of guilt arising from sexual repression as of a passionate desire to vindicate the honour of Christ and of their monastery. Gilbert's biographer, writing at the end of the twelfth century, said of him that, 'The reward of virgins is a hundredfold, and to preserve their state he gave up his property, received a hundredfold, and possessed eternal life.'[36] And according to a modern anthropologist, writing about a Greek mountain people, 'Sex, sin, and death are related; similarly virginity, continence, and life.'[37] The nuns clearly feared that the sin of one of their numbers would be attached to them all and were determined to avenge, as Aelred said, 'the injury of virginity' and 'violated chastity', which for them was clearly communal as well as individual.[38] The punishments therefore also had a communal character, and the association of the woman in the sexual nature of the punishment of the man may support the interpretation of the severed parts in the biblical sense of *feda sanguine*. Be this as it may, Aelred wrote that 'when vengeance had been exacted' the nuns addressed themselves to God, whose miracles obviated the need for further expiation by demonstrating His forgiveness for the nun and, through her, for the entire community. The episode can therefore be seen as an example of what Victor Turner has called a social drama, marked by four successive stages, of a

[35] [J. K.] Campbell, *Honour, [Family and Patronage: A Study of Institutions and Moral Values in a Greek Mountain Community]* (Oxford 1964) p 278, compare pp 183–4, 202–3, and 349–50; Black-Michaud, *Cohesive Force* pp 218 and 227, who stressed the importance of sexual integrity as an aspect of political integrity. 'The dynamics of honour and dishonour in sexual transgressions' in modern Spanish society are discussed by Julian Pitt-Rivers, 'Honour and Social Status', in *Honour and Shame: The Values of Mediterranean Society*, ed J. G. Peristiany (London 1965) pp 45–7, who also emphasized (pp 25 and 74) that 'The laundry of honour is only bleached with blood'.

[36] *Vita*, in *MA* 6, 2 p vii*.

[37] Campbell, *Honour* p 280.

[38] 793A, D and 794A. Aelred twice emphasized the concern of the nuns for their 'shame' (793A and 794A) and their 'verecundia virginalis' (794B).

break of social norms, leading to a crisis, which is followed by redressive action, and, finally, by social reintegration.[39]

The last question to be asked about this story is the light it throws on the life of the community at Watton and on the history of the Gilbertine order, which is obscure because the *Constitutions* and three extant lives of Gilbert of Sempringham all date from the late twelfth or early thirteenth century.[40] Aside from charters, therefore, which shed comparatively little light on the internal affairs of the order, the story of the nun of Watton is the earliest authentic account of life in a Gilbertine house.

Its testimony in part confirms what is known from other sources, such as the facts that Watton was a double house, with both male and female members (which has been questioned by some scholars[41]), and that it was the only such house in the diocese of York in the mid-twelfth century.[42] It also confirms that it was under the direct control of Gilbert himself, whom Aelred called the *magister congregationis*. With regard to the status of the participants, the woman was certainly a nun, since she was said to have taken the veil and was called *sanctimonialis femina* in the contemporary *explicit*; but the status of the man is less certain. He was described as one of 'the brothers of the monastery to whom the care of external affairs is entrusted', which suggests that he was a *conversus* or lay-brother, especially since *frater* was used in contrast with *canonicus* in an almost contemporary letter concerning the Gilbertines.[43] In Henry Murdac's charter confirming the foundation of Watton, however, the canons were said to serve the nuns 'in both divine and secular affairs', and since the young man certainly wore a

[39] Victor Turner, 'Social Dramas and Ritual Metaphors', published in 1971 and reprinted in his *Dramas, Fields, and Metaphors: Symbolic Action in Human Society* (Ithaca/London 1974) pp 39–42.

[40] [Raymonde] Foreville, [*Un*] *procès* [*de canonisation à l'aube du XIII*e *siècle* (*1201–1202*). *Le Livre de saint Gilbert de Sempringham*] (Paris 1943) pp xi–xii; Jane Fredeman, 'John Capgrave's *Life of St Gilbert of Sempringham*', *BJRL* 55 (1972–3) pp 112–45; compare Golding, 'St Bernard and St Gilbert' p 47.

[41] Archbishop Henry Murdac's charter confirming the foundation laid down that there were to be thirteen canons having charge of the nuns and serving them 'in accordance with the institutes of the order of Sempringham'; *MA* 6, 2 p 955. Compare Foreville, *Procès* intro p xi and p 87, where she apparently confused Watton with Malton, on which see the following note.

[42] 789D. In the letter cited p 223 below, archbishop Roger of York and bishop Hugh of Durham wrote that there was one house in the diocese of York where men and women lived honourably within the same wall. This was doubtless to distinguish Watton from Malton, which was for canons only: see *MRHEW* p 198.

[43] [David] Knowles, '[The] Revolt [of the Lay Brothers of Sempringham]', *EHR* 50 (1935) p 481 (no 7).

religious habit and was said after his flight from the monastery to be 'secular not only in mind but also in habit',[44] he may have been a canon.

The principal value of the story, however, is as a source for the internal arrangements of the house. The fact that the nun was accepted at the age of four, for instance, and that Aelred apparently did not question the propriety of this reception, which may impress modern readers as the real source of the subsequent difficulties, shows that the policy of the Gilbertines with regard to the acceptance of children was less strict than that in many contemporary reformed religious orders, including the Gilbertines themselves at a later date.[45] Even more interesting is the relative ease with which the two young people were able to communicate and meet, which contrasts sharply with the later provisions forbidding a woman from so much as seeing a man, let alone from speaking with him or leaving the monastery to meet him.[46] That they were able to do so at Watton may have been owing to laxness there, as Aelred suggested in his rhetorical questions in the second parenthesis.[47] But it may also have been owing to the existence at that time of less rigid controls and of greater freedom of contact between the sexes than is found in the later legislation. The fact that the ex-abbot of Meaux lived as a recluse 'next to the church' at Watton from 1160 until 1167, at the very time of the episode involving the nun, and that he was presumably dependent on the community at least for his food and clothing, likewise suggests a degree of openness. This view is supported by a comparative study of religious houses and orders in the twelfth century, which shows that the process of development from relatively inchoate and flexible origins into highly disciplined institutions often extended over a period of years.[48] This seems to have been particularly true of communities

[44] *MA* 6, 2 p 955; *PL* 195 col 795CD.

[45] See the *Institutiones ad moniales pertinentes* cap 35 (cited n 14 above) and *Scripta de fratribus* cap 4, in *MA* 6, 2 p xxxvii*.

[46] Compare *Institutiones ad moniales pertinentes* cap 4–7, in *MA* 6, 2 pp xlv*–xlvi* and *passim* in the Gilbertine legislation.

[47] Aelred himself was very concerned (perhaps more than Gilbert) about the possibility of contacts between men and women in religious life: see his *De institutione inclusarum* cap 19, ed Charles Dumont, *Sources chrètiennes* 76: *Textes monastiques d'Occident* 6 (Paris 1961) p 92, where he condemned the association of women even with old men whose chastity was secure.

[48] See in particular the important series of articles on early Cistercian legislation by Jean-A. Lefèvre, whose conclusions were summarized by David Knowles, 'The Primitive Cistercian Documents', *Great Historical Enterprises* (London/Edinburgh 1963) pp 198–222 and Polykarp Zakar, 'Die Anfänge des Zisterzienserordens. Kurze Bemerkungen zu den Studien der letzten zehn Jahre', *ASOC* 20 (1964) pp 108–38.

involving both men and women, in many of which an early attitude of freedom and trust was later replaced by a policy of strict separation.

Further research needs to be done on the persistence, or re-emergence at this time, of the practice of men and women leading a chaste religious life under the same roof or within the same community.[49] There are at least two well-known examples of such relationships between individuals. One was between a monk of Vendôme named Herveus and the English recluse Eve, to whom Goscelin of St Bertin addressed his *Liber confortatorius* in 1082–83 and who had been given as a girl to the abbey of Wilton and later moved to the priory of St Eutropius near Angers, where she lived under the spiritual guidance of Herveus.[50] 'There Eve lived for a long time with her companion Herveus,' according to a contemporary poem. 'I sense that you who hear this are disturbed at this statement. Be not suspicious, brother, and banish this thought. This love was not in the world but in Christ.'[51] Christina of Markyate also combined an emphasis on virginity with a practice of spiritual relationships with men, especially abbot Geoffrey of St Albans. The author of her *Vita* admitted that they were the subject of gossip. 'Before they became spiritual friends, the abbot's well-known goodness and the maiden's holy chastity had been praised in many parts of England. But when their mutual affection in Christ had inspired them to greater good, the abbot was slandered as a seducer and the maiden as a loose woman.'[52]

[49] The projected (or lost) second part of the *Libellus de diversis ordinibus et professionibus qui sunt in aecclesia,* which was written probably in the diocese of Liège in the second quarter of the twelfth century, dealt among other subjects with women 'who take up Christ's sweet yoke with holy men and under their guidance': ed Giles Constable and Bernard Smith (Oxford 1972) p 4. On the continued popularity of syneisactism in twelfth-century England, see Louis Gougaud, 'Mulierum consortia. Étude sur le syneisaktisme chez les ascètes celtiques'. *Ériu* 9, 1 (1921) pp 147–56 and Roger E. Reynolds, '*Virgines subintroductae* in Celtic Christianity', *HTR* 61 (1968) pp 559 and 563–4, who defined the practice as 'the chaste living together of a male and female ascetic' (p 554), of which the purpose was both spiritual assistance and a test of chastity. Aelred specifically condemned it in his *De institutione inclusarum* (see n 47 above).

[50] C. H. Talbot, 'The Liber confortatorius of Goscelin of Saint Bertin', *Analecta monastica* 3, *SA* 37 (1955) pp 1–117, esp intro pp 8 and 22–3; compare [François] Chamard, [*Les*] *vies* [*des saints personnages de l'Anjou*] (Paris/Angers 1863) 2 pp 102–19 and 531–41.

[51] Chamard, *Vies* 2 p 535.

[52] *The Life of Christina of Markyate,* ed and trans C. H. Talbot (Oxford 1959) p 175; Compare Otto Pächt, C. R. Dodwell, and Francis Wormald, *The St Albans Psalter, Studies of the Warburg Institute* 25 (London 1960) pp 27–30 and 136–7, suggesting parallels between this life and that of St Alexius. See also pp 196–8 above.

Many religious reformers in the early twelfth century attempted to provide for the religious life of both men and women. They were like Gaucherius of Aureil, who was said by his biographer to have known 'that neither sex is excluded from the kingdom of God. Wherefore he tried to build the heavenly Jerusalem out of the double wall, that is of men and of women, and constructed the habitation of women a stone's throw from his cell, distributing what little he had to both men and women'.[53] The biographer of Gilbert of Sempringham compared his order to the chariot of God, 'which has two sides, that is one of men and the other of women; four wheels, two of men, clerics and laymen, and two of women, literate and illiterate; two beasts dragging the chariot, the clerical and monastic disciplines'. He then went on to praise 'this marvelous unity of persons and churches and this unheard-of community of all things, which made all things one and one thing all in the diversities of so many hearts and such great monasteries'. The ideal was one of paradisiacal harmony in which men and women lived side by side united in spiritual love.[54]

Gilbert was naturally aware of the dangers of this ideal in practice and concerned with regulating the contacts between men and women in the houses under his control, as Aelred's questions in the second parenthesis show, but he appears himself to have enjoyed a high degree of ease in his relations with women. According to his biographer, he was reputed never to have touched a woman from the beginning of his long life until the end, 'and since he overcame the more severe struggle of youth, he was all the more worthy later to assume the steadfast rule of the weaker sex'.[55] William of Newburgh, writing shortly after Gilbert's death, described him as 'a clearly extraordinary man, and of singular grace in the care of women' and as supported in his undertaking 'by the consciousness of his own chastity and confidence in divine grace . . . In my opinion, indeed,' William continued, 'he holds the palm in this region among all those whom we know to have devoted their religious labour to ordering and controlling women.'[56] This confidence is reflected in an extraordinary story—

[53] *Vita b Gaucherii, Nova bibliotheca manuscriptorum librorum,* ed P. Labbe (Paris 1657) 2 p 562.

[54] *Vita, MA* 6, 2 pp ix*–x*.

[55] *Vita, MA* 6, s p v*, compare pp v*–vi*, where he recounted Gilbert's dream of putting his hand on a woman's breast and consequent avoidance of female company.

[56] William of Newburgh, *Historia rerum anglicarum* 1, 16, in *Chronicles of the Reigns of Stephen, Henry II, and Richard I,* ed Richard Howlett, *RS* 82 (London 1884–9) 1 p

almost as extraordinary as that of the nun of Watton—told by Gerald of Wales about Gilbert, who when an old man and, as Gerald put it, 'most unsuited for the purposes of lust', was looked upon with lascivious eyes by one of his own nuns. Gilbert was horrified, and the following day, after preaching in chapter on the virtue of chastity, he disrobed entirely, walked around three times for all to see him, 'hairy, emaciated, scabrous and wild', and then cried, evidently pointing to the crucifix, 'Behold the man who should be duly desired by a woman consecrated to God and a bride of Christ'. He then went on, pointing to himself: 'Behold the body on account of which a miserable woman has made her body and soul worthy of being lost in Hell'.[57] Gerald is an untrustworthy source, and the story may be apocryphal, but it illustrates the spirit of confidence, not to say bravado, that marked Gilbert's relation with his nuns. More generally, it illustrates the relative freedom between men and women that existed in many reformed religious communities, especially in the north of Europe, in the twelfth century, and it therefore helps to explain both the situation of Watton and the savage reaction of the community when the freedom was abused.

While it is impossible to estimate the influence of the episode on the history of the Gilbertine order, it is worth noting that the lay-brothers of Sempringham who revolted against Gilbert in the mid-1160s, a few years after the affair at Watton, specifically raised the question of moral lapses caused by the proximity of nuns and canons, together with the issue of an alleged requirement to make a new profession.[58] Influential

---

54–5. This work was begun in 1196, soon after Gilbert's death, at Newburgh in Yorkshire.

[57] Gerald of Wales, *Gemma ecclesiastica* 1, 17, in *Opera,* 2 p 247–8. This work was written between 1194 and 1199, according to Michael Richter, *Giraldus Cambrensis* (Aberystwyth 1972) p 66. Graham, *Gilbert* p 40 called this story 'gossip'. For Knowles' opinion, see n 2 above.

[58] See *Vita, MA* 6, 2 pp xii*–xiii* and above all Knowles, 'Revolt' pp 485–7, from whom the summary of charges given here derives and who dated the revolt from *c*1166–7 'at the latest', and Foreville, *Procès* pp 83–110, who dated it from late 1165. Both Knowles (pp 475–87) and Foreville (pp 90–110) independently published, from somewhat different sources, the main documents dealing with the affair. They are cited here by number (not page) from Foreville, whose dossier is more complete, but references will be given to Knowles, also by number and especially to his no 7, which was omitted by Foreville. On the possible connection between this revolt and the affair of the nun of Watton, see the thesis of Sharon Elkins cited above; on this and parallel episodes in the histories of other reformed religious orders, see Jean Becquet, 'La première crise de l'ordre de Grandmont', *Bulletin de la Société archéologique et historique du Limousin* 87 (Limoges 1960) pp 283–324, esp pp 298–9.

voices refuted this charge, however. 'All the episcopal testimony,' wrote David Knowles, 'added to that of the king, asserts that no breath of scandal has sullied the new order'.[59] No less than five bishops wrote to pope Alexander III, who seems to have been inclined at first to believe the lay-brothers, and assured him that the nuns and canons in Gilbertine houses in their dioceses lived strictly apart.[60] The prior of Bridlington wrote that no evil rumour concerning the canons had ever reached his ears.[61] Henry II sent two letters supporting Gilbert and threatening to take away the property of the order if it was in any way changed.[62]

The most surprising among these letters are those from archbishop Roger of York, of which one (written jointly with bishop Hugh of Durham) specifically referred to Watton as 'the only house in the diocese of York in which canons and lay brothers live together honourably with nuns within the same walls, which are ample, but separately, as common repute has it',[63] and of which the other (written in Roger's name alone) again denied that the canons, brothers, and nuns lived together in the houses subject to the rule of Gilbert and went on to say that, 'They live separately, eat separately, and are so segregated from each other that access to the nuns is possible for no canon or brother. With regard to the houses that he has in our diocese', Roger continued, 'we dare say with certainty that they are ruled most honestly and religiously'. And he then warned, like the king, that the donors who had given property to the house would take it away if the canons and brothers were separated from the nuns in the manner ordered by the pope.[64]

[59] Knowles, 'Revolt' p 470.

[60] Foreville, *Procès* no 3 (Knowles no 1) from William of Norwich, no 4 (Knowles no 6) from Henry of Winchester, no 5 (not in Knowles) from Robert of Lincoln, and no 6 (Knowles no 2) from Roger of York and Hugh of Durham, and Knowles no 7 (not in Foreville) from Roger of York. The terms of these letters are similar—perhaps suspiciously so—but William of Norwich, Roger of York, and Hugh of Durham emphasized that they had taken steps to ensure the separation of the sexes.

[61] Foreville, *Procès* no 9 (Knowles no 8).

[62] Foreville, *Procès* nos 10 and 13 (Knowles nos 10–11).

[63] Foreville, *Procès* no 6 (Knowles no 2). It is uncertain from the text whether the phrase 'ut fama publica est' belongs with 'seorsum' or 'honeste'. Roger and Hugh went on to deny the other charges against Gilbert but added that they had ordered, and he had agreed, to separate the canons from the nuns in accordance with the papal mandate.

[64] Knowles no 7 (not in Foreville). Some ten years later the cardinal-legate Hugh of Pierleone visited the nuns at Sempringham, 'whose way of life . . .', he wrote to the pope, 'might better and more truly be said to be in heaven than among mankind', and praised Gilbert and his order: Foreville, *Procès* no 16 (Knowles no 9).

It is difficult to explain how Roger could have written these words explicitly about a house where the events described by Aelred of Rievaulx had occurred only a few years earlier.[65] He may really have been ignorant of them, although they were certainly known to a number of people outside Watton itself, including not only Aelred and the distant friend to whom he addressed his account but also the companions who came with Aelred from Rievaulx. It is more likely that Roger knew about the affair but regarded it as uncharacteristic, insignificant, or as effectively settled.[66] He may also have hesitated to provide an excuse for papal interference in the affairs of his diocese. Those scholars who have accepted without question the royal and episcopal exonerations of Gilbert and his order from the charges brought by the lay brothers of Sempringham may not have taken sufficiently into account, in reaching their conclusion, the facts that the revolt came at the height of the quarrel between Henry II and Becket and that Becket, in spite of his high personal esteem for Gilbert, wrote him two severe letters in 1166 ordering him to put into effect the reform mandated by the pope.[67] The bishops who wrote to Alexander III in support of Gilbert all favoured the king against the archbishop. Roger of York, indeed, was one of Becket's strongest opponents.[68] All but one of them were with Henry at Westminster towards the end of 1165, when word of the revolt first spread,[69] and it is not unlikely that they agreed to support Gilbert as a matter of policy.

This is no way to imply that their admiration for Gilbert and his order was insincere or feigned, since he was clearly revered personally

[65] This problem is discussed, and a somewhat different solution proposed, in Sharon Elkins's thesis.

[66] Compare Henry C. Lea, *History of Sacerdotal Celibacy in the Christian Church* (3 ed London 1907) 1 p 343, who commented on the small effect that clerical scandals seem to have had on public opinion in England in the twelfth century.

[67] Foreville, *Procès* nos 1–2 (not in Knowles). Compare *Vita, MA VI*, 2 p xii*, where Gilbert himself was said to have favoured Becket and to have been held for questioning by the royal judges until he was freed at the king's command. The *Vita* was written after the deaths of both Becket and Henry, however, and at a time when all good men were supposed to have supported Becket.

[68] David Knowles, *The Episcopal Colleagues of Archbishop Thomas Becket,* Ford Lectures 1949 (Cambridge 1951) pp 12–14 (Roger of York), 14–15 (Hugh of Durham), 15–16 (Robert of Lincoln, who was linked by family and friendship with Becket's enemy Gilbert Foliot), 31–3 (William of Norwich, also a friend of Foliot), and 34–7 (Henry of Winchester). On Hugh, see also [G. V.] Scammell, *Hugh [du Puiset, Bishop of Durham]* (Cambridge 1956).

[69] C. W. Foster, *The Registrum Antiquissimum of the Cathedral Church of Lincoln* 1, *LRS* 27 (Lincoln 1931) pp 120–1 (no 194); compare R. W. Eyton, *Court, Household, and Itinerary of King Henry II* (London 1878) p 87 and Scammell, *Hugh* p 274.

by everyone involved, including Becket.[70] Henry II and the royal family were said by Gilbert's biographer to have gone out of their way to honour and assist him.[71] The various letters concerning the revolt of the lay brothers reflect not only a pride in Gilbert but also a determination to protect him and the good name and independence of his order. Even Walter Map, who rarely resisted the temptation to score off religious reformers, had only good words for the Gilbertines, though he characteristically warned that, 'There is fear, however, for the frauds of Venus often penetrate the walls of Minerva, and there is no meeting between them without consent'.[72] The testimony of William of Newburgh, and even the story of Gerald of Wales, show Gilbert's high reputation after his death, as above all do his speedy canonization and the impressive dossier compiled to support it in 1201–2.[73]

It is not therefore surprising that in the 1160s, when he was already nearly eighty years old, men of high position and repute came to Gilbert's aid in the affairs both of the nun of Watton and of the revolt of the lay-brothers. They doubtless wanted not only to prevent a public scandal that would have tarnished the reputation of an admired religious leader and the order he had founded—the only native English religious order—but also to forestall any papal interference in the affairs of the English church. These events may well at the same time, however, have contributed to the institutional development of the Gilbertine order, and especially the tendency towards an increasingly strict separation of men and women. Gilbert's biographer may indeed be referring specifically to the affair at Watton when after praising Gilbert's efforts to suppress vice he wrote that, 'He cured by harsh punishment a particular nun who was aroused by the fire of ungovernable lust through the machinations of the Devil'.[74] Events such as this clearly promoted a stricter discipline in the order, which was in a period of institutional development at the time of the affair at Watton. It reflects something both of the early fervour and freedom

[70] Foreville, *Procès* no 1 (not in Knowles).

[71] *Vita, MA* VI, 2 p xiv*, compare p x* on his high repute among contemporaries.

[72] Walter Map, *De nugis curialium* 1, 27, ed M. R. James, *Anecdota Oxoniensia: Mediaeval and Renaissance Series* 14 (Oxford 1914) p 55.

[73] Foreville, *Procès* pp 1–73, including thirty-four letters and two collections of miracles.

[74] *Vita, MA* VI, 2 p x*; compare the *Scripta de fratribus* cap 28 (cited n 29 above) on the treatment of incestuous members of the order and the *Institutiones ad moniales pertinentes* cap 35 and *Scripta de fratribus* cap 4 (cited nn 14 and 45 above) on the age of reception.

of the Gilbertines and of the resulting problems, which contributed to the formulation of the rigid regulations found in the surviving statutes of the order.

Dumbarton Oaks

THE PROBLEM OF THE CISTERCIAN NUNS IN THE TWELFTH AND EARLY THIRTEENTH CENTURIES

by SALLY THOMPSON

THE early Cistercians were remarkable for their hostility to the feminine sex. 'No religious body' wrote Southern, was 'more thoroughly masculine in its temper and discipline than the Cistercians, none that shunned female contact with greater determination or that raised more formidable barriers against the intrusion of women.'[1] The whole tenor of several of the early Cistercian statutes was that women were to be avoided at all costs. One decree enjoined the monks to sing like men and not imitate the high-pitched tinkling of women.[2] Apart from these disparaging references to the female sex in general, an early statute explicitly stated that no Cistercian abbot or monk should bless a nun.[3] In the thirteenth century this was interpreted as applying to the solemn consecration of nuns—a task which pertained to the bishop. It is stated that abbots did have the power to bless nuns at the end of their novitiate.[4] But this later interpretation may well reflect later subtleties. It seems probable that the decree was originally intended to stop the Cistercians concerning themselves with nuns.[5] The view that it was originally a straight-forward prohibition is strengthened by the fact that the same early decree went on to forbid the baptizing of infants. This decree, therefore, is crucial to any analysis of the position of nuns within the Cistercian order in the twelfth century. Dating it is difficult.[6] Van Damme suggested that

[1] [R. W.] Southern, *Western Society* [*and the Church in the Middle Ages*] (Harmondsworth 1970) p 314.

[2] Canivez 1 p 30 cap 73.

[3] *Ibid* 1 p 19 cap 29.

[4] *Ibid* 2 pp 100–1 cap 53 (1231); 2 p 231 cap 5 (1241).

[5] Other historians have also suggested this interpretation. See [E.] Krenig, 'Mittelalterlich frauenklöster [nach den konstitutionem von Citeaux'] *ASOC* 10 (1954) pp 11, 16; [M.] Fontette, *Les religieuses* [*à l'âge classique du droit canon. Recherches sur les structures juridiques des branches féminines des ordres*] (Paris 1967) p 29.

[6] For a summary of the problems surrounding the primitive Cistercian documents see D. Knowles, *Great historical enterprises. Problems in monastic history* (Edinburgh 1963) pp 197–222. He pointed out, p 220, that the first volume of Canivez is largely out dated by new findings.

the second group of statutes in the *Instituta*—of which this is one—dated from 1125.[7] The collection as a whole was probably made in 1151 and this decree was still in the later codification of 1202,[8] although it was omitted from a collection of 1256.[9] It would seem that the assembly of Cistercian abbots was prohibiting their members from taking responsibility for nuns in the early years of the twelfth century, with the decree—technically at least—remaining in force until after the beginning of the thirteenth. Probably as a reflection of this, the early statutes of the Cistercian general chapters virtually ignored the question of nuns and nunneries, and it was not until 1213 that a decree specifically dealt with convents of women.[10] But by the middle of the thirteenth century a large number of nunneries had been formally accepted into the order and this is reflected by the number of decrees dealing with nuns and their convents. In 1241 twenty of the seventy-five statutes of that year were concerned with the needs and demands of religious ladies.[11] So whereas the Premonstratensian and Arrouaisian orders came to repent of their early tolerance of religious women and tried to exclude them,[12] the Cistercians, who at first seem to have thought a Cistercian nun was a contradiction in terms, eventually sheltered and organised a large number of nunneries.

This development raises interesting questions. What were the reasons behind the Cistercians' eventual acceptance of women into their order, and what was the status and position of nunneries which aspired to follow their reforms and customs before *L'efflorescence Cistercienne*[13] in the thirteenth century? The statutes themselves highlight the problem. Later twelfth century decrees of the general chapter

[7] J. Van Damme, 'Genèse des Instituta generalis capituli' *Cîteaux* 12 (1961) pp 42–53.

[8] [B.] Lucet, *La codification Cistercienne* [*de 1202 et son évolution ultérieure*] (Rome 1964) p 39.

[9] BM Additional MS 11294, printed in J. Fowler, *Cistercian statutes ad 1256–7* (London 1890). In this collection, cap 7 p 24 which preceded the prohibition about baptism, merely stated that no bishop was to bless a novice. No mention is made of nuns.

[10] Canivez 1 p 405 cap 3.

[11] *Ibid* 2 pp 230–45.

[12] For the refusal of the Premonstratensians to admit any more sisters, see a bull of Innocent III (1198) *PL* 214 (1890) col 174. See also Southern, *Western Society* pp 313–14. From the end of the twelfth century the Arrouaisians attempted to limit the numbers of women within the order, and in 1233 it was decreed that no more were to be received without the consent of the whole chapter—see [L.] Milis, *L'ordre des chanoines* [*réguliers d'Arrouaise, son histoire et son organisation, de la fondation de l'abbaye-mère* (*vers 1090*) *à la fin des chapitres annuels* (*1471*)], 2 vols (Bruges 1969) 1 p 248.

[13] For a study of this expansion of Cistercian nunneries in the thirteenth century see [S.] Roisin, 'L'efflorescence Cistercienne [et le courant féminin de piété au treizième siècle'], *RHE* 39 (1943) pp 342–78.

contain hints of the existence of women dedicated to the religious life —women who may have had some links with the Cistercian order. A decree of 1194 punished the abbots of La Ferté, Pontigny and Clairvaux for allowing nuns into the choir at the dedication of the basilica of Cîteaux. They had also transgressed in extending the length of time allowed for women to be present at such a dedication beyond the permitted nine days.[14] It is interesting that such important members of the Cistercian order had countenanced the presence of nuns on such an auspicious occasion. Naz argued that the decree showed that by this date Cistercian nuns were already in organised existence.[15] But it is not stated that the nuns were Cistercian, and the abbots were punished for their temerity. Earlier, in 1191, the statutes of the general chapter made a reference to nuns when a decree dealt with the problem of abbesses in Spain attending a chapter of their own. The matter had been raised by Alphonso VIII of Castille, and the Cistercian abbots adopted a cautious tone, stating that they were unable to compel the ladies to attend such an assembly but would be pleased if they did.[16] The Cistercian monks were explicitly prohibited from holding local assemblies[17] and the general chapter's response to the royal request in itself suggests that the status of the nuns requires further study.

Even the early Cistercian fathers, imbued by their zeal for a return to a strict interpretation of the Benedictine rule, and with a stress on manual labour which was hardly appropriate for ladies, could not escape from the importunities of women. Under Robert of Molesme several ladies lived within the shelter of that monastery.[18] Land at Jully was granted to Molesme on condition that it was used to house women called to the religious life, and the priory of Jully may well have been founded, in part at least, to accommodate the wives and dependants of the monks at Cîteaux. The first prioress was Elizabeth, wife of the eldest brother of Saint Bernard, and the saint's sister,

[14] Canivez 1 p 180 cap 55. For an earlier decree about the presence of women at dedications see *ibid* 1 p 61 cap 10 (1157).

[15] *DDC* 3 col 775.

[16] Canivez 1 p 139 cap 27. The tone is in marked contrast with the incisive decrees compelling the attendance of abbots at general chapters held at Cîteaux, for example *ibid* 1 p 128 caps 49–50. See also p 237 of this chapter.

[17] General chapters were to be held annually at Cîteaux, *ibid* 1 p 13. For an example of the general chapter acting against a local chapter of abbots in Lombardy see *ibid* 1 p 136 cap 13 (1191).

[18] [J.] Croix Bouton, ['L'établissement des] Moniales Cisterciennes,' *Mémoires de la société pour l'histoire du droit et des institutions des anciens pays Bourguignons* 15 (Dijon 1953) pp 83–6.

Humbelina, also entered the house and later became prioress. It appears that the priory was influenced by Cistercian reforms: it was not to receive churches or to have servants. But although advice seems to have been obtained from the Cistercian abbots of Clairvaux, Morimond, Pontigny and Fontenay, the priory of Jully remained under the jurisdiction of Molesme.[19]

A house often described as the first Cistercian nunnery is the convent of Tart.[20] Its foundation certainly mirrored the actions of the first Cistercians. Some nuns from Jully, dissatisfied with the religious life in that house, asked Stephen Harding for help in their desire to follow a stricter vocation. The first abbess of Tart was Elizabeth de Vergy, and Croix Bouton suggested that she might have been the daughter of the Elizabeth who gave generous endowments to Cîteaux when the new foundation was struggling to survive.[21] But in some instances the customs of the nunnery showed interesting divergencies from what might be expected of a Cistercian establishment. A document of 1132 showed that the house received the tithes of the church of Tart.[22] A bull of Eugenius III, addressed to the abbess of Tart, made no mention of the nunnery as belonging to the Cistercian order.[23] It was only at the end of the twelfth century that a letter of abbot Guy of Cîteaux stressed Tart's links with the Cistercians and stated that *propria est filia domus Cisterciensis*.[24] It may well be that originally the nunnery's links with Cîteaux were largely due to the initiative of Stephen Harding.[25] The general chapter's decree prohibiting the blessing of nuns would seem to indicate that this was one of the saint's initiatives which the assembly of Cistercian abbots did not wish to follow.

Both Tart and Jully, therefore, had particular historical links with the Cistercians. That did not mean they formed a feminine branch of the order or were fully incorporated into it. This also seems to be true of some other nunneries which entered into a particular relationship with the Cistercian order in the course of the twelfth century.

Stephen, abbot of Obazine, founded a nunnery nearby at Coiroux in 1143. Enclosure was strictly enforced and the convent was kept

[19] *Ibid* pp 88–9.

[20] *Ibid* p 90. See also [P.] Guignard, *Les monuments primitifs* [*de la règle cistercienne publiés d'après les manuscrits de l'Abbaye de Cîteaux*] (Dijon 1878) p lxxxviii.

[21] Croix Bouton, 'Moniales Cisterciennes' pp 94–6.

[22] *PL* 185 bis (1854) col 1410.

[23] *PL* 180 (1902) cols 1199–1200; Jaffé 2 no 9013.

[24] *PL* 185 bis (1854) cols 1413–14.

[25] Krenig, 'Mittelalterlich frauenklöster' pp 15–16 and Fontette, *Les religieuses* p 29 also take this view.

under the abbot's immediate supervision.[26] Problems arose when, in 1147, Stephen wanted to join the Cistercian order. According to the *Vita beati Stephani* the holy man's relationship with the nuns was regarded as the greatest impediment to this step.[27] Manrique interpreted this objection as referring simply to the close proximity of the nuns to Obazine.[28] But, as Boyd pointed out, it does seem to have a wider interpretation than this, and provides further doubts about the exact status of 'Cistercian' nunneries in the first half of the twelfth century.[29] In accepting Obazine into the order, the *Vita Stephani* emphasised the part played by abbot Raynard of Cîteaux who had a great regard for Stephen. As with Stephen Harding and the nunnery of Tart, it may well be that the initiative of the abbot of Cîteaux was important. It certainly seems clear that the acceptance of Coiroux was largely forced on the abbots of the Cistercian order, by the virtual impossibility of accepting Obazine and rejecting Coiroux when the nunnery was so recently founded and so dependent on its mother house.

The houses of Savigny posed similar problems about the position of nunneries linked with an order affiliating to Cîteaux. When these joined the Cistercians in 1147 there were three nunneries in addition to the twenty-eight men's houses.[30] Buhot argued that these nunneries did not pose any problems for the Cistercians, and used this as evidence to support the thesis that there were Cistercian nunneries in the first half of the twelfth century.[31] On the other hand there is the view that the nunneries were not technically incorporated into the order, but remained on the fringe under Savigniac patronage and control.[32] Under the terms of the affiliation it was recognised that the houses of the order of Savigny could keep their particular customs—customs which, as in the case of the acceptance of ecclesiastical revenues, were sometimes contrary to previous Cistercian decrees.[33] It is true that even

[26] E. Baluze, 'Vita beati Stephani abbatis monasterii Obazinensis' *Miscellanea*, ed J. Mansi, 4 vols (Lucca 1761) 1 pp 158–9.

[27] *Ibid* 1 p 160.

[28] A. Manrique, *Cisterciensium seu verius ecclesiasticorum annalium a conditio Cistercio*, 4 vols (Lyons 1642–59) 1 p 430. A decree of 1218 later ordered that nunneries were not to be constructed within six leagues of men's abbeys, see Canivez, 1 p 485 cap 4.

[29] [C.] Boyd, *A Cistercian nunnery* [*in medieval Italy*; *the story of Rifreddo in Saluzzo, 1220–1300*] (Cambridge Mass., 1943) p 80.

[30] The nunneries were Abbaye Blanche, Bival and Villers Canivet.

[31] [J.] Buhot Rambaud, ['L'abbaye Normande de] Savigny, [chef d'ordre et fille de Cîteaux],' *Moyen Age* 7 (1936) p 105.

[32] See J. Van Damme, 'La constitution Cistercienne de 1165', *ASOC* 19 (1963) p 62 n 3.

[33] Buhot Rambaud, 'Savigny' p 188. See also J. O'Donnell, *The congregation of Savigny*,

after the incorporation of the Savigniac houses, new nunneries affiliated to Savigny were founded. The nunnery of Bival in Rouen diocese, founded three houses of women before the third quarter of the twelfth century.[34] These foundations, however, may well reflect the demands of women with a religious vocation[35] and the pressure they exerted on Savigny, rather than a general acceptance of nunneries by the Cistercian order. The evidence which suggests that in the mid twelfth century the Cistercians were not concerned with nunneries and did not regard convents of women as members of the order, is reinforced by the chapter's rejection of Gilbert of Sempringham in 1147—the same year in which the houses of Savigny, and Obazine and Coiroux, were accepted. Although both the pope and Bernard of Clairvaux were impressed by the Englishman and gave him a warm reception,[36] the Cistercians refused to allow his nunneries to affiliate to their order. The main reason for this seems to have been that they were not prepared to undertake the care of nuns.[37]

During the twelfth century, however, apart from the houses with specific links with the Cistercians—tenuous though they may have been—there undoubtedly were other convents which imitated the Cistercian customs and the fervour of their return to the primitive Benedictine rule. The dialogue between a Cistercian and a Cluniac monk written *c* 1153–73, had the Cistercian boasting of the dedication of some women who imitated his order.[38] Herman of Laon described women working vigorously in the fields and imitating the monks of Clairvaux in every way they could.[39] But he made it quite clear that the women adopted the Cistercian customs spontaneously; there is no suggestion of Cîteaux taking any initiative, nor is it shown

---

1147–1344. (Fordham doctoral thesis 1952) p 22. O'Donnell described the union as 'more a marriage than an amalgamation.' For an example of a statute specifically exempting the abbot of Savigny from a ruling which applied to the other Cistercian abbots, see Canivez 1 p 48 cap 22 (1153).

[34] Buhot Rambaud, 'Savigny' p 106.

[35] For evidence of the religious fervour among women in the twelfth and thirteenth centuries see [B. M.] Bolton, 'Mulieres sanctae', *SCH* 10 (1973) pp 77–95.

[36] R. Graham, *S. Gilbert of Sempringham and the Gilbertines* (London 1903) p 13.

[37] Life of Saint Gilbert, *ASB* February 1 p 572. For a different interpretation of the significance of this refusal, see [B.] Golding, 'St Bernard and St Gilbert' [*The influence of St Bernard: Anglican essays with an introduction by Jean Leclercq*,] ed B. Ward (Fairacres Oxford 1976) pp 44–6.

[38] 'Dialogus inter Cluniacensem et Cisterciensem monachum', Martène and Durand, *Thesaurus* 5 col 1639. For the dating of the Dialogue see W. Williams, 'A dialogue between a Cluniac and a Cistercian', *JTS* 31 (1930) p 167.

[39] *Liber de miraculis S. Marie Laudensis, PL* 156 (1880) cols 1001–2.

whether the monks of Clairvaux accepted any responsibility for the nuns who admired them so greatly. Detailed local studies are needed to determine the validity and strength of such nuns' claims to be members of the order in the face of apparent official indifference.

Where such studies do exist, they show that many of the nunneries only made specific claims to be Cistercian in the thirteenth century. Herkenrode has been described as the first example in Belgium of a nunnery claiming to be a member of the Cistercian order. The house was founded in 1182, but the early history of the convent is shrouded in legend and it is the confirmation charter of the founder's son which probably first describes it as Cistercian.[40] A closer study of many of the nunneries traditionally regarded as belonging to the order, may well suggest that such claims had little foundation in the twelfth century. For example Salzinnes, another Belgian house, was thought to have affiliated to Cîteaux in 1154, but Canivez pointed out the difficulties surrounding the early history of the convent[41] and it seems to have first been referred to as Cistercian in 1209.[42] Krenig showed that the nunnery of Wechterswinkel in Bavaria, although it was founded before 1144, did not appear to enjoy the full privileges of the Cistercian order until the pontificate of Alexander IV.[43] The nunnery of Rifreddo in Italy is also interesting. Its foundation charters, dating from 1219, stressed that the house was to follow the Benedictine rule in its entirety, but the foundress, Agnes of Saluzzo, seemed more concerned with placing the nunnery under the protection of the pope than affiliating it to the Cistercian order. It was only in 1244 that the pope, in response to a petition from the nuns, placed Rifreddo under the supervision of the Cistercian monastery of Staffarda and specifically described it as Cistercian.[44]

Such absence of specific claims to be Cistercian in the twelfth century, would not preclude the possibility that some nunneries were unofficially linked to the order through connections with particular monasteries. In the thirteenth century, when nunneries were openly received into the order they were placed under the control and care of a father abbot. The statute of 1213 made several references to this.

[40] [J.] Canivez, *L'ordre de Cîteaux* [*en Belgique des origines* (*1132*) *au vingtième siècle*] (Forges lez Chimay 1936) pp 124–5. See also [J.] Hinnebusch, [*The*] *Historia Occidentalis* [*of Jacques de Vitry*,] *Spic Fr* 17 (1972) pp 263, 265.

[41] Canivez, *L'ordre de Cîteaux* pp 319–20.

[42] Hinnebusch, *Historia Occidentalis* p 263.

[43] Krenig, 'Mittelalterlich frauenklöster' p 19.

[44] Boyd, *A Cistercian nunnery* pp 41–2, 95–103.

Nuns were not to leave the cloister unless by special licence of the abbot responsible for them. The final sentence in the decree enjoined the abbots to see that the disciplinary measures laid down by the chapter were carried out in all the nunneries under their jurisdiction.[45] But the early history of such links between convents of women and Cistercian monasteries is obscure. According to one source Wechterswinkel was associated with the Cistercian house of Bildhausen from the middle of the twelfth century, but the first documentary evidence of the head of Bildhausen acting as father abbot to the nunnery dates from the late thirteenth century.[46] The abbey of Villers in the diocese of Liège, is often cited as an example of a monastery which favoured and supported convents of women.[47] The houses of Parc-les-Dames, Valduc, Roosendael, la Cambre and Ter Beeck all seem to have associated in some way with Villers. But none of these were mentioned as Cistercian before the early thirteenth century.[48] According to the chronicle of the house of Villers, the monastery's concern began with the pleadings of Gila, a Benedictine nun, who wished to lead a stricter form of life.[49] She encountered great opposition from the ecclesiastical authorities in her desire to adopt Cistercian customs. The chronicler recorded how the cowl of Saint Godfrey was given to her by a monk of Villers and this enabled the lady to overcome her opponents. The foundation of her nunnery of La Cambre, is usually dated *c* 1200.[50] Abbot Walter of Villers (1214–21) was certainly an active patron of nunneries. *Nihil aliud in mundo desiderabat* stated the chronicler, *nisi homines ad religionem adducere et monasteria virginum fundare; cumque plurimas domos monialium nostri ordinis in diocesim Leodiensem plantasset.*[51] There is less evidence that the earlier abbot Charles (1197–1209) was particularly concerned with the needs of religious ladies. The tradition that he was may well be partly based on an error of the chronicler who reported that he ended his days in retirement at the nunnery of St Agatha.[52] But at

[45] Canivez I p 405 cap 3. For the role of the father abbot in the care of nunneries see Fontette, *Les religieuses* p 35.
[46] Krenig, 'Mittelalterlich frauenklöster' p 20 n 1.
[47] Roisin, 'L'efflorescence Cistercienne' pp 354–5.
[48] Hinnebusch, *Historia Occidentalis* p 263. See also Canivez, *L'ordre de Cîteaux* pp 149, 198, 212, 231, 255.
[49] *Ex gestis sanctorum Villariensium, MGH SS* 25 (1880) p 230.
[50] [F.] Van der Meer, *Atlas [de l'ordre Cistercien]* (Amsterdam/Brussels 1965) p 274.
[51] *C[hronica] V[illariensis] M[onasterii], MGH SS* 25 (1880) p 199.
[52] *Ibid* p 197.

that date the house of St Agatha (Hocht) was in fact inhabited by monks and only became a residence for nuns in 1215.[53]

Links between a Cistercian monastery and a nunnery in the twelfth century are by no means proven. Krenig, who stressed the importance of the ties between Cistercian nunneries and a father abbot, also pointed out that it is not at all clear how real such links were in this period.[54] The position is further complicated by the fact that even when there was an association with a Cistercian monastery, it is not always clear that the nunnery followed the Cistercian institutes. For example Terbank in Belgium was linked to Villers, but the nunnery seems to have followed the Augustinian rule.[55] In areas where research has been undertaken for the twelfth century, it is the links between the diocesan authority and the nunnery which emerge, rather than control by a father abbot. Krenig has shown the part played by the bishop in the development of many of the German nunneries. At Wechterswinkel, the nuns owed obedience to the bishop from an early date. When the house eventually attained the privileges of the Cistercian order during the pontificate of Alexander IV, the bishops of Wurzburg retained considerable powers of supervision.[56] The part played by the bishops may well in itself reflect lack of concern on the part of individual Cistercian abbots as well as the general chapter in the twelfth century. Once the episcopal authorities had gained certain rights over the nunneries it would not be easy to modify the position[57] even though the Cistercian claims to exemption developed rapidly in the course of the twelfth century.[58]

In spite of lack of evidence in the statutes of the general chapter, and the lack of evidence about the role of individual Cistercian abbots, it is clear that by the opening years of the thirteenth century there were some houses of women which claimed to be Cistercian. The

[53] [E.] Moreau, *L'abbaye de Villers[-en-Brabant aux 12 et 13ième siècles]* (Brussels 1909) pp 49–50. See also Hinnebusch, *Historia Occidentalis* p 267.

[54] Krenig, 'Mittelalterlich frauenklöster' pp 17–18. Southern, *Western Society* p 316, argued that individual Cistercian abbots did play an important part in the expansion of the nunneries before the general chapter took any account of them.

[55] Moreau, *L'abbaye de Villers* p 114. For Villers's patronage of the béguines see Roisin, 'L'efflorescence Cistercienne' pp 363–4.

[56] Krenig, 'Mittelalterlich frauenklöster' pp 19–20.

[57] The problem of freeing nunneries from episcopal control is reflected in the statutes of 1244 and 1245 which decreed that new nunneries could not be incorporated until the diocesan had granted a charter renouncing his claims over them Canivez 2 p 275 cap 7 and p 291 cap 6.

[58] For the question of Cistercian exemption see J. Mahn, *L'ordre Cistercien et son gouvernement* (Paris 1951) cap 4.

decree of 1213 referred to *moniales quae iam etiam incorporatae sunt ordini.*[59] This could simply refer to the houses of Tart, Coiroux, the Savigniac nunneries and their affiliations, which, as I have shown, had particular historical links with Cîteaux. It could also indicate a more widespread breach of the edict that Cistercians were not to accept responsibility for nuns. A suggestion that such responsibility was being accepted is implicit in a decree of 1206 which stated that nuns were presuming to educate boys in the cloister.[60] Before the statute of 1213 only two nunneries were mentioned by name in the Cistercian decrees, and one of these—Villers Canivet—was a Savigniac house.[61] The other reference, in a decree of 1212, was to the nunnery of Brayelle-lès-Annay in the diocese of Arras,[62] a house founded in about 1196.[63] The wording of the decree suggests that it had only recently come under the jurisdiction of Cîteaux, as the problem was over its close proximity to a house of monks. It is also interesting that the question was referred to the abbot of Savigny, who presumably was thought to have had some experience in dealing with nuns.

The impression given by these fragments, is that it was only at the very end of the twelfth and the beginning of the thirteenth century[64] that the Cistercian abbots changed from their former position of indifference and incorporated into the order communities of nuns which may well have earlier imitated their customs. There were probably several reasons behind this change. Jacques de Vitry stated that no houses of women were founded in the early period of the order as they could not hope to reach the Cistercians' height of perfection. He went on to link the expansion of the Cistercian nunneries to the refusal of the Premonstratensians to admit any more women.[65] This may well have added to the number of women with a religious vocation seeking links with the Cistercians and increased the pressure they exerted. The greater number would demand a greater degree of organisation and the contrast would be striking between the disciplined

[59] Canivez 1 p 405 cap 3.

[60] *Ibid* 1 pp 320–1 cap 5. Educating children had long been forbidden by the Cistercians, see *ibid* 1 p 31 cap 78.

[61] *Ibid* 1 p 333 cap 75.

[62] *Ibid* 1 p 403 cap 62.

[63] Van der Meer, *Atlas* p 274.

[64] Compare the view of Boyd, *A Cistercian nunnery* pp 84–5 n 28. She also believed there was a change of attitude but dated it from the last quarter of the twelfth century. The English evidence she used to support this date is questionable.

[65] Hinnebusch, *Historia Occidentalis* pp 116–17. See also note 12 of this chapter.

organisation of the monks and the lack of control over the women on the fringes of the order.[66]

Against this background the importunities of Alfonso VIII of Castille may well have been an important factor in obtaining official recognition of the nuns within the Cistercian order. The famous Spanish convent of Las Huelgas, founded in 1187, seems to have been the earliest nunnery to put forward, from its foundation, vigorous claims to be Cistercian. Alfonso stated that he was founding a nunnery *in quo Cisterciensis ordo perpetuo observetur.*[67] In a letter of 1199 he referred to his intention that Las Huelgas *specialis filia sit ipsius Cisterciensis ecclesie.*[68] He went on to promise that if he entered religion he would choose the Cistercian habit. Alfonso was a powerful patron[69] and the abbot of Cîteaux may well have born this in mind when he promised to send some Cistercians to advise about the foundation. But it is interesting that the preamble to the abbot's letter stressed the royal and episcopal pressure put on him, and the wording suggests that the advice could be taken or rejected by the king and his high-born nuns.[70] The tone is similar to the cautious note adopted by the general assembly about their inability to compel the Spanish ladies to attend a gathering of their own at Las Huelgas.[71] The impression given is that Alfonso was determined that his nuns would be full members of the Cistercian order, but that the assembly of abbots was not so enthusiastic. The king's determination may have benefited other nunneries. It is interesting that it was only after the foundation of Las Huelgas that abbot Guy's letter stressed the links between Tart and Cîteaux.[72] Perhaps the nuns were jealous of the ladies of Las Huelgas appearing to have obtained a greater degree of recognition than they had. It also appears that it was only after the first chapter

[66] Bolton, 'Mulieres sanctae' p 79.

[67] J. Gonzalez, *El reino de Castille en la epoca de Alfonso VIII,* 3 vols (Madrid 1960) 2 p 809.

[68] *Ibid* 3 pp 208–9.

[69] In his will the king made generous grants to Cîteaux, *ibid,* 3 p 346. Alfonso's wife Eleanor, daughter of Eleanor of Aquitaine was, like her mother, a patron of Fontevrault, *ibid* 1 p 191, 2 pp 945–6. The power and aristocratic prestige of Las Huelgas suggests interesting similarities with Fontevrault.

[70] [R.] Lopez, [*El real monasterio de*] *Las Huelgas* [*de Burgos y el hospital del Rey*] (Burgos 1907) p 329 no 4.

[71] Canivez 1 p 139 cap 27. See also p 229 of this chapter. Part of the problem may have been resistance on the part of the nuns to dictation from the all-male general chapter.

[72] *PL* 185 bis (1854) cols 1413–14. For the dating of abbot Guy (1194–1200) see J. Marilier, *Chartes et documents concernant l'abbaye de Cîteaux* (Rome 1961) p 27.

at Las Huelgas in 1189[73] that a similar assembly for daughter houses was held at Tart.[74] The privilege of the Spanish nunnery remained a striking feature. The third abbess, Dona Sanchia Garcia (1207–30) even went so far as to take upon herself the same powers as an abbot —including his sacerdotal authority—and presumed to hear confessions and bless novices.[75] Innocent III was scandalised and pointed out the unworthiness of women for such offices in spite of the virtues of the Virgin Mary.[76] Such actions by the abbess were hardly likely to be pleasing to the Cistercian abbots any more than the pope. It suggests that the counsel given by the nearby abbots was not proving an effective organ of Cistercian authority. But Las Huelgas had put forward definite claims to be Cistercian and was in a real sense associated with the order. The letter of the abbot of Cîteaux stated that *nos sanctum collegium vestrum in fraterna societate recipimus in omnium beneficiorum ordinis nostri plena vobis communione concessimus.*[77] The wording does not necessarily imply formal incorporation but a significant precedent had been established.

The demand for official recognition of nuns and their organisation within the Cistercian order was eventually met by the statute of 1213. But the problems were by no means solved. A mere seven years later a statute of 1220 decreed that no more convents of nuns were to be incorporated into the order.[78] In 1228 this prohibition was repeated but in more precise terms. The Cistercian abbots recognised that they had no right or power to prevent nuns imitating their customs and way of life, but stated clearly that they would not take responsibility for any more such houses or accept the task of visiting them. The decree was strengthened by sanctions against those who contravened it—sanctions directed against monks and lay brothers who sought to obtain the affiliation of nunneries as well as against abbots.[79] In accepting their inability to prevent imitation and yet refusing to accept more nunneries within the framework of the order, the Cistercians may consciously have been returning to the position earlier in the

[73] [A.] Dimier, 'Chapitres generaux [d'abbesses Cisterciennes'], *Cîteaux* 11 (1960) p 272.

[74] Dimier, 'Chapitres generaux' p 270. Compare the view of Fontette, *Les religieuses* p 37 who suggested that the chapters at Tart started in 1188 or 89. This is presumably based on a mis-dating of abbot Guy derived from Guignard, *Les monuments primitifs* p lxxxix.

[75] Dimier, 'Chapitres generaux' p 274.

[76] *PL* 216 (1891) col 356; Potthast 1 no 4143.

[77] Lopez, *Las Huelgas* p 329 no 4.

[78] Canivez 1 p 517 cap 4.

[79] *Ibid* 2 p 68 cap 16.

twelfth century. Their reluctance to accept nuns within the order seems to be linked, at least in part, with their difficulties in disciplining them. Several statutes in the early thirteenth century stressed the importance of enclosure[80] and the decree of 1220 added that nuns who refused to accept this were to regard themselves as beyond the jurisdiction of the order.[81] A further hint of the troublesome nature of some of the religious ladies, and their failure to attain the Cistercian ideals, is implied in a decree of 1249 which stated with a hint of desperation that for nuns who were already incorporated into the order and enjoying its privileges *decens est et honestum ut in iis quae secundum Deum et ordinem fieri possunt, ordini se conforment.*[82] Another problem was the sheer volume of work resulting from the affiliation of nunneries. In 1228 special auditors were appointed to hear cases involving the nuns and so remove from the general chapter *earundem taedium et gravamen.*[83] In 1222 the Cistercian abbots petitioned the pope with the request that they should not be forced to send monks to live with nuns and help them with their temporal affairs for *vergit enim res ista ad praeiudicium ordinis et periculum animarum.*[84] Providing confessors for the ladies posed further difficulties. It was the need to send older, and presumably less susceptible, monks to hear the nuns' confessions which, according to the chronicler of Villers, caused abbot Walter to relinquish the responsibility for some of his nunneries.[85] He felt that the senior men's absence deprived the abbey's younger brothers of a sage and stabilizing influence.

The impression given is that the Cistercians were not able to control the nunneries—or the nuns—wishing to belong to the order. The actual procedure of incorporation is by no means clear, perhaps reflecting the lack of a coherent policy. The statute of 1213 stated that the nuns were not to be sent out to found a new house without the consent of the general chapter.[86] This was in accordance with the general policy, for by the end of the twelfth century the consent of the chapter was necessary for the foundation of a new abbey of monks.[87] But there was no ruling in this statute about the procedure

[80] For example *ibid* 1 p 505 cap 12 (1219).
[81] *Ibid* 1 p 517 cap 4.
[82] *Ibid* 2 p 335 cap 3.
[83] *Ibid* 2 p 69 cap 17.
[84] *Ibid* 2 p 19 cap 30.
[85] *CVM* p 199.
[86] Canivez 1 p 405 cap 3.
[87] For occasions when abbots were reprimanded for acting without this consent see *ibid* 1 p 231 cap 46, 1 p 216 cap 31.

for nunneries already in existence—just an order that the nuns of any convent wishing to join the Cistercian order must be strictly enclosed. Nor, as Fontette pointed out, was the status of houses linked with the order before 1213 ever clarified by any specific ruling of the general chapter.[88] Between 1213 and the prohibition of 1220 only six nunneries are mentioned in the statutes as being incorporated.[89] At least four of these appear to refer to existing foundations which were outside the scope of the 1213 decree. The prohibition of 1220, however, was probably intended to stop the inclusion of any more houses—new or existing foundations—although this was not made explicit until 1228.[90] The decree of that year specifically prohibited both the affiliation of existing nunneries and the foundation of new ones. But from 1220 to 1228 the statutes only provide evidence of a mere handful of incorporations.[91] In some of these, particular Cistercian abbots were ordered to enquire into the suitability of a proposed foundation or an existing nunnery. As no name is given, it is virtually impossible to identify the name and locality of the convent and so discover whether it was accepted or not. In many of the cases where the abbots were ordered to report back at the following general chapter, there is no record of their recommendations. This may, of course indicate that the proposed foundations were not accepted, but it seems evident that many of the incorporations were not recorded in the statutes. Apart from the suspiciously low number of affiliations given specific mention, Boyd noted that the formal incorporation of Rifreddo took place some time between 1244 and 1249,[92] but no record of it is extant and there is no mention of it in the decrees of the general chapter. It may well be that many nunneries were received into the Cistercian order *de facto* rather than *de iure*.

The Cistercian efforts to limit the number of nunneries joining the order proved unavailing—as futile as the attempt of the early monks almost a century earlier to check the number of new foundations.[93]

[88] Fontette, *Les religieuses* p 31.

[89] Krenig, 'Mittelalterlich frauenklöster' p 17 n 4 listed four incorporations but omitted one of 1219, Canivez 1 p 513 cap 51. One decree, *ibid* 1 pp 415–16 cap 59 referred to two nunneries.

[90] Canivez 1 p 517 cap 4 (1220), 2 p 68 cap 16 (1228).

[91] Krenig 'Mittelalterlich frauenklöster' p 17 n 5 cited five. There are a few other examples in addition to these, for example the nunnery of St Pons de Gemenos and its daughter houses were associated in 1223, Canivez 2 p 29 cap 31. It is also possible that Tarrant, Dorset, was incorporated in this year see pp 243–4 of this chapter.

[92] Boyd, *A Cistercian nunnery* p 102.

[93] Canivez 1 p 45 cap 1 (1152).

After the decree of 1228 there was a decrease in the number of nunneries apparently requesting incorporation into the order, but it was short-lived. No incorporations are mentioned in the statutes of 1229, but two nunneries were accepted into the order in 1230,[94] and in the following decades the affiliations were numerous.[95] There is a hint of this failure to restrict the acceptance of nuns in a decree of 1235. It refers not only to convents of nuns already associated with the order but also to those *vel etiam de cetero sociandae*.[96] At the same time the rigour of some of the disciplinary measures taken against abbots who failed to control nuns in their care was modified. The penalty for an abbot who visited nuns who were not enclosed was changed from deposition to a mere diet of bread and water.[97] A large number of the later incorporations were at the petition of the pope or some powerful noble. The statutes stressed that the acceptance of the nunneries in 1230 was in response to a request from the pope, and a clause in one of the decrees made a somewhat vain attempt to ensure that this breach of the 1228 edict would not be regarded as a precedent.[98] In the year 1250 five successive statutes referred to the incorporation of different nunneries. Three of these affiliations were requested by a count or countess, one by a bishop and one by the pope.[99] Canivez's studies of Cistercian nunneries in Belgium showed that at least twenty of the houses founded in the early thirteenth century numbered dukes and countesses as their patrons,[100] Roisin noted the large number of nunneries which were accepted into the order and the absence of definite refusals, and argued that the general chapter willingly accepted the convents of women.[101] But, as already suggested, the statutes do not provide a complete record. The fact that the chapter eventually obtained a promise from the pope not to ask for more nunneries to be admitted to the order,[102] and the prevalence of powerful patrons behind the nunneries which were incorporated, indicates the importance of their influence and prestige. The impression given is that in the first half of the thirteenth century the agreement

[94] *Ibid* 2 p 87 cap 18; 2 pp 85–6 cap 10.
[95] For details of these see Roisin, 'L'efflorescence Cistercienne' pp 342–78.
[96] Canivez 2 p 139 cap 3.
[97] *Ibid* 2 p 76 cap 5 (1229).
[98] *Ibid* 2 p 87 cap 18.
[99] *Ibid* 2 pp 354–5 caps 40–4.
[100] See Canivez, *L'ordre de Cîteaux* for individual nunneries.
[101] Roisin, 'L'efflorescence Cistercienne' p 359.
[102] Canivez 2 p 361 cap 4 (1251).

of the general chapter was the reluctant result of persuasion by powerful patrons

The gradual acceptance of nuns as members of the Cistercian order in the course of the thirteenth century, is reflected in the development in the codifications of the statutes of the general assembly. It was probably only during the years 1221–40 that the decrees concerning nuns were collected under a separate heading. Before this, edicts concerning religious ladies were placed under the title of *de capitulis quae non habet propriam distinctionem*—a heading which in itself suggests their relative lack of significance.[103] Nuns were not allowed to attend the general chapter,[104] and it was only in the fourteenth century that many of the statutes of the general assembly were addressed to abbesses as well as abbots.[105] This does not mean that the nuns were regarded as a separate branch of the Cistercian order. They, like the monks, were under the jurisdiction of the general chapter. A thirteenth century translation of the *Ecclesiastica officia* made specially for nuns is printed in Guignard.[106] *Le povre Martin*, the author, was probably a chaplain to a nunnery. The translation does not reveal significant modifications to the Cistercian customs. The author merely suppressed some chapters dealing with clerics and altered the gender to the feminine as a concession to the nuns. Such minimal changes, however, should not obscure the difficulties inherent in the inclusion of women within the Cistercian order. The early Cistercians at first ignored and then barely tolerated the ladies who wished to share their fervour and imitate their customs. The acceptance of women was a gradual process and even in the first half of the thirteenth century the affiliation of nunneries to the order was beset by difficulties.

The problems revealed by this general survey are clearly illustrated by a study of the English Cistercian nunneries. Knowles and Hadcock listed twenty seven of the English nunneries as Cistercian.[107] Not included in this list are the houses of Stamford, Northamptonshire,

[103] Lucet, *La codification Cistercienne* p 10.

[104] Canivez 2 p 169 cap 4 (1237).

[105] Fontette, *Les religieuses* p 41.

[106] Guignard, *Les monuments primitifs* pp lxxiv–lxxxviii, and pp 407–643.

[107] *MRHEW* p 272. Hutton, Nunthorpe and Baysdale are counted as one convent as it was a single foundation which moved site. Knowles and Hadcock noted that sixteen of these houses belonged at one time to another order.

which claimed to be Cistercian for some part of the thirteenth century,[108] and Langley, Leicestershire, which put forward similar claims at the end of the twelfth.[109] Of all these, only Marham in Norfolk and Tarrant in Dorset are mentioned in the thirteenth century statutes of the order, and were clearly incorporated by that date. Marham was founded as a Cistercian abbey in 1250. A statute of the general chapter of that year referred to the inspection of the nunnery by two Cistercian abbots.[110] It is significant that it was a later foundation than the other nunneries and that its foundress, Isabel, widow of Hugh d'Aubigny, was a powerful lady.[111] In her foundation charter she specifically referred to her nunnery as Cistercian.[112] She consulted the abbot and monks of Waverley about her foundation and tactfully donated them four marks and a cask of wine after her visit.[113] The house of Tarrant was founded sometime before 1175,[114] but the earliest mention of it as being Cistercian is not until shortly before 1228,[115] and what little evidence there is about the early years of the nunnery suggest characteristics of a traditional Benedictine rather than a Cistercian house. It seems to have been dedicated to All Saints, not the Virgin, and it received grants of tithes and churches.[116] It may well be that the links with the Cistercians were forged under the patronage of bishop Richard Poore. There is an entry in the Cistercian statutes of 1223 which referred to the incorporation of an abbey requested by the

[108] *Ibid* p 266.

[109] A bull of Alexander III, Jaffé 2 no 13528, printed in *MA* 4 p 221 no 2, referred to the nunnery as Cistercian. The Augustinian canons of Breedon, however, disputed that they belonged to the order.

[110] Canivez 2 p 355 cap 43.

[111] *The Complete Peerage* by G. E. C., rev ed V. Gibbs, H. A. Doubleday, Lord Howard de Walde, G. H. White and R. S. Lea, 12 vols (London 1910–59) 1 p 238.

[112] *MA* 5 p 744 no 1.

[113] *Annales de Waverleia, Annales Monastici* ed H. Luard, 5 vols, *RS* 36 (London 1864–9) 2 pp 344–5.

[114] Evidence from the pipe rolls suggests that the founder, Ralph de Kahaines, was dead by 1175–6. See *Pipe Roll 21 Henry II* (1174/5) p 23 and *22 Henry II* (1175/6) p 155, *Pipe Roll Society* (London 1897, 1904) The date given in *MRHEW* for Tarrant, p 276, is *c*1186.

[115] The declaration of abbess Claricia to bishop Richard, preserved in the Salisbury diocesan record office, referred to the house as Cistercian, chapter records, press 2 box 1.

[116] A confirmation charter of Henry III, dated 1235 referred to Ralph de Kahaines's grants and those of his son William, and gave the dedication of the convent as All Saints, *MA* 5 p 621 no 6. Dedication to the Virgin was obligatory for Cistercian houses, Canivez 1 p 17 cap 18, and it does occur in later Tarrant charters, for example *MA* 5 p 620 nos 2 and 3.

bishop of Salisbury.[117] The house is not described as a nunnery, but the next decree in the statutes does refer to women,[118] so it is conceivable that the reference to *monialium* was omitted in error. If this were so the decree could mark the incorporation of Tarrant into the Cistercian order in spite of the 1220 decree prohibiting the reception of any more nunneries. Richard Poore was clearly an able and forceful man.[119] According to tradition Tarrant Keynes was his birth place,[120] and he was certainly a patron of Tarrant.[121] The Cistercians viewed him with favour, and on his death the priests of the order said masses for his soul.[122] The possibility that he obtained the incorporation of Tarrant into the Cistercian order is strengthened by the fact that the house was first called Cistercian in an oath taken by abbess Claricia to the bishop.[123] The house had certainly obtained official recognition by 1243 when a decree of the general assembly entrusted the care and correction of the house to two Cistercian abbots.[124]

The position of the other 'Cistercian' nunneries is considerably more confused. As already suggested, the fact that there is no mention in the statutes of their ever being incorporated into the order does not necessarily mean that they were not. Contemporary evidence as to the order of many of the English nunneries is scanty. Private charters rarely made reference to it. Royal records occasionally stated that a house was of the Cistercian order and so exempt from taxation.[125] But such statements could well be the result of pressure from a nunnery

[117] Canivez 2 p 29 cap 30 'petitio Cantuariensis et Domini Sarisberiensis de abbatia iterum Ordini incorporanda exauditur.' The use of the word 'iterum' is puzzling as there seems to be no earlier mention of the petition.

[118] *Ibid* 2 p 29 cap 31.

[119] The constitutions promulgated by him for the diocese of Salisbury acted as a model for several other areas. See *Councils and synods with other documents relating to the English church*, ed F. M. Powicke and C. R. Cheney, 2 vols (Oxford 1964) 1 pp 57–96.

[120] *DNB* 16 p 108.

[121] Matthew Paris described Tarrant as 'domum scilicet sanctimonialium quam venerabilis episcopus R. Dunelmensis a fundamentis construxerat.' *Matthei Parisiensis chronica majora*, ed H. Luard, 7 vols *RS* 57 (London 1872–84) 3 p 392. Richard Poore was translated to Durham in 1228, Le Neve 2, *Monastic Cathedrals* (1971) p 31.

[122] Canivez 2 p 170 cap 11.

[123] Declaration of abbess Claricia to bishop Richard Poore preserved in the Salisbury diocesan record office, chapter records, press 2 box 1.

[124] Canivez 2 p 271 cap 62.

[125] For example Tarrant and Swine are described as Cistercian in the close rolls of 1233 when the nuns were declared exempt from the payment of a tax. *Close Rolls [of the reign of] Henry III [preserved in the Public Record Office]*, 14 vols, *PRO texts and calendars* (London 1903–27) 2 (1905) 1231–34 p 295.

struggling to gain the privileges of the Cistercian order and do not necessarily reflect the views of the Cistercian abbots. An entry on the close rolls of Henry III reveals the abbot of Cîteaux complaining to the dean of Lincoln that although six abbesses wore the Cistercian habit they did not belong to the order and had no right to claim its privileges.[126] The houses listed were Stixwould, Greenfield, Nun Cotham, Legbourne, Gokewell and Stamford. It is interesting that four of these convents featured in a sixteenth century list in the general statutes naming houses which were to be visited by Cistercian abbots and so presumably by this time belonged to the order.[127] But a later description of a house as Cistercian clearly does not prove that it belonged to the order in an earlier period. The abbot's statement certainly suggests that houses which merely adopted Cistercian customs had no real claim to be members of the order.

Several general indications confirm the lack of official recognition given to these English nunneries in the twelfth and early thirteenth centuries. The abbot of Cîteaux was wrong when he described the Lincolnshire houses as abbeys—they were priories. Fontette argued that all Cistercian monasteries were abbeys.[128] It is true that the individual houses had a considerable degree of autonomy, and in the statutes of the general chapter the word abbey is always used.[129] In 1233, however, a decree does provide an isolated example of a priory of nuns being incorporated into the order[130] and there is no suggestion that the status of the house was in this case regarded as an obstacle. It would seem hazardous to argue that the status of a priory automatically excluded the English nunneries from belonging to the order. Fontette herself noted that the women's convents had a more dependent relationship than the men's on the monastery which was entrusted with their visitation and oversight.[131] A priory of Cistercian nuns would seem to be less of an anomaly than a priory of Cistercian monks. Nevertheless it is interesting that the only convents with the status of abbey were Marham and Tarrant. The fact that the others were priories could certainly be an indication of their lack of formal status within the order.

The lack of official recognition given to the nunneries by the

[126] *Close rolls Henry III* 14 (1938) 1268–72 p 301.

[127] Canivez 6 p 719 caps 45–6.

[128] Fontette, *Les religieuses* p 34.

[129] There are no priories among the list of Cistercian houses in *MRHEW* pp 112–15.

[130] Canivez 2 p 117 cap 31.

[131] Fontette, *Les religieuses* p 34.

Cistercian order in the twelfth and early thirteenth centuries is also reflected in their omission from lists of Cistercian foundations.[132] With such a dearth of evidence the *Mappa Mundi*, ascribed to Gervase of Canterbury,[133] increases in significance. In his introduction to the works of Gervase, Stubbs dismissed the *Mappa Mundi* stating that 'it affords some small material for local investigation, but its usefulness is quite a thing of the past'.[134] But when Knowles analysed the list he revealed a considerable degree of accuracy.[135] According to the catalogue in the *Mappa Mundi*, seven houses were of white nuns, *moniales albae*.[136] It is tempting to take this description as meaning the houses belonged to the Cistercian order. White habits certainly came to be regarded as a mark of the followers of Saint Bernard. The author of the *Vita Aelredi* compared the monks to flocks of sea gulls and regarded the colour of their habits as a sign of the whiteness of their souls.[137] But it is not clear how far the clothing of the Cistercians was uniformly white. An early twelfth-century manuscript showed them wearing grey and brown habits,[138] and they are described as grey monks in the dialogue between a Cistercian and a Cluniac.[139] It is also not clear how far the habit of the Cistercian nuns was distinct from other reformed orders. The *Mappa Mundi* listed Amesbury, Wiltshire, as a house of white nuns.[140] Amesbury was refounded in 1177 as a priory of the order of Fontevrault.[141] The ladies

[132] One example of a list probably dating from the early thirteenth century which makes no mention of nunneries is BM Cotton Faustina B VII fol 36—see the article by W. Birch 'On the date of foundation ascribed to the Cistercian abbeys in Great Britain', *Journal of the British Archaeological Association* 26 (London 1870) pp 281–99, 352–69.

[133] [*The historical works of*] *Gervase of Canterbury*, ed W. Stubbs, 2 vols *RS* 73 (1879–80) 2 pp 414–49.

[134] *Gervase of Canterbury* 2 p xlii.

[135] D. Knowles, 'Gervase of Canterbury and the Mappa Mundi', *DR* 48 (1930) p 238.

[136] *Gervase of Canterbury* 2 pp 418–49. The houses are Amesbury p 420; Camesturne p 422; Shouldham p 428; Brewood p 438; Duva (Keldholme), Rosedale and Sinningthwaite p 440. Camesturne may be the same house as Tarrant, the only other priory of nuns in Dorset, but the identification is not certain. It is possible that the white habits worn at Brewood White Ladies, Shropshire, reflect an early imitation of Cistercian customs. It is clear that the house became a member of the Augustinian order, see *VCH* Salop, 2 (1973) p 83.

[137] Walter Daniel, *Life of Ailred abbot of Rievaulx*, ed F. M. Powicke (2 ed Edinburgh 1963) p 10.

[138] C. N. L. Brooke, *The Monastic World 1000–1300* (London 1974) pp 28, 139. A feature of unbleached material is that it can take a variety of muted colours, with whiteness eventually predominating after frequent washing.

[139] Martène and Durand, *Thesaurus* 5 p 1645.

[140] *Gervase of Canterbury* 2 p 420. [141] *MRHEW* p 104.

of this order did wear white habits, as did probably the Arrouaisians, the Premonstratensian nuns and possibly the Gilbertines too.[142].

In addition to the houses of white nuns, the *Mappa Mundi* described thirteen convents as having white canons and nuns—*canonici albi et moniales*. Eight of these were Gilbertine houses[143] and the remaining five are usually classed as Cistercian.[144] The presence of canons in a Cistercian nunnery seems highly unlikely. There is, however, a considerable amount of evidence to support Gervase's statement and suggest that at several of these nunneries there was a sizeable body of canons. This is certainly true of Stixwould in Lincolnshire. Witness lists of charters indicate the presence of at least eight brothers with two others, Thomas and Tori, who were sometimes given the title of canon.[145] A charter dating from *c*1184–9 reveals the donor requesting that the nuns would receive his body and that of his wife and bury them as they would a canon or nun of the house.[146] At Wykeham and Catesby the documents indicate the presence of canons, and at Nun Cotham there seem to have been resident brothers.[147] Other houses beside those listed in the *Mappa Mundi* seem to have canons forming part of the community. This is true of the Yorkshire

[142] For details of the Fontevraldine habit see Fontette, *Les religieuses* p 76 n 78. Very little is known about the clothing of the Arrouaisians. The nuns' habits were probably some combination of black and white, see Milis, *L'ordre des chanoines* pp 489, 491. The Norbertine sisters also wore unbleached wool. A white alb may well have covered most of the dark tunic underneath, see F. Petit 'Les vêtements des Prémontrés au 12 siècle', *Analecta Praemonstratensia* (Tongerloo/Averbode 1925–) 15 (1939) p 23. The Gilbertines may also have worn a fuller white tunic in addition to the black habit, *MA* 6 (2) p lxxix.

[143] Sempringham, Haverholme, Catley, Sixhills, Bullington, Alvingham, Ormsby and Chicksands.

[144] Nun Cotham, Stixwould, Wykeham, Hampole and Catesby. *MRHEW* p 271, suggested that it was the presence of brothers in these houses which explained why they were mistakenly taken to be members of the order of Sempringham. But it was only in the case of Catesby, Northants, that the *Mappa Mundi* specifically described it as Gilbertine, *Gervase of Canterbury* 2 p 431.

[145] Some Stixwould charters are printed in [F. M.] Stenton, [*Documents illustrative of the social and economic history of the*] *Danelaw* [*from various collections*] (London 1920) cap 7. For these witnesses see pp 283–4, p 288 no 385. In a charter transcribed in the Stixwould cartulary, BM Add MS 46701 fol 6^{v}, Thomas and Tori act as witnesses but are not given the title of canon.

[146] Oxford Bodleian MS Linc charter 1167; see also the charter printed in Stenton, *Danelaw* p 286 no 382 which refers to the same grant.

[147] For example a Wykeham charter printed in *MA* 5 p 670 no 2 is witnessed by Nigel, a canon of the house; a letter of bishop Gravesend referring to the canons of Catesby is enrolled in Sutton's register, see *The rolls and register of bishop Oliver Sutton 1280–99*, ed R. M. T. Hill, 7 vols (Lincoln 1948–75) 2 (1950) p 5. The brothers of Nun Cotham are mentioned in a letter of Alexander III see *MA* 5 p 676 no 4.

priory of Swine and of Legbourne in Lincolnshire.[148] It is not clear to what order the canons belonged. Fragments of evidence from the thirteenth century suggest that there may have been links in some cases with nearby communities of Augustinian canons. Magister Hamo of Swine came from Healaugh Park[149] and Catesby seems to have had close links with Canons Ashby.[150] Lack of evidence precludes any firm conclusion about the origin of these canons apparently resident at the nunneries. Gervase of Canterbury's description of them as white canons suggests similarities with the Gilbertines rather than the Augustinians. There is, however, certainly nothing to suggest that the brothers ministering to the nuns were Cistercian monks or that these nunneries had any real claim to be members of the Cistercian order in the twelfth and early thirteenth century.

Several nunneries may have put forward such claims in an attempt to gain the privileges of the order. This is implied in the letter of the abbot of Cîteaux refuting the pretensions of the Lincolnshire houses.[151] It is comparatively well documented in the case of Nun Cotham, one of the houses on his list. Papal letters reveal an interesting progression from the statement that the nuns followed the Benedictine rule to claims that they followed the rule of Saint Benedict and the institutions of the Cistercian brothers.[152] This phrase occurred first in a letter of 1177[153] and was linked with claims for exemption from tithes. An earlier letter of Alexander III, dating probably from c1168–77, not only made no mention of the Cistercians but contained a clause permitting the religious at Nun Cotham to transfer to a stricter monastery[154]—a proviso usually omitted in the case of Cistercian houses. Stamford, also

[148] For example a charter of Henry II to Swine referred to canons and brothers of the house, *EYC* 3 p 78 no 1363. There are occasional references to canons of Legbourne, for example BM Add charter 7524, Oxford Bodleian MS Linc charter 1165.

[149] *Chronicon monasterii de Melsa a fundatione usque ad annum 1396*, ed E. Bond, 3 vols *RS* 43 (1886–8) 2 p 13.

[150] *MRHEW* p 153. See also *VCH* Northants 2 (1906) p 123.

[151] *Close Rolls Henry III, 1268–72* (1938) p 301.

[152] I am grateful to professor Holdsworth for pointing out that, in general, references to Cistercian brothers in papal bulls confirming monastic possessions are comparatively infrequent pre Alexander III. For example, Adrian IV's bull to Rufford, dated ?1156 stated that the monks followed the Benedictine rule making no reference to the Cistercians, while a bull of Alexander III dated 1160 did refer to the 'consuetudinem Cisterciensium fratrum', *Rufford charters*, ed C. J. Holdsworth, 2 vols, *Thoroton Society Record Series*, 29 and 30, (Nottingham 1972–4) 2 pp 364, 366–8.

[153] [W.] Holtzmann, [*Papsturkunden in England*,] 3 vols (Berlin/Göttingen 1930–52) 3 (1952) pp 370–1.

[154] *MA* 5 p 676 no 4. The dating clause of this bull is omitted and it is described in Holtzmann 3 p 31 as a bull of Alexander IV, But the reference to prioress Mathilda

in the diocese of Lincoln, provides an even clearer example of a convent which seems to have put forward claims to be Cistercian in an attempt to gain privileges. It was founded by the Benedictine house of Peterborough, and the nunnery was closely controlled by the monks.[155] But there is extant an inspeximus of a group of documents dating from 1269–73 which stated that Stamford was Cistercian and so exempt from the payment of a tenth.[156] Stixwould seems to have joined with Stamford in making this claim, and the abbot of Cîteaux's letter of 1270 was probably in response to their attempts to avoid paying the tax.[157] Stamford does seem to have later abandoned its claims to be Cistercian, and as Sturman pointed out, tried to obtain exemption from taxes on the ground that they were poor rather than that they were entitled to the privileges of Cîteaux.

It would, however, be cynical to suggest that all nunneries only imitated Cistercian customs in an attempt to gain fiscal privileges. There is some evidence that one or two English nunneries may have had stronger affinities with the followers of Saint Bernard. The founders of Sinningthwaite in Yorkshire certainly favoured the Cistercians. Bertram Haget gave valuable grants to Fountains,[159] and one of his sons became abbot first of Kirkstall and then of Fountains.[160] A letter of Alexander III dated 1172 stated that the nunnery followed the Benedictine rule and the institutions of the Cistercian brothers.[161] But when archbishop Geoffrey took the nunnery under his protection, he made no mention of the Cistercian order.[162] By 1276 the nuns clearly regarded the archiepiscopal interest as irksome and appealed to the pope against the right of the archbishop to visit them, claiming the exemption of the Cistercian order. But the nuns seem to have lost their appeal and archbishop Giffard ordered them to receive friars

---

and pope Anastasius would indicate that it is earlier. It presumably dates from *c*1168–77, as it is very similar to the bull of Alexander III printed in Holtzmann 3 p 366.

[155] *MA* 4 p 261 no 2.

[156] PRO Anc Deeds E 326/B11365 transcribed in [W.] Sturman, ['History of the nunnery of St Michael outside] Stamford.' (unpublished MA thesis, London 1945) appendix 4 p 391.

[157] Compare the view taken in *MRHEW* p 271, that it was in response to a decree of the general chapter.

[158] Sturman, 'Stamford' p 205.

[159] *Memorials of the abbey of St Mary of Fountains*, ed J. Walbran, 3 vols *SS* 42, 67, 130 (1863–1918) 1 (1863) p 123 n 6.

[160] *HRH* p 136 (Kirkstall), p 133 (Fountains).

[161] *EYC* 1 pp 167–8 no 200.

[162] *MA* (1 ed 1655) p 828.

minor as their confessors, in spite of the prohibition of the Cistercian abbots. According to the archbishop, Cîteaux had no jurisdiction over the ladies of Sinningthwaite.[163] Such a lack of official status within the order would not preclude the possibility, indeed the likelihood, that the nunnery had imitated Cistercian customs from an early date.

At Wintney in Hampshire there is a suggestion of a particular link between the nunnery and the Cistercian abbey of Waverley. The house was founded in about 1160 by a Geoffrey fitz Peter.[164] The foundation charters are only preserved in an inspeximus copy of Edward I and do have some features which raise doubts as to their unsullied authenticity.[165] The charter of Geoffrey fitz Peter claimed that the convent was founded by Waverley, and he invoked the whole weight of the monks' authority to bind the nuns to an agreement about the number of masses to be performed for his soul. It is difficult to assess this claim that the nunnery was founded under the auspices of Waverley. The abbot and prior witnessed one of the charters,[166] but there seems to be no other evidence of any link between the houses. The late thirteenth century obituary roll of the nunnery recorded the death of six abbots of Reading but only mentioned one abbot of Waverley.[167] As at Sinningthwaite, the nuns may well have imitated the customs of the Cistercians but these links were probably not supported by any organisational framework.

A study of the English Cistercian nunneries in the twelfth and first half of the thirteenth century reveals a web of uncertainties. Marham

[163] *Register of Walter Giffard* [*Lord Archbishop of York 1266–79,*] ed W. Brown *SS* 109 (1904) p 295.

[164] He cannot be identified with the justiciar of the same name. Apart from the early date, the names of his wife and mother differ from those of the justiciar, see *Calendar* [*of the*] *charter rolls* [*preserved in the Public Record Office,*] 6 vols, *PRO texts and calendars* (1903–27) 4 (1912) p 392. There is further evidence of an earlier Geoffrey fitz Peter in the Pipe Roll of *7 Henry II* (1160/1) p 57. See also a reference in *Winchester in the early middle ages; an edition and discussion of Winton Domesday*, ed M. Biddle (Oxford 1976) p 106 no 509 and note.

[165] For example, a confirmation charter of Henry II has the addition of a thirteenth century dating clause, *Calendar charter rolls* 4 p 391.

[166] *Ibid* 4 p 392.

[167] BM MS Cotton Claud D III fols 140^v–62^v. This is printed in *Annales Edwardi II Henrici de Blaneford chronica et Edwardi II vita Johannie de Trokelowe*, ed T. Hearne (Oxford 1729) pp 384–93. The abbot of Waverley is Adam, see *ibid* p 387. This could either refer to Adam 1 (1216–19) or Adam 2 (1219–36) *VCH* Surrey 2 (1905) p 88.

and Tarrant were formally incorporated into the Cistercian order by 1250. The other houses probably followed some of the Cistercian customs in a variety of ways and with a variety of modifications. Several, like the Gilbertine establishments, were organised in the form of double houses with resident canons. Swine priory in Yorkshire may well have been founded, like Sempringham itself, by a priest who gathered nuns round him and ministered to them.[168] The visitation returns of archbishop Walter Giffard showed the presence of canons, lay brothers and lay sisters as well as the nuns at Swine, and also referred to the windows through which food and drink were passed.[169] This would suggest an arrangement very similar to that in operation at Gilbertine houses. This was not necessarily a betrayal of the Cistercian ideals. There is evidence that the Gilbertines were thought to provide women with a form of life which closely approached the aims and zeal of the Cistercian monks. Bishop Alexander of Lincoln in his foundation charter for Haverholme stated that the Gilbertine nuns seized on the narrow life of the Cistercian order so far as they were able.[170] It is interesting that the Cistercian archbishop, Henry Murdac, placed the small girl who was later to cause such a saga of scandal and edification at the Gilbertine house of Watton.[171] The success of the Sempringham houses and those other nunneries which followed similar forms of organisation, may be a factor in explaining why so few English houses were formally incorporated into the Cistercian order. They were founded at a time when the Cistercians did not recognise nuns, and the presence of canons and resident brothers did not harmonize with the organisation demanded by the general chapter in the thirteenth century. Moreover, most of the houses were small, poor, and without powerful patrons—factors which again lessened their chances of obtaining incorporation. Lacock abbey, founded *c*1229,[172] illustrates the problem. The foundress, Ela, countess of Salisbury, was a great admirer of the white monks. Her abbey was dedicated to the Virgin and Saint Bernard,[173] and she obtained a grant of confraternity with the

[168] The founder is described as a brother Robert de Verli in a notification of Hugh du Puiset, *EYC* 3 p 75 no 1360. He is also described as Magister Robert de Verli in *MA* 5 p 495 no 5. This is probably the same man as the Magister Robert de Swine who featured in several witness lists, for example *EYC* 3 p 59 no 1338; Oxford Bodleian MS Dodsworth 7 fol 256.

[169] *Register Walter Giffard* pp 147–8.

[170] *MA* 6 (2) pp 948–9. See also Golding, 'St Bernard and St Gilbert' pp 44–8.

[171] For the story of the nun of Watton see *PL* 195 (1855) cols 789–96, and above pp 205–26.

[172] *VCH* Wilts 3 (1956) p 303.

[173] *MRHEW* p 281.

Cistercians—granted because of the great devotion which she had for the order.[174] But her nunnery, founded as it was only a year after the prohibition of the general chapter in 1228, had to be content with adopting the Augustinian rule.[175]

University of London

Westfield College

[174] *VCH* Wilts 3 p 303 n 8.
[175] *Ibid* 3 p 303.

VITAE MATRUM: A FURTHER ASPECT OF THE *FRAUENFRAGE*

by BRENDA M. BOLTON

THE prologue to Jacques de Vitry's *Life* of Mary of Oignies introduces us immediately to a situation peculiar to a small part of Europe at the turn of the twelfth century.[1] He draws our attention to a small, like-minded, closely knit group of people, mainly women, whose religious views and experience seemed to have developed only within the confines of the principalities of Brabant-Flanders, an area which the members of this group knew as Lotharingia.[2] In writing the *Life* his aim was to make the group which he had found and indeed which he himself had been eager to develop, known to a much wider audience, with the ultimate aim of establishing a tradition sufficient to allow for its possible institutionalisation and ultimate acceptance by the ecclesiastical authorities.

The prologue shows that he had considered the lives of the early fathers of the church to be important examples; that the accounts of their virtues and noble actions written by Jerome and Gregory the Great were for the edification of future generations, acting also as a means to confirm and strengthen the faith of waverers, to spur the idle to activity and the earnest to imitation.[3] He had come to the conclusion that it was to be his task and duty to write similarly about the inspiration to be found in the lives of the women of the group whom he came to know so well. He was helped in this intention by the encouragement of Fulk of Toulouse who, being impressed by what he had seen when he had visited the area, had wished to use it as an *exemplum* in preaching against the heretics of his own diocese,[4] and by

[1] Jacques de Vitry, *V[ita] M[ariae] O[igniacensis,]* ed D. Papebroeck, *ASB* June 4 (Antwerp 1707) pp 636–66. For various aspects of the whole *Frauenfrage* see Grundmann pp 170–98, 452–56; [E. W.] McDonnell, *The Beguines [and Beghards in Medieval Culture]* (Rutgers University 1954); A. Mens, 'Les béguines et béghards dans le cadre de la culture médiévale', *Moyen Age* 64 (1958) pp 305–15; [S.] Roisin, 'L'efflorescence cistercienne [et le courant féminin de piété au xiii siècle',] *RHE* 39 (1943) pp 342–78 and G. Koch, *Frauenfrage und Ketzertum im Mittelalter* (Berlin 1962).

[2] *VMO* p 666.1.

[3] *Ibid* p 636.1.

[4] *Ibid* p 638.8; Fulk of Toulouse (?–1231), created bishop of Toulouse in 1206, was driven from his diocese by heretics in 1212 and went to preach the crusade in Flanders.

the examples of Augustine and Jerome, both of whom had at various times supervised small groups of wealthy women leading lives of renunciation, celibacy and good works.[5] Jerome, in fact, had produced a flood of pamphlets, widely read and imitated in the middle ages, in which he had inveighed against the fickleness of women in general whilst praising the heroic dedication to the ascetic life of the women in these communities.[6] Jacques de Vitry had been a close friend and admirer of Mary of Oignies and, at least at the time of her death, an enthusiastic patron and promoter of this group of religious women.[7] He therefore used his ability as a narrator of the contemporary scene to follow Jerome and write a biography illustrating his view of what a new or modern saint should be.[8] When he came to write, Jacques de Vitry did not however invoke the early fathers as a mere literary device. He had sound practical reasons for so doing. In addition to being the most important and earliest reliable witness of the Franciscan movement[9] he was also the fervent supporter and sensitive biographer of any group which reflected the new religious enthusiasm of the *vita apostolica*.[10] This women's movement which had emerged from within his own diocese of Liège in Lotharingia, he considered to be no less significant than that of the early fathers in the stress which was laid upon ascetic behaviour, incredible feats of physical endurance, interior silence, intense compassion and great humility.[11] It is possible

---

His interest in religious women's communities as a bulwark against heresy had already led to his support of Dominic's foundation at Prouille. For a useful account of his activities,[R.] Lejeune, 'L'evêque de Toulouse, [Folquet de Marseille et la principauté de Liège',] *Mélanges Felix Rousseau* (Brussels 1958) pp 433–48, and [Brenda M.] Bolton, 'Fulk of Toulouse: the escape that failed', *SCH* 12 (1975) pp 83–93 for more general concerns in Languedoc.

[5] Christopher Brooke, *The Monastic World* (London 1974) pp 20–1, 167.

[6] *Ibid* p 20; J. N. D. Kelly, *Jerome: his life, writings and controversies* (London 1975).

[7] Jacques de Vitry (*c* 1160–70–1240) was a regular canon of St Nicholas of Oignies in the diocese of Liège from 1211–16, bishop of Acre from 1216–27, auxiliary bishop of Liège from 1227–9 and cardinal of Tusculum from 1229–40. For some most illuminating remarks on his career and writings see [J. F.] Hinnebusch, [*The*] *Historia Occidentalis* [*of Jacques de Vitry*] *SpicFr* 17 (1972) pp 3–15. Some other details are given in Bolton, 'Mulieres Sanctae', *SCH* 10 (1973) pp 77–97.

[8] Hinnebusch, *Historia Occidentalis* p 9.

[9] He saw them as he crossed Umbria on his way to Perugia in 1216, ed [R. B. C.] Huygens, *Lettres* [*de Jacques de Vitry*] (Leiden 1960) pp 71–8 and also 'Les passages rélatifs à Saint François d'Assise et à ses premiers disciples', ed Huygens, *Homages à Leon Herrman, Collection Latonius* 44 (Brussels 1960) pp 446–53.

[10] Hinnebusch, *Historia Occidentalis* for his account of several such groups.

[11] *VMO* p 636.1.

that he saw these women, known generically as beguines, as the new mothers of the church.[12]

The *vita* which he wrote on this inspiration has been described as marking a turning point in hagiographical language with a lyrical quality akin to the *Song of Songs* or to a troubadour lyric.[13] He himself said that he had put down only some of the many things which he himself had seen or had known from personal experience.[14] We have much interesting evidence which comes from this *Life* to advance our knowledge of the position of women. Not only was it an *exemplum* dealing directly with Mary and indirectly with other women and young girls, but it was a piece of propaganda to advance their interest. The contribution made by these women was recognised by many male contemporaries to be more dominant and more widespread than that of any previous female grouping but it is not surprising that this large and mainly female movement should have met with hostility. Even in Liège there were shameless men hostile to all religion who called these holy women by malicious names, howling like mad dogs over their devout practices and further damaging their reputations with disparaging 'new names'.[15] The women tolerated with great patience the opprobium which they received and so justification for their lives had to be provided. A saintly old monk from the Cistercian abbey of Aulne who had himself doubted the holiness of these women prayed that he might find out the truth about them.[16] He received the answer directly from the Holy Spirit that they were steadfast in faith and efficacious in works. A further proof of their sanctity occurred during the sack of Liège in 1212.[17] Those women who had not been able to flee into churches flung themselves into the river Meuse or climbed into the

[12] The beguines were essentially urban and extra-regular. An excellent account is given of them in R. W. Southern, *Western Society and the Church in the Middle Ages* (Harmondsworth 1970) pp 318–31. Jacques de Vitry used them in many of his *exempla*. See *The exempla of Jacques de Vitry*, ed T. F. Crane, *Folk Lore Society Publications* 26 (London 1890); *Die Exempla aus den Sermones feriales et communes*, ed J. Greven, (Heidelburg 1914) and G. Frenken, *Quellen und Untersuchungen zur lateinischen Philologie des Mittelalters*, 5 (Munich 1914) pp 1–153.

[13] Lejeune, 'L'evêque de Toulouse', pp 436–7.

[14] *VMO* p 638.11.

[15] *Ibid* p 637.4. Unfortunately we are not told what these names were. He refers to them as being similar to the 'new names given to Christ and his followers by the jews'.

[16] *Ibid*.

[17] Liège was sacked 3–7 May 1212 by the soldiers of Henry I, duke of Brabant, E. de Moreau, *Histoire de l'église en Belgique*, 3 vols (Brussels 1940–5) 2 p 133; McDonnell, *The Beguines* p 43. Mary of Oignies had also prophesied that an army of wicked spirits would come there, *VMO* pp 651–2.57.

sewers preferring rather to be drowned or suffocated than to lose their chastity. 'But Christ himself looked after them and not one was violated or killed'.[18]

The prologue to the *Life* of Mary of Oignies indicates four main categories of religious women in the area.[19] There were the many holy virgins who had given up all the delights of the world for Christ, who lived in poverty and humility with their heavenly spouse and by the work of their hands. They had rejected all the riches their parents had showered upon them, realising that it was only with the greatest danger to themselves that they could remain in the secular world. There were the holy matrons serving God and carefully watching over the chastity of these young girls, directing them by discreet suggestions to desire only a heavenly spouse. There were also widows, serving God in a number of ways, through fasting and prayer, through tears and manual work so that their endeavours to please Christ in the spirit might not fall short of their earlier efforts to please their former husbands but indeed might outstrip them. These widows were performing the corporeal acts of mercy, washing the feet of the poor, offering hospitality and tending lepers. The fourth category of women were those who were living in continence with their husbands' consent and bringing up their children to be as god-fearing as they themselves. Can we identify any of these women? Unfortunately the task is made more difficult by the insistence of Jacques de Vitry that he could not mention any of these women by name while they were still alive lest they should be shown too much honour which would distress them.[20] Since Mary of Oignies had died early he was only able to refer to the others obliquely. Thus whilst some of the actions can only apply to certain individuals and identification is relatively easy,[21] some women can be referred to because other means exist to prove that they were within this circle.[22] This mixture of factual and circumstantial evidence leads us to the *vitae* of five women.

Mary of Oignies (1177?–1213) was born into a rich and highly respected family in Nivelles in the diocese of Liège.[23] She was married

[18] *VMO* p 637.5.

[19] *Ibid* pp 636–7.3.

[20] *Ibid* p 638.9.

[21] *Ibid* p 638.8 certainly must refer to Christina of St Trond.

[22] When he speaks of those who dissolved with joy when the spirit comforted them, *ibid* p 637.6, he may well have been referring to Lutgard of Aywières. See below note 134.

[23] *Ibid* p 639.11.

at fourteen but preferred the religious life and prevailed upon her husband not only to live in continence with her but also to share her labours in the nearby leper colony of Willambrouk probably from *c*1191.[24] Here she gained a great reputation for her holy way of life and became the focal point for a group of likeminded women living in chastity under her guidance.[25] In 1207 to escape the crowds who had heard of her fame, she obtained permission from her husband and her priest to visit the recently founded and little known priory of St Nicholas at Oignies on the banks of the river Sambre near Namur.[26] There she remained attracting many people to that place including Jacques de Vitry and Fulk of Toulouse who visited her between 1212 and her death in 1213.[27]

Christina of St Trond (1150–1224) was known as *Mirabilis* for her amazing exploits.[28] The youngest of three daughters from a very modest background, her task was to watch the family flock and she spent this solitary time in prayer and meditation.[29] In 1182 she seems to have fallen into a cataleptic trance, awakening from it only during her funeral mass.[30] Whilst all but the priest and her sister fled, Christina levitated to the rafters of the church.[31] God had allowed her to come back from purgatory so that she might make expiation for herself and for the souls of others.[32] For several years she underwent a series of alarming activities without hurt to herself and it was only after her total immersion in a baptismal font that she recovered sufficiently to lead a more temperate life in the company of other human beings.[33] Jacques de Vitry himself saw her in this calmer and more peaceful state and mentioned her in the prologue to the *Life* of Mary of Oignies.[34] Thomas de Cantimpré, then a regular canon of Notre Dame de Cantimpré, composed her *Life* in *c*1232, eight years after her death.[35]

[24] *Ibid* p 640.14 *in loco qui dicitur Willambroc.*

[25] *Ibid* p 657.80. Two such women were Heldewide who had been looked after by Mary for twelve years and Beselene.

[26] *Ibid* p 657.80.

[27] Lejeune, 'L'evêque de Toulouse', p 439. Fulk was in Liège in 1212 and again between January and September 1213. Mary died in June 1213.

[28] Thomas de Cantimpré, *V[ita beatae] C[hristinae] M[irabilis Trudonopoli in Hasbania,]* ed J. Pinius *ASB* July 5 (Antwerp 1727) pp 650–60.

[29] *VCM* p 651.4.

[30] *Ibid* p 651.5.

[31] *Instar avis evecta templi trabes ascendit, ibid* p 651.5.

[32] *Ibid* pp 651–2.6–8. [33] *Ibid* pp 654.21. [34] *VMO* p 636.8.

[35] Thomas de Cantimpré, a native of Liège, moved from the canons regular to the Dominican order in 1232, becoming eventually lector and sub-prior of the house in

Ivetta of Huy (1157–1228) was from an affluent family in Huy and it was her parents' main concern that she should make a good marriage.[36] This she did at the age of thirteen much against her inclination and after five years of a marriage unsuccessful even by medieval standards, she was left a widow with three young sons.[37] She avoided pressure to remarry mainly through the intervention of the bishop of Liège, her *adiutior et protector*.[38] After a further five years, she handed her young family over to her father and opened a hostel for pilgrims and guests which contained a strongly charitable element.[39] Feeling still too much in contact with the world, she moved to a very small and poor leper colony on the banks of the river Meuse in *c*1180.[40] Her great humility and extreme fasts had much influence so that her father and two of her sons entered Cistercian monasteries,[41] and many women and young girls came to join here in the colony.[42] Her *vita* was written by Hugh of the Premonstratensian abbey of Floreffe in 1230 and was dedicated to his abbot, John of Floreffe.[43]

Margaret of Ypres (1216–37)[44] was born into an urban, middle-class family in Ypres and when her father died about 1220 she was placed in a convent where she showed an extraordinary and precocious devotion to the eucharist.[45] When she was eighteen she met the Dominican Siger of Lille who warned her to beware of secular things.[46] She then followed a life of penitence with Siger as her spiritual adviser

---

Louvain. See [S.] Roisin, 'La méthode hagiographique [de Thomas de Cantimpré',] in *Miscellanea historica in honorem Alberti de Meyer*, 2 vols (Louvain/Brussels 1946) 1, pp 546–57.

[36] Hugh of Floreffe, *V*[*ita*] *I*[*vettae*] *R*[*eclusae Huyi*,] ed G. Henschenius, *ASB* January 1 (Antwerp 1643) pp 863–87, p 865.8.

[37] *VIR* pp 865–6.13.

[38] Ralph of Liège (1167–91), *ibid* p 866.16.

[39] *Ibid* p 868.25, 26.

[40] *Ibid* p 870.33.

[41] *Ibid* p 871.39–41. Her father went first to Neufmoustier but found the life there to be *laute et laxe tam in vestitu quam in victu* and moved to the monastery of Villers. Her eldest son entered Orval in Luxemburg, *ibid* p 871.42 while her second son, who had gone astray, was eventually converted by his mother's prayers and went to the abbey of Troisfontaines in Catalonia, *ibid* pp 874–5.53–9.

[42] *Ibid* p 877.72.

[43] *Ibid* p 864.5–7; Ivetta had an association with Floreffe for the necrology of the abbey names her as the donor of a hogshead of fine wheat, McDonnell, *The Beguines* p 62 n 18.

[44] Thomas de Cantimpré, *V*[*ita*] *M*[*argarete de*] *Y*[*pres*,] ed [G.] Meersseman, in 'Les frères prècheurs [et le mouvement dévot en Flandre au xiiie siècle',] *AFP* 18 (1948) pp 69–130 to which the *VMY* forms an appendix pp 106–30.

[45] *VMY* p 107–8.2.

[46] *Ibid* p 109.6, *ille admoneret eam cuncta secularia respuere.*

and within the next three years and up to her death in 1237 she became the centre of a group of *amici spirituales*, religious men and women who were directed by the Dominicans.[47] Her *Life* was composed *c*1240 by Thomas de Cantimpré[48] who tells us that despite the marvellous phenomena associated with her, Margaret did not glorify herself as did so many holy women who seemed to have contracted the detestable habit of clucking like hens when they have laid their eggs.[49]

Lutgard of Aywières (1182?–1246) was the child of a noble mother and a middle class father from Tongeren who wished her to make a spectacular marriage.[50] Her mother however was on her side and Lutgard was allowed to enter the Benedictine convent of St Catherine in St Trond when she was twelve years old.[51] After twelve years she was elected prioress.[52] However on the same day as her election she resolved to leave the convent on account of her great humility[53] and was advised by John de Liro[54] to go to Aywières, a Cistercian house where French was spoken. Lutgard herself would have preferred Herkenrode in a Flemish-speaking region[55] but at this point Christina *Mirabilis* intervened, saying in reply to Lutgard's argument that she would find the language difficulties insuperable that 'she would rather be in hell with God than in heaven with the angels but without God'.[56] Lutgard transferred to Aywières in 1206 and remained there until her death forty years later when she would still speak barely enough French to ask properly for bread when she was hungry.[57] She received many distinguished visitors in person and saw many others after their

[47] *Ibid* p 119.25.

[48] Meersseman, 'Les frères prècheurs' p 70. Thomas de Cantimpré based the *vita* on oral information given by Siger of Lille which he wrote down on two little parchments before developing it into a much longer composition for which he used all his skills, Roisin, 'La méthode hagiographique' p 549.

[49] *Ibid* pp 119–20.27 *Multe enim nostri temporis religiose, perniciosum galline habentes modum, statim clamorem produnt cum ovum ediderunt.*

[50] Thomas de Cantimpré, *V*[*ita*] *L*[*utgardis*] *V*[*irgine,*] ed G. Henschenius *ASB* June 3 (Antwerp 1701) pp 234–52; also [S.] Roisin, *L'hagiographie cistercienne* [*dans le diocèse de Liège au xiii*[e] *siècle,*] *Recueil de Travaux d'Histoire et de Philologie*, 3 series, 27 (Louvain 1947) pp 50–4.

[51] *VLV* p 237.1.

[52] *Ibid* p 241.20.

[53] *Ibid* p 241.20.

[54] John de Liro was a friend of Jacques de Vitry and adviser to beguines. He was in very close relationship with Lutgard to whom he appeared after his death. Also Hinnebusch, *Historia Occidentalis*, pp 285–6.

[55] *Ibid* pp 242.22.

[56] *Ibid*, *potius vellem in Inferno esse cum Deo quam in caelo cum Angelis sine Deo.*

[57] *Ut panem recto modo Gallice peteret, ibid* p 243.1.

death in visions.[58] Her *Life* was written by Thomas de Cantimpré in 1249 three years after her death and was dedicated by him to Hawide, abbess of Aywières in order to obtain a relic.[59] There seems to have been an unseemly dispute as to which part of her body would be suitable.[60] Hawide thought that a finger would be sufficient but Thomas de Cantimpré replied that he wanted her head and a hand. The abbess was adamant.

These women are interesting because their lives bring us into contact with most of the possible forms of religious life available to women at the time in this area: a beguine, Mary of Oignies, a recluse Ivetta of Huy, a Dominican tertiary Margaret of Ypres, a Cistercian nun Lutgard of Aywières and Christina of St Trond, called *Mirabilis*, claimed by Benedictines, Cistercians and Premonstratensians alike but who in reality was not attached to any religious order nor to a beguine group.[61] The very close spiritual currents which ran between Cistercians and beguines in Lotharingia and especially in the diocese of Liège[62] have now been shown to have parallels in the almost equally close relationship between the beguines and the Dominicans in the same area.[63] An examination of these *vitae*, showing that for the most part these women whether regular or extra-regular were in close relationship with each other, serves simply to underline this view.[64]

It is in the area of personal and mendicant poverty that we can see most clearly *la contagion béguinale*, this infectious desire on the part of pious women to give up their riches in order to work with their hands or even to beg.[65] Mary of Oignies's family was greatly shocked that she and her husband, of their own accord, should have given up everything for Christ's sake and they put up a violent resistance even though

[58] She stayed with Ivetta, *ibid* p 240.16; she knew Christina, *ibid* p 242.22 and Jacques de Vitry, *ibid* p 244.3. She also saw the following in visions: Simon de Foigny, *ibid* p 244.4; Innocent III, *ibid* p 245.7; John de Liro, *ibid* p 245.8; Mary of Oignies, *ibid* p 245.9; Jacques de Vitry, *ibid* p 257.5 and Jordan of Saxony, former minister general of the Dominicans, *ibid* p 256.3.

[59] *Ibid* p 261.19.

[60] A *conversus* Guido and his friends cut off a finger and extracted sixteen teeth but the abbess only allowed Thomas de Cantimpré to have the finger, *ibid* p 261.19.

[61] Roisin, 'La méthode hagiographique', p 552.

[62] Roisin, 'L'efflorescence cistercienne', pp 361–4; also Roisin, 'Refléxions sur la culture intellectuelle en nos abbayes cisterciennes médiévales', in *Miscellanea Historica in honorem Leonis van der Essen* (Louvain 1947) pp 245–56.

[63] For some illuminating insights into the relationship between beguines, Cistercians and Dominicans, [J. B.] Freed, 'Urban development and the *cura monialium* [in thirteenth century Germany',] *Viator* 3 (California 1972) pp 311–27.

[64] Roisin, 'L'efflorescence cistercienne', p 364.

[65] Roisin, *L'hagiographie cistercienne*, pp 547–8.

as Jacques de Vitry tells us, the young couple would be recompensed a hundred-fold in the next world.[66] Ivetta of Huy also came from a family possessed of considerable wealth. Her father was one of the creditors of the bishop of Liège[67] and was appalled at her disregard for the family property which she gave away only too readily.[68] That Margaret of Ypres's background was far from impoverished we may judge from the threat from the secular world which Siger recognised could corrupt her life.[69] Lutgard too was from a sufficiently affluent background and we see the tension in her early life between her father's secular ambition and her mother's support of her vocation.[70] Christina seems here to be the exception for her origins were far humbler than the others.[71]

That these and many other religious women of the time were largely from the nobility or urban patriciate groupings should not surprise us. These were the classes most accessible to the penetration of new ideas and we should remember that the ideals of charity, renunciation and mendicant poverty in opposition to the avidity for riches were still relatively novel at this period.[72] There were however problems. As lay women, Mary of Oignies, Ivetta of Huy, Margaret and Christina could only express their personal poverty in a limited way and one which was appropriate to their status. Hence Mary of Oignies who was always attended by a maidservant[73] affected a type of dress, midway between negligence and refinement, consisting of an uncoloured woollen tunic and cloak.[74] Beneath these she wore a hair-shirt instead of a linen petticoat.[75] Ivetta handed over all her possessions to her father in trust for her children[76] and Margaret gave all that she had to her mother, abandoning her beautiful clothes in exchange for second-hand ones.[77] Both lived as modestly as possible. Christina had

[66] *VMO* p 640.15.
[67] *VIR* p 866.15.
[68] *Ibid* p 868.25.
[69] *VMY* p 109.6.
[70] *VLV* p 237.1.
[71] *VCM* p 651.1.
[72] For the background to these ideals see M. Mollat, *Études sur l'histoire de la pauvreté*, Publications de la Sorbonne, *Études*, 8, 2 vols (Paris 1974) especially A. Gieysztor, 'La légende de Saint Alexis en Occident: un idéal de pauvreté', 1, pp 125–39.
[73] *VMO* p. 643–28 She used to take a maidservant with her when she went on pilgrimage to a nearby church. The name of one such attendant was Clementia, *ibid* p 662.95.
[74] *Ibid* p 639.11, p 646.37.
[75] *Ibid* p 646.37.
[76] *VIR* p 870.34.
[77] *VMY* p 117.22.

nothing of her own to give up for Christ since she had inherited nothing. All that she could renounce, that is her food and drink, she did.[78] In the *vita* of Lutgard the problem of personal poverty does not appear as so much of an issue for, as a member of a religious order, she was personally poor through the device of corporate possession. However finding the rule of life in St Trond insufficiently harsh, she practised such austerities that she became unpopular with the other sisters there.[79]

This brings us to the whole problem of begging and the attempt to present the *vitae* of these women as examples of absolute orthodoxy. We know that any form of mendicity was regarded with the greatest suspicion by the ecclesiastical authorities and that pious women were neither expected nor allowed to beg. Jacques de Vitry comments with heartfelt relief in the prologue to the *Life* of Mary that even during the great three year famine, there was miraculously not one woman in the whole diocese of Liège who, once she had renounced everything for Christ, either died of hunger or was forced to beg in public. [80] But like her southern contemporary Clare, Mary of Oignies felt a strong attraction for the mendicant life. We are told that her desire for poverty was so great that she would scarcely retain the necessities of life and that she had once thought of going to a foreign country to beg unknown from door to door.[81] She had bidden farewell to her companions and was about to set out with scrip, wooden bowl and old and tattered garments when her friends managed finally to dissuade her from leaving.[82] Christina did go out to beg so that she could share her alms but ceased when it was put forcibly to her that she might inadvertently be accepting money which had been unjustly acquired.[83] Margaret, having given away all that she had, began to beg herself so that she could share her alms with a beggar. She liked poverty so much that she used frequently to escape from the house to go and beg. But her spiritual director, knowing the dangers this might bring to a young woman, ordered her to stay with her mother.[84] Neither Ivetta nor Lutgard were in a position to beg.

[78] *VCM* p 654.22.

[79] *VLV* p 238.7, 8.

[80] *VMO* p. 637.5. On this famine of 1195–98 and some of its social effects see M. Mollat, 'Hospitalité et assistance au début du xiii siècle', *Poverty in the Middle Ages*, ed D. Flood, *Franziskanische Forschungen* 27 (Werl-Westfalia 1975) pp 37–51.

[81] *VMO* pp 648–9, 45.

[82] *Ibid* p 648.

[83] *VCM* p 654.22.

[84] *VMY* p 117.22.

Linked with mendicant poverty was the idea of sharing the sufferings of Christ, and a strong taste for extraordinary mortifications is to be found amongst those women much in contact with the beguine movement.[85] As we should expect we find these self-immolations practised most assiduously and enthusiastically by Mary and Christina. Jacques de Vitry actually goes so far as to compare the immolations of Mary with the maggot-infested wounds of Simon Stylites or the self-inflicted burns of St Antony.[86] The afflictions which Mary made upon herself were inspired by her contemplation of Christ's sufferings which induced in her such a loathing of her own body that she cut off pieces of her own flesh with a knife and buried them in the ground.[87] These scars were witnessed by the woman who prepared her body for burial.[88] Christina whose activities have brought forth a good deal of scepticism[89] believed that she had been able to return to the world after her 'death' so that, by her example and suffering, men would be converted.[90] She therefore proceeded to suffer dramatically, jumping into the icy waters of the Meuse,[91] into cauldrons of boiling water,[92] into ovens[93] or into fires.[94] Once she hanged herself on a gibbet between two robbers[95] and often entered the tombs of the dead to bewail the sins of men.[96]

Neither Ivetta, nor Margaret nor Lutgard imposed upon themselves any mortications as violent as these. However all five practised incredible feats of endurance in fasting, prayer and lack of sleep. When Mary had to eat she took food only once a day and that at night.[97] She ate no meat nor drank wine but instead lived on wild herbs that grew near her cell and the coarsest and blackest bread, unfit even for dogs, which made her throat bleed and distended her stomach.[98] At night she slept little for she saw no merit in sleep but rejoiced instead in watching over the relics in the church.[99] She also practised a 'strange

[85] Roisin, *L'hagiographie cistercienne* p 96.
[86] *VMO* p 642.22.
[87] *Ibid* p 641.21.
[88] *Ibid.*
[89] Roisin, 'La méthode hagiographique', p 552, calls them 'a web of extravagances'.
[90] *VCM* p 652.7.
[91] *Ibid* p 652.10, 12.
[92] *Ibid* p 652.11.
[93] *Ibid.*
[94] *Ibid.*
[95] *Ibid* p 652.13.
[96] *Ibid.*
[97] *VMO* p 642.23.
[98] *Ibid* p 642.24, p 648.44. [99] *Ibid* p 645.33.

and unheard of devotion' by genuflecting hundreds and thousands of times for forty days on end and then reading through the entire psalter while standing.[100] One year from Martinmas to lent she lay on the church floor for the whole of a winter so severe that even the wine in the chalice froze.[101] During one such period of prayer she ate nothing at all for thirty-five days, remaining in a tranquil and happy state throughout.[102] Christina ate the vilest food imaginable when she bothered to eat at all.[103] In her earlier days she used to climb to the tops of trees or towers to pray.[104] Sometimes she would roll up into a ball like a hedgehog when praying or contemplating while at others she would stand for hours in prayer.[105] At one period she left her own home and went to the castle of Loos on the borders of Germany where she spent nine years with Ivetta in prayer and contemplation.[106] Ivetta fasted so much that she became weak and emaciated.[107] Eventually on the advice of her religious friends who quoted passages from Timothy, Augustine and Jerome, she moderated her actions somewhat in accordance with their advice lest she should cause a scandal by having 'overdone it a trifle'.[108] Margaret had begun to fast at the age of seven and also recited the canonical hours.[109] She also said private prayers of which Thomas de Cantimpré distinguishes two sorts, four hundred *paters* and *aves* which she said with numerous genuflections and one hundred and fifty *ave Marias* in three series of fifty, one of which she said prostrate each day.[110] Lutgard too practised great austerities and her entry into the Cistercian order in no way modified her ardour for penance. Three times she imposed on herself a seven year fast and when the third came to an end she fasted until the end of her life.[111] She too once spent a short time in seclusion with Ivetta for we know that the distractions of convent life worried her.[112]

Apart from their ascetic endeavour and incredible feats of physical

[100] *Ibid* p 643.29.
[101] *Ibid* p 645.36.
[102] *Ibid* p 642.25.
[103] *VCM* p 655.25.
[104] *Ibid* p 653.16.
[105] *Ibid, instar ericei conglobotum corpus redibat ad formam.*
[106] *Ibid* p 657.38. Thomas de Cantimpré tells us that he came a long way from France to visit Ivetta and gained much information about Christina from her.
[107] *VIR* p 873.49.
[108] *Ibid* p 873.51.
[109] *VMY* p 108.3, pp 116–17.20.
[110] *Ibid* p 117.21.
[111] *VLV* p 245.9, p 256.4.
[112] *Ibid* p 240.16. They spent two weeks together in prayer and contemplation.

endurance, these *vitae* show that the religious women of Lotharingia shared some other features in common with the desert fathers. In the first place they displayed the same hatred of crowds. It was her fame which forced Mary of Oignies to leave Willambrouk in 1207[113] and fame too which caused Ivetta to move into a cell to escape from the crowds who came to see her.[114] Christina climbed on to roofs and into trees in order to avoid the many who had heard of her wonderful deeds.[115] Nor did Margaret escape the crowd phenomenon for she was visited not only by many women from the urban patriciate, but also by simple people from very remote districts of Flanders.[116] Secondly they engaged in battles with demons who appeared to them in various guises. Christina was constantly tormented by them in the restless stage of her life[117] and Lutgard saw the devil in the form of a young girl.[118] Mary, by her innocent and virtuous life, managed to torment her particular devils to such an extent that they howled at her and ground their teeth.[119] They also observed the long silences associated with the early fathers. Mary's manual work was performed in absolute silence from the feast of the holy cross to easter and we are told several times of the very great value which she placed upon interior silence.[120] Christina and Lutgard both came to Ivetta's cell at different times to share her silence.[121] Yet another feature which they shared with their earlier desert counterparts was their intense compassion often in their case linked with great humility. Mary performed every kind of charitable work, not merely tending the sick but being present at the last moments of the dying and at the burial of the dead.[122] Her humility was sometimes so great that she would run away and hide herself lest she should be called upon to give advice, for which task she felt unworthy.[123] Christina showed wonderful compassion to the jews whose congregation was large in St Trond, offering them the mercy of Christ if they should be converted.[124] Ivetta showed such compassion

[113] *VMO* p 661.93. On the ascetics of the desert see P. R L. Brown, 'The rise and function of the holy man in Late Antiquity', *JRS* 61 (1971) pp 80–101.

[114] *VIR* p 875.60.

[115] *VCM* p. 653.16.

[116] *VMY* pp 117–18.22, 23, p 112.

[117] *VCM* p 655.28.

[118] *VLV* p 237.2.

[119] *VMO* p 643.29.

[120] *Ibid* p 646.39.

[121] *VCM* p 657.38; *VLV* p 240.16.

[122] *VMO* p 650.50.

[123] *Ibid* p 649.47.

[124] *VCM* p 655.25.

towards her lepers, washing their bodies, ironing their clothes and providing charity for them that many people imitated her example or prayed for her well-being.[125] Lutgard was so humble that on the same day that she was elected prioress of St Catherine at St Trond, she decided to leave and in her new house of Aywières, so feared her elevation to high office that she prayed that she would never learn French which was spoken in that convent.[126]

However the *vitae* of these women go beyond the mere imitation and emulation of the early fathers and the simple recounting of lists of miraculous happenings for they introduce a mystical element which is the natural corollary of asceticism. Their physical detachment opens up an immense capacity for loving their Lord and the renunciation of their temporal goods reveals an unassuaged desire for real and eternal goods.[127] Hence we can distinguish two essential characteristics of this mystical piety: its clearly Christocentric nature and an intense eucharistic devotion which is the logical consequence of this ardent love for Christ whether they are beguines, Cistercians or Dominicans. Mary of Oignies who remained almost continuously in the church snatching a short sleep and dreaming always about Christ, found no rest except in his presence.[128] The sacred bread strengthened her heart and the heavenly wine inebriated and gladdened her soul. She was filled with the holy food of Christ's flesh and purified and cleansed by his life-giving blood. This was the only comfort she could not endure to be without. To receive Christ's body was the same thing to her as to die and to die was in her mind to be with her Lord.[129] Jacques de Vitry tells us how he and her priest tried to see if unknowingly she could be made to take a small part of an unconsecrated host but it was so nauseating to her that she spat it out and cried aloud with disgust.[130] Although she rinsed her mouth with water again and again, she was unable to rest that night or for a long time afterwards. Christina too lived only for the sacrament and longed to receive it frequently.[131] Margaret of Ypres made her first communion at the age of five and while under the direction of Siger she was allowed to receive it every fortnight.[132] The eucharist was the principal source of the mystic life

[125] *VIR* p 870.35. [126] *VLV* p 243.1.

[127] Roisin, *L'hagiographie cistercienne* p 127; Meersseman, 'Les frères prècheurs', pp 75–7.

[128] *VMO* p 645.35.

[129] *Ibid* p 659.87.

[130] *Ibid* p 664.105. This example is also used by Jacques de Vitry in his commentary on the sacrament of the altar in Hinnebusch, *Historia Occidentalis* p 207.

[131] *VCM* p 654.22. [132] *VMY* p 111.11, p 118.24.

to her and once Christ himself gave her the host.[133] Lutgard entered a state of ecstacy whenever she considered Christ's redemptive sufferings and on one occasion broke a blood vessel which turned her thoughts to martyrdom.[134] So great was her pleasure in the sacrament that it grieved her to be deprived of it and once at Aywières, out of obedience to the abbess, she was compelled to omit frequent communion, an unheard of penance.[135] In the *Life* of Lutgard we should expect to see the characteristics of female Cistercian piety and we are not disappointed. The *Song of Songs* was very familiar to her[136] and she may possibly have been influenced by the thoughts of St Bernard on the *anima sponsa verbi*, seeing Christ as the husband figure to whom was due all love.[137] Yet it is not possible in these *Lives* to distinguish particular trends in spirituality and to attribute them to one order or to one group. It was here in this union with the mystic husband for whom they sought avidly in the eucharist that the essence of the piety of the beguines and the spirituality of Cistercians and Dominicans lay.[138] It was here in this area of Lotharingia that priests, monks and the patrons of these women were able to share in their frequent and sublime experiences.[139] And it was to this area that Francis had probably decided to journey after the chapter of pentecost 1217 because of the emphasis placed on the sacrament here.[140]

It was this strong evidence of faith and the stress on the eucharist, confession and penance by these women together with the testimony of Fulk of Toulouse which moved Jacques de Vitry away from his general view of women which was essentially little different from that held by the majority of churchmen[141] to a more particular view of these devout women. He frequently referred to Mary as his *mater spiritualis* and acknowledged freely in her *vita* his tremendous debt to her.[142] We know from his own writings as well as from the evidence

[133] *Ibid* p 118.24.

[134] *VLV* p 249.21.

[135] *Ibid* p 246.15.

[136] *Ibid* pp 252–3.42, 43.

[137] Roisin, *L'hagiographie cistercienne* pp 106–13.

[138] *Ibid* p 117.

[139] *Ibid* p 118; *VMO* p 660.90 where St Bernard appeared to Mary of Oignies and *ibid* p 653.63 for her friendship with a Cistercian abbot.

[140] P. Hilarin, 'S. François et l'Eucharistie', *EF* 34 (1922) pp 520–37 and McDonnell, *The Beguines* p 313.

[141] Hinnebusch, *Historia Occidentalis* pp 116–18 and especially p 116 where he states that women are too frail for the rigours of Cistercian discipline.

[142] *VMO* p 655.69; Huygens, *Lettres*, p 72 lines 34–46. Compare with *VLV* p 251.38 where Thomas de Cantimpré refers to Lutgard as *mater specialissima.*

of Thomas de Cantimpré who later wrote the supplement to her *vita* that she had ardently wished God to grant her the merit and office of preaching in the person of someone else.[143] Her request had been granted in his person and he became her special preacher. He saw himself as her instrument, uttering her words and getting through to his audience by her prayers, one hundred *aves* every time that he preached.[144] His account in the *vita* reveals that when he first started to preach to simple people he suffered from nervousness and the fear that he would break down before he finished.[145] He had been accustomed to collect material from all quarters to bear upon the subject and consequently spoke vaguely and loosely. Mary was of tremendous help to him in preparing better sermons and in acting as the source of his inspiration.[146] She also helped to influence his career as a crusade preacher. She had herself taken up the cause of the Albigensian crusade with passionate enthusiasm.[147] Indeed three years before men had taken the cross against the heretics, she had seen a number of crosses descending from heaven and from this had conceived an ardent desire to go to that spot.[148] As she could not without causing scandal, Jacques de Vitry seemed again to be her instrument.

After her death Jacques de Vitry and others made a very real effort to win approval for these women. John de Liro, a friend and counsellor of beguines and other religious women including Lutgard, perished in the Alps probably in 1216 while on his way to the curia to negotiate on behalf of the women of Lotharingia.[149] Jacques de Vitry must have hoped for assistance from Innocent III but his arrival at Perugia in 1216 coincided with the death of that pope.[150] He saw instead Honorius III from whom he only managed to obtain oral permission for the beguines in Flanders, France and the empire to live together in religious communities and to assist one another by mutual exhortation.[151] Jacques de Vitry may have taken the *vita* of Mary with him when he went to Italy but there is no evidence that he showed it to Honorius III.[152] We do know however that Hugolino read it.[153] The

[143] *VMO* p 654.68, 69.
[144] *Ibid* p 654.69.
[145] *Ibid;* McDonnell, *The Beguines* p 23.
[146] *Ibid* p 654.68.
[147] *VMO* p 658.82.
[148] *Ibid.*
[149] *VLV* p 245.8.
[150] Huygens, *Lettres* p 73 lines 61–70.
[151] *Ibid* p 74 lines 76–81.
[152] Bolton, '*Mulieres Sanctae*', p 84. [153] *VMO* pp 674–5.22.

bishop of Ostia who was being attacked by violent temptations of faith to the point at which he feared he might succumb to apostacy, confided his lack of security and confidence to Jacques de Vitry in an intimate conversation possibly in 1226. Jacques de Vitry did what he could to console his friend who had 'long wanted to meet him' and concluded by suggesting that he should read the biography of Mary of Oignies, even going so far as to offer him his relic of her finger which he wore in a silver reliquary around his neck and to which he attributed two miraculous rescues from drowning.[154]

We have no such precise information about the audience of the other *Lives*: indeed it would be most revealing if we had. All that we can say is that they display a tremendous concern to establish the complete orthodoxy of the women in spite of some of their rather strange activities. Although heretics feature in only two of the *vitae*, when both Mary and Lutgard prophesy the Albigensian crusade,[155] the area of Lotharingia had had its share of heresies and it is surely not mere chance that the *vitae* stress again and again the devotion of the women to the sacraments at a time when the heterodox view was to deny them.[156] Further the *vitae* make it plain that the role of the priesthood was in no danger from feminine zeal. Christina understood latin and could fully interpret the meaning of divine scripture, being able to answer the most obscure questions on spiritual matters. Yet she did not wish to do this, saying that the clergy were the correct people to expound the holy scriptures and that the function of interpretation did not belong to her.[157] Lutgard had wished to understand the scriptures and miraculously was able to interpret the psalter clearly but she did not wish to know divine mysteries.[158] *Quid mihi idiotae et rusticae et laicae moniali scripturae secreta cognoscere?* she asked modestly.[159] We do know however that she did not know latin for when she received a divine instruction in that language she did not understand the words and had to have them translated by a sister.[160] On her deathbed Mary had expounded in a new and marvellous way certain passages of

[154] Huygens, *Lettres* p 72 lines 34–46. It was the possession of this relic to which he attributed his safe arrival in Milan in 1216 despite the hazards of crossing rivers in flood in Lombardy, and, *VMO* p 673.16, his safe return from the Holy Land.

[155] *Ibid* p 658.82; *VLV* p 243.2.

[156] R. I. Moore, *The Origins of European Dissent* (London 1977) pp 168–96.

[157] *VCM* p 657.40.

[158] *VLV* p 239.12.

[159] *Ibid.*

[160] *Ibid* pp 245–6.10. This may have been Sybilla de Gages who composed Lutgard's epitaph in Latin. See also McDonnell, *The Beguines* pp 377, 383.

scripture but this is presented as a divine revelation rather than something which she had learned.[161]

The influence and example of Mary of Oignies had as we have seen a great impact on the career development of Jacques de Vitry. The writing of her *vita* and its failure to bring about an independent female order may have turned his mind in other directions. Indeed shortly after Mary's death, Lutgard had had to warn and pray for him because he was displaying 'a too human love' for a religious woman reclining in her cell to the considerable detriment of his preaching.[162] It is left to Thomas de Cantimpré however, in his supplement to Mary's *Life* to raise serious doubts about the wisdom of Jacques de Vitry's acceptance of a cardinal's hat at Tusculum in 1229 thus leaving unfinished the spiritual and institutional advancement of the women of Lotharingia.[163]

The supplement was dedicated to Gilles, prior of Oignies by Thomas de Cantimpré and was written *c*1230 and certainly later than 1227, probably just before his entry into the Dominican order.[164] He admitted that he, a humble canon, might be considered audacious if he added anything to that which Jacques de Vitry, then bishop of Acre and now cardinal of Tusculum had written. However he obviously thought it necessary to stress once more that that part of Lotharingia was an area of special religious enthusiasm and he brings out quite clearly that what took Jacques de Vitry to Oignies in the first place was Mary's renown and the desire to identify himself with her work.[165] Whilst two thirds of the supplement deal with a few interesting additions to the *Life* of Mary and some polite comments about her biographer, the last part is written by a highly indignant young man, full of admiration for the saintly preacher whom he had heard in the region when he was a boy of fourteen,[166] yet bitterly disappointed to find that his former hero had feet of clay. He describes how Jacques de Vitry had taken up the *vita apostolica* with enthusiasm but shows how very soon he had adapted himself to a more official and consequently more luxurious life. When the vestments and relics at Oignies were destroyed by an accidental fire, it was Jacques de Vitry still bishop of

[161] *VMO* p 663.99, 100.

[162] *VLV* p 244.3.

[163] Thomas de Cantimpré, *V*[*itae*] *M*[*ariae*] *O*[*igniacensis,*] *S*[*upplementum*] ed D. Papebroeck, *ASB* June 4 (Antwerp 1707) pp 666–76 and Hinnebusch, *Historia Occidentalis* p 5.

[164] Roisin, 'La méthode hagiographique', p 547. Thomas de Cantimpré refers to himself as *humilis canonicus*, *VMOS* p 666.1.

[165] *Ibid* p 667.2, 3; McDonnell, *The Beguines* p 22.

[166] *VMOS* p 676.27, *nondum enim annorum quindecim aetatem attigeram.*

Acre who replaced the lost objects within ten years.[167] In 1220 he had written to Lutgard and John of Nivelles that for the peace of his soul he was forwarding to Oignies oriental silks taken by the crusaders at Damietta.[168] In 1226 or 1227 he returned to Europe and in 1227, at the request of prior Gilles he dedicated the five altars of the church at Oignies, including one which he had paid for himself.[169] At the same time he consecrated Mary's bones, placed her relics in a shrine and granted an indulgence to all who came to revere them.[170] But in spite of such worthy actions, Thomas de Cantimpré is still able to mark the precise time of Jacques de Vitry's lapse from the ideals of the *vita apostolica*. He recounts how, while still bishop of Acre, Jacques de Vitry sent to cardinal Hugolino a heavy silver cup, finely wrought and beautiful, full of nutmeg. The cardinal 'a consistent spurner of wealth' sent the cup back but kept the nutmeg, adding that it had come from the east whereas the cup was from Rome.[171]

When Honorius III died, Hugolino, as pope Gregory IX, asked his friend to visit him in Rome. In spite of Mary's insistence through a dream that he should ignore the request, he went to Rome and when he was offered a cardinalate he was not dissuaded from his choice by her alleged reproaches.[172] She refused either to appear to him or to accompany him on his journey but instead told him that he would in any case be accompanied by three women from whom he could not escape. These women are identified as *Episcopatus*, *Cardinalatus* and *Ecclesia Lotharingiae*[173]. By her prayers Mary had released him from any obligation to the first two and the point is strongly made that his rightful place is with church of Lotharingia, giving help and wise advise to simple people. Thomas de Cantimpré contrasted the glory which Jacques de Vitry would have in the church with the central idea of the *vita apostolica* that there is no real glory in this world to which the cardinal replied that he would return some of this glory to Lotharingia and to Mary who was poor and deprived. Here Thomas de Cantimpré plays on the idea of Mary's poverty saying that instead she

[167] *Ibid* p 671.13.

[168] McDonnell, *The Beguines*, p 17.

[169] *VMOS* p 674.21. His own altar was dedicated to the Trinity.

[170] McDonnell, *The Beguines* p 38. On the treasures which were collected at Oignies see E. M. Link, *Hugo von Oignies* (Fribourg-im-Breisgau 1964); S. Collon-Gevaert, J. Lejeune, J. Stiennon, *L'art mosan au xi et xii siècles* (Brussels 1951); *Hugo of Oignies: the Goldsmith's Treasure* (Brussels 1978).

[171] *VMOS* p 672.15.

[172] *Ibid* p 675.23.

[173] *Ibid* p 675.25.

was most rich and had received tremendous merit from Christ through her adoption of the *vita apostolica*.[174] He also chooses to play on the contrast between Jacques de Vitry who had spent most of his time abroad and who had left his home of his own accord whereas he himself still chose to rest in that humble place Oignies amongst the *oves Beghinarum*.[175] He goes on to say that there were many cardinals, so many indeed in France that revenues would scarcely support them, but that the world rarely if ever had produced a cardinal who wished to imitate Christ. France had never produced one but now, under the auspices of Christ himself and through the prayers of his handmaiden Mary of Oignies, Lotharingia had the first.[176] Would that the *Ecclesia Lotharingiae* might make him repudiate *Episcopatus* and *Cardinalatus!* In this way by using hagiographic device as well as an argument based on the *vita apostolica*, Thomas de Cantimpré seems to have set out to prove that Jacques de Vitry had committed a serious error, thereby underlining Mary's vital role in his career to demonstrate that his rightful place was back at Oignies.

But perhaps Jacques de Vitry was more realistic than Thomas de Cantimpré and was trying to make a last bid in a different way and in a different place. No independent female order could be formed given the decree of the fourth Lateran council[177] and the opposition of the religious and social attitudes of the day. It might just have been possible with a high status friend such as Jacques de Vitry would have hoped to have become as cardinal.[178] There was, however, no structural support: the high status authority of the church was against them. The general problem of male attitudes to religious women, even when those women were responsible for a new upsurge of contemporary piety and in spite of the fact that they had sympathetic male biographers, could not be overcome in a situation where one biographer at least was to become better known than the subject. In the relationships of the time, men were dominant. It is perhaps now the time to look at these *vitae* again with the hope of reaching a reassessment of

[174] *Ibid.*

[175] *Ibid.*

[176] *Ibid.*

[177] Cap 13, Lateran IV, *COD* (2 ed Fribourg 1962) p 218.

[178] Bolton, '*Mulieres Sanctae*' p 89. The death of Mary of Oignies had deprived the beguines of a leader and by 1229 there was no other such charismatic figure on the scene. Further there were new opportunities for women in the Cistercian and mendicant orders. See Freed, 'Urban development and the *cura monialium*,' p 313 for some most convincing figures for their foundations between 1228–73.

what was written in the early thirteenth century. This would make these women more important and would upgrade their *Lives* to make them worthy of the title *vitae matrum*.

University of London
Westfield College

ST CLARE

by ROSALIND B. BROOKE AND
CHRISTOPHER N. L. BROOKE

St Clare died on 11 August 1253, and the celebration of her seventh centenary in 1953 was accompanied by a revival of scholarly interest in her life and work scarcely to be paralleled since the Bollandists passed through August. Grau established the canon of her writings and published an annotated German translation: Hardick fixed the chronology of her life—born in 1193–4, received into the religious life at the age of 18 in 1212; from 1212 to 1253 head and leader (from 1216 abbess) of the community in San Damiano.[1] Much else occurred besides in 1953 in scholarly publication and popular festivity; and little perhaps remains to be discovered about her life and works. Yet something can still be said of the relation of Clare and her movement to the wider issues of female involvement in the religious movements of the twelfth and thirteenth centuries, and her own record

[1] In this study the following abbreviations are used:

1, 2 Celano	Thomas of Celano, *Vita Prima*; *Vita Secunda, AF* 10, pp 1–117, 129–268.
Eubel	*Bullarii Franciscani Epitome*, ed C. Eubel (Quaracchi 1908).
Legenda	*Legenda Sanctae Clarae Virginis*, ed F. Pennacchi (Assisi 1910), English trans P. Robinson (Philadelphia 1910) and, from the sixteenth-century French version, C. Balfour (London 1910): see below and n 11.
Opuscula	*Opuscula S. patris Francisi Assisiensis* (2 ed Quaracchi 1941).
SL	*Scripta Leonis Rufini et Angeli Sociorum S. Francisci,* ed and trans R. B. Brooke, *OMT* (Oxford 1970).

For a general view of Clare and the early history of her Order, see [J.R.H.] Moorman, [*The Franciscan Order from its Origins to the year 1517*] (Oxford 1968) pp 32–9, 205–15. On the wider context, see the classic study of Grundmann: chapters 3–6 deal specifically with the religious movements among women and the *Frauenfrage*; pp 253–71 with the early Franciscan sisters, including Clare herself; pp 274 *seq* develop the study of the relations of the mendicant orders and their female communities. See also B. Bolton, '*Mulieres sanctae*' *SCH* 10 (1973) pp 77–95.

The main products of 1953 were: *S. Chiara d'Assisi, 1253–1953*; *Studi e Cronaca del VII Centenario* (Assisi 1954); [E.] Grau and [L.] Hardick, [*Leben und Schriften der heiligen Klara von Assisi*] (1 ed actually 1952; 3 ed Werl 1960) and the English version *The legend and writings of St Clare* (St Bonaventure, New York, 1953), including a revised version of P. Robinson's translation—Hardick's study of Clare also appeared in French translation in *Spiritualité de Sainte Claire* (Paris 1961); *AFH* 46 (1953) esp pp 3–43, A. Fortini, 'Nuove notizie intorno a S. Chiara di Assisi'; *FStn* 35 (1953) esp L. Hardick on the chronology of her life, pp 174–210, and E. Grau on the influence of St Francis's *Regula Bullata* on St Clare's rule of 1253, pp 211–73. For the rules, her writings and other early sources see nn 3–5.

leaves many puzzles. In the modern world there are roughly three women in a religious order to every man; in the twelfth century, though our evidence is even more approximate, we can be sure that the men vastly outnumbered the women, and the balance was only redressed in the thirteenth century, and then only in Germany and the Low Countries.[2] Part of the reason was a deliberate constriction or restriction of female initiative, and of this Clare is an exceptionally interesting witness. Her life was outwardly stable and peaceful, save for the occasion when she is said to have routed some Saracen troops of the emperor Frederick II.[3] But the popes and the cardinal protectors found it necessary to provide her own and her sister communities with no less than six rules between 1219 and 1263,[4] which does not suggest that all was peaceful within. Indeed it is commonly assumed that between Clare and the curia, and within her own mind and soul, there was considerable friction and conflict. Perhaps it is possible to see this in a slightly plainer light than hitherto by setting the story of her life and rules in firmer juxtaposition to some other movements of female religious.

[2] See refs to Grundmann and B. Bolton in n 1. Compare C. N. L. Brooke and W. Swaan, *The Monastic World* (London 1974) pp 177–8, 254 (cap 11 n 2). For the very rapid growth of Cistercian houses of nuns in Germany in the thirteenth century see maps and index to F. Van der Meer, *Atlas de l'Ordre Cistercien* (Amsterdam/Brussels 1965); some corrections by E. Krausen and P. Zakar, *ASOC* 22 (1966) pp 279–90; F. Vongrey and F. Hervay, *ASOC* 23 (1967) pp 115–27. On Cistercian nuns see also n 13.

[3] Canonisation process, ed F Lazzeri, *AFH* 13 (1920) pp 403–507, esp 451–2, 455–6, 471; *Legenda* caps 21–2, pp 30–1. These are the chief sources for Clare's life. The process was also edited (modern Italian) by N. Vian, *Il processo di S. Chiara d'Assisi* (Milan 1962). For editions of *Legenda* see n 1: *Legenda* pp xiii *seq* discuss the attribution to Thomas of Celano and produce verbal parallels to his lives of Francis on pp xviii-xxvi; see also on the sources M. Fasslinder, *FStn* 23 (1936) pp 296–335, esp pp 321 *seq* on Celano's authorship (which has been generally accepted in recent studies, though it is far from certain). Modern lives are legion: there is still useful material in [E.] Gilliat-Smith, [*St Clare of Assisi*] (London/Toronto 1914) and relevant chapters of the lives of St Francis by Paul Sabatier and Father Cuthbert; among recent biographies F. Casolini, *Chiara d'Assisi* (Assisi 1953, 3 ed 1954) is the best documented we have seen of those produced in 1953; there is a useful brief summary and bibliography by L. Hardick in *NCE* 3 (1967) p 913; and see n 1.

[4] See excellent summary in Moorman pp 211–15; the most important are edited from the original bulls in Eubel, pp 234–7 (Gregory IX, reissuing in 1239 in revised form his own earlier, lost, rule), 241–6 (Innocent IV, 1247), 251–7 (Innocent IV's confirmation of St Clare's rule, 1253), 269–75 (Urban IV, 1263)—we have made up the number six by adding Urban IV's confirmation in 1263 of the 'Isabelline' rule of 1252 to the two of Hugolino and Gregory, two of Innocent IV and one of Urban IV listed here; but the computation is somewhat arbitrary since there were presumably only minor differences between the first two, and certainly no more between 1239 and 1247. On the rules see esp F. Oliger in *AFH* 5 (1912) pp 181–209, 413–47 (esp on the rule of 1218–19 pp 193 *seq*.); M. Fasslinder in *FStn* 23 (1936) pp 306 *seq*.

Anyone wishing to penetrate to the heart of St Francis's intentions and inspirations naturally starts with his *Testament*; and so it must be with St Clare. We immediately encounter the difficulty that Clare's *Testament* only survives in a transcript from an ancient manuscript in Wadding's *Annales*, from which all later editors have copied it.[5] Early in this century several scholars expressed doubts of its authenticity, but these seem mostly to have been resolved; we have witnesses, if not texts, from the fifteenth century; there are no evident anachronisms; and above all, it bears the kind of relation to the text of her *Rule* that could reasonably be expected. The authenticity of Clare's own *Rule* is guaranteed by the original text of the papal bull of confirmation which quotes it verbatim and was issued two days before her death. In its heart lies a crucial passage with strong echoes of Francis's *Testament* in its style and some of its words; and this passage is almost identical with the central core of Clare's *Testament*.[6] The differences are such as we should expect: Clare's *Testament* is more autobiographical, and summarises two of Francis's letters to her; the *Rule* is terser and yet quotes the letters at length. It is natural to suppose that both represent Clare's own attempt to complete her life's work, as Francis had, by providing her own *Rule* and *Testament*, and it would be unreasonable seriously to question the *Testament's* authenticity. Nonetheless, one is bound to accord a respect for the words of her *Rule* slightly greater than that one gives to her *Testament*—even if one bears in mind that the papal chancery may have tidied up Clare's Latin, as it is likely that they tidied Francis's.[7]

The common core of the two documents deals with the basis of Clare's way of life: she had promised obedience to Francis, and to lead a life of poverty and imitation of Christ and his Mother. Directly before it in the *Testament* Clare describes how Francis, immediately after his conversion, and before he had brothers or companions,

[5] [L.] Wadding, *Annales* [*Minorum*] 2 (Lyon 1628) pp 46–9 (=1253 cap v), whence *ASB*, August II, pp 747–8, *Seraphicae legislationis textus originales* (Quaracchi 1897) pp 273–80. On its authenticity see P. Robinson in *AFH* 3 (1910) pp 442–6, citing also a fifteenth-century French and a sixteenth-century Italian version; M. Fasslinder, *FStn* 23 (1936) pp 304–6; *S. Chiara d'Assisi 1253–1953*, pp 519–20. Apart from the *Rule* and *Testament*, Clare's only substantial surviving writings are her letters to B. Agnes of Bohemia, *AFH* 17 (1924) pp 509–19, also *S. Chiara d'Assisi 1253–1953*, pp 132–43, with Italian translation: see Grau and Hardick for full bibliography.

[6] Rule of St Clare, cap vi (33), ed Eubel pp 254–5.

[7] There is a notable absence of grammatical error in the *Regula Bullata*. Minor errors can be discerned in Francis's autograph and it was alleged that he deliberately allowed errors to appear in his Latin.

laboured to rebuild the church of San Damiano, where he had been inspired to leave the world. 'Climbing then on the church's wall, he spoke in a loud voice in French (*lingua francigena*) to a group of poor folk standing round: "Come and help me in my work on the monastery of San Damiano, since there will one day be ladies there, and by their celebrated, holy way of life Our Father in Heaven will be glorified in all his Holy Church".'[8] The substance of this story is happily confirmed in an earlier source, the *Vita Secunda* of Thomas of Celano, with such differences as make clear that our two witnesses are independent. Clare very likely knew the version in Celano, but if so she corrected it. In the early days after his conversion Francis was begging oil for the lamps in San Damiano, but drew back feeling suddenly shy from a throng of men amusing themselves round the door of a house he wanted to enter. Then he took courage and spoke up fervently *lingua gallica* urging all those present to help with the fabric of San Damiano, saying in the hearing of all that there would be a monastery there of holy virgins of Christ.[9] If we accept the authenticity of Clare's *Testament*, she is an exceptionally reliable source for earlier Assisi tradition, though she might well have had a prejudice in favour of such a tale. Celano's stories mostly came from the saint's companions, and this (though not otherwise recorded)[10] has a distinct flavour of early tradition about it, since no one is likely to have invented stories about Francis hesitating to beg, and the reference to the holy ladies is quite incidental to the point of the story. There seems thus to be exceptionally reliable early evidence that Francis had in mind at the outset of his adventures to provide a home for a community of women. This is consistent with the evidence that the initiative for Clare's conversion came from him rather than from her. It would be relatively easy to imagine a sequence of events starting with an impulsive girl insisting on joining Francis and his companions, insisting on his providing her with a way and means of life—thus facing him from the start with a problem already showing some of the embarrassing ambiguities which many have discerned in later events. But for such a reconstruction there is no evidence. Several witnesses in the canonisation process stated fairly plainly that she changed her

[8] Wadding, *Annales*, 2, p 47.

[9] 2 Celano 13.

[10] For the known sources of 2 Celano, see *SL* introduction esp pp 73–6; J. R. H. Moorman, *The Sources for the Life of S. Francis of Assisi* (Manchester 1940, repr Farnborough 1966) esp pp 90 *seq*, 110–27.

way of life on his advice—*sancti viri monitis ad Deum conversa* as Celano has it in the *Vita Prima*; and the *Legenda S. Clarae* tells of many secret meetings in which Francis's burning words convinced her.[11] The last account may be a little coloured, but the drift of all the evidence is the same: Francis took the initiative in seeking a female companion or supporter, and may well have envisaged at the outset a religious institute in which men and women collaborated.

Most of the new movements and orders of the twelfth and thirteenth centuries had followers of both sexes. One can divide them, with no great precision, into orders in which the women played a part from the start and were welcomed by the founders, and those whose leaders refused to acknowledge the women religious claiming to be their disciples. Robert of Arbrissel, in whose life every impulse of the religious movements of the late eleventh and early twelfth centuries may be discerned, ended by founding the order of Fontevrault in which women played a predominant role.[12] St Gilbert of Sempringham founded a double order of canons and nuns strictly segregated. The Cistercian fathers buried their heads in the sand, ostrich-like, and for two generations or more seem to have claimed, against all the evidence, that there were no Cistercian women.[13] St Norbert inspired a very large number of both sexes to join his order in early days; but his women suffered the fate of the lay brothers in the Franciscan order a century later. There were alleged by Norbert's biographer to be over ten thousand Premonstratensian women in the middle of the twelfth century,[14] but presently recruiting was forbidden and the female communities died of attrition.

St Dominic fostered a house of nuns at Prouille before he founded his own order, and he himself was sometimes looked after in his middle years by some of his holy female disciples, as they gave witness in his canonisation process.[15] But when the order began to form, the Dominican nuns were always kept at a distance, semi-detached at least,

[11] *AFH* 13 (1920) pp 452, 459, 464, 480, 488, 489 (speaks of secret meetings), 493; *Legenda* caps 5–6, pp 8–10; 1 Celano 18 echoed in *SL* no 109, p 280.

[12] Grundmann pp 43 *seq*; [R. B.] Brooke, [*The Coming of the*] *Friars* (London 1975) pp 57–8 and refs; J. von Walter, *Die ersten Wanderprediger Frankreichs*, 1 (Leipzig 1903).

[13] Our own knowledge of this subject owes much to work being undertaken by Mrs S Thompson (above pp 227–52). See also n 1.

[14] Brooke, *Friars*, pp 58–9, esp p 59 and n 1 and refs; *MGH SS* 12 pp, 657, 659; Grundmann p 48 nn 78–9.

[15] Ed [A.] Walz, *M*[*onumenta*] *O*[*rdinis*] *P*[*raedicatorum*] *H*[*istorica*] 16 (Paris 1935) pp 89–194 (text pp 123 *seq*; see esp pp 181–2, Toulouse depositions caps 15–17, on women's evidence); compare Brooke, *Friars*, pp 177 *seq*, esp p 102.

even though friars and nuns could sometimes still be on terms of remarkable spiritual intimacy as the correspondence of Jordan of Saxony and Diana Dandolo reveals.[16]

Francis's story has something in common with Dominic's, but more perhaps, in the end, with Norbert's. The indications are that in early days Friars Minor and Poor Sisters worked hand in hand, that Francis and Clare were much on the terms of Dominic and his sisters. But by about 1218 a Cistercian monk was visitor to the houses inspired by San Damiano,[17] and although relations with the friars were presently restored, the order (if such it can be called) was formally placed under the *Rule* of St Benedict in 1219;[18] Clare herself lived out her later years cloistered and enclosed in San Damiano. Visits from Francis were relatively rare, though there was one famous occasion when he was nursed at San Damiano in a serious illness and composed the *Canticle of Brother Sun*;[19] and Clare survived his death for almost twenty-seven years, nearly a whole generation, which witnessed many vicissitudes in her relations with his order.

What are the indications of a closer bond in early days? There is a famous story in the *Actus-Fioretti* which, if true, belongs to the very early years of Clare's conversion, of how Francis sent brother Masseo to consult her and brother Silvester as to his own true vocation—to serve the world by preaching or to become a contemplative; and how both advised him that Jesus's will was that he should serve many, not himself alone, and preach.[20] The *Actus* is a late and unreliable source; but both this and its neighbour story of how Clare was greatly comforted by a visit to Francis, and how the sisters in San Damiano lived in fear that he would send her away to another house, as Agnes, her sister, had been sent to Florence, have a hint of early tradition about them unusual in this book; and it is evident that Francis needed periods of refreshment in a hermitage, and was tempted to make the Carceri and Fonte Colombo his home;[21] and likely enough that in early years Clare might have been one of his confidants.

[16] *Beati Iordani de Saxonia Epistulae*, ed Walz, *MOPH*, 23 (1951).

[17] [Father Cuthbert], [*Life of St Francis of Assisi*] (2 ed London 1913) p 172 and n.

[18] In Hugolino's rule, for which see n 4. On Hugolino's relations with Clare see below at nn 35–8 and his letter of 1218–19 in *AF* 3 (1910) p 183 (compare *The Legend and Writings of St Clare*, pp 111–13).

[19] *SL* nos 42–3 and 45, pp 162–7, 170–1; compare [P.] Sabatier, *Vie* [*de S. François d'Assise*] (Paris 1893–4) cap 18; Cuthbert pp 418–25.

[20] *Actus* [*b. Francisci et sociorum eius*], ed P. Sabatier (Paris 1902) cap 16, pp 55–9 (=*Fioretti* cap 16); compare the neighbour story cap 15, *Actus* pp 52–4.

[21] See esp F. C. Burkitt, 'Fonte Colombo and its Traditions', in Burkitt and others,

The other indication is more securely based. The earliest evidence about the Poor Sisters is in the well known passage in Jacques de Vitry's letter written in October 1216 as he lay in the harbour of Genoa preparing to sail to Acre.[22] It has often been cited, but has still something to tell us. Jacques de Vitry was one of the great enthusiasts of his age, a fervent preacher, an ardent crusader, and yet a man who reveals his thoughts in a straightforward, attractive manner in his letters. He had lived in the diocese of Liège as a canon regular, and fallen under the influence of St Marie d'Oignies, one of the notable female religious leaders of the Low Countries; the *Frauenfrage* and the rising power of the women in the religious movements of the age were therefore familiar to him. He came south in 1216 to be consecrated bishop of Acre, and gives in this letter (among other details) his impression of Milan, *fovea . . . hereticorum*, and of the papal curia in Perugia, obsessed with worldly business. In each city he found a consolation. In Milan hardly anyone resisted the heretics, save certain 'holy men and religious women', whose enemies maliciously called *Patareni*, but whom the pope has called *Humiliati* and licenced to preach and resist the heretics. They live of the labour of their own hands, and have so prospered in the diocese of Milan that there were one hundred and fifty *congregationes conventuales, virorum ex una parte, mulierum ex altera* . . . established by them, apart from those who have stayed in their own houses. In the region of Perugia he found one consolation too: many of both sexes have left the world, called *Fratres Minores et Sorores Minores*. They are revered by pope and cardinals, but have no care for temporal things, labouring for the cure of souls. 'They live according to the pattern of the primitive church . . . By day they enter cities and towns, giving practical help that they may benefit some; by night they return to a hermitage or lonely houses, devoting themselves to contemplation. The women live together near the cities in separate hostels; they receive nothing, but live by the toil of their hands, and are greatly upset and troubled because they are honoured by clergy and

---

Franciscan Essays 2 (British Society of Franciscan Studies, 1932) pp 41–55. Compare *SL* pp 110–11 and 111 n 1, 134–7, 186–9, 284–7 (compare pp 60 *seq*).

[22] For what follows see *Lettres de Jacques de Vitry*, ed R. B. C. Huygens (Leiden 1960) no 1, pp 71–8 (on Humiliati pp 72–3; on the Franciscans pp 75–6; on the date p 52). For later comments on Francis and his order see no 6, pp 131–3 (1220); Jacques de Vitry, *Historia Occidentalis*, ed J. F. Hinnebusch *Spic Fr* 17 (Fribourg 1972) pp 158–63. On the Humiliati, see Grundmann pp 72–91; B. Bolton, 'Innocent III's treatment of the *Humiliati*', *SCH* 8 (1972) pp 73–82; and 'Sources for the early history of the *Humiliati*', *SCH* 11 (1975) pp 125–33, (p 125 for bibliography, p 129 for Jacques de Vitry).

laity more than they wish.' And he goes on to describe the annual chapter of the order and the promulgation of *institutiones sanctas et a domino papa confirmatas*.

Doubtless Jacques de Vitry was influenced by the experience of his homeland, and by his recent meeting with the *Humiliati*. Yet he was a contemporary witness, and a shrewd one, perfectly capable of distinguishing one religious system from another; his later letter about St Francis's visit to the east shows a penetrating mixture of respect and critical reflection on the Franciscan way of life. His evidence is entirely consistent with the indications that Francis originally intended women to play as central a part in his activities as men, and that their role was at first not so different as it later became.

Yet this makes all the more curious the well-known puzzle: in his later life he very rarely visited the sisters himself, and he altogether prevented the kind of cooperation which Jacques de Vitry seems to be describing. His companions were at pains to emphasise that he rejected all familiarity with women and forbade his brothers to visit the sisters save when specially instructed. In Celano's second *Life* there are two striking passages, which doubtless came from those close to Francis, even though no precise sources are known, expressing the saint's attitude to women. Chapters 112–14 warn sternly against any mingling with women, and in chapter 112 the saint is made to say that he never looked them in the face, and only knew two by sight. They are not named, but it has always been assumed that the reference is to St Clare and the lady Jacoba de Settesoli.[23] In chapters 204–7 Francis is shown instructing by precept and example how the friars are to treat the sisters: they are to visit them indeed, but rarely and unwillingly. When he was at San Damiano being nursed in his sickness the 'vicar' (presumably Elias) frequently admonished him to preach the word of God to the ladies; eventually he did so, but by an acted parable only: he formed a circle of cinders and prayed and did penance in their midst. Celano tells us that they were mightily edified; but doubtless they were disappointed too, for this was a far cry from the collaboration of earlier days.

Celano spells out that Francis's purpose was to teach the friars by example that they should visit the sisters indeed, but reluctantly and occasionally, and thus avoid the snares of female companionship. Doubtless his explanation was basically correct: Francis projected

[23] Cuthbert, p 161 and n 2. But compare Sabatier, *Vie*, p 150 and n 1, who simply disbelieves Celano.

himself, especially in his later years, as an example; he became increasingly aware that what he said and did was noted and followed, and he deliberately fostered this attitude to enforce what he reckoned essential lessons. For a large order trying to establish its respectability before the hierarchy at large in the 1220s—and the 1240s when Celano was writing—it was doubtless essential to avoid the suspicion of excessive familiarity even with holy women. But in what measure can we penetrate to the root of the separation of Francis and Clare, and understand how it began?

We may probably discern two stages in the story. The *Legenda S. Clarae* has a highly coloured account of the efforts of St Clare family's to fetch her back, and their even sterner efforts to recover her sister Agnes.[24] The witnesses at the canonisation process told a calmer story, but as several of them were evidently old family friends, doubtless they were not inclined to show Clare's relatives in too harsh a light.[25] In the event their attitude must have had serious consequences for Francis's plans. At first both he and Clare were rebels, dropouts from their social order. The son of the rich merchant Pietro Bernardone had made public renunciation of his father and his wordly goods,[26] and his presence in Assisi was a constant challenge to the values of his parents' society. Yet in the long run this ceased to be so; the outcast became respectable. Paradoxically, the merchant's son turned rebel found himself, however unwillingly, a guest of honour in the houses of bishops and cardinals and the pope himself; and he had great difficulty in Rome to reconcile the hospitality of the curia and the life of abject poverty he demanded of his followers.[27] He moved in circles where his father could never have entered. It is true that this was strictly a spiritual not a social respectability, but that made it precious, or at least necessary to him. In his *Testament* he was to lay great emphasis on his relation to priests and to the pope;[28] it was this which enabled his order to survive and prosper while the *Humiliati* remained a local order of declining reputation. The story is a very complex one, and many stages in it are imperfectly known. Francis must early have become aware that recognition came relatively easily to him, but while Clare

[24] *Legenda* caps 9–10, 24–6 (esp caps 25–6), pp 14–16, 33–7 (esp 35–7).

[25] *AFH* 13 (1920) pp 487–8, 491–3.

[26] 1 Celano pp 12–15; *Legenda trium sociorum, ASB*, October 2 (ed of 1866 pp 723–42) cap 6 (20).

[27] Compare *SL* no 92, pp 248–53; compare C. Brooke, *Medieval Church and Society*, (London 1971) p 205.

[28] *Opuscula* pp 78–9.

remained his colleague and in a sense his companion, it could never come to her. So much is plain; the rest is conjecture. But it is also likely that Clare's background added to the difficulties. Several of the witnesses in the canonisation process emphasise that she came of noble stock,[29] that is to say, was Francis's social superior. This is quite in the tradition of the *Humiliati*, whose communities contained a substantial element of well-to-do, and highly-born, men and women parading their denial of the material values of their world;[30] and Francis may well have been encouraged in his persuasions to Clare by the effect such an example would have in Assisi. Evidently her family were both pious and conventional: as one witness observed, when she fell under Francis's influence she was of marriageable age (about seventeen) and good-looking, and her parents thought it high time she was married.[31] Her mother had been on long pilgrimages and was noted for her good works.[32] A reaction against such a home was less excusable in the public eye than Francis's; and it may be that some measure of conformity to social prejudice became necessary to Francis and Clare from a fairly early stage.

The other element in the story is the patronage of cardinal Hugolino and the search for a rule. The draconian decree of the fourth Lateran council of 1215 against new orders—or against new rules, as it was interpreted—brought notorious difficulties to all the religious leaders Innocent III had formerly helped.[33] After a pause St Dominic returned to the curia claiming the *Rule* of St Augustine as his foundation deed; Francis himself firmly relied on Innocent's verbal approval of his first rule in 1210. As the years passed and he came to enjoy more and more the help and patronage of Hugolino, pressure was brought to bear—from within the order, if we may believe the *Verba S. Francisci*, but via the cardinal—on Francis to accept an existing rule.[34] This he steadfastly refused, but it was not until 1223, eight years after the council and only three before his death, that the final version of his *Rule* received formal papal approval. Meanwhile, long before, Hugolino himself had been using San Damiano as a recruiting ground for superiors for his own foundations when he was legate in Lombardy

[29] *AFH* 13 (1920) pp 443, 487, 491–2; compare *Legenda* cap 1, pp 4–5.
[30] B. Bolton in *SCH* 11, esp pp 131–2; compare Grundmann, pp 158–69.
[31] *AFH* 13 (1920) p 490.
[32] *Ibid* p 443; *Legenda* cap 1, pp 4–5.
[33] Brooke, *Friars*, pp 86–8, 160–1 and refs; Mansi 22, cols 998–9, 1002–3.
[34] *SL* no 114, pp 286–9 (compare pp 59–60); [R. B.] Brooke, [*Early Franciscan*] *Government* (Cambridge 1959) pp 72–3, 286 *seq.*

and Tuscany;[35] and in a general way giving encouragement to communities inspired by St Clare and her disciples. These needed a rule, and Hugolino provided a rule himself, in 1219, intended for the whole group of houses.[36] We know its text from his own reissue, when he was pope Gregory IX, in 1239; and we have his own word for it that the texts were essentially the same. At its base lies subjection to the *Rule* of St Benedict, strict enclosure, and the right to communal property, for Hugolino evidently reckoned total poverty incompatible with an effectively enclosed life.[37] It has the strange provision which seems to limit the novitiate to a few days;[38] but is otherwise quite a clear, straightforward rule for a strict, austere, utterly retired life, much influenced by Cistercian customs. In all probability Clare had accepted by this date the need for enclosure; and Hugolino's rule was accompanied by a slight renewal of Franciscan contacts, since a Franciscan replaced a Cistercian visitor about the same time.[39] But there can be little doubt that she resisted from the first any suggestion that she was not bound to the rule of St Francis and to poverty.[40] It took Francis eight years to obtain confirmation of his rule, and Clare had to wait another thirty for hers. Her life ended in a quiet but dramatic triumph. Innocent IV, not the pope most noted for sympathy with Franciscan poverty in its more extreme forms, came and settled for a while in Perugia, and he and his cardinals visited the dying abbess, now a figure of great prestige, generally and widely admired.[41] Two days before her death the pope at last confirmed her own version of her own rule.[42] It enshrined the privilege of poverty, which she claimed to have had from Innocent III and which Innocent IV had

[35] On Hugolino as legate, Brooke, *Government*, pp 59 *seq*, esp pp 62–7, 286; E. Brem, *Papst Gregor IX bis zum Beginn seines Pontifikats* (Heidelberg 1911) esp pp 26 *seq*, 111 *seq*.

[36] See n 4.

[37] Eubel pp 234–7; compare p 234 n 1 and refs.

[38] *Ibid* p 234; see refs in n 4 for commentary.

[39] See n 17; brother Philip was visitor for a while in and after 1219, but was removed after Francis's return from the east in 1221 for acting beyond his instructions; he was, however, visitor for a long period in later years—*AF* 10 p 21 n 12 (note to 1 Celano cap 25), and refs; Moorman pp 13, 32, 38n.

[40] This is implicit in her *Rule*—explicit indeed in her claim in the *Testament* to have had the privilege of poverty from Innocent III as well as Innocent IV. On this much of the discussion of the authenticity of the *Testament* has turned (see refs in n 5); we need not doubt that Clare believed she had this privilege from Innocent III, just as we cannot doubt Francis believed that the same pope had confirmed his *Rule*. Gregory IX also confirmed the privilege, for San Damiano alone.

[41] *Legenda* caps 40–2, pp 56–60, esp pp 56–7, pp 44, pp 61–2; for her death and funeral, conducted by the pope and cardinals, *Legenda* caps 45–8, pp 62–72.

[42] *Solet annuere*, 9 August 1253, Eubel pp 251–7; this was also for San Damiano alone.

already confirmed to her; it lays less emphasis than Gregory on enclosure, though the nuns are only allowed to go out in case of necessity; it says nothing of St Benedict; and it is closely modelled on the *Rule* of St Francis and has many echoes and quotations from it.[43] It was a personal privilege for Clare and her community: long since her own fixed enclosure and her resistance to the implications of Hugolino's rule had made it impossible for her to be in any sense an administrative head of her order. She was its inspiration and its link with Francis; and in both these senses, it seems clear, Hugolino as cardinal and as pope Gregory IX had accepted her position. In 1253 she was free to make her own *Testament* and the confession in her *Rule*:[44] *postquam altissimus pater coelestis per gratiam suam cor meum dignatus est illustrare* . . . 'After the most high heavenly Father by his grace deigned to illuminate my heart, so that I might do penance by the example and teaching of our most blessed father Francis, a short while after his conversion, together with my sisters I willingly promised obedience to him'—an obedience, be it noted, which subjected her to Francis's rule, not to Benedict's. 'The blessed father expected us to have no fear of poverty, toil, tribulation, reviling and the world's scorn, but rather to hold them highly delectable things; and so he was moved by *pietas* and wrote for us a pattern of living—*formam vivendi*—in this fashion: "By God's inspiration you have made yourselves daughters and slaves of the most high, supreme king, the heavenly Father, and have wedded yourselves to the Holy Spirit by choosing to live according to the perfection of the Holy Gospel; and so I will and promise, on my own account and my brothers', always to have such diligent[45] care of you as of ourselves, and a particular responsibility." While he lived he diligently fulfilled his promise, and willed his brothers always to fulfil it. Also, to prevent us from anywhere falling off from the most holy poverty on which we had entered—or any of our sisters yet to come—a little before his death he wrote to us his final will, saying: "I, brother Francis, poor and feeble (*pauperculus*), wish to follow the life and poverty of our most high Lord Jesus Christ and his most holy mother, and to persevere in it to the end. And I ask you all, my ladies, and I give you counsel that you always live in this most holy way of life and poverty. And take much care not to draw back from it at all,

[43] See E. Grau in *FStn* 35 (1953) pp 211–73; the *Rule* of St Clare and its main sources are conveniently laid out in Gilliat-Smith pp 287–305.

[44] What follows is the version in the *Rule*, Eubel pp 254–5; for the closely parallel passage in the *Testament*, Wadding, *Annales* 2 pp 46–9 (=1253 cap v). See p 277 and n 6.

[45] *Curam diligentem*, which could mean 'loving care'.

on any man's teaching or advice, for ever." And thus I was ever anxious with my sisters to preserve the holy poverty which we promised to God and the blessed Francis; and thus the abbesses who succeed me in this office, and all the sisters, are bound to observe it unbroken to the end—that is, in not receiving or holding any possession or property by themselves or through any intermediary, nor anything which can reasonably be called property, save only as much land as necessity demands for decent provision and removal of the monastery; and that land shall not be worked except for a garden to serve their own needs.'

Francis was ready to obey Hugolino and the pope so long as they demanded nothing incompatible with his own revelation—'no man showed me what to do, but the most high revealed to me that I should live according to the pattern of the holy gospel'.[46] So also Clare: she would obey Francis so long as he demanded nothing incompatible with his own instruction to poverty; and in the end she would obey no cardinal or pope who made her renounce obedience to Francis and his instructions. What passed between her and Gregory IX is a puzzle and a mystery, just as is much of what passed between Francis and Hugolino between 1215 and 1223.[47] But the essence of the matter was that Francis instructed her to poverty, and doubtless to a life of contemplation; and copious witnesses at the canonisation process confirmed that this kind of life was congenial to her, both because she was by nature a contemplative and because she was obedient to Francis.[48] This betokened, however, a marked change in the attitude both of Francis and of Clare to her vocation between 1212 and 1219; how much this owed to changes in him and in her, how much to social and ecclesiastical pressure, is quite obscure. Yet surely we may conclude that—whether or not Francis owed his own decision to lead an active life to her advice—she owed her own, contrary decision, to him.

University of Cambridge

[46] Francis's *Testament*, *Opuscula* p 79.

[47] See esp Brooke, *Government* pp 59–76 and *SL* pp 59–60; also the refs cited in n 18 above, and *AFH* 13 (1920) p 452.

[48] *AFH* 13 (1920) pp 403–507 *passim*; compare *Legenda* esp caps 19–20, pp 27–9.

Additional note. The great edition of the writings of St Francis by K. Essser (Grottaferrata 1976) and the new edition of *Opuscula S. Francisci et Scripta S. Clarae,* ed J. M. Boccali and L. Canonici (Assisi 1978) came into our hands too late to be used in this chapter. (We have not seen the edition of Clare's *Escritos* by I. Omacchevarría (Madrid 1970).

THE THIRTEENTH-CENTURY GUGLIELMITES: SALVATION THROUGH WOMEN

by STEPHEN E. WESSLEY

FOR the thirteenth-century Guglielmites[1] women were the only hope for the salvation of mankind. These idealists believed that contemporary human failings could be remedied and that all were soon to be saved through the intervention of a female. Yearning for such immanent change, the Guglielmites quickly moved from enthusiasm to heresy. If the false Christians, jews, saracens, and, in fact, all those outside Christianity were still not transformed by grace, according to these zealots, it was the fault of the present form of the *ecclesia* which must therefore be altered to fulfill their utopian expectations. The Guglielmite sectaries proclaimed that a female incarnation of the Holy Spirit, namely, Guglielma of Milan, was presently to establish a new church ruled by a female pope and female cardinals. Only with the advent of this female church would such world-wide salvation be possible.[2] And without it, according to the Guglielmites, there would be complete destruction. Had their incarnation come as a man, they opined, he would have been killed and the entire world would

[1] The chief source of information about the Guglielmites is the inquisitorial process against Guglielma's followers which is printed by [F.] Tocco. 'Il processo [dei Guglielmiti'], *Reale Accademia dei Lincei, memorie della classe di scienze morali, storiche e filologiche, Rendiconti*, 5 Series, 8 (Rome 1899) pp 309–42, 351–84, 407–32, 437–69. The text is a transcription of MS A 227 inf of the Biblioteca Ambrosiana, Milan. *Processus ab inquisitoribus haereticae pravitatis confecti Mediolani anno Domini MCCC contra Guillelmam Bohemam.* Apparently this entire extant manuscript, which includes other inquisitorial cases, was composed as a unit and written in the same hand in or after 1303, the latest date noted. (According to [M.] Caffi, [*Dell' abbazia di Chiaravalle*] (Milan 1842) p 91, this document was preserved by a Carthusian, Matthew Valerio, in the sixteenth century.) A microfilm of this manuscript has been consulted, but references will be to Tocco's printed text. A slightly abbreviated Italian translation of the process in [A.] Ogniben, [*I Guglielmiti del secolo XIII*] (Perugia 1867) is of little use. The record of this inquisitorial activity against the Guglielmites, which lasted from 19 April 1300 until 12 February 1302, is not complete. Thirty-three individuals are examined in the process within which occur references to examinations not extant. Lacking these documents, certain questions concerning the Guglielmites will never receive precise answers.

[2] For various summations of the basic teachings of this sect see Tocco, 'Il processo', pp 319, 320, 329, 332, 336–7, 338, 340, 352–3, 354–5, 358–9, 363–4, 368–9, 377–8.

have perished.[3] This arresting formulation of doctrine cannot fail to elicit a variety of responses from us, and the same was true for earlier writers who investigated these beliefs. Unfortunately for the history of heresy their disparaging appraisals of these heterodox teachings precluded satisfactory discussion of the various motives underlying them. Following a brief review of earlier interpretations of the Guglielmites I will attempt to present a more accurate picture of the development of this doctrine.

Striving to fashion a perfect *ecclesia*, medieval enthusiasts like the Guglielmites never found sympathy or even understanding among churchmen who lived by compromising. Labelled variously as fools, precursors of the Antichrist, or orgiasts, such zealots were dealt with as enemies to be destroyed when both papal and inquisitorial interests determined an investigation. After the extermination of the Guglielmites by the inquisition in 1300 popular writers in the late middle ages depicted Guglielma of Milan, considered the heresiarch, solely as a high priestess of pagan orgies. Gabrio de Zamorei of Parma in his *Sermo de fide*, composed between 1371 and 1375, portrayed Guglielma as a leader of sexual debauchery and quoted some poetic lines he had written in his youth about this notorious episode.[4] The story of her immorality was narrated also by Bernardinus Corio (1459–1519?) and Johannes Trithemius (1416–1562).[5] Supposedly Guglielma gathered her followers in an underground cavern and exhorted them to have sexual intercourse with whomever they wished. These meetings were eventually discovered, according to these chroniclers, by a suspicious husband, Conradus Coppa, who revealed the scandal to other duped husbands at a special banquet.[6] Additionally, Trithemius specified that to make themselves holy new initiates of the sect drank wine mixed with the dust of murdered infants born of their nefarious unions. This type of orgiastic story has an ancient lineage, of course, probably a result of the

[3] *Ibid* p 413.

[4] M. Vattasso, 'Del Petrarca e di alcuni suoi amici', *Studi e testi*, 14 (Vatican 1904) p 53.

[5] B. Corio, *Storia di Milano*, ed E. De Magri, A. Butti and L. Ferrario, 3 vols (Milan 1855–7) 1 pp 684–5 and J. Trithemius, *Annalium hirsaugiensium, opus*, 2 vols in 1 (St Gall 1690) 2 pp 76–8. A manuscript fragment noted by P. Kristeller, *Iter italicum*, 2 vols (Leiden 1965–7) 2 p 268, Venice, Biblioteca Nazionale Marciana MS Marc Lat XIV 235 fols 78^{r}/^{v}, *De sceleribus secte Gulielma et Andree viri sui apud Mediolanum*, told the same story of sexual excesses as found in Corio. This tale was repeated also by J. Foresti in *Novissime hystoriarum omnium repercussiones* [Venice 1503] fols 324^{v}–5^{r}.

[6] Conradus Coppa's wife, Jacoba, actually did belong to the sect. Conradus was *absente et nesciente* while the sectaries met in his house and one leader, Mayfreda, distributed blessed hosts; see Tocco, 'Il processo', p 414.

common belief that non-conformist ideas resulted in immoral acts.[7] Because there is no mention of immorality in inquisitorial records concerning the Guglielmites it is possible that the tales received impetus from the reports about the contemporary Dolcinist apostles, and from a bull of Boniface VIII, *Nuper ad audientiam* (1296) which condemned women who taught new dogma and led immoral lives.[8] The chroniclers then just borrowed old formulas to fill out their story, which may reveal something about human nature but sheds no light on the sect itself.[9]

Among modern historians few attempts have been made to understand what brought these sectaries to their beliefs and attention has mainly been focused on a search for the original heretic among the Guglielmites. One nineteenth-century historian, Andrea Ogniben, who published the greater part of the inquisitorial evidence in Italian, classified the two leaders of the Guglielmite heretics, Andreas Saramita and Mayfreda de Pirovano, with founders of other religions.[10] All these religious innovators, according to Ogniben, were subject to hallucinations and therefore pretended to be the sons of God sent either to rule or free the human race. Guglielma of Milan herself was innocent of any heretical leanings, Ogniben claimed; her so-called followers, Andreas and Mayfreda, were the real heretics.[11] These sectaries were guiltless,

[7] Key elements and descriptive phrases of the stock heretical orgy have been traced back to reports of Justin Martyr, Minucius Felix, and Tertullian. The heretics at Orleans (1022) were perhaps the first medieval actors in what becaame the standard orgiastic scenario. For discussions of sexual orgies and heresy see J. Russell, *Witchcraft in the Middle Ages* (Ithaca and London 1972) pp 88–93 and his 'Witchcraft and the Demonization of Heresy', a paper delivered at the seventh annual conference of the Center of Medieval and Early Renaissance Studies, Binghampton, N.Y. (The proceedings are to be published.)

[8] *Bullarium magnum romanum*, ed A. Taurinorum, S. Franco, H. Fory, and H. Dalmazzo, 25 vols (Turin 1857–72) 4 pp 134–5. In the year of this bull, 1296, one member of the Guglielmite sect was called before the inquisition. See R. Guarnieri, 'Il movimento del Libero Spirito: I. Dalle origini al secolo XVI, II. I "Miroir des simples âmes" di Margherita Porete, III. Appendici', *Archivio italiano per la storia della pietà*, 4 (Rome 1965) pp 387–8 for references to several other groups this bull might have been directed against.

[9] A few writings, such as the *Annales colmarienses* [*maiores*], *MGH SS*, 17 p 226, contemporary with the sectaries, did, however, correctly identify Guglielma's heresy as the claim to be the Holy Spirit incarnate. The content of the Guglielmite heresy was rediscovered in 1676 by J. P. Puricelli, whose unpublished manuscript in the Ambrosian Library in Milan was based on inquisitorial records; see [J. P.] Puricelli, [*De Guillelma bohema . . . dissertatio*], Milan, Biblioteca Ambrosiana, MS sup C[1] inf. His finding was reviewed by C. Amoretti in June 1812 in a paper delivered to the Istituto Storico Lombardo.

[10] Ogniben pp 117–30.

[11] *Ibid* pp 84–90.

however, because they were deceived by their hallucinations. Felice Tocco, who published the latin text of the inquisitorial process at the turn of the century, compared this group to the beguines, beghards, free spirits, and fraticelli, and concluded that the Guglielmite sect was a caricature of heresy and a monstrous confusion of diverse beliefs.[12] Concentrating on its origin, he accused Guglielma herself of founding the heresy; she had enunciated the key dogma proclaiming that she was the Holy Spirit incarnate.[13] Tocco's interpretation was later attacked by an early twentieth-century specialist in Milanese history, Gerolamo Biscaro, who maintained the innocence of Guglielma and implied that her main follower, Andreas Saramita, had fathered the heresy.[14] For Biscaro the heretics were simply fanatics and he seemed to echo the American medievalist Henry C. Lea who had written off this entire episode as a 'spiritual aberration'.[15]

Rather than be dismissed as an aberration, however, Guglielmite doctrine, I propose, should be viewed as part of the continuous development of thirteenth-century enthusiasm. This approach will serve two functions: it will not only illustrate the structure of these teachings, but also allow us to understand more readily their attraction in the thirteenth century. With this in mind I hope to demonstrate that Guglielmite belief derived basically from three contemporary enthusiastic motifs: the *ecclesia spiritualis*, the *imitatio Christi*, and the *vita apostolica*. These ideals were carried to literal extremes by the Guglielmites and given a female bias.

The original ideologue of the *ecclesia spiritualis*, Joachim of Fiore (d 1202), provided an attractive doctrine which could not only give hope to the utopian orthodox, but also engendered an ideology that was the source of both mission and consolation for persecuted zealots. Predicting an age of the Holy Spirit, a third age which followed both that of the Son and that of the Father, Joachim foretold that there was to be a new gospel, an 'eternal gospel', which was to supersede the other books of scripture and which was to be preached by the future *viri spirituales*. Although convinced of the immanence of this epoch, the Calabrian abbot hedged about the exact time of its beginning. And

[12] F. Tocco, 'Guglielma Boema e i Guglielmiti', *Reale Accademia dei Lincei, memorie della classe di scienze morali, storiche e filologiche, Atti*, 5 Series, 8 (Rome 1900) p 28.

[13] *Ibid* pp 25–6.

[14] G. Biscaro, 'Guglielma la Boema e Guglielmiti', *ASL*, 6 series 57 (1930) pp 1, 22, 26, 31, 32, 50, 64, 67.

[15] H. C. Lea, *A History in the Inquisition of the Middle Ages*, 3 vols (New York 1888, repr 1955) 3 p 102.

in the same way he spoke of a transformed papacy, but was unclear about its precise nature in the new age.[16]

For many Franciscans, both conventual and spiritual, this notion of an *ecclesia spiritualis* was useful because it gave a special historical identity to their order. Even after his attempt to limit the radical application of the ideas of the abbot Joachim, Bonaventura, general of the Franciscan order (1257–74), continued to call Francis the angel of the sixth seal of the apocalypse and the engenderer of the new *ecclesia contemplativa*.[17] A number of Franciscan spirituals who were persecuted for their adherence to a strict interpretation of the rule, began to predict events that were to usher in a renovated church within which they were to gain their rightful authority. Gerard of Borgo San Donnino published the three major works of Joachim of Fiore in 1254 and proclaimed that they were, in fact, the awaited 'eternal gospel' and that the new age, foretold by Joachim, had begun. In 1297 concerned with the worsening state of affairs since the resignation of pope Celestine V, whose acceptance of the papacy had been imbued with messianic overtones, the Franciscan Peter John Olivi wrote of a *pseudopapa* and a soon-to-come jubilant third age of the Holy Spirit.[18]

Even more radical formulations concerning the new age were made outside the Franciscan order. The Amalricians, in the early thirteenth century, believed they participated in a new era wherein there were contemporary incarnations of the Holy Spirit.[19] At the end of the same century Dolcino of Novara predicted the beginning of the last period

[16] Contrast Joachim of Fiore, *Tractatus super quatuor evangelia*, ed E. Buonaiuti (Rome 1930) p 80 with *Concordia* (Venice 1519, repr 1964) fol 95^{v}. For arguments that Joachim kept the Petrine and papal elements in the future church see [M.] Reeves, [*The Influence of Prophecy in the Later Middle Ages*] (Oxford 1969) pp 395–7; H. Denifle, 'Das Evangelium aeternum und die Commission zu Anagni', *ALKG*, 1 (1885) pp 55–6; and *Joachim abbatis liber contra Lombardum*, ed C. Ottaviano, *Reale Accademia d'Italia, Studi e documenti*, 3 (Rome 1934) pp 22–5.

[17] Bonaventure, *Legenda sancti Francisi*, *Opera omnia*, 11 vols (Quaracchi 1882–1902) 8 p 504 and *Collationes in Hexaemeron*, *ibid* 5 p 445.

[18] 'Littera magistrorum', ed S. Baluze and J. Mansi, *Miscellanea*, 4 vols (Lucca 1761–4) 2 p 259. Although Reeves, pp 195–8 and R. Manselli, 'La terza età, *Babylon* e l'antichristo mistico', *BISIMEAM*, 82 (1970) p p49 and 58 have debated the meaning of Olivi's unique passage concerning three ages connected with the Trinity, neither has denied that the text is his. See also D. Burr, *The Persecution of Peter Olivi*, *Transactions of the American Philosophical Society*, ns, 66 pt 5 (Philadelphia 1976) p 19.

[19] Amalric of Bena died in 1206 and a number of Amalricians were burned in 1210. For their ideas about the incarnation of the Holy Spirit see Caesarius of Heisterbach, *Dialogus miraculorum*, ed J. Strange, 2 vols (Cologne/Bonn/Brussels 1851) 1 p 305; *Chartularium universitatis parisiensis*, ed H. Denifle and E. Chatelain, 4 vols (Paris 1889–97) 1 pp 70–2. When the heresy was discovered it had just begun to spread from

of the church and the immanent death of the then pope, Boniface VIII, who was to be replaced by a *papa sanctus*. At Carcassonne in 1325 Prous Boneta confessed to the inquisitors her conviction that she was to be the *donatrix* of the Holy Spirit and that the church brought into existence in this way was to be headed by a new pope, an associate of hers named Guillelmus Guiraudi.[20]

Placed in this context several doctrines of the Guglielmites can be seen to be an extreme and literalist version of the *ecclesia spiritualis*. Guglielma of Milan was believed by the Guglielmite sectaries to be the Holy Spirit, the third person of the Trinity, incarnate in the female sex. With the abolition of the Roman papacy a new church was to be inaugurated by her, and the earthly vicar of Guglielma as the Holy Spirit was to be the sectary Mayfreda de Pirovano,[21] who would celebrate mass both on Guglielma's grave site, equal to the holy sepulchre in Jerusalem, and in Rome.[22] Both the rites of the Roman church and the *curia* would be superseded. The gospels were to be abolished and four new evangels would become the holy testament.[23] Obviously, there would be new cardinals, one of whom had already been named, and also new orders.[24] In this dispensation Mayfreda, the Guglielmite pope, and all the followers of Guglielma were to baptist the jews, saracens, and all others outside the *ecclesia*.[25]

The enthusiastic motif of the *imitatio Christi* in the thirteenth century is so dominated by the exemplar Francis of Assisi that similar contemporary figures are often neglected.[26] Not only was Francis

---

the university of Paris to other areas; consult M.-T. d'Alverny, 'Un fragment du procès des Amauriciens', *Archives d'historie doctrinale et littéraire du moyen âge*, 26 (Paris 1951) pp 325–36. M. Reeves and B. Hirsch-Reich, *The 'Figurae' of Joachim of Fiore* (Oxford 1972) p 298, observed that the author of the *Contra Amaurianos*, Werner of Rochefort, used Joachim of Fiore's ideas against the Amalricians because he felt they had misapplied the ideas of the abbot. Hence, Reeves and Hirsch-Reich opened up the possibility of an interconnection between these intellectual currents.

[20] W. May, 'The Confession of Prous Boneta Heretic and Heresiarch', *Essays in Medieval Life and Thought*, ed J. Mundy, R. Emery, B. Nelson (New York 1965) pp 11, 27; 19–20. For information about another contemporary who considered himself the apostle of a new dispensation see R. Lerner, 'An "Angel of Philadelphia" in the Reign of Philip the Fair: The Case of Guiard of Cressonessart', *Order and Innovation in the Middle Ages*, ed W. Jordan, B. McNab and T. Ruiz (Princeton 1976) pp 343–64.

[21] Tocco, 'Il processo', p 340.

[22] *Ibid* p 321. [23] *Ibid* p 333.

[24] *Ibid* pp 318, 320.

[25] *Ibid* pp 338, 342, 353, 370, 373.

[26] Gilbert of Tournai in his *Collectio de scandalis ecclesiae* wrote about the stigmata of a contemporary German woman, who has been identified as Elizabeth of Erkenrodt in A. Stroick, ' "Collectio de scandalise cclesiae". Nova editio', *AFP*, 24 (1931) p 62.

charismatic in his life of poverty and the report of his stigmata a most dramatic reminder of his efforts to parallel the life of Jesus, but also his more ardent followers hoped for his resurrection and appearance among them in times of their travail.[27] A less famous practitioner of the *imitatio Christi* was Gerard Segarelli of Parma who was described, in his own day, with little sympathy by the hostile Franciscan chronicler Salimbene. After being refused admission to the friars minor, according to Salimbene, Gerard foolishly attempted to live literally like Christ. Beyond preaching the gospel and living in poverty, Segarelli re-enacted specific events from Jesus's life. Salimbene asserted that Gerard had himself wrapped in swaddling clothes, circumcised, and even suckled as a baby.[28]

Similar to the accounts of both Francis and Gerard Segarelli, the story of Guglielma of Milan's life was made to mirror details of the life of Jesus.[29] Believed by her followers to be of the same flesh as Jesus.[30] she was reputedly marked with the stigmata [31] and considered a miracle-worker. The beginning and end of her life were averred to have followed the gospel events. After learning from Guglielma that she had been born on pentecost, Andreas and Mayfreda, her two chief followers, said that they both believed and thought it ought to be so, that as the archangel Gabriel had announced the incarnation of Christ to Mary, thus it seemed to them that there would clearly have had to have been a parallel annunciation by the archangel Raphael to Guglielma's mother to foretell the incarnation of the Holy Spirit.[32] Immediately after her death Guglielma was supposed to have visited her disciples[33] and was expected to ascend bodily to heaven in their presence.

Widespread enthusiasm for the *vita apostolica* in the twelfth and thirteenth centuries brought into existence new orders and groups

[27] His stigmata was used by both the conventuals and the spirituals as absolute proof of Francis's sanctity, and it also played a role in their apocalyptic symbolism; see S. Bihelf 'S. Franciscus fuitne angelus sexti sigilli? (Apoc. 7, 2)', *Ant*, 2 (1927) pp 59–90. For the belief in Francis's resurrection and subsequent appearance see 'Auszüge aus des Petrus Johannes d'Olive Postille über die Apokalypse', *Beiträge zur Sektengeschichte des Mittelalters*, ed I. v. Döllinger, 2 vols (Munich 1890, repr [1960]) 2 p 549.

[28] Salimbene, [*Chronica*], *MGH SS*, 32 pp 255–8.

[29] Tocco, 'Il processo', p 372, ' . . . quod ipse Andreas credebat, quod dicta sancta Guillelma esset spiritus sanctus, et quod ipsa Guillelma faceret multa similia hiis que fecerat Christus.'

[30] *Ibid* pp 415, 418, 420.

[31] *Ibid* pp 329, 441 for the belief; pp 371–2 for the lack of proof.

[32] *Ibid* p 373.

[33] *Ibid* pp 321, 375, 413.

which stressed their evangelical *religio* as the way to implement the fullest kind of Christian life. Whichever aspects of the *ecclesia primitiva* they emphasised those became the highest paths to moral perfection. In the latter part of the thirteenth century the Franciscans, in this regard, were rivalled by groups of enthusiasts which not only stressed poverty, but also professed to carry out the gospel injunctions in a more literal way. Accepting each biblical example as a general rule, the *Apostoli* founded by Gerard Segarelli, owned only one tunic, had no permanent resident, begged for a living, and made no provision for the future.[34] Segarelli's devotees, who were obviously named after the original disciples and at times were, in fact, grouped as the twelve, revered their founder as a type of Saint Peter even to the extent of being able to walk on water and heal the sick.[35]

Convinced of the immanent advent of their own *ecclesia*, the Guglielmites followed practices and upheld beliefs derived from the concept of primitive Christianity. Fortified by Guglielma's supposed appearances after her death, the Guglielmites undertook to write new gospels, epistles, and prophecies that were plainly imitative of Christian scripture.[36] Remaining together on account of their devotion to Guglielma, who wished that the group stay as a family and that they love and honour one another, the sectaries partook of commemorative meals and praised the miracles worked through Guglielma.[37] Amongst themselves they were to have a Judas who was to betray them and a Peter, Mayfreda de Pirovano, who was to be the vicar of the Holy Spirit. This 'second Peter', who attempted to heal the sick, was reputedly commanded by Guglielma boldly to preach the new dogma.[38] Offering mass and performing other liturgical duties, Mayfreda awaited a future pentecost when Guglielma, the paraclete, was to establish her formally as the head of the church and begin the conversion of all non-Christians.[39]

Although various enthusiastic motifs can be delineated within thirteenth-century heresies, it is not always clear to us why the heretics

[34] Salimbene pp 280–4, 286.

[35] L. Aldrovandi, 'Acta Sancti Officii Bononiae ab anno 1291 usque ad annum 1309', *Atti e memorie d.r. Deputazione di storia patria per le provincie di Romagna,* 3 Series, 14 (Bologna 1896) pp 259, 260; *Historia Fratris Dulcini heresiarche di Anonimo Sincrono,* ed A. Segarizzi, Muratori, 9 pt 5 p 57.

[36] Tocco, 'Il processo', pp 317, 322, 329–30, 331, 333, 373–4.

[37] *Ibid* pp 424, 425.

[38] *Ibid* pp 422, 426; 370, 326.

[39] *Ibid* pp 353, 369.

carried their enthusiasm to such lengths. Because the Milanese Guglielmites were not widely diffused but were located in a comparatively small area and maintained close contact with one another, I think certain observations are possible concerning conditions that helped both to initiate and sustain this heresy. And the observations I wish to discuss here are those that should bring us closer to an understanding of the religious motivations of the Guglielmites.

The genesis of the sect may be clarified by a seemingly obscure statement ascribed to Guglielma of Milan by one of her followers, Franceschinus de Garbagniate. Guglielma declared, according to Franceschinus's testimony before the inquisitors, that after 1262 the body of Christ was not consecrated alone but together with the body of the Holy Spirit which was hers.[40] Guglielma asserted that she did not care to see the body of Christ sacrificed because she saw herself. When these remarks attributed to Guglielma are placed in the context of thirteenth-century Milan, they are given new meaning. For fifteen years, from 1262 to 1277, Milan's validly ordained archbishop, Otto Visconti, was not permitted to enter his city.[41] After the death of the previous archbishop, Leo of Perego, in 1257, a dispute had arisen over the election of a new archbishop. An impasse later developed between the candidates of both the ruling della Torre family in Milan and the papacy probably because of papal resentment over the granting to the Ghibelline and fautor of heretics Uberto Pallavicino of the captaincy of Milan for a four-year term in 1259. As a result of the conflict, the della Torre would not allow Otto to enter the city, and the castles and lands of the church were confiscated. To counter these actions archbishop Otto Visconti placed Milan under interdict, and censures against the Milanese government were renewed during the course of the dispute.[42] Therefore, it seems probable that Guglielma's statement about the consecration of the eucharist after 1262 was prompted by the interdict and the repeated penalties imposed by the prelates of the church.

[40] *Ibid* p 415. Guglielma's statement resembles the assertions of the free spirit mystics; see R. Lerner, *The Heresy of the Free Spirit in the Later Middle Ages* (Berkeley, Los Angeles/London 1972) pp 115, 211, 218, 222.

[41] The career of Otto Visconti may be studied in E. Cattaneo, 'Ottone Visconti arcivescovo di Milano', *Contributi dell' istituto di storia medioevale*, 3 Series, 1 (Milan 1968) pp 129–65.

[42] Galvanno Fiamma, *Chronica Mediolani seu manipulus florum*, Muratori, 11 col 692; [O.] Raynaldus, [*Annales ecclesiastici*], 15 vols (Lucca 1747–56) 3 p 389. The full involvement of the whole city in this controversy can be seen in A. Ratti, 'A Milano nel 1266', *Memorie del reale istituto lombardo di scienze e lettere*, 3 Series 12 (Milan 1899–1907) pp 205–35.

She apparently worried about the validity of the Milanese church denied its ordained archbishop. Strife within the *ecclesia* could have made Milanese enthusiasts discontented and disillusioned with the church and led to the desire for an *ecclesia spiritualis*.

Later controversies, both those involving the entire *ecclesia*, and those within the Milanese church can also be seen to have affected the development of the Guglielmite sect. Making good use of the questions concerning the legality of the election of Boniface VIII, the sectaries asserted that he was not the true pope because he was elected while another pope was living.[43] Likewise, Franciscus Fontana of Parma, archbishop of Milan from 1296 to 1308, was not able to absolve or condemn, according to the Guglielmites, because he was appointed by Boniface. For those members of the sect who were also Humiliati quarrels between the previous archbishop and the Humiliati order in the late 1280s over jurisdiction, and also a conflict within the order itself that resulted in the punishment of five members for sedition and rebellion must have confirmed their need for a new dispensation.[44] In fact, the Humiliati sister and Guglielmite, Mayfreda de Pirovano, in her moment of triumph as the new pope, planned to celebrate mass, preside and preach in Saint Mary Major in Milan.[45]

The unlikely association of the Guglielmites with female Humiliati and even with Cistercian monks allows us further opportunities to gain insight into the growth of the sect. The Guglielmites were sustained, in part, by the Milanese Humiliati house of Biassono which supplied the largest cohesive group of sectaries—six Humiliati sisters—and sheltered the proposed future Guglielmite pope, Mayfreda de Pirovano. Emblazoned on a banner above Biassono's altar was a picture representing the Trinity with Guglielma and, presumably, Christ, releasing captives from prison. On the altar itself was placed the liquid which remained after the washing of Guglielma's dead body and this water was used as chrism to anoint the sick by the Guglielmite leader sister

[43] Tocco, 'Il processo', pp 320–1, 411.

[44] *Les registres de Martin IV*, ed L'École francaise de Rome and F. Olivier-Martin (Paris 1901–35) pp 267–71; D. Arnoldi, 'Le carte dello archivio arcivescovile di Vercelli', *Biblioteca della società storica subalpina*, 85 (Turin 1917) pp 324–35; *HVM*, 2 pp 32–29; and pp 317–18, '. . . quod non sine mentis turbatione referimus, religionis quidem gestantes habitum, sed a religionis actibus discrepantes, in eodem ordine pacis emulo instigante, seditiones multiplices excitarunt, et assumpto rebellionis spiritu contra magistrum ejusdem ordinis et suos prelatos se in superbiam erexerunt, ac horrendis ab eis nimium excessibus perpetratis, plurima in predicto ordine scandala suscitarunt, in suarum animarum periculum, et ipsius ordinis maximum detrimentum . . .'

[45] Tocco, 'Il processo', p 333.

Mayfreda.[46] This sectary had first enjoyed religious prestige in preaching to her Humiliati sisters at Biassono,[47] and then apparently desiring an even more important role, sought to exercise sacerdotal power. Assuming the office of priest, she consecrated hosts on Guglielma's grave, and with sectaries as acolytes recited the mass according to Roman ritual.[48] Although within the sect Mayfreda was second to another leader Andreas Saramita, because of the feminine bias of Guglielmite teachings the sectaries paid special devotion to Mayfreda, and she, not Andreas, was to be the supreme pontiff in the new age.[49]

Because of their peculiar requirement, under the aegis of a female Holy Spirit, that only women hold higher office the preponderent female membership among the Guglielmites cannot be surprising. Adherence of women to medieval heresies has often been ascribed to their search for economic security.[50] It has recently been suggested that growing prosperity in the late thirteenth century resulted in parents giving female infants better care and thus increased their chances for survival.[51] And statistically women then lived longer than men[52] so this meant, together with other causes, more widows and spinsters for whom the new thirteenth-century heretical and orthodox organizations could provide social position and income. Among the twenty-eight female Guglielmites there were seven widows for whom the sect offered companionship and social stature. An explanation for the Guglielmite ideology should not be adapted, however, to the classic models of economic struggle. Even the Marxist historian Ernst Werner

[46] *Ibid* p 376.

[47] *Ibid* pp 316–17, 324.

[48] *Ibid* pp 320, 337, 339, 340, 352, 359, 412–14, 415. The hosts were given to the sick and consumed out of devotion to Guglielma. Any recoveries were ascribed, of course, to her; see *ibid* pp 326 and 366. When the sectaries were cited by the inquisition, Mayfreda particularly feared the disclosure of this priestly activity; she warned those cited to say nothing about the mass in *ibid* p 412.

[49] *Ibid* pp 318, 332, 333.

[50] G. Koch, *Frauenfrage und Ketzertum im Mittelalter* (Berlin 1962) pp 31 and 32. For Koch the most important impulses that drove women into beguine houses and cathar groups were economic and social, but he did not deny religious motivation. E. McLaughlin, 'Les femmes et l'hérésie médiévale. Un problème dans l'histoire de la spiritualité', *Concilium*, 111 (Paris 1976) pp 73–90, failed to consider the Guglielmites in her discussion of the presence of women in medieval heretical groups.

[51] E. Coleman, 'Infanticide in the Early Middle Ages', *Women in Medieval Society*, ed S. M. Stuard ([Philadelphia] 1976) p 64 and D. Herlihy, 'Life Expectancies for Women in Medieval Society', *The Role of Women in the Middle Ages*, ed R. T. Morewedge (Albany 1975) pp 14, 20. I am grateful to John Mundy of Columbia University who originally offered this suggestion to me.

[52] *Ibid* pp 10–16.

has backed away from labelling the first decades of the fourteenth century in Italy a true revolutionary period; thus for Werner, the followers of an heretical leader like Dolcino were only groping toward a revolutionary ideology.[53]

As motivation for joining an heretical sect a woman's desire for spiritual importance cannot be excluded.[54] If orthodox Christianity allotted to women only a minor rule in its organization, some heresies provided avenues for female advancement. Catharism established a female *perfecta*, though its eastern European counterpart Bogomilism gave greater scope to female ambitions.[55] Some Waldensians made women priests,[56] and the heresiarch Prous Boneta, in 1325, declared herself to be the bearer of the Holy Spirit. No sect, however, had the grandiose visions of the Guglielmites: female cardinals under a female pope who was the vicar of a female Holy Spirit. Salvation came through a female, divinised to redeem all men through her suffering. Grace was to be dispensed by the female hierarchy of the true church of the future.[57] The Guglielmite ideology, which we can interpret as a reaction to an exclusively male priesthood based on a male incarnation, offered female enthusiasts justification for exercising priestly office and promised them ecclesiastical roles far beyond their limited opportunities in the medieval church.

Confidence in the advent of their female church of the future was bolstered, indirectly, by another segment of the thirteenth-century Milanese church: the Cistercian monastery of Chiaravalle.[58] Located near the city, this monastery, from 1281 until 1300, promoted, with the usual elements of partisanship and rivalry, an orthodox saint cult of Guglielma of Milan. Probably an oblate of Chiaravalle, Guglielma

[53] E. Werner, 'Messianische Bewegungen im Mittelalter', *Zeitschrift für Geschichtswissenschaft*, 10 (Berlin 1962) p 396.

[54] E. Werner, 'Die Stellung der Katharer zur Frau', *Studi medievali*, 3 Series, 2 (Turin 1961) pp 295–301.

[55] In practice catharism did not provide equality for its *perfectae*, as Werner, *ibid* p 300, tells us.

[56] Bernard Gui, *Manuel de l'inquisiteur*, ed G. Mollat, 2 vols (Paris 1964) 2 p 42; *Summa fratris Renerii . . . de catharis et Leonistis seu Pauperibus de Lugduno*, Martène and Durand, *Thesaurus*, 5 col 1775.

[57] E. Aegerter, *Les hérésies du moyen âge* (Paris 1939) p 98, wrote drolly, 'Telle (*sic*) quelle la doctrine apparaît comme une sorte de Joachimisme pour suffragettes'. Although the hierarchy seems to have been limited to women, their priesthood was, in fact, open to men.

[58] For information about Chiaravalle, located near Milan, see especially Caffi; also R. Bagnoli, *L'abbazia di Chiaravalle milanese nella storia e nell' arte* (Milan 1935), and G. Ottani, *L'abbazia di Chiaravalle milanese e la sua storia* (Milan 1942).

had lived in a house provided by the monastery in the parish of Saint Peter all' Orto.[59] When she died in 1279 Guglielma was buried first at the church of Saint Peter; two years later a delegation of Cistercian monks was able to secure Guglielma's remains for Chiaravalle.[60] At the monastery her body was ceremoniously washed with a mixture of water and wine in the church of the lay brothers,[61] then dressed in Cistercian garb and reburied. To encourage devotion an altar[62] was erected at Chiaravalle and a fresco was painted in her honour.[63] Cistercian monks participated in all these activities and clearly they were aided by an ardent devotee, Andreas Saramita, who was later exposed by the inquisitors as a leading member of the Guglielmite sect.

Devotees of this venerated saint travelled to the monastery especially in October to celebrate the feast of the translation of her body and on Saint Bartholomew's day, 24 August, for the anniversary of her death. The abbot of Chiaravalle provided some food for the festivities,[64] and the monks preached laudatory sermons which, comparing Guglielma to the moon and the stars, asserted that she had healed sick monks of the monastery.[65] Proclaiming that Guglielma had lived a good life, engaged in wholesome conversation, and performed miracles, on 24 August a monk, Marchixius de Veddano, preached about Guglielma to more than one hundred and twenty-nine men and women.[66]

[59] Tocco, 'Il processo', p 461. In the purchase of this house for the monastery Andreas Saramita acted on behalf of Chiaravalle.

[60] According to the inquisitorial process Guglielma was alive in 1276, but was not mentioned in the proceedings of 1284 when the sect was investigated. The exact date of her death can be computed as 24 August 1279. Guglielma was originally buried at Saint Peter's and later exhumed and brought to the house of a sectary. Then, the monks of Chiaravalle claimed her remains for their monastery. When the translation of the relics to Chiaravalle took place, an escort was necessary because Milan and Lodi were at war (1281). Between Guglielma's burial at Saint Peter's and the war of 1281, according to the testimony before the inquisitors, two years had elapsed. The anniversary of Guglielma's death was celebrated yearly on 24 August. The evidence is not completely clear, however, and sparse in details; see *ibid* pp 364–5.

[61] Although Guglielma was brought to the church of the lay brothers, both *fratres clerici* and *conversi* were present, see *ibid* p 376.

[62] *Ibid* p 339.

[63] Puricelli fols 11r/v; Caffi pp 10 and 69, described the fresco painted at Chiaravalle in honour of Guglielma, and represented its configuration with a line drawing.

[64] Tocco, 'Il processo', pp 360, 361, 364.

[65] *Ibid* pp 331, 357, 360, 361, 362, 364, 367, 379–80, 381.

[66] *Ibid* p 378. In a list of the abbots of Chiaravalle, Marchixius de Veddano, who was elected abbot in 1305, was noted as the one under whom the notorious Guglielma was buried; see A. Ratti, 'La miscellanea chiaravallese e il libro dei prati di Chiaravalle', *ASL*, 3 Series, 4 (1895) p 127.

Guglielma's cult at Chiaravalle served as a focal point for the sectaries, and through the acts of veneration and reports of her miracles it also worked to reinforce their belief in the worthiness of Guglielma. At her grave site Mayfreda said mass and consecrated hosts. Other members of the sect travelled to Chiaravalle to offer private devotions and prayers to Guglielma. While the reputed miracle convinced her orthodox devotees of her saintliness, they were confirmation of her divinity for her heretical followers. And during the trial in 1300 two sectaries indicated that the more they thought Saint Guglielma answered their prayers that much more they believed in her divinity.[67]

The saint cult lasted until 1300 when the inquisitors determined that many of those devoted to Guglielma had used it as a type of camouflage for the heretical sect.[68] Of the more than one hundred and twenty-nine people who had participated in the ceremonies honouring this putative saint, forty-six were Guglielmites,[69] including three oblates of Chiaravalle,[70] the monastery's sole connection with the heresy. Condemned by the inquisition, three sectaries were put to death, and also Guglielma's remains were exhumed and burned.[71]

[67] Tocco, 'Il processo', pp 340–2.

[68] Some contemporaries suspected that such inquisitorial investigations of putative saints supported by older orders aided mendicant interests. When a Brescian, Guido Lacha, was exhumed for heresy by the inquisition, according to the report of the Dominican Bernard of Luxemburg, the people demanded the death of the bishop and friars because these men wished out of jealousy to burn a saint; see Bernard of Luxemburg, *Catalogus hereticorum* ([Cologne] 1526) H, fol 4v; and R. Creytens, 'Le manuel de conversation de Philippe de Ferrare, O. P. (†1350?)', *AFP*, 16 (1946) pp 120–1. (I am grateful to Fr Kaeppeli of the Istituto Storico Domenicano in Rome for pointing out to me the mention of Guido Lacha in Philip of Ferrara's work.) The investigation of Armanno Pungilupo of Ferrara by the inquisition fits this same pattern; see M. da Alatri, 'L'eresia nella Cronica di Fra Salimbene', *Coll Franc*, 37 (1967) p 372). On the other side, however, the Franciscan chronicler Salimbene gave the mendicant viewpoint concerning these cults when he listed the all-too-human motives for the veneration of several 'false' saints of his day; see Salimbene pp 503–4.

[69] From the inquisitorial records it can be concluded that there were at least twenty-eight female sectaries, eighteen of whom were examined during the trial, and eighteen male sectaries, eight of whom were also examined. It is important to note that among the sectaries there were adherents of both the rival Visconti and della Torre factions, and also that the attempt of John XXII in the 1320s to use this heresy as part of his anti-Visconti propaganda campaign does not give the sect itself any political overtones.

[70] G. Biscaro, 'Il contratto di vitalizio nelle carte milanesi del secolo XIII', *Rivista italiana per le scienze giuridiche*, 41 (Rome and Turin 1906) pp 28–32.

[71] Although the document that sentenced Guglielma's body to be burned is lost, and although the incomplete process against the Guglielmites does not declare that Guglielma was a heretic, other evidence indicates this fate for her remains; see Tocco, 'Il processo', p 462; *Annales colmarienses* p 226; Raynaldus, 5 p 262; and *Chronique*

Although the Guglielmite sect has arresting features—salvation through women and involvement with a Cistercian saint cult—it must be understood not as a spiritual aberration but rather as a specific fulfilment of thirteenth-century enthusiastic aspirations. What led these enthusiasts to heresy was disillusionment with both the Milanese church and the papacy over prolonged ecclesiastical controversies. Continually assured of the necessity of its proposed dispensation by recurrent turmoil in the church, sustained by women seeking priestly rank, and aided by an orthodox saint cult, the Guglielmite sect flourished in the latter part of the thirteenth century.

York College of Pennsylvania

---

latine de Guillaume de Nangis de 1113 a 1300 avec les continuations de cette chronique de 1300 a 1368, ed H. Géraud, 2 vols (Paris 1843) p 5.

ALLEGORICAL WOMEN AND PRACTICAL MEN: THE ICONOGRAPHY OF THE *ARTES* RECONSIDERED

by MICHAEL EVANS

AMONG the best-known mediaeval women are literary and pictorial personifications of abstract concepts: Virtues and Vices, Fortune and Philosophy, and the Seven Liberal Arts. Male embodiments of these subjects are exceptional, flouting both iconographic convention and the gender of the Latin nouns. The *artes liberales* in particular might be expected to remain a female preserve. In literature, from their first appearance as personifications in Martianus Capella's *De nuptiis Mercurii et Philologiae*,[1] they are uniformly female. Even when writers describe them as engaged in such virile activities as military combat (Henri d'Andeli)[2] or coachwork assembly (Alanus ab Insulis)[3] they are indubitably feminine; and when the *artes* themselves marry (Jean le Teinturier)[4] it is their spouses, the normally female Virtues, who have apparently changed sex to accommodate them. In art, too, the *artes* are generally regarded as feminine, and conventionally represented as seven allegorical women identified by attributes.[5] However, a miniature prefacing an early fourteenth-century copy of the *Livre du Trésor* of Brunetto Latini[6] exhibits a completely different treatment (Pl 1). There are twenty-one, not seven *artes*; the *artes liberales*, which occupy the central column, are represented by two or more male figures engaged in activities which are occasionally obscure but identified by inscriptions; they are flanked by pictures of fourteen other activities, some manual, some intellectual,

1 *Martianus Capella*, ed A. Dick, rev J. Préaux (Stuttgart 1969); English translation and commentary: W. H. Stahl, [R. Johnson, E. L. Burge], *Martianus* [*Capella and the Seven Liberal Arts*] (New York 1971, 1977).

2 *The battle of the seven arts. A French poem by Henri d'Andeli, trouvère of the thirteenth century*, ed L. J. Paetow (Berkeley 1914).

3 *Alain de Lille, Anticlaudianus*, ed R. Bossuat (Paris 1955).

4 *Le mariage des sept arts par Jehan le Teinturier d'Arras*, ed A. Langfors (Paris 1923).

5 For the most recent general survey of the iconography of the *artes*, see P. Verdier, 'L'iconographie des arts libéraux dans l'art du moyen âge jusqu'à la fin du quinzième siècle', *Arts libéraux et philosophie au moyen age, Actes du quatrième congrès international de philosophie médiévale* (Montréal/Paris 1969), p 305.

6 BL MS Add 30024; a description of this MS is given in the appendix.

and all but one again portrayed by males. In scope, this miniature is unique; diagrammatic *divisiones scientiae* of comparable complexity exist, but none is illustrated.[7] Its components, though combined in an original way, are less unprecedented; specifically, the use of males engaged in the practice of the *artes* instead of females personifying them is found elsewhere. The hegemony of allegorical women as representatives of the *artes liberales* is a myth; what might be described as practical men were frequently combined with them and occasionally, in illustrations to popular summaries of universal knowledge like the *Trésor*, preferred to them.

The male *artes* in general, and the Brunetto miniature in particular, will be considered later. Before that it will be helpful to submit the female personifications of the *artes* to a reconsideration. Handbooks of iconography tend to give the impression that this is one of the major secular allegories of the middle ages, that it depends on a literary source, and that there is a fairly consistent way of representing each *ars*.[8] None of this is so. Compared with themes like the Virtues and Vices[9] or the Labours of the Months,[10] the *artes* were rarely represented. Before the twelfth century there are hardly any examples: a Boethius MS in Bamberg,[11] and two MSS in Paris, one a Martianus Capella,[12] the other including verses on the *artes*,[13] contain the only extant pictorial cycles of these personifications prior to 1100. The theory that verses by Theodulf of Orleans,[14] Hibernicus Exul[15] and other early mediaeval writers are descriptions of, or tituli to, lost representations

[7] The development of the *divisio scientiae* in the middle ages is described in J. Mariétan, *Problème de la classification des sciences* (Paris 1901); for examples of diagrammatic *divisiones*, see J. Folda, *Crusader manuscript illumination at Saint-Jean d'Acre, 1275–1291* (Princeton 1976) figs 24, 25.

[8] For example E. Mâle, *L'art religieux* [*du XIII*e *siècle en France*] (6 ed Paris 1925) pp 75 *seq.*

[9] A. Katzenellenbogen, *Allegories* [*of the virtues and vices in mediaeval art*] (London 1939)

[10] J. C. Webster, *The labours of the months in antique and mediaeval art* (Evanston/Chicago 1938).

[11] Staatl Bibl MSC Class 5, fol 9v; W. Köhler, *Die Schule von Tours*, 1, 2 (Berlin 1933), pp 65 *seq*, and Tafel 90.

[12] BN MS lat 7900A; K.-A. Wirth, '[Eine illustrierte] Martianus [-Capella-Handschrift aus dem 13. Jahrhunderts]', *Städel-Jahrbuch* NF 2 (1969) p 43 and figs 15–19.

[13] BN MS lat 3110, fol 60r; M.-T. d'Alverny, 'La Sagesse et ses sept filles', *Mélanges Félix Grat* 1 (Paris 1946) p 245. Arras, Bibl de la Ville MS 559, t. iii, fol 1r (*c*1070) shows seven heads on the entablature of a building, and it has been suggested that these represent the *artes*; the identification is plausible but unprovable; see S. Schulten, 'Die Buchmalerei des 11. Jahrhunderts im Kloster St-Vaast in Arras', *Münchner Jahrbuch* 7 (1956) p 80.

[14] *Carmen* 46; *MGH Poet* [*aev car*] 1, p 544.

[15] *Carmen* 20; *ibid* 1, p 408.

of the *artes* is unconvincing.[16] There is no evidence for the existence of such pictures, a visual realization of the descriptions is impossible, the verses are clearly literary in inspiration and they confirm to orthodox poetic forms – some of the so-called tituli, for instance, are probably verse enigmas.[17] From about 1150 the *artes* appear in a variety of contexts and materials, but infrequently—there is no one place where they can normally be found as, for example, the Labours of the Months can be found in calendars. The relatively small number of monuments makes it difficult to isolate, still less to generalize about, an iconographic tradition.

The theory that this tradition depends on the personifications of the *artes* described in Martianus Capella's *De nuptiis* was first advanced by Corpet, with reservations, in 1857.[18] It was unreservedly adopted by such popularizers of iconographic studies as Emile Mâle and is still current,[19] despite the blatant difference between images of the *artes* and those invented by Martianus. His personifications are essentially literary creations, making their effect as much by word-play as by descriptive reporting, and employing devices that are incapable of being reproduced visually. His descriptions of *grammatica* as a Roman physician, *geometria* as a traveller, *arithmetica* emanating rays, the winged *astronomia* with her inlaid metal book and *musica* with her circular stringed instrument are unfamiliar in pictorial art, and would not be recognized for what they are—as was demonstrated when Hermann published a drawing in Vienna showing *geometria* as traveller and captioned it 'Pallas'.[20] Pictures of *dialectica* and *rhetorica*, it is true, often employ imagery found in *De nuptiis*: both the serpent common in representations of the former[21] and the armour sometimes worn by the latter are mentioned by Martianus. But these features are only

[16] J. von Schlosser, *Beiträge zur Kunstgeschichte aus den Schriftquellen des frühen Mittelalters* (Vienna 1891) pp 128 *seq.*

[17] For example those published as an 'Appendix ad Theodulfum' in *MGH Poet* 1, p 629; compare the stanza on *sapientia,* beginning *me pater ingenitus,* with the riddles *de glacies* (beginning *me pater ex gelido*; *ibid* 1, p 21) and *de sale* (beginning *me pater ignitus*; *ibid* 4, p 738, 3).

[18] E.-F. Corpet, 'Portraits des arts libéraux d'après les écrivains du moyen âge', *Annales archéologiques* 17 (Paris 1857) p 89.

[19] Compare J. J. M. Timmers, *Christelijke symboliek en iconografie* (rev ed Bussum 1974) p 194.

[20] H. J. Hermann, *Beschreibendes Verzeichnis* [*des illuminierten Handschriften in Oesterreich*] 8, 1 (Leipzig 1928) p 183; the identification was perpetuated by F. Saxl, *Verzeichnis des astrologischer und mythologischer illustrierter Handschriften . . . in Wien* (Heidelberg 1926) p 79; compare Wirth, *Martianus*, p 57.

[21] *Reallexikon zur Deutschen Kunstgeschichte, sv Dialektik.*

details of his more complex personifications, in which they are presented differently: the armour is covered by an embroidered mantle, while the serpent is concealed in *dialectica*'s sleeve—the whole point of the attribute is that it cannot be seen.

If Martianus had any connexion with the iconography of the *artes*, one would expect a tradition of illustrated copies of his book.[22] No such tradition is discernible in the middle ages, and with one exception the few MSS of the work that contain pictures reveal that even when Martianus's text was in front of him, the artist was unwilling or unable to realize it pictorially. The exception, a French MS of about 1100,[23] confirms the irrelevance of *De nuptiis* to portrayals of the *artes*, as the personifications depicted in this book are unlike any others in the middle ages. They represent an ingenious attempt to find a compromise between the bizarre verbal fantasies of a fifth-century author and the conventions of mediaeval art—for instance, *astronomia*'s inlaid book and *cubitalis mensura* (whatever that may be)[24] are omitted, but the fiery globe she arrives in is rationalized as a diagram of the spheres.[25] The influence of the pictures in this MS, which belonged to Niccolô Niccoli, can be seen in two humanist copies of Martianus;[26] but the sole hint of this iconographic type elsewhere in mediaeval art is the mis-identified *geometria* in Vienna, which may have formed part of a similar series: as only a few pages of the MS to which it belongs are extant, it is not possible to tell. In any case, these illustrations were not integral to the MS tradition of *De nuptiis*, and it is evident that illustrators of other copies had no pictorial exemplar associated with the text to draw on. The earliest illustrated copy of the work, a French MS of about 900,[27] contains pictures of only five *artes* of markedly different types. This suggests that the artist, lacking a model showing the seven *artes*, assembled his series from whatever was available. Only in one case did he turn to Martianus's description: his *dialectica* is an unusually conscientious attempt to depict the personification as presented in the text. For *grammatica* and *rhetorica*, however, he

[22] The MSS of Martianus are catalogued in C. Leonardi, 'I codici [di Marziano Capella',] *Aevum* 33 (1959) p 433; 34 (1960) 1 p 411.

[23] Florence, Bibl Mediceo-Laurenziana, MS S. Marco 190; L. H. Heydenreich, ['Eine illustrierte] Martianus [Capella-Handschrift,'] *Kunstgeschichtliche Studien für Hans Kaufmann* (Berlin 1956) p 59; Wirth, *Martianus*, figs 23–9.

[24] See Stahl, *Martianus*, 1, p 172, n 8.

[25] Alternatively this may represent her *siderens vertex*; either way it is not a literal interpretation of the text.

[26] Vat MS Urb lat 329; Venice, Marciana MS Cl XIV, 35; Heydenreich, *Martianus*, figs 7–12. [27] See note 12 above.

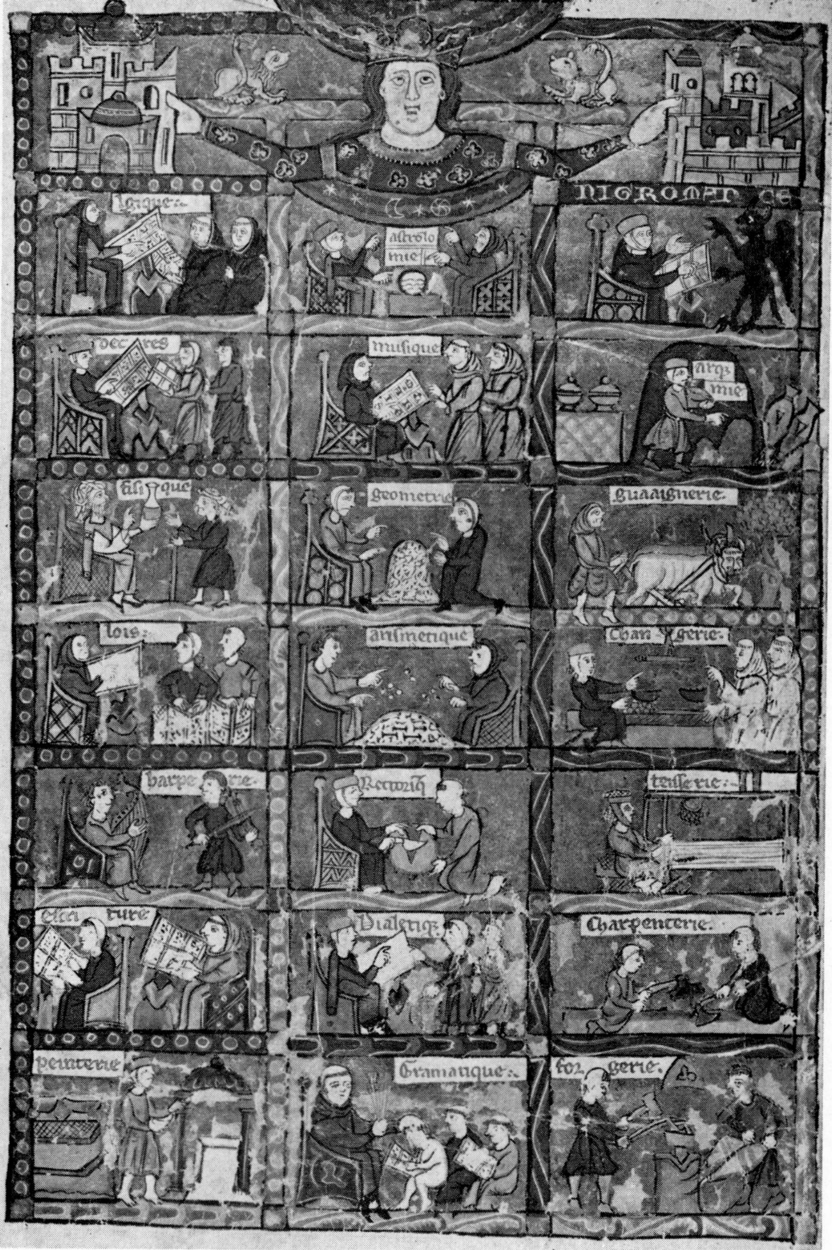

Plate 1 BL Add 30024 fol 1v.

Plates 2, 3 Munich Staatsbibl Clm 17405 fols 3^{r}, 4^{v}.

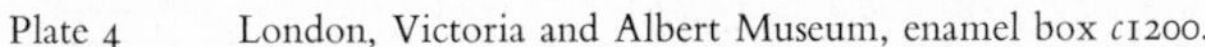

Plate 4 London, Victoria and Albert Museum, enamel box *c*1200.

Plate 5 Laon cathedral, west front, north window.

Plate 6 Sens cathedral, central portal, left embrasure, detail.

Plate 7 Clermont-Ferrand cathedral, north transept portal, gable.

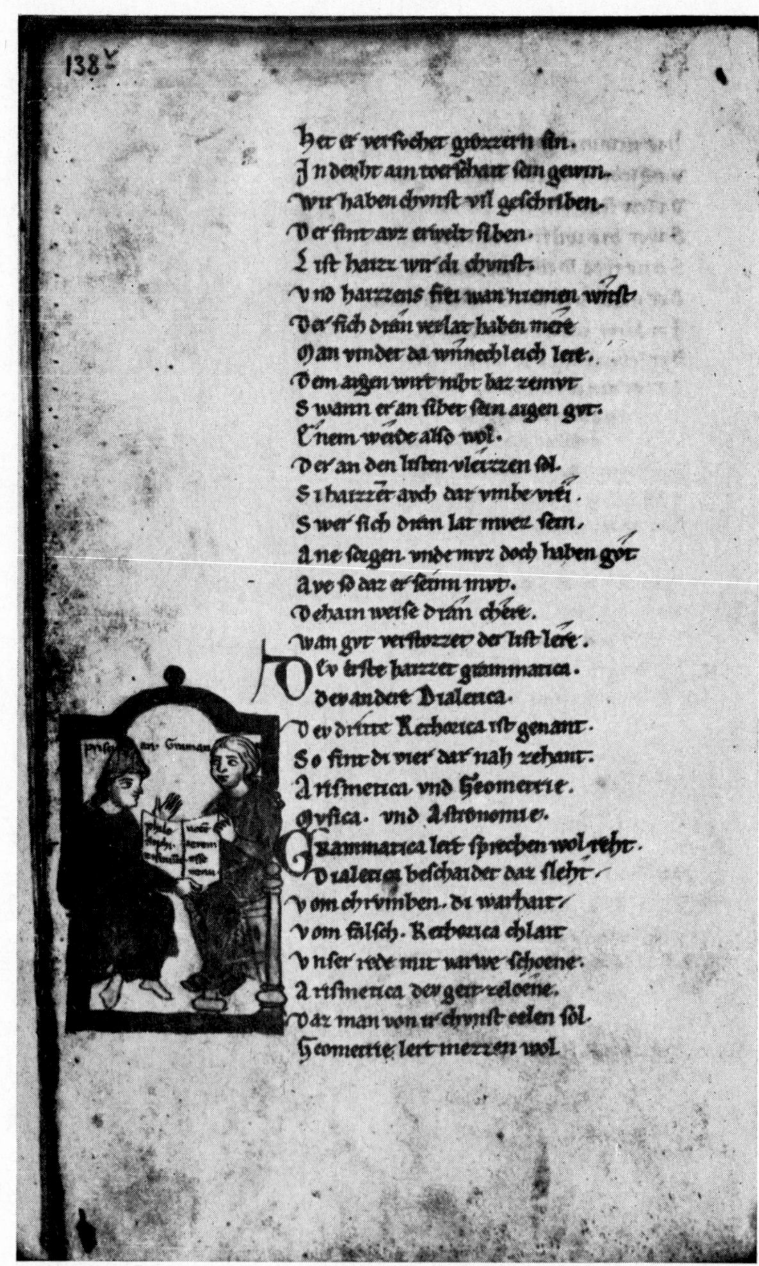

138v

het er versuochet grozzern sin.
Jn deiht ain toerschait sin gewin.
Wir haben chunst vil geschriben
Der sint auz erwelt siben.
List haizz wir di chunst.
Vnd haizzens frei wan niemen wirst
Der sich dran verlat haben mere
Man vindet da wunechleich lere.
Dem aigen wirt niht daz zemvt
Swann er an sibet sein aigen gvt.
Enem weide also wol.
Der an den listen vleizzen sol.
Si haizzent auch dar vmbe vrei.
Swer sich dran lat muez sein,
Ane sorgen vnde muz doch haben gvt
Ave so daz er seinn mvt.
Dehain weise dran chere.
Wan gvt verstozzet der list lere.
Dev erste haizzet grammatica.
Dev andert Dialectica.
Dev dritte Rethorica ist genant.
So sint di vier dar nah zehant.
Arismetica vnd Geometrie.
Mvsica. vnd Astronomie.
Grammatica lert sprechen wol reht.
Dialectica beschaidet daz sleht.
vom chrvmben. di warhait.
vom valsch. Rethorica chlart
vnser rede mit varwe schoene.
Arismetica dev gert zeloene.
Daz man von ir chunst zelen sol.
Geometrie lert mezzen wol.

Plates 8, 9 Heidelberg Univ Bibl Pal Germ 389 fol 138v, 139r.

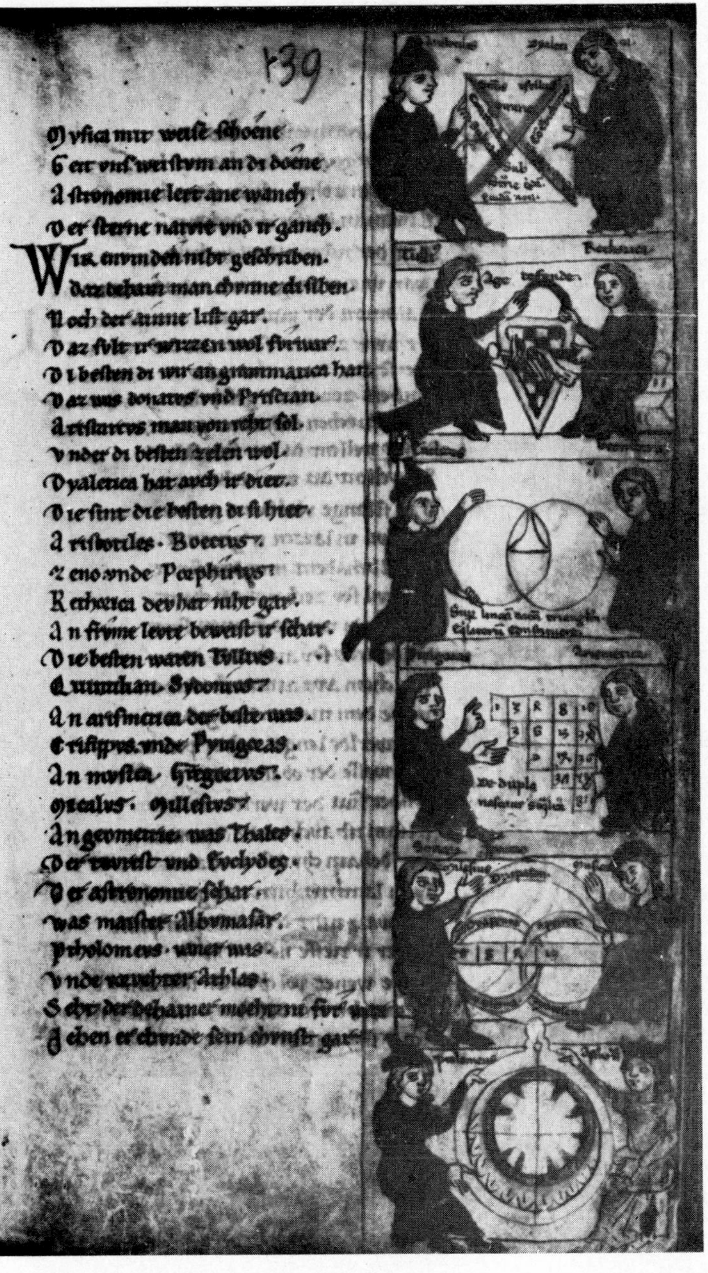
139

Mvsica mit weise schoene
Get vns weistvm an di doene.
Astronomie lert ane wanch.
Der sterne natvre vnd ir ganch.
Wir vinden niht geschriben.
daz dehain man chvnne di siben.
Noch der ainne list gar.
Daz sult ir wizzen wol firwar.
Di besten di wir an grammatica han.
Daz was donatus vnd Priscian.
Aristarcus was von reht sol.
Vnder di besten zelen wol.
Dyaletica hat auch ir diet.
Die sint die besten di si hiet.
Aristotiles. Boetius.
Zeno vnde Porphirius.
Rethorica dev hat niht gar.
An fume leute beweist ir schar.
Die besten waren Tullius.
Quintilian. Sydonius.
An arismetica der beste was.
Crisippus. vnde Pytagoras.
An musica Gregorius.
Micalus. Millesius.
An geometrie was Thales.
Der wiest vnd Euclydes.
Der astronomie schar.
was maister Albumasar.
Ptholomeus. winer was
Vnde warchter Athlas.
Sehr der dehainer mochte fur was
Jeben er chunde sein chunst gar

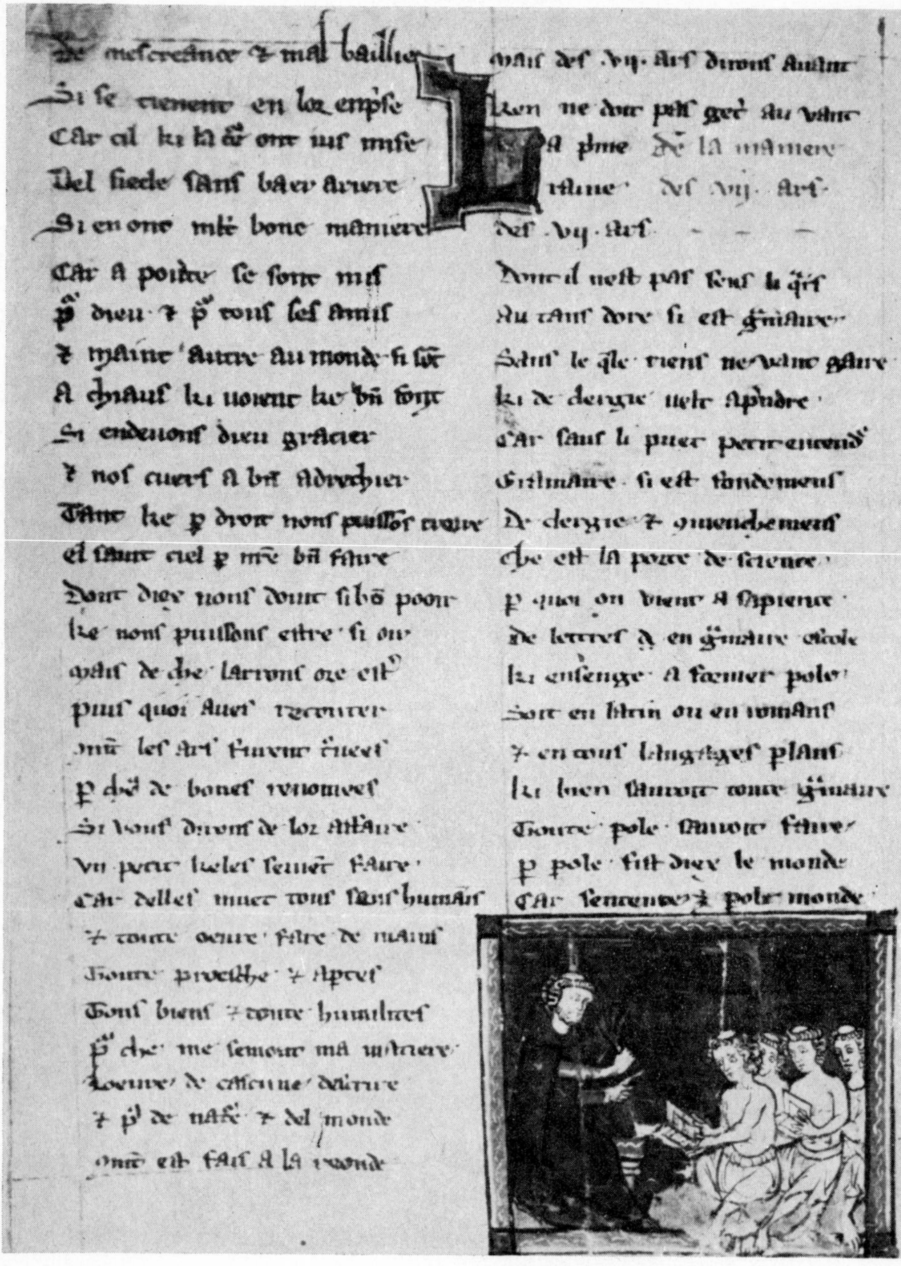

Plates 10, 11 Paris, Ste-Geneviève 2200 fols 57v, 58r.

La seconde ars si est logique
ke on appelle dyalectique
Ceste si prove voir et faus
par quoi on conoist bien et visce
ki bien savroit logique toute
bien et mal prouveroit sans doute
par bien fu criez paradis
et par mal enfer establis

La tierce rethorique est nom
ki est droiture de raison
et ordenee de parole
kele ne soit tenue a fole
de cesti sont li droit estrait
par quoi li iugement sont fait
ki esgardes sont par raison
en court de roi et de baron
et sont iugie des cites [illegible]
de cest art furent decretales
decretes et decres et lois
ki mestier ont en maintes lois

Si conoistroit et tort et droit
ki rethorique bien savroit
par tort faire est li mons perdus
et par droit sauve ses vertus

La quarte est nom arismetique
Ceste vient apres rethorique
et en mi les .vii. ars est mise
Car sans lui ne puet estre assise
Chascune des ars proprement
se lui seue entierement
Devant ke on sache cest art
Car toutes respondent lor pre-
se ne porent estre sans lui
por che fu elle mise en mi
les .vii. ars en qui [illegible]
de cesti muevent tout li nombre
par quoi tout croist et tout nest
Car sans nombre nule riens n'est
[illegible] peu [illegible] puet est
li des .vii. ars [illegible]
[illegible] quis en saiche [illegible] dire

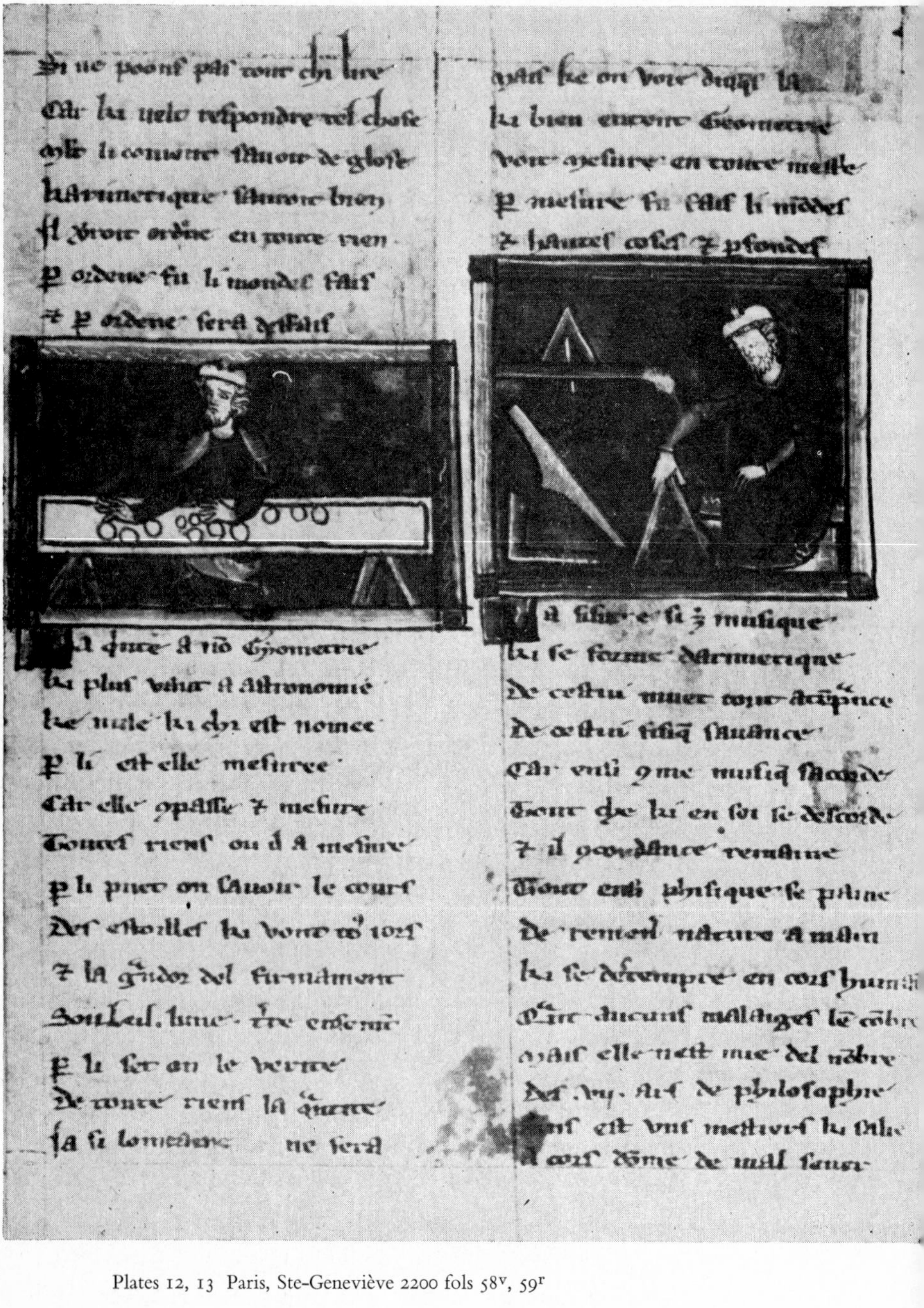

Plates 12, 13 Paris, Ste-Geneviève 2200 fols 58^{v}, 59^{r}

7 de maladie garder
Tant com il se maintient en vie
7 por che liberaus n'est mie
Car elle sert del cors garir
Chascune fors paroir pour
7 nule riens liberal n'est
Se france ki de cuer n'est
7 por che science quiert
A cors humain franchise pr
mais celes ki a l'ame tienent
liberal non du mont deservent
Car l'ame doit liberal estre
Si comme cose de noble estre
Comme cele ki de dieu muet
7 a dieu revenir s'en veut
7 por che art liberal sont
Ki l'ame toute franche font
7 ensengner comment doit faire
Aprendre en chascune afaire
Sa verité est la droite raison
Por quoi ars liberal a non
Ki le fait l'ame liberal
7 delivre estre de tout mal
De cestes est musique l'une
Ki si bien s'acorde a chascune
Ke par lui acordees furent
Les vii ars si come elles durent

De cestes sont li chant estrait
Ki en sainte glise sont fait
Toute acordance 7 estrument
Li ont de .ii. acordement
De toute riens set l'acordance
Ki de musique a la science
Toute riens ki de bien se paine
A acordance se remaine.

A septisme est astronomie
Ki est fins de toute clergie
Ceste ensengne raison a estre
Des coses du ciel 7 de terre
Ki par nature faites sont
Ja si ...ones ne seront
Ki astronomie savroit bien
Raison savroit en toute rien
Dieu fist toutes riens par raison
Ki chascune dona son non
Par cest art fu premiers encerchie

Plate 14 BN fr 574 fol 27^{r}.

Plate 15 Baltimore, Walters Art Gallery 199 fol 29

Plate 16 BN fr 574 fol 27^{v}.

Plate 17 BN fr 25344 fol 27^{r}, detail.

Plate 18 Paris, St-Geneviève 2200, fol 50^{v}.

Plate 19 BN fr 25344 fol 27^{v}, detail.

Plate 20 *(left)* Stuttgart, Landesbibl MS Poet et Phil 2^{0} 33 fol 31^{r}.

Plate 21 *(right)* Vienna, Nat Bibl 1196 fol 209^{r}.

Plates 22, 23 Rhetorica and Musica, from *Caxton's mirrour*.

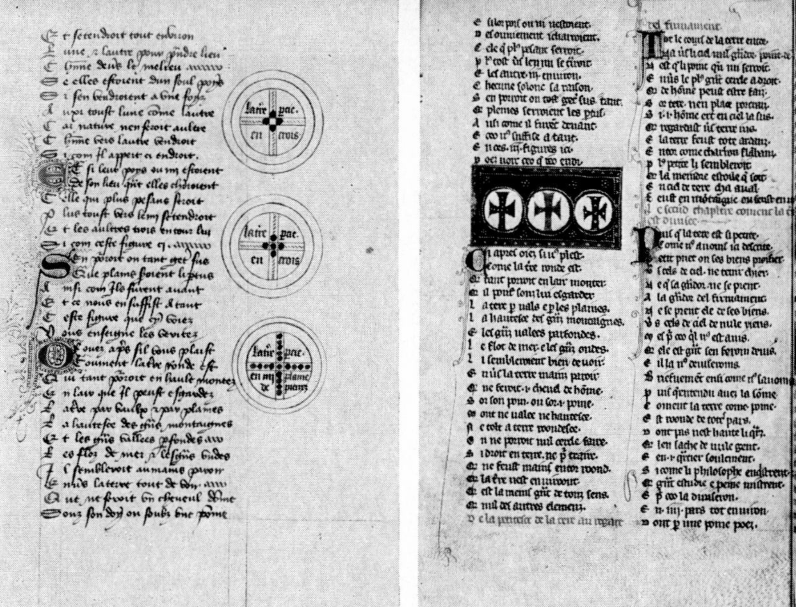

Plate 24 BN fr 14965 fol 30[r].

Plate 25 BN fr 1607 fol 41[v].

Plate 26 *(left)* Berlin, Staatsbibl Hamilton 675 fol 82[v].

Plate 27 *(right)* Salzburg, Univ Bibl M III 36 fol 239[v].

Plates 28, 29 New Haven, Yale University Beinecke 404 fols 6v, 7v.

Plate 30 *(left)* Leipzig, Univ Bibl 1253 fol 3r.
Plate 31 *(right)* BL Arundel 83 fol 12r.

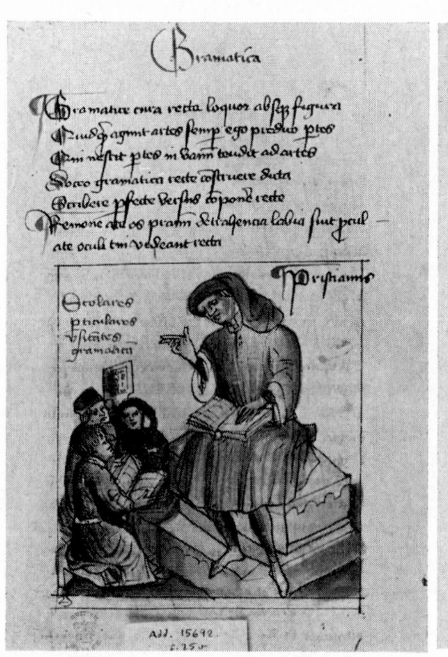

Plates 32, 33 BL Add 15692 fols 24v, 36v.

used school scenes, for *musica* a muse and two musicians, and for *astronomia* an astronomer standing within a schema of the elements. Other illustrated MSS of *De nuptiis* contain more uniform cycles of images, but these differ in appearance from one another and from the textual account.[28]

The disparity between these sequences of illustrations is matched by the variety found in the iconography of the *artes* elsewhere. Recognizable types were slow to develop, and the iconography remained labile. Most of the early personifications are literary, and apparently unrelated to pictorial art. They too are varied, and sometimes grotesque. For instance, Walther of Speyer (late tenth century) identifies *astronomia* with Urania;[29] according to Adelard of Bath (early twelfth century) she carries a rod and an astrolabe;[30] while one of the supposed tituli describes her as having five breasts, representing the terrestrial zones.[31] In contrast, the early pictorial representations such as the illustration to the verses in Paris, or the early twelfth-century mosaic in Ivrea,[32] barely distinguish one *ars* from the next. The miniature of the *quadrivium* in the Bamberg MS includes distinctive attributes, but this is because these figures are modelled on the muses, and although the *artes liberales* functioned to some extent as the muses of the middle ages,[33] there is no iconographic connexion between the muses and later mediaeval representations of the *artes*. When during the twelfth century the *artes* became established as a recognized if occasional element in the iconographic repertory, their appearance was influenced by the formula already established to personify the Virtues: a female figure with an emblematic attribute.[34] An inscribed diagram of about 1150 from Admont[35] specifies one or more attribute for each *ars*: a flaming jar for *grammatica*, a key and a half-concealed dragon for *dialectica*, etc. Although a number of pictures exists showing the influence of this programme,[36] the less allusive personifications

[28] The illustrated MSS are listed in Leonardi, *I codici*, p 477 n 202 and addenda.

[29] *Der Libellus Scolasticus des Walther von Speyer*, ed P. Vossen (Berlin 1962) 1, p 206.

[30] *Des Adelard von Bath Traktat De eodem et diverso*, ed H. Willner (Münster 1903) p 31.

[31] *MGH Poet* 1, p 629, 2.

[32] *L[exikon der] C[hristlichen] I[konographie]* (Freiburg etc 1968–) *sv* Künste fig 2.

[33] L. D. Ettlinger, 'Muses and liberal arts', *Essays [in the history of art presented to Rudolf] Wittkower* (London 1967) p 29.

[34] For the attributes of the Virtues, see Katzenellenbogen, *Allegories*, p 55.

[35] Chicago, Newberry Library MS F 9, fol 65v; M. Masi, 'A Newberry diagram of the Liberal Arts', *Gesta* 11/2 (1972) p 52.

[36] See R. Green, M. Evans, C. Bischoff, M. Curschmann, *The Hortus deliciarum [of Herrad of Hohenbourg]* (London 1979) p 104.

apparently first employed on the west facade of Chartres cathedral (1145–55)[37] were more widely accepted. *Grammatica* here has the more direct emblem of a whip, and instructs children; *dialectica* keeps her symbolic animal, but there is no attempt at concealment. The other *artes* seem to have been similarly explicit (some have now lost their attributes) and imitations of the Chartrian type were produced until the early fourteenth century.[38]

From the fourteenth century, a more allegorical recension of this type was current:[39] *grammatica* does not teach children but suckles one, and *dialectica* bears a small face signifying reason on her breast. The source of these images is a set of verses[40] describing each *ars*—the priority of the text over the pictures is suggested by the fact that, for instance, the face on *dialectica*'s breast is a literal interpretation of the words *in medio ratio profundo de pectore manet* rather than a conventional iconographic motif. The verses also specify an appropriate author or scholar to accompany each personification. The practice of further characterizing the *artes* by linking them with distinguished exponents of each discipline goes back to the twelfth century. The *artes* at Chartres alternate with seven male figures using writing implements, though as they are not labelled (their traditional identifications are guesswork)[41] they do not assist in identifying the individual disciplines. But in other cases the exponent is named: the Admont diagram, for instance, prescribes an appropriate scholar for each *ars*, and a sequence of thirteenth-century coloured drawings from Aldersbach[42] shows the *artes* accompanied by an almost identical series of authors. There was, however, no established canon of seven scholars, comparable to the Seven Sages of antiquity, and the choice, within limits, seems to have been arbitrary. A bifolium of miniatures prefacing a

[37] A. Katzenellenbogen, [*The sculptural programs of*] *Chartres* [*cathedral*] (Baltimore 1959) pp 15 *seq.*

[38] The reliefs of the *artes* on the west facade of the cathedral at Auxerre (1280–1310) are untimately dependent on Chartres; F. Nordström, *The Auxerre reliefs* (Uppsala 1974).

[39] Exemplified by the miniature in Milan, Bibl Ambros MS B 42 inf, fol 1^{r}; see L. Coletti, 'Un affresco, due miniature e tre problemi', *L'Arte* 37 (1934) p 101.

[40] Transcribed in J. von Schlosser, 'Giustos Fresken [in Padua und die Vorläufer der Stanza della Segnatura'], *Jahrbuch der Kunsthistorischen Sammlungen des allerhöchsten Kaiserhauses* 17 (1896) p 92.

[41] Compare Katzenellenbogen, *Chartres*, p 20.

[42] Munich, Staatsbibl MS Clm 2599, fols 102^{r}–4^{v}, 106^{r}; W. Hörmann, 'Probleme einer Aldersbacher Handschrift', *Buch und Welt, Festschrift für G. Hofmann* (Wiesbaden 1965) p 335; E. Klemm, 'Artes liberales und antike Autoren in der Aldersbacher Sammelhandschrift Clm 2599', *Z*[*eitschrift für*] *K*[*unstgeschichte*] 41 (1978) p 1; *The Hortus deliciarum* p 104.

thirteenth-century *Historia scholastica* from Scheyern[43] has two exponents for each *ars*, but this is exceptional (Pls 2, 3); the usual practice was to show one only, either at the feet of the personification or beside it. As Voge observed, exponents are rarely found in mediaeval sculptured cycles of the *artes*;[44] but there are very few such cycles, and exponents occur frequently elsewhere, sometimes incongruously. Heinrich von Mugeln (fourteenth century), who made a German adaptation of Alanus ab Insulis's *Anticlaudianus*,[45] also wrote a set of verses *Von allen frien künsten*,[46] which unlike the *Anticlaudianus* specifies an appropriate scholar for each *ars*. These verses accompany a series of fifteenth-century pictures showing *artes* and exponents;[47] the *artes* are not holding attributes indicative of learning but busy building a chariot, as described in Alanus's poem (Pl 27). Here, the conventional accoutrements of scholarship are associated with the exponents, while the personifications are overtly mere artisans. This blurring of the rôles of *ars* and exponent ultimately results in pictures omitting the personification altogether, and showing, for instance, Priscian as grammarian instructing the group of pupils appropriate to the personified *grammatica* (Pl 32). Since the exponents are invariably male, the effect is to create a cycle of masculine *artes*; but the MS in which these pictures occur is late (1438) and, as will be seen, atypical. It was more usual for both *ars* and exponent to be present. Although the latter is sometimes a subservient figure crouched at the feet of the personification, it frequently shares in displaying the attribute of the *ars* and occasionally, as in some of the Scheyern pictures, assumes sole responsibility for it (Pl 2).

One example of particular significance is found in illustrations to Thomasin von Zerclaere's didactic poem the *Welsche Gast* (1215–16).[48] Pictures of the *artes* appear in nine MSS of the work, dating from the mid-thirteenth to the fifteenth centuries (Pls 8, 9, 26).[49] The earliest

[43] Munich, Staatsbib MS Clm 17405, fols 3r–4v; J. Damrich, *Ein Künstlerdreiblatt des XIII. Jahrhunderts aus Kloster Scheyern* (Strassburg 1904) pp 24, 84; A. Boeckler, 'Zur Conrad v. Scheyern-Frage', *Jahrbuch für Kunstwissenschaft* 1 (1923) p 83.

[44] W. Vöge, *Jörg Syrlin der Altere und seine Bildwerke*, 2 (Berlin 1950) p 176.

[45] *Der meide kranz*, ed W. Jahr (Borna/Leipzig 1908).

[46] *Vier Meistergesänge von Heinrich von Mügeln*, ed U. Kube (Berlin 1932) p 92.

[47] Salzburg, Univ Bibl MS M III 36, fols 239v–42v; K.-A. Wirth, 'Neue Schriftquellen zur deutschen Kunst des 15. Jahrhunderts', *Städel-Jahrbuch*, NF 6 (1977) p 319, figs 15–21.

[48] *Der Wälsche Gast des Thomasin von Zirclaria*, ed H. Rückert (Quedlinburg/Leipzig 1852); F. W. von Kries, *Textkritische Studien zum Welschen Gast Thomasins von Zerclaere* (Berlin 1967).

[49] A. von Oechelhaeuser, *Der Bilderkreis [zum Wälschen Gast]* (Heidelberg 1890); H. Fühmorgen-Voss, *Text und Illustration im Mittelalter* (Munich 1975) p 36.

of these copies, now in Heidelberg,[50] employs iconographic types that are used consistently in the other MSS: the *artes* are represented by confronted personifications and exponents holding attributes between them; the attributes are unconventional and peculiar to this text. *Grammatica* and Priscian hold a book open at the first sentence of the *Institutiones*; *dialectica* and Aristotle hold a figure of the square of opposition; *rhetorica* and Cicero hold a sword in front of a shield; *geometria* and Euclid hold the first proposition from the *Elementa*; *arithmetica* and Pythagoras hold a triangular schema showing double, triple and sesquialteral proportions; *musica* and Timotheus of Milesius hold a figure of the perfect consonances; and *astronomia* and Ptolemy hold an astrolabe. The unusual and effective device of basing attributes on technical diagrams is not accounted for by anything in the text of the *Welsche Gast*. Most of the hundred or so pictures with which the MSS are illustrated must have been specially invented for the work—the allegories and exempla are not appropriate to any other context—but the pictures of the *artes* were probably taken over from another source; the *Welsche Gast* belongs to the tradition of mediaeval courtesy-books,[51] and allusions to Euclidian geometry and Pythagorean proportions are out of keeping. They differ from the other illustrations not only in their relation to the text, but also in their layout—while most of the other scenes float freely on the page without any kind of surround, the pictures of the *artes* are framed. The implications of this will be considered later.

In almost all the examples mentioned so far the *artes* are female while the exponents are male. The exception is the *Historia scholastica* from Scheyern: here the personification of *arithmetica* is a bearded man, and that of *geometria* is probably male too (Pl 3). As well as being iconographically odd, this bifolium is ill-suited for inclusion in a codex. If detached from the book, it would show *philosophia* and the *trivium* on one side of a wide sheet of parchment, and the *quadrivium* on the other. Folded and bound into a volume, however, the *quadrivium* is split between the recto of the first leaf and the verso of the second, with the *trivium* and *philosophia* coming between them. This suggests that the pictures were copied from a model that was not intended as a book-illustration, a suspicion that is endorsed by the composition of

[50] Cod Pal Germ 389; facs with commentary by F. Neumann and E. Vetter (Wiesbaden 1974) – [*Facsimilia Heidelbergensia* 4].

[51] E. Oswald, 'Early German courtesy-books', *Queene Elizabethes Achademy*, ed H. Furnivall, *EETS*, extra series 8 (1869).

the individual scenes. All the personifications except *musica* are shown frontally. *Philosophia*, the *trivium* and *astronomia* are absolutely symmetrical, holding matching attributes in each hand or making the same gesture with each; the pair of exponents which flanks the personifications reinforces this apparently needless structural parallelism. This sequence of rigorously symmetrical compositions makes its full effect only if the miniatures are placed one above the other: then they create a balanced design with a strong vertical emphasis. A likely medium for such a composition would be stained glass—a lancet illustrating the *artes* such as has been conjectured for Lausanne cathedral,[52] but with *philosophia* at the bottom. This hypothetical window would be formally similar to a Jesse Tree like that at St Denis,[53] with authors flanking *artes* instead of prophets flanking ancestors. The anomolous pose of *musica* (Pl 2) and her lack of exponents could be explained by her position at the top of the design, in the ogive.

Whatever the model, the Scheyern artist made only a superficial attempt to adapt it to its new format, from which it might be inferred that the male *artes* were present in the prototype. If he did decide to change their sex, his motive is obscure. Petrus Comestor's text[54] ascribes the invention and transmission of the *artes* to patriarchs and wise men, and the preface to his work faces the page with the two male *artes*; but it is hard to believe that the artist would prefer male personifications on this account. On the other hand, he was a careless copyist—he omitted stools for some of the seated exponents—and he may simply have misunderstood his model. But there were precedents for occasional male figures among female *artes*. A late twelfth-century enamel box in the Victoria and Albert Museum[55] is decorated with personifications of the *artes*, *philosophia* and *natura* (Pl 4); *rhetorica* is a man holding scales. The attribute is as unexpected as the personification's sex, and but for the inscription above the figure its identity would be doubtful even in this context. There are other peculiarities in this cycle: *astronomia* is seen from the back—not even the personification's face is visible—while *dialectica* has an arrow in her mouth and *natura* suckles an infant identified as *scientia*. In this elegant and iconographically abstruse *objet d'art*—perhaps made to hold the writing-materials of a courtly scholar—the *artes* seem to have been introduced as a

[52] E. J. Beer, *Die Rose der Kathedrale von Lausanne* (Bern 1952) p 68.
[53] A. Watson, *The early iconography of the Tree of Jesse* (London 1934) p 77 and pl 24.
[54] *PL* 198 col 1053.
[55] M.-M. Gauthier, *Émaux du moyen age occidental* (Fribourg 1972) pp 14, 315.

decorous ornamental motif, as they probably were on church portals, despite the efforts of some scholars to associate their presence there with renowned local schools.[56] The designer of the box evidently felt free to treat them with unusual liberty and inventiveness. On façades they were more stereotyped, but here too male figures were introduced. The reliefs of the *artes* on the left embrasure of the portal at Sens cathedral[57] begin and end with a pair of men (Pl 6), and the voussoirs of the north window on the west front of Laon cathedral[58] include a writing man among the personified *artes, philosophia* and *medicina* (Pl 5). In the absence of labels it is futile to attempt to identify these figures; but whatever they stand for—*artes* outside the canonical seven, or an allusion to the scholars depicted at Chartres—it is clear that by the early thirteenth century it was not thought incongruous to have an allegory of learning that included male figures on equal terms with female ones.

It is nevertheless surprising to find, beginning in the thirteenth century, a uniformly male cycle of *artes* attached to one particular text. The text is the *Image du Monde*, a popular summary of universal knowledge by Gossouin of Metz, who finished the first version of the work in 1246.[59] It was a very successful compilation—it exists in several redactions, adaptations and translations—and one of the reasons for its popularity must have been that it was illustrated. The author states at the beginning that his argument cannot be understood without reference to the twenty-eight *figures* or diagrams which accompany the text. These diagrams were frequently treated as illuminated miniatures and executed in body-colour and gold; they form a most attractive feature of the book (Pls 24, 25). The most ambitious MSS of the *Image* contain further pictures, not essential to the comprehension of the content: these include pictures of the seven *artes liberales*. The earliest and most extensively illuminated of the

[56] For example Mâle, *L'art religieux*, p 82; but the *artes* also appeared on the facades of churches at places of no academic importance, like Déols and Loches. Furthermore, it has been suggested that the 'School of Chartres' was in fact based on Paris [R. W. Southern 'Humanism and the School of Chartres', *Mediaeval Humanism and Other Studies* (Oxford 1970) p 61; the reliefs of the *artes* on the central west portal of Notre-Dame are a nineteenth-century fabrication.

[57] W. Sauerländer, *Gotische Skulptur in Frankreich 1140–1270* (Munich 1970) p 99.

[58] Viollet-le-Duc, *Dictionnaire raisonné de l'architecture* (Paris 1854–) *sv Arts*; L. Broche, *La cathedrale de Laon* (Paris 1926).

[59] *L'image* [*du monde de maitre Gossouin*], ed O. H. Prior (Lausanne/Paris 1913); for a list of MSS and discussion of the problem of the author's name, see M. Destombes, *Mappemondes* [*AD 1200–1500*], *Monumenta cartographica vetustioris aevi* 1 (Amsterdam 1964) p 117.

extra-illustrated copies is in the Bibliothèque Ste-Geneviève in Paris, and dated 1277 (Pls 10–13, 18).[60] The iconographic types established in this MS were preserved with remarkable consistency throughout the fourteenth and fifteenth centuries; they are found, for example, in a large and splendid copy of the work from the library of Jean de Berry (Pls 14, 16),[61] executed about 1325, and in a Netherlandish copy made in Flanders and dated 1489 (Pl 15)[62] *Grammatica* is represented by what is in all respects but one the conventional scene of education: however, the teacher holding the whip is male, bearded and tonsured (Pls 10, 14). *Dialectica* in the Ste-Geneviève MS is another school scene (Pl 11); in later MSS a more distinctive image was employed, a dispute between two groups of figures (Pls 16, 19). *Rhetorica* is another dispute, but one figure against several (Pl 11). Again, in the later MSS this was refined and made more precise: the single figure is crowned, while those disputing with him hold a document with a seal dangling from it (Pls 16, 19). The *quadrivium* is represented by single personages engaged in the relevant disciplines, similar to the conventional type exemplified at Chartres except that all the figures are men (Pls 12, 13, 18).

An examination of the text of the *Image* reveals little that would account for these invariably masculine *artes*. The seven short chapters on the sciences which the miniatures illustrate[63] do not describe or mention female personifications, but this in itself is no explanation—texts like the *Welsche Gast* and the *Historia scholastica* do not do so either. These chapters are prefaced by two longer ones, *Pour quoi et comment les vii arz furent trouvées. Et de leur ordre*, and *Des trois manieres de gens, et comment clergie vint en France.*[64] The former extols the wise men of antiquity who established the *artes* after 2400 years of study, and contrasts their selfless pursuit of knowledge with the mercenary attitude of modern scholars; the latter emphasises the importance of learning to society. It is possible that the artist decided to complement the author's factual and practical treatment of the *artes* by employing a literal rather than an allegorical mode of representation. The picture of *rhetorica* as a confrontation between clerics and a ruler is consonant with Gossouin's remarks on the links between scholarship and the

[60] MS 2200; *Bulletin de la société Française de reproductions de manuscrits a peintures,* 5 (Paris 1921) p 47.

[61] BN MS fr 574; Destombes, *Mappemondes* p 137.

[62] Baltimore, Walters Art Gallery MS 199; *Illuminated books of the middle ages and renaissance* (ex cat) (Baltimore 1949) p 50.

[63] *L'image* 1, vii (pp 80–6).

[64] *Ibid* 1, v, vi (pp 67–80).

state: *Car se clergie s'en aloit de France, chevalerie s'en iroit après, comme ele a toz jours fet. Car touz jours se tient près de lui. Si la retiengne li rois de France pour son preu. Car il porroit bien perdre son riaume, se clergie se departoit de France.*[65] Much later in the work Gossouin returns to the *artes. Comment l'en sauva les clergies pour la deluge*[66] describes how the *genz qui sorent le sens des vii arz que Diex leur envoia en terre* preserved them from destruction; *De ceuls qui trouverent les clergies après la deluge*[67] tells how the *artes* were re-established after the Flood by Sem, Abraham, Plato, Aristotle and Boethius. This emphasis on historical practitioners of the *artes*, and the omission of any female contribution, may have made the traditional feminine allegories seem rather irrelevant. The word Gossouin uses for 'learning', *la clergie*, could conceivably have suggested to the artist *le clergié*, a cleric; certainly the pictures often show tonsured figures. But it is unlikely that any of this would have been sufficient to bring about a complete rejection of conventional iconography.

A more probable explanation is that the artist had access to a model containing pictures appropriate to the whole *Image* text, including figures which would serve to illustrate the chapters on the *artes*, and that these figures were male. The wide range of subjects covered by the *Image*, embracing cosmology, geography and zoology, would have called for an illustrated exemplar of encyclopaedic scope; but texts of summaries of universal knowledge were seldom illustrated. There is some evidence that the standard handbook of the earlier middle ages, the *Etymologiae* of Isidore, contained an extensive cycle of illustrations, reflected in the pictures in the copy of Rabanus's *De universo* in Montecassino.[68] But such MSS must have been exceptional, and the only graphic material commonly found in copies of Isidore and Rabanus consists of technical diagrams and schemata. Nor were the great scholastic compendia, like the *Speculum major* of Vincent of Beauvais, illustrated with anything like the exhaustiveness that would match the text. The 'pictorial encyclopaedias' of the middle ages, like the *Liber floridus* and the *Hortus deliciarum*, turn out on closer inspection to be not summaries of learning but books developing a particular

[65] *Ibid* 1, vi (p 79).
[66] *Ibid* 3, ix (p 181).
[67] *Ibid* 3, x (p 182).
[68] F. Saxl, 'Illustrated mediaeval encyclopaedias 1', *Lectures* (London 1957) p 228; E. Panofsky, 'Hercules agricola: a further complication in the problem of the illustrated Hrabanus manuscripts,' *Essays Wittkower*, p 20.

argument.[69] A systematic handbook with a full cycle of illustrations is very rare.

There is however one type of illustration that may occur in any kind of handwritten book. This is the historiated initial. The capital letter embellished with human figures may be purely ornamental, but often it alludes to the text it prefaces. So while copies of the great mediaeval summaries of universal knowledge seldom contained a sequence of miniatures, they could and did have pictures in the initials of the text itself. An early twelfth-century Isidore MS from Swabia,[70] for instance, has a historiated initial for most of the books into which the work is divided, and for some of the major divisions within the books. These contain simple designs appropriate to the content: a bust of Christ for book 7, *De Deo*; a scribe for book 6, *De veteris et novis testamentis*; a doctor and patient for book 4, *De medicina*. Book 3, *De mathematica*, is divided into four parts dealing with the *artes* of the *quadrivium*. Each begins with an initial showing a figure engaging in a relevant activity. The A of *arithmetica* contains a man counting on a tally; the G of *geometria* shows a man with rod and dividers; the M of *musica* has a man with a monochord; the A of *astronomia* shows a man looking at the sky (Pl 20). These are not personifications: they are simply the figurative elements in historiated initials establishing a connexion between capital and text. A volume like this, surpassing the *Image* in extent of subject-matter and offering a wide variety of images in initials, would have been a useful model for an artist attempting to augment the twenty-eight *figures* of the *Image du Monde*. The result, deriving from the tradition of ornamental capitals rather than illuminated miniatures, would include designs appropriate to the chapters on the *artes*, but featuring male rather than female figures.

This is not to suggest that female personifications never appear in historiated initials: the Swabian Isidore includes personifications of *Ecclesia* and *Synagoga* to preface book 8. But when no special identity is attached to the figures in the letters, when they are differentiated only so far as to make the design apt for the following text, they are usually male. In some thirteenth-century bibles, for example, the Book of Proverbs is prefaced by an initial containing a teacher with a whip instructing a naked pupil (Pl 21);[71] the iconography is that of the

[69] H. Bober, 'The Liber Floridus: structure and content of its imagery (summary), '*Liber Floridus colloquium*, ed A. Derolez (Ghent 1973) p 19; *The Hortus deliciarum* p 24.

[70] Stuttgart, Landesbibl MS poet et phil 2° 33; K. Löffler, *Schwäbische Buchmalerei in romanischer Zeit* (Augsburg 1928) p 69.

[71] For example Vienna, Nat Bibl MS 1196, fol 209^r; Hermann, *Beschreibendes Verzeichnis*

conventional scene of *grammatica*, but the figures are male, and bear a strong resemblance to those of the *grammatica* picture in the *Image* (compare Pl 14).

The *Image* iconography of the *artes* is consistently employed in most of those copies of the text that include pictures of them. Exceptionally the artist may revert to the orthodox female personification. A MS of *c*1350, evidently copied from the one belonging to Jean de Berry,[72] begins the sequence with a feminine *grammatica* but reverts to male figures for the rest of the *artes* (Pls 17, 19); the anomaly is inexplicable, unless the artist had started to execute a conventional series of *artes* and was corrected as soon as the first miniature was completed. Caxton translated the work into English *c*1480 and brought out two editions including woodcuts of the *artes*.[73] Six of these cuts preserve the peculiar iconography, even to the seal on the document in the picture of *rhetorica* (Pl 22). *Musica*, however, is an innovation: a male recorder-player accompanies a female vocalist (Pl 23). Caxton claimed that his edition was derived from a MS 'whiche was engrossed and in alle poyntes ordeyned by chapitres and figures in ffrenshe in the toun of Bruggis the yere of thyncarnacion of Our Lord .M.CCCC.lxiiii'.[74] This MS is usually assumed to be one of the Royal MSS in the British Library[75] which is dated Bruges 1464; however, it is not the only MS bearing this inscription[76] and it lacks pictures of the *artes*, so it is more likely that Caxton's archetype was another MS. Whether this contained the eccentric *musica*, or whether Caxton for some reason substituted it, is unknown; but the pictures of the other six *artes* are powerful testimony to the close connexion between these images and the text they illustrate.

Occasionally this iconographic type is found elsewhere. A fourteenth-century relief on the gable of the north transept portal of the cathedral at Clermont-Ferrand[77] shows seven crowned male *artes* in simplified versions of the *Image* pictures, with only one or two figures to represent the *artes* of the *trivium* (Pl 7). The *arbor sapientiae* in the

---

8, 7, (Leipzig 1935) p 62. Such initials to Proverbs are often described as showing Solomon and a scholar, but when the teacher is uncrowned this is questionable.

[72] BN MS fr 25344; *La libraine de Charles V* (ex cat) (Paris 1968) p 82.

[73] *Caxton's mirrour* [*of the world*], ed O. H. Prior, *EETS*, extra series 110 (London 1913).

[74] *Caxton's mirrour* p 7.

[75] *Caxton's mirrour* p viii.

[76] It is also found in Baltimore MS 199.

[77] H. du Ranquet, *La cathédrale de Clermont-Ferrand* (Paris nd) p 81.

late thirteenth-century MS called *Virgiet de solas* in Paris[78] contains pictures of the *artes* that are also abbreviated recensions of the *Image* types. The so-called 'Rothschild Canticles' (early fourteenth century)[79] includes two facing pages devoted to the *artes* (Pls 28, 29). The extraordinary imagery of some of the pictures of the Trinity in this book uses elements derived from the *figures* of the *Image*, so it is not surprising to find that the *artes* are predominantly male. They are in fact the *Image artes* adjusted to form a balanced tableau—*musica* has been expanded, and *rhetorica* (here called *logica*) is a dispute between a man and a woman, but otherwise the characteristic iconography of the *Image* is faithfully preserved, even to the seal on the document in the picture of *rhetorica*.

If the Rothschild Canticles miniatures represent a recasting of the *Image* iconography to fit a two-page format, an even more ambitious mutation of the model occurs in the frontispiece to the Brunetto Latini MS (Pl 1). Here the male *artes* of the *Image* are conflated with the confronted figures of the *Welsche Gast* illustrations and the imagery of Boethius's *De consolatione philosophiae*; these concepts are expanded to include a wider range of learning and iconographic references. The *Livre du Trésor*,[80] compiled in the 1260s, was one of several vernacular summaries of knowledge that followed the success of the *Image*. It is in three parts; the first deals with the division of the sciences, and with theology, history, geography and natural history; the second deals with ethics, and the third with rhetoric and politics. BL Add MS 30024 is an early fourteenth-century copy of the first version of the *Trésor*, probably made in the south of France; it is unique among Brunetto MSS in being prefaced with two full-page paintings. Fol 1^v shows the *artes*, appropriate to the opening chapters of book 1 on the *divisio scientiae*; fol 2^r shows a tree of Virtues and Vices, appropriate to book 2.[81] The only other illustrations are seven historiated initials. The full-page miniatures are not at present integral to the volume: they have been laid on paper. However, they are by the same hand that executed

[78] BN MS fr 9220, fol 16^r; illustrated in J. Levron, 'La naissance des encyclopédies', *Le siècle de Saint Louis* (Paris 1970) p 100.

[79] New Haven, Yale University, Beinecke Rare Book and Manuscript Library MS 404; M. R. James, *Description of an illuminated manuscript in the possession of Bernard Quaritch* (London 1904).

[80] *Li livres dou tresor de Brunetto Latini*, ed F. J. Carmody (Berkeley/Los Angeles 1948). Carmody mentions the BL MS on p xlviii, but confuses it with a fifteenth-century copy of the text, MS Royal 17 E i. His remarks on the codicology of the MS refer to Add 30024, those on the text to the Royal MS.

[81] *LCI sv Tugenden und Laster*, fig 6.

the historiated initials and there is no doubt that they belong to this text. Two miniatures by the same artist illustrate another copy of the *Trésor* in Carpentras.[82] There is substantial loss of gold and pigment in the *artes* miniature, which makes some of the scenes hard to interpret, and it is inexpertly executed, but in intention it is a grand design.

The core of the miniature is an image based on a well-known passage from the beginning of *De consolatione*.[83] Although it lacks an identifying label, the bust at the top of the page must be *philosophia*. Its head penetrates a conventional representation of the sky, just as that of Boethius's apparition seemed to. Brunetto paraphrases this passage in book I, I of the *Trésor*, after explaining that philosophy is the root from which all sciences grow: *Pour çou dist Boesces el livre de la consolation que il le vit en samblance de dame, en tel abit et en si très mervilleuse poissance qu'ele croissoit quant il li plaisoit, tant que son chief montoit sor les estoilles et le sour le ciel, et porveoit amont et aval droit et selonc verité*. The two lions and the stylized towns, one with its gate open, that flank *philosophia* do not belong to Boethius's allegory but to the iconography of the Throne of Solomon.[84] The connexion between Solomon's throne, the *sedes sapientiae*, and *philosophia* is logical but surprisingly is found nowhere else.[85]

Boethius's *philosophia* bore an emblematic allusion to education in the form of a robe inscribed with steps ascending from practice to theory, represented by the letters *pi* and *theta*: *Atque inter utrasque litteras in scalarum modum gradus quidam insigniti videbantur quibus ab inferiore ad superius elementum esset ascensus*. This feature was sometimes realized pictorially as a ladder—incongruously propped against the personification in the archivolt showing the *artes* at Laon cathedral (Pl 5), more subtly treated as a kind of frogging on the garment in a miniature from a thirteenth-century MS of *De consolatione* in Leipzig (Pl 30).[86] Boethius does not specify what the degrees mean, but in the Leipzig miniature they are identified with the *artes liberales* and the rungs of

[82] MS 269, fols 1^r, 108^r; *Catalogue général des manuscrits des bibliothèques publiques de France, départements*, 34, I (Paris 1901) p 142.

[83] *A.M.S. Boethii Philosophiae consolatio*, ed L. Bieler (Turnhout 1957) I pr I; [P.] Courcelle, *La consolation* [*de philosophie dans la tradition littéraire*] (Paris 1967).

[84] I. Ragusa, 'Terror demonum and terror inimicorum: The two lions of the throne of Solomon and the open door of paradise', *ZK* 40 (1977) p 93.

[85] There is, however, a Solomonic allusion in the Admont diagram and the Aldersbach miniatures: *philosophia* tramples on Nebuchadnezzar and Antiochus, the two destroyers of the Temple.

[86] Leipzig, Univ Bibl MS 1253, fol 3^r; R. Bruck, *Die Malereien in den Handschriften des Konigreichs Sachsen* (Dresden 1906), p 59.

the ladder are inscribed accordingly. In the Brunetto miniature the *artes liberales* are ranged below *philosophia* in the same order as indicated in the Leipzig Boethius. They occupy the middle column of the tripartite design, which is emphasized by being extended over *philosophia*'s shoulders like a yoke—or like a ladder, an image that becomes more recognizable if the lateral columns of *artes* are ignored, as they will be initially. It is not normal for pictures of the *artes* to be set out in a ladder-like frame; one of the few instances where they are is in MSS of the *Welsche Gast* (Pls 8, 9). Since the pictures of the *artes* in the extant MSS are divided into two unequal columns, or may even extend over two pages, the borders to the miniatures do not immediately suggest a ladder. However, since these are the only miniatures in the *Welsche Gast* that are customarily framed, it would seem that a frame was regarded as peculiarly appropriate to this subject; and the fact that the frames are conjoint and arranged vertically suggests that this may have been because the border was an iconographically significant element, an allusion to the ladder of *artes* ultimately dependent on Boethius. Admittedly, *grammatica* is at the top of the *Welsche Gast* 'ladder' whereas one would expect her to be at the bottom; but this means that the *artes* appear in the order in which they are discussed in the text.

This is not the only link between the *Welsche Gast* and the Brunetto miniature: it extends to the iconography of the *artes*. This is most evident in the picture of *rectorique*, where confronted figures hold a sword and shield—though without the evidence of the *Welsche Gast* illustrations it would be hard to identify the attributes, as the artist has reduced them to toy proportions. His distortion of other items is even more drastic. The striated disk is a poor substitute for the astrolabe in the picture of *astrolomie*, but at least it conforms to the shape of the original instrument. The speckled mounds in the scenes of *arismetique* and *geometrie*, however, bear no relation to the mathematical diagrams of the *Welsche Gast* illustrations: the only similarity with the proposed model is the confronted pair of figures. But it is significant that none of the *Welsche Gast* MSS reproduces either of these diagrams accurately and that draftsmen were capable of reducing scientific diagrams to nonsensical scribbles even when, as in the *Image du Monde*, they were supposed to be essential to the understanding of the text. If the elegant *figures* demonstrating gravity that illuminate some MSS (Pl 24) could be travestied as a row of Greek crosses (Pl 25),[87] it would be reasonable

[87] BN MS fr 14965, fol 30r (fifteenth century); BN MS fr 1607, fol 41v (thirteenth century).

to suppose that a yet less talented artist could pervert more complex images into heaps of rubble. Some of the other *Welsche Gast* MSS approach this level of incomprehension—one transforms Euclid's proposition into a pair of quatrefoils (Pl 26)[88] while in another the Pythagorean triangle becomes a rectangle.[89]

The seated, facing pairs of figures in the Brunetto miniature confirm the influence of the German work—yet here both figures are male. The artist's inadequacy is such that determination of gender is questionable, but a comparison of the figures on this page with the author-portrait in the initial on fol 8^{v}—a figure wearing *béguin* and cap inscribing a book with the name 'Brunetto'—suggests that they are all men except for the exponent of *tesserie*, whose coiffure is contained by a hair-net and scarf. That the sex of these *artes* depends on the *Image* is suggested by the picture of *grammatique*, which is very close to the scene in the Ste-Geneviève MS: the tonsures, the two books held by the pupils and the anguished attitude of the foremost student in the *Image* picture are all found in the Brunetto miniature—where, however, the pupil in front has more reason to be anguished. *Dialectique* in the Brunetto picture, too, is similar to the corresponding Ste-Geneviève miniature; but this is a composition the Brunetto artist uses several times—a figure with a book facing two other figures. He uses it for *musique*, where the book is inscribed *maistre*; he also uses it three times in the left-hand column, where the inscriptions on the books are meaningless ciphers.

Flanking the *artes liberales* are two columns of miniatures depicting other disciplines. The *divisio scientiae* which begins Brunetto's book divides philosophy into three parts, but they do not correspond to the subjects presented here. According to the *Trésor*, the first part of philosophy is *theorike*, which divides into *phisike*, or the natural sciences, and *mathematique*, the *quadrivium*. The second part is *practique*, which has three subdivisions: *etique*, *yconomique* and *politique*. *Politique* is further divided into *oevre* and *paroles*; the latter consists of the *trivium*, the former are *li mestier ke l'en oevre tousjors des mains et des piés, ce sont sueurs, drapiers, cordewaniers, et ces autres mestiers ki sont besoignable a la vie des*

[88] Berlin, Staatsbibl MS Hamilton 675 fol 82^{v} (fifteenth century).

[89] Heidelberg MS Pal Germ 320, fol 67^{v}; Oechelhaeuser, *Bilderkreis* Tafel VI. The frames here are circular, but still serve to distinguish these pictures from others in the book. The only MS of the *Welsche Gast* in which all the miniatures are framed is the unusually luxurious copy made for archbishop Kuno von Falkenstein of Trier, New York, Pierpont Morgan Library, MS Glazier 54; J. Plummer, *The Glazier Collection of illuminated manuscripts* (New York 1968) p 33.

homes, et sont apielès mecaniques. The third part is *logike*, which divides into *dialetique*, *fidike* and *sophistique*. Thus *dialetique* appears twice, once as a part of *politique*, and again as a part of *logike*. At the top of the left-hand column of the Brunetto miniature is a picture labelled *logique*; in composition it is similar to the picture of *dialetique* in the central column: the only difference is that the participants are cowled and tonsored in *logique*, while those in *dialetique* appear to be laymen. It is not possible to equate *logique* in the miniature with any of the parts of philosophy mentioned in the text. Below this scene are *decres*, *fisique* and *lois*. *Decres* and *lois*, which employ the same kind of compositional formula as *logique*, are canon and civil law, subjects which Brunetto ignores in his *divisio*; *fisique* is here not natural science but medicine: the physician with his urine-flask and the bandaged patient with his stick admit of no other interpretation. The three lower scenes on this side are again neglected by Brunetto: music-making, writing and painting. The distinction between the mathematical discipline of *musica* and practical musicianship is seldom illustrated: the pictures of *musica mundana*, *musica humana* and *musica instrumentalis* in Florence MS, Laur Plut 29 I are the closest analogue,[90] but no other image differentiates the liberal art, which was entirely theoretical, from performance. The picture illustrating *escriture* is also of interest, as it shows a lay scribe working alongside a tonsured one. The bottom picture of *peinterie* is paradoxically so damaged and, as far as can be seen, so badly executed that it is impossible to say what the painter is doing: he appears to be holding a container of paint in his right hand and decorating the capital of a baldachin with an implement in his left.[91]

These occupations belong to no known *divisio scientiae* or list of accomplishments, and it is not clear on what grounds they have been selected: they certainly do not form a parallel series to the *artes liberales*. The seven scenes in the right-hand column also seem to represent an arbitrary selection, but from a more banausic class of occupation. The bottom three show craftsmen at work: smiths, carpenters and, as the sole woman in the series, a weaver. Above them is a money-changer —a layman dealing with two clerics—and above that a ploughman representing agriculture. The two scenes at the top depict activities respectively suspect and damnable: alchemy and necromancy. These seven professions bear only a remote resemblance to Brunetto's

[90] *Die Musik in Geschichte und Gegenwart* (Kassel etc 1949–) *sv Musik*, Tafel 61.

[91] For contemporary pictures of painters in the middle ages, see V. W. Egbert, *The mediaeval artist at work* (Princeton 1967).

mestiers ki sont . . . apielès mecaniques, and again correspond to no classification of learning or members of society.

Comparable cycles of non-liberal *artes* are rare in mediaeval art. From the thirteenth and fourteenth centuries only three are known: drawings in a model-book from Reun, five statues on the socles of the north porch of Chartres cathedral, and some reliefs on the campanile at Florence.[92] The Reun model-book[93] (*c*1210) contains a set of twelve drawings, uniformly framed, most of which show workers or craftsmen. Some of these are straightforward *genre* scenes of the kind found in pictures of the Labours of the Months; others are more eccentric: a herdsman asleep amidst a disorderly collection of animals, a cook whipping his assistant; others have nothing to do with occupations at all: a couple embrace while a child hits a swaddled baby. There are no elucidatory inscriptions, and the meaning of the cycle is obscure; it may not even be a cycle, for model-books typically contain a disparate selection of images. The figures at Chartres[94] (*c*1225) are equally enigmatic, though here there are inscriptions identifying two of them as *philosophus* and *magus*. The other three have attributes: one holds a right-angle, another a tablet, and the third stands among plants. The likelihood that these are an allegory of *artes* outside the liberal canon is strengthened by the fact that they are next to figures of the Children of Lamech, who were associated with the invention of various skills[95] and by whom, according to a much later source, *omnes artes vel scientiae seculares liberales vel mechanicae . . . leguntur.*[96] But exactly what the three figures with attributes mean is unclear, as is the precise significance of the cycle as a whole. The reliefs at Florence[97] also include the Children of Lamech, as well as other scenes from Genesis, mythological figures and scenes of trade, crafts and learned professions. Above them are four groups of seven smaller reliefs showing the planets, the Virtues, the sacraments and the *artes liberales*. Only on the west side of the campanile do the lower reliefs form a similarly

[92] The reliefs on the soffit of the outer arch of S. Marco in Venice belong to the same class, but seem to have a specifically local significance; see O. Demus, *The church of S. Marco in Venice* (Washington 1960) p 161.

[93] Vienna, Nat Bibl MS 507; see R. W. Scheller, *A survey of mediaeval model books* (Haarlem 1963) p 84.

[94] M. J. Bulteau, *Monographie de la cathédrale de Chartres*, 2 (2 ed Chartres 1892) p 255; S. Abdul-Hak, *La sculpture des porches du transept de la cathédrale de Chartres* (Paris 1942) p 144.

[95] Genesis 4, 20–22; *Historia scholastica, Genesis* 28; *PL* 198 col 1079.

[96] H. Schedel, *Liber chronicarum* (Nuremburg 1493) fol 10ʳ.

[97] Schlosser, *Giustos Fresken*, p 53.

coherent sequence: they present, in chronological order, biblical scenes of creation and the beginnings of occupations, from the creation of Adam to the drunkenness of Noah (admittedly Noah is properly the first tiller of soil rather than the inventor of alcohol, but the story suggests a lack of previous knowledge of the product). No such system is discernible in the other reliefs: those on the east side, for instance, begin with men rowing a boat, followed by Hercules, a ploughman, and a man in a horse-drawn cart.

It is by no means certain that any of these works is intended to represent a cycle of non-liberal *artes*; but they have points in common with the Brunetto miniature. They show predominantly male figures engaged in, or embodying, a variety of vocations. They are set out in what is overtly an orderly sequence but one which, on examination, defies analysis. This is despite the fact that there existed a theoretical system of seven *artes mechanicae*, corresponding to the *artes liberales*.[98] They were first codified by Hugh of St Victor in his *Didascalicon*[99] (*c*1125). They consisted of *lanificium*, *armatura* and *navigatio*, which provided external protection and were equated with the *trivium*; and *agricultura*, *venatio*, *medicina* and *theatrica*, which were concerned with inward benefits and corresponded to the *quadrivium*.[100] This system was rapidly adopted by other writers[101] and became almost as invariable as the *artes liberales*; it was still in use in the seventeenth century.[102] It was certainly well-known during the middle ages, and is frequently included in diagrammatic *divisiones scientiae*; yet it was not illustrated until the fifteenth century. The ingenious attempt to identify some of the reliefs in Florence with the *artes mechanicae*[103] is unconvincing: too many of the identifications of individual reliefs are tenuous, and the alleged *artes* are out of sequence and interspersed with subjects which cannot be interpreted as Victorine *artes*. The little evidence there is suggests that programmes for pictorial cycles of non-liberal *artes* in

98 F. Alessio, 'La filosofia e le "artes mechanicae" nel secolo xii', *Studi Medievali* 6, 1 (1965) p 71.

99 *Hugonis de Sancto Victore Didascalicon de studio legendi*, ed C. H. Buttimer (Washington 1939); English translation and commentary: J. Taylor, *The Didascalicon of Hugh of St Victor* (New York/London 1969).

100 *Didascalicon* bk 2, caps 20 *seq.*

101 See L. Baur, *Dominicus Gundissalinus, De divisione philosophiae* (Münster 1903) p 349.

102 For example Richard Blome, *The gentleman's recreation* (London 1686): 'The Seven Servile Arts were known by their several Professors, viz. the Agriculture, the Huntsman, the Military Person, the Navigator, the Chirurgeon, the Weaver, and that sort of Artificer which the Latins call Faber . . .'. Only the last is non-Victorine.

103 Schlosser, *Giustos Fresken*, p 70.

the thirteenth and fourteenth centuries ignored the Victorine canon, and deliberately employed a selection of occupations that did not correspond to scholastic theory or to the *artes liberales*, even when the latter were included in the programme.

It is not until the late middle ages that there is evidence for the existence of pictures of the Victorine *artes mechanicae*. An account dating from 1462–4 of some frescoes formerly in Brandenburg[104] records their use on a monumental scale, but before that they had been illustrated in a German MS compiled by Andreas Drutwyn in 1438.[105] This is the MS that conflated the personified *artes liberales* with their exponents (Pl 32); these *artes* are followed by seven *artes mechanicae*, identical to the Victorine cycle except for the substitution of *theatrica* by *ars fabrilis*. Each *ars* is represented by a scene of activity, as it was at Brandenburg, though on a much reduced scale (Pl 33). Although all but one of the scenes are inscribed with the names of the Victorine *artes*, they do scant justice to the concept as described in the *Didascalicon*. According to Hugh of St Victor, each *ars* embraced a wide range of activities: *armatura*, for instance, included building and metal-working as well as military skills. The picture in the Drutwyn MS (Pl 33) is not only inadequate—it is positively misleading. It may have been this difficulty in representing the *artes mechanicae* that inhibited earlier illustration of the sequence and obliged artists who wished to portray *artes* outside the liberal canon to chose an arbitrary selection of occupations.

The *artes* presented in the Brunetto miniature are a curious collection: some are shared with the Chartres sculptures and the Reun drawings, some with the Victorine series, but as a group they are inchoate. Yet they are deployed in a rigorously schematic framework totally at variance with their seemingly random choice. Triple-columned designs like this were used to set out groups of interrelated concepts[106]—for instance the articles of the creed with the twelve prophets who adumbrated it and the apostles who preached it (Pl 31).[107] But there is no horizontal correspondence in the Brunetto miniature and the potential of the schematic layout is ignored. None of the diagrammatic

[104] *Ibid* p 84.

[105] BL MS Add 15692; the *explicit* giving Drutwyn's name and the date occurs in MS Add 15693, a copy of the *Etymachia* in the same hand as the *artes* MS, and possibly once part of it.

[106] F. Saxl, 'A spiritual encyclopaedia of the later middle ages', *Journal of the Warburg and Courtauld Institutes* 5 (London 1942) pp 107 *seq*.

[107] BL MS Arundel 83, fol 12^{r}; L. F. Sandler's PhD thesis on this MS (New York University 1964) is being prepared for publication.

divisiones scientiae is tabular like this: they are always set out as stemmata, like a genealogical tree.[108] But an emblematic tree does not provide much space for illustration; the branches can bear figured panels or medallions, but unless these are few and small they obscure the articulation of the stemma. The miniature of the tree of Virtues and Vices facing the picture of the *artes* demonstrates the limitations of the format;[109] it is almost unintelligible, a jumble of tiny pictures and cramped inscriptions. A tabular layout offers a more rigid but also a more spacious setting for illustrations. Although the tree's properties of limitless subdivision are antithetical to the circumscribed exposition of the columnar table, the latter was occasionally used as a substitute for the former. For instance the genealogy of Christ, which was normally set out in the arboreal form of the Tree of Jesse, could appear as a schematic design in three columns,[110] permitting the ancestors to be depicted in a less congested ambience. If this transformation could overtake a religious image as hallowed as the Tree of Jesse, it could certainly have happened to the *arbor scientiae.*

Whatever the source of the Brunetto miniature—and an inscribed diagram, following the precedent of the Admont one, seems likely —it can hardly have been created to preface the *Trésor*. The discrepancy between the *artes* shown and those described in the text is too great. However, by introducing imagery devised for two other popular didactic texts, the *Welsche Gast* and the *Image du Monde*, the artist has created a frontispiece that is appropriate to the literary *genre* if not to this particular book. His choice of male figures to represent the *artes* reflects not only the influence of the cycle devised for the *Image* on a similar text, but also what appears to have been the practice when depicting figures of the non-liberal *artes*. The fact that the only female figure is the representative of weaving again accords with what was apparently established practice: in both the Florence reliefs and in the Drutwyn MS the cloth-working scenes include women. This may be an acknowledgement of the prominent part played by women in this industry, but it may be connected with the tradition that this *ars* was invented by Noema, Lamech's only daughter.[111] By using males

108 For examples see note 7 above and Courcelle, *La consolation* pl 27.

109 See above note 81.

110 For example Aschaffenburg, Schlossbibl MS 13, fol 18r; H. Swarzenski, *Die lateinischen illuminierten Handschriften des XIII. Jahrhunderts* (Berlin 1936) p 101 and fig 222.

111 *Historia scholastica, Genesis* 28; *PL* 198 col 1079. Noema is the only specific female exponent of the *artes* to be represented by mediaeval artists (for example in the Egerton Genesis, BL MS Eg 1894, fol 2v). They totally ignored women scholars; I am glad of

to represent all the other *artes* united under the outstretched arms of *philosophia* the artist subtly lessens the distinction between the *artes liberales* and the other disciplines: the *trivium* and *quadrivium* are in the more prominent position, but iconographically they are of the same kind as the non-liberal occupations. The result is a uniquely comprehensive image of the intellectual and manual activities of mediaeval men and women.

University of London

The Warburg Institute

this opportunity to offer congratulations to so distinguished a one, and would also like to thank Carla Lord, Elizabeth McGrath and Elizabeth Sears for their advice in the preparation of this paper.

Appendix: description of BL MS Add 30024.

246 vellum leaves, one paper quarter-leaf; fols 9–245 numbered 1–241 on recto in a mediaeval hand. Page measures 335 x 225 mm, writing area 220 x 150 mm. Text in two columns, 13 mm apart, 29 lines. *c*1300, south French.

Binding: nineteenth-century morocco by Townsend of Sheffield; edges gilt.

Collation: text on 32 quires, numbered at ends, all originally of 8; 7^7, ^{8}, 9^8, 10^1 are missing after fols 48 and 63. Catchwords. After 32^7 a quarter-leaf of paper has been inserted. Two vellum leaves with miniatures precede quire 1; they are laid on paper with a parchment fillet in the gutter, and it is not possible to tell if they are conjoint.

Ruling: in pencil, above top line. Pricking in inner margin.

Contents: Brunetto Latini, *Livre du trésor*, first redaction (Paris, before 1266) with some omissions (for example book 1, 139) and compression (for example book 1 93–8 form one short chapter).

fol 3^r *Ci comence le Livre dou Tresor . . . De phelosophie . . .*

Table of contents, indexed to mediaeval pagination as far as fol 47.

fol 8^v *Ci comence le Livre dou Tresor . . . Cest livres est apeles Tresor* . . . book 1, prologue.

fol 245^v [explicit] . . . *et t'en iras chief toi a gloire et a henor amen.* Book 3, 105.

fol 245^v blank.

fol 246^r quarter-leaf; two prayers in a fifteenth-century hand; verso blank.

fol 247 blank.

Provenance: William Bragge (1823–84), of Birmingham; sold at Sotheby's 7 June 1876, lot 44; entered British Museum in the same year.

Writing: *littera textualis formata,* the same hand throughout. Chapter headings in red.

Decoration: two full-page miniatures:

fol 1^v: *philosophia* and 21 *artes.*

fol 2^r: tree of Virtues and Vices.

seven historiated initials:

fol 8^v: C: author-portrait (book 1, 1: *Ci comence* . . .). Filigrane border in red, blue and gold at left and bottom of page enclosing an inscription in capitals: *Ci comence le Livre dou Tresor, de Sapience, et d'Aristote et de Rectorique.*

fol 54^v: T: confronted hybrid animals (book 1, 121: *Ci comence tout le devisement de mappamonde . . . Terre est sainte . . .*).

fol 64^v: P: the sea, with fishes and a ship (book 1, 130: *Ci comence de la nature des animaus . . . Poissons sont sanz nonbre . . .*).

fol 91^r: L: Aristotle inscribing his name in a book, seated before a king (book 2, 1: *Ci comence le segont livre de Aristotes . . . La premiere partie . . .*).

fol 124^r: L: a scholar at his desk, inscribing *le maistre* in a book (book 2, 50: . . . *les enseignemenz des vices et des vertus . . . Le livre de Aristotes . . .*).

fol 181^r: A: a geometer with compasses (book 3, 1: *Ci comence rectorique . . . Apres ce que maistre Brunet . . .*).

fol 220^v: E: a scholar at his desk, inscribing random letters in a book (book 3, 73: . . . *les gouernemens des cites. Es premiers livres . . .*).

Alternate blue and red two-line initials for each chapter, with red or blue filigranes extending vertically, sometimes to the full height of the page; they occasionally include human or animal heads.

Catalogue of additions to the manuscripts in the British Museum in the years 1876–1881 (London 1882) p 21.

H. Varnhagen, 'Neueste Erwerbungen des Brit Mus.', *Zeitschrift für romanische Philologie,* 1 (1877) p 548.

WHITE ANNAYS AND OTHERS

by DOROTHY M. OWEN

IN 1364 a cause of divorce *a vinculo*[1] was brought in a York court by a certain Edmund Dronesfeld against his reputed wife Margaret de Donbarr, on the grounds of her previous marriage in Scotland. The story unfolded by the witnesses, whose depositions are the only remaining record of the cause, is a strange one, which reflects the unsettled conditions of life on the border and in northern England during the long-drawn-out Scottish wars, and the further confusion introduced by the Black Death. The questions put by Edmund's side were intended to prove that Margaret's name was originally Agnes, that she had married in Scotland, eighteen years before, a man named William de Brighan, who was still alive, and that Edmund himself had not known this when he had 'married' her at Bedale six years later. He learned the truth, and took measures to establish his innocence, after William, now a household knight of the king of Scots, had come to York in the royal train at Christmas 1363. There he had met various Scottish acquaintances, from whom he learned that his wife was still alive, and whom he commissioned to make search for her; in the course of the enquiries Edmund was evidently warned, and removed himself from his 'wife's' company.

The first witness was Agnes/Margaret's first cousin Gilbert son of Henry de Whelpdale, called Henry of Dunfermline. He had known William and Agnes, whose father was John de Bawnes, all his life (he was thirty or more), and Edmund for the past four years. He had been present in the little church of St Mary of *Lauthean* near to the vill of *Lauthean* in Scotland,[2] when at dawn on a Friday after Easter, eighteen years before, William and Agnes had been married. He

The sources of this paper are to be found in the first series of cause papers at the Y[ork] B[orthwick] I[nstitute], and are listed below in appendix one. I have described these records in SCH 11 (1975) pp 199–222, and hope to treat them more fully in a forthcoming *Borthwick Paper*.

[1] Richard H. Helmholz, *Marriage Litigation in Medieval England* (Cambridge 1974), has discussed the forms of pleading in matrimonial causes in some detail and has quoted some of the material used here.

[2] I owe to Professor D. E. R. Watt of St Andrews the suggestion that this place may be identified with Leitholm, now a chapelry in the parish of Eccles.

believed that they lived together for the next seven years, and had three or four children; to the certain existence of three children he was prepared to swear. Then Agnes had left Scotland in the company of an Englishman called Robert Corbet, and was not again seen by Gilbert. He had never seen William again until the previous Christmas when they met in York, and being asked by him about his wife's whereabouts, told about her second marriage, but professed himself unable to say where she was to be found. William 'swore vehemently' at the news.

Gilbert was followed by Thomas Scott, otherwise known as Thomas de Thorpearche, a skinner born at Peebles, who had been in England since 1346, when he was captured at the battle of Neville's Cross. The examiner of the court, who was writing the depositions, recorded that little trust could be placed on this witness because he changed his style of speech too often: pretending sometimes to be an Englishman from the south, sometimes to be a north countryman, and occasionally pronouncing English words in a Scottish way.[3] Thomas had known Edmund for the last four years in France and England, and his wife, whose name he knew to be Agnes, and not Margaret, ever since she had married William de Brighan. He said that William and Agnes had lived together in Caerlaverock castle after their marriage, and had two children before Agnes left Scotland with 'a certain English squire'. Thomas, too, had seen William in York, and had received forty silver pennies from him to make search for Agnes.

John de Sadbery, who was a native of the diocese of Durham, but was now a cook in the Dominican friary at York, had also been present at the first wedding, which had taken place during his five years captivity in Scotland, when he was William's prisoner. He had held a torch at the wedding and had more details to give about the bride, who was known as Agnes de Donbar, and sometimes White Annays, because the countess of Dunbar had been her godmother,[4] her parents being John de Bawnes and his wife Maria. Agnes was abducted by Robert Corbet about a year after the battle of Neville's Cross, and soon after, John himself was freed, and never saw her again until one day in the last lent, when he met and recognised her on the Ouse bridge in York.

[3] In a previous reference to this paper *SCH* 11 p 218, I suggested incorrectly that this criticism applied to Agnes/Margaret.

[4] Professor Watt has pointed out to me that the countess Agnes of Dunbar was known later in the middle ages as 'Black Agnes'.

The next two witnesses were concerned with the second marriage. John Tyas a chaplain now living in Ripon, had known Edmund all his life, and twelve years before had seen him married in Bedale church to Margaret de Donbarr. The marriage took place at cockcrow, the church doors were shut, no banns had been called, and no one was present except himself and Walter de Ellerton who celebrated the marriage. Robert de Acastre had served Margaret as her servant for three years, and had known both her and Edmund for thirteen years. He had been present in Margaret's chamber at Patrickbrompton on a day twelve years before, when at a very early hour Edmund and two chaplains came to take her to church. Robert de Floketon, who had also known Edmund all his life, was aware that a clandestine marriage had been celebrated between him and his wife Margaret twelve years ago, just before Corpus Christi and that they afterwards lived together as man and wife until Edmund was told of the previous marriage in Scotland, since when he had refused to regard her as his wife.

Agnes/Margaret's story is more dramatic than that of most of the women whom we meet in these York causes, if only because it is set against the background of changing fortunes in the Scottish wars. Her marriage seems to have taken place in 1345, or thereabouts, at a time of Scottish triumph, when her husband, who perhaps formed part of the Randolph following, had captured at least one prisoner, and was helping to garrison a stronghold in the southwest, very close to the border.[5] When the war was resumed at Neville's Cross in 1346, and king David was captured, the border territories were overrun, prisoners were released, and Agnes left for England with one of the invaders. After this her movements were uncertain for a few years; no doubt the disruption of the Black Death helped her successfully to cover her tracks, and she did not reappear until 1351, when she was living in Patrickbrompton, with a servant in attendance. This is a village close enough to the line of the Great North Road to make it likely that she had moved southwards into Yorkshire by this route, and had settled sufficiently to acquire a local man as her servant. A year later she married Edmund with a series of precautions which suggest that she, at least, was aware of the possibility that William was still alive. As time passed she evidently became secure enough to reveal herself to her cousin Gilbert, and to Thomas Scott, but the flocking of expatriate

[5] I owe this suggestion to Professor Watt. See also *An Historical Atlas of Scotland*, ed Peter McNeill and Randal Nicholson, Conference of Scottish Medievalists (St Andrews 1975) maps 63–6.

Scots to York, when their king came there in 1363, and William's unexpected presence in the royal retinue allowed the second marriage to become more widely known, and so brought it to an end. It is hard to believe that in this series of adventures Agnes had remained passive. Was she willingly abducted? Did she allow Edmund to be deceived about the first marriage? Why, above all, did she let her presence be known to the fellow Scots who would betray her? Her nickname White Annays suggests that she had some personal attractions, and, perhaps, some force of character: it seems unlikely that she waited for things to happen to her.[6]

This is an unusual story however one looks at it, and no other cause of the same period provides so dramatic a view of female activities. It is true that no ecclesiastical court ever affected all the inhabitants of its area of jurisdiction, and that women do not figure as litigants and deponents except in matrimonial causes, and very occasionally in testamentary and defamation suits. Even though the York cause papers survive in greater quantity for the fourteenth century than in any other court except perhaps Canterbury, a great deal has been lost. It is impossible to use them to draw any 'total' picture of fourteenth century female life, and hopes that they might provide material for a miniature study emulating *Montaillou*[7] have vanished. It seemed nevertheless worth while to examine such evidence as they provide for the life of women involved in the cases.

The type of family from which the women who concern us are drawn seems, with few exceptions, to be of the merchant or small landowner class, with sufficient wealth to be concerned about increasing it by suitable marriages, living in fairly large houses, with servants, horses, gardens, brew-houses and garners. The size of the family units is uncertain, witnesses are reluctant to pronounce on the numbers of children in any one marriage, many children die early, there are many one-parent families and, after 1349, many orphans living with relatives. No mention is made of education or upbringing after infancy, though at least one girl was in a household for educational purposes, and her boy-husband was being reared in a clerical establishment at the same time. Evidence of literacy is sparse, although Dame Margery Rouclif could evidently read and understand legal documents. Light on social life in any class higher than that of tavern frequenters, is equally sparse, and any rounded picture of fourteenth-century female life seems impossible.

[6] For a transcript of this cause see appendix two.

[7] E. Le Roy Ladurie, *Montaillou, Village Occitan de 1294 a 1324* (Paris 1975).

Some facts about the attitudes and experiences of these women can nevertheless be extracted from the evidence they give, and what follows is a summary of what can be deduced from their own words, or those of their friends. For the most part none of the parties in the causes, men and women alike, move any great distance from their bases: Bolton Percy to Acaster Malbys, Hook and Newland to Rawcliffe, Rawcliffe to York, Bridlington and Middleton to Beverley, are the extent of their movements. A divorce cause brought in 1373 by John de Thetilthorp against Joan daughter of Philip atte Enges of Patrington shows that such lack of experience was not universal. Thirteen years before the cause began, Joan who was born at Patrington, married Richard son of Henry Carter of Nunmonkton, who was her fellow servant in the house of Philip Fysch at Clementhorpe, just outside York. Eight years later, and five years before the cause began, Joan had reached Althorpe in Lincolnshire, was working there, and had married John de Thetilthorpe, who must have travelled fifty miles from his own birthplace, if he really was born at Theddlethorpe, while her first husband was still alive. There is no explanation for Joan's removal from a York suburb, across the Humber in this fashion, and it seems certain that it was done of her own volition. Elen Layremouth and Isabella de Holm, who each brought causes of prior contract against William de Stoketon in 1382, form part of a Newcastle group which had migrated to York, where they were servants in the St Saviourgate house of a merchant and burgess Roger de Morton. Alice de Bridelingeton had come to Beverley from her birthplace to work as a spinster, and her fellow spinster Joan del Hille originated in Aike. Some few women actually undertook long journeys, when circumstances called for them: a Swinefleet widow was said to be going on pilgrimage to Canterbury before she would consider a second marriage, and the mother of a not very considerable Rawcliffe heiress travelled to London to seek the help of the privy council in circumventing her daughter's guardian.

Most women were far less enterprising, however, and their ideas about any places outside their immediate knowledge were very imprecise. They know very well the location of events they actually witness, such as the sighting of Agnes/Margaret on the Ouse bridge at York, or the making of a marriage contract in Mirfield, in a place called Hatclyffe below a big rock called Stoupandston. Agnes de Huntinton contracted herself to Simon de Monketon in words spoken from a window in her father's house in Fotergate, while he stood in the garden of the next house; later she made other vows to John de Bristow in a garden called Moubraygarth in Petergate, which belonged to the mansion known as Moubrayhalle, which lay in Stonegate. A large family supped together in a ground floor room of Emmota Erle's inn at Wakefield, and Agnes Lovel spied on her sister and a suitor first in the brewhouse, and later in a gatehouse chamber of her father's house.

Not all witnesses are as precise as this, however, and one set of witnesses, male and female alike, were all uncertain of the existence of a well into which an old man had threatened to throw his great-niece if she declined a marriage he had arranged for her. When they moved beyond the immediate neighbourhood of home there was even more uncertainty: the women of Bootham spoke of it as a community quite separated from York, the inhabitants of Rawcliffe on the south bank of the River Aire knew nobody living further away than Newland, a mile away on the north bank, and those of Patrickbrompton did not range beyond Bedale three miles away.

A sense of time, and of chronology was equally hazy in most of the witnesses. Less than a century later York people could and did quote the time told by the Minster clock,[8] but only one woman, who came from Newcastle, mentions clock time in these documents. Otherwise, cockcrow, after dawn and before sunrise, in the dark of the night, was the nearest most of the witnesses came to a precise hour. They were equally imprecise about dates, although the day of the week was often known. A Monday between Michaelmas and Martinmas, somewhere after St John Baptist, lent (because we were eating fish) was the closest that most of them could come to month or season. It is true that Dame Margery de Rouclif, who was seventy, could recall the dates of various writings concerning her property, and that a Newland witness described events she had witnessed on the Tuesday in easter week last, about the ninth hour. For the most part witnesses could never agree about the date of birth of an heiress, or a party in a matrimonial cause. Sometimes, no doubt, they had good reason to feign uncertainty, but this cannot have been true about the large number of variants in one cause which turned on the age of an heiress at marriage. Some of the witnesses on both sides concentrated on the birth of John de Rouclif, older brother of the heiress Alice. Isabella de Strensall was pregnant herself at the same time and remembered that it was fourteen years before; Agnes de Richemond remembered the churching of his

[8] YBI, CPF 33.

mother; Elena Taliour was invited to be his wet-nurse; Amabilia Pynder was also pregnant, but could not say how long ago it was; Dame Margery Rouclif was his godmother and remembered that she had a grandson of the same name born the same year; Lecia de Melsay, whose husband was John's godfather, was ill at the time of the baptism, but recalled its date because her own son was born two years later. None of these witnesses, except the first, clearly declares how long ago this took place, nor is it certain what interval separated his birth and that of Alice, nor what Alice's present age could be. The abbot of St Mary's York, the plaintiff's uncle, deposed that Alice looked as if she were of marriageable age; various witnesses recalled the birth of a bastard son to one of the family servants at the Bartholomewtide after Alice was born, and her godmother knew that the baptism took place the year after her son became a Carmelite, 'that is, fourteen years ago, when William La Zouche was archbishop'.

One point which clearly emerges from all the causes is the closely knit bonds of the family, and the overriding importance of the blood relationship, especially between siblings, or between parents or grand-parents and their descendants, but almost equally between uncles and aunts and their nieces and nephews. It was Agnes/Margaret's first cousin who witnessed, and later testified to, her first marriage. John Trayleweng of Swinefleet called his brother William to witness his contract with the widow Agnes Jacson, and later took an oath that he knew of no pre-contract, on tables with a crucifix painted on the cover which belonged to his cousin Richard Trayleweng. Children were particularly subject to the power of their relatives. In a divorce plea which succeeded because the parties had made the contract before they were of age, and because the husband could prove that he had neither consented to the marriage, nor had intercourse with his wife, the witnesses demonstrated that the husband's maternal uncle who had fostered him after his parents died in the Black Death, persuaded him into the marriage, having been bribed to do so by the bride's father. The marriage was celebrated in the chapel of Fenwick Hall, where the bride was an inmate of Lady Hastings' household, and her grandfather was steward, and immediately afterwards the bride's uncle, William Malcake took the bridegroom south with him to his church of Mablethorpe and kept him first there, and then at Elsing in Norfolk.[9]

[9] Lincolnshire Archives Office, episcopal register 9, fol 65, William de Swynflet resigned Mablethorp St Mary 17 September 1349.

In another child marriage the bride had never consented despite her great-uncle's threats to throw her into a well, and the persuasions of her mother and grandfather. The mother, aunt, and great-aunt of another heiress, Alice de Rouclif, were all said to have tried to promote an unsuitable marriage with John Marrays, who was himself supported in the project by his relative William Marrays, the abbot of St Mary's York, and by his sister, to whose inn he took her after the ceremony. It was Elizabeth de Waldegrave's brother Richard who led a group of men with swords and knives, into a bakehouse where she and John de Penesthorpe were together, and the whole scene was watched from behind a straw-stack by servants of John's father who had sent them in search of him. When Katherine Paynell brought a successful action for divorce against her husband Nicholas de Cantelupe, on the grounds of his impotence, her parents tried for a long time to make her stay with him, and no doubt the complications of dower, and of other family arrangements, would encourage the elders of an important landed group such as the Paynells were, to adopt such an attitude. Even for the relatively unfettered widow, family support and participation were needed for her re-marriage: when Emmota Erle discussed with John de Topclyf the marriage he was urging upon her, it was at a family meal which was shared by her mother and her son, the wife of her first husband's nephew and her daughter's godfather, a literate layman who was evidently there to give legal advice.

In several of these family set-pieces, the mothers seem to have played unsympathetic parts. Agnes de Huntinton's mother, eager to promote a second and more desirable marriage for her, threatened to curse her if she refused to swear that an earlier contract had been conditional on her parents' consent. Alice Bellamy's mother ignored her daughter's plea against a distasteful marriage, even though the child knelt to her, and Alice Rouclif's mother, who was in conflict with her daughter's guardian, prepared to seek legal redress against him in London, despite the girl's protests. Perhaps Agnes/Margaret is the most puzzling of mothers. *Did* her children survive in Scotland, and, if so, what had happened to them after she left for England?

More natural mothers are to be found, of course. Alice de Beleby's memory of her Carmelite son strikes a warmer note, and so do the words of another deponent in the same cause. Elena Taliour of Skelton, who was a servant in the Rouclif family circle, was asked while she was suckling her own son, to be wet-nurse to John de Rouclif. She refused the urgent plea of his mother, another Elena, because she loved her own son as much as Elena loved hers, and could not bear to see him die on account of Elena's child.

Most of the witnesses in this Rouclif cause were concerned, as we have seen, with the birth of Alice and her brother John and the depositions present a series of pictures of female life in which pregnancy loomed very large. Two women, Amabilia Pynder, who had no husband, and lived with her mother at Rawcliffe, and Elena Taliour, refused to nurse the heir while suckling their own children, but Elena two years later nursed Alice, carried her to church for baptism, and suckled her until her milk failed after a fever; she remained in the household for the whole of the year for which she had been hired. This common experience of pregnancy and child-rearing which bound together all the women in a community is implicit in the testimony of Dame Margery de Rouclif that John's birth coincided with that of a grandson who was baptised at the point of death, and with those of various children in Rawcliffe, and in Amabilia Pynder's story that a few days before the birth of her son, John's mother, who had just been churched, sent her a writing which was said to be good for women in labour. Other women of the village, or in Bootham, where the family was well known, recalled the births of the two children because they too were pregnant, or remembered other women who were, or were servants with the family and had discussed the news with their father. A pathetic note is struck by a Bootham woman Beatrix de Morland, because just after she had borne a child herself, in the same year, when the Rouclif family was living in her house, her husband John de Midford had been killed.

In any society where marriages were carefully negotiated, a go-between of some sort was called for and often wielded considerable power. In one of these causes the godmother of the man bringing a plea of divorce from a child bride, was said to have terrorised him into marrying the girl, by threatening to cut off his ear if he refused the alliance she had arranged. More often, however, it was a clerical relative or the parish priest, who seemed to take the lead in arranging marriages or in initiating prosecutions. Two priests, Walter de Ellerton and William, presided over Agnes/Margaret's second marriage, another priest Richard Trayleweng supported his cousin in an attempt to marry a widow and made the crucifix on his tablets available when she required an oath. The rector and parochial chaplain of Mirfield witnessed and swore to a contract of marriage made in a field, and yet another clerical relative, who was abbot of St Mary's

York allowed a chamber in the abbey to be used for a secret exchange of vows. The local rector, the parish priest, even the diocesan, were all involved in Katherine Paynell's escape from her impotent and unpleasant husband, and the bride's clerical uncle after the Malcake marriage, took charge of the husband in what looks very like protective custody.

The servants of a household and their visitors, had an important and often decisive rôle as witnesses of events, transmitters of news, and givers of advice. Women servants and their friends moved freely about the houses where they worked or visited; they went to the stair-foot to listen to incriminating words, they visited their mistresses in childbed and they missed nothing that passed. If they were employed about an ale-house, a tavern, or an inn, they were incomparably well-placed for such observation and their horizons in such circumstances were surprisingly wide. The Rouclif cause reveals many details about the composition and regular visitors of a household of middling size and wealth. At different times it included two temporary wet-nurses, Joan Symkinwoman who had a bastard child while there, Margery Thewe who worked in the garden, Matilda de Herthill, Agnes called Gervauswoman and Isabella de Rouclif who was the master's niece. Another household group, employed by a York merchant, included Geoffrey de Hebston, John de Flaynburgh, William de Stoketon, Elen Layremouth, Isabella de Holm and Cecilia de Hessay, most of whom hailed from Newcastle.

Relations between master or mistress and their servants were rarely explicitly stated, apart from the views of the wet-nurse already quoted. Alice Pypynell was capable of defending the status of her master Thomas Maltster from the rough jokes of a Newland tavern company who called him a churl, even though they pursued the attack with the charge that she herself was a priest's whore, and threatened to throw her in the river. Alice was probably defending her own status as much as that of her master, but Katherine Paynell's servant Margery de Halton was more disinterested. She repeated in evidence the advice she gave her mistress, who after the marriage looked very sad . . . 'Why do you look like that? Show that you are a great lady, and will be able to do what you like'.

Margery's rather worldly advice undoubtedly coincided with that of her mistress' parents and her view of marriage, as something to be borne with, and exploited, does not differ essentially from that of another woman, Margery Scot, who endured twenty years of violent treatment from her husband Richard, before she fled in her nightclothes to the hospital at Newcastle. Not all matrimonial violence was as persistent or pathological as this: more often it took the form of Simon de Monketon's when he sought to drag his wife out of the church of St Michael le Belfrey at York to prevent her bearing witness against him. Some women were not to be intimidated in this way: when Adam de Helay said that he would break his ward's neck if she did not marry his son, she escaped him and married elsewhere. Other women might even try violent means themselves, or subtlety, like Alice de Flecton, who according to some witnesses tried to poison an unwanted husband, but who, in fact, induced another man to pretend that he had made an earlier contract with her, and so enabled her to procure a divorce.

Perhaps the best example of this sort of female aggression can be seen in a matrimonial cause heard in the York courts on appeal from Beverley against Thomas de Midelton, a Beverley chapman, who although he had been convicted in the Charnel, which was the peculiar court of the minster, of carnal knowledge of Margery de Merton, had uccessfully pleaded that no contract had been made with her. He had not only denied Margery's assertions but impugned the evidence of her two female witnesses, and all three appealed to a higher jurisdiction. The witnesses produced during the appeal prove that Margery was on her own confession pursuing Thomas in the courts to make him look silly, and there is even a suggestion that the judge of the peculiar court was suborned by her. All told, the evidence in this cause provides an interesting vignette of small town life in 1365, and is worth repeating as an indication of the rôle of some women at the time.

Thomas Carter, who was the employer of the two female witnesses, Alice de Bridelingeton and Joan del Hill, who worked for him as spinsters, first testified to the hearing in the Charnel and to the good reputation of Alice and Joan. He was followed by four chaplains who alleged that Joan had left her husband and was not to be trusted as a witness, and that Margery herself had influenced Mr. Ralph de Waleys, the judge of the Charnel. Three Beverley men testify to the hearings in the Charnel, where Thomas was represented by his clerk Henry de Axilholm. Then Alice de Bridelingeton and Joan del Hill gave evidence, that they were both at a window in the house of Richard de Midelton, Thomas's brother, next the Shambles, when they heard Thomas and Margery talking together, and Margery saying, in reply to Thomas's inquiry as to why she was making him waste his money in law-suits, that she did so to make a fool of him. Margery, the women said, had been fetched by Thomas's nephew and they themselves by Richard's wife, to witness the meeting. Finally Thomas's own witness was brought in to deny that he was in Beverley on the day when he was alleged to have contracted himself to Margery: William atte Keld of Midelton had drunk with William in a tavern at Middleton on that very day, had bought three ells of russet cloth from him and had gone with him to the house of William Gamelston the tailor, where he had stabled his horse. Apart from that excursion he and William had spent the whole day, which was wet, drinking old ale in the tavern, on a bench before a fire of straw, with a 'talocandel' on the table.

University of Cambridge

Appendix 1: Cause papers used in this study:

YBI/CPE
18.1328 Lovel v Martin. (H)
23.1332 Draycote v Crane. (H)
25.1332 Flexton v Brun.
26.1334 Penesthorpe v Waldegrave. (H)
28.1335 Dalton v Driffield
37.1338 Forster v Staunford.
61.1348 Traylweng v Jacson.
62.1348 Hopton v Broun.
70.1355 Shippen v Smyth.
72.1356 Ward v Pypynell.
76.1357–8 Aunger v Malcake. (H)
85.c1364 Thomson v Bellamy.
87.1364 Dronesfeld v Dunbarr.
89.1368 Marrays v Roucliff.
102.1366 Merton v Midleton.
124.1380 Erle v Topclyf.
126.1382 Holm v Stoketon.
128.1382 Layremouth v Stoketon.
155.1372 Thetilthorp v atte Enges.
171.1364 Austerfield v Arnewe.
248.1370 Huntinton v Munketon.
257.1349 Devone v Scot.
259.1368 Paynell v Cantelupe.
(H) indicates cause papers printed in whole or in part by Helmholz.

Appendix 2: text of CPE 87, Dronesfeld v Dunbarr. (This material consists of two membranes stitched into a single continuous roll. Words missing on the edge of the membrane are indicated thus . . .)

Gilbertus filius Henrici de Whelpdall vocatus de Donfermlyn de regno Scocie etatis xxx annorum et amplius. Et primo respondit de noticia personarum inter quas agitur: dicit quod novit Willelmum de Brighan et Agnetem de quibus in primo articulo fit mencio ab infancia sua. Et dicit interrogatus quod vocatur Agnes de Donbarre sive Agnes filia Johannis de Bawnes quem Johannem patrem bene novit ut dicit quia est advunculus istius iurati ut dicit. Et non vocatur Margareta. Et dicit quod novit Edmundum partem actricem per quatuor annos proxime preteritos. Super primo articulo dicit quod continet veritatem in omni parte. Interrogatus per quid scit dicit per hoc quod presens fuit in ecclesia parva sancte Marie in Lauthean iuxta villam de Lauthean Scocie set cuius diocesis nescit quodam die veneris per quatuor septimanas proxime festum Pasche ultime preteritum sequentes fuerunt octodecim anni elapsi ubi et quando in aurora dicti diei veneris dicti Willelmus et Agnes prout continetur in hoc articulo per verba hic accipio te etc. matrimonium adinvicem contraxerunt et illud in facie dicte ecclesie publice solempnizari fecerunt et bene scit ut dicit quod dictum matrimonium carnali copula subsecuta consummarunt quia post dictum diem veneris dicti Willelmus et Agnes ut vir et uxor per septem annos proxime tunc sequentes adinvicem cohabitarunt et tres vel quatuor proles inter se suscitarunt quarum tres iste iuratus bene novit ut dicit. Et dicit ulterius super dicto articulo quod prefatus Willelmus fuit superstes in festo Natalis domini ultime preteriti et hoc scit quia vidit eum superstitem in comitiva domini regis Scocie in civitate Ebor' qui explorabat de isto iurato si prefata Agnes esset superstes qui sibi respondebat quod sic et quod coniugata esset in partibus istis referendo se ad comitatum Ebor' sed nescivit quo loco unde dictus Willelmus tunc adiurabatur vehementer. Super secundo articulo dicit quod de contractu habito inter Edmundum et Agnetem de quibus agitur nescit deponere nisi quod audivit et vidit dictum Edmundum iurare super librum quod a tempore quo constitit sibi de contractu matrimoniali et solempnizacione inter ipsos Willelmum et Agnetem habita prout in hoc articulo continetur idem Edmundus nunquam consenciit in eam ut in uxorem suam. Super articulo ultimo dicit quod super dicto contractu matrimoniali inter ipsos Willelmum et Agnetem ut premittitur habito a tempore solempnizacionis eiusdem matrimonii in regno Scocie laboravit et nunc in diocesi Ebor' laborat publica vox et fama. Et dicit quod predicta Agnes post contractum matrimonialem et solempnizacionem eiusdem cum dicto Willelmo habitum de regno Scocie et comitiva dicti Willelmi tunc mariti sui cum quodam Roberto Corbett depatriavit.

IIus testis

Thomas Scott aliter dictus de Thorparche arte pelliparii de diocesi sancti Andree in villa de Pebels oriundus ut dicit qui moram traxit in Anglia a tempore belli commissi apud Dunolm' quia ibi fuit captus ut dicit, iuratus et examinatus super premissis dicit quod novit Edmundum de quo agitur per quatuor annos proxime preteritos et amplius in regnis Francie et Anglie et illam mulierem quam idem Edmundus nunc habet in uxorem que vocatur Agnes uxor Willelmi de Brighan et non Margareta a tempore quo ipse Willelmus cum dicta Agnete matrimonium per verba de consensu hic accipio etc. contraxit et illud in facie ecclesie in ecclesia sancte Marie de Lauthean in regno Scocie quodam die veneris inter festa Pasche et Pentecostes ultime preterita fuerunt octodecim anni elapsi prout bene recolit ut dicit solempnizavit et per duos annos ante et eundem Willelmum similiter, cui solempnizacioni iste iuratus una cum dictis contrahentibus, Johanne patre et matre ipsius Agnetis, Gilberto conteste suo, quodam Johanne nunc morante in Bramham et quodam capellano ipsum matrimonium solempnizando, et non pluribus personaliter interfuit et fuit ipsa solempnizacio facta in aurora diei veneris. Interrogatus quantum tempus est effluxum a tempore dicti belli dicit quod nescit nec an dictus contractus sic habitus sit quatuor quinque vel sex annos proxime precedentes dictum bellum set bene scit quod precessit tempus istius belli et dicit quod dicti Willelmus et Agnes ut vir et uxor simul cohabitabant in castro de Carlaverok et super eadem prout bene scit iste testis suscitabant duas proles ut dicit. Et dicit ulterius quod locutus fuit cum dicto Willelmo de Brighan in civitate Ebor' in festo Natalis domini ultime preterito in comitiva regis Scocie qui quidem Willelmus ut dicit dedit quadraginta denarios argenti isto iurato ut querat dictam Agnetem. Super secundo articulo nescit deponere ut dicit. Et eciam quod a comitiva dicti Willelmi mariti sui a Scocia cum quodam armigero anglicano dicta Agnes recessit. Interrogatus per quantum tempus post dictum matrimonium sic contractum se recessit dicta Agnes dicit quod nescit nec recolit. Iste testis in deposicione sua sepius mutuavit modum loquendi fingendo se aliquando anglicum australem aliquando borialem mere et aliquando Scoticum per modum Scotorum sonando ydioma Anglicanum et ideo videtur examinatori quod minor fides est sibi adhibenda.

iii^us testis

Johannes de Sadbery oriundus in diocesi Dunolm' cocus fratrum predicatorum Ebor' iuratus et examinatus super premissis dicit quod circa festum nativitatis beate Marie virginis ultime preteritum fuerunt octodecim anni elapsi ipse iuratus fuit captus in guerra per Willelmum de Brighan tunc armigerum nunc militem et fuit captivus suus per quinquennium proxime tunc sequens et quadam die veneris post festum Pasche proxime sequens capcionem istius iurati quidam Willelmus de Brighan tunc armiger et nunc miles et Agnes de Donbarre aliter dicta White Annays filia cuiusdam Johannis ut dicebatur de Bawnes et Marie uxoris sue matrimonium per verba mutuum consensum exprimencia de presenti adinvicem contraxerunt sic dicendo hic accipio te etc. Interrogatus de loco contractus et solempnizacionis dicti matrimonii dicit quod in ecclesia beate Marie in villa de Lauthean situata. Interrogatus de tempore dicti contractus dicit quod infra mensem festum Pasche ultime preteritum proxime subsequentis fuerunt octodecim anni elapsi ut credit et quatenus scit modo computare. Et dicit interrogatus quod nominata fuit Agnes de Donbarre eo quod comitissa de Donbarr ipsam de sacro fonte levavit. Interrogatus a quanto tempore et per quantum tempus novit dictam Agnetem dicit quod nunquam novit eam antequam vidit et audivit dominum Willelmum et Agnetem predictam contrahere matrimonium ut prefertur et ab illi tempore requisitus quando morabatur cum dicto Willelmo quod fuit per biennium ut credit antequam fuit abducta per quendam Robertum Corbett qui ipsam Agnetem abduxit per annum post bellum commissum apud Dunolm'. Dicit eciam interrogatus quod infra annum et dimidium proxime sequentem tempus dicti belli fuit iste iuratus de captivacione totaliter liberatus. Interrogatus quando vidit dictam Agnetem post dictum contractum matrimonialem dicit quod a tempore quo recessit a dicto Willelmo et abducta fuit per dictum Robertum nunquam vidit eam ante quadragesimam ultime preteritam et tunc vidit eam super pontem Use in civitate Ebor'. Interrogatus qualiter scit quod fuit eadem Agnes cum qua predictus Willelmus matrimonium contraxit dixit quod hoc scit per relationem Gilberti contestis superius nominati et aliter nescit ut dicit. Requisitus an dictus Willelmus adhuc sit superstes dicit quod sic quia vidit eum in civitate Ebor' in comitiva regis Scocie in festo nativitatis domini ultime preterito. Super secundo articulo nescit deponere ut dicit nec super articulo sequenti ut dicit. Dicit eciam quod presentes fuerint in dicto contractu ipsi contrahentes ipse iuratus qui tenuit ibidem unum torche ardentem in dicta solempnizacione Gilbertus et Thomas contestes sui superius nominati capellanus ipsum matrimonium solempnizans et alii.

Fuerunt exhibita xii^o die Junii anno domini etc. lxiiii^to per Co. et Hak.

iiii testis

Dominus Johannes Tias capellanus manens in Rypon etatis xl annorum ut dicit iuratus et examinatus super premissis dicit quod Edmundum de quo agitur novit ab infancia et Margaretam contra quam agitur per duodecim annos proxime preteritos et amplius. Super primo articulo nescit deponere ut dicit. Super secundo articulo dictus R. dicit quod continet veritatem in omni parte. Interrogatus per quid scit dicit per hoc quod presens fuit quadam nocte cuiusdam diei de quo pro certo non recolit, modicum post primum gallicantum eiusdem noctis in estate iam instante fuit duodecim annos elapsos in ecclesia parochiali de Bedall ubi quando vidit et audivit dictos Edmundum et Margaretam ad ostium revestiarii in dicta ecclesia stantes matrimonium adinvicem contrahentes. . . . informacionem domini Walteri de Ellerton capellani qui celebravit matrimonium tunc inter eosdem ostio predicte ecclesie clauso. Interrogatus in qua forma verborum matrimonium tunc contraxerunt dicit quod dictus Edmundus cepit Margaretam per manum dextram sic sibi dicendo hic accipio te Margaretam in uxorem meam tenendam et habendam usque ad finem vite mee si sancta ecclesia hoc permitterit et ad hoc do tibi fidem meam. Et statim eadem Margareta dicto Edmundo respondens dixit Hic accipio te Edmundum in virum meum habendum et tenendum usque ad finem vite mee si sancta ecclesia hoc permitterit et ad hoc do tibi fidem meam. Interrogatus qui fuerunt presentes in huiusmodi solempnizacione et contractu matrimoniali sic inter eos habito dicit quod dicti contrahentes dictus dominus Walterus ac istemet iuratus et non plures prout bene scit. Examinatus an idem Edmundus consensit in ipsam Margaretam prout continetur in hoc articulo nescit deponere ut dicit nisi ex relatu dicti Edmundi. Interrogatus an banna inter dictos Edmundum et Margaretam ut moris est fuerunt edita in facie ecclesie ante huiusmodi solempnizacionem dicit quod non. Et dicit quod presens fuit . . . publica notoria et manifesta in parochia de Bedall et locis vicinis et super hiis ibidem laborat publica vox et fama. . . . vel predicto corruptus ut dicit.

v testis

Robertus de Acastr'manens ad hospitalem sancti Leonardi Ebor' etatis xl annorum ut dicit iuratus et examinatus super premissis dicit quod novit Edmundum et Margaretam de quibus agitur per tresdecim annos proxime preteritos et amplius. Super primo articulo respondens dicit quod super eodem nescit deponere. Super secundo articulo respondens dicit quod continet veritatem. Interrogatus qualiter hoc scit dicit per hoc quod istemet iuratus fuit serviens dicte Margarete per tres annos hinc a duodecim annis elapsis et amplius et fuit presens ut dicit in camera dicte Margarete in villa de Patrikbrompton nocte [?] diem mercurii proxime ante festum de Corpore Christi ultime preteritum fuerunt duodecim anni elapsi proxime precedente ubi ante auroram dicti diei mercurii Edmundus de quo agitur et duo capellani videlicet quidam vocabatur dominus Walterus de Ellerton et alius Willelmus prout recolit venerunt ad dictam cameram ipsius Margarete et duxerunt eam ad ecclesiam ut matrimonium inter eosdem Edmundum et Margaretam esset solempnizatum. Et istemet iuratus. . . . fuit solus dimissus in dicta camera ut dicit, nec tamen presens fuit ut dicit in solempnizacione huiusmodi matrimonii set bene scit ut dicit quod est publicum notorium et manifestum quod dictus Edmundus duxit ipsam Margaretam in uxorem prout continetur in hoc articulo in parochiis de Patrikbrompton et Bedall et locis vicinis et super hoc ibidem laboravit et laborat publica vox et fama.

vi testis

Robertus de Flokton manens in Flokton in parochia de Thornhill etatis xxx[a] annorum ut dicit iuratus et examinatus super premissis dicit quod novit Edmundum de quo in articulo memorato ab infancia ipsius Edmundi et Margaretam contra quam agitur per duodecim annos proxime preteritos. Super primo articulo nescit deponere ut dicit nisi ex relatu aliorum. Super secundo articulo dicit quod. . . . dicit quod predicti Edmundus et Margareta matrimonimum clandestinum bannis non editis adinvicem contraxerunt et illud in ecclesia de Bedale quadam die mercurii circa festum de corpore Christi proxime preteritum fuerunt xii anni elapsi et vidit ut dicit quod postmodum habitaverunt ut vir et uxor quousque constitit dicto Edmundo quod quidam dominus Willelmus Brighyne de Scocia ipsam Margaretam. . . . duxerat in uxorem et ab illo tempore idem

Willelmus [*sic:* for Edmundus] nullatenus quod iste iuratus scit ut dicit consensit in eandem ut in uxorem sed eam habere in uxorem dissenciit et aliter super contractibus matrimonialibus nescit deponere ut dicit nisi quod super contractu inter dictos Edmundum et Margaretam habito ut prefertur a tempore solempnizacionis eiusdem in archidiaconatibus Ebor' et Rich' laboravit et laborat publica vox et fama.
Examinata . . . snno domini lxiiii.

THE PIETY OF JOHN BRUNHAM'S DAUGHTER, OF LYNN

by ANTHONY GOODMAN

THE historian chips eagerly in search of veins of psychological truth behind the autobiographer's polished facade. But the latter's Roman art held little appeal in the medieval west. Medieval autobiographers had no generally favoured literary stereotype on which to model their fragments of experience. Familiar with confessional practices, and with preachers' *fabliaux*, they often wrote with a frank, engaging air. Yet, since they were inclined to conform to what they considered seemly for *exempla*, the historian needs to be as much on his guard against seduction by their apparent artlessness as by the polished suavity of the antique self-portrait.

This is certainly true of *The Book of Margery Kempe*.[1] There is good reason to believe that the one surviving manuscript of its text, though not the original, is an accurate copy.[2] To what extent is the *Book* likely to have been the illiterate Margery's composition, rather than that of her amanuenses? Since her first amanuensis was a layman with a limited ability to express himself in English, it is probable that his draft of Liber I, the bulk of the *Book*, was a highly literal transcript of her words. But its linguistic and orthographic patterns in its final form are, it has been argued, mainly those of her second amanuensis, the priest who, with her assistance, performed the arduous task of deciphering and making sense of his predecessor's work, and drafted Liber II.[3] The priest may have felt a compulsion to reproduce *verbatim*, as far as possible, the words of one whom he considered to be outstandingly holy. Margery, a forceful and literal-minded person, is likely to have insisted that he should record Christ's dialogues with her soul in the words in which they were conceived, with the literary model of St Bridget's *Revelations* in mind.[4] The *Book's* insistence that Margery

1 Ed[S. B.] Meech and [H. E.] Allen, *EETS* (1940); version in modern English by W. Butler-Bowden (London 1936).

2 Meech and Allen, pp xxxii *seq*.

3 *Ibid* pp vii *seq*.

4 For her emulation of Bridget, *ibid* p 47. The *Book*'s composition as a series mainly of short, self-contained episodes and contemplations, often tenuously linked, suggests that it was dictated. The priest wrote Liber II 'after her own tongue' (*ibid* p 221)

acquired gifts of scriptural exposition and devotional insight which repeatedly confounded clerks and drew layfolk to a more devout way of life, makes it unsafe to attribute passages to the priest simply on the grounds that they are priestly in manner and matter. The *Book* does, indeed, have features which are more readily attributable to an illiterate laywoman. It lacks chronological order—a defect likely to have jarred on a cleric, and for which an explanation is given.[5] It is frequently abrupt in expression, awkward in sequence and homely in imagery. Mention is made in it, in different contexts, of recurrent anxieties which ring true as the obsessions of a habitual penitent.

But there are two chapters in Liber I which clearly owe a great deal to the priest's influence. They are concerned with the resolution of his doubts about her sanctity. Chapter 24 tells how he compelled her, through threats not to write for her, to demonstrate her prophetic gift, and gives his own detailed account of how her demonstration of it in a particular instance convinced him that her 'feeling was true'.[6] Chapter 62 tells of his changes in attitude towards the long-continued controversy in Lynn as to whether or not her public exhibitions of weeping and crying out were tokens of sanctity. A notable Franciscan preacher's criticisms of her led him to reject his belief in their holiness. But he reversed his opinion again after studying a literary parallel drawn to his attention by a 'worshipful clerk'. At this point in the *Book* other biographical examples which helped the priest to accept her behaviour as holy are cited at some length.[7] By writing out a tract over several years to publicise Margery's sanctity, the priest was committing his reputation in a matter of more than local controversy. He could not disinterestedly copy her random scribbled or verbal musings, for he now also had a vital stake in proving that her spirituality was real and valuable, and that she was not hypocritical, sick, heretical or affected by malignantly inspired illusions, as she had often been accused of being. The *Book's* content and argument are probably deeply influenced by the evolution of his thought about the nature of Margery's spirituality, and slanted to what he considered appropriate to it, acceptable to the devout, and necessary to convince his sceptical or hostile colleagues in Lynn and elsewhere.[8]

[5] *Ibid* p 5. For a recent comment on Margery's illiterate bookishness, M. Aston, 'Lollardy and Literacy', *History*, 62 (1977) p 349.

[6] Meech and Allen pp 55 *seq*.

[7] *Ibid* pp 152 *seq*. For personal testimony supporting Margery's performance of a miracle by 'he that wrote this book', *ibid* pp 178–9.

[8] Often, whilst Margery was 'occupied about the writing', he 'could not sometimes

The *Book* cannot be viewed as the unalloyed composition of Margery Kempe, nor solely as an expression of secular piety. It is a distillation of her matured devotional experiences, made by her in conjunction with a cleric who mulled over them for a number of years. Yet he was not the only cleric to have done so. As the *Book* amply bears witness, Margery had painstakingly related her 'feelings' to a succession of confessors, whose frequently strong reactions undoubtedly shaped her concepts. *The Book of Margery Kempe* bears, besides the marks of a woman's dilemmas, the stamp of clerical analysis and controversy. It is a deeply polemical work, in a way which her literary models were not.[9] It is a justificatory treatise not only for Margery, but for the regulars and seculars at Lynn and Norwich who supported her against the strictures and qualms of their colleagues and against popular *canards*. More generally, it is a manifesto in favour of one sort of clerical reaction to current manifestations of feminine piety which were provoking alarm and controversy.

Therefore, despite the *Book*'s plausible naivetés of expression, the autobiographical material in it has been shaped in a sophisticated and highly selective way. Much of this material was recalled and written down long after the events described. Many of these occured between Margery's marriage to John Kemp *c*1393, when she was aged about twenty, and her return to more or less permanent residence in Lynn *c*1418. The first draft of Liber I was not made till *c*1431, and the final one was commenced in 1436.[10] According to Margery, it was over twenty years after her first 'feelings and revelations' that any writing was done, and she had 'forgotten the time and the order when things befell'.[11] Here, then, we have autobiographical fragments recalled, some of them from a hazily distant context, by an ailing woman of about sixty, caught up in continued controversy and intensity of personal emotion. How far can we trust her recollections? The fact that she had a remarkable memorising capacity, schooled by oral learning, is reflected in her knowledge of the new testament and devotional literature. Vivid factual and conversational shafts of recollection in her *Book* spring from a retentive rather than an inventive mind. The

keep himself from weeping' (*ibid* p 219). He 'held it expedient to honour of the blissful Trinity that his holy works [through Margery] should be notified and declared to the people when it pleased him, to the worship of his holy name' (*ibid* p 221).

[9] For her models, *ibid* pp 39, 143.

[10] *Ibid* pp vii–viii, xlvii–li.

[11] *Ibid* pp 3, 5.

work is, indeed, a monument to her lack of originality. *Its* originality —its peculiar mixture of devotion and controversy—springs from the circumstances and purposes of its composition. As it demonstrates, Margery lacked the intellectual robustness to strike out into unorthodoxy like her contemporary Margery Baxter, the wright of Martham's outspoken wife convicted of heresy in 1428.[12] Her imaginings of divine scenes painstakingly copied visual imagery such as the easter ceremonies at Lynn, and did not flower into the arresting allegories of St Bridget's revelations. Margery's spiritual dilemmas and interior dialogues were heavily influenced by those in Bridget's treatise. But though Christ speaks refreshingly to Margery, in the grave but familiar tones of the Lynn élite, his words lack the singular and magisterial profundity with which he addressed Bridget.[13]

Margery's mental banality provides some assurance for the reliability of her vivid recollections of incident and feeling. But it is possible that she unconsciously distorted the significance of events in her early life. The brightness of an individual's spiritual illumination and the force of the need to enlighten others can magnify the natural tendency to impose new perspectives on greying experience. When Margery's *Book* was written, she had long lived on a dizzy plateau of intimacy with Christ and his saints. The alarming physical symptoms of this interior life were by then confidently accepted by her and her supporters as tokens of her habitation on this rarified plane. Like some self-made Victorian engineer, she gazed down from her towering mental construction on early days of sordid, gruelling lessons in learning to overcome her worldly lusts and to bear the world's stripes. To provide an integrated interpretation for herself and for the *Book*, early episodes in her life were extrapolated, such as struggles to live in chastity, to bear witness to the love between Christ and herself, and to wear white raiment at his command. The dramas of confrontation which Margery recounted may have been touched up by an imagination long dyed by the Passion, and the martyrdom of saints, such as those eloquently defiant virgins tormented by pagan officers and crowds, whose legends the Augustinian friar, Osbern Bokenham was soon to versify in English for East Anglian layfolk, particularly for ladies.[14]

[12] For Margery Baxter, *Heresy Trials in the Diocese of Norwich 1428–31*, ed N. P. Tanner, *CSer* 4 ser 20 (1977) pp 41 *seq*; J. A. F. Thomson, *The Later Lollards 1414–1520* (Oxford 1965) pp 123 *seq*.

[13] Compare *The Revelations of Saint Birgittal* [ed W. P. Cumming], *EETS* (1929).

[14] *Legendys of Hooly Wummen*, ed M. S. Serjeantson *EETS* (1938); compare the *Life*

Despite this mature tincturing Margery's accounts probably do contain valid insights into the evolution of her pre-meditative personality. Her development of the habit of meticulously analysing her feelings kept alive echoes of earlier anxieties, which appear appropriate to a coltish young housewife rather than to a widow 'somdel stape in age'. She remembered the terror of damnation which she had experienced, but had long shrugged off, and her resort to pious remedies which later appeared to her as elementary, such as fasting—'good for young beginners—'and telling beads—'good to them that can no better do'.[15] Her memories of faltering steps along the devotional path provide reliable material with which to seek an answer to the question of why she did not remain conventionally devout, contentedly hair-clothed, but attained distinctive heights as a religious phenomenon.

Margery's original standing had derived from the fact that she was, as the bishop of Worcester put it, 'John of Brunham's daughter of Lynn'.[16] Brunham arguably played a more important part in the government of Lynn than any other individual in the later fourteenth century. He was a leading member of a small, close-knit group of burgesses which had to show a politic care to preserve its privileges and power against both episcopal and internal challenges.[17] Brunham's administrative skill was appreciated in government circles under Richard II.[18] In her *Book* Margery displayed a just, even boastful appreciation of her father's standing and achievements.[19] There is a bleak contrast in her references to her own repeated failures to fufil her secular roles as a burgess's wife. For months she was totally incapable of running her household.[20] She for long failed to accept her husband's counsel,

---

of St Catherine of Alexandria written by John Capgrave, Augustinian friar of Lynn (1394–1464), ed C. Horstmann and F. J. Furnivall, *EETS* (1893).

[15] Meech and Allen pp 7, 12, 17, 89, 208–9.

[16] *Ibid* p 109.

[17] For Brunham's career, *ibid* pp 359–62. For tensions between bishop Despenser of Norwich and the men of Lynn, *Anglo-Norman Letters and Petitions*, [ed M. D. Legge] (Oxford 1941) nos 1, 2, 5, 8, 44, 58, 63, 302, 304, 305. For Lynn's internal tensions in the early Lancastrian period, *Calendar of Inquisitions Miscellaneous (Chancery), 1399–1422*, no 517; *HMC, Eleventh Report, Appendix, Part III* (London 1887) pp 191 *seq*.

[18] For some of the royal commissions on which Brunham was appointed, *Calendar of Patent Rolls, 1381–5*, p 349; *ibid 1385–9*, pp 181, 259; *ibid, 1391–6*, p 157. He may have been the 'J. B' whom Richard II referred to in a signet letter of 1396–8 as having been replaced in his long-held office of customer at Lynn without reasonable cause (*Anglo-Norman Letters and Petitions*, no 14).

[19] Meech and Allen pp 9, 111.

[20] *Ibid* pp 7–9.

and answered him disrespectfully. She caused adverse comment among neighbours by excessive array, and by her business ambitions and failures.[21] Brunham died a few months either before or after his daughter at last persuaded her long-suffering husband to ratify what kinsfolk and neighbours might well have judged her scandalous attempts to withdraw from married sociability and obligation.[22] Brunham in his advanced years probably knew and grieved about some of his daughter's social failures. Indeed, they may have compounded earlier acts of disobedience to him and her mother—the habit of defiance was deeply ingrained in Margery. As an older woman, after she had ground her husband's authority to a shadow, she tended to bridle at the commands of confessors whose direction she had eagerly sought, playing out with them, perhaps, long past family dramas.[23]

Some of her problems as a wife may have stemmed from her previous relationship with a masterful and awe-inspiring father. She found it hard to respect and obey a husband whose amiable qualities she recognised, but whom she portrays as timid, a slave to his lusts, and unable to withstand the force of her personality.[24] In her unregenerate days she had found it hard to bear that as Kempe's wife she was less 'worshipful' than as Brunham's daughter: she reproached Kempe with his lower status and his failure to provide for her in the style she desired.[25] In fact Kempe was one of the sons of a leading burgess of Lynn and started to be elected to high office there at about the time of his marriage. But he does not seem to have been as commercially successful as his father, and his promising career in urban government soon faded.[26] Perhaps he was distracted by his wife's problems. These may have been complicated by a fundamental difficulty in coping with her marital role. Her account of her first pregnancy emphasises the exceptional pain which she believed herself to have experienced during it and in labour. After the birth, she says, she was near to death: while

[21] *Ibid* pp 9–11. For her extravagant headgear and the reactions which it provoked, compare F. E. Baldwin, *Sumptuary Legislation and Personal Regulation in England* (Baltimore 1926) pp 76 *seq*, 85, 91–2.

[22] Meech and Allen pp xlix, 361–2. Their vows of chastity were, as canonically required, mutual, but Margery makes clear that John agreed to them reluctantly, as a result of her constant pressure, *ibid* pp 11–2, 21, 23–5, 34; compare [E. M.] Makowski ['The conjugal debt and medieval canon law'], *JMedH*, 3 (1977) pp 99 *seq*.

[23] Meech and Allen pp 82 *seq*, 91–2, 103, 116, 226–8, 246–7.

[24] *Ibid* pp 21 *seq*, 28–9, 104. For difficulties which she experienced in relations with her son, and with her widowed daughter-in-law, *ibid* pp 221 *seq*, 228, 231.

[25] *Ibid* pp 9–10. It is unlikely that Margery was an heiress (*ibid* pp 361–2).

[26] *Ibid* pp 362 *seq*. For his debts, *ibid* p 25.

she was seriously ill, what she considered an unwarrantedly harsh reproof from her confessor precipitated a total nervous breakdown, with strong feelings of religious guilt and despair, and suicidal tendencies, which lasted over eight months.[27] She described herself as travelling to Norwich after one of her pregnancies in a dazed and depressed state, and apparently suffering physical collapse there.[28] It may be, then, that her repeated pregnancies inflicted on her a degree of physical and mental suffering which she found hard to bear, and that her intense revulsion from the sexual relations which she had enjoyed with her husband, leading to the crisis of her marriage, resulted from fear of these sufferings.[29]

Therefore, at the root of Margery's conversion to a lonely and prickly way may have lain the reactions against her marriage role of a forceful and determined woman, whose emotional patterns and physical constitution inhibited her from fulfilling it satisfactorily. Her new way, carried to extremes of perfection, assuaged her guilt at failing the conventional expectations of her father, husband and kinsfolk. As a substitute for failed kinship relations, she developed filial ones with confessors. Pointedly she elevated one of them in her prayers above her father, or husband.[30] Above all, Christ became the father who instructed her soul, the husband who embraced it, and the son who doted on it.[31] She could recollect in tranquillity the transcending drama of how Christ once allowed her to be tormented in her soul because she had doubted the genuineness of his revelations to her, and shown a rebellious spirit, and of how she had wholly submitted and achieved perfect reconciliation.[32]

Margery owed her ability to construct such spiritual dramas, with more satisfying conclusions than family ones sometimes had, to the instruction provided in 'mystical' treatises. Her eventually erudite knowledge of their methodology was derived from communings with and readings by both secular and regular clerics at Lynn and Norwich, such as those which a young priest of Lynn carried on with her for seven or eight years.[33] Orthodox interest in revelatory phenomena may have quickened in the 1410s, the period of her conversion to their

[27] *Ibid* pp 6 *seq*.
[28] *Ibid* pp 38–9.
[29] *Ibid* pp 11–12, 115, 181.
[30] *Ibid* pp 20–1.
[31] *Ibid* pp 29 *seq*, 85 *seq*.
[32] *Ibid* pp 144–6.
[33] *Ibid* pp 142 *seq*.

methods, as a result of current fervour for St Bridget—to whom Margery's revelations probably owed more in form than to anyone else.[34] Once Margery developed an interior life dedicatedly biased on these lines, she commanded rapt confessorial attention. Priests were agitated or excited by what she claimed as real spiritual experiences, such as they had only read about in modish treatises. Some of those inclined to accept the validity of her revelations were nevertheless prey to suspicions that she was a pious fraud, suspicions stirred by the oddity of her physical symptoms and the scepticism of colleagues. Some critics were probably scandalised that a married woman, whose past worldliness was notorious in Lynn, laid claim to superior enlightenment, which they considered appropriate only to those who, like Dame Julian at Norwich, were *reclusa*. But the celibate sympathies of other priests were engaged by the dilemmas of wives such as Margery who grieved for their lost virginity and the necessity of fulfilling marital obligations. They probably considered that Margery had set up a worthy model in Lynn of how to live as a 'maiden in the soul', involved in but not defiled by secular society—a model worthy of encouragement and promotion.[35]

Ambivalent clerical reactions to her claims (perhaps stimulated by rivalry among the Orders and between them and the seculars in Lynn) are reflected in the waverings of confessors, and the probable disagreements in the Dominican and Carmelite houses there, involving among the Carmelites their provincial, Thomas Netter.[36] Clerics' doubts were often reinforced, and their opposition was often provoked, by Margery's suspect facility in quoting and glossing holy writ, and in telling homilies. She threatened to usurp priestly prerogatives, and,

[34] *The Revelations of Saint Birgitta*, pp xxix *seq*; Knowles, *RO* 2 (1961) pp 176 *seq*. In 1415 Bridget's canonisation was confirmed at the council of Constance, and the foundation-stone of the Bridgettine convent of Syon (Middlesex) was laid (*Acta Sanctorum*, October 4, p 475; Knowles, *RO* 2 p 177). Margery was in Rome, seeking memorials of Bridget, and concerned that the saint should be 'had in more worship than she was at that time' possibly within months of the process at Constance (Meech and Allen pp 95, 304–5). Margery's Carmelite confessor Alan of Lynn, who died probably in the 1420s, made indexes to Bridget's *Revelations* (*ibid* pp 259, 268; compare for his career, Emden (C) pp 381–2). For Margery's later visit to Syon Abbey, Meech and Allen pp 245–6, 348–9.

[35] *Ibid* pp 50 *seq*. For contrary reactions of confessors to Margery's revelations, *ibid* pp 43–5. Capgrave's model of St Catherine, though in important respects different from Margery, is worthy of comparison: his heroine is resolute in defence of her virginity and religion, literate and steeped in erudition, and adept at worsting in public debate the nobles who put forward the conventional views of secular society.

[36] Meech and Allen pp 37–8, 168, 328.

like Bridget, denounced priestly faults. Her behaviour touched on current clerical apprehensions about assertively devout women. In Henry V's reign the preacher John Swetstock denounced those who asked 'Why should not women be priested and enabled to celebrate and preach like men?' and Netter in his anti-Wycliffite *Doctrinale* (completed 1426–7) denounced such feminine presumption.[37] Clerics were concerned about the anger which Margery provoked in noble circles by, allegedly, counselling a lady to leave her husband.[38] Members of archbishop Bowet's *familia* were alarmed by the popular influence which she gained in York, fearing that she might lead the people astray.[39] Basic to much clerical opposition to her was an appreciation—a just one, on the *Book*'s evidence—of how her behaviour could disrupt parochial rituals, divide the opinions of parishioners, and encourage among some dangerously singular and unsocial conduct, tendencies inimical to the reconciliatory and socially binding roles of religious rites in towns.

Similar criticisms animated opposition to her among urban élites. At Lynn—in contrast to York and some other places—there was a generally unfavourable reaction among the people, centred on her effusive disruption of rituals. This may have been intensified because she was Brunham's daughter, and was consequently despised by social inferiors as well as equals because she was acting eccentrically, and, in the eyes of some, oppressively, since she aroused superstitious dread.[40] Her references to the kindnesses and hospitality of 'worshipful' friends in Lynn indicate that many of Margery's natural allies did not repudiate her.[41] But she sorely tried their patience. Leading families were surely ashamed that a proverbial tale about her spread through the realm implying that she was 'a false feigned hypocrite in Lynn'.[42] Their alarm at the way she excited the people is seen in the advice of her friends—advice which she ignored—that she should leave town.[43] They criticised her indebtedness, resulting from her charitable gifts of other people's money as well as her own. Though some of them were willing

[37] R. M. Haines, 'Wilde Wittes and Wilfulness: John Swetstock's Attack on those Poyswunmongeres, the Lollards', *SCH* 8 (1972) p 152; Meech and Allen pp lvii, 259, 329.

[38] *Ibid* p 133; compare the mayor of Leicester's fears *ibid* p 116.

[39] *Ibid* p 125.

[40] *Ibid* p 154.

[41] *Ibid* pp 105–6, 151, 170, 202.

[42] *Ibid* pp 243–4.

[43] *Ibid* p 154.

to give her alms to finance her as a pilgrim (perhaps in eager anticipation of her departure), the readiness of a burgess's wife to wander abroad without her husband, and, on occasion, to beg in public and perform menial tasks must have been hard for them to accept.[44] Her residence in separate accommodation from her ageing husband, in order to protect their reputation for chastity, provoked her condemnation when he was badly injured in a fall.[45] Common opinion attributed her son's ailments to her prayerful wrath.[46]

Thus Margery's rejection of bourgeois norms of familial, parochial and commercial life were viewed by many folk in Lynn with irritation or distrust. They were, indeed, accustomed to the repudiation of their way of life by kinsfolk and neighbours. But these did not pose a threat, because they opted out, withdrawing to the regular or eremitical life. Margery remained, an anti-social virus in the body politic. Why did she stay? One reason may have been that conventual communities who, like the Minoresses of Denny, were glad to listen to her spiritual communings, would have been alarmed at the threat to their peace of mind if they had provided her with chamber and board.[47] Another reason may be that the constant experience of popular denigration had become a necessary 'fix' for Margery's spiritual life. Moreover, as concern about securing her own salvation lessened, she developed a patrician interest in saving the people through her prayers, to which daily contact with their sinfulness may have provided a stimulus.[48]

Yet another incentive for her continued residence in Lynn was the support and protection which she received from influential seculars, Benedictines, Dominicans and Carmelites there. They approved her visions and way of life, defended her sanctity against doubting colleagues and explained it to visiting priests, chided popular slurs, and provided extra-parochial facilities for her worship in their chapels when urban feeling ran high against her. These mentors do not appear to have set a high value on the need for the devout layman to be discreet and inoffensive to convention in pursuing personal devotions,

[44] *Ibid* pp 85–6, 92, 96–7, 102, 105–6.
[45] *Ibid* pp 179–80.
[46] *Ibid* pp 221 *seq*.
[47] *Ibid* pp 202, 337. Margery could have taken conventual vows after her husband's death, which probably occurred in 1431 (*ibid* pp 332, 342; compare Makowski p 110). For a case commissioned by bishop Alnwick of Norwich in 1436, in which a Norfolk lady's escape from an unhappy marriage by profession as a nun was adjudged licit, R. Virgoe, 'The Divorce of Sir Thomas Tuddenham', *Norfolk Archaeology*, 34 (Norwich 1966–69) pp 406 *seq*.
[48] Meech and Allen pp 20, 186.

unlike the confessor who wrote a set of instructions probably for a Warwickshire urban husband in the early fifteenth century.[49] Their relative lack of concern about Margery's disruptions of urban sociability is surely reflected in the *Book's* unashamed admissions about the trail of controversy and restlessness which Margery stirred up in the towns of England.[50] This insensitivity to certain prized contemporary values is perhaps an indication of the development of a radical trend of opinion among Lynn religious nourished on devotional literature in the early fifteenth century, which the behaviour of Margery Kempe may have helped to crystallise. The patronage which they extended to her shows their interest in how revelatory methodology might effect personal reformation among those who were firmly part of secular society. But this way, founded on intensive individual study and discipline, was unlikely to have a wide popular appeal.[51]

The Book of Margery Kempe reveals a glimpse of what may have been a significant division of opinion between conservative-minded burgesses and people of Lynn, encouraged by like-minded clerics, and a group of clerical radicals drawn together from various religious disciplines. The latter backed what were to turn out to be losing modes of piety, too individual and unsocial to appeal widely within, and to regenerate spiritually, a tense, fissured urban society, looking for modes of religious expression which affirmed rather than threatened its secular values, and strengthened its fragile communal cohesiveness. In this context Lollard reformation had some winning potential, for its proponents, though slated hard as another divisive threat, conceived the working-out of the individual's salvation within a tightly-knit community. Sadly but perhaps not surprisingly, *The Book of Margery Kempe*, that abrasive feminine and clerical cry aganist bourgeois values, survived in entirety only in a manuscript owned by the remote, austere Carthusians of Mount Grace. When Henry Pepwell came in 1521 to reprint the brief, anodyne selection from the *Book* issued by Wynkyn

[49] *Ibid* pp 132, 138–9, 148 *seq*, 155, 165 *seq*; W. A. Pantin, 'Instructions for a devout and literate layman', *Medieval Learning and Literature. Essays presented to Richard William Hunt*, ed J. J. Alexander and M. T. Gibson (Oxford 1976) pp 398 *seq*.

[50] In Canterbury, Bristol, Leicester, York, Hull, Lincoln and London (Meech and Allen pp 27–9, 107–9, 111 *seq*, 118, 120 *seq*, 129, 245).

[51] One aspect of her rejection of secular values which may have seemed most shocking to Lynn folk was her readiness to act without or against the counsel of her friends (*ibid* p 247). In her own eyes, she had already been received into the celestial *familia*, and the counsel she received there took priority—perhaps one could see this as a sort of conflict of 'bastard feudal' loyalties.

de Worde, he transposed Margery to where the secular world always wants to put spiritual dissidents—out of it. He entitled her 'a deuoute ancres'.[52]

University of Edinburgh

[52] *Ibid* pp xlvi *seq.*

'GREAT REASONERS IN SCRIPTURE': THE ACTIVITIES OF WOMEN LOLLARDS 1380–1530

by CLAIRE CROSS

RECENT historians have drawn attention to the influence of women in later lollardy, and it may also be that in parts of England as soon as lollardy moved out from the university some women immediately adopted its tenets, their involvement being largely hidden by the inadequacies of the contemporary sources.[1] The attractions of lollardy for lay people in general and women in particular are not hard to understand. After a millennium during which a priestly caste had more and more been distancing itself from the laity certain discontented lay people, excluded from the mysteries of the church and especially from direct access to the scriptures, could scarcely have failed to respond to novel doctrines which stated that a lay man predestined to life stood equal in the eyes of God to any priest. These revolutionary ideas first propagated by Wyclif continued to be disseminated by some heretical clergy throughout the fifteenth century. One such priest, John Whitehorne, parson of the parish of Coombe Bisset in Wiltshire, in 1499 confessed to having taught, in addition to much else, that 'when Christ should ascend into heaven, he left his power with his apostles and from them the same power remaineth with every good true Christian man and woman living virtuously, as the apostles did, so that priests and bishops have no more authority than another layman that followeth the teaching and good conversation of the apostles'.[2] It would be misleading to claim that in the century and a half between the death of Wyclif and the reception of the reformation among the populace in some forward areas women

[1] I am heavily indebted to [K. B.] McFarlane, [*John*] *Wycliffe* [*and the Beginnings of English Nonconformity*] (London 1952) and *Lancastrian Kings* [*and Lollard Knights*] (Oxford 1972); [C.] Kightly, ['The Early Lollards 1382–1428'] unpubl University of York DPhil thesis (1975); [J. A. F.] Thomson, [*The Later Lollards 1414–1520*] (Oxford 1965), and [J.] Fines ['Heresy Trials in the Diocese of Coventry and Lichfield 1511–12'] *JEH*, 14 (1963). Without their pioneering work this attempt to assess the contribution women made to lollardy would have been impossible.

[2] C. Jenkins, 'Cardinal Morton's Register', *Tudor Studies presented . . . to A. F. Pollard*, ed R. W. Seton-Watson (London 1924) pp 47–50. Spelling in quotations has been modernised throughout.

became the dominant force in lollardy, on the contrary where it flourished lollardy can more properly be described as a family sect, but through their very importance within the family women may well have achieved a degree of active participation in this very amorphous movement greater than any they had previously attained within the orthodox church in England.

Late in the fourteenth century the chronicler Walsingham conveyed the clergy's alarm at the intrusion by heretical lay people and above all heretical women in the sphere hitherto strictly reserved for the ordained ministry in the possibly apocryphal story of how one 'John Claydon had made his son [or daughter] a priest to celebrate mass in his own house for his wife, rising from childbirth'.[3] These stories apart, some firm evidence does exist to substantiate the activities of women in lollardy from the earliest days of its diffusion among the population at large. When archbishop Courtney began investigations into lollardy in Leicester in 1389 the leaders who emerged were William Smith and Roger and Alice Dexter. Smith had clearly amassed the most detailed information concerning Wyclif's teaching: he possessed books, epistles and gospels in English which he had been compiling for eight years. Courtney discovered that in addition all three held heretical ideas on the sacrament of the altar, believed that tithes should not be paid to priests in mortal sin, that images might not be worshipped, that laymen might preach and teach the gospel and that every good man, though unlearned, was a priest. Besides Alice Dexter, the archbishop's officials had their suspicions about a Leicester anchoress called Matilda or Maud who lived in a cell in St Peter's churchyard. Because of her 'sophistical answers' to their questions Courtney summoned her to appear before him personally in Northampton in November 1389. On that day she submitted completely and he allowed her to return to her celibate life.[4] The fate of a Northampton anchoress proved entirely different. In 1393 Anna Palmer came to the notice of the ecclesiastical officers on suspicion of receiving lollards at night and of being present at illegal lollard conventicles. When cited before the bishop of Lincoln she did not scruple to refer to the bishop as antichrist and to his clerks as antichrist's disciples. She refused to answer the articles alleged against her and in consequence was im-

[3] Quoted in M. Aston, 'Lollardy and Sedition 1381–1431', *PP* 17 (1960) p 13.

[4] J. Crompton, 'Leicestershire Lollards', *Transactions of the Leicestershire Archaeological and Historical Society*, 44 (Leicester 1968–9) pp 11–14; [J.] Foxe [*Acts and Monuments*], 1 (London 1684) pp 576–7; McFarlane, *Wycliffe* p 140.

prisoned and eventually sent to London for examination. Also in 1393 the authorities heard that an apostate nun, Agnes Nowers, had been seen in Northampton consorting with lollards. They imprisoned her, like Anna Palmer, for her association with heretics.[5]

These early, tantalisingly brief mentions of links between lollardy and unsettled female religious apparently did not outlast the first decades of the movement. Lollardy subsequently found more permanent roots among women in secular life. When Richard Wyche, the Herefordshire priest, succeeded in forming a lollard cell in Newcastle on Tyne at the turn of the fourteenth century the circle of lay people who supported the lollard clergy included John Maya and his wife, one Green and his wife, and an unnamed layman, his wife and his mother-in-law.[6] This phenomenon of women acting together with their husbands persisted wherever lollardy managed to entrench itself. Rather more information about the positive contribution made by these women comes to light at the time of Oldcastle's revolt. In Bristol Christina More shared an interest in heretical activities jointly with her husband, William, a member of the governing class of the city, indeed she may just possibly have assumed the lead. For several years husband and wife kept a lollard chaplain, William Blake, in their household. Left a widow in 1412, Christina More took over both the running of her late husband's estate and his patronage of lollards, even to the extent of equipping Blake and another servant, James Merrshe, and perhaps others at the time of the rising. On this account she was among the eight heretics from Bristol prosecuted by bishop Bubwith in 1414 and it may be that her social position alone saved her from a worse penalty than trial and purgation.[7] A Derbyshire lawyer, Thomas Tickhill and his wife Agnes, came from a somewhat similar background. They also had protected a lollard chaplain, William Ederick, and in their house at Aston upon Trent provided him with a base for his evangelising missions. At the time of Oldcastle's revolt men set out from Aston for London and though Tickhill prudently remained at home he nonetheless had to answer to the authorities for harbouring a notorious heretic, and spent some months imprisoned in the Tower.[8]

[5] A. K. McHardy, 'Bishop Buckingham and the Lollards of Lincoln Diocese', *SCH* 9 (1972) pp 131–45.

[6] M. G. Snape, 'Some Evidence of Lollard Activity in the Diocese of Durham in the early Fifteenth Century', *Archaeologia Aeliana*, 4 ser 39 (Newcastle-upon-Tyne 1961) pp 355–61.

[7] Kightly pp 242–9; Thomson pp 22–3.

[8] McFarlane, *Wycliffe*, p 175.

In the present state of knowledge it seems impossible to state with any certainty whether lollardy at this period ever obtained a foothold among women at the most elevated levels of society. K. B. McFarlane assembled a little evidence that some of the wives of the lollard knights may perhaps have sympathised with their husbands' beliefs. Dame Anne Latimer in 1402 made one of the knights, Sir Lewis Clifford, an overseer of her will and the lollard parson of Braybrooke, Robert Hook, another. In her will, in what may be lollard phraseology, she left to God 'so poor a present as my wretched soul'. Dame Alice Sturry, widow of Sir Richard Sturry, in 1414 wished that there should be no elaborate display at her funeral, while years later the widow of Sir William Beauchamp, Joan Lady Bergavenny, in 1435 ordained that her 'simple and wretched body' should be buried without 'pomp or vainglory'. At the very most the case concerning the lollard inclinations of high born women remains not proven.[9]

Information about the implication in lollardy of women among the populace, however, though still sporadic, is much more clear cut. In Lincolnshire about 1415 one Katherine Dertford stood trial accused of holding heretical opinions concerning the eucharist, and of deriding images and pilgrimages. In the slightly better documented exposure of heresy in the Tenterden area of Kent at approximately the same time the sixteen lay people cited to appear before the archbishop's officers included William Somer and his wife, Marian, and John Wadnon and Joan, his wife. The lack of detailed records of these early lollard trials compares unfavourably with the much fuller amount of material which happens to have survived relating to a lollard community in East Anglia in the 1420s: there can be no shadow of doubt that there women took a vigorous part in heresy alongside men.[10]

The lollards of the valley of the Waveney, which forms the county boundary between Norfolk and Suffolk, had been converted to their heretical opinions by a man and his wife from Kent, William and Joan White. William White had been a university scholar and follower of Wyclif who had entered the church but had subsequently given up his benefice and married. He had already once abjured his beliefs in Canterbury in 1424, clearly insincerely for he began propagating his opinions as actively as ever as soon as he reached Norfolk. He was burnt as a relapsed heretic in Norwich in 1428. According to Foxe, Joan White taught and sowed her husband's doctrine, for which she received

[9] McFarlane, *Lancastrian Kings*, pp 214–15.
[10] Foxe, 1, pp 730–1.

punishment at the hands of the bishop. The group of lollards William and Joan White helped to create contained at least thirteen women out of the eighty-nine named as having recanted before episcopal officers in 1425. One of the chief of these women was Margery Baxter, the wife of the wright of Martham. She no longer accepted the catholic doctrine of transubstantiation, refused to honour images, expressed scepticism concerning the saints, especially Thomas Becket, and had scruples over swearing oaths. She owned a lollard book which had belonged to William White which her husband read to her, and her husband had also held readings from other books in their house. Their servant Alice as well had associated herself with the sect; she had been left a new testament and may just possibly have been able to read. Margery Baxter abjured like her fellow lollards in 1428, but again obviously deceitfully for she had to make a second recantation in 1429 and may in consequence have been put to death as a relapsed heretic.[11]

Thomas Moon, his wife, Avice, and their daughter illustrate particularly well how some as families committed themselves to lollardy. They had given hospitality to William and Joan White in their house in Loddon. Very interestingly, their daughter could read English, and had almost certainly been reading for the benefit of the illiterate the lollard books circulating in this community. They had acquired the *Pater Noster*, the *Ave* and the creed in English, a book of the new law in English, and one member, Nicholas Belward, had paid four marks and forty pence in London for a new testament. The ecclesiastical authorities required all three members of the Moon family to renounce their heresy in 1428. Matilda Fletcher seems to have been an equally convinced lollard. Both she and her husband, Richard, abjured their beliefs in 1428 but she appeared again before the bishop on 18 April 1430, suspected of having returned to her former opinions. She submitted, however, and the officials prescribed no more serious a penalty for her than a beating. Nicholas Belward had confirmed Margery Wright and her husband in heresy, and they may have been related to Katherine Wright, the wife of William Wright, who recanted her heretical opinions in 1428. She was yet another who almost immediately reverted to her old beliefs: on 20 December she admitted to the bishop of Norwich's vicar general to having held erroneous beliefs concerning baptism, confirmation, confession and matrimony.[12]

[11] *Ibid* pp 750–8; Thomson pp 123–8.

[12] Foxe, 1, pp 750–8; E. Welch, 'Some Suffolk Lollards', *Proceedings of the Suffolk Institute of Archaeology*, 30 (Bury Saint Edmunds 1964) pp 154–65; Thomson p 131.

Apart from their names nothing is known about the other seven lollard women in this community which apparently did not continue after 1430. While it existed, it seems to have enjoyed the articulate support of its adherents who in reaction to catholic teaching placed a special emphasis on the superiority of the married to the celibate state. John Skilly, in particular, the miller of Flixton, asserted defiantly 'that it is lawful for priests to take wives, and nuns to take husbands . . . holding that life more commendable than to live chaste'. By their succour of Joan and William White, by their family conventicles and family readings, by their instruction of their children in lollardy, these Norfolk and Suffolk lollards had in a very literal sense been living out their beliefs.[13]

Joan and William White had moved to East Anglia from Kent about 1424 and there may well have been a more or less continuous tradition of lollardy in parts of Kent from the time that Oldcastle brought lollard priests to the neighbourhood of Cooling Castle until protestant ideas began to penetrate into England during the Lutheran reformation. Because of the paucity of the evidence, however, the composition of lollard groups in Kent cannot be examined after 1416 until 1511 when a determined investigation by the archbishop's officers uncovered lollard congregations of some antiquity. William Carder of Tenterden stands out as the dominant force behind early sixteenth century Kentish lollardy, but a figure of almost equal influence was Agnes Grebill, then aged sixty, tried at the same time as Carder and one of the five lollards burnt in Kent in 1511. According to information drawn from her own family Agnes Grebill had been led into heresy by John Ive about the end of the reign of Edward IV, and she had then proceeded to teach her doctrines to her husband and sons. The views attributed to her differed little from the opinions current in the lollard community in East Anglia two generations earlier: that the sacrament of the altar remained bread after consecration; that auricular confession should not be made to a priest; that priests had no more power than laymen to say divine service; that marriage did not constitute one of the sacraments; that another sacrament of the catholic church, extreme unction, was not necessary; that images should not be worshipped, and that pilgrimages had no merit; that prayer should be made to God alone and that holy bread and holy water contained no special virtue. Joan Grebill, who may have been Agnes Grebill's daughter, also did penance in 1511; she had to wear a badge of faggots

[13] Foxe, I, p 751; *EHD 1327–1485*, ed A. R. Myers (London 1969) pp 864–5.

on her garments for life to mark her out as a one time heretic, and was prohibited from leaving the parish where she then lived without the permission of the archbishop.[14]

Next to Agnes Grebill the episcopal officers clearly considered Agnes Chitenden of St George's parish in Canterbury one of the most notorious of the women lollards. They induced her to confess to having held similar beliefs to those of Agnes Grebill and, as part of her punishment, made her witness the burning of William Carder. Agnes Ive, perhaps related to John Ive who had converted Agnes Grebill, came from the same parish as Agnes Chitenden and made an equally full confession of heretical beliefs. She, too, had to watch the burning of Carder, appear both in Canterbury cathedral and in her own parish church bearing faggots, wear the faggot badge for life, and could not leave her present parish without the archbishop's consent. Elizabeth White, also of Canterbury, received almost the same form of penalty, although she did not have to see Carder die. At first the archbishop's officers imposed an even more severe punishment upon Joan, wife of William Olbert of Godmersham, sentencing her to perpetual imprisonment. This they subsequently mitigated to public penance in Canterbury cathedral and her home parish and to wearing the faggot badge for life. The Hills family of Tenterden closely resemble the East Anglian Moon family of fifty years earlier. In 1511 both Robert Hills and his wife had to renounce their heresy: in addition, their twenty year old daughter, Alice, made a full abjuration of lollard beliefs, and as part of her penance was forbidden from wearing a smock on Fridays. Altogether the heresy proceedings in Kent in 1511 involved seventeen women; some indeed appeared as the supporters of their husbands, but others, like Agnes Grebill, had clearly initiated their families into heresy. Only standardised confessions have survived for this episode of heresy in Kent and consequently these women seem rather less individual and less enterprising than lollards elsewhere. Verbatim accounts of an exactly contemporaneous inquisition exist for Coventry and these demonstrate just how confident some lollard women could be in the essential righteousness of their cause.[15]

A woman lollard, Joan Washingby (or Ward), provided a direct connection between the lollard community in Coventry and that in

[14] Foxe, 2 (1684) pp 531–3; Thomson pp 184, 187–8; *B[ritish] Mag[azine]*, 23 (London 1843) pp 401–2.

[15] Foxe, 2, p 533; *BMag*, 23, pp 394–5, 398–402, 631–3; 24 (1843) pp 638–41; 25 (1844) pp 142–5.

Kent. In 1511 she admitted having learnt her heresy twenty years previously from Alice Rowley in Coventry. When still a young woman she had moved away from the west Midlands first to Northampton and then to London, perhaps going from lollard household to lollard household. She may have brought a lollard book from Agnes Johnson in Coventry to Joan Blackbyre in London; and this Joan Blackbyre had already associated with heretics before Joan Washingby came to live with her. Joan Washingby remained in London for three years and met her husband there. They then went to Maidstone where in 1495 she had to abjure her lollard beliefs. She subsequently returned to Coventry and despite her recantation participated actively once more in the lollard movement in the town. She certainly had at least one lollard book in her possession, *De mortuo aut egrotante*, which she had acquired from Robert Silkby. After twenty years of dissembling the churchmen at last discovered the extent of her deception: on 11 March 1512 they condemned her as a relapsed heretic and handed her over to the secular arm to be burnt.[16]

Joan Washingby typifies the enterprise of the Coventry lollards. Out of the seventy-four people examined in the city for lollardy in 1511 and early in 1512 a third were women, and some of these had evidently been active in propagating their beliefs. 'Little mother Agnes' had taught heresy to Rose Furnour, and Rose in her turn had served in the house of another lollard, Robert Hachet. Thomasina Viller's mother had taken her as a child to Roger Landesdale's house where she had heard readings out of a large book. Years later, after her marriage to Richard Bradley, she had persuaded her husband to go to Landesdale's house to receive instruction. The leadership of the Coventry women, however, remained over the two decades with Joan Washingby's mentor, Alice Rowley. Although apparently illiterate, she seems to have been attracted to lollardy particularly because of its writings, and a considerable number of lollard books passed through her hands. She herself had a volume of Tobit, the epistle of St James, and, at least for a time, St Paul's epistles which her husband read to her. On one occasion she had lent St Paul to Roger Landesdale and, even more significantly, on another a book concerning the new law to James Preston, DD, vicar of St Michael's, Coventry, who left a very Wyclifite will when he died in 1507. Furthermore she confessed to destroying many of her books when the heresy hunt had begun.

[16] L[ichfield] R[ecord] O[ffice] B/C/13 fols 16r, 21r; Fines pp 163–4; Thomson pp 113–15.

When accused of heresy in 1511 she had at first defied the ecclesiastics, asserting 'my belief is better than theirs, save that we dare not speak it . . . I care not, they cannot hurt me, my Lord knoweth my mind already'. Rather pathetically, she believed that God would protect her 'because of our good steadfast belief, and good books'. Despite this brave show, imprisonment broke her resolve, and she abjured like her fellow lollards.[17]

Joan Smith attained a very similar standing in the community to that of Alice Rowley. She had learnt her heresy from her first husband, Richard Landesdale, and had later passed his books on to a probable relation, Roger Landesdale, though in 1511 she had still kept a copy of Acts. When her servant married John Cropwell, she brought her husband to her mistress to be instructed. She, too, recanted in 1511. The widow Smith burnt in Coventry in 1520 together with six other relapsed heretics may perhaps be identified with this same Joan Smith, especially since in 1520 the bishop's officials had initially dismissed her, but then re-arrested and condemned her when they found her in possession of English books. Agnes Corby, like Alice Rowley, only acknowledged her lollard beliefs after a period in prison. Another woman lollard, Joan Gest, had become acquainted with lollardy through her master, John Smith, and then had led her husband, John Gest, a Birmingham cobbler, into heresy.[18]

The confessions made by the Coventry lollards in 1511, though detailed, do not reveal much directly about the competence and social status of these women. That it was in their own interest to conceal their capabilities complicates matters yet further. At the beginning of the heresy investigations Juliana Young denied that she could read, but when the bishop's officers confronted her with Robert Silkby's testimony, she admitted that she could. She may well not have been the only Coventry woman to try to hide her education. Even if illiterate, these women obviously had no difficulty in a city like Coventry in finding others within the sect to read the prohibited books to them. Some of the women employed servants and seem to have been members of fairly substantial households. In addition, further evidence suggests that in Coventry lollardy not only touched some of the civic clergy such as Dr Preston but may also have percolated right to the apex of the city's hierarchy. William Pysford, who was mayor in 1501,

[17] LRO B/C/13 fols 1r, 6v, 14v, 22r; Fines pp 162, 165, 168; Thomson pp 110, 133; [I.] Luxton, ['The Lichfield Court Book; a postscript'], *BIHR*, 44 (1971) pp 120–5.

[18] LRO B/C/13 fols 4r, 18r; Foxe, 2, pp 181–2; Thomson pp 110, 111, 113, 116.

acted as the overseer of the will of Richard Cook, mayor in 1486 and 1503, an almost certain lollard who left two English bibles on his death in 1507. Both William Pysford and his two sons made wills which contained lollard terminology: Pysford's daughter, Agnes, married the extremely wealthy Leicester merchant, William Wigston the younger, and in 1511 some of the lollards said before the ecclesiastical investigators that Master Wigston and Master Pysford had 'beautiful books of heresy'. It may be that their wives also shared their interests.[19]

The fortunate survival of the Lichfield court book for 1511–12 makes possible the partial reconstruction of the Coventry lollard community in the late fifteenth and early sixteenth century: circumstantial accounts are even more full concerning the lollards who lived at this time in the Chilterns. This community certainly numbered several hundreds and may possibly have risen to as many as a thousand adherents: while particularly strong in the Amersham area it took in groups of lollards from as far west as Burford in Oxfordshire and Newbury in Berkshire, and as far east as Uxbridge and some London parishes, all in some sort of association through travelling evangelists. Heresy in the Chilterns proper certainly went back well into the fifteenth century; Robert Collins of Asthill had learnt his opinions from his father and had been of the sect in 1480. As in Kent, there may have been a continuous tradition of lollardy in the area from the time of Oldcastle's revolt. As had happened earlier in East Anglia, the Chilterns also profited from the attentions of married missionaries, in this case Thomas Man and his wife, who succeeded in ministering in the Chilterns and beyond for a generation before being captured. They taught at Amersham, London, Billericay, Chelmsford, Stratford Langthorn, Uxbridge, Burnham, Henley-on-Thames, Newbury and in Norfolk and Suffolk. They had been spreading their opinions in Amersham for twenty-three years, and having found a company of well disposed people in Newbury had settled there for fifteen. The ecclesiastical authorities who examined several hundred suspects in the Chilterns first at the time of the great abjuration of about 1511 and later at a new investigation in 1521 considered that Man and his wife alone had won over six or seven hundred people to their sect. When the persecution came to a climax in 1511 Thomas Man with his wife had helped five families to escape from the Chilterns to places of refuge in Norfolk and Suffolk. Both abjured in 1511, but both soon reverted to

[19] LRO B/C/13 fols 14^r, 15^v, 18^v; Fines p 169; Luxton pp 120–5; Thomson p 110.

their heresy. Man was burnt as a relapsed heretic in 1518; little else has been preserved about his wife apart from the fact that she with others discussed books of scripture with some of the leaders of the Chiltern lollards including Robert Pope.[20]

With Thomas Man and his wife directing the community and providing links between the scattered cells, it is scarcely surprising that the women of the Chilterns themselves participated eagerly in the sect. In the early sixteenth century Alice Sanders of Amersham seems to have been among the most forceful. She boasted that she had persuaded her husband to dismiss Thomas Houre from his service when he had come to her and told her that the churchmen were condemning many for heresy and that he would lean that way no more. She resented Houre's apostacy to such an extent that she went on pursuing him, and later got him deprived from his new post as holy water clerk in the town. Joan Collingbourn showed a rather similar lack of discretion in proclaiming to Joan Timberlake and Alice Tredway that she did not believe in pilgrimages or in worshipping saints; this led to her being reported to the bishop. The wife of Thomas Africk had revealed her sympathies by consulting Robert Pope about the gospel of St Matthew. At least a dozen women, and probably many more, received punishment for their heretical activities in 1511 and these included Joan Clerk, whose father, William Tilseworth, was burnt at Amersham in that year.[21]

Information about the persecution in the Amersham area in 1511 which the lollards themselves called the great abjuration can now only be gleaned from the infinitely better documented heresy proceedings of 1521. The extremely full confessions which date from this year make it abundantly obvious that the ecclesiastical authorities had failed to curb heresy in the Chilterns in 1511 and incidentally show in unprecedented detail the eager participation of the local women in teaching lollardy, acquiring lollard books, learning lollard tracts by heart and demonstrating their dislike of catholic ceremonies. In disseminating lollard beliefs these women on occasion did not hesitate to take the initiative. Alice Harding of Amersham advised Richard Bennett what to do to conceal his opinions when the priest came. She dissuaded Joan Norman from going on pilgrimages or venerating images of saints and told her that she might break her fast before going to mass, and had no need to confess to a priest. Isabel Tracher brought her daughter to

[20] Foxe, 2, pp 18–21, 34, 36; Thomson pp 53–76.
[21] Foxe, 1, pp 877–8; 2 pp 31–3.

Alice Harding for instruction, and this girl subsequently influenced Alice Holting. Isabel Morwin, the wife of John Morwin, displayed a comparable independence of mind. Not only did she teach Copland's wife her errors and to speak against images, but also at the time of their father's death took the opportunity of correcting her sister's views on the fate of the soul. Denying the existence of purgatory, she claimed that at death the souls of all men passed straight to heaven or hell, and so by implication repudiated the late medieval reliance upon masses for the dead.[22]

The quality of the teaching of some of these women can be gauged from the work of Agnes Ashford of Chesham. She first helped James Morden learn

> We be the salt of the earth; if it be putrified and vanished away, it is nothing worth. A city set upon an hill may not be hid. Ye tende not a candle, and put it under a bushel, but set it on a candlestick, that it may give a light to all in the house. So shine your light before men, as they may see your works, and glorify the father which is in heaven. No tittle nor letter of the law shall pass over till all things be done.

Morden needed to visit Agnes five times until he had this lesson word perfect. He then progressed to the next, Agnes still acting as his guide.

> Jesus seeing his people, as he went up to a hill, was set, and his disciples came to him; he opened his mouth, and taught them, saying, Blessed be the poor men in spirit, for the kingdom of heaven is theirs. Blessed be mild men, for they shall weld the earth.

After only two attempts, Morden got this lesson by heart. Agnes herself in the course of the persecution was called upon to repeat both these passages from the new testament to six bishops, who enjoined her never to teach them again and especially not to her own children.[23]

Agnes Ashford, the investigators soon discovered, had been only one among many women teachers of heresy. Joan Gun had taught John Hill in the epistle of St James. Joan Steventon had learnt from Alice Collins the ten commandments and the first chapter of St John, and the same Alice passed on her beliefs to Margaret House. Much as the women in Coventry had done, Agnes Edmunds had brought Richard Collins to her father's house to be instructed in God's law. Mrs Cottismore, alias Dolie, on one occasion told her maid that she would have as much merit for praying in her chamber as for going on a pilgrimage to Walsingham. She would not agree to her servant's making

[22] *Ibid* 2, pp 26, 29. [23] *Ibid* p 26.

a proxy pilgrimage for her dead husband, and maintained that images were no more than carpenter's chips. At a later date the maid informed on her mistress to the bishop of Lincoln's official, swearing that Mrs Dolie had also said that John Hacker, the London lollard, 'was very expert in the gospels and all other things belonging to divine service and that he could express and declare it, and the *Pater Noster* in English, as well as any priest'. Furthermore, she had kept several heretical books in her chamber upon which she had set great store. Of all these women, the daughter of John Phip, a lollard instructor in Hughenden, made the most outrageous claims in the ears of the orthodox: she had been heard publicly stating that 'she was as well learned as was the parish priest, in all things, except only in saying mass'.[24]

Perhaps partly because of illiteracy, but perhaps even more to avoid being found in possession of incriminating books, much learning of lollard scriptures by heart went on in this community, and here women indisputably dominated the scene. In Burford Allice Collins was frequently called upon to recite at conventicles the ten commandments and the epistles of Peter and James, and she brought up her daughter Joan to do the same. Alice Atkins had learnt from John Morden the *Pater Noster*, the *Ave Maria*, the ten commandments, all in English, the five marvels of St Austin, and a piece in English beginning 'here ensueth four things by which a man may know whether he shall be saved'. Alice Brown had also got by heart the beatitudes and other sayings of Jesus, instructed by John Tracher of Chesham. Similarly Agnes Edmunds knew the ten commandments, the five wits bodily and ghostly, and the seven deadly sins. The community particularly cherished the epistle of St James, and Agnes Wellis memorised this through her brother, Robert Bartlett, another prominent lollard. Thurston Littlepage came to knowledge of the creed through his grandmother: indeed, the women in this family developed a very considerable commitment to lollardy for Thurston's wife, Alice, later taught William Littlepage the ten commandments in his father's house. The wife of John Morden could also with her husband recite the ten commandments in English, while Marian, the sister of James Morden, burnt as a heretic in 1521, had learnt the *Pater Noster* and *Ave* from her brother as well as the creed.[25]

Despite the danger, women lollards in the Chilterns seem to have set as high a value on lollard books as the lollard women of Coventry.

[24] *Ibid* pp 26, 30, 31, 33, 34, 37, 38, 194–5.
[25] *Ibid* pp 23, 27, 28, 29, 30, 37.

John Colins and his wife of Asthill had contrived to procure a bible for twenty shillings. Robert Pope's wife acquired a small collection of English books, one bound in boards, and three in parchment covers, a book of the service of the Virgin Mary in English, and four sheets written in English against the catholic religion. Mrs Dolie's small library of books, one containing the twelve articles of the creed, covered in red board, another black book which she especially prized, together with other unspecified books, came to the notice of the church authorities in 1521. Alice Sanders, so intolerant of backsliders from the sect, exercised much ingenuity, if not sharp practice, to obtain these sort of books. She once gave Thomas Holmes 12d. to buy a certain book in English for her daughter even though Holmes had told her it would cost at least a noble: on another occasion she gave him 6d to get another English book worth at least five marks.[26]

When they could not buy books these women borrowed them, or attended meetings where they were discussed. Joan Burgess, at whose wedding the gospel of Nichodemus had been read, had subsequently been present at a debate upon the book with seven clasps at her house in Burford. John Harris and his wife in the same way had talked on the Apocalypse, had sponsored readings in their own house at Upton, and had attended readings elsewhere. In addition to taking Thomas Man into their house at Rickmansworth when he was flying from persecution, Marion Randal, her husband and father-in-law had all read Wyclif's *Wicket*. The wife of Henry Ulman of Uxbridge had left home to go with one Carpenter and his wife to hear readings at a goodman's house in Friday Street in London. Thomas Spencer and his wife borrowed a book of gospels in English and both used to read it.[27]

The enterprise of some of these women extended in yet other directions. Katherine Bartlett, the mother of Robert and Richard Bartlett, feigned sickness to avoid having to attend church. Isabel Tracher, her neighbours alleged, also did not go to church, being in fact in good health. Having been made to abjure, Agnes Frank and her husband went to church, but once there sat mum. On the whole these women seem to have emphasised the constructive elements in lollardy, particularly in their reading of scripture and other lollard texts, but occasionally they, too, descended into the scurrility always to some degree present in the movement. Eleanor Higgs bragged that she would burn the sacrament of the altar in the oven, her protest somewhat

[26] *Ibid* pp 31, 36, 195.
[27] *Ibid* pp 27, 31, 32, 35–6.

resembling that of Alice Rowley in Coventry who had asserted that priests would buy a hundred wafer cakes for a penny and sell them again one for two halfpennies. In much the same tradition at Great Marlow in 1541 Eleanor Godfrey poked scorn at a fellow parishioner who showed reverence to the priest at the time of mass. In these instances lollardy may chiefly have acted as a vehicle for the expression of that age old jealousy which some of the laity from time immemorial had felt for the priesthood.[28]

Very much the same type of lollardy, in most respects positively founded on books and readings but also occasionally negative and destructive, surfaced in East Anglia in the early sixteenth century. Some heresy seems to have become entrenched in Colchester and its surrounding area by the beginning of the reign of Henry VIII. In 1511 William Sweeting who had served the prior of St Osyth for sixteen years was burnt at Smithfield for lollardy together with John Brewster of Colchester, an illiterate carpenter who had listened to readings given by Sweeting which Woodruf, a netmaker, and his wife had also attended. Around 1516 Mrs Girling who then lived in the household of Sir Thomas Eyers, the curate of Skells in the diocese of Norwich, had to recant and the priest himself died for his heretical opinions. In 1504 Dorothy Long was convicted of lollardy in London and some time between then and 1524 migrated to the parish of St Giles in Colchester where she reverted to her old beliefs: in the early 1520s together with Thomas Parker she passed on the four evangelists and the gospels in English to another lollard. Detailed knowledge of this community, however, only emerged as a result of bishop Tunstall's persecution of 1528.[29]

The confessions procured by Tunstall's officers confirm yet again that some East Anglian women displayed as keen an interest in lollardy as their sisters in the Chilterns and that they had been equally prominent in furthering the sect. More clearly than at Coventry some Essex women seem to have been opening their houses as lollard centres. The London evangelist John Hacker visited Mother Beckwith and her three sons at Braintree and the important Steeple Bumpstead lollard, John Tyball, stopped at her house on his way to make contact with the lollard community in Colchester. Other women made their houses available for heretical meetings: some of these assemblies took place

[28] *Ibid* pp 27, 32, 35, 453; LRO B/C/13 fol 2r; Fines p 166.

[29] [A. F.] Pollard [*The Reign of Henry VII from Contemporary Sources*], 3 (London 1914) pp 237–8; *CalLP*, 4, 2, no 4175.

at Mother Bocher's house at Steeple Bumpstead, others at Mother Charte's at the adjacent settlement of Birdbrook.[30]

There is no doubt at all that on occasions these women took the initiative in spreading heresy. About 1522 as she was sitting at dinner in her house William Rayland put a leading question to Mrs Girling who he knew had been convicted of heresy in the diocese of Norwich some six years before. To his query 'What is the sacrament of the altar?' she replied 'that the sacrament of the altar was but an host; and that the body of Almighty God was joined in the word; and that the word and God was all one, and might not be departed'. She also broadcast her opinion that the images of saints were no more than idols. Like Mrs Girling, Alice Johnson and her husband had come to Essex to escape persecution, though they had travelled considerably further, from Salisbury to Boxstead. They had a copy of Wyclif's *Wicket* and heard readings from it in their house. Johnson or his wife once 'moved a question of the Father, the Son and the Holy Ghost'. Most of the women teachers, however, seem to have been local women. As in the Chilterns, several wives converted their husbands. Mrs Hemstead passed on to her husband knowledge of the *Pater Noster*, the *Ave Maria* and the *Credo* in English, which she had learned from Gilbert Shipwright. Around 1524 at a time when she was contracted to him in marriage Joan Dyer, daughter of one Dyer of Finchingfield, instructed Thomas Hilles in the first chapter of James. Even more momentously for the history of lollardy in Essex, Agnes Pykas began the process which ended in her son's joining the sect. About 1523 Agnes who lived in Bury St Edmunds sent for her son John, then a baker in Colchester, 'and moved him not to believe in the sacraments of the church, for that was not the right way. And she gave him a book of Paul's epistles in English, and bade him live after the way of the epistles and gospels, and not after the way the church teaches'. Convinced partly by his mother, partly by the books he read Pykas went on to become one of the leaders of lollardy in the Colchester area.[31]

In Colchester Pykas often held meetings at the house of Thomas Matthew where Tyball also stayed. Matthew must have been a man of some substance since at the time of his abjuration in 1528 the bishop's official ordered him to contribute 6s. 8d. to the poor of Colchester for

[30] *Ibid* nos 4029, 4850; Strype, *Memorials*, 1 (London 1721) appendix, pp 36–7; Foxe, 2, p 268.

[31] *Cal LP*, 4, 2; nos 2095, 4029, 4175; Strype, *Memorials*, 1, app pp 36–7, 43; Foxe, 2, pp 266–8.

each of the five remaining weeks in Lent. He had a step-daughter, Marion Westden, as ardent a lollard as her father: according to Pykas in 1528 Marion had in her own house spoken many times of the epistles and gospels which she had well by heart. She had also frequently said to him in the previous three years that men should not go on pilgrimages since they were meaningless. She claimed to have set up as few candles to images as any woman had, as that also was not lawful. She had been a 'known woman' and of the brotherhood for three years by his certain knowledge and for twelve years as he had heard say. Not even Tunstall's severe measures could irradicate this sort of religious individualism. When in 1532 John Wily, his wife, Katherine, their children and grandchildren appeared before an ecclesiastical court on the comparatively minor charge of eating pottage on fast days the authorities discovered that they had a treatise of William Thorpe and Sir John Oldcastle: still in the old lollard tradition one of their daughters aged ten could recite by heart most of the twenty-fourth chapter of Matthew and the *Disputation between a Clerk and a Friar*. At least in some parts of East Anglia lollardy survived, partly through the activities of these women, to merge with Lutheran ideas penetrating the area from Cambridge and perhaps also directly from the continent.[32]

The lollard communities in East Anglia, the Chilterns, Coventry and Kent all at some time had connections with lollards in London where women again had a significant part in the sect's preservation. London, indeed, in the 1490s had the distinction of contributing one, if not two, lollard women martyrs. Foxe could supply little information about Joan Boughton aged over eighty when burnt at Smithfield in 1494 for holding eight of Wyclif's opinions. She was, however, the mother of Lady Young, wife of a former lord mayor of London, Sir John Young, and Lady Young herself just possibly may have followed her mother to the fire. In 1511 Joan Baker, wife of a London merchant taylor, Gervais Baker, had to answer the charge that she had asserted that Lady Young had died a martyr.[33]

The influence of Joan Boughton and Lady Young clearly inspired other London women and in 1509 Elizabeth Sampson, wife of John Sampson, junior, of Aldermanbury stood accused of holding blasphemous opinions, and having been a sower of evil seed against

[32] *Cal LP*, 4, 2, nos 4029, 4175; Strype, *Memorials*, 1, p 84, app pp 36–7; Foxe, 2, pp 268–9; R. A. Houlbrooke, 'Persecution of Heresy and Protestantism in the Diocese of Norwich under Henry VIII', *Norfolk and Norwich Archaeological Society*, 25 (Norwich 1972) pp 308–26.

[33] Foxe, 1, p 829; 2, p 5; Thomson p 156.

pilgrimages, adoration of images, the sacrament of the altar, Christ's ascension, and the general resurrection to the perturbation of the faithful and to the vilification of God, the blessed Virgin Mary, and All Saints. She admitted uttering obscene words concerning various local images and pilgrimages and having said 'I will not give my dog that bread that some priests doth minister at the altar when they be not in clean life', asserting that she herself 'could make as good bread as that was; and that it was not the body of our Lord, for it is but bread, for God cannot be both in heaven and earth.' She further confessed to having said 'in so much that God Almighty was buried here bodily in earth, it is impossible that he should come bodily to heaven'. The special heresy proceedings in London as well as in Kent, the Chilterns and the Midlands in 1511 confirmed bishop FitzJames in his conviction that the case of Elizabeth Sampson indicated the existence of widespread lollardy in the city.[34]

Foxe culled the names of six women from the twenty-three recorded in the bishop of London's register as having abjured in 1511 or 1512. These included Joan Austy (or Austin), the daughter of Thomas Vincent who in his turn had instructed the notable lollard evangelist, John Hacker. A fellowship of lollards comprising Joan and her husband Thomas Austy, Joan and Lewis John, and Christopher Ravin and his sister Dyonise faced trial for having read a very impressive collection of lollard translations and lollard books, the four evangelists, Wyclif's *Wicket*, the book of the ten commandments, the Revelation of St John, and the epistles of Paul and James. The episcopal officers also suspected them of having spoken against the sacraments, images, and pilgrimages. Joan Baker, in addition to revering Lady Young as a martyr, had called the crucifix a false god, denied the pope's power to grant pardons and had asserted that she could hear at home a better sermon than any doctor or priest could make.[35] A few years later the diocesan authorities called upon Elizabeth Stamford, the pupil of Thomas Beele who had once lived at Henley in the Chilterns, to answer the familiar charges of speaking against the sacraments and praying to saints, and of reviling the pope. She had made her own Beele's teaching on the eucharist which she could still repeat by heart eleven years later. In a statement, which incidentally reveals the spiritual attractions of lollardy, she told her judges

That Christ feedeth and fast nourisheth his church with his own

[34] Pollard, 3, pp 244–6; Thomson pp 160–1.

[35] Foxe, 2, pp 5, 6, 17; *CalLP*, 4, 2, no 4029; *VCH, London*, 1 (London 1909) pp 234–5.

precious body, that is, the bread of life coming down from heaven: this is the worthy word that is worthily received, and joined unto man to be in one body with him. Sooth it is that they be both one, they may not be parted: this is the wisely deeming of the holy sacrament, Christ's own body: this is not received by chewing of teeth, but by hearing with ears, and understanding with your soul, and wisely working thereafter. Therefore, saith St Paul, I fear me amongst us, brethren, that many of us be feeble and sick; therefore I counsel us, brethren, to rise and watch, that the great day of doom come not suddenly upon us, as the thief does upon the merchant.[36]

In a further spate of abjurations in 1520 and 1521 more links emerged between London and the Chilterns. Joan Barrett, wife of a London goldsmith, had attended the wedding of Durdant's daughter at Henley where St Paul had been read aloud to the assembled company. Her husband could recite St James without book and she had herself lent John Scrivener the gospels of St Matthew and St Mark. Before the great abjuration of 1511 another London goldsmith, William Tilseworth, used to go to Thomas Man's house at Amersham, and it may be his wife who was subsequently condemned for not thinking catholicly of the sacrament of the altar. Yet again later in the decade when the bishop directed his investigations chiefly against East Anglian lollards his officials exposed six more London women. Mother Bristow at the Castle in Wood Street had a book of Hacker's 'of the evangelist St Luke in English, which Mother Bristow did hear his doctrines and teachings, and had delectation in the same; and was of his sect and learning, and well learned in the same opinions'. Coney, the clerk of St Anthony's, and his wife had also been of the sect for six years and had another of Hacker's books called *The Bayly*.[37]

These lollard attitudes and beliefs seem to have lingered among some Londoners for years after new protestant doctrines had been openly disseminated. About 1540 the churchwardens of St Botolph's without Aldgate presented Margaret Ambsworth for not reverencing the sacrament, for instructing her maids, 'and being a great doctress'. The curate of St Benet Fink reported Martin Bishop's wife for not being shriven in lent, for not receiving the sacrament at easter and of making light of his admonition. Notable among the many citizens who had been despising the mass and the ceremonies of the church were Robert Plat

[36] Foxe, 2, p 17.
[37] *Ibid* pp 29, 32; *CalLP*, 4, 2, no 4029.

and his wife, also of St Benet Fink, accused of being 'great reasoners in scripture, saying that they had it of the spirit; and that confession availeth nothing; and that he, not able to read, would use no beads'. With their lollard tradition of illicit (and undirected) bible reading some of these Londoners would not willingly accept a clerically dominated form of protestantism.[38]

Late medieval lollardy never more than a minority movement, if so ill defined a body could even be called a movement for much of its existence, did not recruit an undue number of women among its adherents. Nevertheless, the admittedly incomplete evidence suggests that many of the women who joined the sect did so as far more than passive members. The English church towards the end of the middle ages made little specific provision for women: far fewer religious houses had been founded for them than for monks or friars, and they enjoyed considerably less opportunities for expressing their particular interests and needs than men. In general in ecclesiastical matters the laity seemed greatly underprivileged when compared with churchmen: lay women in their turn formed the least privileged sector of the laity. It is, therefore, not difficult to account for the marked interest some women in certain parts of England showed in lollardy despite all its dangers. The prominence which Joan Collins and her daughter achieved when summoned to recite the scriptures at conventicles in Burford must have exceeded the recognition they would have attained in women's activities in an orthodox parish. These women had every reason to conceal their skills from enquiring clerics: it may be that considerably more women than the churchmen suspected acquired the ability to read in order to peruse lollard books. Certainly a reverence for books characterise women in a majority of communities and in several lollard women took a major part in organising book distribution. As mothers and grandmothers they had unique authority over impressionable children and far more women than have been recorded may have been responsible for helping educate succeeding generations in heresy. The way in which the daughters, rather than the sons, of lollard missioners tried to continue their father's work merits a special mention. Joan Clerk loyally cherished the opinions of her father William Tilseworth burnt for heresy at Amersham in 1511. Thomas Vincent's daughter, Joan, perpetuated her father's teaching in her assiduous reading of lollard books while the daughter of Thomas Moon, or, a century later, the young daughters of John Wily at their

[38] Foxe, 2, pp 449, 450.

fathers' prompting learnt passages of scripture to recite at meetings. The joint evangelism of husband and wife, moreover, such as Roger and Alice Dexter seem to have carried out in Leicester in the 1380s and as William and Joan White undoubtedly pursued in Norfolk and Suffolk a generation later, and Thomas Man and his wife all over the southern part of England at the close of the fifteenth century and into the next two decades had no parallel outside lollardy in England in the later middle ages. It only became fairly prominent again among the sects a hundred and fifty years later at the time of the civil war and interregnum.[39]

When exposed by the ecclesiastical authorities lollard women, like their male counterparts, almost invariably recanted, though also like them, many seem to have done so with every intention of reverting to their former opinions. Probably not as many as a dozen women were burnt as relapsed heretics, and these include, besides Joan Boughton and perhaps her daughter, Lady Young, one Ellen Griffith who died at Lydney about 1495 (and was not recorded by Foxe), an unnamed woman from Chipping Sodbury put to death in the reign of Henry VIII, Agnes Grebill who suffered in Canterbury in 1511, the two Coventry women, Joan Washingby and widow Smith, and Joan Norman almost certainly killed in the Chilterns in 1521. Perhaps the churchmen, who do not otherwise emerge particularly well from the heresy investigations, should at least be given some credit for the paucity of lollard women martyrs, since there seem to have been far more women who returned to opinions deemed erroneous by the church than were ever put to death as relapsed heretics. Not considering the generality of women capable of comprehending the higher mysteries of the faith, and horrified at the very idea of the bible being laid open to the mean understanding of women, the higher clerics tended persistently to underestimate the influence of women in spreading lollardy.[40]

Difficult as had been the problems of ecclesiastics in those parts of southern and central England where lollardy continued in the fifteenth and early sixteenth centuries, they appeared as nothing when compared with the complexities confronting the more conservative of the Henrician bishops after the influx of new protestant doctrines especially in some southern dioceses in the 1530s. In the city of London

[39] *Ibid*, 1, pp 576–7, 751, 752–5, 877; 2, pp 18–19, 37, 268–9; *CalLP*, 4, 2, no 4029; C. Hill, *The World Turned Upside Down* (London 1972) esp chapters 9, 10 and 14.
[40] Foxe, 1, p 880; 2, p 40; J. F. Mozley, *John Foxe and his Book* (London 1940) p 205.

alone around 1540 reports reached the bishop of Brinsley's wife, of St Nicholas, Flesh Shambles, who, like many more had been 'busy reasoning on the new learning and not keeping the church'. The churchwardens of St Andrew's Holborn informed on Mistress Castle, 'a meddler and a reader of the scripture in the church'. Ralph Clervis and his wife had drawn suspicion to themselves by maintaining preachers of the new learning while Mistress Elizabeth Statham had given clear proof of her sympathies by providing hospitality to Latimer, Barnes, Garret, Jerome and other advanced protestants. From this date churchmen could no longer ignore the part being played by English women in promoting potentially heterodox religious movements. Perhaps, however, the activities of women lollards in the later middle ages in helping to perpetuate their sect have not yet fully received their due.[41]

University of York

[41] Foxe, 2, p 448.

BIBLIOGRAPHY OF THE WRITINGS OF ROSALIND M. T. HILL

by JOHN FUGGLES

1937 *Ecclesiastical Letter-Books of the Thirteenth Century*, Oxford B Litt thesis, pp 297.

1943 'Bishop Sutton and the Institution of Heads of Religious Houses in the Diocese of Lincoln', *EHR* 58 pp 201–9.

1946 'A Letter-book of S. Augustine's, Bristol', *Transactions of the Bristol and Gloucestershire Archaeological Society* 65 (Gloucester) pp 141–56.

1947 'Two Northamptonshire Chantries', *EHR* 62 pp 203–8.

1948 *The Rolls and Register of Oliver Sutton 1280–1299*, 1, *LRS* 39 pp xxvii, 295.

1949 'Oliver Sutton, Bishop of Lincoln, and the University of Oxford', *TRHS* 4 ser 31 pp 1–16.

1950 *The Rolls and Register of Oliver Sutton 1280–1299*, 2, *LRS* 43 pp xix, 205.

Oliver Sutton, Dean of Lincoln, later Bishop of Lincoln (1280–1299), Lincoln Minster Pamphlets 4 (Lincoln) pp 36.

1951 'Bishop Sutton and his Archives', *JEH* 2 pp 43–53.

'Public Penance: Some Problems of a Thirteenth-Century Bishop', *History* ns 36 pp 213–26.

1952 REVIEW

English Bishops' Chanceries, 1100–1250, by C. R. Cheney, *History* ns 37 p 238.

1953 *Both Small and Great Beasts*, (London) pp 16.

1954 *The Rolls and Register of Oliver Sutton 1280–1299*, 3, *LRS* 48 pp lxxxvi, 250.

1955 'Some Beasts from the Medieval Chronicles of the British Isles', *Folk-Lore* 66 (London) pp 208–18.

1956 'The Lost Settlement of Brige', *Papers and Proceedings of the Hampshire Field Club and Archaeological Society* 20 (Winchester) pp 3–13.

REVIEWS

The Religious Orders in England, 2, by M. D. Knowles, *History* ns 41 pp 207–8. *A Handlist of the Records of the Bishop of Lincoln and of the Archdeacons of Lincoln and Stow,* compiled by Kathleen Major, *JEH* 7 pp 90–1.

1957 'The Theory and Practice of Excommunication in Medieval England', *History* ns 42 pp 1–11.

REVIEWS

A Royal Imposter—King Sverre of Norway, by G. M. Gathorne-Hardy, *History* ns 42 pp 145–6.

Hugh de Puiset, by G. V. Scammell, *History* ns 42 pp 220–1.

1958 *The Rolls and Register of Oliver Sutton 1280–1299*, 4, *LRS* 52 pp viii, 221.

REVIEWS

The Register of Thomas Longley, 1–2, ed R. L. Storey, *SS* 164 and 166, *Archives* 3 (London) pp 188–90.

The 'Dignitas Decani' of St. Patrick's Cathedral, Dublin, ed N. B. White, *JEH* 9 p 239.

1959 REVIEW

The Registrum Antiquissimum, 8, ed Kathleen Major, *LRS* 51, *History* ns 44 pp 46–7.

1960 REVIEWS

Early Franciscan Government, by R. B. Brooke, *History* ns 45 pp 45–6.

The Register of Thomas Langley, 3, ed R. L. Storey, *SS* 169, *Archives* 4 pp 241–2.

1962 *Gesta Francorum et Aliorum Hierosolimitanorum* (London) pp xlv, 1–103 × 2, 107–13.

REVIEWS

The Register of Thomas Langley, 4, ed R. L. Storey, *SS* 170, *Archives* 5 p 173.

Carte Nativorum: a Peterborough Abbey Cartulary of the Fourteenth Century, ed C. N. L. Brooke and M. M. Postan, *Northamptonshire Record Society* 20, *JEH* 13 pp 232–3.

1963 'The Northumbrian Church', *Church Quarterly Review* 164 (London) pp 160–72.

REVIEW

Sidelights on the Anglo-Saxon Church, by Margaret Deansley, *JEH* 14 pp 123–4.

1964 REVIEWS

A History of the Crusades, 2, The Later Crusades, by R. L. Wolff and H. W. Hazard, *EHR* 79 pp 106–7.

Aspects of the Crusades by J. J. Saunders, *EHR* 79 p 823.

1965 *The Rolls and Register of Oliver Sutton 1280–1299,* 5, *LRS* 60 pp vii, 255.

REVIEW ARTICLE

'The English Church in the Thirteenth Century', *History* ns 50 pp 329–31.

REVIEWS

The Crusade. Historiography and Bibliography, by A. S. Atiya, *EHR* 80 p 378.

Crusade, Commerce and Culture, by A. S. Atiya, *EHR* 80 p 379.

The Early Rolls of Merton College, Oxford, ed J. R. L. Highfield, *JEH* 16 pp 122–3.

1966 'Christianity and Geography in Early Northumbria', *SCH* 3 (Leiden) pp 126–39.

REVIEWS

Crusaders as Conquerors, by H. E. Lurier, *EHR* 81 pp 146–7.

Historical Interpretation: Sources of English Medieval History, by J. J. Bagley, *History* ns 51 p 73.

Institutions Ecclésiastiques de la Chrétienté Médiévale 1st pt, 2–6, by G. Le Bras, *History* ns 51 p 203.

L'Age Classique, 1140–1378. Sources et Théorie du Droit, by G. Le Bras, *History* ns 51 pp 342–3.

1968 *The Labourer in the Vineyard: the Visitations of Archbishop Melton in the Archdeaconry of Richmond,* Borthwick Papers 35 (York) pp 21.

'The Stockbridge Elections', *Papers and Proceedings of the Hampshire Field Club and Archaeological Society* 23, pp 120–7.

REVIEWS

The Register of Thomas Langley, 5, ed R. L. Storey, *SS* 177, *Archives* 8 pp 161–2.

Orbis Britanniae and other Studies, by Eric John, and *The Early Charters of Eastern England,* by C. R. Hart, *JEH* 19 pp 96–7.

1969 *The Rolls and Register of Oliver Sutton 1280–1299,* 6, *LRS* 64 pp ix, 236.

REVIEWS
The Knights of St. John in Jerusalem and Cyprus 1050–1310, by J. Riley-Smith, *EHR* 84 pp 348–50.
Saint Louis, the Life of Louis IX of France, by M. W. Labarge, *History* ns 54 pp 85–6.
Excommunication and the Secular Arm in Medieval England, by F. D. Logan, *History* ns 54 p 260.

1970 REVIEWS
The English Parish 600–1300, by John Godfrey, *History* ns 55 pp 98–9.
Christianity in Britain 300–700, ed M. W. Barley and R. P. C. Hanson, *JEH* 21 pp 172–3.

1971 '"*A Chaunterie for Soules*": London Chantries in the Reign of Richard II', *The Reign of Richard II: Essays in Honour of May McKisack*, ed F. R. H. Du Boulay and C. M. Barron (London) pp 242–55.
'Some Hertfordshire Clergy of the Thirteenth Century', *Hertfordshire Past and Present* 11 (Chichester) pp 16–21.
REVIEW
A History of the County of Middlesex, 1, ed J. S. Cockburn, H. P. F. King and K. G. T. McDonnell, (*VCH*), *EHR* 86 pp 147–8.

1972 *Unfashionable History. An Inaugural Lecture* (London) pp 15.
'Belief and practice as illustrated by John XXII's excommunication of Robert Bruce', *SCH* 8 (Cambridge) pp 135–8.
REVIEWS
The Early Christian Archaeology of North Britain, by Charles Thomas, *JEH* 23 pp 348–9.
Church and Society in Medieval Lincolnshire, by Dorothy M. Owen, *JEH* 23 pp 355–6.

1973 REVIEW
The Crusades, by H. E. Mayer, *JEH* 24 pp 218–19.

1974 *The Labourers in the Field*, The Jarrow Lecture (Jarrow on Tyne) pp 15.
REVIEWS
Libellus de diversis ordinibus et professionibus qui sunt in aecclesia, ed Giles Constable and B. Smith, *History* ns 59 p 89.
Durham Priory, 1400–1450 by R. B. Dobson, *JEH* 25 pp 341–2.

1975 *The Rolls and Register of Oliver Sutton 1280–1299*, 7, *LRS* 69 pp xv, 192.

'Uncovenanted blessings of ecclesiastical records (*Presidential address*)', *SCH* 11 (Oxford) pp 135–46.

'Holy kings: the bane of seventh-century society', *SCH* 12 (Oxford) pp 39–43.

REVIEWS

The Feudal Nobility and the Kingdom of Jerusalem 1174–1277, by J. Riley-Smith, *EHR* 90 pp 167–8.

The Templars in the Corona de Aragón, by A. J. Forey, *JEH* 26 pp 325–6.

1976 'Bede and the Boors', *Famulus Christi: Essays in Commemoration of the Thirteenth Century of the Birth of the Venerable Bede*, ed Gerald Bonner (London) pp 93–105.

'Pure air and portentous heresy', *SCH* 13 (Oxford) pp 135–40.

'The Manor of Stockbridge', *Papers and Proceedings of the Hampshire Field Club and Archaeological Society* 32, pp 93–101.

1977 *The Register of William Melton Archbishop of York 1317–1340*, 1, *CYS* 70 (London) pp ix, 178.

'The Christian view of the Muslims at the time of the First Crusade', *The Eastern Mediterranean Lands in the Period of the Crusades* ed P. M. Holt (Warminster) pp 1–80.

'The Borough of Stockbridge', *Papers and Proceedings of the Hampshire Field Club and Archaeological Society* 33, pp 79–88.

'From 627 until the Early Thirteenth Century' (with C. N. L. Brooke), *A History of York Minster*, ed G. E. Aylmer and R. Cant (Oxford) pp 1–43.

REVIEW

Medieval Women, by Eileen Power ed M. M. Postan, *JEH* 28 pp 101–2.

1978 REVIEW

Women in Medieval Society ed S. M. Stuard, *JEH* 29 pp 120–1.

ABBREVIATIONS

AASRP	*Associated Archaeological Societies Reports and Papers*
AAWG	*Abhandlungen der Akademie* [*Gesellschaft* to 1942] *der Wissenschaften zu Göttingen*, (Göttingen 1843–)
AAWL	*Abhandlungen der Akademie der Wissenschaften und der Literatur* (Mainz 1950–)
ABAW	*Abhandlungen der Bayerischen Akademie der Wissenchaften* (Munich 1835–)
Abh	Abhundlung
Abt	Abteilung
ACO	*Acta Conciliorum Oecumenicorum*, ed E. Schwartz (Berlin/Leipzig 1914–40)
ACW	*Ancient Christian Writers*, ed J. Quasten and J. C. Plumpe (Westminster, Maryland/London 1946–)
ADAW	*Abhandlungen der Deutschen* [till 1944 *Preussischen*] *Akademie der Wissenschaften zu Berlin* (Berlin 1815–)
AF	*Analecta Franciscana*, 10 vols (Quaracchi 1885–1941)
AFH	*Archivum Franciscanum Historicum* (Quaracchi/Rome 1908–)
AFP	*Archivum Fratrum Praedicatorum* (Rome 1931–)
AHP	*Archivum historiae pontificae* (Rome 1963–)
AHR	*American Historical Review* (New York 1895–)
AKG	*Archiv für Kulturgeschichte* (Leipzig/Münster/Cologne 1903–)
AKZ	*Arbeiten zur kirchlichen Zeitgeschichte*
ALKG	H. Denifle and F. Ehrle, *Archiv für Literatur- und Kirchengeschichte des Mittelalters*, 7 vols (Berlin/Freiburg 1885–1900)
Altaner	B. Altaner, *Patrologie: Leben, Schriften und Lehre der Kirchenväter* (5 ed Freiburg 1958)
AM	L. Wadding, *Annales Minorum*, 8 vols (Rome 1625–54); 2 ed, 25 vols (Rome 1731–1886); 3 ed, vol 1– , (Quaracchi 1931–)
An Bol	*Analecta Bollandiana* (Brussels 1882–)
Annales	*Annales: Economies, Sociétés, Civilisations* (Paris 1946–)
Ant	*Antonianum* (Rome 1926–)
APC	*Proceedings and Ordinances of the Privy Council 1386–1542*, ed Sir Harris Nicolas, 7 vols (London 1834–7)
—	*Acts of the Privy Council of England 1542–1629*, 44 vols (London 1890–1958)
—	*Acts of the Privy Council of England, Colonial Series* (*1613–1783*) 5 vols (London 1908–12)
AR	*Archivum Romanicum* (Geneva/Florence 1917–41)
ARG	*Archiv für Reformationsgeschichte* (Berlin/Leipzig/Gütersloh 1903–)
ASAW	*Abhandhungen der Sächischen Akademie* [*Gesellschaft* to 1920] *der Wissenschaften zu Leipzig* (Leipzig 1850–)
ASB	*Acta Sanctorum Bollandiana* (Brussels etc 1643–)
ASC	*Anglo Saxon Chronicle*
ASI	*Archivio storico Italiano* (Florence 1842–)
ASL	*Archivio storico Lombardo*, 1–62 (Milan 1874–1935); ns 1–10 (Milan 1936–47)
ASOC	*Analecta Sacri Ordinis Cisterciensis* [*Analecta Cisterciensia* since 1965] (Rome 1945–)

ABBREVIATIONS

ASOSB	*Acta Sanctorum Ordinis Sancti Benedicti*, ed. L' D'Achery and J. Mabillon (Paris 1668–1701)
ASP	*Archivio della Società* [*Deputazione* from 1935] *Romana di Storia Patria* (Rome 1878–1934, 1935–)
ASR	*Archives de Sociologie des Religions* (Paris 1956–)
AV	Authorised Version
AV	*Archivio Veneto* (Venice 1871–): [1891–1921, *Nuovo Archivio Veneto*; 1922–6, *Archivio Veneto-Tridentino*]
B	*Byzantion* (Paris/Boston/Brussels 1924–)
Bale, *Catalogus*	John Bale, *Scriptorum Illustrium Maioris Brytanniae Catalogus*, 2 parts (Basel 1557, 1559)
Bale, *Index*	John Bale, *Index Britanniae Scriptorum*, ed R. L. Poole and M. Bateson (Oxford 1902) *Anecdota Oxoniensia*, medieval and modern series 9
Bale, *Summarium*	John Bale, *Illustrium Maioris Britanniae Scriptorum Summarium* (Ipswich 1548, reissued Wesel 1549)
BEC	*Bibliothèque de l'Ecole des Chartes* (Paris 1839–)
Beck	H-G Beck, *Kirche und theologische Literatur im byzantinischen Reich* (Munich 1959)
BEHE	*Bibliothèque de l'Ecole des Hautes Etudes: Sciences Philologiques et Historiques* (Paris 1869–)
Bernard	E. Bernard, *Catalogi Librorum Manuscriptorum Angliae et Hiberniae* (Oxford 1697)
BF	*Byzantinische Forschungen* (Amsterdam 1966–)
BHG	*Bibliotheca Hagiographica Graeca*, ed F. Halkin, 3 vols+1 (3 ed Brussels 1957, 1969)
BHI	*Bibliotheca historica Italica*, ed A. Ceruti, 4 vols (Milan 1876–85), 2 series, 3 vols (Milan 1901–33)
BHL	*Bibliotheca Hagiographica Latina*, 2 vols+1 (Brussels 1898–1901, 1911)
BHR	*Bibliothèque d'Humanisme et Renaissance* (Paris/Geneva 1941–)
Bibl Ref	*Bibliography of the Reform 1450–1648, relating to the United Kingdom and Ireland*, ed Derek Baker for 1955–70 (Oxford 1975)
BIHR	*Bulletin of the Institute of Historical Research* (London 1923–)
BISIMEAM	*Bullettino dell'istituto storico italiano per il medio evo e archivio muratoriano* (Rome 1886–)
BJRL	*Bulletin of the John Rylands Library* (Manchester 1903–)
BL	British Library, London
BM	British Museum, London
BN	Bibliothèque Nationale, Paris
Bouquet	M. Bouquet, *Recueil des historiens des Gaules et de la France. Rerum gallicarum et francicarum scriptores*, 24 vols (Paris 1738–1904); new ed L. Delisle, 1–19 (Paris 1868–80)
BQR	*British Quarterly Review* (London 1845–86)
Broadmead Records	*The Records of a Church of Christ, meeting in Broadmead, Bristol 1640–87*, HKS (London 1848)
BS	*Byzantinoslavica* (Prague 1929–)
Bucer, *Deutsche Schriften*	*Martin Bucers Deutsche Schriften*, ed R. Stupperich and others (Gütersloh/Paris 1960–)
Bucer, *Opera Latina*	*Martini Buceri Opera Latina*, ed F. Wendel and others (Paris/Gütersloh 1955–)
Bull Franc	*Bullarium Franciscanum*, vols 1–4 ed J. H. Sbaralea (Rome 1759–68) vols 5–7 ed C. Eubel (Rome 1898–1904), new series vols 1–3 ed U. Höntemann and J. M. Pou y Marti (Quaracchi 1929–49)

ABBREVIATIONS

BZ	*Byzantinische Zeitschrift* (Leipzig 1892–)
CA	*Cahiers Archéologiques. Fin de L'Antiquité et Moyen-âge* (Paris 1945–)
CaF	*Cahiers de Fanjeaux* (Toulouse 1966–)
CAH	*Cambridge Ancient History* (Cambridge 1923–39)
CalRev	Calumy Revised, ed A. G. Mathews (Oxford 1934)
CalLP	*Calendar of the Letters and Papers (Foreign and Domestic) of the Reign of Henry VIII*, 21 vols in 35 parts (London 1864–1932)
CalSPD	*Calendar of State Papers: Domestic* (London 1856–)
CalSPF	*Calendar of State Papers: Foreign*, 28 vols (London 1861–1950)
Calvin, *Opera*	*Ioannis Calvini Opera Quae Supersunt Omnia*, ed G. Baum and others *Corpus Reformatorum*, 59 vols (Brunswick/Berlin 1863–1900)
Canivez	J. M. Canivez, *Statuta capitulorum generalium ordinis cisterciensis ab anno 1116 ad annum 1786*, 8 vols (Louvain 1933–41)
Cardwell, *Documentary Annals*	*Documentary Annals of the Reformed Church of England*, ed E. Cardwell, 2 vols (Oxford 1839)
Cardwell, *Synodalia*	*Synodalia*, ed E. Cardwell, 2 vols (Oxford 1842)
CC	*Corpus Christianorum* (Turnholt 1952–)
CF	*Classical Folia*, [*Folia 1946–59*] (New York 1960–)
CGOH	*Cartulaire Générale de l'Ordre des Hospitaliers de St.-Jean de Jerusalem (1100–1310)*, ed J. Delaville Le Roulx, 4 vols (Paris 1894–1906)
CH	*Church History* (New York/Chicago 1932–)
CHB	*Cambridge History of the Bible*
CHistS	*Church History Society* (London 1886–92)
CHJ	*Cambridge Historical Journal* (Cambridge 1925–57)
CIG	*Corpus Inscriptionum Graecarum*, ed A. Boeckh, J. Franz, E. Curtius, A. Kirchhoff, 4 vols (Berlin 1825–77)
Cîteaux	*Cîteaux: Commentarii Cisterciensis* (Westmalle 1950–)
CMH	*Cambridge Medieval History*
CModH	*Cambridge Modern History*
COCR	*Collectanea Ordinis Cisterciensium Reformatorum* (Rome/Westmalle 1934–)
COD	*Conciliorum oecumenicorum decreta* (3 ed Bologna 1973)
Coll Franc	*Collectanea Franciscana* (Assisi/Rome 1931–)
CR	*Corpus Reformatorum*, ed C. G. Bretschneider and others (Halle etc. 1834–)
CS	*Cartularium Saxonicum*, ed W. de G. Birch, 3 vols (London 1885–93)
CSCO	*Corpus Scriptorum Christianorum Orientalium* (Paris 1903–)
CSEL	*Corpus Scriptorum Ecclesiasticorum Latinorum* (Vienna 1866–)
CSer	*Camden Series* (London 1838–)
CSHByz	*Corpus Scriptorum Historiae Byzantinae* (Bonn 1828–97)
CYS	*Canterbury and York Society* (London 1907–)
DA	*Deutsches Archiv für* [*Geschichte*, –Weimar 1937–43] *die Erforschung des Mittelalters* (Cologne/Graz 1950–)
DACL	*Dictionnaire d'Archéologie chrétienne et de Liturgie*, ed F. Cabrol and H. Leclercq (Paris 1924–)
DDC	*Dictionnaire de Droit Canonique*, ed R. Naz (Paris 1935–)

ABBREVIATIONS

DHGE	*Dictionnaire d'Histoire et de Géographie ecclésiastiques*, ed A. Baudrillart and others (Paris 1912–)
DNB	*Dictionary of National Biography* (London 1885–)
DOP	*Dumbarton Oaks Papers* (Cambridge, Mass., 1941–)
DR	F. Dölger, *Regesten der Kaiserurkunden des oströmischen Reiches* (*Corpus der griechischen Urkunden des Mittelalters und der neuern Zeit*, Reihe A, Abt I), 5 vols: 1 (565–1025); 2 (1025–1204); 3 (1204–1282); 4 (1282–1341); 5 (1341–1543) (Munich/Berlin 1924–65)
DRev	*Downside Review* (London 1880–)
DSAM	*Dictionnaire de Spiritualité, Ascétique et Mystique*, ed M. Viller (Paris 1932–)
DTC	*Dictionnaire de Théologie Catholique*, ed A. Vacant, E. Mangenot, E. Amann, 15 vols (Paris 1903–50)
EcHR	*Economic History Review* (London 1927–)
EEBS	Ἐπετηρὶς Ἑταιρείας Βυζαντινῶν Σπουδῶν (Athens 1924–)
EETS	*Early English Text Society*
EF	*Etudes Franciscaines* (Paris 1899–1938, ns 1950–)
EHD	*English Historical Documents* (London 1953–)
EHR	*English Historical Review* (London 1886–)
Ehrhard	A. Ehrhard, *Uberlieferung und Bestand der hagiographischen und homiletischen Literatur der griechischen Kirche von den Anfängen bis zum Ende des 16. Jh*, 3 vols in 4, *TU* 50–2 (=4 series 5–7) 11 parts (Leipzig 1936–52)
Emden (O)	A. B. Emden, *A Biographical Register of the University of Oxford to 1500*, 3 vols (London 1957–9); *1500–40* (1974)
Emden (C)	A. B. Emden, *A Biographical Register of the University of Cambridge to 1500* (London 1963)
EO	*Echos d'Orient* (Constantinople/Paris 1897–1942)
ET	English translation
EYC	*Early Yorkshire Charters*, ed W. Farrer and C. T. Clay, 12 vols (Edinburgh/Wakefield 1914–65)
FGH	*Die Fragmente der griechischen Historiker*, ed F. Jacoby (Berlin 1926–30)
FM	*Histoire de l'église depuis les origines jusqu'à nos jours*, ed A. Fliche and V. Martin (Paris 1935–)
Foedera	*Foedera, conventiones, litterae et cuiuscunque generis acta publica inter reges Angliae et alios quosvis imperatores, reges, pontifices, principes vel communitates*, ed T. Rymer and R. Sanderson, 20 vols (London 1704–35), re-ed 7 vols (London 1816–69)
Franc Stud	*Franciscan Studies* (St Bonaventure, New York 1924–, ns 1941–)
Fredericq	P. Fredericq, *Corpus documentorum inquisitionis haereticae pravitatis Neerlandicae*, 3 vols (Ghent 1889–93)
FStn	*Franzikanische Studien* (Münster/Werl 1914–)
GalC	*Gallia Christiana*, 16 vols (Paris 1715–1865)
Gangraena	T. Edwards, *Gangraena*, 3 parts (London 1646)
GCS	*Die griechischen christlichen Schriftsteller der erste drei Jahrhunderte* (Leipzig 1897–)
Gee and Hardy	*Documents illustrative of English Church History* ed H. Gee and W. J. Hardy (London 1896)
GEEB	R. Janin, *La géographie ecclésiastique de l'empire byzantin*; 1, *Le siège de Constantinople et le patriarcat oecumenique*, pt 3 *Les églises et les monastères* (Paris 1953); 2, *Les églises et les monastères des grands centres byzantins* (Paris 1975) (series discontinued)

Golubovich	Girolamo Golubovich, *Biblioteca bio-bibliografica della Terra Santa e dell' oriente francescano:* series 1, *Annali*, 5 vols (Quaracchi 1906–23) series 2, *Documenti* 14 vols (Quaracchi 1921–33) series 3, *Documenti* (Quaracchi 1928–) series 4, *Studi*, ed M. Roncaglia (Cairo 1954–)
Grumel, *Regestes*	V. Grumel, *Les Regestes des Actes du Patriarcat de Constantinople*, 1: *Les Actes des Patriarches*, I: 381–715; II: 715–1043; III: 1043–1206 (Socii Assumptionistae Chalcedonenses, 1931, 1936, 1947)
Grundmann	H. Grundmann, *Religiöse Bewegungen im Mittelalter* (Berlin 1935, 2 ed Darmstadt 1970)
Guignard	P. Guignard, *Les monuments primitifs de la règle cistercienne* (Dijon 1878)
HBS	*Henry Bradshaw Society* (London/Canterbury 1891–)
HE	*Historia Ecclesiastica*
HistSt	*Historical Studies* (Melbourne 1940–)
HJ	*Historical Journal* (Cambridge 1958–)
HJch	*Historisches Jarhbuch der Görres Gesellschaft* (Cologne 1880–, Munich 1950–)
JKS	Hanserd Knollys Society (London 1847–)
HL	C. J. Hefele and H. Leclercq, *Histore des Conciles*, 10 vols (Paris 1907–35)
HMC	Historical Manuscripts Commission
Holzapfel, *Handbuch*	H. Holzapfel, *Handbuch der Geschichte des Franziskanerordens* (Freiburg 1908)
Hooker, *Works*	*The Works of . . . Mr. Richard Hooker*, ed J. Keble, 7 ed rev R. W. Church and F. Paget, 3 vols (Oxford 1888)
Houedene	*Chronica Magistri Rogeri de Houedene*, ed W. Stubbs, 4 vols, *RS* 51 (London 1868–71)
HRH	*The Heads of Religious Houses, England and Wales, 940–1216*, ed D. Knowles, C. N. L. Brooke, V. C. M. London (Cambridge 1972)
HS	*Hispania sacra* (Madrid 1948–)
HTR	*Harvard Theological Review* (New York/Cambridge, Mass., 1908–)
HZ	*Historische Zeitschrift* (Munich 1859–)
IER	*Irish Ecclesiastical Record* (Dublin 1864–)
IR	*Innes Review* (Glasgow 1950–)
JAC	*Jahrbuch für Antike und Christentum* (Münster-im-Westfalen 1958–)
Jaffé	*Regesta Pontificum Romanorum ab condita ecclesia ad a. 1198*, 2 ed S. Lowenfeld, F. Kaltenbrunner, P. Ewald, 2 vols (Berlin 1885–8, repr Graz 1958)
JBS	*Journal of British Studies* (Hartford, Conn., 1961–)
JEH	*Journal of Ecclesiastical History* (London 1950–)
JFHS	*Journal of the Friends Historical Society* (London/Philadelphia 1903–)
JHI	*Journal of the History of Ideas* (London 1940–)
JHSChW	*Journal of the Historical Society of the Church in Wales* (Cardiff 1947–)
JIntH	*Journal of Interdisciplinary History* (Cambridge, Mass., 1970–)
JLW	*Jahrbuch für Liturgiewissenschaft* (Münster-im-Westfalen 1921–41)

JMH	*Journal of Modern History* (Chicago 1929–)
JMedH	*Journal of Medieval History* (Amsterdam 1975–)
JRA	*Journal of Religion in Africa* (Leiden 1967–)
JRH	*Journal of Religious History* (Sydney 1960–)
JRS	*Journal of Roman Studies* (London 1910–)
JRSAI	*Journal of the Royal Society of Antiquaries of Ireland* (Dublin 1871–)
JSArch	*Journal of the Society of Archivists* (London 1955–)
JTS	*Journal of Theological Studies* (London 1899–)
Kemble	*Codex Diplomaticus Aevi Saxonici*, ed J. M. Kemble (London 1839–48)
Knowles, *MO*	David Knowles, *The Monastic Order in England, 943–1216* (2 ed Cambridge 1963)
Knowles, *RO*	——, *The Religious Orders in England*, 3 vols (Cambridge 1948–59)
Knox, *Works*	*The Works of John Knox*, ed D. Laing, Bannatyne Club/Wodrow Society, 6 vols (Edinburgh 1846–64)
Laurent, *Regestes*	V. Laurent, *Les Registes des Actes du Patriarcat de Constantinople*, 1: *Les Actes des Patriarches*, IV: *Les Regestes de 1208 à 1309* (Paris 1971)
Le Neve	John Le Neve, *Fasti Ecclesiae Anglicanae 1066–1300*, rev and exp Diana E. Greenway, 1, St Pauls (London 1968); 2, Monastic Cathedrals (1971) *Fasti Ecclesiae Anglicanae 1300–1541* rev and exp H. P. F. King, J. M. Horn, B. Jones, 12 vols (London 1962–7) *Fasti Ecclesiae Anglicanae 1541–1857* rev and exp J. M. Horn, D. M. Smith, 1, St Pauls (1969); 2, Chichester (1971); 3, Canterbury, Rochester, Winchester (1974); 4, York (1975)
Lloyd, *Formularies of faith*	*Formularies of Faith Put Forth by Authority during the Reign of Henry VIII*, ed C. Lloyd (Oxford 1825)
LRS	*Lincoln Record Society*
LQR	*Law Quarterly Review* (London 1885–)
LThK	*Lexicon für Theologie und Kirche*, ed J. Höfer and K. Rahnes (2 ed Freiburg-im-Breisgau 1957–)
LW	*Luther's Works*, ed J. Pelikan and H. T. Lehman, American edition (St. Louis/Philadelphia, 1955–)
MA	*Monasticon Anglicanum*, ed R. Dodsworth and W. Dugdale, 3 vols (London 1655–73); new ed J. Caley, H. Ellis, B. Bandinel, 6 vols in 8 (London 1817–30)
Mansi	J. D. Mansi, *Sacrorum conciliorum nova et amplissima collectio*, 31 vols (Florence/Venice 1757–98); new impression and continuation, ed L. Petit and J. B. Martin, 60 vols (Paris 1899–1927)
Martène and Durand *Collectio*	E. Martène and U. Durand, *Veterum Scriptorum et Monumentorum Historicorum, Dogmaticorum, Moralium Amplissima Collectio*, 9 vols (Paris 1729)
Thesaurus	*Thesaurus Novus Anedotorum*, 5 vols (Paris 1717)
Voyage	*Voyage Litteraire de Deux Religieux Benedictins de la Congregation de Saint Maur*, 2 vols (Paris 1717, 1724)
MedA	*Medium Aevum* (Oxford 1932–)
Mendola	*Atti della Settimana di Studio*, 1959– (Milan 1962–)
MF	*Miscellanea Francescana* (Foligno/Rome 1886–)

ABBREVIATIONS

MGH	*Monumenta Germaniae Historica inde ab a.c. 500 usque ad a. 1500*, ed G. H. Pertz and others (Berlin, Hanover 1826–)
AA	*Auctores Antiquissimi*
Ant	*Antiquitates*
Briefe	*Epistolae 2: Die Briefe der Deutschen Kaiserzeit*
Cap	*Leges 2: Leges in Quart 2: Capitularia regum Francorum*
CM	*Chronica Minora* 1–3 (=*AA* 9, 11, 13) ed Th. Mommsen (1892 1894, 1898 repr 1961)
Conc	*Leges 2: Leges in Quart 3: Concilia*
Const	4: *Constitutiones et acta publica imperatorum et regum*
DC	*Deutsche Chroniken*
Dip	*Diplomata in folio*
Epp	*Epistolae 1 in Quart*
Epp Sel	4: *Epistolae Selectae*
FIG	*Leges 3: Fontes Iuris Germanici Antique*, new series
FIGUS	4: , *in usum scholarum*
Form	2: *Leges in Quart 5: Formulae Merovingici et Karolini Aevi*
GPR	*Gesta Pontificum Romanorum*
Leges	*Leges in folio*
Lib	*Libelli de lite*
LM	*Ant 3: Libri Memoriales*
LNG	*Leges 2: Leges in Quart 1: Leges nationum Germanicarum*
Necr	Ant 2: *Necrologia Germaniae*
Poet	1: *Poetae Latini Medii Aevi*
Quellen	*Quellen zur Geistesgeschichte des Mittelalters*
Schriften	*Schriften der Monumenta Germaniae Historica*
SRG	*Scriptores rerum germanicarum in usum scholarum*
SRG ns	, new series
SRL	*Scriptores rerum langobardicarum et italicarum*
SRM	*Scriptores rerum merovingicarum*
SS	*Scriptores*
SSM	*Staatschriften des späteren Mittelalters*
MIOG	*Mitteilungen des Instituts für österreichische Geschichtsforschung* (Graz/Cologne 1880–)
MM	F. Miklosich and J. Müller, *Acta et Diplomata Graeca medii aevi sacra et profana*, 6 vols (Vienna 1860–90)
Moorman, *History*	J. R. H. Moorman, *A History of the Franciscan Order from its origins to the year 1517* (Oxford 1968)
More, *Works*	*The Complete Works of St Thomas More*, ed R. S. Sylvester and others Yale edition (New Haven/London 1963–)
Moyen Age	*Le moyen âge. Revue d'histoire et de philologie* (Paris 1888–)
MRHEW	David Knowles and R. N. Hadcock, *Medieval Religious Houses, England and Wales* (2 ed London 1971)
MRHI	A. Gwynn and R. N. Hadcock, *Medieval Religious Houses, Ireland* (London 1970)
MRHS	Ian B. Cowan and David E. Easson, *Medieval Religious Houses, Scotland* (2 ed London 1976)
MS	Manuscript
MStn	*Mittelalterliche Studien* (Stuttgart 1966–)
Muratori	L. A. Muratori, *Rerum italicarum scriptores*, 25 vols (Milan 1723–51); new ed G. Carducci and V. Fiorini, 34 vols in 109 fasc (Città di Castello/Bologna 1900–)

NCE	*New Catholic Encyclopedia*, 15 vols (New York 1967)
NCModH	*New Cambridge Modern History*, 14 vols (Cambridge 1957–70)
nd	no date
NEB	*New English Bible*
NF	Neue Folge
NH	*Northern History* (Leeds 1966–)
ns	new series
NS	New Style
Numen	*Numen: International Review for the History of Religions* (Leiden 1954–)
OCP	*Orientalia Christiana Periodica* (Rome 1935–)
ODCC	*Oxford Dictionary of the Christian Church*, ed F. L. Cross (Oxford 1957), 2 ed with E. A. Livingstone (1974)
OED	*Oxford English Dictionary*
OMT	*Oxford Medieval Texts*
OS	Old Style
OHS	*Oxford Historical Society*
PBA	*Proceedings of the British Academy*
PG	*Patrologia Graeca*, ed J. P. Migne, 161 vols (Paris 1857–66)
PhK	Philosophisch-historische Klasse
PL	*Patrologia Latina*, ed J. P. Migne, 217+4 index vols (Paris 1841–64)
Plummer, *Bede*	*Venerabilis Baedae Opera Historica*, ed C. Plummer (Oxford 1896)
PO	*Patrologia Orientalis*, ed J. Graffin and F. Nau (Paris 1903–)
Potthast	*Regesta Pontificum Romanorum inde ab a. post Christum natum 1198 ad a. 1304*, ed A. Potthast, 2 vols (1874–5 repr Graz 1957)
PP	*Past and Present* (London 1952–)
PPTS	*Palestine Pilgrims' Text Society*, 13 vols and index (London 1896–1907)
PRIA	*Proceedings of the Royal Irish Academy* (Dublin 1836–)
PRO	Public Record Office
PS	Parker Society (Cambridge 1841–55)
PW	*Paulys Realencyklopädie der klassischen Altertumswissenschaft*, new ed G. Wissowa and W. Kroll (Stuttgart 1893–)
QFIAB	*Quellen und Forschungen aus italienischen Archiven und Bibliotheken* (Rome 1897–)
RAC	*Reallexikon für Antike und Christentum*, ed T. Klauser (Stuttgart 1941)
RB	*Revue Bénédictine* (Maredsous 1884–)
RE	*Realencyclopädie für protestantische Theologie*, ed A. Hauck, 24 vols (3 ed Leipzig, 1896–1913)
REB	*Revue des Etudes Byzantines* (Bucharest/Paris 1946–)
RecS	Record Series
RGG	*Die Religion in Geschichte und Gegenwart*, 6 vols (Tübingen 1927–32)
RH	*Revue historique* (Paris 1876–)
RHC,	*Recueil des Historiens des Croisades*, ed Académie des Inscriptions et Belles-Lettres (Paris 1841–1906)
Arm	*Historiens Arméniens*, 2 vols (1869–1906)
Grecs	*Historiens Grecs*, 2 vols (1875–81)
Lois	*Lois. Les Assises de Jérusalem*, 2 vols (1841–3)
Occ	*Historiens Occidentaux*, 5 vols (1844–95)
Or	*Historiens Orientaux*, 5 vols (1872–1906)
RHD	*Revue d'histoire du droit* (Haarlem, Gronigen 1923–)

ABBREVIATIONS

RHDFE *Revue historique du droit français et étranger* (Paris 1922–)
RHE *Revue d'Histoire Ecclésiastique* (Louvain 1900–)
RHEF *Revue d'Histoire de l'Eglise de France* (Paris 1910–)
RHR *Revue de l'Histoire des Religions* (Paris 1880–)
RR *Regesta Regum Anglo-Normannorum*, ed H. W. C. Davis, H. A. Cronne, Charles Johnson, R. H. C. Davis, 4 vols (Oxford 1913–69)
RS *Rerum Brittanicarum Medii Aevi Scriptores*, 99 vols (London 1858–1911). *Rolls Series*
RSCI *Rivista di storia della chiesa in Italia* (Rome 1947–)
RSR *Revue des sciences religieuses* (Strasbourg 1921–)
RStI *Rivista storica italiana* (Naples 1884–)
RTAM *Recherches de théologie ancienne et médiévale* (Louvain 1929–)
RV Revised Version
Sitz *Sitzungsberichte*
SA *Studia Anselmiana* (Roma 1933–)
sa *sub anno*
SBAW *Sitzungsberichte der bayerischen Akademie der Wissenschaften*, PhK (Munich 1871–)
SCH *Studies in Church History* (London 1964–)
ScHR *Scottish Historical Review* (Edinburgh/Glasgow 1904–)
SCR *Sources chrétiennes*, ed H. de Lubac and J. Daniélou (Paris 1941–)
SF *Studi Francescani* (Florence 1914–)
SGra *Studia Gratiana*, ed J. Forchielli and A. M. Stickler (Bologna 1953–)
SGre *Studi Gregoriani*, ed G. Borino, 7 vols (Rome 1947–61)
SMon *Studia Monastica* (Montserrat, Barcelona 1959–)
Speculum *Speculum, A Journal of Medieval Studies* (Cambridge, Mass. 1926–)
SpicFr *Spicilegium Friburgense* (Freiburg 1957–)
SS *Surtees Society* (Durham 1835–)
SSSpoleto *Settimane di Studio sull'alto medioevo*, 1952– , Centro Italiano di studi sull'alto medioevo, Spoleto 1954–)
STC *A Short-Title Catalogue of Books Printed in England, Scotland and Ireland and of English Books Printed Abroad 1475–1640*, ed A. W. Pollard and G. R. Redgrave (London 1926, repr 1946, 1950)
Strype, *Annals* John Strype, *Annals of the Reformation and Establishment of Religion . . .during Queen Elizabeth's Happy Reign*, 4 vols in 7 (Oxford 1824)
Strype, *Cranmer* John Strype, *Memorials of . . .Thomas Cranmer*, 2 vols (Oxford 1840)
Strype, *Grindal* John Strype, *The History of the Life and Acts of . . . Edmund Grindal* (Oxford 1821)
Strype, *Memorials* John Strype, *Ecclesiastical Memorials, Relating Chiefly to Religion, and the Reformation of it . . . under King Henry VIII, King Edward VI and Queen Mary I*, 3 vols in 6 (Oxford 1822)
Strype, *Parker* John Strype, *The Life and Acts of Matthew Parker*, 3 vols (Oxford 1821)
Strype, *Whitgift* John Strype, *The Life and Acts of John Whitgift*, 3 vols (Oxford 1822)
sub hag *subsidia hagiographica*

sv	*sub voce*
SVRG	*Schriften des Vereins für Reformationsgeschichte* (Halle/Leipzig/Gütersloh 1883–)
TCBiblS	*Transactions of the Cambridge Bibliographical Society* (Cambridge 1949–)
THSCym	*Transactions of the Historical Society of Cymmrodorion* (London 1822–)
TRHS	*Transactions of the Royal Historical Society* (London 1871–)
TU	*Texte und Untersuchungen zur Geschichte der altchristlichen Literatur* (Leipzig/Berlin 1882–)
VCH	*Victoria County History* (London 1900–)
VHM	G. Tiraboschi, *Vetera Humiliatorum Monumenta*, 3 vols. (Milan 1766–8)
Vivarium	*Vivarium: An International Journal for the Philosophy and Intellectual Life of the Middle Ages and Renaissance* (Assen 1963–)
VV	*Vizantijskij Vremennik* 1–25 (St Petersburg 1894–1927), ns 1 (26) (Leningrad 1947–)
WA	*D. Martin Luthers Werke*, ed J. C. F. Knaake (Weimar 1883–) [*Weimarer Ausgabe*]
WA Br	*Briefwechsel*
WA DB	*Deutsche Bibel*
WA TR	*Tischreden*
WelHR	*Welsh History Review* (Cardiff 1960–)
Wharton	H. Wharton, *Anglia Sacra*, 2 parts (London 1691)
Whitelock, *Wills*	*Anglo-Saxon wills*, ed D. Whitlock (Cambridge 1930)
Wilkins	*Concilia Magnae Britanniae et Hiberniae A.D. 446–1717*, 4 vols, ed D. Wilkins (London 1737)
YAJ	*Yorkshire Archaeological Journal* (London/Leeds 1870–)
Zanoni	L. Zanoni, *Gli Umiliati nei loro rapporti con l'eresia, l'industria della lana ed i communi nei secoli xii e xiii, Biblioteca Historica Italica*, 2 series, 2 (Milan 1911)
ZKG	*Zeitschrift für Kirchengeschichte* (Gotha/Stuttgart 1878–)
ZOG	*Zeitschrift für osteuropäische Geschichte* (Berlin 1911–35) = *Kyrios* (Berlin 1936–)
ZRG	*Zeitschrift der Savigny-Stiftung für Rechtsgeschichte* (Weimar)
GAbt	*Germanistische Abteilung* (1863–)
KAbt	*Kanonistische Abteilung* (1911–)
RAbt	*Romanistische Abteilung* (1880–)
ZRGG	*Zeitschrift für Religions- und Geistesgeschichte* (Marburg 1948–)
Zwingli, *Werke*	*Huldreich Zwinglis Sämmtliche Werke*, ed E. Egli and others, *CR* (Berlin/Leipzig/Zurich 1905–)

SUBSCRIBERS

The Library, the University College of Wales, Aberystwyth
Dr. John Addy
Dr. Joan P. Alcock
Olive Anderson
Phyllis Auty
Derek Baker
Melanie Barber
John M. Barkley
Professor Frank Barlow
Miss Christina Barratt
Dr. Caroline M. Barron
Mrs. Sheila Barthes
Mary R. Barton
Dr. Mary Beare
Judy Behennah
Miss Heather Bell
Dominic Bellenger
Miss Diana Bennett
The Reverend Joyce M. Bennett
Nicholas Bennett
The Reverend Canon Ronald Bircham
Dr. Ernest Blake
Brenda Bolton
Gerald Bonner
The Gurney Library, the Borthwick Institute, York
Leonard E. Boyle
Mrs. J. M. Bradshaw
Professor Dr. Walter Brandmüller
Dora K. Briggs
Reginald Brocklesby
Christopher N. L. Brooke
Rosalind B. Brooke
Professor R. Allen Brown
The Reverend R. F. G. Burnish, BA (Theol), MTh.
Janet Burton
Dr. L. H. Butler, the Royal Holloway College, University of London
Mrs. M. C. Butler
James K. Cameron
James Campbell
Mrs. June Card
Katherine Carr
Mrs. Irene Carrier (née Wheatley)
Miss Gwen Chambers
Professor Christopher Cheney
Mrs. Mary Cheney
Dr. Marjorie Chibnall
Mary Clayton
Giles Constable
The Reverend Professor Robert T. Coolidge
Joyce Coombs
Mrs. K. Coutin
The Reverend Dr. L. W. Cowie
Claire Cross
Mrs. K. Jane E. O. Cross
Dr. C. M. D. Crowder
Norhann Crowley
Melville E. Carrell
Marie D'Aguanno
Susan J. Davies
David P. Davison
Rosemary Devonshire Jones
Anne Dewe
Professor Barrie Dobson
Miss Barbara Dodwell
The Reverend James Dollard
John E. Donnelly
Professor T. S. Dorsch
The Reverend Professor C. W. Dugmore, DD
Louisa J. V. Dunlop
F. I. Dunn
Marilyn Dunn
Robert W. Dunning
Professor G. R. Dunstan
The Library, University of East Anglia
The Library, University of Edinburgh
The Reverend Arthur Edwards
Caroline Elam
Fiona Ellis
C. R. Elrington
Professor G. R. Elton
Richard Emms
Michael Evans
David Hugh Farmer
The Right Honourable Lord Fletcher
Sister Helen P. Forshaw
Miss Daphne Fraser, MTh.
John Fuggles
A. R. B. Fuller
Phyllis E. Gibson
John Godfrey
A. E. Goodman
Dr. Joan Greatrex
Dr. R. Gerald Guest
Mrs. Hermione Gullard
Dr. Roy Martin Haines

SUBSCRIBERS

Dr. Elizabeth M. Hallam Smith
Bernard Hamilton
The Reverend Edward R. Hardy
C. G. Harlow
Dr. Christopher Harper-Bill
Mrs. Christopher Harper-Bill
The Reverend James Martin
Barbara F. Harvey
Margaret M. Harvey
Professor Denys Hay
Dr. Felicity Heal
Dr. Muriel Heppell
Jane L. Herbert
Kathryn Hill
Christopher J. Holdsworth
The Reverend Professor R. F. G. Holmes
Anne Hudson
Dr. Gordon Huelin
Joan Hunter
Ailsa Inckle
R. T. Jääskeläinen
Carolyn Jenkins
Bridgett Jones
Carol Jones
Susan Judson
The Reverend H. A. Lloyd Jukes, MA, Sth, FRHistS
The Reverend Dr. David J. Keep
William Kellaway
M. J. Kennedy
Professor Edward B. King
Christopher Kitching
Mrs. K. Knight
Miss Lucy Knox
Mrs. Margaret Laird
M. D. Lambert
Miss Joan C. Lancaster, CBE
Hugh Lawrence
Mrs. K. E. Leddy
The Librarian, the Brotherton Library, the University of Leeds
Gordon Leff
Dora M. Leonard
John Le Patourel
Miss G. Mary Lewis
Lester K. Little
F. Donald Logan
Professor H. R. Loyn
Mrs. Mary Ludlow
David Luscombe
Jeffrey A. H. Lynan
Miss C. McCue
Leslie J. Macfarlane
Dr. P. McGurk
A. K. McHardy
Dr. E. K. Mackenzie
Dr. Rosamond McKitterick
John McManners
John Macnab
Alice Mackrell
John Mackrell
Brian Mains
Miss Kathleen Major
R. A. Markus
John Martell
Evelyn Martin
Dr. Emma Mason
Dr. W. B. Maynard
Anne Mayne
H. M. R. E. Mayr-Harting
Bernard Meehan
R. I. Moore
D. A. L. Morgan
Professor Colin Morris
Joan Morris
Jocelyn Morris, FSA
Richard Mortimer
Sister Anne Murphy, MTh, BA
Mr. A. Murray
Mrs. A. I. Mussett
Professor A. R. Myers, MA, PhD, FSA, FRHistS
Janet L. Nelson
Miss Sarah Newman
Joan Nicholson
Duncan Nimmo
Eileen M. North
G. F. Nuttall
A. E. B. Owen
Dorothy M. Owen
W. B. Patterson
The Reverend Dr. T. M. Parker
Joan M. Petersen
Mary Pettman
Hugo Petzsch
Miss Anne Philpott
A. J. Piper
Lucie Polak
Margaret A. Powell
Christine I. Markham Pressley
Marjorie Booth Pritchard
Ralph B. Pugh
Martyn Rady
Miss Rosalind Ransford
Dr. P. Revell
Dr. Michael Richter

SUBSCRIBERS

The Honourable Mrs. Roberts
Olivia Robinson
The Library, Rolle College, Exmouth
Professor Ivan Roots
R. K. Rose
Dr. Harry Rosenberg
Joel T. Rosenthal
Professor Nicolai Rubinstein
The Honourable Sir Steven Runciman
Julie Ryan (née Williams)
The Library, St Anne's College, Oxford
Dr. J. E. Sayers
Mrs. Mana Sedgwick
Seeley Historical Library, University of Cambridge
Michael M. Sheehan, CSB
Ian Short
Miss Elizabeth Siberry
Dr. Grant G. Simpson
Eileen M. Sindell-Wright
Miss M. D. Slatter
R. C. Smail
Miss Beryl Smalley
David M. Smith
Jacqueline Smith
R. Mary Smith
Janet Sondheimer
Dr. Margaret Spufford
Pauline Stafford
Beryl E. Stevens
Miss Janet H. Stevenson
Professor E. L. G. Stones
Mrs. J. M. B. Stones
Dr. Enid Stoye
Neil Stratford
Dr. R. N. Swanson
Mrs. Virginia Syvan
Audrey Tank
Eric Tappe
The Reverend Brian Taylor
Mrs. Joan Taylor
L. A. Thomas
Dr. D. M. Thompson
Sally Thompson
Dr. J. A. F. Thomson
Dr. Andreas Tillyrides
Victoria Tudor
Joan Varley
Mrs. Antoinette Wale
Canon David Walker
A. F. Walls
Sister Benedicta Ward
Professor W. R. Ward
Mrs. D. B. M. Warren (née Lesley Odom)
Miss B. G. Watson, MA, BA
Dorothy Bruce Weske
Stephen E. Wessley
Christopher M. Wheeler
Professor Beatrice M. I. White, DLit, FSA
Kathleen M. Whiteley
M. J. Wilks
The Reverend C. P. Williams
Diana Wood
I. N. Wood
Ann-F. Woodings
The Library, Worcester College, Oxford
The Reverend Dr. J. Robert Wright
Marianne Wynn
George Yule
Dr. Georgianna Ziegler